The Chatham Hou
and other Middle-Ea

BY THE SAME AUTHOR

*England and the Middle East: The Destruction
of the Ottoman Empire*
Nationalism
*Afghani and 'Abduh: An Essay on Religious Unbelief and
Political Activism in Modern Islam*
Nationalism in Asia and Africa
Arabic Political Memoirs and Other Studies
*In the Anglo-Arab Labyrinth: the McMahon-Husayn
Correspondence and Its Interpretations, 1914–1939*
Islam in the Modern World and Other Studies

EDITED BY THE SAME AUTHOR

The Middle-Eastern Economy
The Jewish World
Modern Egypt (with Sylvia G. Haim)
Towards Modern Iran (with Sylvia G. Haim)
Palestine and Israel in the 19th and 20th Centuries
(with Sylvia G. Haim)
Zionism and Arabism in Palestine and Israel
(with Sylvia G. Haim)

The Chatham House Version and other Middle-Eastern Studies *New Edition*

ELIE KEDOURIE
Professor of Politics in the University of London
and Fellow of the British Academy

We in that land begin our rule in courage,
The seal of peace gives warrant to intrusion;
But then our grin of emptiness breaks the skin,
Formless dishonour spreads its proud confusion.
                              James McAuley

 Published for Brandeis University Press by
UNIVERSITY PRESS OF NEW ENGLAND
Hanover and London

UNIVERSITY PRESS OF NEW ENGLAND
Brandeis University
Brown University
Clark University
Dartmouth College
University of New Hampshire
University of Rhode Island
Tufts University
University of Vermont

Originally published by Weidenfeld and Nicolson, London, and Praeger Publishers, New York

LIBRARY OF CONGRESS CATALOGING IN PUBLICATION DATA
Kedourie, Elie.
  The Chatham House version, and other Middle-Eastern studies.
  Bibliography: p.
  Includes index.
  1. Near East—History—20th century—Addresses, essays, lectures.
I. Title.
DS62.4.K4   1984   956   83-40553
ISBN 0-87451-304-9 (pbk.)

Printed in the United States of America

Contents

Foreword

The studies which make up this book – with the exception of the last one, published here for the first time – were originally published in the course of the last seventeen years in *The Cambridge Journal, Commentary, The Historical Journal, Journal of the Royal Asiatic Society, Middle Eastern Studies, Orient, The Political Quarterly, St Antony's Papers,* and in the volume on *Political and Social Change in Modern Egypt* edited by P. M. Holt. Most of them have now been enlarged, sometimes considerably, to take account of material which became available after their first publication. I am much obliged to the various publishers and editors who have kindly allowed republication.

I am very grateful to the Librarian of Birmingham University, the Librarian of the School of Oriental Studies, Durham University, the Librarian of the University of Newcastle, the Librarian of New College, Oxford, and the Librarian of Pembroke College, Cambridge, for allowing me access to the Austen Chamberlain Papers, the Sudan Archive including the Wingate Papers, the Gertrude Bell Papers, and the Ronald Storrs Papers in their respective custodies. I would like also to thank the staff of the Public Record Office, London, and of the foreign affairs branch of the National Archives, Washington and the Director and staff of the Israel State Archives, Jerusalem, for their ready helpfulness.

Crown copyright records appear by permission of the Controller, Her Majesty's Stationery Office.

I am indebted to the Central Research Fund of the University of London and to the Government Research Division at the London School of Economics for making it possible for me to obtain books, periodicals and documents not available in this country. I am also particularly indebted to the Warden and Fellows of St Antony's College, Oxford, and especially to Mr Albert Hourani for having made it possible for me to spend some time at Washington in order to consult documents at the National Archives.

It was as a scholar of St Antony's College in 1951–53 that I was first able to pursue my interest in middle-eastern history; and, in fact, of the studies republished here, the first which I wrote – now chapter 10 of the book – was written in the College library in the long vacation of 1952. My debt to the College is thus extensive; in token of which I would inscribe these studies to St Antony's.

London School of Economics, August 1969   E.K.

Introduction to the New Edition

The twelve studies included in *The Chatham House Version* relate to a period when British power and influence in the middle east were at their most extensive. Thus, many of the episodes and issues considered here arise out of the British presence in the middle east, and are examined with the purpose of elucidating the manner in which this great power and influence were employed, what assumptions ministers, high officials and military leaders made about middle-eastern politics and society, what their strategic calculations were, how they dealt with challenges and emergencies and what, usually unexpected and undesired, consequences their policies and actions had, both for British interests and for the countries and the social groups which these policies and actions affected.

Whether it is British officials in Cairo and Khartoum seeking to build a regional policy on Sharif Husain and his sons; or Allenby prohibiting his troops from entering Damascus in order that the Sharifians should claim to have conquered it themselves; or Samuel being persuaded to appoint, in an irregular manner, Hajj Amin al-Husaini as Mufti of Jerusalem and affording him unchallenged and unaccountable control over all Muslim institutions in Palestine; or Allenby, Milner, and Lloyd George allowing themselves to be out-manoeuvred by Egyptian politicians whom Cromer and Kitchener had known how to control; or the successive ministers who set up the ramshackle, sanguinary, and ill-fated kingdom of Iraq; or Eden, Spears, and Altrincham elbowing the French out of the Levant and seeking to preserve control over the middle east by the promotion and encouragement of pan-Arabism; all these episodes show successive and cumulative manifestations of illusion, misjudgment, maladroitness, and failure. Such at any rate is the picture which emerges from the evidence examined in this book.

The evidence is evidence of what was said and done in particular circumstances, at a given time and place. From it cannot be inferred that what was done was inescapable. On the contrary: McMahon and his officials in Cairo in 1915 could have reached a different conclusion about the prospects of an Arab revolt led by the Sharif of Mecca; Allenby could have issued different orders about the occupation of Damascus; Milner could have refused to be entangled in compromising negotiations with Zaghlul; the British government could have decided that the importation of an outsider to rule Mesopotamia was ill-judged and dangerous. The historical enterprise does indeed assume that what was done need not have been done at all, or need not have been done in the manner in which it came to be done. And if things had been done differently, it is a safe assumption that the consequences would have been different, even though we cannot possibly know what these other consequences would have been, how those involved would have responded, or how their different interests would have benefited or suffered. The historian, again, cannot take the actions and thoughts which he narrates to be instances of a law, nor can he consider them to be simply an epiphenomenon deriving its meaning and significance from a hidden structure which, so to speak, bodies it forth.

These remarks are inspired by some reactions which *The Chatham House Version* attracted when it was first published in 1970. The points made in two review articles, by Professor Arnold J Toynbee and Sir Alec Kirkbride ('Was Britain's Abdication Folly?', *The Round Table,* April and July 1970), may usefully sum up these reactions. The writers attribute what they call Britain's abdication of rule in the middle east during the period covered by *The Chatham House Version* to its decline as a world power and to its diminished military capacity. The forces of nationalism simultaneously became irresistible, and the British Empire therefore uncontrollable. In the circumstances, so it is alleged, the British people were unwilling to embark on a reconquest of empire. But this argument is muddled, because it is anachronistic. It transports a state of affairs and a state of mind which came to exist in the decades following the second world war, and particularly after 1956, to the period between 1919 and 1945. In fact, during this earlier period there is no evidence that policy-makers were guided in their decisions by a belief that the empire was on the decline, or that nationalism was an uncontrollable force which rendered the empire ungovernable. It is true that immediately after the first world war military expenditure began to be scaled down considerably. But this was because the British government believed that there was little prospect of a major European war. Ministers, however, did not believe that Britain was too weak to control either India or the middle east, and the record between the wars proved them right. There were of course some disturbances in India—chiefly in the Punjab—in Egypt, Iraq, and Palestine during 1919 and 1920. But these were short-lived and they were quelled with relative ease. So far as the middle east was concerned, it was after these disturbances were put down that policy-makers decided that British interests could be preserved more economically and with less trouble if local leaders were to be installed in power and if British imperial interests were secured through treaties, the ultimate guarantee of which would, of course, be British military and naval preponderance in the area.

Toynbee is particularly insistent on the inevitability of what he called British abdication in the middle east. This is a curious paradox in someone for whom challenge-and-response is the motor of history. Such a notion *ipso facto* rules out the foreordained and the inevitable. The response to a challenge can never be anything mechanical or automatic. Implicit in the very idea of a response is that it could have been other than what, in the event, it was. Toynbee believes for some reason that Western rule over non-Westerners was bound to be short-lived, that like the North American colonists, malcontents in the middle east would have been sure to resort to force, that British policy-makers saw the red light and conceded before being willy-nilly evicted from the middle east. In the absence of evidence, such arguments, one must conclude, seem to be justifications for political positions associated with what I have called the Chatham Version, rather than genuine historical judgments.

As the evidence shows, British policies discussed in this book were not adopted under compulsion. They were a matter of choice. They are of interest to the historian precisely because they were a matter of choice, not an automatic and unthinking reaction. There would indeed be little point in exploring the assumptions, implications, and consequences of British responses to middle-eastern conditions during the period covered by this book if Toynbee, Kirkbride, and others are right, if—to mention episodes discussed in this book—there was really no alternative to what Allenby and Milner did over Egypt between 1919 and 1922, to what Churchill decreed about Mesopotamia in 1920, to Cornwallis refusing to allow British troops to enter Baghdad in 1941 in order to quell looting and murder. History would then lose its savour and the historical enterprise would be a pointless recital of inevitabilities.

Toynbee and the others are wrong and doubly so: not only did the British Empire have a lot of elbow-room in the middle east between the wars, but also the policy-makers themselves believed that this was the case—indeed continued to do so even when, with India gone, their room for manoeuvre had shrunk considerably. For as late as 1956, Eden was convinced that Great Britain could take action on its own in order to bring Egypt to heel, and safeguard the real preeminence which he believed his country still enjoyed in the middle east.

Two other volumes, *Arabic Political Memoirs and Other Studies* and *Islam in the Modern World and Other Studies,* published in 1974 and 1980 respectively, contain chapters which complement and augment the studies published in this book.

E. K.

January 1984

The Chatham House Version
and other Middle-Eastern Studies

The Middle East and the Powers

Ever since the nineteenth century, when so-called reforms were initiated in the Ottoman empire, there have not been wanting western ministers and diplomats to look on middle eastern politics with hope and expectancy. It is quite common knowledge that in the last hundred years the middle east has seen no quiet, that disturbance has suceeded disturbance, and that violent, categorical men have followed each other to prescribe and apply drastic but unavailing remedies. It might therefore seem more prudent to assume that the distemper of the modern east is not a passing one, that its political instability is rather the outcome of a deep social and intellectual crisis which the schemes of the reformer and the goodwill of the philanthropist can scarcely assuage or modify. And yet the sober assumption that middle eastern instability is today endemic has found little favour either in Britain or in America. The prevalent fashion has been to proclaim the latest revolution as the herald of a new day, and the newest turbulence as the necessary and beneficent prelude to an epoch of orderliness and justice.

The meliorism of western liberals, the activist categories and the hopeful concepts of their political science go far to explain such an attitude, as also their conviction that a stable, universal peace will ensue only when the world is composed of democratic and progressive nation-states. Whatever the truth of this dogma, it is not one which a statesman should entertain, and indeed it is irrelevant to him whether the events with which he has to cope are milestones on a road leading somewhere, or mere variations on an eternal theme eternally repeated.

The ultimate significance of social and political change, and the remote consequences of action, are dim and uncertain. The power of chance, the accident of personality, the ritual of tradition, and the passions of men are always at work to mock benevolence and denature its contrivances. It is enough for practical men to fend off present evils and secure existing interests. They must not cumber themselves with historical dogmas, or chase illusions in that maze of double talk which western political vocabulary has extended over the whole world.

But when recent British and American policies in the middle east are considered, together with the doctrines and principles which justify them, then it is realised what a large part verbal traps and dubious dogmas have had in the construction of doctrines and the shaping of policies. The reasons for this are many. The fact that the middle east is remote, that its traditions and its codes of behaviour are alien, should not by itself have necessarily led to misunderstanding. The unfamiliar may invite caution as well as recklessness. But in this case the remoteness meant that it was difficult and in many cases impracticable to judge and to criticise in the light of common sense and experience certain interpretations of middle eastern history and politics offered to the Americans and the British by interpreters who seemed expert and well placed. Among the most influential of these in America are the missionaries. Their case is curious: they went out to proselytise and have stayed to sympathise. To America they began, since some fifty years ago, to present a picture of Islam as a strict unitarian version of Protestantism, democratic and egalitarian. The task before Christians, they said, was not to make converts from Islam to Christianity, it was rather to lean over middle eastern society with compassion, to take it by the hand, and rescue it from centuries of superstition, corruption and tyranny. Essentially and basically, Islam was enlightened and progressive. The western education which they, the missionaries, provided would serve to make Muslims aware of the true value of their religion and to inculcate in them a sense of brotherhood towards the Christians who, after all, worship – albeit in their own manner – the same true God as the Muslims. And in fact, it is asserted, this is what is more and more happening in the middle east. Enlightenment is spreading, the rulers are acquiring a public conscience, and democracy becomes stronger every day. To take a recent instance of the attitudes of these missionaries: 'The time seems ripe', writes the Reverend Erich W. Bethman,[1] director of the Department of Research and Publications of the American Friends of the Middle East, 'to usher in the era of cooperation – a cooperation based on mutual respect for and esteem of the deep spiritual qualities inherent in both religions. These

2

qualities are a part of every believing Muslim and every believing Christian, finding in each their deepest realisation in prayer, "and where prayer, love and mercy dwell, there God is dwelling too".'

Such an interpretation of the middle eastern situation is difficult to dislodge, and not only because its sponsors are authoritative and well placed. Two other factors at least allow such an interpretation to go unchallenged. The first, as has been said, is that of remoteness. One of the simplest and yet most effective means known to mankind of keeping touch with reality is to contrast what people say with what they do, to compare professions with performance. In one's own society, with a clear conception of one's position and interests, with a familiar knowledge of the meaning of words and the significance of behaviour, a test such as this seldom fails. But a Power such as America is unlikely to have a clear and settled conception of its interest in every distant part of the world where events compel her to have a policy. Alien conventions and unfamiliar speech add to the confusion. Reports are uncertain, actions dissolve in a haze, causes and consequences alike shadowy and unsubstantial, and those in power seem more the emanations of current legend and fashionable doctrine than solid men of flesh and blood, who take bribes and make conspiracies, who deport, imprison and kill. All too often, therefore, assumptions are not tested on the pulse of experience, they remain mere abstract doctrins, and men   are taken up and praised for what they say rather than for what they are. This tendency is reinforced by a second, powerful factor. The language of modern English and American politics is now adopted by the whole world and, divorced from the tradition in which it has value and dignity, becomes a debased, inflated jargon, a showman's patter by which tyranny is made to seem constitutional, and crookedness to look straight. The snare of this familiarity, more than any exotic remoteness, entraps the mind with smooth explanations and plausible theories. 'Therefore,' we read of our condition in Holy Scripture, 'is the name of it called Babel because the Lord did there confound the language of all the earth.'

The missionary arguments have their equivalents in Britain. They are not identical, but they tend to the same conclusions. Influential orientalists and commentators on oriental affairs have been successful in spreading a deep sense of guilt among the English intellectual and political classes. The west, they have argued, has sinned grievously. It has sinned from ignorance and presumption, and it has sinned from

3

cupidity. It has been contemptuous of eastern values, and it has taken advantage of eastern weakness to impose its domination. In its pure condition, the academics have said, Islam is more wholesome than western civilisation. It forbids drunkenness, prohibits usury, and makes very difficult the war of the classes. And what has the west, what has Britain done? It has let vice loose in the east, it has made cupidity attractive and has shattered the harmony of the classes. These assertions contain sufficient truth to make them plausible, but the passion and the tenacity with which they have been held and advanced vindicate neither the judgment nor the discretion of their authors. For they have not been content merely to expound a theory on the nature and history of Islam. They have condemned, rebuked and recommended. They have said that the action of France and Britain after the first world war twisted and deformed the political development of the Arab countries. There were then upright, moderate Arab nationalists who were prepared to cooperate with the west and to set up modern, enlightened and progressive polities. They were thwarted, betrayed, and driven to violence and extreme courses. Britain conspired with France and the Zionists, to deny the Arabs their just claims and to bring ruin on them. The least that the west could now do was to make amends for their sins, to repair the moral and material damage it had sinfully wrought. It had to promote and guarantee Arab unity, to provide political support for Arab nationalism, and to give ample, unconditional economic aid. This, of course, is now a familiar weapon of Arab propaganda, but the weapon was forged and perfected by English writers and scholars.

Their work was made easier by two circumstances. The first lay in the nature of Anglo-American historiography dealing with recent political events. Some of the most influential versions of the origins and consequences of the first world war were based on the assumption or rather the conviction, that the war and the unsatisfactory settlement which followed it were both due to the operations of powerful and sinister interests trying to realise their aims by secret diplomacy. Had diplomacy been open, it was argued, many disastrous consequences would have been averted, and governments would not have dared to avow, much less try to secure, their illicit and dangerous ambitions. Now it was of course the case that the Allies had concerted the settlement of the eastern question by means of secret agreements, and this was enough therefore to denounce this settlement – which was not particularly concerned with pan-Arab ambitions – as immoral, dishonourable and worthless. This explains, for instance, the extraordinary currency which, even today, George Antonius' tendentious history still enjoys as an authority on the transactions of the Allies with the Arabs and the Zionists.

The other circumstance which has confirmed the current picture of modern middle eastern history, as it obtains in Britain, is the outcome of an accident, the consequences of which are prodigious and inexhaustible. This accident is the involvement of Lawrence and his friends in British middle eastern policy. Lawrence was an outsider who suddenly rose to fame and power in the space of a very few years. He had neither the *esprit de corps*, nor the understanding of the state's position and interest which comes from the constant and regular practice of government and diplomatic negotiation. His impassioned apologetic was therefore violently eccentric and out of all relation to the facts. This in itself is not surprising; what is surprising is that powerful and influential men, neither outsiders nor eccentrics, accepted and embraced a version of history so subversive of their country's position and so contemptuous of traditional instruments of its welfare such as the army and the civil service. The burden of Lawrence's complaint, and the refrain of his party, was that a great act of injustice had been committed against the Arabs by reactionary politicians and their ridiculous civil servants. This had happened because these men were ignorant of the new forces in the east, and because of their criminal weakness in the face of the satanic designs of France. Lawrence and his friends spoke not as mere students of politics, but with authority. They had been there, in this new east, they were acquainted with the new men, and they recommended them heartily to the British public. And this again is a matter for surprise. What surprises is not so much Lawrence's own extravagance as that of his friends, who took up and sponsored little conspiratorial officers devoid of political style and filled with tedious political fanaticisms.

The result of all this has been to establish as a commonplace of political discussion that the two most important issues confronting statesmen in the middle east are Zionism and imperialism. It is asserted that these two factors are at the root of instability in the area. If these two factors could somehow be removed, or if the Arabs could be convinced that they have been removed, or at least neutralised, then there would be a hopeful prospect of peace and prosperity. How sound is such an analysis? Two questions arise at once. Are these,

5

in the first place, issues capable of settlement; and, in the second, even if they were settled, would peace and progress establish their dominion in the middle east?

What may one properly mean by a settlement of the Palestine problem? Because of the shape and history of the dispute, one cannot mean a settlement of the dispute which arose between the Palestinians, Zionist and Arab. This dispute has become secondary and, indeed forgotten. The dispute now lies between Israel and the Arab states; but to put the matter in this way is to confuse the accidental with the essential; for in this wider dispute Israel is the immediate but not the most important factor. This lies in the rivalries of the Arab states which led them to form an Arab League in which each party tried to gain the ascendancy. Of this game Palestinian Arabs – together with the oriental Jewries – were the hapless victims. A solution of the Palestine problem, we may therefore say, will accomplish little even if all the Israelis were exterminated and their state destroyed. For then would perhaps come a quarrel about the spoils and issues even more intractable, but certainly not peace.

Imperialism, as an issue of practical politics, is even more deceptive and irrelevant. For what can it mean to say that imperialism has to be eliminated before peace can be assured in the middle east? For some time now it has meant that what remains of British and French influence in the middle east had to be destroyed. This obviously does not entail the elimination of the influence of the other Great Powers, on the contrary. But to replace British and French influence and rivalries by American and Soviet ones is not necessarily to secure greater prosperity or a firmer peace. If, however, the contention means that peace cannot be secured in the area until all great Powers cease to have influence in the middle east, then it is a nonsensical one, the outcome of fashionable western sentimentality which holds that Great Powers are nasty and small Powers virtuous. Further, since Great Powers necessarily must always wield influence in this area, the contention becomes an empty slogan further to confuse and debase the language of political discourse.

The elimination of British and French power and influence in the middle east may, of course, have been thought to redound to the benefit of the United States, and indulgence in current political jargon, it may be argued, was a convenient smoke-screen the better to reach this objective. If use of jargon implies no doctrinal commitment, then we may enquire whether the elimination of British and French

6

influence had to remain a permanent aim of United States policy, and how far the acceptance, and further propagation, of such a jargon could help to establish the influence of the United States in the area. The elimination of Britain and France, however, has strengthened not merely the United States but also the Soviet Union. This is not only the unwitting result of a particular policy, as was the case with American action at the time of the Suez expedition, but is inherent in the very logic of the situation. Short of enforcing her claim by war, the United States cannot be the only patron in the area; and with Britain and France eliminated, some clients at least, in the hope of satisfying their local ambitions, will find attractive the patronage of the only other Great Power remaining, namely, the Soviet Union. Such a situation, as Britain eventually found to her cost, provides a temptation which it is difficult to resist, and which may lead to great loss. The fortuitous and temporary absence of Russia from the middle east after 1917 meant that Britain and France remained there face to face, and the traditional triangular or quadrilateral game of the Eastern Question as it was perfected in the nineteenth century could no longer be played. Anti-French prejudices, which coloured so much of British political attitudes between the wars, made it seem, therefore, safe, reasonable and attractive to edge the French out of the Levant, so that Britain would remain the sole dominant power. In the event, this led to the undoing not only of the French position but of the British position as well. The very same arguments that were used, with British encouragement and applause, against the French, were later turned against Britain with equal effect. History, it is true, neither teaches lessons nor repeats itself, and where Britain failed the United States may well succeed. However, if the United States and the Soviet Union are the only patrons, they are likely both to be forced into the same posture. They must try to outbid one another. But with the Soviet Union as competitor, it does not seem profitable for the United States to ride, out of conviction or convenience, the anti-imperialist wave. Neither has the Soviet Union found much profit in becoming the patron of pan-Arabism. Britain tried to do it and promoted the Arab League, but like the Old Man of the Sea the extravagant rhetoric and inflated ambitions conjured up on that occasion remained inexorably to cramp and cripple all attempts to follow a saner policy. Anti-imperialism in the middle east as an issue of practical politics is either irrelevant or nonsensical. It increases misunderstandings, and promotes illusions, to the benefit of agitators and those who know how, and do not scruple, to use them. In such a game the losers are the peaceable and the civilised.

Tidy doctrines, then, will not help, and simple answers will deceive. The disorder of the east is deep and endemic, and the disappearance neither of Israel nor of so-called imperialism will cure or even mitigate it. The very attempts to modernise middle eastern society, to make it western or 'democratic' must bring about evils, which may be greater than the benefits. Today it is fashionable to say that the prosperity coming to certain countries in the middle east from oil, from foreign aid and from increased economic activity will in the end mean the development of that middle class hitherto so notoriously absent from Muslim history and which will prove a bulwark of constitutionality and freedom. This hope is presumably based on an analogy with European and American history, an analogy, which is, however, quite false. The middle classes in Europe and America attained their greatness by their own efforts, without the help of government as in America, sometimes against the obstruction of aristocrats and absolutists as in Europe. But whereas economic enterprise was in the west predominantly the affair of individuals, in the middle east it is predominantly the affair of governments. The British government neither opened up the coal mines of the British Isles nor claimed to share the profits of the enterprise with the mine owners; similarly the government of the United States did not claim that every Texan who found oil in his backyard should give up half the value of his property to the state. It may be argued that this has caused great discrepancies in wealth, and that the benefits of wealth were distributed at random, in proportion neither to merit nor to need. This may well be, but such a state of affairs is inseparable from the libertarianism, the independence and the mistrust of authority which are traditionally associated with the qualities of the middle classes in the west, and which, it is now hoped, can somehow be transplanted in the middle east. But in this area government is the chief entrepreneur. It is the recipient of oil royalties and of foreign aid, and it is through its decisions and its favours that prosperity filters through to the generality of the people. Again, it may be argued that this arrangement is the one most conducive to the greatest welfare; but in this case, it has to be recognised that it does not diminish, but rather magnifies and exaggerates, the power of government. In Europe, the middle classes attained political power after becoming economically predominant. In the middle east it looks as though modern economic processes will lead to no such result, since these processes only accentuate what has always been a character of Muslim society, namely the dependence of all ranks and classes on the central political authority. Now, as in the past, wealth generally depends on access to political power, on the benevolence or at least the acquiescence of those in power. In an area where political power is traditionally capricious in the transmission, acquired by violence and established by repression, it is the caprice of those in power rather than the impersonality of the economic process which gives society its predominant character and its characteristic visage. And what must also tend to confirm habits and an established character is that this new wealth is not the product of local enterprise, but seems a sudden, capricious windfall, the tribute which a miraculous Providence has compelled the Powers of Europe and America to press upon the east.

Another modern development which tends in the same direction is an outcome of westernisation. European administrative techniques have been put at the disposal of the local governments who have been thus enabled, as never before, to exert a minute systematic control over social and economic activities. New methods of import licensing, exchange control, and fiscal supervision have made private persons quite dependent on the goodwill of those in authority who are able, when they choose, to punish the object of their malice and ill-will swiftly and effectively. It is by such means that the Iraqi government was able efficiently to spoil and loot the Jews of Iraq, and by similar means that the government of Egypt has been able recently to follow in its footsteps. This new power of government makes even more complete the dependence of the economic on the political, and must thus hinder the emergence of that independent middle class on which so much hope is set. This increase in the power of government affects not only the economic sphere, but extends in all directions. The modernisation of society in the middle east has not been the result of private initiative and the gradual adaptation of a local tradition to changing conditions. Rather, it has been imposed from above, by decree, and implemented, as far as possible, by officials. This meant that the traditional articulation of middle eastern society had either to bend to the will of the reformer or be completely dislocated. Such has been the fate of Muslim as well as non-Muslim religions and communal organisations, of provincial particularisms, of

9

local and vested interests. Individuals are now equal under the law, corporations the creatures of statute, and law and statute the irresistible will of a central and sovereign authority.

This increase and concentration in the power of government is the most striking consequence, so far, of the attempt to westernise middle eastern society. It has given new life to the political attitudes prevalent in Muslim society, it has confirmed the subject in his passive obedience to the effective ruler, and the ruler for the time being in the amplitude of his power. Political stability in such a situation is, of necessity, chancy and precarious. The traditional checks and balances have grown progressively weaker, habits of liberty are unknown, and the subject has more reason than ever to fear the displeasure of his masters. To get hold of power, it is sufficient to get hold of the central mechanism, and the rewards of power are prodigious. This instability is increased by the character of the men who now compete for power. They are new men whose earliest and deepest political impulse is contempt for the ways of their fathers. Youth, which in most countries and ages has been a disqualification for the practice of government, has become, since the days of the Young Turks, an advantage in the contest for power. The dislocation of society is made more acute by estrangement between the generations. The young are those who possess the techniques of Europe which middle eastern society – so they insist – must adopt or perish. Therefore they know better than their fathers, and they have the key to political salvation. The passion and presumption of youth, their rooted belief in their ancestors' ignorance and folly, their inexperience and clumsiness in the exercise of power, combine to deprive them of that decorum and *gravitas* which impressed foreign observers in the Muslim ruling classes of past centuries, and which served to put a decent check on the full expression of greed and cruelty. Heaven knows that sedition, treason and civil war are common enough in middle eastern history, but only in the present age is revolution glorified as a necessary part of the political process, violence proclaimed beneficent and treason holy.

The institutions and the men who control them combine together to make these unfortunate middle eastern polities the victims of instability and the sport of civil commotion. This has been the case ever since the Young Turks came to power, and there is no sign of change. If only because of these factors it would be prudent to expect trouble, and not to put too much faith in simple solutions and neat explanations. But there are also other reasons which concern more intimately the conduct of foreign policy. The Muslim theory of international relations recognises two possible situations only: war on the infidel or his subjugation to the faithful. Peace with him *de jure* is impossible; there can only be various grades of active or passive hostility until he recognises the authority of the Muslim ruler. Such indeed has been not only the theory but the practice in the relations of Muslim and Christian powers. The disturbed frontiers between Israel and her neighbours today are nothing exceptional; they exemplify rather what has normally been the case on the frontier between Christendom and Islam. The concepts therefore of international law and practice which have been current for centuries in the Christian west, concepts such as the concert of the Powers, the comity of nations, or the sanctity of treaties, the rules of natural justice, or 'decent respect for the opinions of mankind', are quite alien and largely unintelligible to the middle east. It is significant that the Ottoman empire was formally made a member of the concert of Europe only after the Crimean war, when it had lost its superiority and was being gradually overwhelmed by the Christian Powers. It is not surprising then that to Muslim minds the western vocabulary of international relations should appear little relevant to their most important preoccupation, namely, the steady encroachment by Christian Powers over the domain of Islam. The same may be said of the Muslims' attitude to the two creations of the western theory of international relations: the League of Nations and the United Nations. For by the time these institutions came to be set up the Christian Powers seemed more powerful and dominating than ever. The Muslim states thought of themselves not as mere quiescent members of the comity of nations, but as fighters engaged in an active struggle against the very Powers who claimed to set the tone and establish the rules of behaviour in international relations. Their adherence to the western principles of international relations is as formal as the admittance of the Ottoman empire to the concert of Europe in 1856.

These traditional Muslim attitudes have been confirmed and fortified by nationalist doctrine, which of all western political doctrines has been the most popular and the best understood in the middle east. The international theory of nationalism is as little disposed as the Muslim theory to envisage a stable international order as a practical possibility. The Muslim theory postpones this to the day when the last infidel shall have made his obeisance to the Caliph,

while nationalist theory postpones it to the day when national vindi-
cations shall have been all satisfied. Both are subversive of international stability, both are activist, both consider conflict not a
regrettable evil, nor even the continuation of diplomacy by other
means but, so long as a single imperfection subsists in the world, or
so long as a single principle remains unrealised, a duty the discharge
of which is exhilarating and rewarding. Against all this turbulence
a simple strategy does not avail. Resource, cunning, patience, and
steadfastness can scarce contend with it. But even they will fail once
it is thought they can do more than keep disorder at bay.

Cairo and Khartoum on the Arab Question, 1915-1918

The Arab question in British diplomacy, it is remarkable to observe, has conjured up, both among those directly involved and among subsequent commentators, an amount of passionate discussion, of anguished retrospection, of accusation and self-denunciation quite out of proportion to its intrinsic importance. For after all, compared to the great issues of Europe, America, the Commonwealth and India, the Husain–McMahon Correspondence, the Sykes–Picot Agreement, the Balfour Declaration are small and paltry transactions which, as luck would have it, have turned out, it is true, to be inopportune and profitless and the cause of much loss and tribulation. For the historian of the middle east, of course, the British connection must loom very large by reason of its immediate impact and of its ultimate consequences, but in British history can the short-lived middle-eastern episode be more than a passing incident in the Indian summer of the empire? For they are perhaps right, those who assert that had Britain been able to retain India, her middle eastern position could probably have been maintained, regardless of mistakes and confusions in middle eastern policy itself, and that India once gone, neither virtue nor virtuosity would have availed to preserve Suez, Haifa and Habbaniyya. But this cool, sceptical view is rarely met in the writings either of the participants or of the subsequent commentators, whose mode is one of burning regret and vehement lamentations, and who are for ever weighing good faith against bad faith, promises kept and promises broken, scrutinising motives and examining scruples, like the diligent followers of some strict pietism, oppressed by sin and dolefully thirsting for justification.

It is curious to trace this feeling of sinfulness to its earliest origins, to see whence it could have arisen, to elucidate the now forgotten transactions which engendered it, and the confusions and ambiguities which nurtured it. On 12 September 1916 there was held in Cairo a conference at which were present many British high officials, including the high commissioner, the commander-in-chief of the Egyptian Expeditionary Force, Colonel G. F. Clayton, who was then Sudan agent in Cairo and in charge of Intelligence in Egypt, and Colonel C. E. Wilson, governor of the Sudan Red Sea province, then representing the British government in Jedda. At this conference, held to consider the critical position of the Sharifian rebellion which then seemed on the point of collapsing, Sir Henry McMahon, seeming much exercised by this difficult situation, and vexed by the unhelpful and contradictory suggestions of his interlocutors, was moved to put on record how it came about that he should now be saddled with the sharif of Mecca and his problems.

It was the most unfortunate date in my life when I was left in charge of this Arab movement [he said] and I think a few words are necessary to explain that it is nothing to do with me: it is a purely military business. It began at the urgent request of Sir Ian Hamilton at Gallipoli. I was begged by the Foreign Office to take immediate action and draw the Arabs out of the war. At that moment a large portion of the [Turkish] force at Gallipoli and nearly the whole of the force in Mesopotamia were Arabs, and the Germans were then spending a large amount of money in detaching the rest of the Arabs, so the situation was that the Arabs were between the two. Could we give them some guarantee of assistance in the future to justify their splitting with the Turks? I was told to do that at once and in that way I started the Arab movement.[1]

Sir Henry McMahon's blunt and cursory account indicates the precise date at which the possibilities of Sharifian rebellion began to be taken seriously, and the military exigencies which gave rise to this new attitude. Before the autumn of 1915, British ministers did not think that a Sharifian movement would be efficient or useful in the short run, and they were afraid that in the long run encouragement of the sharif would be troublesome and costly. This, certainly, was Lord Curzon's view. In the spring and summer of 1915 Lord Cromer was plying him with suggestions emanating from Sir Reginald Wingate in Khartoum that the sharif of Mecca be encouraged with liberal promises of future aggrandisement, to secede from the Ottoman empire and put himself at the head of a movement for Arab independence. In a letter to Cromer of 22 April 1915, Curzon deprecated the idea that promises and declarations be made to the Arabs. The British, he pointed out, were not yet in Constantinople; and further, what evidence had the Arabs shown that they would be able to administer an Arab state extending from the Persian gulf to Egypt? Again, was it not futile, he asked, to proclaim a new state which would be without territory, capital or ruler? Why, lastly, should the British government prejudge the issue of the war and at once promise Basra and Baghdad 'to a people who are at this moment fighting against us as hard as they can and known to be in the pay of the Germans?'[2] A few months later, in reply to further talk about an Arabian caliphate, Curzon expressed great scepticism about the capacity of the sharif. The sharif, he agreed, was a descendant of the Prophet, but this apart, what could he accomplish? If the British government recognised him as caliph, would they not be bound to go to his support 'when his khalifate begins to totter or crumble'? He was not greatly attracted to the perils of oriental politics where, as he remarked, 'we usually put our money on the wrong horse'.[3] Lord Curzon's views were not peculiar to himself. Official opinion at that time viewed with misgivings any plan to partition the Ottoman empire. The committee on Asiatic Turkey set up in April 1915 by the prime minister under the chairmanship of Sir Maurice de Bunsen regarded partition as by far the least satisfactory solution of the Eastern Question; the solution which they themselves favoured was for the Ottoman empire to remain substantially intact and its ad ministration decentralised.

That the sharif, as leader of an Arab union and as caliph, was not the wrong horse to back, was emphatically the view of Sir Reginald Wingate. In a letter to Lord Stamfordham of 5 September 1915, he indicated what moved him to 'push the future Arab union for all it is worth'. Before the war, he wrote, he had supported and upheld the Turkish connection on utilitarian grounds. But when the Turks took the German side

I joined more vehemently perhaps, than others in the hue and cry against them. . . . Besides [he continued], I had to govern a country in which the very name of 'Turk' stinks in the nostrils of the people. They have been ground under the heel of the Turk and Egyptian (to them the names are synonymous) and were in close proximity to the Arabs of Arabia, who entertain very similar feelings to their own in regard to their Turkish masters. For these reasons, I – who so warmly supported the Turk on utilitarian grounds — now espoused the Arab cause with still greater warmth and with more real sympathy.[5]

This sympathy and preference for the Arab over the Turk which, as

Wingate explains, came from service in the Sudan, was to leave its mark on British policy during the war and long afterwards. Indeed, Wingate's words express some of that sentimentality, so much in contrast with Curzon's scepticism, and so misplaced in politics, which was yet to colour official British attitudes until the sixth decade of the twentieth century, to disappear, perhaps finally, only at the murder of the Hashimites and of Nuri al-Sa'id in Baghdad on 14 July 1958. This sentimental bias was reinforced by arguments from policy. On the outbreak of war with the Ottoman empire, British officials in Egypt and the Sudan had to cope with widespread Muslim hostility, and to guard against its possibly serious consequences on internal security and military operations. A British understanding with the sharif, advertising a split in Muslim ranks, would bring them welcome relief and enable them to rebut Ottoman charges that Britain was waging an anti-Muslim war. Hence they were concerned to open and maintain negotiations with the sharif and would not want them abandoned.[6] It followed that they had to refute any allegations tending to throw doubt on the sharif's standing and capacity. Thus both Wingate in Khartoum and Clayton in Cairo were ready to answer the objections to the sharif raised by the India Office, by the government of India and by others. Clayton, in a note of July 1915 declared emphatically that the sharif possessed most of the attributes considered by Muslims essential for the caliphate, and was also undoubtedly the most suitable from the British point of view.[7] Wingate equally emphatically supported Clayton's view and added that the consensus of the Sudanese *ulama* was that the sharif was in every way qualified for the caliphate.[8] The sharif, he said in answer to the objections from the India Office, was not a nonentity; the India Office exaggerated the differences between Arab chieftains, and in any case Husain was well able to compose such differences.[9]

The urgent tone of the officials in Khartoum and Cairo is easily appreciated. Their responsibility for internal security, their proximity to the Ottoman theatre of war, made them eager to close a deal with the sharif and impatient with the delays and objections to which they were subjected from London. There was a grave risk, they were convinced, that if their aspirations were not satisfied, the Arabs would irrevocably side with the Turks. When, at the end of October 1915, negotiations with the sharif were at last begun in earnest, Clayton wondered whether it was not already too late; but if not, it was a near thing, he thought. By the middle of the following November, when the India Office were still objecting to the sharif's demands, McMahon telegraphed to warn the authorities that the matter brooked no more delay, and to reinforce his argument cited a letter from the sharif to Sayid Ali al-Mirghani, the Sudanese religious dignitary, to the effect that if the British did not hasten to make an agreement, the Arabs would give their support to the Turks and the Germans.[10] But even if we bear in mind their anxiety about Egypt and Muslim opinion, yet such haste and urgency in a case which was by no means so pressing or so dangerous as they represented, such eagerness at once to concede the patently inflated claims which the sharif must have advanced in expectation of long and arduous bargaining, still remain surprising in cautious and experienced officials. The exigencies of the hour do not completely account for their attitude. They were worried certainly about the immediate future, but they also wanted to seize the opportunity of the war to advance a scheme, which were it to succeed, would greatly increase Great Britain's power and influence in the middle east, would indeed make it the arbiter of the destinies of Islam in the world. A passage in a letter of March 1915 from Storrs to Colonel FitzGerald, Kitchener's military secretary, gives a hint of their hopes and ambitions. 'A North African or near eastern vice-royalty including Egypt and the Sudan and across the way from Aden to Alexandretta would surely', Storrs enthusiastically affirmed, 'compare in interest and complexity, if not in actual size, with India itself'.[11] Such a design goes far to explain their readiness to grant with little haggling or discussion what the sharif demanded. Their views are cogently put in a letter from Wingate to Lord Hardings, then viceroy of India, dated 26 August 1915. He was, he said, increasingly drawn to a pan-Arab scheme as an antidote to the aggressive pan-Islamism of the Ottoman empire. Pan-Arabism would bring about a balance of power in the central area of Islam. The historic position of the Arabs within Islam made them the only effective counterpoise to the anglophobia of the Ottomans which, he feared, would increase after the war. He had, he said, no illusions about the difficulties of his scheme, 'but I conceive it to be not impossible that in the dim future a federation of semi-independent Arab states might exist under European guidance and supervision, linked together by racial and linguistic bonds, owing spiritual allegiance to a single Arab primate, and looking to Great Britain as its patron and protector'.[12] Wingate was therefore in favour of expressing 'pious aspiration on the subject of the sharif's idea of an Arab union', and even of encouraging *salafis* like Rashid Rida, who not only aspired to an Islamic union in which the Arabs would have the primacy, but also desired that the political life of the Islamic state should be regulated according to the religious law.[13] 'After all', he observed to Clayton a year or so later, 'once we decided to encourage the sharif to act, we should have done all we possibly could to meet his demands without demur – this I *constantly* urged. Instead of this, we have made twenty bites out of the cherry'.[14] With Wingate's knowledge and approval, hints on these lines were conveyed to the sharif. Sayyid Ali al-Mirghani, who was then being used as an intermediary in communicating with the sharif, employed remarkably direct and clear language. In a letter of 17 November 1915 he urged the sharif to restore to the Arabs the stolen caliphate and the independence and civilisation which the Turks had destroyed; the sharif was to rise and take over the 'holy Arabian Koreishite Khalifate', and there was no man better qualified.[15] To the sharif, who knew that his correspondent was agent and not principal, these words must have seemed the categorical, unmistakable confirmation of the ambiguous hints which British official communications had earlier carried.[16] Husain thereafter persisted in believing that Britain promised him kingship over all the Arabs together with the caliphate. Since official British promises of Arab independence were addressed exclusively to him, as Hogarth wrote in a paper of March 1918, the sharif was persuaded that Arab independence necessarily meant unity under him;[17] since, further, the suggestion of an Arab caliphate had come, as he correctly pointed out to Colonel C. E. Wilson, not from him, but from the British, and what is more, had come quite unsolicited,[18] it may well have appeared to Husain that if these earlier hints were ambiguous, this was only because their authors, as non-Muslims discussing such a matter, did not think it seemly to be more explicit.

When one considers the position and prospects of the British empire as they appeared to its officials in Cairo and Khartoum, Wingate's scheme of a pan-Arab union presided over, in some fashion, by an Arab caliph, and the whole under the aegis and protection of Great Britain – a scheme which Clayton also supported – seems to be cogent and feasible. Both Wingate and Clayton advanced an attractively prudential calculation which, in their eyes, served considerably to minimise the risk of such a scheme. 'After all', Wingate argued in a letter to Clayton of 15 November 1915, 'what harm can our acceptance of his [the sharif's] proposals do? If the embryonic Arab state comes to nothing, all our promises vanish and we are absolved from them – if the Arab state becomes a reality, we have quite sufficient safeguards to control it and although eventually it might act towards its "Allied" creators as Bulgaria has acted towards Russia – I think it is in our power to erect such barriers as would effectively prevent its becoming the menace which the Indian Government appears to fear'.[19] McMahon and Clayton in Cairo, for their part, were also of exactly the same mind.[20]

One particular argument which served to confirm the Cairo and Khartoum officials in their views constituted, however, a considerable misreading of the situation. In a telegram to the Foreign Office of 3 December 1915, McMahon, still trying to overcome India Office objections, adduced in support of his position the idea that the Arab movement was 'less religious than national', and that therefore an Arab state was less dangerous to British interests than the Ottoman empire.[12] Some two months before, when Clayton had interviewed Muhammad Sharif al-Faruqi, the Ottoman officer who had deserted at Gallipoli,[22] he had been relieved to find that the claims of the Arab nationalist societies, as represented by al-Faruqi, though similar in point of territorial extent to those of Rashid Rida and his followers, were yet devoid of 'Moslem fanaticism'. Al-Faruqi and his fellow-officers were not, Clayton reported, carried away by the dream of an Arab empire; they appeared to be reasonable men, willing to compromise, and only asking for 'a general recognition of their aspirations by England and the promise of a fair measure of self-government in the various countries concerned under the guidance and with the help and support of England'.[23] This beguiling contrast between 'Moslem fanaticism' and nationalism was as wrong in theory[24] as it was useless in practice. It imported an element of doctrine which served, in an incalculable and far-reaching manner, to distort and falsify the calculations of policy. The belief that nationalist aspirations were benign and beneficial was of course no invention of Clayton's. It had become the creed of Gladstonian Liberalism, and, applied to the British empire, formed an essential part of 'Liberal Imperialism', so-called, which infected so many British statesmen at home and so many British officials overseas, at least from the beginning of the twentieth century until the liquidation of the empire. In the middle east itself the doctrine made attractive such policies as the support of Faisal both in Damascus and Baghdad, Milner's policy towards Zaghlul, Allenby's Declaration of 28 February 1922 in Egypt (supported and advocated by Clayton, among others) and, in a later decade, the encouragement of an Arab League. The outcome of these diverse policies is sufficient commentary on the doctrine.

Al-Faruqi, Clayton reported, looked to the support of England, *'but of no other Power'*. One other Power was here meant, namely France, and France indeed represented then the most serious obstacle to the scheme of Arab unity under British patronage as mooted in Cairo and Khartoum. The officials here were aware of French claims, and were indeed kept regularly informed of the Anglo–French negotiations which issued in the Sykes–Picot Agreement of 1916, and which began in London in November 1915. The records of these negotiations in the *Wingate Papers* are too fragmentary for a complete and coherent account, but the evidence unmistakably shows that Cairo and Khartoum views were continuously put before the Foreign Office by Sir Herny McMahon, and before the War Office by General Maxwell, the G.O.C., Egypt. Further, Wingate himself in extensive private correspondence with Lord Stamfordham, Sir Clive Wigram, Lord Cromer and others endeavoured to expound and advance their views. In the War Office, Cairo and Khartoum had a valuable and zealous sympathiser, Lieutenant-Colonel A. C. Parker, Kitchener's nephew,[25] who had served in Egypt and was later to take part in the Hijaz operations and to be the civil governor of al-Arish in 1917, during Allenby's advance into Palestine. His views are set out in a note on *The Arab Movement*, which shows him to have been a strong advocate of a descent on Alexandretta and the occupation of Aleppo, and of satisfying Arab claims by buying the French out.[26] This idea was put to a committee composed of representatives from the Foreign Office, the India Office and the War Office, set up to concert a policy against Picot's forthcoming visit to London. Sir Arthur Nicolson, the permanent secretary at the Foreign Office, rejected the idea as impossible and, Parker reported to Clayton, expressed the view that the sharif's movement was incoherent and unreal.[27] Indeed, the Foreign Office and the India Office were at one in their hostility to any pan-Arab scheme under British auspices. Grey agreed with Austen Chamberlain that such a scheme would be a useless and embarrassing liability and would make agreement with France impossible. Picot met the committee on 23 November 1915, and declared himself sceptical of any Arab movement. He claimed for France the whole of Syria and Palestine, less the Holy Places, and declared that Mosul, Baghdad and Basra should satisfy the Arabs. His move was a shrewd one. Since the British were so keen on Arab support, should they not themselves make some effort to satisfy Arab claims? He, for his part, offered Mosul which he claimed to be in the French sphere; let the British offer Baghdad and Basra. The prospect, held out to him, of a large-scale desertion of Arab troops from the Ottoman armies, failed to tempt him, and an *impasse* was reached.[28] Immediately afterwards Parker, as he wrote to Clayton, began preparing a paper, to be signed by General Callwell, who was not, as he put it, 'exactly red hot yet' for the Arab movement, which threatened dire catastrophes – Mohammedan uprisings in British possessions, withdrawal of British forces from France, etc. – if the sharif's demands were not immediately granted.[29] These exaggerations – if they indeed met with Callwell's approval – failed to move Picot, and we find Clayton writing to Parker on 10 December that if progress was to be made Picot had to be replaced.[30] In the event, of course, as is well known, a compromise was reached which, in Syria, meant that the territory of the four towns of Damascus, Homs, Hama and Aleppo would constitute an Arab state under French influence.[31]

It is this latter provision, that the French were to be the predominant power in the territory of the four towns, which, from the beginning, gave the Sykes–Picot Agreement a bad name with the officials in Cairo and Khartoum, not because it conflicted with the so-called 'McMahon pledge' to the sharif or prevented, or even delayed, agreement with him; but rather because it meant a setback to their scheme of a middle east entirely under British tutelage. From the very start of Anglo-Sharifian negotiations, the British side were quite aware that the sharif's demands, in respect of territory, were, for the purposes of bargaining, pitched very high. 'He knows', wrote Storrs in a note of 19 August 1915, in a comment on a letter which set out the sharif's demands, 'he is demanding, possibly as a basis for negotiation, far more than he has the right, the hope, or the power to expect'.[32] The ambiguities of Anglo–Sharifian diplomacy were to be the occasion, in later years, of much controversy, but at the time the British officials in Cairo, made aware by the Foreign Office of possible French claims and of the need for caution, framed their proposals to the sharif in such a manner that they could be consistent with any possible Anglo–French agreement – which at the time still remained to be negotiated. Reporting on his 'pledge' to the sharif that the four towns of Damascus, Homs, Hama and Aleppo would form part of the Arab state, Sir Henry McMahon stated that by adding the qualification that Great Britain could give assurances only in regard to these territories 'in which she can act without detriment to the interests of her ally, France', he was trying to provide for possible French claims, the extent of which he did not know.[33] Al-Mirghani's letter to the sharif, mentioned above, for all its rhetoric was yet careful and deprecatory about discussing precise territorial boundaries. 'In what they told you before', al-Mirghani wrote, 'that the discussion of the frontier question was premature, they meant by saying this that the Arabian government had not yet come into existence and that the most important problem was first to have it brought to life and that any other question was secondary'.[34] Commenting on the course of the Anglo–French negotiations – and, it would seem, before the French made their concession on Syria – Wingate wrote that even if the French demands were all conceded, the British could not be accused of a serious breach of faith with the sharif.[35] In a letter to Clayton of the following April, Wingate reiterated that he was not a believer in 'a consolidated Arabian kingdom under the sharif': 'Of course', he went on, 'any such notion is altogether remote from my real views, and it has suited me, as I believe it has suited all of us, to give the leaders of the Arab movement this impression'; but impressions had to be distinguished from actual undertakings: 'we are quite sufficiently covered by the correspondence which has taken place to show that we are acting in good faith with the Arabs as far as we have gone'.[36] When agreement was finally negotiated, Clayton grudgingly admitted that there was no conflict between the two sets of undertakings. 'Luckily', he wrote, 'we have been very careful indeed to commit ourselves to nothing whatsoever [i.e. in respect of Sharifian claims]'.[37] Again Hogarth, who had intimate knowledge of the situation, writing ten years after these events, recorded that 'few of us' believed that the sharif was 'the spokesman of one united Arab nation about to rise from the ashes of the war'. 'We did not believe', he continued, 'that, either under him or under anyone else, would it so rise united. Therefore neither to him nor to any other Arab did we ever explicitly guarantee or even promise anything beyond liberation from the Turk'. 'We are guiltless, therefore', he concluded, 'of any betrayal of King Husein. The sole condition of his action – that he be freed from his Ottoman overlords and recognised as an independent sovereign – has been fulfilled'.[38] Furthermore, it is doubtful if the sharif was really much interested in territorial commitments. When he replied to McMahon's 'pledge' he refused, it is true, to concur in the former's conditions and qualifications, but it is highly interesting to note that his messenger reported to Storrs that his son Abdulla strongly emphasised the point – obviously with the intention that his words should reach the British authorities – that the 'reservations contained in the written message should not be taken too seriously'.[39] The impression is strong that the sharif, aware of his weak and isolated position in the Muslim world, and yet strongly tempted by the prospect of a caliphate, was willing, on any terms or no terms at all, to start something, provided he could involve the British government in his own fortunes. Is this not the most consistent explanation of his willingness to join the British side, even when his correspondence with McMahon showed that the tangible advantages of such a course were minimal? The weakness of his position and the temptation of the caliphate may have inclined him to disregard, and dismiss for the moment, the unsatisfactory and unsubstantial character of McMahon's pledge, but he may also have been tempted into this easy opportunism by the weakness and duplicity of his servants. Towards the end of 1916 the sharif had himself proclaimed king of the Arabs, and when the British queried the title he replied that according to his agent in Cairo, al-Faruqi, the high commissioner himself had approved it. Investigation showed that al-Faruqi, to enhance his own importance and the value of his services, had a habit of occasionally reporting to the sharif interviews with the high commissioner which had never taken place and, what is even more interesting, that he was 'apt to put into the mouth of Sir Henry things said to him by more junior people'.[40] Since the sharif himself cancelled written messages by means of oral, it would have seemed natural to him that the British government should use his agent for messages which it did not care to send in writing. The schemes which the sharif mooted before proclaiming his rebellion in June 1916 are sufficient indication of the drift of his policy. In February 1916 the messenger bringing a letter from the sharif also brought a verbal message from Abdullah. Abdullah, said the messenger, wanted £3,000 for a scheme. The scheme consisted in choosing a powerful Islamic committee who would proceed to offer his father the caliphate.[41] A little while later, the sharif asked for British help to start operations in Syria. Discussing the scheme – which was turned down – Wingate allowed that it was more convenient for the sharif to confine his operations to the Hijaz but, he observed, 'it must be remembered that his desire to strengthen his position in the Syrian hinterland is intimately connected with his aspirations to the khalifate, and that these latter aspirations are at best as important an influence on his actions as his hostility to the Turks'.[42]

Clayton, as has been seen, granted that between the Sykes–Picot Agreement and McMahon's offer to the sharif there was no contradiction, and if he knew – as he must have – the methods and ambitions of the sharif, he need have had little to exercise him about a breach of faith. Yet during the negotiations in London he expressed his disquiet and dissatisfaction at the course they were taking. In a letter of 14 January 1916 to Wingate he remarked that the proposed settlement made things very difficult and that it was 'hard to see how we can go on negotiating much longer, without laying ourselves open to a charge of a breach of faith, unless we honestly tell the Arabs that we have made Syria over to the French. The ways of our government', he concluded, 'are truly marvellous'.[43] A few days later, he was writing that 'some of our Syrian friends' seem to have realised that 'we have handed Syria over to the French', and that he was expecting trouble. They should, he thought, be told so direct and advised to settle with the French.[44] Yet when agreement was finally reached in May 1916, he was all for keeping the arrangement for the time being secret 'from our Arab friends'.[45] This embarrassment over the Sykes–Picot Agreement as at some shameful and dishonourable thing is the first intimation of a later and widely prevalent British attitude. How to account for it in Clayton? He speaks, we may notice, of 'our Arab friends', of 'some of our Syrian friends'; can it be that his embarrassment was not so much over contradictory undertakings as over hopes – now doomed – which may have been earlier aroused among Syrian Muslims like Rashid Rida or Syrian Christians like Faris Nimr, who were either keen for the British connection *per se* as the latter, or wished to use it as a defence against French ambitions like the former, hopes which were based on what Clayton himself attempted to bring about? But there was no need for concealment, for a letter from Rashid Rida of February 1916 to Wingate's Arabic secretary tells us that 'the English people here say openly that France insists on the occupation of Syria or the northern part of it and that it is quite impossible to break up with her on this account'.[46] Clayton's talk of 'our Arab friends' and 'our Syrian friends' brings into view another ambiguity in Anglo–Sharifian diplomacy. Formal negotiations, such as they were, had been carried on with the sharif, but the sharif, however much he claimed to represent all the Arabs, had in fact no authority or standing to do so. The sharif, said a note on the *Arab question* which seems to date from the beginning of 1916, 'though he has always written as spokesman of the Arab nation, is not, so far as we know, supported by any organisation of Arabs nearly general enough to secure throughout, or indeed in the larger part of the Arab area, the automatic acceptance of terms agreed to by him'.[47] The sharif, furthermore, was by no means the first, on the Arab side, to initiate contacts with Britain. These contacts, in Cairo, had been made by Syrian immigrants and their organisations, such as the Decentralisation Party, which at the outbreak of war had sent, with the knowledge of British officials, two agents to Syria and Mesopotamia to gather intelligence and carry out anti-Ottoman activities.[48] The importance of these Syrians in British eyes is indicated by the fact that, later on in the war, they were the recipients of an important declaration of policy – the Declaration to the Seven.[49] Important as these men were, yet they too could hardly claim to be fully representative, so that Clayton was justified in observing that 'no Arab central committee exists in a form capable of putting forward definite proposals, or appointing delegates, who could be considered representative of Arab as distinct from Sharifian views'.[50] This absence of a single authoritative body, this multiplicity of opinions and claims able to command official attention could not but darken counsel and blur the line between official undertakings and unofficial wishes, leading, in the end, to a maze in which were inextricably confused hints and declarations, disappointed hopes and conscientious scruples. And here may lie the explanation of Clayton's embarrassment.

The progress of the war and its uncertain prospects made Clayton recur – after policy had been settled for the time being by the signature of the Sykes–Picot Agreement – to the vital importance of the Arabs. He was on a visit to London in the summer of 1916, and there, as he wrote to Wingate, 'made the texts of any sermons which I was able to deliver at home. "Do not forget that Germany would sacrifice much (indeed almost anything) to keep her hold on Turkey – Berlin to Baghdad, Basra, Persia, Afghanistan, India, is the keynote of German Welt-Politik . . . Granted the above, our Arab policy is one of the big cards – if not the biggest in our hand and our main weapon against the habitual Moslem sympathy for the Turk" '.[51] The next opportunity to attempt an alteration of Arab policy came in the spring of 1917 when Sykes and Picot proposed to visit Egypt and the Hijaz to display Anglo–French unity and jointly to deal on the spot with difficulties and contentions. Clayton then pointed out that the sharif had not been officially informed of the Sykes–Picot Agreement and that, as an alternative to telling him about it, he should be told that Sykes and Picot were coming to examine the Syrian question *de novo*. The Foreign Office rejected the advice.[52] One may speculate on the results of such a step, had it been taken; official ignorance not-withstanding, the sharif would have drawn quite interesting con-clusions from this denial of the understanding between France and Britain which he already knew to exist. Clayton knew that the sharif was aware of the Sykes-Picot scheme, and would take advantage of the absence of such official notification to pretend that the matter was not settled, and thus open a door to possible concessions.[53] Sykes and Picot went to Jadda, saw the sharif, and put the Agree-ment in his hand; the three then came to the understanding that the French position in Syria should be similar to that of the British in Mesopotamia.[54] Clayton was quick to see the drawbacks of such an arrangement, which were indeed real enough if one assumed Anglo–French disagreement rather than agreement.

Had it only been a question of the British in Baghdad [he wrote] I do not think any difficulties would have arisen as the king probably realises that he has but little influence there, and would have been content to allow us to do pretty well as we liked. A new element has been introduced, however, by making the French position in Syria dependent on our position in Baghdad, and this is likely to make the king and the Arabs very much more attentive to what they may consider their rights and interests in Baghdad than would have ever been the case before, and I think may easily be a source of considerable embarrassment to us in Mesopotamia.[55]

Here was another bad mark against the Sykes–Picot scheme.

At the time of Sykes's and Picot's visit criticism and dislike of the Agreement swelled into a chorus. Colonel C. E. Wilson, the British representative in Jadda, had been a fervent partisan of the sharif. Urging more financial help for him in August 1916, he had said he was convinced that the sharif was the right horse to back, being probably the next caliph, and that to help him was a unique oppor-tunity to acquire influence and control.[56] He now sent a letter full of indignant pity for the poor sharif who was being asked to give his consent to things he did not understand, and of solemn warning about Sykes's 'heavy responsibility' in getting him to do so. This simple, trusting sharif who kept on saying that the word of Great Britain was enough for him, that he would do what Sir Mark Sykes wanted because he knew that Sykes would fight for the Arabs better than he himself could do, that 'he was putting the whole weight and responsibility of the future of the Arabs on Sir Mark Sykes',[57] was also capable of asking Sykes, through Faisal his son, in exchange for the arrangement on Syria, to make Ibn Sa'ud and the Idrissi acknowledge him as their king; Wilson records the episode, but does not seem to appreciate its comedy. 'If we are not going to see the sharif through', he warned, 'and we let him down badly after all his trust in us, the very "enviable"(?) post of Pilgrimage Officer at Jeddah [his ostensible office there] will be vacant because I certainly could not remain'.[58] Newcombe's voice was joined to Wilson's. Newcombe, of the Military Mission, had a conversation with Fuad al-Khatib on Sykes's and Picot's transactions, and his generous indignation was aroused. The sharif could not understand these complicated matters which they debated with him; four hours were not enough for him to decide;[59] therefore responsibility lay on the British government 'to see the sharif or Arab Cause through to the end: otherwise we are hoodwinking the sharif and his people and playing a very false game in which officers attached to the sharif's army are inevitably committed and which I know causes anxiety in several officers' minds: in case we let them down.'[60] The muddle of Anglo–Sharifian relations is again illustrated by this episode, for the same Fuad al-Khatib whose piteous tale so moved Wilson and Newcombe apparently also managed to convince Sir Mark Sykes that to him should go the credit of getting the sharif to agree to the Sykes–Picot scheme. When in 1920 Rashid Rida taxed him with this behaviour, Fuad swore a heavy oath (bi'l-talaq) that he would now at last divulge the truth, and stated that the sharif was in reality quite content with the Sykes–Picot scheme, that he himself attempted to oppose it by informing the British that the sharif was against it, and that only when he found himself unable to make the sharif oppose the scheme did he go to the British and convince them that it was really through his intercession that the sharif came to accept the scheme.[61] What to us seems a labyrinth of cunning and double-dealing was, however, to Wilson and Newcombe, a clear and straightforward issue: the Arabs, wronged and betrayed, were exhaling their plaint by the mouth of Fuad al-Khatib, and to this plaint it was their duty chivalrously to respond.

27

Later, it became the mark of a tender and liberal conscience to be pained at the mention of the Sykes-Picot Agreement. We here witness a first manifestation of the sentiment. The voice of conscience has always seemed quite loud in these Arab affairs. To those who invoked it, it was always audible, unambiguous and imperious. The case of Colonel Lawrence is well known. But it is surprising to see the politic and well-informed Clayton speaking like a Wilson, or a Newcombe: 'I cannot conscientiously', we find him declaring in the spring of 1918, 'carry out any line of policy which will go against our pledges to the Arabs, and I can always return to Egypt [he was at G.H.Q. in Palestine] if they don't want me, and should in many ways prefer it as I have no axe to grind here'.[62] As usual when conscience is invoked we find, on further inquiry, that the moral and political aspects of the question are by no means so clear-cut as to call for such desperate, uncompromising manifestos. In the present case it was Palestine and the activities of the Zionist commission which had stirred Clayton's ire, and the ease with which he seemed to discriminate what did from what did not go 'against our pledges to the Arabs' in this matter is very remarkable.

As the war went on, objections to the Sykes–Picot Agreement were pressed again and again with the authorities in London. In the summer of 1917, D. G. Hogarth, the director of the Arab Bureau, prepared a note for them which argued the impolicy of proceeding with the Agreement in the circumstances then obtaining. The Agreement, Hogarth said, had favoured France to the detriment of her allies not only in point of territory, but also because France stood to gain her share of the Ottoman empire without being obliged to fight in the middle east. Hogarth accepted that cogent reasons had existed for signing the Agreement the year before, but he himself was inclined to think that the situation was now quite altered and that 'much water had run under the bridge'. This, he noted, was not the view of Sir Mark Sykes and Sir Ronald Graham, who were for upholding the Agreement, but he would point out that Mesopotamia was now under British occupation, that Russia was no longer as important as she was a year before, and that democratic America had joined the war. Further, the Arabs and the Jews both wanted the British rather than the French. Therefore, while certainly not desiring entirely to exclude the French from the area, and disclaiming any belief in Arab capacity for self-government, he yet wished to revise the Agreement, principally so as to give Britain a stronger position both in Palestine and in Arabia proper.[63] Wingate himself kept on pressing at that time for the amendment of the Sykes–Picot Agreement.[64] Again, in the autumn of the same year, Clayton, professing anxiety at what the Turks might offer in order to detach the Arabs, suggested that the French government should be urgently asked to announce that they had no annexatory designs either in Syria or in the Lebanon.[65] The Balfour Declaration – later to join the Sykes–Picot Agreement in common execration by right-thinking persons – was also invoked, and Clayton informed London that the understanding between Faisal and Weizmann would remain barren of results until the two surviving parties to the Sykes–Picot Agreement should recognise that it was no longer a practical instrument.[66] The Cairo officials' continuing dislike of the Sykes-Picot Agreement was at last given public expression when Wingate, answering a query from the sharif, disowned the Agreement in June 1918.[67] Justifying his action to the Foreign Office he said that the Sharif had never been officially informed of the Agreement; this of course was not exactly the case, since Sykes and Picot had shown it to him, and the effect of Wingate's message was stronger and ultimately more disastrous to the sharif than if this had really been so. Concluding his telegram, Wingate asked permission to tell the sharif without more ado that the Agreement was dead for all practical purposes.[68] Permission was refused, but in a dispatch of the following September he could state that he was not aware to what extent the terms of the Sykes–Picot Agreement were still binding.[69]

The existence of this dispatch indicates that by that time the long-held misgivings of the Cairo officials over the Sykes–Picot Agreement had communicated themselves to the government in London. In April 1917 a committee of the imperial war cabinet which included Curzon, Lord Robert Cecil, Austen Chamberlain, and Smuts, and which considered British territorial *desiderata* at the end of the war, concluded that Palestine – which under the Sykes–Picot scheme was to be internationally administered – as well as Mesopotamia should be under British control as this was necessary for the safety of the empire.[70] By the summer of 1918 'private advices' from London, as a contemporaneous note by Symes put it, indicated that the Agreement was in abeyance and practically defunct. A specimen of such 'advices' survives in the *Wingate Papers*: a letter from George Lloyd of 10 October 1918 in which he tells Wingate that the Sykes–Picot Agreement was dead and that, had it not died, it would have created increasing difficulties in the future.[71] This letter most accurately reflected the official view. In answer to a request from the secretary of state at Washington to provide information on the Sykes–Picot Agreement, O. B. Laughlin, counsellor at the American embassy in London, telegraphed on 10 October – the very day Lloyd wrote his letter to Wingate – as follows: 'I ascertained from the Foreign Office that the agreement was actually made relative to spheres of influence, but that conditions have rendered it practically a dead letter'. Four days later, Lord Robert Cecil himself confirmed the statement of his officials for, as Laughlin reported, he said 'that this arrangement has been rendered practically unworkable in its larger aspects by change of conditions particularly by our entry into the war and that the British government now naturally wishes to consult us with respect to any such joint action in the Turkish empire'.[72]

The note by Symes gives an idea of the future policy envisaged by the Cairo officials. The Zionists and the Arabs would join in common opposition to the French, the Zionists supporting the Arabs in Syria, and the Arabs making way for the Zionists in Palestine. As for Mesopotamia, the British meant to stay there, but since open annexations were now debarred by all kinds of solemn declarations, the substance rather than the shadow of power would be secured there if the sharif were installed as nominal ruler, and lip-service were paid to the ideal of Arab unity. This was preferable to a mandate which allowed intervention by European powers. Renunciation of formal rule in Mesopotamia also meant that the British could strengthen their hands against French political penetration in Syria and would allow 'Syrian prejudice, Moslem partiality and Zionist opportunism to combine and operate on behalf of pro-British and anti-Hun influences throughout the Arab countries'.[73] In one way or another this prescription was tried in the middle east in following decades, but British interests did not conspicuously benefit. Lloyd George inaugurated the series of experiments by trying – in vain – to talk the French into believing that the Sykes–Picot Agreement was no more, or perhaps had never really existed.

The views and attitudes of the Cairo and Khartoum officials had an appreciable influence on the conduct of policy in 1919, but this does not exhaust their interest. The Middle Eastern Question in Britain from 1919 to 1948 was by and large an affair of officials: it did not arouse any great public debate, as the Eastern Question did in the nineteenth century, and ministers on the whole seem to have accepted and to have been guided by the views of the officials: Chur hill in 1921, Austen Chamberlain in 1925–9, Passfield in 1929, Eden and Malcolm Macdonald in 1937–9, Bevin in 1945–8 – the record of all these seems to give substance to such an impression. And the Cairo and Khartoum officials of the first world war seem to have been quite prominent in middle eastern administration and policy in the following decades. Sir Stewart Symes, who during this period was Wingate's private secretary, and who was to become chief secretary of Palestine and governor-general of the Sudan, has a significant passage in his memoirs:

It is noteworthy [he writes] how the members, at different periods, of Sir R. Wingate's personal staff at Khartoum were distributed subsequently in the Arabic-speaking world. Of his private secretaries, Sir Lee Stack was governor-general of the Sudan and Sirdar up to the date of his assassination in Cairo; Clayton proceeded on a special mission to Ibn Saud and was chief British representative in Irak when he died; I followed Clayton [as chief secretary, Palestine government]. Of our assistants (Sir) Kinahan Cornwallis at this time was chief adviser to King Feisal and, after the outbreak of war, returned as British Ambassador to Baghdad; (Sir) A. Keown-Boyd held key posts for a number of years in the Ministry of the Interior in Egypt. . . . Each one of us [he continued] had been given his initiation into oriental policies and the conduct of public business by the same kindly and experienced chief.[74]

When to this list are added the names of subordinates, associates and successors, one can appreciate how a particular view of Arab policy was transmitted, upheld, defended and publicised from decade to decade until it acquired the venerable sheen of orthodoxy. The literary Arabophiles, Colonel Lawrence and Miss Bell, cannot sustain comparison with such weighty and durable influence: they supplied the myth and the *panache*, but little would have been accomplished had the officials themselves not been the convinced and confident upholders of the policy. Two examples, relating to officials with Sudanese connections, may be given in illustration. The first concer..3 Sir Harold MacMichael, who became high commissioner in Palestine, and it indicates for how long heavy disapproval of the Sykes–Picot scheme persisted. In 1939 he was host in Jerusalem to his French counterpart in the Levant, M. Puaux. MacMichael, according to Puaux, expressed his regret over the parcelling out of the near east. He did not believe in a great Arab empire, yet he nonetheless deplored the existence of frontiers which did not favour economic or cultural traffic. ' "They were wrong to partition this region" ', Puaux reports him as saying, ' "it would have been better to entrust the whole of it to one country"; after an interval, he added, "To you, or to us".'[75] The second concerns a man in many respects quite different from Sir Harold MacMichael: Sir Douglas Newbold, whose Sudan career culminated in the civil secretaryship. Readers of his *Life and Letters* will note with interest how fervent a supporter he was of pan-Arabism: his simple creed was that 'the Zionists and the French are the real stumbling blocks in the middle east'.[76] Could we not, on this showing, conclude that Arabophilia – whether sentimental or utilitarian – as a doctrine and a line of policy, found its main source and strength in the Anglo–Egyptian Sudan?

3

The Capture of Damascus,
1 October 1918

When Colonel Lawrence renounced the world his ambition, as readers of his *Letters* know, was to become a great writer, to exchange the uncertain and treacherous triumphs of war and politics for the sure and lasting reward of artistic creation. The attempt does not come off, and *Seven Pillars* is a work seething with rancour and resentment, full of advocacy and rhetoric, firmly imprisoned in the world of practice from which its author ceaselessly proclaimed his yearning to escape. As a work of art *Seven Pillars* is deeply flawed, but since it is impregnated with that demonic quality which is manifest in Lawrence's career in war and politics, it exerts the same powerful fascination over those who come into contact with it. Consider, for instance, the illustrations which Eric Kennington executed for *Seven Pillars* on Lawrence's commission: they are pictures of heroes and paladins, exemplars of loyalty and chivalry, in drawing which Kennington was entirely influenced and governed by what Lawrence wrote. But when we compare what these men really were, the mediocrity of some, the duplicity of others, the ordinariness of most, with Kennington's superior beings we are repelled as by a piece of deception which the artist not so much practised as, medium-like and in the measure of his sensitivity, was wished into practising by a potent but impure spirit. Terence Rattigan's play, *Ross*, at a much greater distance has been touched by the same influence to the detriment both of factual and of imaginative truth. In a scene where Allenby and Lawrence dramatically confront one another, the latter comes to mention the Sykes–Picot Agreement and the dialogue proceeds as follows:

Allenby: I've never heard of it.
Lawrence: No? Nor, for the moment, has Feisal, but if he finds out there'll be hell to pay. So it's vital that he and his people should continually be

fed, from now on, the right kind of lies by the right kind of liar. Therefore this man of yours has to be a very senior officer. Then his lies will
have real weight.[1]

The rejoinder is meant to be a rapier-thrust dealt by one consummate duellist to another, its purpose is to illuminate a situation which
is extraordinary and characters who are exceptional. The tension
within and between the protagonists depends on the truth of the
assumption that the Sykes–Picot Agreement was a shameful betrayal
of the Arabs; since this is not the truth, but merely a slogan which
Lawrence found useful to propagate, the drama becomes histrionics
and the taut dialogue sags into the tedious rhetoric of political
controversy.

Seven Pillars conforms to the canons of dramatic art: the small,
accidental beginnings, the vision in the desert, the years of organising,
contriving, fighting, willing and imposing mastery, culminating at
last in the investment and capture of Damascus, terminus and fulfilment of a superhuman effort. It is as if this event were the pre-
ordained consummation through which all the past incidents of the
desert war acquire their meaning and coherence. If *Seven Pillars*
were the true history it purports to be, this would be a remarkable
example of nature imitating art. Its climax has inspired Mr Rattigan
to give us a picture of Lawrence at the gates of Damascus dictating a
dispatch to Allenby in which, after telling him that he and his
Arabs had destroyed the Fourth Turkish Army, the sardonic and
jocular hero goes on to say:

> In view of this situation it is my intention to enter the City of Damascus
> at first light tomorrow and to hold it in the name and authority of Prince
> Faisal. I assume this action will meet with your approval – an assumption
> forced on me by the fact that should it not it will anyway be too late for
> you to inform me.[2]

The film *Lawrence of Arabia*, plodding ham-handed in Super Pana-
vision through its cinematic commonplaces, has naturally fallen for
Seven Pillars' magic ending and allows its audiences to assume that
Lawrence captured Damascus. But it is precisely in respect of this
crucial episode of the book that we have Lawrence's clear admission
that his account, in part at any rate, is fictional. Commenting on a
book by Mr Robert Graves which described his Arabian adventures,
Lawrence had this to say about the Damascus section: 'I call this
section extremely good. Swift and fine in its writing and simple too.

But I was on thin ice when I wrote the Damascus chapter and any-one who copies me will be through it, if he is not careful. S.P. [*Seven Pillars*] is full of half-truth: here'.[3] Nature, then, has not imitated art; rather it has been doctored and touched up with a story-teller's skill; but we remember that Lawrence claims to tell not just a story, but a true story.

The Damascus episode as narrated in *Seven Pillars* is, then, a crux in judging whether Lawrence succeeded in his attempt to find in art the fulfilment which eluded him in war and politics, to distil out of the bitter discordance of his adventures, for his own solace and the world's admiration, a transparent thing of truth and beauty. He seems to have failed since, on his own admission, this episode – the keystone of his narrative – is heavy and opaque with deliberate suppression. To establish what happened at the capture of Damascus is necessary in order to understand Lawrence and his literary artefact; also, since the episode is of some importance, it is worthy of the historian's attention both for its own sake and for the light it throws on the Syrian question at the end of the first world war and the behaviour of the different parties involved in it. In a book on *England and the Middle East*, published in 1956, I brought together a certain amount of circumstantial evidence to show that Damascus could not have been captured by the Sharifians, but rather that, after the evacuation of the city by the defeated Ottomans, they were allowed to occupy it and to claim that they had captured it; I then went on to argue that this act of commission – whoever was responsible for it, was – more than any number of ambiguous or contradictory pledges and agreements – instrumental in eroding the British position in Mesopotamia and in creating the bitter and tangled situation be-tween British, French and Sharifians in Syria which General Gouraud resolved by force of arms at Khan Maisalun in July 1920. The evidence, it is true, was neither direct nor definitely conclusive, but it was fairly strong and deserved – because of the substantial conclusions which flowed from it – careful and critical scrutiny. It is curious however that writers on this period of middle eastern history have continued in their wonted way exclusively to balance and weigh carefully agree-ment against undertaking and pledge against intention as though Anglo–Arab relations were a branch not of political history but of ethical theory. In her *Britain's Moment in the Middle East 1914–1956*, published in 1963, Miss Elizabeth Monroe devotes no attention to the capture of Damascus or to the events which immediately

35

followed it. It is true that in discussing the subsequent acrimonious exchanges at the Peace Conference she quotes a sentence from a report by Sir Gilbert Clayton, Allenby's chief political officer, to the effect that 'Our permitting the occupation of Damascus by the Sharifians has allayed some of the suspicion of British intentions' but Miss Monroe does not discuss the significance of the statement which remains in her narrative odd and unexplained.[4] Professor Z. N. Zeine who published *The Struggle for Arab Independence* in 1960, claiming, in his preface, that there was 'actually no serious historical work, entirely and exclusively devoted to a detailed study of this period, based both on European and Arabic sources', again does not attempt to elucidate the sequence of events leading to the capture and occupation of Damascus but states: 'At midnight [on 30 September 1918], the Desert Mounted Corps was at the gates of the city. At dawn the next day, Arab troops of the emir Faisal's army, under the command of Nuri Pasha al Sa'id, followed at 6.00 a.m. by the 3rd Australian Light Horse Brigade with General Wilson in command, occupied Damascus'. This highly misleading statement is then followed by a passage in which the complicated events are so telescoped, garbled and hopelessly confused that considerable labour is required to restore their proper sequence and significance.[5] In his *Syria and Lebanon under the French Mandate* published in 1958, Mr S. H. Longrigg is considerably briefer than but as misleading as Professor Zeine. 'By the evening of 30th September', he writes, 'a senior Sharifian representative (the amir Nasir), with tribal escort, reached the outskirts of Damascus. Led by the Iraqi officer Nuri al Sa'id, Arab forces entered the town early on 1 October, followed a few hours later by British troops'. But what distinguishes Mr Longrigg's narrative is that he goes out of his way to dismiss, in a footnote, as though it were an idle tale of the bazaar, the idea that Damascus was deliberately left to the Sharifians to occupy: 'There does not seem to the writer to be adequate foundation', he asserts, 'for the oft-repeated story that the entry of troops into Damascus was purposely delayed so as to enable the amir to have the honour.'[6] The source and the exact tenor of the story which Mr Longrigg so dismisses are unspecified, but it is fair to observe that his language implies, if it does not outright assert, that if the Sharifians occupied Damascus, it is because they captured it.

But a review of the recent literature, instructive though it may be, is not my chief purpose here. This is to examine some fresh evidence which bears on the capture of Damascus and the events which followed it. At the end of September 1918, Allenby, having defeated the Ottoman forces in northern Palestine, prepared to march on and take Damascus. To achieve his aim he had at his disposal two main bodies of troops, namely the Australian Mounted Division under the command of Lieutenant-General Sir Harry Chauvel, who also, directly under Allenby, commanded the Desert Mounted Corps – as the combined body of troops marching on Damascus was known – and the Indian 4th and 5th Cavalry Divisions under the command, respectively of Major-General Sir G. de S. Barrow and of Major-General H. J. M. Macandrew. These troops were supplemented by a small French contingent and by Faisal's so-called 'Northern Arab Army' which consisted of a small regular contingent – six hundred according to Sir Hubert Young[7] – accompanied by an indeterminate and fluctuating number of irregulars and camp-followers. All these troops were approaching Damascus in a fanlike movement from the south. Their operations are lucidly described in the official British and Australian War histories but these narratives may be supplemented and amplified with the help of the details contemporaneously recorded in the War Diary of the General Staff of the Australian Mounted Division and of those of its units who most directly participated in the capture of Damascus.[8] The interest of these Diaries is enhanced by the fact that the Australian contingent had been allotted the task of cutting the enemy's retreat north of Damascus and that Australian units were much involved in the events inside Damascus which took place after the capture of the city.

Orders for the march on and the capture of Damascus were issued at Kuneitra on 29 September early in the afternoon. 'Chauvel's immediate purpose, as his divisions advanced from the Jordan and up the Pilgrim's road further east, was', in the words of the Australian war history, 'to isolate the city by seizing the Barada gorge and the northern route to Homs. This was the mission of the Australian Mounted Division, while Barrow and Macandrew, when the exits were closed, were to press into the city from the south'.[9] From the Diaries it appears that among the orders issued at Kuneitra was one to the effect that care was to be taken to avoid entering Damascus if possible; that unless forced to do so for tactical reasons, no troops were to enter Damascus; and that pickets were to be posted on all roads into Damascus to ensure performance of this order. By the afternoon of 30 September the Australian troops were in the vicinity

37

of Damascus. The War Diary of the 3rd Australian Light Horse Brigade – commanded by Brigadier Wilson — shows that the brigade was then ordered to move north-east of Damascus as rapidly as possible and on to the Homs road, as it was not the policy to enter Damascus if it could be avoided. But Brigadier Wilson decided, in the words of the British war history 'that it was impossible for him to carry out the instructions he had received to avoid Damascus'.[10] He was convinced, explains the Australian war history 'that, if he persisted in carrying out his orders to work round Damascus, his brigade would become unduly scattered, and he would probably fail either to cut the road to Homs in time to prevent a heavy withdrawal of troops and material from the city, or to intercept the troops of the Fourth Army'.[11] In the early morning of 1 October, therefore, the 3rd Brigade crossed the northern part of Damascus, and it is to them that Damascus may be said to have formally surrendered.[12]

Neither the War Diaries nor the official war histories – which latter mention the order to avoid Damascus not in relation to the general plan of attack issued at Kuneitra, but only when discussing the movements of the 3rd Light Horse Brigade – explain why Damascus was to be avoided. The reason could, of course, have been either military or political. It may have been decided not to go into Damascus from the south, but rather to encircle the city and prevent the escape of Ottoman troops. This may explain why the orders issued at Kuneitra allowed entry into the city for *tactical* reasons, but it does not explain why Wilson of the 3rd Brigade, deploying his troops from the north-west to the north-east, should have been reluctant to do so through the only practicable road (which crossed the northern end of the city) until he referred the problem to divisional headquarters. The war diaries are silent about any military considerations which might have made Brigadier Wilson, for instance, nervous of entering a city swarming with hostile troops whose reactions might be strong and unpleasant. On the contrary, as we see from the Australian war history, Brigadier Wilson was concerned lest he might not be allowed to cross Damascus, and thus become incapable of accomplishing his task. From this it would seem that avoidance of Damascus was based on political rather than military reasons and that at least at one point military necessity conflicted with what must have been political calculation. The war diary of Bourchier's Force – composed of the 4th and 12th regiments drawn from the 4th Light Horse Brigade and commanded by Colonel Bourchier – affords further support for the view that the reason for avoiding Damascus was political rather than military. The force was deployed against Damascus on the south of the city. On the afternoon of 1 October, when it was quite clear that the city was no longer in the hands of the enemy, we read in the war diary that Colonel Bourchier was forced, in the interests of discipline, and on account of the extraordinary noise and apparent unrest in Damascus, to place guards on public institutions, consulates, hospitals and the like, but that since the complete control of the town was in the hands of the Sharifian forces, Colonel Bourchier was ordered, in the early evening, to get in touch with them and arrange for them to take over guard duties. It would seem then that its presence within Damascus was not part of the original instructions of the force, that Colonel Bourchier was compelled to intervene by the emergency and that divisional headquarters were anxious to hand over the city to those on whom complete control of Damascus had been bestowed. We thus find that both the 3rd Brigade and Bourchier's force, confronted with different problems at different stages of the battle had yet to be guided by an identical directive quite unrelated to their actual situation, and from which, in the end, they had to depart; namely, the general directive, issued at Kuneitra to avoid entering Damascus. That the order was political in character is clearly the implicit view of the official Australian war historian when, in the course of his narrative, he writes: 'Meanwhile, as the Arabs, under their compact with the Allies, proceeded to take over control of the city . . .'.[13]

There was, however, no such compact. But there was the so-called Declaration to the Seven, an official statement made in July 1918 to seven Syrians in Cairo in which the British government pledged itself to recognise 'the complete and sovereign "independence" of any Arab area emancipated from Turkish control by the action of the Arabs themselves'.[14] Whatever the original status and significance of this unilateral declaration to seven individuals – on a matter which did not concern Great Britain alone – it seems to have been later used – whether on Allenby's authority, or on that of superiors in London is still to be established – as a convenient peg on which to hang territorial claims which the Sharifians were to be allowed – and encouraged – to make. Hence, it may be suspected, the order to the Australians to avoid Damascus, hence the necessity to prove that the Arabs were the first to enter the city. The Sharifians – and therefore Lawrence – must have known the role for which they had been cast.

39

Nasib al-Bakri, Faisal's Damascene follower who was with him in this campaign, later informed the historian Muhammad Kurd Ali that, following the Declaration, he was sent to recruit Druzes and Hauranis so that the Northern Arab Army might enter Damascus in force and in proper style.[15] In *Seven Pillars* Lawrence taunts these Druzes with their mercenary motives and says that they started rioting and looting after he had 'sharply refused' to reward them for their 'tardy services'.[16] Nasib al-Bakri's account explains Lawrence's enigmatic reference to their tardiness, and if these Druzes were at the last minute recruited for purposes of representation, it was imprudent to refuse to pay for their services and unkind to hold them up to ridicule before his literate and sophisticated audience.

As has been seen, the order not to enter Damascus had, owing to the accident of battle, unavoidably to be disregarded in two instances: once in the early morning of 1 October when the 3rd Light Horse Brigade had to cross the north of the city, and once in the afternoon of the same day when Bourchier's force had to intervene in order to protect life and property. It could not therefore be unequivocally said – as might have been originally desired – that the Sharifian forces had been the first in Damascus. The official War Office communiqué as published in *The Times* on 3 October declared that 'Troops of the Australian Mounted Division entered Damascus during the night of September 30' and added that 'At 6 a.m. on October 1 the city was occupied by a British force and by a portion of the Arab army of King Hussein'. It is instructive to set out side by side with this communiqué other contemporary official records. They indicate well the uncertain and equivocal situation in Damascus which the communiqué glossed over. An official bulletin seen by Captain William Yale, who was then in or near the theatre of war, is instructive. 'On the morning of October 1st', it said, 'the town was entered by our mounted troops and the Arab army. After guards had been posted, the troops were withdrawn from the town'.[17] An Admiralty information bulletin declared: 'Damascus was entered by Australian troops during the night of the 30th September. . . . After the surrender all the Allied troops, with the exception of the necessary guards were withdrawn, the administration of the city being left in the hands of the local authorities'.[18] In a telegram from the U.S. consulate general at Cairo the Department of State was informed on 5 October: 'The representative of the Hedjaz government took over Damascus from the British on October 1st'.[19] It is curious, lastly, to quote a footnote in the British war history which adds yet another version of the capture of Damascus. 'There has been some controversy', the foot-note reads, 'as to which troops were the first to enter Damascus. It seems clear that a number of Sharifian irregulars were in the city by midnight on the 30th September. They did not, however, venture to attack the Turks to whom they were indistinguishable from the local Bedouin who had been demonstrating for some days'. So true and so convenient is it that *la nuit tous les chats sont gris*. 'The advance guard of the 3rd L.H. Brigade', concludes the footnote, 'entered the city before 6.30 a.m. on 1st October'.[20] To the ambiguities of official communiqués and the judicious hesitations of official histories may be added ministerial reticence. On 31 October 1918, Lord Robert Cecil, answering a Member, Theodore Taylor, who had asked 'under what flag the city of Damascus now lives', declared: 'General Allenby was authorised on 1st October to allow the Arab flag to be hoisted at Damascus'.[21] But these ambiguities and hesitations and reticences have, of course, been swept aside by the bold claim that Damascus was an Arab conquest. The claim began to be made very early. *The Times* of 17 October published an article which came 'From a Correspondent' and which purported to deal with 'the final Arab advance on Damascus'. Sent from Cairo on 8 October, it was most probably written by Lawrence. It displays a touch of his usual meretricious flamboyance when it describes the incompetent ex-Ottoman official who for a few days was head of the Sharifian administration in Damascus as 'the senior descendant of Saladin'. Entitled 'The Arab March on Damascus', it stated that Damascus was entered on the night of 30 September, 'the Arabs being the first troops in'.

Let us now turn to *Seven Pillars* and see how Lawrence's account tallies with the evidence here reviewed. We notice a paucity of actual detail but many hints here and there that Damascus was an Arab, was Lawrence's, conquest. The brief summary of its conquest which is prefixed to Book X says: 'We moved behind Deraa to hasten its abandonment. General Barrow joined us; in his company we advanced to Kiswe, and here met the Australian Mounted Corps. Our united forces entered Damascus unopposed'; the coda which concludes the whole work begins: 'Damascus had not seemed a sheath for my sword, when I landed in Arabia; but its capture disclosed the exhaustion of my main springs of action'; reporting an interview he had with Allenby on 20 September 1918, he makes the general persuade him 'not to carry out my saucy threat to take Damascus, till we were all together'; 'we, the Arab leaders', he writes when the armies had reached the gates of Damascus on 30 September, 'had waited for the slower British';[22] after the entry into Damascus on 1 October he meets General Chauvel: 'I described the excitement in the city, and how our new government could not guarantee administrative services before the following day, when I would wait on him to discuss his needs and mine. Meanwhile I made myself responsible for public order: only begging him to keep his men outside, because tonight would see such carnival as the town had not held for six hundred years, and its hospitality might pervert their discipline'; Chauvel – who under Allenby was in command of the whole campaign – 'had no instructions what to do with the captured city'; he asks Lawrence's permission to drive round the town, and is only concerned with empty points of ceremonial which are occasion for Lawrence to poke fun at him: 'In place of an "entry" he would make a "march through": it meant that instead of going in the middle he would go at the head, or instead of the head the middle. I forgot, or did not well hear, which: for I should not have cared if he had crawled under or flown over his troops, or split himself to march both sides'.[23] This passage is clearly Kennington's source for his drawing called 'Caesar', which shows a gigantic pompous and monocled officer, a drawn sword in his hand, strutting astride a crowd of marching soldiers. But apart from such hints and jeers all that we gather from Lawrence's narrative is that 'Allenby hoped that we would be present at the entry' because 'he knew how much more than a mere trophy Damascus was to the Arabs'. The next thing we are told is that Lawrence is driving in the streets of Damascus, surrounded by crowds, 'joy shining in their eyes'.[24] There is nothing about the orders to the Australians not to enter Damascus, nothing about the 3rd Brigade, or Bourchier's force; indeed the way he speaks of Chauvel, of keeping the Australians out lest their discipline be perverted, manages to convey an impression the exact opposite of what, if the Australian war diaries are to be believed, really happened. And it is difficult to imagine that these diaries have falsified the course of events. It remains to add that the manuscript of *Seven Pillars* contains a brief but candid and explicit sentence which goes a long way to reconcile Lawrence's account with that of the War Diaries.

According to *Seven Pillars*, Allenby had another reason for desiring the Sharifians to be present at the entry to Damascus. It was a 'prudential' one: 'In their envelopment of Damascus the Australians might be forced, despite orders, to enter the town. If anyone resisted them it would spoil the future. One night was given us to make the Damascenes receive the British army as their allies'.[25] The reference to orders not to enter the town is left vague and unexplained, and the reader gathers the impression that Damascus was placed out of bounds to the Australian soldiers because they might meet with disagreeable incidents from which Allenby designed the Northern Arab Army to shield them. In view of the exertions of the Australians to restore order in Damascus which the Sharifians could not preserve, Lawrence's account seems an offensive travesty of the facts. What is established is that, once Damascus was captured, it was to be given over to the Sharifians to control and govern; for one night, says Lawrence; for twenty-four hours, says his companion Colonel Stirling.[26] On the morning of I October the official and ostensible conqueror of Damascus was Sharif Nasir, the nominal leader of the Sharifians in the vicinity of Damascus. He entered the city and made his way to the municipality, where he found a Sharifian flag flying and a committee sitting which acknowledged the authority of King Husain and claimed to act on his behalf. It was this committee which had been sitting when the advance guard of the 3rd Light Horse Brigade arrived in Damascus, and had surrendered the city to them. This committee seems to have been formed by the Ottoman authorities on 30 September before their withdrawal from the city, to preserve law and order. It was composed of notables representing different quarters and presided over by Amir Sa'id al-Jaza'iri, who had an Algerian following in the city. The Ottoman commander issued arms to the committee and Amir Sa'id armed his Algerians and put them under the command of his brother, Amir Abd al-Qadir. At the same time, so one Damascene writer states, the Ottomans seem to have appointed Shukri al-Ayyubi, a high-ranking officer in the Ottoman army, military governor of Damascus.[27] Whether this was so or not is, in fact, unclear. What does seem to be the case is that Lawrence dismissed the Jaza'iris and appointed or confirmed Ayyubi as military governor. This was an injudicious move. Then and subsequently Ayyubi proved to be quite incompetent. A later estimate by a British Intelligence officer sums up the character of Lawrence's nominee: 'He is not intelligent, said to be fanatical and is ... a little queer mentally. He is pleasant mannered but useless.'[28]

Some light on Lawrence's activities at this juncture is thrown by an autobiographical sketch which Chauvel wrote some time after the War. Early in the morning of 1 October, Chauvel writes, General Barrow informed him that Lawrence had ridden into Damascus with a small Arab following on the heels of the advanced guard of the 14th Cavalry Brigade. Chauvel considered Lawrence as his 'liaison officer' – presumably with the Sharifians – and was looking to him to assist in the civil administration of Damascus. On hearing Barrow's report, he decided to go into Damascus accompanied by his Chief-of-Staff. He found Lawrence in the *saray* of Damascus accompanied by a 'magnificently attired individual' whom Lawrence introduced as Shukri Paska, the military governor of Damascus. Chauvel declares that as Ayyubi looked obviously like an Arab, he demanded to see the Turkish *wali*; Lawrence told him that the *wali* had fled and that Ayyubi had been appointed military governor by a meeting of residents. At this juncture Chauvel knew nothing of the Jaza'iris and their committee which had in fact surrendered Damascus earlier that morning to the Australians, and he confirmed Ayyubi in his post. It was only after returning to Corps headquarters, so Chauvel states, that he received the 'disquieting' information that Ayyubi only represented the supporters of the Sharif, 'a comparatively small section', that the Damascenes were alarmed at the prospect of Sharifian domination, that the 'Arabs' were pouring into Damascus, and were 'looting freely'. But as he had already informed Allenby of his appointment of Ayyubi, Chauvel decided to let it stand.[29]

As might be expected, in consequence of these manoeuvres, relations between Ayyubi and the Jaza'iris were not good. Acting under the authority which Lawrence had talked Chauvel into conferring on him, Ayyubi took a step which had serious consequences: he had the prisons opened and the prisoners, some four thousand of them, among whom, declared an eye witness, were 'murderers, robbers, opium addicts and forgers', set free. These prisoners started looting and killing, particularly Ottoman soldiers who were either wounded or sick or fugitive and thus contributed to the troubles which compelled Bourchier to intervene on the afternoon of 1 October.[30] If Ayyubi had not been put in authority, or if he had taken steps to control the Sharifian camp-followers who were moving on Damascus, and had not opened the prisons, appearances might have been saved, a Sharifian government ceremoniously proclaimed and quietly established. But the advent of the Sharifians found Damascus in turmoil, easily quelled, to be sure, by a trained and numerous force such as the Australians, but quite beyond the Sharifians to deal with. On this disorder *Seven Pillars* is silent; one word merely: 'The day was drawing in, the world was in the streets: riotous'.[31] What this actually meant we have the war diary of Bourchier's force to tell us; also the memoirs of Sir Alec Kirkbride, who was with Lawrence on that and the following day. 'His tastes', writes Kirkbride of Lawrence,

were anything but bloodthirsty, and he appeared to be genuinely shocked by the free use which I made of my revolver during the evening after we entered Damascus, when he would insist on rescuing Turkish stragglers from being murdered by the local populace, and, during the next morning, when a small Arab army detachment was called upon to quell some nasty street fighting and looting in the bazaars. Before going to tidy up the Turkish military hospital that evening he asked me to go out with him and help in stopping the killing of Turks in the streets. I expressed my willingness to go, but suggested that we should take an armed party along. He said, 'Oh no; you and I can manage, I am sure!'

We must have looked an ill-assorted couple, he short and in Arab robes with no arms but an ornamental dagger, and myself long and lanky in khaki, wearing a large service revolver. When we found anyone butchering Turks he went up and asked them in a gentle voice to stop, while I stood by and brandished my firearm. Occasionally, someone turned nasty and I shot them at once before the trouble could spread . . .

We returned to Arab headquarters leading some twenty Turkish prisoners whom we had rescued and who refused to let us go until we had found a guard to whom they could be handed over.[32]

Lawrence is more forthcoming about the events of 2 October. But he attributes them to the machinations of the Jaza'iri brothers, who incited their armed Algerian followers, and to the greed of the mercenary Druzes, who, denied payment, joined forces with the Algerians. The Druzes, however, did not create the disorders, they only aggravated them. And, in any case, they were in the city as part of the Sharifian force, in order to prove to the world that Faisal was the conqueror of Damascus. As for Lawrence's enmity towards the Jaza'iris, its reasons are not clear.[33] When they took over from the Ottomans the Jaza'iris had proclaimed that they were merely the agents of King Husain, and when Sharif Nasir came into the city he seems to have accepted their claim at face value and, as Faisal's representative, to have confirmed them in their authority.[34] Had everything gone well their committee, recognised by Sharif Nasir, would have been presented by Allenby to the world as a Sharifian administration already constituted and functioning well before the capture of the city. That this was his intention is made clear by a telegram which he sent to the War Office on 29 September in which he said that 'As far as the "A" area, and notably the city of Damascus is concerned, I shall recognise the local Arab administration which I anticipate finding already in existence, and shall appoint French liaison officers as may be necessary.'[35] A letter from Faisal to Amir Sa'id al-Jaza'iri – which the recipient, however, did not receive at the time – confirms Allenby's plan. Faisal instructs Sa'id that if the Ottomans evacuated Damascus peaceably, he, together with the municipality, was to take over the city in the name of the 'Arab government'; but if they did not give up without a fight, Faisal hoped that Sa'id would hoist the 'Arab flag' before anyone entered the city, would proclaim a provisional government in the name of His Majesty the 'King of the Arabs', and receive the Allied armies 'with the Arab flags in your hands'.[36] It is in the light of such plans that we must look at Allenby's instruction, issued at Kuneitra on the same day, that Damascus was to be left under the existing civil administration.

A statement made later by Amir Sa'id also indicates what Allenby wanted to happen. Writing in 1934, he declared that towards the end of the war he had asked Faisal what pledges and conditions relating to Syria had been negotiated with the British and that Faisal had replied:

> There are no pledges or conditions, O my brother, but what has been agreed upon is that we will attack Syria and Palestine; and any of the three forces, British, French or Arab, which first occupies a town will exercise control over it until the Allies consider its fate. Therefore if you want to ensure your country's independence, do not wait; but when you hear of the armies approaching, declare independence even though this might entail a sacrifice. Because the Arab army might be delayed and another advance in its place.[37]

The Jaza'iris' pro-Sharifian sentiments may have been merely opportunistic, but the fact remains that, as *The Arab Bulletin* stated, Amir Abd al-Qadir had offered allegiance to the Sharifian cause in 1917,[38] that King Husain had entrusted him with a Sharifian standard which was now floating over the government offices, and that Sa'id had been on good terms with Faisal who had used him in 1917 to conduct negotiations with the Ottomans.[39] Lawrence, however, took exception to them and dismissed them from their functions immediately following his entry into Damascus. Whatever his reasons for this step, by antagonising both the Jaza'iris, with their armed following, and the Druzes, and by appointing Ayyubi instead of alleviating, he increased disorder in a city already given over to large numbers of criminals on the rampage. By his action Lawrence frustrated Allenby's design and made it difficult to claim that Damascus on its capture was under the undisputed and effective control of a 'local Arab administration'.

Seven Pillars gives the impression that the disorders of 2 October were easily quelled by Sharifian regulars. This was not so, as clearly appears from the Australian sources, from the reports of the U.S. special agent William Yale, the testimony of the journalist W. T. Massey and other evidence cited in *England and the Middle East*.[40] In fact, Chauvel decided to march his troops into Damascus in order to intimidate the rioters, but useful though this measure was it could not affect conditions in the maze of narrow streets which branched off the main thoroughfares. There, as Kirkbride points out, a fairly strong force was necessary in order to come to grips with the rioters, but the police force had ceased to function 'and there was political objection to calling in the British forces, who were camped on the outskirts of the town, and so admitting that the new Arab administration was incapable of controlling its own people'. So the small number of Sharifian troops were employed 'to shoot up any street in which there was fighting in progress and then, when people ran for safety, to double up and fire a few parting shots to keep the other side moving. This,' Kirkbride pointed out, 'meant the killing and wounding of a number of persons which would have been avoided had the forces of law and order been more numerous'.[41]

Thus, messily and inelegantly, the Sharifians were enabled to gain control of Damascus. Ultimately to no purpose, for two years after these events they were dislodged by the French. Some twenty-three year later, British troops once again captured Damascus, and once again were deliberately prevented from entering the city. In 1918, the device was used to forestall French claims to a privileged position in Syria; in 1941, ironically enough, this was done to enable the Free French formally to claim its capture, and thus in effect to assert the French privileged position in Syria.[42] It was of course Anglo-French rivalry in the Levant which explains these extraordinary incidents of 1918. Now, only a few decades later, we find this rivalry to belong to a vanished world, of which nothing remains. Nothing but whatever satisfaction the historian feels when, out of the confusion and the inexactitude, the distortions, the garbled reports and the surviving fragments, he makes for himself a coherent intelligible picture.*

* See postscript, page 51 below.

Appendix

Précis of the Australian War Diaries

Shortly after midnight 27–8 September 1918, orders were received for the Australian Mounted Division to move at six o'clock in the morning with the object of relieving Damascus on the 29th. An engagement was fought with the enemy at Jisr Banat Yakub, the enemy was routed and Kuneitra occupied on 28 September. On the evening of 28 September orders were received from the Desert Mounted Corps that the move from Kuneitra to Damascus would be postponed until the evening of 29 September. At 2 o'clock in the afternoon on September 19 orders were issued at Kuneitra for the march on and the capture of Damascus. Care was to be taken to avoid entering the city if possible; unless forced to do so for tactical reasons, no troops were to enter Damascus; pickets were to be posted on all roads into Damascus to ensure performance of this order; Damascus was to be left under the existing civil administration and no national flags were to be flown. Further, the Beirut railway was to be barricaded and telegraph lines were not to be cut.

At 3 o'clock the 3rd Australian Light Horse Brigade moved off from Kuneitra, the rest of the division following it at 5 o'clock. The 9th Light Horse Regiment and 6th Machine Guns were advanced guards. The advanced guards encountered the enemy at 8 o'clock in the evening, who proved too strong for them. The 10th Light Horse Regiment was sent in reinforcement, and an attack mounted against the enemy's right flank at Nahr Mughaniye. The operation proved very difficult owing to the rocky country making it almost impossible for mounted men to move across country in the dark; further, the enemy's right flank was protected by an impassable boggy creek. The brigade was ordered by divisional headquarters to push on as quickly as possible. It forced its way through the enemy's position astride the road, but was fired on by machine guns from a hill about twelve hundred yards to the east. As it could not pass on and leave the remainder of the corps exposed to this fire, the operation had to be extended to the east. The 8th Light Horse Regiment (less one squadron) was sent in reinforcement at 2 o'clock on the morning of 30 September, and by 3 o'clock the enemy's position was captured, and he retreated into Damascus. The 4th Light Horse Brigade now constituted the divisional advanced guard

In the morning of 30 September orders were received for the 5th Australian Light Horse Brigade to endeavour to close all exits from

48

Damascus to the north-west and the north-east, by moving via Katana north-easterly along the foothills of Kalabat El Mezze. The 3rd Australian Light Horse Brigade was closely to support the 5th Brigade. Bourchier's force formed at Kuneitra on 29 September and composed of two regiments (the 4th and the 12th) from the 4th Light Horse Brigade was to move directly on the town via Daraya.

Bourchier's force encountered the enemy – estimated at about 2,300 with numerous machine guns – that morning holding Kaukab and the ridge to the east of it. Colonel Bourchier tried to work round the enemy's right flank, but decided that unnecessary casualties would be entailed without heavy artillery support. An attack was mounted after a bombardment which was seen to affect the morale of the enemy; the 12th Light Horse Regiment worked round the Turkish left flank and the 4th Regiment attacked the front. The enemy was defeated about midday; prisoners were taken and the Turkish cavalry escaped into Damascus.

The 5th Australian Light Horse Brigade moved forward but was halted at El Mezze about midday by enemy guns and machine guns. At 1 o'clock in the afternoon the 19th Royal Horse Artillery Brigade arrived and succeeded in silencing the enemy. His position was difficult to force; hills and woods made the ground too narrow for a mounted attack in the face of so many machine guns. In the afternoon, the French regiment arrived to help and the enemy was finally defeated by 6 o'clock; four thousand prisoners, caught between the French regiment and the 14th Light Horse Regiment, were captured.

At 3.30 in the afternoon the 3rd Australian Light Horse Brigade was ordered to move north-east as rapidly as possible and cut the Homs road as it was not the policy to enter Damascus if it could be avoided. The brigade reached the village of Dumar and reconnaissance soon showed that the nature of the terrain was such that an advance across country over Jabal Kasiun was impossible. The only alternative was the main road from Dumar through El Rabwa and the northern end of Damascus itself. Divisional orders were received for the brigade to bivouac for the night, and to march at five o'clock on the following morning for the Homs road and capture the enemy escaping via the north-east from Damascus.

By 5 o'clock on the morning of 1 October the 3rd Australian Light Horse Brigade was on the move. The column descended to the main road at Dumar and moved towards Damascus. It passed on without opposition through the northern end of the city. The enemy in the city showed no sign of opposition. All lines of retreat were closed to them, and the brigade passed them by in order to get on to the Homs road. At this spot the 4th Light Horse Brigade later collected twelve thousand prisoners.

In the afternoon of 1 October, the divisional headquarters and the divisional troops were established in Salahiye, the 3rd Australian Light

Horse Brigade was on the Aleppo road, the 5th Brigade was on the Beirut road, and Bourchier's force was partly in the city maintaining order and the remainder guarding prisoners. Colonel Bourchier was forced, in the interests of discipline, and on account of the extraordinary noise and apparent unrest in Damascus, to place guards on many of the public institutions, consulates, hospitals, etc. Arabs were looting and murdering Turkish wounded and stragglers. But as the complete control of the town was in the hands of the Sharifian forces, Colonel Bourchier was ordered, in the early evening, to get in touch with them and arrange for them to take over the duties of guarding the various public institutions. The Desert Mounted Corps were informed that Colonel Bourchier had consulted with the Sharifian authorities, and that as Sharifian troops were fully engaged clearing up the town, they could not relieve his troops on guard at public buildings. At 12 noon took place the official entry into Damascus by the G.O.C. accompanied by the G.S.O.I., staff and a detachment from the Australian Mounted Division. Very shortly afterwards Colonel Bourchier was ordered to keep his force at Hamidiah Barracks with one squadron ready to be placed at the disposal of Colonel Lawrence to assist the Sharifian authorities to maintain order in the town, as considerable trouble had been experienced during the morning on account of irregular bodies of Druzes looting.

In the early afternoon the 5th Australian Light Horse Brigade at Dumar reported the arrival of some two hundred native soldiers who claimed to belong to the Sharifian forces, who began breaking into houses, shooting cattle and horses and looting property. The Desert Mounted Corps were asked for information to assist in discriminating between Sharifian and other Arab troops, since it was impossible to tell regular from irregular Arabs. The corps answered that all Sharifian troops were in Damascus and its immediate vicinity; other soldiers were Bedouin or Druze irregulars who, in the event of breaking the peace, or looting, were to be treated as hostile.

On 3 October Bourchier's force was disposed picketing the town and guarding prisoners. On the following day orders were issued placing Damascus out of bounds to the troops. The Fourth Cavalry Division were ordered by the Desert Mounted Corps to post a squadron in the Christian quarter of the town. On 6 October orders were received from the Desert Mounted Corps to relieve one squadron Stafford Yeomanry on guard on Christian and Jewish quarters of Damascus. On 8 October Colonel Bourchier was ordered to reconnoitre and report on the best route for ambulances between the Victoria Hotel and the British and French hospitals, because the existing route passed through the bazaar quarter which was to be avoided if possible. On 30 October, a message was received from the Desert Mounted Corps that the 10th Light Horse Regiment had been ordered to rejoin the division. It left Damascus on

31 October. (Narrative based on the War Diary of the General Staff of the Australian Mounted Division, Australian Imperial Force in Egypt, on the War Diary of Bourchier's Force, and on the War Diary of the H.Q., 3rd Australian Light Horse Brigade.)

Postscript. An examination of war office papers at the Public Record Office which I was able to make only after this book went to press makes it possible, in spite of the fragmentary nature of these papers, and of the fact that some of them are closed for 100 years, to settle definitely some crucial questions concerning the capture of Damascus. Two telegrams from the war office to Allenby both sent on 1 October 1918 – the culmination of exchanges which began on 25 July previous – make it clear that it was the desire of the British Government that 'the authority of the friendly and allied Arabs should be formally recognised in any part of the areas "A" and "B" [as defined in the Sykes-Picot Agreement] where it may be found established, or can be established, as a result of the military operations now in progress' (W.O.33/960, no. 10177), and that Allenby was 'authorized by His Majesty's Government to hoist Arab flag in Damascus when you arrive there' (*Ibid.*, no. 10178). The exact manner of carrying out these instructions was presumably left to Allenby. How he proceeded may be seen from an order sent to Lawrence on 25 September in which he was desired to inform Faisal that 'there is no objection to Your Highness entering Damascus as soon as you can do so with safety'. (Appendix M to War Diary of General Staff (Operations), G.H.Q., Egyptian Expeditionary Force, W.O.95/ 4371.) This, of course, contrasts with the order to the other troops not to enter Damascus, the political purpose of which this document amply indicates. Allenby's purpose in forbidding Damascus to non-sharifian troops becomes even clearer from an exchange between the Fourth Cavalry Brigade and the Desert Mounted Corps in the afternoon of 1 October. The Brigade, who obviously knew of no exception to the order forbidding troops to enter Damascus, asked: 'Are Hejaz regulars to be allowed to enter?' The reply was: 'Hejaz regulars are to be allowed to enter Damascus.' (Appendices 7 and 11 to War Diary of the General Staff, Desert Mounted Corps, W.O.95/4473.) A few hours earlier, at 11.25 a.m., the Australian Mounted Division had already informed the Desert Mounted Corps that 'Arabs are apparently looting and setting fire to parts [of] Damascus'. (Appendix 2, *ibid.*) Thus the chief responsibility for what took place at Damascus on 1 and 2 October falls on Allenby, who chose to carry out his instructions in this particular manner, and on Lawrence who misled Chauvel into ratifying his choice of Ayyubi as governor.

4

Sir Herbert Samuel and
the Government of Palestine

When, in April 1920, Lloyd George asked Herbert Samuel to undertake the government of Palestine the mandate for which had just been assigned to Great Britain, he was quite deliberately offering the appointment to someone who sympathised with Zionism and would try to make a success of the Zionist programme. Samuel's interest in and involvement with Zionism dated at least from the outbreak of the war in 1914. When in November of that year the Ottoman empire joined the Central Powers, he was quick to suggest to Grey, the foreign secretary, the possibility of establishing a Jewish state in Palestine; the following January, he sent Asquith a memorandum on this subject, its romantic rhetoric startling and somewhat amusing the prime minister. 'The Jewish brain', declared the chairman of the local government board,

is a physiological product not to be despised. For fifteen centuries the race produced in Palestine a constant succession of great men – statesmen and prophets, judges and soldiers. If a body be again given in which its soul can lodge, it may enrich the world. Till full scope is granted, as Macaulay said in the House of Commons 'let us not presume to say that there is no genius among the countrymen of Isaiah, no heroism among the descendants of the Maccabees'.[1]

The following March a revised version of this memorandum was circulated to the cabinet, of which Samuel was a member. In it, he argued that British imperial interests required a British protectorate over Palestine, and that this might provide an opportunity for Jews to immigrate, found colonies and develop the country so that in due course a majority would become settled in and rooted to the land.

Let a Jewish centre be established in Palestine [he urged], let it achieve, as it may well achieve, some measure of spiritual and intellectual greatness, and insensibly the character of the individual Jew, wherever he might be, would be raised. The sordid associations which have attached to the Jewish name would be, to some degree at least, sloughed off, and the value of the Jews as an element in the civilisation of the European peoples would be enhanced.[2]

These, clearly, are the words of a convinced Zionist, who accepts and takes for granted the Zionist analysis of the Jewish predicament and how to surmount it. And for the rest of the war, indeed until his appointment as high commissioner at the end of April 1920, whether in or out of office, though he was not a member of the Zionist Organisation, he remained helpful and sympathetic to the movement. In 1918 and 1919, in particular, as he says in his *Memoirs*, he was 'co-operating closely' with the Zionist leaders,[3] and even ready, at times, to use his influence and connections to further their cause. Thus we find him, for instance, writing to Balfour in March 1919 to express his disquiet at the news of an inter-Allied commission being sent to investigate conditions in the near east. This news, he writes, 'has caused much anxiety to those who are interested in Palestine' and who were afraid that delay and indecision would be harmful to the Zionist cause.[4]

He became the chairman of the Advisory Committee on the Economic Development of Palestine, and as such was consulted by the government on ways of furthering the Zionist programme. In February and March 1920 he was in Palestine on behalf of the Foreign Office, to investigate the 'financial and administrative conditions there, and to advise concerning the line of policy to be followed in future in these respects, should the mandate fall to Great Britain'. If it be asked how Samuel reconciled his Zionist sympathies with an active career in British politics, the answer is that he saw here no contradiction which needed to be reconciled or resolved. In his final report as high commissioner in Palestine there is a paragraph which deals with this subject and which seems an echo of those war-time controversies in which the notables of Anglo-Jewry adopted sharply divergent attitudes. In this passage Samuel refers to the fear of many Jews that the Balfour Declaration would undermine their position as established and fully-fledged citizens. This fear, he declared, led these Jews to regard Zionism and the Balfour Declaration 'with embarrassment, and sometimes with hostility'. Others, however, equally patriotic – and it is among these others that he undoubtedly counted himself – had a contrary view:

They refused to engage in fine-drawn discussions as to the meaning of 'national' and 'people'. They were deeply interested in the return of a body of their co-religionists to Palestine; they wished to see the movement succeed, and were ready to help in promoting it; and at the same time [he went on] they saw no reason why they should not remain, in spirit and in action, as loyal citizens of the states to which they belonged as if Palestine had not entered the field of political discussion and as if the Balfour Declaration had never been made.[5]

It was, then, as an avowed and indeed ardent sympathiser with Zionism that Samuel was chosen by Lloyd George to inaugurate the administration of Palestine under British mandate. Samuel's record as high commissioner may be held to have amply justified Lloyd George's choice. When Samuel left Palestine in 1925 the country was at peace and had been so for four years, Palestine was endowed with a modern and generally efficient administration, and the land was beginning to know some prosperity. Justifiable as it proved to be, Lloyd George's choice was also natural. From the start the prime minister had sympathised with Zionism. His motives were no doubt mixed, some of them even devious, but it is certain that he believed the enterprise of a Jewish National Home in Palestine both feasible and beneficent – beneficent alike to the British empire and to the Jews. Furthermore, it was as a patron of Zionism, as the author of the Balfour Declaration, that the British government publicly justified its case to be the mandatory of the League of Nations in Palestine, and who better than a sympathiser with Zionism to carry out a pro-Zionist policy and thus show the British government to be in earnest over its professions?

On hearing Lloyd George's offer, Samuel's first impulse was, as he tells us in his *Memoirs*,[6] to ask the prime minister whether 'such an appointment was open to the danger that measures, which the non-Jewish population would accept from a British Christian governor, might be objected to if adopted by a Jew'. He therefore did not accept the offer on the spot. It was only after giving the matter further thought, and consulting Weizmann and Sokolow, that he wrote to Lloyd George accepting the post. The objections which he himself had raised, he now came to think, could be overcome. In the long run, he came to believe, the attitude of the non-Jewish population depended upon the reasonableness of his measures and upon the manner in which they were presented. Very soon after taking up his post another consideration began to have weight with him, to become

54

with the years gradually uppermost in his mind. In his *Memoirs*[7] he puts it as follows: 'I had been appointed with full knowledge on the part of His Majesty's Government of my Zionist sympathies, and no doubt largely because of them. But,' he adds, 'I was there to administer the country, not for the benefit of one section of the population only, but for all; not commissioned by the Zionists but in the name of the King.' Samuel, as anyone who looks at his record must agree, was essentially a fair-minded and a punctiliously honourable man. It is therefore not surprising that the duties of his public office should have, very quickly, begun to weigh more with him than the advancement of a scheme which, however near it was to his heart, was yet the private dream and ambition of one section only of the population for which he was responsible.

In a debate in the House of Lords in May 1939 he declared that immediately after the war he, like other figures such as Neville Chamberlain, Winston Churchill and General Smuts, had contemplated that some day or other a Jewish state might be established, but that fuller experience convinced everyone that a Jewish state covering the whole of Palestine was not possible.[8] How quickly he himself became so convinced may be seen from a gloss on the Balfour Declaration which he wrote after the Jaffa riots of May 1921, in consultation with the Colonial Office, and which he made public in a speech delivered at Jerusalem on 3 June. What the Balfour Declaration meant, said Samuel, was 'that the Jews, a people who are scattered throughout the world, but whose hearts are always turned to Palestine, should be enabled to found here their home; and that some among them, within the limits which are fixed by the numbers and interests of the present population, should come to Palestine in order to help by their resources and efforts to develop the country to the advantage of all its inhabitants'.[9] It is, again, instructive to note what he had to say about Zionist aims and ambitions in the Report published in August 1921, in which he reviewed his first year as high commissioner. In it, he referred to those Zionists 'who sometimes forget or ignore the present inhabitants of Palestine', who, intent as they are on realising the Zionist dream, suddenly 'learn with surprise and often with incredulity, that there are half-a-million people in Palestine, many of whom hold, and hold strongly, very different views'. Some of these Zionists, he went on, would 'ride rough-shod' over this opposition and condemn anything else as a weak surrender to violence. He himself did not share such views: 'The policy of His Majesty's

Government', he declared, 'contemplates the satisfaction of the legitimate aspirations of the Jewish race throughout the world in relation to Palestine, combined with a full protection of the existing population. For my own part,' he went on, 'I am convinced that the means can be found to effect this combination. The Zionism that is practicable is the Zionism that fulfils this essential condition'.[10] How far removed from mere Zionist advocacy his attitude became may be instanced by an exchange in which he was involved during the House of Lords debate on the Peel Report. Lord Strabolgi had remarked in passing how 'the case for the Jewish people throughout the world' had been put with force and clarity by Lord Reading, Lord Melchett and Lord Samuel. Samuel at once interjected: 'I hope the noble Lord will allow me to disclaim having stated the Jewish case'.[11]

The Zionism, then, which fulfilled the essential condition laid down in his Report of 1921, was the only Zionism which it was both safe, politic and just to encourage and support. For though his duty embraced much more than the mere sponsorship of Zionism, yet after all, it was part of his duty – as well as his inclination – to promote Zionism.

The duty, thus, to govern Palestine in the interest of all its inhabitants as well as solicitude for Zionism – for that practicable Zionism which to him was now the only acceptable one – required that the existing inhabitants of Palestine should be conciliated and reassured. Other, more immediate and pressing reasons reinforced this attitude. When Lloyd George offered him Palestine Samuel, as we have seen, considered whether his being a Jew ought not to preclude him from accepting. Others also thought similarly. When Allenby, the supreme head of the military administration which had governed Palestine since the end of 1917, heard that Samuel was to become the first civil governor of the country, he hastened to telegraph to Curzon, the foreign secretary: 'I think the appointment of a Jew as first governor will be highly dangerous'. The Muslims, he went on, were in a state of great excitement, having heard that the Balfour Declaration was to be included in the peace treaty. 'The only restraining factor being assurance which has been given by chief administrator that government of country would be a British government. They will regard appointment of a Jew as first governor, even if he is a British Jew, as handing country over at once to a permanent Zionist administration'. Allenby went on to prophesy doom and destruction on Samuel's arrival in Palestine with 'outrages against Jews, murders, raids on Jewish villages, and raids into our territory from east if no wider movement'. The Christians, whether Protestant, Catholic, or Greek Orthodox, would also 'deeply resent transfer of government to Jewish authority', and being quite influential, by throwing their weight against the administration would make 'government of any kind very difficult'.[12] These highly alarmist prognostications, characteristic as they are of Allenby's defective political judgment, surely also reflect the advice and information which the commander-in-chief was receiving from his subordinates in Palestine. Zionists have always vehemently complained of the lack of sympathy shown to their cause by the military administration in Palestine from the fall of Jerusalem until Samuel's appointment, and it must be said that the evidence of the official records in the archives does bear out their complaints. This lack of sympathy, and sometimes downright hostility of course could not remain concealed from the Palestinians. The chief administrators who succeeded one another, Generals Money, Watson and Bols, refused – no doubt for reasons which to them seemed convincing – to publish officially the Balfour Declaration in Palestine. Some two years after the publication of the Balfour Declaration in London, for instance, we find the Chief Political Officer writing from Cairo to the Chief Administrator in Jerusalem that the Declaration 'is to be treated as extremely confidential, and is on no account for any kind of publication'.[13] This, of course, did not mean that the Palestinians were unaware of Zionist ambitions or of the support which the occupying Power was likely to give them. In the circumstances, therefore, the refusal to publish the Balfour Declaration was, as the Court of Enquiry into the Easter riots of 1920 at Jerusalem concluded, a mistake. The people, as the court argued, were never squarely faced with a *chose jugée*, a thing which in the east, they observed, often works miracles in persuading people to accept the inevitable.[14] The dangers of this equivocal situation were no doubt increased by Sharifian propaganda in favour of proclaiming Faisal king of Palestine – a project which Bols, the chief administrator, Waters-Taylor, his chief of staff, and Allenby himself, actually took up and pressed strongly on the government.[15] Their attitude cannot have remained unknown to the Sharifians or their sympathisers in Palestine. All these, then, were reasons why the Palestinians should feel encouraged to hope that their natural and long-standing opposition to Zionism could perhaps deflect the British government from a policy the very vagueness of which magnified, for them, its dangers and terrors. The Easter riots which broke out in Jerusalem less than three months before Samuel took up his post showed what fear and hatred Zionism inspired and what methods could be used to persuade the British government to cease promoting it.

This situation, which was not of his making, provided an urgent and compelling reason for Samuel to embark on a policy of conciliation which would show the Palestinians that while Zionism was being encouraged, they had nothing to fear for their rights and their position.

How then were the Palestinians to be conciliated? To ask the question is immediately to realise how difficult – indeed perhaps impossible – such a policy would be. For who were the Palestinians, and how did one set about conciliating them? The Palestinians were in their overwhelming majority Muslims. Conciliating the Palestinians meant, to all intents and purposes, conciliating the Muslim Palestinians. These Muslims had hitherto formed part of the dominant religion in the Ottoman empire. For long centuries they had been accustomed to look upon the state as being peculiarly their own; and while there were among them, naturally, notables and powerful families, the Muslims of Palestine neither had a political organisation exclusively their own nor were they accustomed to negotiate with the government through representatives duly elected and formally appointed. The British military administration must have found it inconvenient in many ways to deal with this, so to speak, acephalous society and hit on the idea of considering the mufti of Jerusalem as the head of the Muslim community in Palestine and of giving him the title of Grand Mufti. This was in many ways a curious proceeding. In Islam a mufti, originally, was a man learned in the law, the analogue of the *prudens* of Roman law. He was, to start with, in no sense a public official; his standing rather depended on his learning and integrity and it was these qualities which gave weight to his opinions or *fatwas*. In some Muslim states the mufti did become in due course a public official appointed by the ruler to deliver legal opinions. In the Ottoman empire, notably, the right to issue *fatwas* came, from the fifteenth century (of the Christian era) onwards, to be vested in Shaikh-al-Islam in Istanbul who was appointed by the sultan. Muftis were also to be found in the Ottoman provinces. In contrast to the *qadi*, or religious judge, who was a transient and a stranger to the district to which he was appointed, the provincial mufti came from a local family. He was usually an elderly person locally respected who sanctioned the judgments of the *qadi* not so much by his legal learning – which may have been minimal – as by his unimpeachable character. A provincial mufti was thus clearly a notable in the Muslim society of his province; but far from representing his community, he was by no means the most important notable. So much is this the case that it would entail considerable labour to ascertain the names of the muftis of Damascus or Jerusalem or Baghdad or a comparable provincial Ottoman city in the last hundred years. Indeed the only mufti of some renown in recent times who comes to mind is Muhammad Abduh, the mufti of Egypt from 1899 to 1905; and his reputation owed nothing to his office, being the outcome of previous political and literary activities quite removed from religion and jurisprudence. Had the question ever arisen, it would surely never have occurred to anybody to consider Abduh as the head of the Muslim community in Egypt. The circumstances in which Abduh assumed office are also useful in showing how cavalierly Muslim rulers could treat muftis and other religious dignitaries; for Abduh's appointment followed his predecessor's abrupt and instant dismissal by the khedive for having presumed to oppose on religious grounds some legislation sponsored by the Egyptian government.[16] The decision therefore of the military administration to treat the mufti of Jerusalem as head of the Muslim community in Palestine and to give him the title of Grand Mufti – a title hitherto unknown in Islam[17] – was a new departure from which were to issue the most momentous consequences. It is most probable that it was Storrs, the governor of Jerusalem, with his weakness for sonorous ecclesiastical titles, who invented the title; and that it was an English adaptation of the French title, *Grand Rabbin* (though the English 'grand' implies much more than the French '*grand*'), a translation of the Ottoman title *Hakham-bashi* which was well-known and familiar all over the middle east. By 1920, the title Grand Mufti was firmly established in the usage of the military administration. It has to be said, however, in the first place that in so magnifying the position of the mufti, the military administration may have been influenced by the fact that the incumbent mufti at the occupation of Jerusalem was Kamil al-Husaini, member of a large, influential – indeed powerful – family, and in the second place that this aggrandisement of the mufti remained something informal, at best semi-official, and was never given the sanction of law.

The mufti Kamil al-Husaini died on 21 March 1921, some nine

59

months after Samuel had become high commissioner, and the events connected with the choice of his successor may throw some light on Samuel's policy of conciliation, which was perhaps the most important and difficult issue facing him in the government of Palestine. Shortly after the Young Turk Revolution of 1908 the Ottoman government had promulgated a law regulating the election of provincial muftis.[18] According to this law, the mufti of a province such as that of Jerusalem was to be appointed by the government from a list of three candidates selected by a college of electors comprising: 1. Imams, preachers and teachers of the great mosques; 2. The elected Muslim members of the municipal councils in the province, and 3. The elected Muslim members of the administrative council of the province.

In 1921, by reason of the war and its aftermath, no administrative council existed in the Jerusalem province and the members of the municipal councils were not elected but had been nominated by the military administration. The electoral college prescribed by the Ottoman law could therefore not be convened, but arrangements were put in hand to call a meeting of imams and other religious persons together with the Muslim nominated members of the municipalities in the Jerusalem province, in the belief obviously that such a meeting was the nearest approximation to the electoral college required by the law.

Kamil al-Husaini's death immediately precipitated a struggle for his succession. Writing to Storrs, the district governor, to notify him of the mufti's death, the *qadi* of Jerusalem added: 'His brother Hajj Amin efendi is his successor'. This was obviously not a statement of fact but the expression of a wish, and in the days following many petitions were sent to the district governor from shaikhs of tribes, notables and private persons urging that Hajj Amin was the people's choice.[19] This was obviously a concerted move organised by the Husaini interest and designed to pressure the high commissioner into choosing Hajj Amin as mufti out of the list of three candidates to be elected by the electoral college, where it was clearly hoped that his name would figure. Hajj Amin was the late mufti's younger brother, and he was very young indeed for the position to which he aspired. Born in 1895 or 1896,[20] he was therefore in 1921 either twenty-five or twenty-six years of age. He is said to have attended al-Azhar in Cairo, but his religious studies cannot have been either long or arduous, for he is also said to have served as an Ottoman officer during the war. After the British occupation of Jerusalem we find him employed – in what must have been a subordinate capacity – in the district governor's office. We then hear of him in 1918 helping to recruit Palestinians for the Sharifian army under the direction of Captain C. D. Brunton. He was then described as 'very pro-English'. But his attitude changed when he came to learn of British support for Zionism, to which he reacted with 'surprise and anger'.[21] He became one of the leaders of the Easter riots in Jerusalem in 1920, and for his part in the disturbance a court martial sentenced him to ten years' rigorous imprisonment. The sentence was pronounced *in absentia*, since Hajj Amin had fled from Jerusalem and taken refuge among the Trans-Jordanian tribes. The high commissioner visited the area in August 1920 and at a meeting at as-Salt a number of shaikhs requested him publicly to pardon Hajj Amin and Arif el-Arif, another Jerusalemite also implicated in the Easter riots. As he wrote in a letter of 26 August to general headquarters, Cairo, 'For political reasons I considered it desirable to announce at the meeting that both the offenders might be pardoned'.[22] By the following October Hajj Amin was back at Jerusalem where we see him included in a police black list of people to be actively watched, and described as 'agitator'.[23]

This then was the record of one of the contenders for the post of mufti of Jerusalem. His main rival was Shaikh Hisam al-Din Jarallah, the inspector of the religious courts, who in fact also began to collect suffrages for himself as soon as the mufti Kamil had died. He must have been a force to contend with, for two days after the mufti's death the deputy director of public security was reporting that 'the efforts of Sheikh Husam al-Din Jarallah on his own behalf may lead to faction strife'.[24]

On the face of it, Shaikh Hisam al-Din was much more than his turbulent and colourful rival the kind of person who had traditionally been chosen as mufti: a man of respectable reputation and with some knowledge of the law. And yet there are indications that Samuel was prepared, before the meeting of the electoral college, to use his prerogative in favour of Hajj Amin. In a note dated 11 April, the day before the meeting of the electoral college, he recorded a discussion with Hajj Amin 'at considerable length' 'on the political situation and the question of his appointment to the office of Grand Mufti' – and we notice that Samuel seems to have accepted 'Grand Mufti' as a proper title for the mufti of Jerusalem. At this interview, at which Storrs was present, Hajj Amin 'declared his earnest desire to cooperate with the government, and his belief in the good intentions of the British government towards the Arabs. He gave assurance that the influence of his family and himself would be devoted to maintaining tranquility in Jerusalem ...'.[25] It is quite clear that this interview was meant to prepare the way for the high commissioner to select Hajj Amin's name from the list of three candidates among whom he probably felt sure to be included, at the election which was to be held on the morrow.

Why, we may ask, was Samuel prepared to appoint as mufti a man of this kind and with such a record? And the answer probably lies in the situation with which he was confronted – a situation which was not of his making. At the Easter riots of 1920 the mayor of Jerusalem happened to be the head of the Husaini family, Musa Kazim Pasha al-Husaini. During the riots, Storrs tells us, 'he became first intractable and then defiant' and the district governor decided to dismiss him. In his place he appointed someone from a rival family, the ex-Ottoman deputy Raghib al-Nashashibi.[26] This happened before Samuel took up his post, and it may well have been represented to him – perhaps by Storrs – that it would be impolitic for both the mayor and the mufti of Jerusalem to be drawn from outside the Husaini clan, and therefore Hajj Amin – such as he was – should be chosen.

The meeting of the electors took place at the governorate on 12 April; to the surprise of the government, Shaikh Hisam al-Din Jarallah was given the largest number of votes, whilst Hajj Amin came at the bottom of the poll – he received only eight votes – and thus could not be included in the list of three candidates from which the high commissioner was to choose the mufti.[27] The result, as a report from the deputy director of Public Security (dated 14 April) informs us, incensed the members of the Husaini family and a meeting was immediately held at the house of Jamil al-Husaini to organise protests and deputations.[28] A powerful attack on the election and its results was in fact soon mounted. Numerous petitions and telegrams were sent to the government; rumours were put about that the *ulamas* who voted in the election had received bribes from the government, that the Jews, or else Raghib al-Nashashibi, had exerted their sinister influence against the Husaini candidate. A graphic example of the lengths to which this campaign was taken is provided by a notice posted on 19 April in the Old City. Entitled 'Wake up Moslems, The Jews are interfering in the election of the mufti', it began:

'Awake and prevent danger before it occurs. The accursed traitors whom you all know, have combined with the Jews, to have one of their party appointed mufti . . .'

Such a mufti, the notice went on to say, would assist the Jews by selling to them *waqf* property and particularly the *waqf* of Abu Midian which included the Western Wall; he would agree to all Zionist claims and kill the national spirit in the country; he would hand over to the Jews the Dome of the Rock and the Aqsa mosque so that they might pull them down and rebuild the Temple, 'as stated by Alfred Mond and the president of the Zionist Commission, Dr Eder.' 'The pride of Islam is dead', concluded the notice, 'but God wants to punish you for having opposed the Moslem government of the caliphate which protected the religion. Will you accept the shame to have a Jewish Zionist mufti and that your religious affairs should become a plaything in their hands?'[29] Finally the election was attacked as invalid on the ground that the membership of the electoral college was not as stipulated in the law. This powerful onslaught soon produced its effect on the government. A dispatch of 9 May informed the Colonial office that 'learned opinion, represented by the law courts, has not favoured the popular candidate Al Haj Amin al-Husseini' but that technical flaws in the constitution of the electorate had delayed the appointment of the mufti,[30] and by the end of the month it was quite clear that the election was to be disregarded, and Hajj Amin allowed to become mufti.

This outcome was determined largely, perhaps decisively, by the advice of one member of Samuel's secretariat, Ernest T. Richmond. Ernest Richmond was by profession an architect and had been employed before the war in the Egyptian Public Works Department. He was Storrs' intimate friend, and it was Storrs who, in 1918, rescued him from the Imperial War Graves Commission where he was then 'eating out his heart',[31] and brought him to Jerusalem in order to survey the damaged fabric of the Dome of the Rock and advise on restoration. He seems in due course, to have become some kind of assistant to Storrs,[32] with whom he shared a house in Jerusalem – as he had shared a flat with him earlier in Cairo. When Samuel was appointed high commissioner he chose Brigadier Wyndham Deedes as his civil secretary, and on the latter's suggestion the Foreign Office were asked at the beginning of August 1920 to release E. M. B. Ingram, then acting as private secretary to Lord Milner – who was then engaged in negotiations with Zaghlul – so that he might serve as political secretary in the newly-organised secretariat at Jerusalem.

The Foreign Office were not willing to release Ingram, and suggested instead James Morgan of the Levant Consular Service. At this point Storrs seems to have suggested Richmond for the post, and with the high commissioner's approval on 3 September he sent this telegram to Richmond who was then in London:

> Post vacant in civil secretary's office salary 1000 plus 100 allowances. Duties general administration and of nature agreeable and suitable to yourself. I recommend.

The telegram did not reach London at the time, and failing to receive an answer, Storrs wrote again to Richmond who now made enquiries at the Foreign Office. Eventually the telegram was repeated on 24 September and at last communicated to Richmond. A telegram from the Foreign Office on 27 September informed Samuel that his offer was accepted.[33]

Richmond was appointed assistant secretary (political). His duties in this office were of the highest importance. He was to maintain liaison between the government and the Muslim community and, in effect, to be the high commissioner's chief adviser on Muslim affairs. Towards the end of 1922 the Colonial Office proposed to change his title from assistant secretary (political) to second assistant secretary. Richmond took this to be a downgrading of his office and contemplated resigning unless his original title was maintained. Samuel wrote a dispatch on 27 December, urging his case and accompanied it by a private letter to Shuckburgh of the Middle East Department in which he stated that Richmond's resignation 'would have considerable political consequences. In the absence of any Arab in the higher ranks of the administration, Richmond who is in close and sympathetic touch with the Arabs, acts as a most useful intermediary. If he were to go', the high commissioner concluded, 'there is no one to take his place'.[34] By the following July the question of Richmond's official title had still not been settled and Sir Gilbert Clayton, the chief secretary, who on Samuel's absence on leave was then officer administering the government, took the matter up in another dispatch. His description of Richmond's function in the administration was somewhat different from Samuel's, and it is interesting to see how the duties of the assistant secretary (political) had by then developed. 'With regard to Palestine itself', wrote Sir Gilbert Clayton, 'rightly or wrongly, the Political Section, and more especially the present head thereof, has become the principal medium of personal approach to the government available to the Arab elements and is regarded in that respect as to some extent the counterpart of the Zionist Organisation'.[35]

The anomaly of a high British official in the secretariat being regarded as the Arab counterpart of the Zionist Organisation was noted by someone at the Colonial Office who pencilled this comment on the margin of Clayton's dispatch: 'but the Arabs don't pay for it'. As the minutes on Samuel's earlier dispatch and letter show, the Department in London was well aware of Richmond's sympathies and how their overt expression was little consonant with British policy. A minute by Mr Clauson is particularly noteworthy:

I must admit [he wrote] that I should not personally have one minute's regret if Mr Richmond resigned, he is by trade an architect, not a Secretariat officer at all, and he has entered the latter profession too late in life to make it possible for him to adapt himself to it. Moreover [Clauson added] he has not taken any particular pains to adapt himself to it; he is a declared enemy of the Zionist policy and almost as frankly declared an enemy of the Jewish policy of H.M.G. . . . Indeed [he concluded] I think that the government, so far from losing would gain very greatly by excluding from its Secretariat so very partisan a figure as Mr Richmond and starting again on a strictly non-partisan basis.[36]

In the event Richmond did not resign until March 1924 and when he did, addressed to the high commissioner a remarkable letter. The letter, dated 13 March 1924, appears to be an answer to an invitation to a dinner. In it Richmond says that he had been led 'gradually and most reluctantly, but definitely' to believe that the Zionist commission, the Middle East Department of the Colonial Office and Samuel's own administration 'are dominated and inspired by a spirit which I can only regard as evil'. He finds himself completely opposed to these policies, but his opposition is not merely political, but moral or even religious. He had tried to alter the machine, but had completely failed and now had to go. He found repugnant any act which implied fellowship with this evil. Such an act would be dishonest 'because there is no fellowship of spirit; on the contrary there is enmity; not, I hope, personal, but still enmity'. If, knowing all this, Samuel still wanted him to come to the dinner, he would do so, but he would do so in the knowledge that he was committing a dishonest act, 'that, in coming, I am sacrificing something of right conduct to the duty I still owe you as my chief for the time being'.[37]

During his three-and-a-half years in the Secretariat, then, Richmond was as he said, trying to alter the machine. This may explain and justify his activities on behalf of Hajj Amin in the year 1921. As has been seen, by the end of April the high commissioner was disposed to delay the appointment of the mufti on the ground that the election of 12 April was technically imperfect. An unsigned note of 3 May which is most probably by Richmond suggested that the post of 'Grand Mufti' should not be left open any longer, that a quick settlement would have a good effect, and proposed the issue of a notice to the effect that

the recent election having been shown to be irregular is null and void, that in the view of the reception by the government of Mazbattas from the Mudarisin, Imams, Ulemas and numerous individuals throughout Palestine in favour of the appointment of Al Hajj Amin al-Husseini, the government considers it to be clearly proved that the people of Palestine desire the nomination of Al Hajj Amin and consequently nominate him.

At the bottom of this note the civil secretary Wyndham Deedes wrote: 'I don't agree'.[38] The suggested notice was never issued, but by means which are as yet unclear, by 10 May Shaikh Hisam al-Din Jarallah **was** prevailed upon to withdraw his candidature.[39] Furthermore, Hajj Amin organised on 31 May a meeting of nine religious dignitaries and notables before whom the mufti of Nablus delivered an opinion that the election of 12 April was invalid. We may add that the same mufti of Nablus delivered on the following day an opinion – which is also on the file – that this election was quite valid. The minutes of the meeting of 31 May were written and signed by Hajj Amin and translated by Richmond. The high commissioner was still not prevailed upon to announce officially the election of Hajj Amin, but from a memorandum by Richmond dated 7 June we learn that on a date not specified – probably after 10 May – Samuel and Deedes privately assured Hajj Amin that he was appointed mufti. This memorandum, a long and remarkable document, was therefore devoted to obtaining for Hajj Amin a formal and public letter of appointment. The memorandum, in the first place, emphasises the overwhelming desire of the people to see Hajj Amin appointed mufti. Richmond produces an imposing list of Muslim divines, notables and beduin shaikhs who, according to him, were all for Hajj Amin, and adds to them the Orthodox patriarch, the Syrian bishop, the *locum tenens* of the Armenian patriarch, the head of the Armenian part of the Church of the Holy Sepulchre, the bishop of the Coptic convent

66

and monks of the Orthodox church. In contrast to this overwhelming support, opposition to Hajj Amin, Richmond tried to show, was most suspect. It consisted of the Jews who were believed by 'a very large number of people' to be against Hajj Amin and to have arranged the election so that he might be set aside; their efforts were seconded by what he called the 'intrigues of the Nashashibi faction' which were favoured by the legal secretary. In the circumstances, this was clearly meant to be a telling, indeed a clinching argument. The legal secretary was Mr Bentwich, not only a fellow-Jew but also a relative of the high commissioner's. About him Richmond was outspoken. As has been seen, the mufti of Nablus having declared on 31 May that the election of 12 April was invalid, proceeded the very next day to change his mind and produced an opinion that the election was valid. This opinion the legal secretary seems to have sent to Deedes. Richmond now pronounced it obscure – which it was – and he questioned the legal status of the mufti of Nablus to pronounce on such a matter; 'but the chief point to bear in mind', he added, 'is that no opinion emanating from the legal secretary or his entourage or from any one dependent in any degree on the favour of his Department will at the present time be regarded as other than suspect by a very large majority of the people in this country'.[40] What effect such an argument had on a high commissioner jealous of his honour and determined to avoid the slightest aspersion on his uprightness and equity we can only conjecture. Moreover, as a minister Samuel had hitherto dealt with civil servants who avoided political commitment and whose primary purpose in tendering advice was to ensure the carrying on of the king's government. Most probably, he had so far never had to deal with a senior civil servant who believed passionately that it was his duty to alter the machine which his superiors expected him to maintain, and he may therefore have taken for granted that advice received in Jerusalem would rest on the same tacit assumptions which obtained in London.

The upshot of the Husaini campaign supported by Richmond from inside the Secretariat was that Hajj Amin was allowed tacitly to assume the office of mufti. He received, however, no official letter of nomination and his appointment was never gazetted,[41] which may indicate that Samuel had misgivings over the whole affair. But Hajj Amin did occupy the office of mufti of Jerusalem, did style himself 'Grand Mufti', and did claim that he was the head of the Muslim community in Palestine. Richmond himself, in one memorandum

after another from August to October 1921 did his best to enhance
Hajj Amin's position by arguing that his salary should be higher
than that of other muftis – he quoted an argument of Storrs' to the
effect that after all the bishop of London was paid more than the
bishop of Chichester – and by insisting time and again – and it was
sheer insistence buttressed by no evidence – that the mufti of
Jerusalem was the head of the Muslim community, that to treat him
on an equality with other muftis would not be received 'with quiet
acquiescence' by the Muslims of Palestine, and that such a step would
be likely to be regarded as 'a deliberate attempt to slight the Moslem
community'.[42] What in retrospect Richmond thought about it all, or
at any rate what he would have wanted the world at large to think is
indicated by a letter which he drafted in August 1923, in answer to
one which Colonel Kisch, chairman of the Palestine Zionist Executive
had sent to the chief secretary the previous January. In this letter
Kisch had said that 'if, by arranging the appointment of the present
mufti, through means involving a direct departure from the established procedure, the government hoped to earn the collaboration of
this party in matters not connected with the Jewish National Home,
it must by now have been gravely disillusioned'. Richmond's draft
answer constituted an utter rebuttal of Kisch's argument: 'While I
do not recognise the existence of any obligation on the part of the
government to reply to criticisms in respect of its appointments,
nevertheless I think it worthwhile in this instance to put you in
possession of the facts'. 'The facts', according to this draft were that
'His appointment was desired by a great majority of the Arabs of
Palestine and took place in accordance with existing regulations. To
have thwarted that desire would not have reacted favourably on the
welfare of Palestine or on that of any section of the inhabitants, not
excluding the Jews'. Clayton, at the time officer administering the
government, ordered that the draft should not be sent, and the
question allowed to drop.[43]

In protesting against the appointment of the mufti, Kisch of course
was concerned with the effects of this appointment on Zionist work in
Palestine. These effects are widely known and need not be laboured.
But it is worth while considering briefly its effect on the Arabs of
Palestine. If Hajj Amin had received enough votes on 12 April
1921 to be included in the list of candidates from which the high
commissioner was to choose the mufti, and if Samuel had chosen
him, the appointment, while admittedly bizarre, would have indi-

cated respect for the due process of law and would thus have perhaps served to conciliate the Palestinians by showing them that here was a government which respected elections and the wishes of the Muslims in the management of their communal affairs. Again, if the high commissioner had chosen to disregard the election and by an exercise of free arbitrary power appointed Hajj Amin – or anybody else – as mufti, he would have been behaving like the generality of Muslim rulers whose cavalier treatment of the religious institution is an abiding theme of Islamic history. From such an exercise of prerogative, the Palestinians would have concluded that a high commissioner was only a sultan writ in Frankish letters, and would have adjusted their behaviour accordingly. But to have tacitly allowed Hajj Amin, in response to agitation engineered by the Husaini clan to become mufti, and that without a letter of appointment defining the length and conditions of his tenure, was to invite the Palestinians to conclude that in Palestine rent-a-crowd was king; and to allow the Husainis, already powerful enough in Palestine, to become the self-appointed exclusive and irresponsible spokesmen of the Palestinians, whose power their fellow-countrymen could, as the sequel showed, challenge only at their peril. It was the Husainis who directed the political strategy of the Palestinians until 1947, and they led them to utter ruin.

The establishment of Husaini dominance over Arab Palestine was made easier by another development which followed shortly after Hajj Amin's elevation. This was the creation of the Supreme Muslim Council. Speaking in a debate on Palestine in the House of Lords in December 1938 Samuel pointed out that the system of *millet* or communal organisation as developed in the Ottoman empire was something suited to middle eastern conditions and that on taking over from the military in Palestine he had come to the conclusion 'that this system of communities was in the main the right one'.[44] This was a shrewd and judicious appreciation. From it the conclusion naturally followed that just as the Jews and the Christians had their long-established communal organisations so the Muslims, who had not needed such an organisation under the Ottoman regime, should now also have theirs. Such a communal organisation was necessary to manage the extensive Muslim religious endowments or *waqfs*, hitherto administered by the Ottoman government, to choose and appoint imams and preachers for the mosques, and *qadis* for the religious courts – these functions also having been previously discharged by the Ottoman administration. 'For the British administration to assume control of the endowments and make appointments to the offices', remarked Samuel in his *Memoirs*, 'we did not consider advisable'. And he added: 'particularly an administration pledged to promote in Palestine the establishment of a Jewish National Home'.[45] Here then was another consideration adding weight to Samuel's general preference for communal organisation. It is worth examining what it is which specifically gave point to Samuel's belief that it was undesirable for an administration pledged to promote the establishment of a Jewish National Home to supervise and regulate Muslim religious affairs. At the beginning of 1918 the British government decided that a Zionist commission headed by Weizmann should go to Palestine. It was not quite clear what exactly it was to do there, or what powers it had, but its presence in the country, its access to the commander-in-chief and to other senior officers, rightly or wrongly gave the impression that it was a privileged body with extraordinary powers which no authority in Palestine was able to restrain. The Palestinians could not help but contrast the humble and difficult position of the Zionist settlers in Ottoman times, with their seemingly exalted position under the British occupation, with this Zionist commission to protect them and advance their interests. It was not simply the mere existence of the Zionist commission which gave rise to fear and antagonism; the activities of some of its members helped to intensify dislike for it. There was, for instance, the aggressive and persistent Jabotinsky, Ussishkin, whose attitude Meinertzhagen – not an enemy of Zionism – described in a dispatch of November 1919 as 'one of overbearing intolerance with a contempt for compromise',[46] and Weizmann himself. Though more subtle and politic than his colleagues, Weizmann was yet not averse from trying to make British authorities act as though the Balfour Declaration meant much more than they were prepared to concede, and he also must have found it difficult to restrain a legitimate feeling of triumph. His behaviour at the period may be illustrated by two significant episodes. 'As to Weizmann and Palestine', wrote Curzon in a letter to Balfour on 26 January 1919, 'I entertain no doubt that he is out for a Jewish government, if not at the moment then in the near future', and he went on to describe how, in the draft mandate for Palestine, to the words 'all necessary arrangements for the establishment in Palestine of a Jewish National Home', Weizmann had added the words: 'or Commonwealth'. 'You meant the first', Curzon observed, 'but he

interpreted it as meaning the second'.[47] It is reasonable to suppose
that the tactics he tried in his dealings with Balfour, Weizmann
would also employ in Palestine. The second episode dates from
November 1921, and may give us an idea of the impression which the
Zionist leader made in the years immediately following the Balfour
Declaration. The Colonial Office had succeeded in arranging a private
meeting between the Arab Delegation then visiting London and the
Zionist Organisation and we have a report on the proceedings in a
minute by Mr E. Mills, who was later to serve in Palestine and who
is not known for anti-Zionist prejudice. 'Doctor Weizmann', recorded
Mills, 'while his speech was conciliatory, adopted an unfortunate
manner in delivering it. His attitude was of the nature of a conqueror
handing to beaten foes the terms of peace. Also I think he despises
the members of the delegation as not worthy protagonists – that it is
a little derogatory to him to expect him to meet them on the same
ground'.[48] It is fair to assume that if such was the impression gathered
by a not unfriendly observer in 1921, then the same impression could
have been derived by others, two or three years before.

The Zionist commission and the reactions to which it gave rise
were not anything for which Samuel was responsible. Rather, he had
to take account of them when he came to administer the country.
And we do know that the widespread notion that the Zionist commission and the Palestine government were one and the same body
gave him considerable worry. In November 1921 his civil secretary
Wyndham Deedes wrote to Shuckburgh at the Colonial Office a
private letter. He stated that he was writing at the high commissioner's
suggestion, and went on to express alarm at the growing mistrust
manifested by the Arab population for the administration; he attributed it to the fact that every administrative measure was believed
to be inspired by the Zionists 'and impotently to have been accepted
by the administration'. In the eyes of the Arabs, he declared 'the
administration and the Zionists are one'. To remedy this situation,
Deedes suggested, the anomalous position of the Zionist Organisation
in the mandate 'should be abolished' and the administration should
be 'left to govern this country with the help of a body in which all
sections of the community should be adequately represented'.[49]
Deedes' suggestion was not feasible; hence it was all the more important that an administration which laboured under such suspicion
should allow Muslims freedom in the management of their religious
affairs. At a conference of notables, muftis and principal *ulamas* in

November 1920 it was agreed to set up a Muslim communal organisation, but it was also agreed that the government should retain financial control over the administration of Muslim religious endowments (which had hitherto been exclusively the affair of the Ottoman government).[50] But we find that in subsequent negotiations, after Hajj Amin became mufti, this stipulation totally disappeared. Regulations promulgated at the end of 1921 provided for the setting up of a Supreme Moslem Council to be composed of a Rais al-Ulema who was to hold office permanently and of four members elected for a period of four years each. This council was to have unfettered control over the management of religious endowments and the expenditure of income therefrom, over the appointment and dismissal of all *shari'a* and *waqf* officials and over the nomination – and virtually the appointment – of *qadis*. And all these enormous powers which touched innumerable Palestinians in their livelihood and welfare were almost totally exempt from official inspection and control. Samuel's object in agreeing to these regulations may be gathered from a passage in his dispatch transmitting the regulations to London: 'I believe', he wrote, 'that the final settlement of the Moslem religious question will be acceptable to the Moslem population of the country and will bring them assurance that the government desires in every way that they should have complete control of their own religious affairs and religious endowments'.[51]

Those who were to elect this powerful body, as the regulations stipulated, were the secondary electors who had been elected at the last Ottoman elections which had taken place in May 1914. This committee met on 9 January 1922. Out of fifty-six electors, fifty-three were present. A motion supported by Raghib al-Nashashibi proposed postponement of the elections; it was lost by forty-three votes to ten, whereupon Nashashibi and five others withdrew from the meeting in protest. The remaining forty-seven electors proceeded to elect the council and Hajj Amin was by forty votes chosen Rais al-Ulema, or president of the council. It was a life appointment and it gave him an income of over £100,000 a year to dispose of and extensive patronage which enabled him to set up and head what the Peel Commission in their *Report* called a third parallel government in Palestine[52] – the other two of course being the government of Palestine and the Jewish Agency. Of these three governments, the Supreme Moslem Council was the most irresponsible, the least fettered by the rule of law, and the least amenable to public agitation or pressure. In spite of the regulations which provided for periodical election of members – but not of the president – the members elected in 1922 remained in office until late in 1937 when the Palestine government at last brought itself to disband the council and thus publicly to recognise – though never explicitly – to what despotism its own policies had abandoned the Arabs of Palestine.[53]

By the mid-1920s, then, both the Jews and the Arabs had, as H. J. Simson put it in *British Rule and Rebellion* (one of the most percipient books written on Palestine under the mandate), succeeded 'in growing crocodile skins round their respective communities, through which the rule of the government of Palestine hardly penetrated at all'. And the same author went on:

> Though there were plenty of representatives of the civil power throughout the country, they dealt in all cases with one, or possibly with two communities, each having an organisation of its own, and each with a voice speaking in Jerusalem. The voices were seldom silent, and were usually complaining of or objecting to something. As a result, rule in Palestine was over-centralised, the voices in Jerusalem were heard too often, and conciliation took the place of rule. So there was order, followed by counter-order, and, in consequence, disorder.[54]

Samuel also devised another strategy to conciliate the Palestinians and wean them of their fears. This was to allow them a say in government through representation in a legislative council. The Palestine Order-in-Council, issued in August 1922, provided for a legislative council to consist of ten official and twelve elected members. Of these eight were to be Muslim, two Jewish and two Christian. Elections were to be conducted according to the Ottoman law. The Palestinian leaders at once declared that unless they were given a clear majority over the officials and the Jews, they would refuse to cooperate in the elections. These leaders no doubt calculated that by being intransigent they would obtain more from the British government than by cooperating, and thus tacitly acquiescing in the mandate and the Zionist programme which it incorporated. Their attitude may also have been more than mere tactical calculation. For neither then nor later did the Palestinian leaders (who were of course largely Muslim) accept the fact that they were no longer the masters in the country and members of a ruling group which dominated not only Palestine, but also an extensive empire. They formed part of the Muslim world and their attitude was governed to some extent by their relation to

73

this world. This preoccupation comes out clearly in a letter from the mufti of Haifa reporting to Hajj Amin on the results of a journey to India which he undertook after the boycott of the legislative council elections in 1923.

We reached the country [wrote Muhammad Murad, the mufti of Haifa, on 17 December 1923] and found repugnance by every Muslim towards anyone who was Arab; if told, Here is an Arab, they took him to be like the Sharif Husain of whom they say that he betrayed Islam and caused the ruin of the caliphate. We were conscious of this situation immediately we arrived in the country, even though the leaders tried to disguise it out of politeness and kindness. We began to rebut this notion and to show all that Palestine had done in giving total aid to the Turkish army and how she fought to the end, etc. We explained to some of them the situation in Palestine, and the success in the boycott of the elections and of the advisory council was of the greatest help in rebutting these allegations. The truth is that this boycott, and our success in it, compelled everybody to respect us at the start, especially the leaders who greatly admired this success.[55]

We must also remember that this consciousness of belonging to a ruling, an imperial group, played its part in making the Palestinian leaders adopt the rigid and cutting attitude towards Zionism, which was characteristic of them from first to last.

At the beginning of 1923, then, the government announced that elections for the legislative council would be held shortly. The Palestine Arab Congress immediately mounted a vigorous campaign against it, which succeeded in frightening off both candidates and electors. Those participating in the elections were branded as traitors, to be cursed publicly and boycotted by their community.[56] The campaign was all the more successful in that the government remained utterly passive in face of it. In his Final Report on the Administration of Palestine, Samuel remarked that 'the government did not regard it as its duty to exercise any pressure on the people to participate';[57] but the government not only did not regard it its duty to put pressure on the electors to vote, it also did not consider it its duty to take action against those who were using pressure to prevent voting. The secretary of the executive committee of the Palestine Arab Congress, Jamal al-Husaini, could insolently taunt the government with its inaction. The government, he wrote, had promulgated laws with special penalties against intimidation: 'But so far', he went on, 'the government brought up only one single case where three of the accused were acquitted and the fourth condemned to pay a fine of £E25. What made the government shrink from applying its own laws when they cherish such beliefs we cannot tell'.[58]

The results of the election were such that the high commissioner was compelled to announce that the scheme to set up a legislative council was being suspended because the people 'have not fully availed themselves of the opportunity offered to participate in the government of the country through elected representatives'.[59] This, of course, was for the Palestine Arab Congress a considerable – though an easy – victory. A minute of 23 February 1923 by Mr Moody – who had served as an administrator in Palestine and who was then seconded to the Colonial Office – was acute and sagacious in describing the situation: 'In order to effect a boycott of the elections', Mr Moody wrote in comment on the Political Report for January, which gave an account of the boycott, 'resolution is not required on the part of the Arab populace; only apathy and inertia. The executive committee of the Arab Congress is flogging a dead horse. If the elections fail they will claim the result as a victory for themselves, and a defeat for the government. It is a pity to have given them such an easy mark'.[60] But one could go further and say that even if there had been no boycott and a legislative council had been elected, yet this would not have ensured the representation of the Palestinians and their involvement in the process of government which Samuel desired. As elections in Ottoman times showed, the result of electoral exercises followed the wishes not of the population but of the government. If, as in this case, the government did not interfere and even allowed or condoned a boycott, to the people this only meant either that the government was secretly opposed to elections or was so weak that its wishes had better be disregarded and its opponents supported. In such circumstances, as Moody observed in a later minute, nomination was more suitable than election. 'I have tried', he remarked, 'to conduct elections in villages for the mukhtarship and uniformly failed'.[61] But elections had been ordained; a boycott had then been proclaimed which the government had done nothing to counteract. Those leaders therefore who had advocated an extreme line were now triumphant. It was a situation which was to be repeated again and again during the mandate. To confine ourselves to Samuel's time, the failure of the elections led him to propose the setting up once again of the nominated advisory council which he had formed shortly after his arrival in Palestine.

75

Invitations to serve on the council were sent to ten Muslems and Christians (who included Raghib al-Nashashibi, Arif al-Dajani, Sulaiman Tuqan, Amin al-Hadi and Isma'il al-Husaini). They started by accepting, but withdrew when agitation against them was organised by the Palestine Arab Congress.[62] A few months later, still in an attempt to provide the Palestinians with representative institutions, the government offered to set up an Arab Agency, to be the counterpart of the Jewish Agency. On this occasion the 'moderates', knowing that the 'extremists' would reject the proposal, 'decided to forestall them by publishing their own non-acceptance'.[63] In his minute of 23 February, when all these developments were still in the future, Moody had written with prescient common sense: 'In Palestine a politician cannot hope to be successful unless he is an extremist. The personal influence of the Arab extremists on the *effendis* in the towns is great. The personal influence of the *effendis* over the *fellaheen* in the villages is even greater . . .'. The government's quest for representative Palestinians had put it – and the Palestinians – at the mercy of the 'extremists'.

If this was so – and beyond any doubt, it was so – the attempt to introduce European representative devices among the Palestinians was hopeless. It is of course perfectly true that the people of Palestine were at one with those who claimed to speak for them in their utter opposition to Zionism. But this was not enough to make these leaders representative, for they were neither properly or periodically elected, nor were they amenable to the checks and controls which representation normally entails. One of Samuel's successors, Sir Arthur Wauchope, once asked a delegation of the Palestine Arab Congress how they had come to be appointed representative of the Arab population. He was answered by Jamal al-Husaini who said that

from the government point of view they were not elected officially, but the Arabs accepted them as their representatives and since 1920, government had also recognised the Arab executive as representative. They represented both the townspeople and the village population. The actual executive was composed of forty persons, who represented the three hundred members of the [Palestine Arab] Congress.[64]

Jamal al-Husaini's claim was, of course, untenable; but the Palestine government, anxious to balance Arab against Jewish representatives, and trapped by its own long and futile quest for representative institutions, was in no position to contest it.

76

There remains one device to be considered, by which Samuel hoped to conciliate the Palestinians and make Zionism more acceptable to them. His partiality for it appears very early in his connection with Palestine, and he continued to favour it long after his period as high commissioner. The device was to involve in one way or another Palestine's Arabic-speaking neighbours with Palestine and its problems, in the belief that this would lessen friction in the country and reassure the Palestinians. Samuel, in other words, was an early believer in pan-Arabism. It was immediately following his first visit to Palestine that Samuel broached to Curzon the scheme of an Arab union in which Palestine would be included. While in the country he had heard that the military administration, alarmed at the doings of Faisal's followers in Damascus and at the anti-Zionist sentiments of the Palestinians, was advocating that Faisal should be recognised as the king of a united Syria, including Palestine.[65] Samuel rightly considered this scheme a threat to Zionist interests, and proposed an alternative scheme: 'I think', he wrote to Curzon, 'the solution lies in the formation of a loose confederation of the Arab-speaking states, each of which should be under its own appropriate government, but all of which should be combined together for common and economic purposes. The seat of such a confederation should be Damascus, and Faisal might be recognised, not only as sovereign in his own state, but also as the honorary head of the confederation'. As Samuel envisaged it, the union would be 'principally economic and not political'; and Palestine, ruled by Great Britain under a mandate embodying the provisions relating to the Jewish National Home, would form part of it. Curzon's immediate reaction to the proposal was to dismiss it briefly. He minuted Samuel's letter: 'A federal council at Damascus with the League of Nations behind it fills me with no sort of enthusiasm'.[66]

Samuel's scheme of confederation was not a mere passing response to a momentary threat. On the contrary. The idea that Palestine's difficulties would be less intractable if her neighbours took an interest in her affairs seems a recurrent one in his thoughts. In his letter to Curzon where he commented on Allenby's fears regarding his appointment to Palestine he insisted on the importance of an understanding with Faisal. 'If that could be effected', he wrote, 'the Arab extremists in Palestine would have no ground on which to stand'.[67] This, of course, was an illusion since the Sharifians had neither power nor following to control or influence events in Palestine. The illusion was widespread among both British and Zionists and took a very long time a-dying.

Some two years after suggesting the Arab economic union, Samuel once more put forward a scheme of Arab unity by which, he hoped, the situation in Palestine would be eased. In a letter to the secretary of state of 12 December 1922, Samuel suggested that the government should promote a confederation of Arab states to include the Hijaz, Syria, Palestine, Trans-Jordan, Iraq and possibly Najd. The president of the confederation would be the king of the Hijaz, and there would be a council to look after the common interests of the confederation, such as communications, customs, extradition, culture, and religion. 'More important, however, than any specific functions of the council', he went on, 'would be the fact of its existence. This in itself would give satisfaction to Arab national aspirations. The confederation would be a visible embodiment of Arab unity, and a centre round which the movement for an Arab revival – which is a very real thing – could rally; it would give leadership and direction to that movement, especially on its cultural side'. The Zionists, he declared, would welcome such a scheme, as they 'would regard the advantage of satisfying the reasonable national aspirations of the Arabs and of securing cessation of open and persistent Arab opposition to Jewish expansion in Palestine, as far outweighing the possible future risks that would be involved in Palestine becoming a member of a distinctively Arab polity'. With Samuel's letter was included a memorandum by his chief secretary, Wyndham Deedes, in which he argued that because the Jewish question was restricted to Palestine, this tended to make the feeling on both sides intenser and more bitter: 'If the question of a Jewish National Home were envisaged as part of the revival of eastern civilisation in which both Arab and Jewish national life were to be fostered by England and France, there would be more hope of cooperation and good understanding . . .'. These proposals were received with much scepticism in the Colonial Office. In forwarding them to Curzon for his comment, the duke of Devonshire wrote, in a letter of 10 January 1923, that Samuel's scheme would irritate the French; would arouse Ibn Sa'ud's suspicion; and would not give the Palestinians what they wanted, namely abandonment of Zionism, but merely 'furnish them with a convenient machinery for further protest and agitation'. He concluded: 'As an attempt to promote cooperation between a number of people who have little in common with one another and are torn by mutual jealousies, it would be very unlikely to succeed'. Curzon's criticism proved even more scathing. The objections to the scheme, he wrote in a letter of 18 January, were 'overwhelming'. As things stood in Palestine, the British government had only two stark alternatives: 'either to rely on Arab support which involves the renunciation of the Zionist policy, or to rely on Jewish support which entails facing the persistent hostility of the Arab element of the population'. Samuel's method of squaring the circle would simply not work. Curzon had a few observations to add concerning the feasibility of relying on the Arabs which exemplify the shrewd, informed judgment which he usually brought to bear on issues of eastern policy – but which, it is true, was not always matched by resolute execution. 'Reliance on the Arabs', he wrote, 'seems to me a policy fraught with considerable danger. It is true that their present hostility is ascribed to our Zionist policy but I feel by no means confident that were that policy to be abandoned we could permanently count on Arab friendship. Our difficulties in Iraq, which no one can attribute to Zionism, should warn us against staking everything on friendly Arab collaboration'.[68] Here, surely, stated in a nutshell, we find expressed the essential objection to the pan-Arab adventure on which successive British governments embarked in the decade which began with the Palestine Round Table Conference of 1939.

This conference came about as a consequence of the Palestine Arab rebellion which began in 1936. Almost from the start of the rebellion offers of mediation were made to the British government. But both the Palestine administration and the Colonial Office firmly rejected these attempts to interfere in a territory under British mandate. Mediation by Iraq, declared the chief secretary of the Palestine government, would implicate her too closely in the affairs of Palestine 'and thus strengthen claim of king of Iraq and associates of Arab rulers to intervene directly in the mandated territory'.[69] 'His Majesty's government', the Foreign Office categorically informed the British ambassador at Baghdad, 'clearly cannot agree to any foreign statesman negotiating or mediating between them and the Palestine Arabs'.[70] In response again, to an offer by the prime minister of Egypt to use his good offices in Palestine, the foreign secretary informed Sir Miles Lampson at Cairo that 'while I have no desire to appear as if administering a rebuff to Nahas Pasha I do not wish to let His Excellency think that by influencing Palestine Arabs to co-operate with the Royal Commission he would be placing His Majesty's Government under an obligation to him. Nor generally do

I wish in any way to encourage his intervention in this matter'.[71]

It was at this juncture, after the announcement of the Royal Commission, but before its departure for Palestine, that Samuel proposed to get in touch with Nuri al-Sa'id and endeavour to find some way out of the difficulty. He informed the colonial secretary, Ormsby-Gore, of his plan. Ormsby-Gore was not enthusiastic and advised Samuel not to commit himself too far to Nuri, as negotiations of this kind might 'reopen the bargaining attitude of the Mufti & Co'.[72] In company with Lord Winterton, Samuel met Nuri at Paris on 19 and 20 September. A note of the discussions which he drew up shows that Nuri's interest in these negotiations was only to advance a pan-Arab scheme in which Iraq would have the primacy. A union between Iraq, Palestine and Trans-Jordan, he told Samuel, would make the Palestinians look with equanimity upon a large Jewish immigration; and he pressed upon Samuel and Winterton his proposal that he, acting officially on behalf of Iraq, should mediate between the Palestinians and the British government. Commenting on these talks, Winterton shrewdly observed that Nuri 'seemed to have the *arrière pensée* that he will some day become the *deus ex* ... for a federation of all Arabia' and that he made any compromise solution impossible.[73]

The Royal Commission on Palestine, reporting in the summer of 1937, proposed the partition of the country into a Jewish and an Arab state. The proposal was open to all kinds of objections, and in a speech in the House of Lords Samuel set them out in a masterly fashion. To partition he himself preferred a 'great Arab confederation – not to be built up in a day or a year, but gradually perhaps, built up, including Saudi Arabia, Iraq, Transjordan, Syria, Lebanon and Palestine as well'. In this confederation Jews and Arabs would cooperate 'as they did in the great days of Arab civilisation, when Jewish statesmen, philosophers and scientists helped the Arabs to keep alight the torch of knowledge'. To this Lord Swinton replied sharply: 'As he knows from his experience, and I know from my four years at the Colonial Office, the difficulty was to get them to cooperate on a Board of Works: are they likely to cooperate in an Arab federation?'[74]

Samuel, however, remained convinced that the solution to the Palestine problem lay through pan-Arabism. While on a visit to Palestine and Egypt in the spring of 1938, he met, among others, the Palestinian leader 'Awni Abd al-Hadi and the Egyptian heir to the throne, Prince Muhammad Ali. The latter told him that a form of union between Palestine, Trans-Jordan, Syria and the Lebanon would assuage the fear of the Palestinians of being swamped by Jewish immigrants. Samuel went away convinced that since there was nobody among the Arabs to speak on their behalf, action to break the deadlock could be initiated only by the Arab rulers. He realised the objection to foreign intervention in the affairs of a territory under British mandate; but the advantages of such intervention clearly outweighed the disadvantages, and indeed he saw no 'better line of approach towards a possible agreement than through the princes'.[75]

By the autumn of 1938, things were no better, indeed worse, in Palestine. Samuel saw Malcolm MacDonald, the colonial secretary, and again proposed a course of action which would invite intervention by neighbours of Palestine in the country's affairs. He suggested the dispatch of a British mission to Egypt, Saudi Arabia, Iraq, and Trans-Jordan 'with a view to securing their cooperation on lines that would be acceptable to the Jews'.[76] In the end, things worked out as Samuel desired. The British government itself decided – but not, of course, in order to facilitate a solution acceptable to the Zionists – that it would be advantageous to recognise outside Arab interest in Palestinian politics. They convened the Round Table Conference, which Samuel welcomed in a speech in the House of Lords as 'a visible proof that His Majesty's Government recognise that Palestine is not merely a local question and that just as it interests Zionists all over the world outside Palestine, so also it interests Arabs outside Palestine wherever they may be, and particularly in the contiguous countries'. And he went on to say that 'There should be extended encouragement to the creation of a confederation of Arab states, in which Palestine and Trans-Jordan should form part'.[77] The Round Table Conference was of course only the beginning of a policy which culminated in the sponsorship of Arab unity and the Arab League. This encouraged and made possible the continuous and systematic interference in Palestine affairs by Iraq, Egypt, Trans-Jordan and the others – each of course, in exclusive pursuit of its own interests. It was an illusion to believe – as its various advocates did – that this policy would either promote peace in Palestine, or advance British interests. As the sequel showed, it also led the Palestinians, within a short space of time, to stark and utter ruin.

5

Sa'd Zaghlul and the British

An nescis, mi fili, quantilla prudentia mundus regatur
OXENSTIERNA

and, whosoever considers that the nature of men, especially of men in
authority, is inclined rather to commit two errors than to retract one,
will not marvel that from this root of unadvisedness, so many and tall
branches of mischief have proceeded.
CLARENDON, History of the Rebellion

When Sa'd Zaghlul went to see Sir Reginald Wingate, the high
commissioner in Egypt, on 13 November 1918, to ask to be allowed to
go to London to demand independence for Egypt, he was already an
old man with a crowded political past behind him. He had been born,
probably in 1857, in Ibiana, the son of a local well-to-do family with
some official connections in the province; he had been sent to Cairo
to study at al-Azhar, and there became a disciple of Muhammad
Abduh who made him literary editor of the *Egyptian Gazette*, of which
Abduh was editor for a few years, between the accession of Tawfiq
Pasha to the Khediviate and the fiasco of the 'Urabi rebellion. While
he was literary editor, Zaghlul contributed an article to the *Gazette*
on constitutional government, which provides a remarkable indication of the views he then held, and with which both Egyptians and
British continued to associate him for many years later.

The tyrant [wrote Zaghlul] is usually defined as he who does what he
pleases irresponsibly, who rules as his passions incline him, whether this
agrees with the *shar'*, or is contrary to it, whether it conforms to the
sunna or differs from it. Because of this you see that when people hear
this vocable or something similar to it, they attribute to it this meaning
and are seized with displeasure at its mention, owing to the great misfortunes they have derived from it, and to the great damage it has done

to peoples and nations. They are justified in their displeasure and disgust because they have derived from it nothing but misfortune and from its rule nothing but mishaps. They have indeed seen that tyranny makes souls perish unjustly, that it eats the possessions of men greedily, sheds blood without due cause, and brings utter destruction on the country. Therefore men are not to be blamed if they are disinclined to praise it, even though some might understand by it something which is not its usual meaning.

It is clear from what we have said above that the Divine Law does not allow it, and that it makes mandatory the limitation of rule by tradition and law. But it is clear and obvious that the rules of the Divine Law by themselves cannot limit rule, because they are but concepts present in the mind of doctors and learned men, or else are indicated by means of symbols set down in books. They are not sufficient to control the ruler if he only has knowledge of them. For limitation of rule to be efficient, there must be men who actually conduct themselves according to its tenets, and who behave as these rules require, men who are ready to set right the ruler, should he deviate from the true path, to exhort him to keep to it and walk in its ways. It is for this reason that our Lord 'Umar, may God be pleased with him, asked the people, in his well-known address, to set him right whenever he erred in applying the rules of the noble *shar'*, and for this reason God, the most high, said: 'Let there be formed among you a group who call for good deeds, who prescribe that which is customary to consider good, and who prohibit evil, and these shall prosper'. It cannot be denied that this noble verse calls generally on kings and others to do good, it orders them to follow what it is customary to consider good, and it forbids them the doing of evil, so that religion may be firmly based, and nobody trespass his prescribed bounds whether he rules or is ruled. This duty cannot be delegated, but is obligatory and incumbent on all, as the doctors have stated – it was made obligatory on the Muslim community that an *umma* – meaning a *ta'ifa* [group] – drawn from it should arise, whose duty would be to call for good actions, to prescribe that which it is customary to consider good, and to prohibit evil, in order that the Divine Law may be safeguarded, and in order that those who are tempted to transgress should not trespass its limits, and those with wayward passions should not haughtily disregard it.[1]

The article, with all its limitations of style and argument, is, for its time and place, a remarkable attempt to deduce the necessity of constitutional government from the prescriptions of Islam. Whether the attempt is convincing or not, the fact remains that Zaghlul continued to be associated with such views after the 'Urabi rebellion, when he became a lawyer with a private practice, and subsequently a judge in the civil courts. It was on the strength of these views, of his association with the disciples of Muhammad Abduh, and of his reputation for uprightness and honesty, that Cromer chose him in 1906 to become minister of education. Cromer had a high regard for Muhammad Abduh, and considered that his disciples, whom he called 'the Girondists of the Egyptian national movement'[2] were the only group with whom lay any hope of constitutional advance in Egypt. Zaghlul was also known to be opposed to Mustafa Kamil, whom he described as 'mad'.[3] His advancement was thus a deliberate move to checkmate the khedive Abbas Hilmi, by encouraging those to whom he was opposed. It was well-known at the time that the khedive hated Muhammad Abduh, who had died in 1905; it is reported, for instance, that when he heard that some of his court officials had attended Muhammad Abduh's funeral, he became very angry and said: 'He is, as you know, the enemy of God, the enemy of the Prophet, the enemy of religion, the enemy of the prince, the enemy of the *'ulama*, the enemy of the Muslims, the enemy of his people, the enemy even of himself, why then show him such regard?'[4] The khedive did not like Zaghlul's appointment, and subsequently came into conflict with him over the separate institution of a School of Religious Law, which would not be under the control of al-Azhar, a project which Zaghlul advocated and the khedive opposed. He liked him even less when he suspected that Zaghlul, together with his brother Fathi, was instrumental in organising *Hizb al-umma*, the People's Party, a party which stood for constitutionalism and opposed the khedive's autocratic leanings.[5] Zaghlul continued a minister for a number of years, and went out of office in 1912. While in office, and also out of it, he showed in public the same moderation which for Cromer was the hallmark of Muhammad Abduh's followers. Thus, in 1909, he was one of those who defended, against nationalist clamour, the extension of the Suez Canal Concession;[6] and when he stood for membership of the Legislative Assembly in 1913 his address to the electors of the Cairo constituency where he was a candidate confined itself to four points: he promised that, if elected, he would press for judicial reform, for educational reform, for municipal reform in Cairo, and that he would try to see that more attention was given to the needs of agriculture.[7]

This was, by and large, the public reputation of the man who in November 1918 went with Abd al-Aziz Fahmi and Ali Sha'rawi, both connected with the People's Party of pre-war days, to see Sir Reginald Wingate to demand Egyptian independence. It is true that, by then, he was generally identified as a leader of the Opposition. His activities in the two years preceding the war had caused the residency to include him in its bad books. When he had resigned as minister of justice in March 1912, it was owing to a clash with the khedive. 'He is', wrote Kitchener to Grey recounting the events which led to Zaghlul's resignation, 'a very trying person to work with, owing to a complete want of tact, and he does not get on well with his colleagues or the khedive. Ever since his appointment, Saad Pasha has been on more or less bad terms with His Highness.' Zaghlul, it seems, had offered to resign the previous May, but the differences were then patched up. Kitchener had tried to compose their quarrels; 'I must say however that Saad Pasha's character is very difficult if not impossible'. Zaghlul, claiming to base his conduct on honest conviction, had continued to apply pinpricks to the khedive. To start with, Kitchener had tended to be in his favour; but the incident which now led to Zaghlul's resignation made him change his mind. It seems that he accused of corruption Husain Muharram Pasha, who had recently been appointed by the khedive as the trustee of a *waqf*. These charges he could not substantiate and 'I could not help thinking', Kitchener wrote, 'that the fact that Hussein Pasha had replaced Saad Pasha's brother-in-law in the post of under-secretary for war had a good deal to do with the latter's attitude'. The khedive took grave offence at Zaghlul's accusation, holding it to be an attempt to besmirch his reputation in Kitchener's eyes and said he would take no further part in the administration if Saʿd remained a minister. Zaghlul had then to resign.[8]

If Zaghlul's later career is any guide, his querulous parade of principle may have stemmed from jealousy and disappointed ambition, since he may have held that on Butrus Ghali's assassination in 1910, it was he rather than Muhammad Saʿid who should have been appointed chief minister.[9] His subsequent activities quickly showed that here was a man quick to invoke his 'honest conviction' but quite flexible in changing it as circumstance required. When he went out of office, he seems to have coquetted with the Nationalist Party, whose late leader he had called mad. This party, which was then opposed to the khedive Abbas, promised to support him in the forthcoming elections for the Legislative Assembly. The Nationalists, as one of them wrote to their exiled leader, Muhammad Farid, believed that they had bound him to their cause heart and soul[10] (*qalban wa qāliban*). Zaghlul, however, soon abandoned them for a more profitable

connection. In a memorandum of June 1914, Sir Ronald Graham, adviser to the Ministry of the Interior, wrote that during these elections
Zaghlul was 'in constant communication with the palace'; and a
powerful press campaign was mounted in his favour. When the
Assembly met, he succeeded, with the active help of the palace, in
becoming the elected vice-president and became, as Graham put it,
the embodiment of the spirit of mistrust and hostility to the government then being energetically promoted by the khedive. The khedive's
purpose then was to have his own way in regard to the sale of the
Mariut railway by which he stood to make a great deal of money.
Kitchener was adamantly opposed to what he considered to be a piece
of blatant corruption. Kitchener was also determined to transfer the
waqf administration from the khedive's unfettered discretion. Control
over the *waqf* gave Abbas Hilmi access to considerable power, influence and riches, and he was therefore equally determined to resist
Kitchener's schemes. His resistance was such that Kitchener at one
point thought he would have to be deposed. It is therefore interesting
to see that Zaghlul and other followers of Abbas Hilmi organised in
the Legislative Assembly a noisy and strenuous opposition to the
proposal of transferring control of the *awqaf* from the khedive to the
government. In the event, these and other attempts availed Abbas
Hilmi nothing, and he was compelled to follow Kitchener's wishes.[11]
'His Highness the khedive', wrote Graham in the memorandum above-
mentioned, 'had been hard hit both in his pride and in his pocket, by
the frustration of the Mariut railway scheme and the formation of the
Waqfs ministry. He bore a bitter grudge against Mohammed Pasha
Said. Although worsted for the moment he was determined to show
that no Egyptian Ministry which did not enjoy his confidence could
carry on government for any length of time. In the new Assembly he
found a weapon ready to his hand, and in Saad Zaghlul a man who
could make good use of it'. Graham's description of Zaghlul's behaviour in the Assembly indicates how even then, and even on such a
restricted stage, Zaghlul showed talents and powers which were to
bring him to the fore some five years later: 'Saad Pasha Zaghlul',
Graham went on, 'was the dominating personality throughout the
session, and he has the makings of a successful demagogue. Able and
eloquent, he was able to sway the House by his speeches, and the lax
rules of procedure in force enabled him to speak again and again at the
same sitting on the same subject. In debate he was more than a match
for any of the ministers, none of whom could stand up to him'. But

when the khedive left Egypt at the end of the session, Zaghlul's 'chief support' was withdrawn, and there were signs of revulsion against him.[12]

Muhammad Sa'id was not able for long to withstand Abbas Hilmi's displeasure and was dismissed in the spring of 1914. The khedive suggested to Kitchener that his successor should be Mustafa Fahmi. This, on the face of it, was a surprising choice since Mustafa Fahmi, who had served for many years as chief minister in Cromer's and Gorst's time had, as Kitchener put it, always loyally supported the British government, and had never been known as a friend of the khedive. He was also Zaghlul's father-in-law, and it soon transpired, as Kitchener reported, that he had fallen under his son-in-law's influence, that he proposed to make a 'clean sweep' of pro-British ministers, and substitute for them others who 'were chiefly distinguished for their devotion to Saad'. Kitchener tried without success to make Mustafa Fahmi change his attitude, 'which I can only ascribe to some promise given to his son-in-law in the matter'.[13] It was Husain Rushdi who, in the end, was appointed chief minister. When he was in Istanbul just before his deposition, Abbas addressed a telegram of condolence to Zaghlul on the death of his father-in-law, which, as Husain Rushdi reported to the khedive, created a bad impression at the residency, being interpreted as an incitement to opposition.[14]

When Abbas was deposed and Husain Kamil appointed sultan in his place, he and Husain Rushdi seemed to have thought it prudent to get Zaghlul on their side by offering him office, but in view of his 'factious opposition and relations with khedive in last session of Legislative Assembly', Milne Cheetham who was in charge of the residency, refused, with Grey's approval, to entertain such a proposal.[15] With this refusal, and with the Legislative Assembly prorogued since the outbreak of war, Zaghlul had for the time being no public role to play. But he made a show of loyalty to the deposed khedive and thus indicated that he was an opponent of the protectorate and of those Egyptians who supported it. In a conversation with Sir William Brunyate, the judicial adviser, some time before Sultan Husain Kamil's death in 1917, he protested against the continued prorogation of the Assembly; when Brunyate said that he would have been in favour of convoking it so that it might swear allegiance to Sultan Husain, Zaghlul replied that 'having upon election sworn allegiance to the khedive, he would not personally have felt at liberty at that time to swear allegiance to the new sultan.'[16]

Towards the end of November 1917, Sultan Fu'ad, who had that year unexpectedly succeeded his brother, twice asked that two ministers who were in office at his accession should be dismissed because of their alleged corruption or moral turpitude, and that Zaghlul and Abd al-Aziz Fahmi, a well-known lawyer, should be substituted for them. This request was supported by Husain Rushdi who was still the chief minister. Wingate, who had succeeded McMahon as high commissioner, was not inclined to oppose an immediate and categorical rejection to Fu'ad's request. 'That the inclusion of Zaghlul and Fahmi will give the reconstituted Ministry a somewhat stronger Nationalistic tendency', he wrote to Lord Hardinge at the Foreign Office, 'is undoubted, but on the other hand I am not alto-gether averse to this. As matters stand at present Zaghlul as vice-president of the Legislative Assembly and with his powers of oratory has acquired a very predominant position and I am not at all sure that we would not be wise to secure his support on the side of the government rather than have him in opposition'.[17] But his appoint-ment was once again turned down. This was due to Wingate's suspi-cion that in proposing this change of ministers both Fu'ad and Rushdi were trying to challenge British control and enlarge their own power and Egyptian autonomy. Resistance to this was a matter of principle, and Wingate therefore was told that if the sultan continued to press for the changes he should agree to one minister only being dismissed and to Abd al-Aziz Fahmi being appointed for a probationary period as an under-secretary.[18] There, for a year or so, matters rested. But it would seem that Fu'ad continued privately to maintain close relations with Zaghlul who together with Isma'il Sidqi, 'Abd al-'Aziz Fahmi and Amin Yahya, constituted what Wingate called Fu'ad's *officine nocturne* and which, he added, the ministers did not like.[19]

These were the immediate antecedents, as they were known to the high commissioner, of the man who came to visit him on 13 November 1918. They were, of course, quite unknown to the general public, among whom Zaghlul's reputation remained as that of an inde-pendent, opposition-minded politician, who had for years kept aloof from court, residency and public office. But Wingate knew, if not at the time then soon afterwards, that Zaghlul's visit had been concerted with the sultan and his ministers.[20] Fu'ad's accession to the sultanate had been unexpected. But for the deposition of Abbas Hilmi, the early death of his successor Husain Kamil, the refusal of his son to succeed him (and his unacceptability to the British government), Fu'ad would not have become sultan. Wingate was not very enthusiastic about his candidature and would himself have preferred outright annexation of Egypt.[21] But the Foreign Office, concerned with the possibility of discontent among the Egyptian official classes if Egypt were to be made into a crown colony, and swayed by Sir Ronald Graham's view that Fu'ad was generally acceptable and 'at any rate not Anglophobe in his sympathies',[22] decided that he should be offered the succession. When he became sultan, then, Fu'ad had a position to make secure and consolidate, an authority to sustain and increase, and this in the face of Abbas Hilmi's still unextinguished claim to the throne, his ministers' greater experience of affairs, and of a British control which, since the outbreak of war, had become even more burdensome, demanding and meticulous. Even the most Anglophil sultan, placed in Fu'ad's position, would sooner or later, in attempting to consolidate his position, have been bound to create difficulties for Britain. And in fact, soon after his accession signs began to multiply that he was not the complaisant puppet which some had expected him to be. Indications were not wanting that Fu'ad was determined to aggrandise himself at the expense both of his ministers and of the British. His *officine nocturne* was one straw in the wind; but there were others. When Edwin Montagu, the secretary of state for India, visited Egypt in the autumn of 1917, Fu'ad received him and (as he informed Wingate) told Montagu that 'he hoped that Egypt would be granted full autonomy in due course'.[23] 'The etiquette of a reigning sovereign or something like it', wrote Sir Milne Cheetham in August 1918, 'has been introduced at Abdine and on one occasion the sultan withdrew without bidding farewell to the high commissioner at all.' The general tone of his reception of British officials and residents had aroused 'outspoken discontent', and it was clear, Cheetham also remarked that Fu'ad wanted to make himself 'the active head of society' in Egypt.[24] Fu'ad also began to profess dissatisfaction with his chief minister, Husain Rushdi, and other ministers complained vehemently to the residency about him. Adli was quite contemptuous of the sultan; Tharwat complained of the interference of the palace in cases before the religious courts in which Amin Yahya, a member of the *officine* was involved; Sirri, the minister of works, also complained that credits for the decoration of Abdine palace were being exceeded on Fu'ad's instructions.[25]

At the same time as he reported these difficulties, Wingate also took the view that Fu'ad's relations with Husain Rushdi were on the mend, but he warned that:

... judging from the tendencies the sultan is now exhibiting, I should be rather afraid that, with a return to more normal times, he might be tempted to encourage the opposition of a more or less Nationalist character with which the government in all probability will have to deal. A development of this kind would be a repetition of the situation in 1914, when Abbas Hilmy supported any elements in the Chamber which were opposed to the government. The present sultan [he went on] is little known in Egypt. He was brought up abroad, and when residing here has chiefly lived among foreigners. It is commonly believed that we put him in as a weak man who would serve our own ends. Hitherto he has failed to gain the public esteem which Hussein Kamel enjoyed, and he may be likely therefore to take a line which would bring him popularity and the position which he lacks.[26]

As the war was coming to a close, less than a month before Zaghlul's fateful interview, Fu'ad again reiterated to Wingate his dissatisfaction with his ministers, and gave expression to his desire for Home Rule for Egypt on the lines of President Wilson's Fourteen points.[27] Wingate had already warned that Fu'ad's thoughts were running in this direction. In his dispatch of 31 August 1918 he had reported that Haines, the adviser to the Ministry of the Interior, visiting the sultan, had remarked that there was no need – as had once seemed the case – for British commandants of provincial police: 'The sultan interrupted him at this point and said that such questions were for his ministers, and did not concern an adviser. It is of course', added Wingate, 'one of the theories of advanced Nationalism that British advisers should have purely technical functions, and not take any part in administration in its executive aspects.'[28] Now, exactly a week before Zaghlul's interview, Fu'ad spoke to Wingate of his desire for a purely Egyptian Ministry, for a national assembly, and for a constitutional monarchy.[29] As the sequel was to show, it is most unlikely that Fu'ad, in speaking thus to Wingate, was moved by a sincere desire to diminish the legally unlimited prerogatives of the sultanate. His history indicates that he was, as Austen Chamberlain described him, 'sly, scheming, corrupt and autocratic'.[30] What is more likely, then, is that he saw in Zaghlul's move, which he no doubt hoped to control and use for his own ends, a means of increasing his stature and power, just as Abbas Hilmi had done in the case of Mustafa Kamil and his Nationalist

Party before he broke with them in 1904. In this autocrat invoking the Fourteen Points, then, we see the first partner in the prolonged game of chess which lasted from 1919 to 1922, when Allenby, extorting his famous Declaration from a reluctant government in London, began the long, painful and humiliating liquidation of the British position in Egypt, which ended at last in the unlikely events of November 1956.

Zaghlul was acting in concert not only with Fu'ad but with his ministers as well. These ministers, the principal of whom were Husain Rushdi and Adli Yakan, had been in office since the outbreak of war. They had shown loyalty to the occupying power, had acquiesced in the deposition of Abbas and the declaration of the Protectorate, and had done their best to comply with the needs of the military. Now that Fu'ad was on the throne, that peace was about to return, they found their situation extremely weakened. They could be attacked for subservience to the British, for disloyalty to the Ottoman suzerain of Egypt and to the ex-khedive, and they had to take action to protect themselves and to parry the attacks that were bound to come. So that, even if they had had no desire to claim independence, once they found Zaghlul and Fu'ad engaging on such a tactic, willy-nilly they had to follow suit and associate themselves with their demands. But in any case they themselves had cause for complaint and a desire to change the modalities of the Protectorate as these had developed in the years from 1914 to 1918.

In 1914 Kitchener was consul general. When war broke out he was on leave in London, and was persuaded to remain there and become secretary of state for war during the hostilities. But the war was not thought likely to last very long, and Kitchener did not want to abandon his Egyptian post. This was why Sir Henry McMahon, an Indian civilian, who had just retired from the position of political secretary to the Government of India, was appointed high commissioner—as the British representative came to be known after the declaration of the Protectorate – as a stopgap measure, to keep the post open for Kitchener. McMahon had spent all his official life in British India and had no intimate knowledge of Egypt. Now Egypt was not India. India was ruled by a tightly-knit, compact civil service, in which there was an unbroken chain of command from the district officer in his remove province to the central seat of authority in Delhi; Egypt under British occupation, on the other hand, was a much more complicated and delicate mechanism to operate. While there could of course be no question that the last word lay with the British representative, yet his authority was not and could not be exercised directly. There was the khedive, who was the legal ruler of the country, there were his ministers who were supposed to control and direct the native officials; these ministers were flanked by British advisers at the centre, and their subordinates by British inspectors in the provinces; it was by means of this peculiar dyarchy that the views and desires of the occupying power were supposed to be transmitted and enforced. This meant that the British representative had to manage and humour khedive, ministers and other official persons, and that his position precluded him from that direct exercise of authority which, in an hierarchical civil service such as that of British India, was customary as between superior and subordinate. The declaration of the protectorate, the coming of McMahon, the concentration of large bodies of British and Allied troops in Egypt – events all of them precipitated by the outbreak of war – could not but exercise the greatest influence on the modes of British control of Egypt; and this in turn could not but greatly disturb the Egyptian ministers and official classes, accustomed as they had been to the political and administrative traditions which had grown up from 1882 to 1914. In a private note written in October 1919 Sir Reginald Wingate recorded an interview he had with Sultan Husain Kamil, while McMahon was still high commissioner, in which the sultan bitterly complained of the increased power of the British officials and stated that Egypt was then being ruled by a *camorra*,* of which they were the head. From that same note it appears that the sultan complained to Lord Hardinge, who was passing through Egypt, and that his complaint, coinciding with Kitchener's death, resulted in Sir Reginald Wingate, then governor-general of the Sudan, being appointed to replace McMahon.[31] Writing to Hardinge shortly after assuming his new office, Wingate described how Lord Edward Cecil, the financial adviser, had been given great authority by McMahon, and how everybody, British and Egyptian, was looking up to him for advancement and promotion.[32] McMahon, it would seem, used Cecil as a kind of prime minister.

The chief minister, Husain Rushdi, became particularly restless. At the end of 1917, when Fu'ad proposed to appoint Zaghlul as a minister, Wingate was somewhat concerned to see Husain Rushdi put into question the protectorate and its working. In conversation

* A Neapolitan secret society.

with Brunyate he declared that he wanted British supervision limited to finance, foreign relations, justice and the army, and that the advisers should be subordinated to their ministers. He went so far as to suggest that ministers should not exercise power without obtaining parliamentary support. But when Wingate taxed him with harbouring such views, Rushdi hastily disclaimed any immediate intention of introducing a new political programme and dismissed his conversation with Brunyate as entirely private and of no official significance. Wingate was inclined not to attach too much importance to Rushdi's outburst, thinking that it was merely an attempt to test the ground, but he warned Hardinge that 'we must expect a very frank *exposé* of national aspirations when the war is over'.[33]

But Wingate must have misjudged Rushdi's tenacity of views, or the strength of the pressures which led him to demand a reconsideration of the protectorate. The lengths to which he was ready to go – or to which he was driven – may be seen from the way in which he dealt with some proposals of Brunyate's dealing with the future of the Capitulations and with other constitutional issues. In this confidential document, which had been prepared at the request of the Egyptian ministers and was no more than a draft put up for discussion, Brunyate proposed the creation of a senate where the foreign communities of Egypt would be substantially represented and which would have large powers over legislation. Husain Rushdi took – or professed to take – violent exception to this proposal. He wrote a vehement rejoinder which, together with Brunyate's memorandum, was distributed in the provinces and given very wide publicity.[34]

Rushdi's behaviour is simple to understand. Once the protectorate was called into question, Rushdi could not afford, out of mere self-protection, to seem indifferent or tepid in such a cause, if only because he realised how easy it was for his rivals to brand him as a traitor for having acquiesced in the policies of the British and collaborated with them for so many years.[35] And as the armistice approached it began to be increasingly clear that various people, each with his own particular motive, were thinking of requesting a reconsideration of the protectorate. Wingate, as has been seen, warned London that some such move could be expected from Fu'ad and from his chief minister. Who, in fact, thought of a specific move is not entirely clear. Prince 'Umar Tusun, a grandson of Sa'id Pasha, the third of Muhammad Ali's sons to succeed him as vali of Egypt, claims that the idea of challenging the protectorate occurred to him after the publication of

President Wilson's Fourteen Points in January 1918. He consulted Muhammad Sa'id who broached the matter to Zaghlul early in October 1918; and the latter promised to discuss it with his friends. Later in October, 'Umar Tusun himself met Zaghlul who told him that £100,000 were required to organise a campaign against the protectorate. Zaghlul and the prince agreed to meet and discuss the matter further. 'Umar Tusun then happened to be in Cairo – on 11 November – when he heard of the forthcoming interview with Wingate; he tried to take part in the movement, but the sultan objected to his participation.[36] And it is a fact that Fu'ad, unsure as he was of his position and afraid of being superseded either by Abbas Hilmi or by some other member of his family, did sharply forbid 'Umar Tusun from taking any further part in the movement against the protectorate.[37] He also took positive steps himself – apart, that is, from what he may have inspired his coadjutors in the *officine nocturne* to do – to show obliquely yet unmistakably that he did not like the protectorate. He sent President Wilson a telegram praising him for his Fourteen Points, but the telegram was sent not through the U.S. consul general but through the telegraph company; he assured his Egyptian visitors that he was in favour of convoking the Legislative Assembly;[38] he is said to have interested himself very much in the collection of money for the use of Zaghlul's delegation which at Alexandria was organised by his man, Amin Yahia; he is also said to have issued a circular 'which was distributed in all towns and contained many open and concealed ambiguities together with a notification of his wish to be associated with the people in all their desires and to share their aspirations'.[39] If 'Umar Tusun and Fu'ad seem to have had a hand in the events which led to Zaghlul's visit to Wingate, so most probably did Rushdi and Adli. Abd al-Aziz Fahmi, who accompanied Zaghlul on the visit to Wingate, stated later that Zaghlul was quite averse to visiting Wingate and that he only changed his mind when Rushdi and 'Adli told him that they and the sultan were agreed on a journey to Europe to demand the rights of Egypt and that it was advisable to have by their side 'a part of the nation on whom we may rely for the defence of its rights, so that we may obtain something from the English'.[40]

Thus it came about that Zaghlul, free of official responsibilities, was pushed forward by Fu'ad and Rushdi. Given this opportunity, Zaghlul was able to set the pace and his backers, whether they liked it or not, had to endorse his demands. As for themselves, it is doubtful

94

whether they really wanted full independence, or whether – as is more likely – they would have been content with a definition of the protectorate which would circumscribe the authority of the British officials and allow the Egyptians more elbow room. In an eloquent note which he wrote for Wingate in December 1918, Husain Rushdi declared that the protectorate was a label which could be used to designate either outright annexation or a reconciliation of British and Egyptian interests. He wanted to know which it was to be; this was the purpose of the talks which they wanted to hold with the British government in London, and he disclaimed any desire to make the Egyptian question international or to seek to present it before the Peace Conference.[41] If this was Husain Rushdi's view, the views of the other Egyptians concerned in Zaghlul's move of November were, at the outset, hardly more clear-cut. Fu'ad, it is safe to say, had started something, and was waiting to see how the cat would jump; he had been careful not to commit himself categorically, and at the worst had only to disclaim responsibility and to say that it was the fault of his ministers, of Zaghlul, of public opinion . . .; if, however, the British were ready to parley, he would put himself at the head of the movement and so manoeuvre as to obtain the greatest benefits for himself and his house. If such was the calculation he was to be sorely disappointed, to find that in Zaghlul he had an old, wily partner, and that the forces he helped to unleash were no longer under his control. As for Zaghlul and his unofficial associates, they also seem to have ventured hopefully, without really knowing the true extent of their demands or what they would consider a satisfactory outcome. This was the attitude of Ahmad Lutfi al-Sayyid, who was a member of Zaghlul's group which soon came to be known as the *Wafd*. He told Muhammad Husain Haikal at the time that the plan, as he saw it, was for Zaghlul's *Wafd* to proceed to Paris and lay the Egyptian demands before the Peace Conference; if they succeeded in this, well and good; if not, then Husain Rushdi and 'Adli Yakan would go to London on their own and endeavour to make precise the conditions of the protectorate and to set up a true constitutional government for the country.[42] Whether these were the precise views of Zaghlul himself we do not know, but his subsequent behaviour would indicate that he was a man ready to extract the maximum benefit from any favourable opportunity.

The answer by the British government to Zaghlul's move came quickly. It was a categorical refusal. No Egyptian leader, official or unofficial, was to move out of Egypt, to go either to Paris or London; further, Wingate was rebuked for allowing himself to be trapped into receiving Zaghlul's delegation and giving them scope for making these demands. In a telegram of 2 December 1918 Wingate was told that his reception of Zaghlul and his colleagues, which was being exploited by them in order to show that their movement was lawful, 'was unfortunate'. The rebuke was less than just, for, as has been seen, Wingate had given plenty of warning of Fu'ad's and Husain Rushdi's state of mind, and he could hardly have refused, unless he were to behave like an oriental despot, to receive three men as prominent in Egyptian society as Zaghlul and his two friends; it was, further, Cromer's policy, and a tradition which he bequeathed to his successors of whom Wingate was one of the worthiest, that the British representative in Egypt was accessible to all classes of men and ready to look into and redress the grievances of the most insignificant of Egyptians. When Wingate subsequently protested against the reprimand which the Foreign Office had administered, he was told that 'what struck the authorities here as somewhat unaccountable was the fact that Saad Zaghlul and his friends should have (at least so it appears) concerted their action with the sultan and probably Rushdi Pasha if not others of the ministers and then have come to you as a deputation without your having any previous knowledge of the objects and aims of their visit.'[43] There is little substance in this complaint, which reflects, rather, the prejudice which, as will be seen, ministers and high officials in London entertained against Wingate. For even if Wingate had known exactly beforehand what demands Zaghlul and his friends were going to make,[44] and had refused to receive them, this would hardly have put an end to a movement which had the sultan's and the chief minister's support. For the same reason, the refusal of Zaghlul's request was misconceived. If Zaghlul, the ministers and the sultan were acting in concert, and if they maintained a united front, what then would the British government do? For, then, it would come to a trial of strength; were they prepared for it? There is no indication that the consequences of refusal were seriously considered. For not only was Zaghlul himself refused permission to go to Europe, the ministers were also forbidden to do so. It might be that had they been allowed to go to London, as Wingate himself urged that they should, they would have been adroit enough to take the initiative away from Zaghlul, and thus enable the British government to break the united front which Zaghlul, the ministers and the sultan maintained, each for his own particular ends. But it is doubtful whether they would have been adroit enough, or daring enough, to proceed on their own, while knowing that the sultan would be obscurely manoeuvring behind their backs and Zaghlul ready to denounce any settlement in which he did not have a part. In the event, faced with the British refusal, they resigned, and were soon declaring that they would not go to London without Zaghlul, obviously fearing that if they left him in Egypt he would be in a strong position to outbid them.[45]

The ministers were prevailed upon to hold back their resignation for the time being, but Wingate found himself in a difficult position, between an equivocating sultan alternately saying that Zaghlul and his friends were justified in their demands, and his ministers right to resign, and then again saying that the ministers were indispensable and should be prevailed upon to stay in office, and that he himself had no sympathy with Zaghlul but dare not disown him; and ministers, in part genuinely offended by London's behaviour and, again in part, fearful of seeming less extreme than Zaghlul.[46] All this while, Zaghlul, now in the limelight, together with his committee, was organising opposition to the occupying power. The text of a petition asking that Zaghlul and his delegation be allowed to travel to Europe to present the Egyptian case was spread throughout the land and signatures collected for it. The provincial authorities, acting on the instructions of the Ministry of the Interior, attempted to confiscate these petitions. Zaghlul, in what may have been a concerted move,[47] protested to Husain Rushdi against the confiscations. What followed throws light not only on the course of the so-called Egyptian revolution of 1919 but on the quality of the British administration of Egypt in those years. Husain Rushdi went with the protest to the adviser of the ministry of the interior and asked him what reply should be made. The adviser was then Mr Haines, who had been an inspector and then a chief collector of taxes; he had been made adviser to the interior by McMahon on Lord Edward Cecil's advice. 'In this post', writes Lord Lloyd, 'he displayed little of his former zeal or competence, and refused to listen to any sort of criticism or advice, thus cutting off the high commissioner from his chief source of information.'[48] Mr Haines, as he explained to Wingate, now told Husain Rushdi to answer Zaghlul by saying that the petitions were being confiscated by the order of the adviser of the ministry of the interior.[49] Husain Rushdi replied in this sense: the letter was made public and it was plain for

97

all to see that the sultan's ministers had no part or lot in putting down Zaghlul's movement, that it was purely the doing of the British. But this dissociation of the Egyptian ministers from their British advisers, facilitated by Haines's extraordinary move, was not the only sign by which the ministers conveyed their approval of Zaghlul's movement. There is evidence to show that they took positive steps to facilitate his work. The petition had been sent, writes Muhammad Husain Haikal, to lawyers, doctors, engineers and other professional people: 'for these, it was not difficult to sign the petitions, since their culture and their appreciation of the meaning of independence were enough to make them eager to sign. But copies of the petition had also been sent to local elected bodies, such as provincial councils, and to 'omdas and notables, and lo and behold, thousands and hundreds of thousands of these signatures began to come in from every side; this is because Rushdi Pasha's Ministry encouraged the *mudirs* and the *ma'murs*, and made them encourage people who were afraid of the power of government, to sign the petitions.'[50] Ahmad Shafiq Pasha, in his *Survey of Egyptian Politics*, also mentions that the government exerted its influence on behalf of Zaghlul's movement and confirms his argument by a speech which Husain Rushdi made a few years after these events recounting the help which he gave to the *Wafd* while in office.[51] It was not only the ministers but the palace as well which exerted its influence in the same direction; so Abd al-Khaliq Tharwat – one of Husain Rushdi's fellow ministers who, it seems had not been consulted about the resignation[52] – told Brunyate, adding that false rumours were being spread by the palace staff.[53] A curious effect of these tactics emerges from the story told in a note by Sir Ronald Graham on unrest in Egypt to the effect that an influential provincial notable loyal to the British connection told a British inspector that he had subscribed £10,000 to Zaghlul's movement because he understood it had the support of the British, and that he gladly cancelled his subscription when he learned to the contrary.[45] Later, in the disturbances which followed the banishment of Zaghlul and his friends, some provincial officials took the part of the rioters, others remained passive, the police in some places showed indiscipline, and in at least one recorded instance Egyptian troops incited the mob to destruction.[55] It would seem, then, that the Egyptian revolution of 1919 was, at least, in instigation and at the beginning, a revolution directed from above.

While effervescence was mounting in the country, Wingate was endeavouring to make the British government change its policy and make some less categorically negative reply to the Egyptian ministers. The government went so far as to say that they would, some time, discuss the issue with Husain Rushdi and his colleagues, but that Zaghlul was on no account to move out of Egypt. Early in the crisis, however, Husain Rushdi and 'Adli had declared that they would not go without Zaghlul. Their reason was precisely what it had been when they discreetly joined Zaghlul in objecting to the protectorate, namely self-protection. Immediately after Zaghlul's visit to Wingate, Rushdi himself saw the high commissioner, declared that he had known of Zaghlul's scheme, and that he and his friends should be given a hearing in London 'as in the event of their request being refused, charge of inadequate representation of Egyptian questions could not then be brought against responsible Egyptian ministers as might be the case if only the latter went to London'.[56] They continued to argue that it was necessary both for them and Zaghlul to go to London, so that the latter might be discredited by his failure to gain a hearing from the British government – than which, they told Wingate, they wished nothing better.[57]

Wingate was summoned for consultations to London, arriving there at the end of January 1919. He was left to cool his heels for a fortnight or so, before Curzon, who was in charge of the Foreign Office while Balfour was at the Peace Conference in Paris, found the time to see him. Wingate then argued that it would be politic to allow both the ministers and Zaghlul to come and present their grievances in London; 'otherwise it was difficult to form an Egyptian government, and whatever government was formed would be very weak'. 'The departmental view on the other hand', said a memorandum of 20 February 1919, which Curzon sent to Balfour in Paris, 'is that the Nationalist leaders, who have placed themselves at the head of a disloyal movement to expel the British from Egypt, have no claim to be allowed to come here, and that to accede to the demands of the ministers on this head would only be regarded throughout Egypt as a sign of weakness.' Further, Egyptian ministers should not be allowed to dictate the terms on which they would come to London; it was quite possible to carry on in Cairo without an Egyptian ministry, and contrary to what Wingate had represented, his views were by no means universally shared in Egypt. Balfour agreed with the departmental view and a telegram, the draft of which was amended and approved by him, was accordingly sent to Cheetham on 26 February. This telegram, which Balfour's amendment made even more stringent and categorical, refused permission to any Egyptian to leave Egypt for any reason whatever.[58] Thereupon Rushdi and 'Adli made their resignation public and final, on 1 March 1919.

One argument which the Foreign Office adduced in favour of its own views was a telegram from Cheetham of 3 February previous in which he stated that, in spite of the ministerial crisis, administration had continued without serious inconvenience during the past fortnight. Sir Milne Cheetham had been counsellor at the residency since 1911. His dispatches show him to have been a competent if colourless subordinate; Gertrude Bell, who met him in Egypt in 1919, described him as a typical Foreign Office man of the bloodless type.[59] Events were now to show that the responsibility which he had to shoulder during Wingate's absence was quite beyond him. He began by being over-confident, allowed himself to be manoeuvred by Fu'ad into taking a rash action, and when its results proved untoward he gave way to panic. He started by sending reports which represented Zaghlul and his ministerial sympathisers as having lost popularity and the country as quiet and peaceful. There seems no reason, he said in a telegram of 24 February, why Zaghlul's movement should affect the decision of the British government on constitutional questions and the proper form to be given to the protectorate.[60]

A few days later, however, Zaghlul took an action which had the most far-reaching repercussions. When the ministers' resignation was made known, he visited the royal palace at the head of a delegation and delivered a minatory letter for the Sultan to deter him from trying to form another Ministry:

We know [the letter said] that Your Highness may have been compelled by family reasons to accept the throne, but the nation, on the other hand, believes that your acceptance of the throne during the temporary and illegal protectorate – out of regard for those family circumstances – should not turn Your Highness away from working for the independence of Your country. People, therefore, have wondered how Your Highness's counsellors did not pay regard to the nation in this difficult period. The nation asks that Your Highness be the first one to come to its help in attaining independence, however much this might cost Your Highness. How can it have escaped Your Highness's counsellors that the terms of Rushdi Pasha's resignation do not allow any honourable and patriotic Egyptian to take his place? How can it have escaped them that a Ministry formed on a programme contrary to the will of the people is doomed to failure? We do not advise our Lord falsely when we beg Him to acquaint Himself with the opinion of His nation before taking a final decision concerning the present ministry. To stand between the nation and its demands is a responsibility which the counsellors of our Lord have not scrutinised with the requisite precision.[61]

The erstwhile member of the *officine nocturne* was giving notice to his coadjutor that he could not so easily wriggle out of his schemes, that even if he were tempted to give in to the obstinacy of the British, Zaghlul would not allow it. Cromer's girondist was turning jacobin.

Fuʾad refused to see the delegation which brought this letter and immediately appealed to Cheetham – 'for protection from further insults'. In a telegram of 6 March the latter stated that he had consulted the principal advisers who agreed with him that the proper course was to intern Zaghlul and his followers outside Egypt: 'I recommend', Cheetham concluded, 'his immediate arrest and deportation, and for the sake of the sultan's prestige, which is a political interest to us, I would beg for an early decision.' And a prompt decision he did get. Entirely guided by Cheetham's estimate of the situation during the past month, the Foreign Office on 7 March authorised the deportation of Zaghlul and three of his companions who, on 9 March, were arrested and sent to Malta. Reporting the deportation, Sir Milne Cheetham opined that 'this action, for which sultan has expressed his warm thanks, will be sufficient for the moment'.[62]

Fuʾad's gratitude was very short-lived. At the end of March, in answer to a Parliamentary question, the government stated that His Highness had appealed to the acting high commissioner for protection against further insults and intimidations, hence the deportations. By then, extensive disorders had broken out in Egypt, Allenby had superseded Wingate, and Zaghlul and his friends were being widely acclaimed as liberators and martyrs. The sultan therefore rejected with indignation this slur on his patriotism: What he had done was merely to show the petition of 5 March to Cheetham, and it was the latter and not himself who had recommended action. His Highness therefore demanded that it should be made clear that it was the British government who, acting on the advice of their representative, were wholly responsible for the deportations. Curzon was not willing to concede this without further discussion; but with his characteristic impatience Allenby cut short the debate and issued a statement in

Cairo magnanimously accepting full responsibility on behalf of the British government: 'I have done this in agreement with sultan', he told Curzon in a telegram of 1 April.[63]

Cheetham's *coup de force*, then, had immediately been followed by widespread and serious disorders: mobs rioting in Cairo, Alexandria and the principal provincial cities, telegraph wires cut, rail tracks destroyed, Englishmen killed. To judge by his dispatches immediately previous to the rising, Cheetham did not have the slightest suspicion of impending trouble. His deportation of Zaghlul and his companions makes sense only on the assumption that here was a handful of mere agitators who, once out of the way, would be deprived of any power for mischief. And yet Cheetham must have known that Zaghlul was acting in concert with the sultan and the Ministry, that officials and notables taking their cue from Cairo had, ever since the previous November, been spreading petitions and propaganda in favour of Zaghlul's delegation. Deporting Zaghlul and his friends was not, then, to strike at the basis of the agitation. To have done it furthermore at Fu'ad's instance showed a dangerous readiness to be bamboozled.

Cheetham also must have known – or, if he did not, he ought to have known – that after four years of war, conditions in Egypt were such as to make the country dangerously responsive to the agitations. Those conditions were, either directly or indirectly, largely the outcome of Egypt being made to supply the demands imposed on it by the British army which naturally was concerned first and foremost to fight the war against the Ottomans. When Egypt had been declared a protectorate the British government solemnly stated that 'Egypt would not have to bear any burdens by reason of the war'. This was presumably done in the expectation of a short war; but as the conflict lengthened and extended, the army began to press for the supply of labour and animals. An Egyptian labour corps was set up, entry into which was supposed to be voluntary. But as the demands of the army increased, though the voluntary principle was not overtly abandoned, yet pressures began to be applied through the Egyptian administration and ultimately through the village *'omdas* to obtain more recruits. These pressures, haphazardly, capriciously, corruptly and abusively applied, gave a bad name to British rule among the *fellahs*. For was this not a return to the *corvée*, the ending of which had been one eloquent vindication of British rule? How little consonant with British methods these practices were was realised at the time. In a dispatch of 15 September 1918 Wingate admitted that such methods were 'not in agreement with the general sentiment and character of our occupation in Egypt' and that they 'obviously' opened the door to abuses which British officials could not possibly prevent. [64] The *ʿomdas* were given this large and discretionary power not only in respect of labour recruitment but also in respect of requisition both of animals and of produce, and there is little doubt that they used these large and arbitrary powers to enrich themselves, to settle old scores and generally to tyrannise over the villages. [65] If there is a ground for blaming Wingate for the events of March, then it is this, that he did not resist with sufficient vigour the insatiable demands of Allenby and of the War Office for manpower and supplies, or at any rate did not organise recruitment and requisition in a way which was not open to abuse.

The war also led the authorities drastically to restrict the acreage of cotton – the most lucrative crop – so that more foodstuffs could be grown. Imports also became scarce, prices rose and an inflation set in which bore heavily on the poorer classes in the cities who, in the words of a memorandum by the financial secretary of the Egyptian ministry of finance, 'have been enabled to cope with the higher cost of living only by the exercise of severe economy and by a reduction in the consumption of necessaries to an extent incompatible with the maintenance of an adequate standard of existence'. [66]

The very war which produced these strains in Egypt at the same time weakened British control over the administration. British officials found their energies absorbed by the over-riding demands of the war, their numbers were depleted, and the high standard of recruitment, hitherto customary, could no longer be maintained. The resulting administrative slackness did not redound to the credit of the British name. This slackness also became apparent at a time when the country was filled with a vast military base through which moved large conscript proletarian armies who knew nothing about the rules of behaviour current in a Muslim society. Their conduct frequently scandalised the population and contrasted strongly with the decorum which Egyptians had been accustomed to associate with Englishmen, whom they now began to see with new, much less respectful eyes. One of the most perceptive witnesses to appear before the Milner Mission, an inspector of the interior, Mr A. Wellesley, drew attention to the decline in respect for the British in Egypt. He attributed it both to the lower standards – and the lower class – of the British official appointed to Egypt in late years, and to the influx of large numbers of soldiers whose manners were, at best, indifferent. 'The sort of English official who did harm', he said, 'was the official of what he might call the N.C.O. class. Of course the war had done incalculable damage to the prestige of British officials. The Egyptians now had experience of ill-mannered and disorderly British officers whom they saw associating with officials and they were not apt to differentiate.'[67]

Beyond these conditions there were others, perhaps less tangible, which served further to complicate and aggravate the disturbance brought about by the war. The very peace and prosperity which accompanied the British occupation had perhaps unleashed the Malthusian devil in Egypt. The population was constantly on the increase, and it pressed ever more relentlessly on the limited resources of an essentially agrarian economy which, moreover, was at the mercy of world economic conditions. It may be, therefore, that even without the war and the strains it occasioned, Egypt was becoming gradually more difficult to manage and govern. This general increase in population necessarily also led to an increase in the size of the cities, which – in a process accelerated by the war – were becoming gradually swollen with migrants from the countryside. These constituted a miserable and volatile mass, easy to rouse and difficult to control. The disturbances of March 1919 saw their ominous emergence on to the scene of Egyptian politics. In Cairo, in Alexandria, in the tightly packed towns of the Delta they rioted, killing and looting, providing a vivid illustration of the problem of government which the increase in population was creating.

Egypt then was going through a serious malaise which the sultan, his ministers and Zaghlul had begun to exploit. Cheetham, as has been said, seemed to have no inkling of this malaise, of its character, or of the way in which it was being manipulated. Having displayed an excess of confidence before Zaghlul was deported, after a few days of disorder he went to the other extreme and assumed that the disorders were the expression of a movement which, as he put it in a telegram of 17 March, was 'national in the full sense of the word', a movement which had 'apparently the sympathy of all classes and creeds, including the Copts'.[68] In speaking thus, Cheetham showed a readiness to accept at face value the slogans of the Cairo politicians. He assumed, uncritically, that the city mob and the peasants on the rampage were moved not by specific distempers and concrete – albeit obscure – discontents, but by the abstract clichés the use of which the official classes had so readily learnt from Europe.

Cheetham had deported Zaghlul on 9 March. Disorders had almost immediately broken out in the cities and villages of the Delta, and in Upper Egypt. By 15 March the acting high commissioner had completely lost his nerve. On that day he sent two telegrams. In the first, marked 'very urgent', he reported that the disorders were continuing and went on to make a suggestion which clearly demonstrated his utter lack of judgment: '. . . would it', he asked, 'represent any inconvenience from wider political point of view if so-called Egyptian patriots were to visit France and England, whether or not any of them were granted official recognition in London?'[69] The second telegram, also 'very urgent', announced that disorders were continuing, that a 'grave situation' was developing and that General Watson, commanding the troops in Egypt, agreed that there was a danger of an 'outbreak of fanaticism'. This danger made it necessary 'to discover some ground for reconciliation' and he might want to recommend 'a concession to native feeling'. He therefore wanted an 'urgent' answer to his previous telegram.[70] Two days later, he again insisted that 'a concession' was necessary.[71] In his panic, Cheetham went further. He tried to enlist the help of the United States in persuading his government to authorise a concession. He sent for the American consul general on 18 March and told him that 'at no time since the Araby rebellion in 1882 has the state of affairs been so critical'. He was, he said, unable to obtain instructions from London and 'intimated', so the consul general reported in a telegram, 'that he desired me to report the serious conditions to my government in the hope that it would exert promptly some influence over his own government and thus make them appreciate the gravity of the situation'. Cheetham also wanted to enlist the help of the consul general in restoring order in Egypt. In a later addition to his telegram, the consul general reported that Cheetham had called him to the residency 'to tell me that the situation is getting beyond control and to ask if I will be prepared to help in the matter if the worst comes'.

Curzon at the Foreign Office did not receive Cheetham's suggestions well. To allow the Egyptians to come to London after these disturbances, he sensibly told Cheetham in a telegram of 17 March 'would make it appear that we were yielding to force when persuasion has failed of its effect.'[73] Curzon also informed Balfour in Paris that he was opposed to Cheetham's proposals, adding that he felt the acting

105

high commissioner was not fully able to cope with the situation.[74] Balfour's advisers in Paris agreed with Curzon. Vansittart – who knew Egypt, having served in the residency before the war – minuted Cheetham's telegram of 15 March advising concessions: 'Having originally refused, it is now more difficult for us to give way without loss of prestige.'[75]

In his telegram of 16 March, informing Balfour of his reaction to Cheetham's suggestions, Curzon also proposed letting Cairo know that the British government was prepared to receive the Egyptian ministers – but not Zaghlul and his friends – in London; this, observed Vansittart in a minute, might have met the situation a few months before; whether it would now was doubtful; but it was at any rate worth trying.[76]

Such, it would seem, was the tenor of the advice which Balfour received. This, at any rate, is what the available papers show. The action which Balfour now took thus becomes quite inexplicable. Answering Curzon on 18 March, he began by saying that the restoration of order and the formation of a competent government must be immediately and unconditionally carried through. Once this was done, the British government would be ready to discuss with the Egyptian ministers the grievances of Egypt. Then Balfour added the following: 'If they [i.e. the Egyptian ministers] think their task would be better performed if they were accompanied or immediately followed by persons qualified to represent the Nationalist case even in its extreme form, I can see no objection.' This telegram, drafted in Balfour's own hand, seems to concede what Husain Rushdi had demanded and what the British government had hitherto resisted, namely that in any negotiations with the British government, Zaghlul should accompany the ministers. Why did Balfour propose making such a vital concession? Curzon, he knew, advised against it, and so did Vansittart. Could he have been impressed by one of Cheetham's telegrams of 15 March in which he stated that General Watson also believed a concession necessary? All that can be said is that this particular telegram adjoins, in the file, Balfour's draft of the telegram of 18 March.[77] The matter becomes all the more puzzling, when another telegram of Balfour's, which immediately followed, is considered. Sent as an urgent, private and personal telegram, it informed Curzon that the preceding telegram contained 'the best personal advice I can give in the circumstances, but I am fully conscious that I have but an incomplete knowledge of the Egyptian situation, and I have not with me in Paris any member of my staff who is fully equipped to assist me.'[78] If this was the case, why did Balfour feel it incumbent on him to give these instructions? Was it that, as Curzon complained, behind his charm and intellectual distinction there lay ignorance, indifference and levity, that he never studied his papers, or knew the facts or looked ahead, that 'he trusted to his unequalled powers of improvisation to take him through any trouble and enable him to leap lightly from one crisis to another'?[79] Was this episode perhaps yet another instance of the ruinous consequences which the war and its aftermath had on the machinery of government? Would it have happened had ministers and officials not been scattered between London and Paris, rushed, harried and overworked? How else to explain this zig-zag of conflicting policies and divergent views of which ministers and their advisers seemed sometimes to have only the haziest notion? On 18 March, as has been seen, Balfour confessing his inability to reach an informed decision yet orders a sudden, quite unexplained and most injudicious reversal of policy. But the permanent under-secretary of state, who was there at his side in Paris, does not seem to have known of his decision. For we find Hardinge on 19 March, that is, the following day, writing from Paris to Wingate to say that he and Balfour had discussed Cheetham's proposed concessions 'and we were strongly of opinion that there could be no question of any concession until order had been restored and a government formed. We both of us felt that no concession is possible so long as disorders prevail and no government has been formed.'[80] We must conclude that unless Hardinge wanted deliberately to mislead Wingate, he himself was in the dark as to Balfour's actual views.

Balfour's intervention, however, did not have any immediate consequences. When his two telegrams of 18 March were received at the Foreign Office, Sir Ronald Graham minuted: 'With all respect I submit that this does not help us. We are and always have been ready to discuss matters with Egyptian ministers, but we cannot allow them to bring the Nationalist leaders with them without reversing our whole previous attitude. It seems . . . that Mr. Balfour desires to leave the whole question in Lord Curzon's hands and that further reference to Paris will be unnecessary.'[81] Curzon agreed, and to another telegram of 19 March from Cheetham insisting that the only solution lay in allowing 'extremists' to leave Egypt and present their case where they wished, he replied on 22 March that the first and essential consideration was to restore law and order, that Cheetham was to transmit all proposals coming from Egyptians and to say that they could not receive consideration until law and order was restored.[82]

When Wingate learned of the disorders and of Cheetham's proposed concessions his own advice – recorded in a memorandum of 21 March – was that immediate repressive measures were necessary: 'I do seriously doubt', he asserted, 'the soundness of giving way to the nationalists' demands *after* they have committed such gross acts of lawlessness.'[83] But though Cheetham was not to remain much longer in authority, the high commissioner's advice did not override his own. For Wingate and his views had become of little account at the Foreign Office and he was soon to be superseded. His sudden and brutal relegation, and the appointment of Allenby over his head as special high commissioner, had remote causes little connected with the present emergency. They dated rather from the time of his transfer to Cairo where he replaced McMahon. The latter, having had no previous experience of Egypt, seems to have relied on and been guided to a large extent by the senior British officials of the Egyptian government, particularly Lord Edward Cecil, the financial adviser and Brunyate, the judicial adviser. On succeeding him, Wingate seems to have been determined to restore to the high commissioner the power and influence which McMahon had allowed to pass into the hands of the advisers. This seems to have been resented and to have created enmities for Wingate. There was, in particular, friction between him and Cecil, which no doubt came to the notice of his uncle Balfour and his brother Lord Robert Cecil. Brunyate too may have put it about that Wingate was not in control of the situation. This certainly was the tenor of a memorandum which he later sent to the Milner Mission describing Wingate as having been 'too tired' for his responsibilities and 'too unacquainted with modern Egyptian conditions'.[84]

Among the officials at the Foreign Office, Sir Ronald Graham, who dealt with Egyptian affairs, was one of his detractors. Graham had served as adviser to the ministry of the interior at Cairo, and had had the ambition of succeeding McMahon, and this may have played its part in shaping his attitude of extreme deprecation towards the language which Wingate had adopted in dealing with Zaghlul and his friends at the interview of 13 November 1918. 'It is regrettable', he wrote in a minute of 25 November 1918, 'that these three Egyptians received any encouragement from the sultan . . . but this confirms the recent reports we have had that the residency and the palace are not working in as close harmony and contact as they ought to be. I also regret that Sir R. Wingate did not turn down these Nationalists in much firmer language than he seems to have used.' The only feature of the agitation in Egypt which caused him some misgiving, he wrote in another minute of 29 November, was 'the half-hearted attitude adopted by the residency towards it. The extremist leaders ought never to have been received by Sir R. Wingate except for the purpose of being told not to make fools of themselves.' Again, in a minute of 7 December, he asserted that 'the root of the whole trouble' was that Wingate did not know how to manage Fu'ad and secure his whole-hearted support; for without 'the sultan's tacit acquiescence, if not approval, we should never have had any open Nationalist agitation still less resignation of ministers'.[85] In this last assertion Graham was undoubtedly right, but he had no ground for thinking that Wingate could have cajoled or persuaded Fu'ad into giving up his ambitions or his intrigues. He was even further out when in a memorandum on 'The Unrest in Egypt', quoted above, which was written in April 1919, he asserted that Wingate's handling of his interview with Zaghlul had placed the British government 'at the outset, in a position from which it was difficult to recover'. For at that interview Wingate had committed neither himself nor his superiors, and it was mere fault-finding to argue that his reception of Zaghlul at the residency encouraged the agitation and made it look respectable. But at the Foreign Office it was not Graham alone who disapproved of Wingate. Graham's minute of 29 November, mentioned above, is followed on the file by a minute of the same date in which Sir Eyre Crowe recorded that 'Sir R. Wingate seems deplorably weak'. And it was Crowe who added in the draft of the telegram sent to Wingate on 2 December 1918 (which is quoted above) the phrase to the effect that his reception of Zaghlul was 'unfortunate'.

A fortnight or so before Wingate's supersession, Symes, his private secretary, told him of 'reports' emanating from Cairo that he was tired out, that he was encouraging natives, that a change of high commissioner was inevitable, and that when Wingate left Cairo and did not resign a suggestion was actually put up to the cabinet that a change in Cairo was desirable.[86] These rumours were significant and indicated with reasonable accuracy the direction into which things were tending. For as early as the beginning of January 1919, Wingate's removal from Egypt was being seriously considered. 'I have sent this telegram to Wingate', wrote Lord Robert Cecil to Balfour on 4 January 1919, 'preparatory to his recall if you decide on that course. Before sending it I spoke to the prime minister and suggested that if Wingate was recalled, Allenby would be a suitable successor. This he warmly approved and so did the CIGS to whom I mentioned it confidentially. But the prime minister wanted nothing done which would preclude Wingate's return to Egypt if that were decided on. I hope the telegram leaves the matter quite open. But I ought to add', he concluded, 'that everyone to whom I have spoken about Wingate is confident that he is not up to the job.'

The outbreak which followed Zaghlul's deportation forced a decision on Wingate's future. In his telegram to Balfour of 16 March, quoted above, Curzon, while noting Cheetham's incapacity, did not propose that Wingate should return to Cairo. He too wanted Allenby to take charge of Egypt, obviously in the belief that he would be more firm and decisive. 'I understand', he told Balfour 'that he arrives in Paris tomorrow and will not be free to return for a few days. Will you consult with him as to steps to be taken?' A few days later, on 19 March, Curzon sent another telegram (drafted by Graham), reminding Balfour that Allenby was arriving in Paris on that day, adding: 'I am sure you will agree that his early return to Egypt is advisable'.[88]

Balfour and Lloyd George acted very promptly. The next day, 20 March, Curzon was told that Allenby was appointed special high commissioner in Egypt – the title being an echo of the title of special commissioner which Lord Dufferin was given when he was sent to investigate conditions in Egypt after the 'Urabi movement – and that he was proceeding to Egypt forthwith. In his memoirs Hardinge has stated that, in appointing Allenby, both Balfour and Lloyd George desired to restore British prestige by administering strong measures and that the prime minister imagined 'that in him he had found a strong man who would impose the views of the British government upon the sultan and would defeat the Nationalists'. That this was Lloyd George's expectation is most probable, but whether Balfour was of the same mind is more doubtful. His telegram of 18 March is not easy to reconcile with a firm or coherent policy. What is more likely is that he had come to entertain a prejudice against Wingate, the necessity of whose removal loomed perhaps larger in his eyes than the exact character and policy of his successor. In his memoirs Hardinge asserts that he was doubtful of Allenby's ability to rule Egypt which, he thought, required a skilled diplomatist and administrator, and that he pressed these considerations 'very strongly' on Balfour.[89] Of such representations the available papers afford us no evidence, but if Hardinge opposed Allenby's appointment his language here indicates that this was not done in Wingate's cause; it was Graham's merits which Hardinge must have pressed.

When Balfour informed Curzon of Allenby's appointment, he added to his telegram a 'secret and personal' paragraph to the effect that Allenby's appointment as special high commissioner 'would not of itself displace Wingate who would for the present retain the post of high commissioner. It is probable', Balfour added, 'that he will not return, though an immediate decision on this point is not necessary.'[90] Wingate himself was told in a telegram of the same date that the emergency in Egypt made it necessary for Allenby to be given both civil and military authority, but that this 'makes no technical change in your position'.[91] For many months Wingate was left in suspense. The only information he was vouchsafed – if such it can be called – was contained in a letter from Balfour the terms of which, deliberately obscure and ambiguous, were carefully designed to mislead its recipient. So long as Allenby was dealing with the existing crisis, the foreign secretary informed the high commissioner on 26 March 1919, 'your services will hardly be required. How long this exceptional period will continue and what shape the future government of Egypt will take neither I nor any other man can say with confidence'.[92] Wingate remained until the autumn of 1919 formally the high commissioner, but he was completely ignored and kept aside. On one crucial occasion shortly after Allenby's appointment, as will be seen, Curzon did ask for his advice; but its soundness did not prevent it being once again dismissed.

Wingate did attempt once to extract an explanation of the treatment to which he had been subjected. He went to Curzon in June 1919 and demanded that an official enquiry should be held into his conduct of affairs in Egypt. Not surprisingly, Curzon found the demand embarrassing. He wrote to Balfour in Paris that he proposed to tell Wingate that no reflection whatever had been cast on his conduct and that Allenby had originally been sent because of his military prestige. The movement in Egypt, however, had proved wider than anticipated. Normality was not yet restored and it was undesirable therefore, and impossible to suspend Allenby from the discharge of his duties. Since this might involve a revival of the troubles, he was proposing to confirm Allenby in his position, and to him, Wingate, he was offering a peerage. All this, Curzon added, was on the assumption 'which I gathered in Paris, that it is not desirable that Wingate should go back as high commissioner to Cairo'. Balfour replied on 9 June that he had consulted the prime minister who agreed to the offer of a peerage provided Wingate undertook not to raise the question of his dismissal in the House of Lords. 'It is not', Balfour went on, 'an easy situation to handle. Wingate is a good fellow, and has been a very valuable and distinguished public servant. He gave specific advice on a difficult problem, warning us that if his advice was not followed trouble would ensue. Thereupon we practically tell him that he is not the man most competent to deal with the situation thus created, and that somebody else must be put in his place! This, I take it, is the skeleton of the story, and it is not one very easy to clothe in attractive flesh and blood.' In extenuation of the government's behaviour, Balfour adduced two points: '1. That the rejection by the government of Wingate's advice was justified by the facts as then known, and that the subsequent troubles were not its results; 2. That Wingate after all that has passed, is not the man to deal with this particular kind of crisis at this particular moment.'[93] Neither point has much weight. It is quite difficult to see how 'the facts as then known' justified the government's rejection of Wingate's advice, unless by 'facts' is meant the prejudice against Wingate that had accumulated in the minds of ministers and officials. As for Balfour's second point, if Wingate was not the man to deal with the crisis, then Allenby, to judge by his record, was even less qualified. Wingate was not in the end offered a peerage. He was made a baronet and offered the governorship of the Straits Settlements, which he turned down. He had also to engage in a long, wearisome and petty controversy with the War Office about the amount of pension due to him.

Allenby reached Cairo on 25 March. Both Lloyd George and Curzon looked to him to use that firmness in which they believed Wingate to be deficient. There is no evidence to show whether Allenby was given in Paris an idea of Balfour's rather different attitude, or whether he was informed of the text of Balfour's telegram of 18 March which, as has been seen, was disregarded by the Foreign Office and not transmitted to Cairo. The fact remains that immediately on arrival at Cairo, he espoused the policy of that telegram and made his own Cheetham's proposals, which both Curzon and Wingate had condemned as ill-judged and dangerous. In so doing, he may have been influenced by the views of his chief political officer, Sir Gilbert Clayton. As early as 17 March, Clayton 'considered that the movement [in Egypt] should be met by a generous recognition of legitimate Egyptian aspirations and a readiness to consider reasonable requests'. He submitted to Cheetham proposals which might serve as a basis for settlement. Among them was one to the effect that if suitable delegates wanted to go to London no objection would be offered 'and those individuals of the [Nationalist] committee who were recently deported will not be prevented from accompanying the delegation – if so desired'.[94] A letter of his to Wingate written the following April makes clear the assumptions on which he proceeded. 'I cannot disguise from myself', he wrote, 'that the principles of Nationalism and the desire for independence have bitten deep into all classes, and I am convinced that our policy in Egypt must be very carefully reconsidered on lines of increased sympathy with national aspirations so far as they keep *within* legitimate limits.'[95] Clayton, then, believed that the unrest of Egypt was caused by the denial of independence or autonomy – as Zaghlul and the politicians claimed – and that therefore the remedy for the unrest lay in treating with Zaghlul and his friends and in working towards a political settlement on the lines which these politicians had adumbrated. It thus followed that for him Zaghlul's deportation had been a mistake and his release by Allenby a necessary measure, as it was better to cut losses rather than persist in the error.[96] Clayton's views, as Allenby would soon have discovered, were now faithfully echoed at the residency, where Cheetham, in order to persuade his masters in London, had in a telegram of 17 March – already quoted – held out the prospect of cooperation by 'Moderates' if the concessions he advocated were authorised.[97]

Immediately on his arrival at Cairo, Allenby adopted Clayton's and Cheetham's views. He was clearly out of his depth in Egyptian politics and accepted uncritically the opinion that, as he put it in a telegram of 20 April 1919, Zaghlul represented the 'opinion of majority of Egyptian intellectuals';[98] as though 'Egyptian intellectuals' were a known or intelligible entity, as though their opinions – whatever they were or however ascertained – had overriding or primordial importance, and as though it made the smallest sense in such a situation to speak – except in the loosest and most misleading manner – of representation or representativeness. But Allenby's mind was made up almost as soon as he reached Cairo, and perhaps even before. Mr Patterson, then director general of State Accounts, testifies to this in a memorandum which must have been written shortly afterwards. 'The release of the four [i.e. Zaghlul and his fellow-deportees]', he wrote, 'was I think in Sir Edmund's mind from the beginning. I saw him . . . within twenty-four hours of his arrival, and he hinted as much. I respectfully pointed out that I thought their return would make all government impossible, and as the high commissioner made no comment on my remark I received the impression that he disagreed with it.'[99]

On 31 March Allenby informed Curzon that he had sent for the ex-ministers Rushdi and Adli, and that they had asked him to remove restrictions on the departure of would-be travellers from Egypt, including the deportees. 'This concession', he said, 'without conferring any official recognition generally from me, would automatically restore tranquillity, andg uarantee formation of a Ministry' with whom 'fruitful' discussion would be possible.[100] This precipitate proposal, buttressed as it was by glib and unconvincing arguments was received with dismay by Curzon in London. He was, he wrote in a letter of 1 April to Balfour 'much startled' by this advocacy of a policy which had been resisted since the previous November. Allenby, he thought was 'misjudging the situation in its wider aspect' by putting all the emphasis on the necessity of forming an Egyptian Ministry.[101] But he was to find no support either from Balfour or from Lloyd George. Allenby's appointment was their doing and they did not dare – as Hardinge points out[102] – disavow or even oppose his policies. 'Prime Minister and I' Balfour telegraphed to Curzon on 2 April, 'are of opinion that as Allenby was appointed special high commissioner of Egypt . . . his advice cannot be disregarded.' 'It is important', he emphasised, 'to avoid any appearance of mistrusting his present policy.' And Balfour ended his telegram by saying that Allenby's policy was not 'in essence' inconsistent with the suggestions he had made in his own telegram of 18 March.[103]

Curzon now called Wingate to his aid. The high commissioner – and this was his last intervention in Egyptian affairs – now wrote a note in which he stated that he differed 'most strongly' from Allenby's advice: 'The Nationalists', he pointed out prophetically, 'will say, and with justice, that by agitation and intimidation they have forced the hands of His Majesty's Government, and I do not think it is going too far to say that we shall have practically abandoned the position in Egypt which we have acquired after years of patient toil and labour.

'. . . our real power and authority will have practically gone and we shall be at the mercy of agitators at any time they care to repeat the methods by which they will say they have obtained their ends in the present crisis.'[104] Curzon sent this note to Balfour with a letter in which he told him that his telegram of 2 April 'caused much consternation here'. Balfour, as has been seen, spoke there of the importance of not disregarding Allenby's authoritative advice; 'if it comes to a question of disregarding authoritative advice', rejoined Curzon, 'let it be borne in mind that Allenby is a soldier of great ability and experience, but no experience of Egypt or its political and administrative problems'. Wingate himself, Curzon went on, who had originally suggested allowing an Egyptian delegation to come to London, considered Allenby's policy 'a disaster'. The consequences 'of this rapid and complete abandonment of our position', Curzon warned, would be catastrophic in Egypt and elsewhere.[105] Curzon, also accompanied by Wingate and Graham, visited Bonar Law, then acting prime minister, to try and enlist his support in opposing Allenby. They were not successful: 'Wingate', wrote Bonar Law to Lloyd George, 'makes a poor impression and I would have no faith whatever in his judgment. On the face of it I should be inclined to agree with Allenby'.[106]

Allenby, then, had his way. He sent another telegram on 4 April, in that urgent and peremptory tone which he was to adopt whenever the government showed the slightest hesitation in ratifying his decisions. It was essential, he now told Curzon, that 'a favourable reply' should be given to his proposals which constituted 'the least concession that will suffice'; otherwise the situation would again 'become bad', as every day's delay augmented his difficulties and increased the gravity of the situation.[107] The CIGS, Sir Henry Wilson, probably instigated by him, added his pressure to Allenby's. In a minute on the latter's telegram of 4 April which he sent to Balfour through Hardinge he stated that 'unless Egypt is kept quiet we shall be called on for more troops, and we shall have to send them which, under present conditions, will be a matter of extreme difficulty'.[108] Lloyd George and Balfour gave in. The utmost that Curzon obtained was that they should propose to Allenby that, as an alternative to Zaghlul's release, he should announce the setting up of a commission under Milner which would immediately set about investigating

Egyptian grievances. But, they added, they were not in a position to judge whether this was wise, and would 'leave this matter to your discretion, but in any event and whatever your decision we shall give you our fullest support'. Allenby promptly replied that though a commission would be desirable later, it was 'useless' now and that he was announcing forthwith the removal of travel restrictions and the release of the deportees from Malta.[109] In a minute of 7 April, Graham wrote that this step, taken even before the formation of an Egyptian Ministry, represented 'a complete surrender'.[110]

Why did Allenby act in this precipitate manner? When he reached Egypt the worst of the disorders was over, and the threat to the British hold over Egypt had been decisively overcome. GHQ's 'Historical Summary', mentioned above, states that when Allenby arrived the Nationalists had begun to despair of success, especially because of the severe attitude of Bulfin – who was in charge of operations – and his refusal to have anything to do with them. Allenby's arrival therefore was interpreted as a forerunner of annexation and as indicating an intention to deal firmly with agitators.[111] 'The release of Zaghlul', wrote G. C. Delaney, Reuter's correspondent in Egypt in a memorandum sent to Graham, 'was a concession never anticipated. In fact the impression I gained was that the leaders were greatly alarmed at the turn of events, had been particularly impressed by General Bulfin's warning that he intended to take repressive measures which would bring tremendous suffering upon the country, and that, at any rate for the moment, they were prepared to obliterate Zaghlul from their minds, and to concentrate their energies on helping to form a Ministry, which they declared was the first vital necessity for the restoration of tranquillity.'[112] To decree Zaghlul's release Allenby no doubt thought a bold master-stroke, allying clemency to firmness, thus eliminating what he took to be the main obstacle to an Egyptian settlement.

In this he proved utterly wrong. For as Delaney pointed out in the memorandum quoted above, the Egyptians 'misunderstood the whole situation, translating General Allenby's action in releasing Zaghlul into a concession wrung from the British authorities. It led to truculence never hitherto experienced or even imagined, and Egyptians naturally think that they have only to repeat their tactics to wring still larger concessions.' Zaghlul and his companions, released from Malta, had gone to Paris where they bickered and wrote inef-fective memoranda to the Peace Conference and to the Powers.

Whatever hopes they had had of diplomatic action were soon dashed by the international recognition of the British protectorate. But in Egypt itself Zaghlul absent proved, as a result of Allenby's action, much more effective and powerful than Zaghlul present. As Vansittart put it in a minute of 25 April 1919: '. . . The whole country is going over to him [Zaghlul] under the impression that he is on the winning side, and *we* have conveyed that impression to the Egyptians.'[113] The extent of Allenby's miscalculation became speedily apparent. The so-called moderates whom his policy was supposed to attract became very dubious of collaborating with the protecting power since it showed itself so inept, so hesitant and so ready to give in to violence. Though Zaghlul's memoranda could make little impression in Paris, yet his denunciations of anybody helping the British had their effect in Egypt. For his supporters grew powerful after his release. Donations to the *Wafd*, whether given in self-protection or whether extracted by threats, became usual. Thus immediately after Zaghlul's release the well-known notable Badrawi 'Āshūr donated ten thousand pounds; a member of the royal family, Prince Yusif Kamal, gave two thousand; so that in a short while, says a chronicler, large amounts of money came to be at the disposal of the *Wafd*. Allenby tried to put a stop to what a proclamation of his termed illegal and forced collections, but he was unable to suppress the evil.[114]

The British were as unsuccessful in putting down another, far more serious, evil. This was the *Wafd*'s terrorist apparatus, directed by Abd al-Rahman Fahmi (1870–1946), who himself acted as the secretary of the *Wafd* committee in Cairo. Abd al-Rahman Fahmi, ex-official and uncle of Ali Mahir and Ahmad Mahir, showed great skill in organising demonstrations, riots, intimidation of public men and newspaper editors, in addition to the forced collections which Allenby was unable to prevent. Also under his control was a 'supreme Council for Assassinations' composed, among others, of Ahmad Mahir, Mahmud Fahmi al-Nuqrashi, Abd al-Latif al-Sufani, and Abd al-Rahman al-Rafi'i.[115] Assassinations were, of course, the ultimate and most powerful weapon which the *Wafd* did not scruple to use.

Contrary, therefore, to Allenby's expectations, the so-called moderates, as much out of fear as out of political calculation, became more intractable after Zaghlul's release. Rushdi and Adli did indeed form a Ministry, but tranquillity did not – as Allenby had confidently asserted – 'automatically' ensue. The Ministry soon had a civil service strike on its hands, in which Ali Mahir took a prominent part. Rushdi and Adli proposed to deal with it by officially announcing that Zaghlul and his friend 'represented' the Egyptian nation. Unwilling, or afraid, to withstand Zaghlulist agitation, Rushdi and Adli resigned on 21 April 1919, after less than a fortnight in office. The main benefit which Allenby anticipated from his policy was thus speedily shown to be illusory.

Muhammad Sa'id was persuaded to form a Ministry. He also showed the same unwillingness to shoulder responsibility or adopt a firm policy. His 'desire to avoid unpopularity among Egyptians and his anxiety to placate his countrymen by measures involving a show of concessions obtained from myself', Allenby wrote in a dispatch of 10 July 1919, 'have led at times to positions of some difficulty.'[117] Among the concessions which Muhammad Sa'id succeeded in obtaining were a relaxation in the censorship of the press and the discontinuance of military courts for the trial of offences against public security (other than those committed against members of the British army).[118] Both concessions gave greater scope to agitation and subversion and thus increased unease and disquiet in Egypt. By the end of 1919, and as a consequence of Allenby's policy, Egypt was in a more parlous situation and was more difficult to govern than when he had taken over. But a new element now appeared which was further to complicate a situation almost hopelessly tangled.

As has been seen, when Allenby at the end of March proposed to release Zaghlul, he was asked to consider as an alternative policy the dispatch of a mission to investigate Egyptian grievances. He dismissed such an alternative, insisting that only his policy would answer. But he agreed that it would be useful to send a mission later. It was Lord Milner, the colonial secretary, who had served in Egypt under Cromer, who was now appointed to head a Special Mission to Egypt. Milner, however, was not in favour of going out to Egypt immediately. In a most interesting letter which he wrote to Curzon on 25 April 1919, he referred to 'the great blunder made by Allenby, when, to save himself from being left without an Egyptian Ministry, he made the concession about passports and the release of Zaghlul and Co. For thirty years we have governed Egypt because of the conviction in the minds of the intriguing Pasha class that in the last resort we could and would do without them. That conviction, for some reason or other, has been weakened of late years. Hence the present troubles, which are simply a "try on" on the part of the caste.' This being so, Milner concluded, it would be a mistake to send a mission just then: 'It looks as if we were flustered, afraid of the situation created by the non-existence of an Egyptian Ministry and the naked assertion of British authority, and felt that something must be done to get us out of a hole.'[119] Milner was inclined, therefore, to postpone the mission to the following September. Allenby started by deprecating this delay. But the Egyptian prime minister, Muhammad Sa'id, wanted the mission postponed until the signature of the peace treaty with Turkey which should finally consecrate the British position in Egypt. In urging postponement Muhammad Sa'id was clearly afraid of the attacks being mounted on him by the *Wafd* as a tool of the British, and he did his best, by means of public declarations, to show himself as opposed to the Milner Mission as his Zaghlulist opponents.[120] He was no doubt encouraged in this attitude by an attempt on his life organised by the *Wafd*'s apparatus. When the coming of the Milner Mission was finally announced, Muhammad Sa'id found it more advantageous – or perhaps safer – to announce his resignation.[121] He was succeeded by a Copt, Yusuf Wahba, who was politically of no account but who – in the circumstances – showed a rare courage in agreeing to take office. Muhammad Sa'id's behaviour once more showed Allenby's impolicy in thinking to attract so-called moderates by making concessions to extremists.

Milner, as has been seen, was at the outset for postponing the visit of his mission. But as time went on, he came to see that delay too had its disadvantages: 'Personally', we find him writing to Graham on 26 August 1919 'I should not object to postponement. But politically I think it would be a mistake. . . . The mission is based on the assumption that the protectorate exists. Would not its postponement in itself suggest that we were not sure about it?'[122] In this Milner spoke better than he knew; for he and his mission were to show precisely that fatal uncertainty about the legitimacy of the British position in Egypt which, added to Allenby's initial blunder, largely ruined the edifice which Cromer had built with such skill and pertinacity. Delay in any case had a serious immediate consequence. It gave time to Abd al-Rahman Fahmi to set on foot and perfect a system of threats and agitation – the so-called boycott – which was quite efficient in isolating Milner's Mission and in seriously cramping its style.[123]

The Milner Mission finally arrived in Egypt in December 1919. It left the country the following March, having heard much evidence from British officials and businessmen, from foreign residents and a few Egyptians, and having conducted discreet conversations with some leading Egyptians. The purpose of the mission, as defined in a letter from Curzon to Allenby of 15 October 1919, was to devise the details of a constitution which would define the respective provinces of the British protecting power and of the Egyptian government.[124] Milner himself seems to have set out with the idea that the purpose of the mission was not to liquidate but rather to buttress the protectorate. The way to do this, he came to believe quite clearly, was by negotiating a treaty between Great Britain and Egypt which would secure to the former the powers of control deemed absolutely necessary. But he was quite emphatic that such a treaty was not a substitute for the protectorate but only a definition of it, its chief purpose being to save Egyptian face.[125] During his stay in Egypt, however, his ideas seem to have gradually changed. The change which they suffered is most clearly seen in a conversation which he had with a European businessman in Egypt, E. R. Fischer, who took the line that the welfare of Egypt required more, not less, British control. Milner did admit that British control was in the interest of the Egyptian masses. But these masses were mute, and the only clamour to be heard was that of politicians abusing and reviling the British. In such circumstances what Fischer recommended was 'a fine ideal, but I cannot say that I feel convinced that Great Britain would have the power or the will to pursue it'. What Fischer said, Milner noted in his diary, 'rather tended to shake the conviction, at which I have been gradually arriving, that the right line for us to take is gradually to draw out of the administration of Egypt and put more real power and responsibility into native hands'.[126] As his colleague on the mission, J. A. Spender, later put it, Milner had come to believe that 'if the Egyptians did not want us to govern them and could keep order and maintain solvency without us, we were under no obligation to undertake the invidious, difficult and very expensive task of governing them against their will'.[127] The more Milner got involved in the quicksand of Egyptian negotiations, the more he came to lull himself with mere words and to believe that in giving up power to the benefit of Zaghlul, or of Fu'ad, or of the so-called moderates, he was actually conferring a benefit on the Egyptians, that this, in fact, was the crown and culmination of Cromer's work which in days gone by he had celebrated in a well-known work, *England in Egypt*. In 1920 a new edition of this book, the thirteenth, came to be published, for which Milner wrote a new Preface. In it he said:

That it should be possible to contemplate so large a measure of independence as is now proposed for Egypt, is surely the most striking tribute to the efficacy of Great Britain's reforming work.

Strangely enough, the view has been expressed in some quarters that any relaxation of British control over the administration of Egypt would be an abandonment of the objects which we have been hitherto pursuing in that country. Nothing could be further from the truth. The establishment of Egypt as an independent state in intimate alliance with Great Britain, so far from being a reversal of the policy with which we set out, would be the consummation of it. . . . . That we should attempt [it] at all, is evidence at once of our good faith and of our confidence in the soundness of the work which we have been doing in Egypt for the last eight and thirty years.[128]

And in a debate in the House of Lords he said, on 4 November 1920:

My belief is that a course of action is possible which will enable us to ensure all that we need in Egypt, including the maintenance of order and progress of which we ourselves are the authors, without involving ourselves in permanent hostility with the Egyptian nation. My intimate conviction is that, while there is undoubtedly an element of Egyptian nationalism which is anti-British, the better and stronger elements of it are not anti-British but simply pro-Egyptian.[129]

These passages, as the evidence shows, are not mere rhetoric designed for the public defence of a policy. They represent an actual conviction. Their fanciful character and sentimental tone therefore indicate a loss of contact with reality, the outcome not so much perhaps of intellectual debility, as of that failure of nerve, that weakening of the will to rule, which became manifest among the British ruling classes in the aftermath of the first world war, and which was to make the dissolution of the British empire so ugly and ruinous, to subjects and rulers alike.

Commenting in his diary on his conversation with Fischer, Milner recorded that the latter's views 'were in some respects inconsistent with the conclusions at which, I think, we have most of us arrived'. The papers of the Milner Mission confirm this judgment in respect of some at any rate of its members, notably J. A. Spender and Cecil Hurst. An undated memorandum by Spender probably written while the mission was still in Egypt argued that if the Egyptians were left to themselves it was 'extremely probable that the government of Egypt would become an oligarchy in which the poor would be entirely at the mercy of a small governing class'. 'The best hope of correcting these tendencies', Spender went on, 'is that the political quarrel between Britain and Egypt should be healed, and that in giving up formal control the British should be able to strengthen their influence with the younger Egyptians and to induce them freely to accept their help and guidance'. It was, Spender insisted, 'of the highest importance that concessions should not be made with the *arrière pensée* that they will fail, but that the utmost help and good will should be shown by the British in making them succeed.' It is difficult to see how exactly Spender thought that the misgovernment of Egypt could be prevented by a policy of concessions, or who 'the younger Egyptians' were on whom he pinned such faith. But it remains the case that he believed that the nationalist movement was 'beyond doubt, deep and genuine', and that this fact should govern all future policy.[130] Hurst's views were less high-flown, more down-to-earth. In a memorandum of 20 February 1920, he advocated 'spontaneous concessions' because, if the legitimate grievances of the Egyptians were met, the cry for complete independence might die away. The argument seems plausible but is really fallacious since the legitimate grievances of the Egyptians and the pretensions of Zaghlul were by no means identical. Hurst had other, quite cogent, arguments in favour of concessions. Relations with the United States and with the Muslim world might deteriorate if Egypt were held down by force; again, limited concessions now might avert others, more far-reaching, which a different British government might feel inclined to concede in the face of continued disorder in Egypt. The guiding principle of a settlement, according to Hurst, ought to be that Egypt should have control over all sections of the administration which were not vital to British interests and which were not necessary for the discharge of obligations to foreign powers. Egyptian ministers were to be responsible to an Egyptian Chamber of Deputies, and the sultan was to become a constitutional monarch. The nationalists might reject this as not the complete independence which they were demanding, but experience would show them that their demand was not realistic: 'Experience', Hurst asserted, 'is the only argument that will convince the Egyptians that they are not all-competent, and I think that experience ought to be forced upon them. British control ought to be withdrawn [from ministries which were of no vital interest to Great Britain] whether the Egyptians like it or not.'[131] Whether the Egyptians like it or not: the Egyptians must be given Zaghlul and Fu'ad to gulp down like an unpleasant, but salutary medicine. But since the exercise of power is quite remote from the practice of medicine, Hurst's liberal, high-minded and confused metaphor had the most sinister of consequences. What these might be can be illustrated from a remark attributed to Hurst and Spender in the papers of the Milner Mission. They had been hearing evidence about the manner in which Zaghlulists, by means of pressures and threats, were managing to force village *omdas* to collaborate with them: 'Mr Spender and Mr Hurst', we read in the minutes of evidence, 'observed that the principle might be adopted of allowing the Egyptian government to do things shocking to us as long as they did not affect foreign interests.'[132] If this was what a policy of concessions meant, then it was a policy which, sooner rather than later would destroy whatever loyalty and respect the British had managed to inspire in Egypt and make their position meaningless and untenable. This policy Milner and his mission, and later Allenby and his advisers, unhesitatingly recommended.

The views of Milner, Spender and Hurst became very much those of the mission as a whole. On their departure from Egypt they drew up a number of General Conclusions, dated 3 March 1920, which on 17 May Milner sent Curzon with a covering letter stating that these were the unanimous views of the mission. In these General Conclusions the mission proposed the conclusion of a treaty with Egypt: 'In determining the measure of control which Great Britain must continue to exercise over Egypt, and for her right to exercise which any treaty must provide,' the mission stated, 'we should be guided by the principle to restrict the direct exercise of British authority to the narrowest possible limits, and outside these limits to rely upon the moral influence of British officials serving under Egyptian ministers in a genuinely Egyptian administration.' Couched in the fashionable euphemisms of the time, this proposal embodies essentially Milner's failure of nerve, Spender's liberal fanaticism, and Hurst's low and misguided common-sense. Side by side with this key passage we find other statements which seem like meaningless relics from a past age, asserting British responsibility for the good government of Egypt. The mission recognised that 'owing to the backwardness of the mass of the people, of whom ninety per cent are quite illiterate, it will be many years before any elected Assembly is really representative of more than a comparatively limited class. Parliamentary government under the present social conditions', they went on to say, 'means oligarchical government, and, if wholly uncontrolled, it would be

likely to show little regard for the interests of the Egyptian people.'
Therefore, the mission considered that 'any treaty or convention
regulating the relations of Great Britain and Egypt must at the same
time define the general character of the future constitution of Egypt.'
'In doing so', they bravely asserted, 'we must seek to safeguard individual liberty and the interests of the mass of the people'. Whether
the proposed treaty which restricted British authority 'to the
narrowest possible limits' was compatible with such aspirations,
whether 'the moral influence of British officials' was alone sufficient
to protect individual liberty and the interests of the mass, the mission
do not discuss. Even more difficult to reconcile with the mission's
main proposal, and with what we know of their attitude is the passage
in which they discuss what would happen if no treaty were to be concluded. In this event 'no relaxation of British control is either possible
or desirable. Indeed', they assert, 'it may be necessary for Great
Britain to undertake fresh responsibilities. It is impossible to allow
the decline of governmental authority, due to the inherent weakness
of the present system, to continue.' The evidence, such as it is, shows
that there was no disposition at all on the part of Milner and his
colleagues to contemplate 'fresh responsibilities' in Egypt. This
passage, therefore, figuring in a confidential document, indicates that
Milner and his colleagues were either not fully aware of their own
assumptions, or else that behind the professed unanimity there were
unresolved disagreements of which these incompatible proposals are
the sign.[133]

In their General Conclusions the mission declared that the proposed
treaty would have to be confirmed by a representative assembly. But
it had first to be negotiated. With whom, then, to negotiate? The
Ministry, headed by Yusuf Wahba, manifestly had no authority,
and was moreover itself anxious to avoid involvement in any negotiation whatever. In an interview with Milner on 29 February 1920
Wahba stated that ministers preferred not to be consulted about any
proposals which might be made by the Milner Mission, and begged,
moreover, not to be quoted publicly by name. 'I have always felt',
wrote Milner, 'that ministers were only anxious to see us go away
without their having committed themselves in any way.'[134] Fu'ad,
likewise, much as he would have liked to be recognised as the proper
authority to negotiate on behalf of Egypt, manifestly could not make
good such a claim.

There remained the other public men, ex-ministers and notables.

They, indeed, abounded in suggestions and advice and were visibly hungry for office and power. But they were unwilling to shoulder responsibility on their own, and terrified of Zaghlul and his apparatus in Egypt. The straits to which the British were now reduced may be summed up in this, that now they had to treat on equal terms with men whom, before 1914, they were accustomed to manage; with men moreover who, unused to the rough-and-tumble of real politics, were bound in any negotiation to prove broken reeds. They had to treat with courtiers, with obedient bureaucrats, with tame and safe administrators who at the slightest squall were likely to scurry for safety. Milner confessed himself disappointed. No one, he wrote to Curzon on 17 February 1920, had sufficient courage to break with the extremists and come forward to meet him halfway.[135]

The exception to all this was Zaghlul. His ambition gave him a force of spirit, a frenzy which cowed and intimidated his rivals. The blunders of these rivals, and of the British, of course gave him many opportunities, but it was his character which enabled him to seize these opportunities and shape them to his own purposes. So, in the end, the Milner Mission had to recognise that if Muhammad would not go to the mountain, the mountain had to come to Muhammad. Those who seem to have mainly helped it towards this conclusion were Zaghlul's rivals, Rushdi and Adli. It was they, as will be remembered, who acting in concert with Zaghlul had precipitated the crisis of November 1918. They now saw a possibility of regaining power with enhanced prestige by getting Milner to agree to autonomy or independence. In a letter to Spender of 1 February 1920, Milner said he was quite sure that Adli and his friends were anxious to get rid of the Wahba Ministry and take their places at once.[136] But as at the end of 1918, Rushdi and Adli now prudently refused to take power or assume responsibility on their own. Adli was in touch with Abd al-Rahman Fahmi in Cairo and Zaghlul in Paris. He suggested that Zaghul should come back to Cairo and join him in negotiating officially with the Milner Mission. But Zaghlul, as wily as his correspondent, would not limit thus his own freedom of manoeuvre. He declined in February to join an administration to be formed by Adli, lest, as he told Adli, the uprightness of the *Wafd* might become suspect, and in order that the confidence which they enjoyed among the people might be of use in providing support and smoothing the path for Adli.[137] Adli and Rushdi now hit on another plan. On 26 February Milner recorded in his diary that Adli had broached the idea of an unofficial delegation 'approved of but not appointed by the sultan and the government' which would 'talk the matter over with the mission'. This unofficial delegation was to include Adli, Tharwat, Rushdi, Sidqi, together with Zaghlul and one or two of his friends. The essential, Adli insisted, was that Zaghlul should be a party to the move. He, Adli, was willing to go to Paris and induce Zaghlul to agree. The advantage of this scheme according to him, was that negotiations would commit neither government. Milner proved quite favourable to the idea and told Adli that if Zaghlul was willing the mission would raise no difficulty.[138]

Thus, shortly after the mission's departure from Egypt, Adli himself left for Paris in order to organise this 'unofficial' delegation. From Paris Adli plied Milner with hopeful reports. Zaghlul and his friends, he wrote on 26 April were 'dans les meilleures dispositions pour arriver à un accord'; therefore Milner should send to Paris a 'personne de votre confiance' who would carry out preliminary negotiations.[139] Adli's bulletins were supported and confirmed by those of Walrond. Osmond Walrond had served in South Africa at the turn of the century and had there known and become friendly with Milner. During the war he was in the Arab Bureau in Cairo and afterwards became an agent of the Secret Intelligence Service in Egypt. Milner listened to and trusted his advice which, as will be seen, was often erratic and injudicious. When Adli left for Paris, Walrond followed him to provide liaison with Milner. On 28 April he reported to Milner that he had seen Adli, who was 'surprised' to find Zaghlul and his friends in 'such a conciliatory and chastened frame of mind'. Again, on 8 May he wrote that Adli was trying to persuade Zaghlul to come to London with one or two other members of the *Wafd* and 'to say that it is a private invitation from yourself'.[140] Such reports now made Milner, who had been rather sceptical of Adli's chances of success, quite hopeful as to the outcome of negotiations with Zaghlul: 'As far as I can gather,' he wrote in a minute of 8 May, 'Adli and Zaghlul are working together and may be regarded as the moderate wing of the Nationalist party. The chances of coming to a good understanding with the Egyptians are brighter than they were.'[141] And two days later he went so far as to write to Walrond that in the last resort he was willing to go himself to Paris as he was 'very anxious to meet Zaghlul', but that a meeting in London, if it could be arranged, would be more convenient.

But such optimism notwithstanding, it was proving rather difficult

to entice Zaghlul to London. He was now being wooed, and was therefore in no hurry to oblige. Also, his basic strategy was to commit
himself to nothing, and to leave himself free to criticise and attack any
agreement which Adli or anybody else might negotiate with the
British. Before coming to Paris, Walrond had clearly seen this. On
29 March he had written to Milner from Cairo that since Zaghlul
claimed to have received from the Egyptians a 'mandate' for nothing
less than 'complete independence', he wanted to shift responsibility
for any compromise with the British on to Adli and his friends.[143]
But now in Paris, in his eagerness to bring Zaghlul and Milner together, he seems to have forgotten this. Milner likewise seems to have
attached no importance to this situation. His neglect of its implications was shortly to prove quite ruinous to British interests in Egypt.
Walrond, then, enthusiastically believing in Zaghlul's readiness to
negotiate an agreement, strongly urged that Milner should do his
utmost to overcome his hesitations. Milner had proposed that
Zaghlul and Adli should go to London for private discussions. This
would have been consonant with Adli's original suggestion of an
'unofficial 'delegation. But Walrond now pointed out that Adli and
Zaghlul did not want to do this because 'their conduct in going to
London uninvited and unrecognised would be criticised and turned
to their detriment, especially if they came back without result'. Adli
also did not wish to make a false move and assume responsibility
alone. He could not afford to have it said that the *Wafd* had obtained
less than they might have because of him. If it was not possible to
recognise the *Wafd*, then Zaghlul and his colleagues should be invited
privately to London, together with Adli. Alternatively, Milner himself
might come to Paris or send Sir Rennell Rodd or Mr Hurst. 'The
Wafd, wrongly called Nationalists', asserted Walrond, 'are not unfriendly, if we reason with them.' He thought it quite possible '*with
Adli Pasha's help*' to get the *Wafd* 'on our side'; it was quite possible,
he continued, compounding his misjudgment, that once the Milner
Mission and the *Wafd* came together, for the latter to prove 'reasonable'. Walrond went on to say that he had shown this letter to Adli
who 'thoroughly approves of it', and who suggested that Hurst, who
was then in Paris, should be taken to see Zaghlul privately: 'He need
not discuss the vital points but talk sweet nothings and if possible
impress them with his liberal views in general.'[144]

Milner, therefore, instructed Hurst to get in touch with Adli and
Zaghlul who were 'nervous of coming here on the score of publicity',

to 'try and persuade them of the importance of doing so'.[145] When Hurst visited Zaghlul, the latter asked whether he was invited to go to London as the representative of the Egyptian people and whether the invitation would be a written one. Hurst demurred to both of these suggestions. All he was prepared to do was to extend an oral invitation. 'En ma qualité de membre de la Mission Milner, j'invite Votre Excellence à se rendre à Londres pour causer avec Lord Milner et les membres de la Mission et trouver les bases d'une entente.' Zaghlul then asked whether he was at liberty to write to his followers and tell them that Hurst had visited him and extended such an invitation. Hurst declared that he would have to consult Milner on this point.[146] These proceedings made Walrond impatient. Hurst, he told Milner, was not 'supple' enough. 'I have seen nothing in any of the *Wafd*', he insisted, 'to change my views or think them anything but well disposed to us and all anxious to bring about an accord. They are the Hisb el-Umma, the "Party of the People", and it was an evil day when they were first dubbed "Nationalists". I do not think they will in the end prove "difficiles" to manage.' 'The *Wafd* organisation in Egypt', he asserted, 'if we win them over, contains the intellectual class. We can win them', he assured Milner, 'I am certain of what I say.' But Walrond was not only inclined to show too much of that *zèle* against which Talleyrand has warned diplomats; he was also, for a secret agent, dangerously gullible: 'I hope', he went on to tell Milner, 'you have got Curzon to ask Allenby to go slow for the moment. Of course the attempts on ministers are not anything to do with the *Wafd*. But only indirectly. I mean they are not directly responsible and are absolutely ignorant of the organisations for assassination.'[147]

Having consulted Milner, Hurst told Zaghlul that he was at liberty to write and tell his followers of Hurst's visit and invitation, with this proviso that the invitation was to Zaghlul in his personal capacity and not as Chief of the Egyptian Delegation.[148] But these subtle and alembicated distinctions in the end availed the British nothing. Zaghlul's telegram to Cairo announcing his forthcoming visit to London was for him a distinct triumph. 'Mission Milner', it said, 'invita Delegation Egyptienne par entremise Hurst membre de la Mission à se rendre à Londres pour discuter avec elle les bases d'un accord entre Egypte et Grande Bretagne.' This was not what Milner had authorised and Hurst had conveyed to Zaghlul; but to have publicly contradicted Zaghlul at this stage on a point which seemed so unimportant would have jeopardised the talks which Milner – following Adli's and Walrond's assurances – expected to resolve the whole Egyptian difficulty. Zaghlul's telegram went on to say that three of his colleagues were travelling ahead of him to London 'pour s'assurer des dispositions de Grande Bretagne concernant les aspirations Egyptiennes pour l'indépendance complète'. This last phrase, Walrond informed Milner, 'means nothing.'[149]

Milner's conduct of his negotiations with Zaghlul was, from first to last, unbusinesslike in the extreme. He does not seem at any stage to have consulted either Curzon or the cabinet. Equally surprising is Curzon's behaviour. In a cabinet memorandum of 11 October 1920 he discloses that the General Conclusions of the Milner Mission written in March 1919 and sent to him the following May were only then being circulated to the cabinet. He also reveals that it was only at the end of August 1920 that Milner sent him the proposals he had made in the negotiations with Zaghlul, and by that time the cabinet was already dispersed and unable to discuss them.[150] And it would seem that at no stage, from Zaghlul's arrival in London towards the end of May until the end of August, did Curzon inform himself about the character or the progress of the negotiations.

Milner, again, showed an anxiety for conciliation – even when prospects of an agreement seemed quite remote – which was so extreme as to be taken for pusillanimity and gullibility. Scott, who was acting high commissioner in Allenby's absence during the summer of 1920, suggested on 10 August that in the event of negotiations with Zaghlul failing, steps should be taken against Zaghlulists in Egypt. Milner refused to countenance even the discussion of such plans. 'We cannot', said a telegram of 14 August drafted by him, 'approve of any action which would exacerbate local situation and, by once more making Zaghlul and his followers our enemies, consolidate all sections of Egyptian Nationalists against us. Of course we must be prepared sternly to repress disorder, but the idea of breaking up the Zaghlulist committees or forbidding the Zaghlulists over here to return to Egypt does not commend itself to us at all.'[151] No wonder that Scott was shortly to report that the *Wafd* appeared 'to continue its somewhat high handed methods of extracting money from the fellaheen. From a series of petitions and personal visits to the residency', Scott continued, 'it would appear that its agents, working in some cases it is alleged with the mamours, do not hesitate to use threats in the event of the natives being unwilling to contribute'.[152] In August, it might be thought, there was a real hope of an understanding with Zaghlul. By the following November this hope had utterly disappeared. And yet we find Curzon telegraphing to Allenby at Milner's suggestion: 'I do not favour the idea of publicly announcing our intention to keep troops in Egypt until we get the terms we want, as this would look like using military pressure to enforce our conditions, whereas it is of the essence of the proposed settlement that it should be a bargain into which the Egyptians entered with their eyes open and of their free will.'[153]

Milner's attitude to the Zaghlulist terrorist apparatus shows even more clearly his misjudgment of the situation and of the men with whom he had to deal. It might be argued that a desire to show goodwill prompted him to instruct Allenby to allow during the negotiations cypher communications between Zaghlul and his followers in Egypt, and not to subject to censorship articles in the Egyptian press inspired by the Zaghlulists,[154] but his attitude to the arrest, trial and condemnation of Abd al-Rahman Fahmi and some of his coadjutors betrays in this experienced statesman a simple-mindedness which is simply astonishing. On 27 June 1920 Allenby reported that Abd al-Rahman Fahmi was under suspicion of organising terrorism and that he proposed to arrest him and search his house. Approval was given the following day, but on the day after another telegram was sent ordering Allenby to defer action until further instructions. Approval was at last given, but the requisition of Abd al-Rahman Fahmi's house was delayed for a fortnight, because it was feared that the search might disclose documents embarrassing to Zaghlul. On 17 July Allenby telegraphed once more asking for permission to search, and J. Tilley at the Foreign Office in a minute of the same date expressed his opposition to such a search which he feared might end all negotiations with Zaghlul. He admitted that failure to perquisition might result in Abd al-Rahman Fahmi's acquittal, which would make the residency look foolish; but at least negotiations with Zaghlul would not be interrupted. Allenby was instructed to defer action. But the following day the high commissioner returned to the attack. He sent a 'very urgent' telegram, 'earnestly begging' authority for the search. On 19 July a telegram dictated by Milner expressed doubts whether a perquisition would produce documentary evidence 'of any value'. but at last gave Allenby a free hand. By then it was entirely too late and the search produced nothing.[135]

Abd al-Rahman Fahmi was found guilty and condemned to death

in October 1920. Zaghlul and his friends, then in Paris, protested against the trial and against the prosecutor's allegation that Abd al-Rahman Fahmi was the intermediary between Zaghlul and the terrorists. Walrond made himself the willing and eager mouthpiece of these protests. In a telegram of 10 October from Paris he expressed the conviction that Zaghlul was 'genuine in the matter'; Adli also thought that something ought to be done, otherwise 'present atmosphere of fraternity and good feeling in Egypt might be damped'. By then, of course, as will be seen, such professions were utterly empty, since Zaghlul had already done his best to ensure the failure of his negotiations with Milner. However, in a minute on this telegram, Tilley took the view that the death sentences pronounced against Abd al-Rahman Fahmi and his accomplices were 'a mistake', and should be reduced to imprisonment. The War Office was asked to instruct the Commander-in-Chief, Egypt, not to confirm the sentences, pending further instructions.[156]

Allenby was then in London and he was consulted about a possible commutation of the sentences. In a letter to Tilley of 13 October he rejected Adli's opinion as transmitted by Walrond and insisted that Abd al-Rahman Fahmi and the other ringleaders should pay the full penalty. To follow Adli's advice, he said, 'would be to desert those who stood by us and our friends, and would be a surrender to the party of intimidation and murder'. Milner's minute on this letter is curious and instructive. He said that he regarded the business with the greatest misgiving; he had 'good reason' for not feeling sure that the findings of the military court were 'unimpeachable'; if the sentences were to be simply confirmed 'I should feel that we were running the risk of something much graver than the failure of the present negotiations, viz. a permanent source of bitter and envenomed feeling, as bad or worse than Denshawai.'[157] We see thus the Conservative statesman governed in his actions by the clichés which a decade and more of Radical agitation had spread and made familiar. The papers show that Milner and the Foreign Office tried hard to find a way of upsetting the convictions or the sentences. The trial was scrutinised by the judicial adviser to the Egyptian government who, Scott reported in a telegram of 24 October, concluded that he could not advise quashing the verdict, since he found that the trial was regularly conducted and the evidence adequate.[158] Hurst, at one point, tried to find a technical ground for upsetting the trial, but this came to nothing. In the end, however, Abd al-Rahman Fahmi's sentence was commuted to fifteen years' hard labour. When Zaghlul came to power in 1924 he was released from prison, but the two quarrelled and fell out the following year.[159]

Milner went even further in preventing action against terrorists, and this at a time when all hope of agreement with Zaghlul had vanished. On 21 October 1920 Scott reported that since the arrest of Abd al-Rahman Fahmi, terrorist outrages had ceased. He asked for authority to carry out further investigations which might affect a large number of suspects. The matter was left pending in London for a month and more. On 25 November, Milner minuted: 'My advice would be strongly to drop the pursuit of these real or imaginary criminals.' Egypt, he went on, was now tranquil. Why risk a disturbance by such investigations? These might connect 'some of Zaghlul's more extreme followers more or less directly, with some of the past outrages. I feel sure,' he added however, 'that Zaghlul himself has had nothing to do with them.' Allenby was informed on 27 November that further investigations of suspected terrorists should be discontinued.[160] In the meantime, Allenby had, as he reported in a telegram of 25 November, directed that Fakhri Abd al-Nur, 'suspected leader of seditionists, prime mover of campaign of intimidation and attempted corruption of witnesses for prosecution' should be interrogated by the military authorities. He proposed that other suspects should be similarly dealt with. This proposal J. Murray, of the Egyptian Department, termed 'unfortunate', and Milner minuted, on 29 November, that so long as Egypt was quiet it was better to discontinue these investigations.[161]

Was so much tenderness towards Zaghlul and his apparatus, we may ask, warranted by the negotiations and their outcome? Milner and his colleagues approached these negotiations with the aim of concluding a treaty. 'The mission', Milner wrote to Adli on 23 June 1920, 'has publicly declared that its object is to reconcile Egyptian aspirations with the special interests of Great Britain and the legal rights of all foreign residents in the country.

'I have been, and am, of opinion, that this object might be achieved by the conclusion of a treaty between Great Britain and Egypt.'[162] At the very outset, then, Milner was abandoning the British position and abandoning it to a set of self-appointed politicians who had no formal authority to negotiate on behalf of Egypt. In effect Milner was making them a gift of Egypt and its people to milk and misgovern. This was pointed out by the minister Isma'il Sirri who happened to be in London at the time of the negotiations. He had an interview with Rodd on 2 July 1920 which the latter reported to Milner. Sirri pointed out, Rodd informed Milner, that 'we have assumed responsibility which we must not in common fairness to the bulk of the Egyptian people surrender'. An autonomous Egypt ruled by a Parliament, etc., Sirri also argued, would deliver Egypt 'into the hands of the dominant class, who would manipulate elections and purchase votes – the whole system of administration by baksheesh would start afresh and the fellah would undoubtedly be oppressed.'[163] This, of course, is what came to pass, and it did not require great divinatory powers in order to prophesy such an outcome. But it may be argued that the mission, having decided that there was no reason 'why Great Britain should be the party primarily responsible for the internal administration of the country inasmuch as no vital British interest is served thereby' and that 'such responsibility entails a great burden on the British taxpayer'[164] had discounted Sirri's objections in advance and was willing to tolerate the state of affairs he prognosticated in exchange for a treaty.

But did Milner get the treaty he wanted? While he was in Egypt Milner refused repeatedly and categorically to concede, in any conceivable treaty, control by Egypt of her foreign relations. 'Our determination to control the foreign affairs of Egypt was', as he told Adli, 'absolute'.[165] He was still of the same opinion at the start of the negotiations with Zaghlul. But he found the latter equally adamant that the control of foreign affairs, 'a question of capital importance', must be conceded to Egypt, or else no agreement was possible. Zaghlul made this demand on 22 June. By 5 July Milner had already conceded it.[166]

Did this concession ensure a treaty for Milner? It could not possibly do so, since Zaghlul and his so-called Delegation were really nobody's delegates and had no power to sign a treaty. In justifying its curious proceedings, the Milner Mission argued in its Report that since a treaty would have to be approved by 'a genuinely representative Egyptian Assembly', since a 'popularly elected body' became therefore necessary, and since the Zaghlulists would command 'a substantial if not an overwhelming majority' in such a body, negotiations with Zaghlul became necessary.[167] The argument has the sophistical plausibility which has distinguished recent official British thought on imperial matters; but however plausible it clearly offered no scope for the conclusion of an actual treaty. So that Milner's negotiations with his resourceful and obstinate opponents issued not in a treaty but in a document which came to be known as the Milner–Zaghlul Agreement, 'but which', the Milner Report notes with a fine discrimination, 'on the face of it, was not an agreement, but merely an outline of the bases on which an agreement might subsequently be framed'.[168]

This so-called agreement stipulated that a treaty would be concluded 'under which Great Britain will recognise the independence of Egypt as a constitutional monarchy with representative institutions'. In exchange for this abolition of the protectorate and the virtual abandonment of the British position, the agreement envisaged that Egypt would concede to Great Britain the right to protect the privileges of foreigners and to safeguard imperial communications and strategic interests.[169]

In conceding so much, Milner no doubt hoped that he would settle the Egyptian problem once and for all. But he seems to have forgotten that the agreement was yet not an agreement, and that his opponent was a wily opponent. For having secured all these concessions, Zaghlul now argued that since the agreement did not fulfil all the demands that he had been mandated to pursue, it was necessary for him to go back to his principals, the Egyptian people, and seek their approval! Milner allowed himself to be duped by this gambit, and Zaghlul retired to take the waters in France, with Milner's concessions in his pocket and himself uncommitted. He felt he could do better; with a little management, he would probably be able to improve his terms and to emerge as the one undisputed leader. He had assured Milner that his agents would recommend the agreement to the Egyptians and Milner had believed him;[170] but, in fact, with them went a secret letter to the Zaghlulists in Egypt, explaining that whatever these agents might say in support of Milner's proposals, he himself was against them. He knew, he said, that his colleagues, in a compromising spirit which he fully understood, wished the agreement ratified, but he himself preferred to go on with the struggle rather than accept a diminished sovereignty.[171] Zaghlul's attitude to the agreement did not long remain secret. A dispatch from Cairo in the *Daily Mail* of 7 September revealed that his objections to the agreement had been published. The agreement, Zaghlul claimed, did not satisfy the demands of the Delegation and they had not accepted it. If now the Egyptian people chose to reject it, Zaghlul also would reject it. Tilley minuted, ingenuously: 'It appears to be extraordinary bad faith on the part of Zaghlul'! But Milner chose to shrug off Zaghlul's public repudiation of the agreement: 'I don't think much is to be gained by worrying about Zaghlul', he minuted, 'the control has really passed out of his hands and he will come into line right enough if things go well in Egypt.'[172]

But how could things go well in Egypt, in the face of Zaghlul's triumphant intransigence? The British authorities seem, at first, to have been deluded by the hope that Zaghlul's emissaries would genuinely recommend the agreement and that their doing so would actually decrease Zaghlul's popularity and increase that of Adli's.[173] They also believed that Zaghlul might be appealed to 'to show a little courage' and back the agreement! Acting on this suggestion the Foreign Office sent on 17 September a telegram (approved by Milner) to Walrond in Paris in which he was asked to enquire from Adli whether Zaghlul could be induced to support the agreement, or whether Adli himself could not intervene 'and instruct delegates to support proposed agreement and publish his approval of its terms'.[174]

The telegram exhibits vividly the crass misunderstanding of Egyptian politics which reigned in the Cairo residency, in the Foreign Office, and among the Milner Mission. From November 1918 it had been Adli's settled resolve to do nothing unless he could carry Zaghlul with him, or unless his opposition could be neutralised. By September 1920 this should have been amply apparent, and that it was futile to ask Adli to endorse publicly a set of proposals which Zaghlul was publicly attacking. Similarly, Zaghlul's attitude towards Adli should by then have been surmised. Zaghlul was determined to use Adli if possible, but not to afford his rival the slightest advantage. His attitude to Adli and Rushdi was as he expressed it in 1921 to Ali Mahir: 'I will cut their throats before they cut mine.'[175] He now let it be known that had it not been for Adli he would have obtained much better terms from Milner. Telegrams, which he did nothing to disavow, were sent by his followers from Paris to Egypt, claiming that Adli had impeded negotiations and had been a 'disaster' for the *Wafd*.[176] These tactics led to a scission within the *Wafd*. Those prominent politicians who had been originally associated with Zaghlul now quarrelled with him. The *Wafd* became Zaghlul's thing, and he was surrounded by hitherto obscure men like Nahhas, Makram 'Ubaid, Nuqrashi, etc. who rose to prominence as his devoted followers and the servants of his cult.

Some responsibility for the abysmal misunderstanding of Egyptian affairs must again be laid on the erratic and mercurial Walrond. As has been seen, he had been a most enthusiastic advocate of negotiations between Milner and Zaghlul, the previous May. When these difficulties arose a few months later, we find him abruptly altering his tone and pinning all his hopes not on Zaghlul but on Adli. 'Zaghlul Pasha, it is true,' we see him writing in a minute of 12 October, 'is a despot and a savage wild man but he is sincere and has a certain rugged kind of honesty. He is a mere child at negotiations.' Zaghlul, he went on, was intensely vain and ambitious: he was going to be a trouble, and Adli alone could control him.[177]

Adli could do nothing of the kind. Zaghlul and his colleagues returned to London at the end of October 1920 and told Milner that if he wanted an agreement he had to concede more. In order to make his proposals palatable to the Egyptian people, he was told, Zaghlul's emissaries had had to say not that the protectorate would be abolished upon the conclusion of a treaty but that it had already been abolished and that Egypt would have complete autonomy in internal as in external affairs. Would Milner confirm this interpretation of the agreement? His credulity and patience at last exhausted, Milner refused to do so.[178] His policy was in ruins and the Egyptian problem as far as ever from a solution.

Indeed, Milner's mismanagement had prodigiously complicated it and had seriously damaged the British position. The Milner–Zaghlul Agreement was supposed to be, strictly speaking, not an agreement. But this distinction proved to be purely academic, and in actual fact the British government found itself committed in advance to concessions which should have been the outcome of a hard-and-fast treaty. Clayton, then adviser to the interior in Cairo, made the point in a minute of 20 September, that is before the negotiations broke down. If the British government were to refuse to sanction the Milner proposals, he wrote, 'a serious situation would arise. H.M.G. may not be committed to the scheme technically, but I am convinced that public opinion throughout Egypt and elsewhere in the near east would regard any drawing back now as a complete breach of faith.'[179] With Zaghlul and his followers on the rampage, every Egyptian negotiator, whether Adli or anybody else, would be bound to demand more than what Zaghlul had rejected. And the vexing thing was that no one in Egypt had seriously expected Milner to offer such concessions. When Fu'ad was first told of them he, according to Scott 'confessed to a feeling of surprise that there should be a disposition to make concessions of so extensive a nature at the instance of men who had fomented a revolution directed against himself, and had caused so much embarrassment to H.M.G. last year.'[100] We need not take seriously Fu'ad's protestations of injured innocence which no doubt were meant to hide his jealousy of, and dismay at Zaghlul's success.[101] But we need not doubt that the surprise was genuine. Again when the Report of the Milner Mission was published in the spring of 1921, Allenby reported (in a telegram of 16 April) that the Egyptians were astounded at the extent of the British concessions.

The cost of Milner's impolicy fell due immediately. Having embarked on informal negotiations with Zaghlul, the British government could not suddenly turn round and refuse further negotiation. And such negotiation had to start from Milner's concessions. Allenby warned, in a telegram of 12 January 1921, that a wide modification of Milner's proposals 'would bring extreme party once again into prominence'. Three days later he informed Curzon that the sultan required a public declaration setting out the official British attitude to the Milner scheme. Two days afterwards Allenby proposed two alternative lines of policy. The government had either to accept immediately Milner's proposals or it had to declare that the status of the protectorate was 'not a satisfactory relation in which Egypt should continue to stand to Great Britain', and that a treaty would be discussed with an official delegation. Though there was no gainsaying the damage to the British position done by Milner's negotiations, yet it could be argued that the best way to limit the damage was by refraining for the moment from negotiations, abstaining from declarations, and putting down the Zaghlulist apparatus in Egypt. And in the cabinet which met on 22 February to consider Allenby's suggestions it was indeed argued that the matter was not urgent and that it had been made perfectly clear that neither government nor Parliament were committed to Milner's scheme. But Curzon was in favour of declaring that the protectorate was not satisfactory and of holding out to the Egyptians the prospect of a treaty. In a cabinet memorandum of 21 February he argued that if the protectorate was abolished, the Egyptians would be pacified and, by means of a treaty, the British could secure all their interests 'as we did with the Indian princes a century ago'. Milner was also present at the cabinet by invitation, and he urged that the present moment was favourable for a treaty and that delay might worsen matters. The cabinet therefore

adopted Curzon's view and authorised a declaration to the effect that
a protectorate had ceased to be a satisfactory relation between Great
Britain and Egypt and that another relationship had to be negotiated.[182] By this declaration the British government officially
accepted and ratified Milner's view of the Egyptian problem and unconditionally conceded what Zaghlul and his associates had been
claiming for more than two years. To show anxiety for further talks
after Milner's failure was bound to weaken the British position; to
admit at the same time that the Zaghlulists had been right to denounce the protectorate was, gratuitously, to weaken this position
still further.

The declaration of 22 February 1921 made further negotiation
necessary. With whom, then, to negotiate? One of Milner's assumptions was that Zaghlul and Adli were the only two Egyptian personalities with whom agreement could be reached. Negotiations with
Zaghlul having broken down, therefore, it was to Adli that Milner
looked for success. When the split between Adli and Zaghlul became
apparent towards the end of 1920 we find him writing: 'I believe the
success of the "Entente" policy [i.e. between Britain and Egypt]
depends on Adly's maintaining the lead.'[183] His views found an echo
in the Foreign Office where Murray, of the Egyptian Department,
declared (in a minute of 20 November 1920): 'I should have thought
the situation was ripe for a moderate man like Adly Pasha to rally all
the more sensible elements to the support of an agreement on the
lines of Lord Milner's proposals without reservations.'[184] But Adli
had been out of power since the spring of 1919, and if he was to
negotiate officially he had to be appointed by the sultan as prime
minister, or at least as head of a delegation. Now Fu'ad did not like
Adli, and saw no reason why he should get all the credit of having
obtained Egyptian independence. Thus, when Allenby brought up
Adli's name at an interview with Fu'ad on 24 February, the latter
replied that 'he was not of the opinion that he represented any real
party in the country and expatiated on the danger of relying too
much on him'. Parties in the western sense, the sultan said, were
nonexistent in Egypt and Adli 'could not be regarded as controlling
a coherent and important section of public opinion'. Fu'ad's advice
was no doubt self-interested, but it happened also to be sound.
Fu'ad tried hard to avoid making Adli prime minister, naturally preferring someone who would be clearly his own nominee. The Foreign
Office, however, were determined that Adli should become prime

minister. Adli, Sir Ronald Lindsay thought, 'quite rightly' insisted that Fu'ad should behave like a constitutional monarch, and jealousy for Egyptian constitutionalism no doubt impelled him to instruct Allenby to enforce this choice.[185] Allenby acted accordingly. On 14 March he sent a message to Fu'ad advising against the appointment of Muhammad Sa'id whom Fu'ad had wanted to make prime minister, adding that 'my advice once given was not my own but the opinion of His Majesty's Government which they would expect should be followed'. In his dispatch recounting this episode, Allenby stated that Fu'ad accepted Adli with resignation: 'If', Allenby went on, 'he was unwilling at first to admit the claims of the party to whom the country had come to look for leadership, some allowance must be made for the fact that the blood of Mohammed Ali runs in his veins. It is with difficulty that members of that house can be persuaded that the old order of things has passed away, and that even in Egypt the ruler must conform to democratic practice, and in matters affecting the fate of the country accept the expression of the people's will.'[186] It was rather bizarre to mistake the voice of Sir Ronald Lindsay, speaking through the mouth of Lord Curzon, for that of the Egyptian people.

Adli, then, was forced on the unwilling Fu'ad. But was it to any purpose? Did he have it in him to withstand Zaghlul, with whom he had broken and who now became vociferous in his denunciations? As soon as Adli formed his Ministry, Zaghlul issued a manifesto from Paris demanding the primacy in any negotiation with the British. Soon thereafter he returned to Egypt and published his demands in Cairo. He demanded complete control over Adli and his Ministry and declared that the Milner proposals had to be turned down, martial law abolished, Abd al-Rahman Fahmi released from prison, British troops not to be stationed west of the Suez Canal, and the Sudan declared Egyptian territory. These demands, of course, went further than anything Zaghlul had put before Milner; they were clearly designed to cramp Adli's style and to pave the way for an attack on any conceivable agreement which Adli might reach with the British. Zaghlul's preface to his demands is revealing. He declared: 'I have done all the work. I have suffered, and I have the confidence of the Egyptian people. I will not see credit for what I have done taken away from me by Adly or anyone else. It is true that Adly has the support of a certain amount of opinion, but his support is mainly semi-foreign.[187]

Adli tried to reach an accommodation with Zaghlul, but he failed. Zaghlul – as Harry Boyle, who was then on a visit to Egypt, reported – looked upon himself 'as though he was absolute ruler of the country and almost seemed to be under the control of some sort of megalomania'.[188] To show his power he began inciting the country against Adli, whom he denounced as a British agent and a traitor to Egypt. Riots and demonstrations again inflamed the country; one particularly bloody affray took place in Alexandria on 20 and 21 May, in which foreigners were murdered and their houses looted. This riot was investigated in some detail by a commission of enquiry, whose report is a classic of its kind.[189] This report makes it possible to form an accurate idea of Zaghlulist political methods and organisation. At the outset of the riot the following circular was distributed among the populace:

You have known who are the members of the official delegation. They are the lowest of God's creatures on God's earth. They are people who have neither conscience nor honour. They are people who sacrifice their honour for the sake of filling their bellies and for filling governmental positions. Where are your students? Where are your fellaheen? Where are your devotees? Where is he who offers himself to redeem his homeland and save his country from disaster? Let you be rising. Rise, you heroes, and generously give what is dear and cheap for the sake of your Fatherland, and for the consolidation of the throne of the nation and its faithful agent Saad Pasha Zaghlul. Know ye that heavenly laws and worldly laws allow killing and shedding of blood in this circumstance. Let the Prophet – may Allah bless Him! – be the best example. He killed many in the way of spreading the Mohammedan call and exterminating the influence of *murtaddin* [backsliders], and the night resembles the preceding night. We defend the dearest thing on earth; defend our life or death; defend our children and grandchildren. Remember the Prophet's word, 'The love of home is part of the faith'. What have you decided upon? History is on the alert, Long live Saad! No chief except Saad! Down with the Government's Delegation! Down with the dissentient members![190]

The follower of Muhammad Abduh then, the believer in constitutionalism and reform, did not scruple, in his pursuit of power, to appeal to the fanaticism of the mob and its savage instincts. Cromer foresaw some such development when he said in his Report for 1906 that whilst some enlightened Egyptians might wish to divorce politics from religion, yet '[unless] they can convince the Moslem masses of their militant Islamism, they will fail to arrest their attention or attract their sympathy'. 'Appeals', he went on, 'either overt or covert, to racial and religious passions are thus a necessity of their existence in order to insure the furtherance of their programme.'[191]

It was a few weeks after the Alexandria riots that Walrond, now back in Egypt as an agent of the Secret Intelligence Service, proposed that Curzon should invite to London an unofficial delegation to be headed by Zaghlul. Zaghlul, Walrond added, was willing to go, provided the invitation did not come from the Egyptian government.[192] This proposal seems to conclude Walrond's active involvement in Egyptian politics.

Adli came to London in the summer of 1921 under the shadow of Zaghlul's threats and fulminations. He came pledged, as he stated in a letter to the sultan, to ensure that the negotiations would issue in Egypt becoming 'an independent state both from the external and the internal point of view'.[193] From the start the prospects of an agreement seemed doubtful. In a telegram of 7 May Allenby warned that to arrive at an agreement with a delegation led by Adli and to secure its ratification by an Egyptian assembly 'will be both matters of great difficulty'.[194] The Foreign Office had prepared, against Adli's visit, a draft convention which the cabinet discussed at a meeting on 11 July. The draft convention, in its main provisions, terminated the protectorate; allowed the re-establishment of an Egyptian ministry of foreign affairs and the appointment of Egyptian consuls (but not of diplomatic representatives); gave the British government the right to maintain troops in Egypt and to control the administration of the Debt; and established a judicial commission to protect the rights of foreigners in Egypt. Curzon warned the cabinet that 'Lord Milner's Commission had so far prejudiced the situation that the freedom of the government in negotiations was severely hampered', but he undertook not to make concessions regarding Egyptian diplomatic representation without consulting the cabinet. Negotiation proved very difficult. 'In reporting the separate points discussed', wrote Lindsay, who took a prominent part in the discussions with Adli, 'I find difficulty in expressing any opinion with confidence as to what Adli would really accept or definitely reject. He is so often prepared to admit his personal concurrence with a view without admitting his official acceptance of it that I can do little more than admit impressions.'[195] But the fundamental difficulty lay not in Adli's character or his manner of negotiation. It lay in his inability to agree to any treaty which might give

Zaghlul an opening to attack and discredit him. Curzon had, in the end, to concede diplomatic representation, but the talks broke down on the military clause of the draft convention, Adli declaring that it constituted 'occupation pure and simple'.[196] It became clear by mid-November that Adli's failure would mean his resignation.[197]

In a final attempt to avert failure, Adli saw Lloyd George. Their interview is most interesting in showing the real causes of the break-down, and Adli's limitations in the exercise of power – limitations which Milner, the Foreign Office and the residency had long and adamantly refused to take into consideration. Lloyd George spoke to Adli of the urgency of dealing with Zaghlul and his agitations, and threw out the suggestion that he might be deported from Egypt. He proposed that the talks should now be adjourned and resumed after Zaghlul's removal. Adli's reaction clearly indicated that he had no stomach for actions of this kind. He was, he told Lindsay, 'unable to associate himself with any such policy. He had no love for Zaghlul, and if H.M.G. decided to proceed against him now, it must be their affair, though he himself doubted the advisability of action at this moment.' This would 'merely increase the agitation'. As for himself, he could not go back to Egypt, shelter behind Allenby's bayonets, crush Zaghlul and come back to accept terms which he now rejected.[198] In a final interview with Curzon, again, Adli asked why the British should not themselves put into operation the terms of their own draft convention: 'For the very obvious reason, I replied,' wrote Curzon to Allenby, 'that this could only be done with Egyptian cooperation; and yet he himself, the man most competent to give it had told me at our previous meeting that his first step on returning to Egypt would be to resign.' Curzon protested that the Egyptians could not have it both ways, pose as heroes by rejecting the British proposals on one hand, and on the other expect Great Britain by herself to put into operation the scheme of very considerable independence which they had chosen to reject.[199] Curzon had, of course, reason to be exasperated, but after all it was the British themselves who had forced Adli's appointment and chosen to negotiate with him.

The failure of the talks with Adli left the British government even more committed to concessions than the breakdown of the Milner–Zaghlul Agreement. In a cabinet committee which considered the British proposals and the Egyptian counter-proposals Churchill declared that in any offer then made the parts favourable to Egypt would be remembered and used as the basis of any future discussion, whilst the distasteful parts would be forgotten. Lindsay thought that this could be met by telling Adli that all offers were withdrawn if he rejected the present one.[200] This, however, was easier said than done and Churchill's fears proved, in the event, to be justified.

Curzon's failure with Adli, as will be seen, transferred the initiative from the Foreign Office to Allenby and his advisers in Cairo. It was they who dictated the settlement embodied in the declaration of 28 February 1922. Their proposals were resisted – albeit ineffectively – by some members of the cabinet, but at the Foreign Office their views were, more often than not, echoed and approved by those to whom the foreign secretary principally looked for advice on Egyptian matters. Of these the principal were Lindsay and Murray. In a minute of October 1920 on the Milner proposals, Murray declared that it was safe to assume that a treaty on the lines of the Milner–Zaghlul Agreement would secure that mutual confidence and collaboration between British and Egyptians without which an orderly and lasting regime was impossible. It was true that the Milner–Zaghlul Agreement departed widely from the original views of the Milner Mission and that the risks it entailed might be held to be excessive, but it was difficult to discover an alternative course. If the government failed to endorse it, this would be seen as a sign of bad faith, 'and will permanently alienate the sympathies which the result of the negotiations had secured for us'. Murray was silent on the character or importance of such sympathies, but he urged that the alternative to Milner's policy was coercion, which meant the maintenance of a costly army and much obloquy for Great Britain in the east.[201] When the negotiations with Adli were nearing breakdown, in a memorandum of 1 November Murray did consider that the possibility of outright annexation should not be set aside and that nothing should be said which might be interpreted as a pledge not to annex.[202] Also, as will be seen, at the very outset of the crisis which Allenby precipitated following Adli's resignation, Murray, on one solitary occasion, questioned the wisdom of the high commissioner's policy. But in general he advocated the view that the dangers involved in making wider concessions than either Milner or Curzon had contemplated were less formidable than those entailed by a failure to reach agreement. For after all, as he argued in a joint minute with Duff Cooper of 14 October 1921, the worst likely consequences of a policy of concessions were 'the gradual decay and corruption of the administration of Egypt which would lead to financial difficulty, outbreaks of disorder, massacre of Europeans', whilst the alternative was a prospect of continuous repression depending on a large British army at least 12,000 strong maintained in Egypt for an indefinite period; and such a policy ran the risk of losing the support of Parliament. Murray and Cooper thought then that the irreducible minimum on which Great Britain had to insist (and which Adli might still reject) was the right to maintain troops in the Canal and for a limited period in Alexandria; the continuation of the *status quo* in the Sudan; a veto on the appointment of foreigners in the Egyptian service; compensation for British officials whose services were to be terminated; the enactment of an indemnity law to protect British officials against the legal consequences of actions taken during the uprising of 1919; and a guarantee for the payment of loans secured on the Ottoman Tribute.[203]

Lindsay was exactly of the same mind. Commenting in a minute of 15 October on Murray's and Cooper's views, he argued that if no agreement with Adli was possible, then the British would have to govern Egypt with bayonets. But the British could not do this well, and for it to be done at all required the unflinching support of government, Parliament and public opinion. This Lindsay did not think forthcoming and he therefore refused to enter into a path which led to 'ultimate disaster'. The proper objects of British policy in Egypt were the safeguard of imperial interests and of British predominance. This meant that they had to abandon 'the solicitude we have displayed for forty years for the orderly conduct of Egyptian domestic affairs – a solicitude,' he added, showing how influenced he was by the clichés of the time, 'which Egyptians have come to resent very strongly.' Such a policy, Lindsay thought, 'places squarely on Egyptian shoulders the exclusive responsibility for the internal administration of Egypt, with all that it implies'. It is here that the essential fallacy of this view is most apparent. For in the first place there was no way of separating internal from external affairs, and 'squarely' placing responsibility for the former on the Egyptians, while maintaining British predominance in respect of the latter. And if, *per impossibile*, such a separation could be managed, and the Egyptians administered Egypt well, how then would the British justify their military predominance in the country? If, alternatively, the Egyptians failed in their attempt to administer Egypt, this might require British intervention, as Lindsay recognised, and would not this lead, by another road, to the 'ultimate disaster' which he was determined to avoid? Lindsay also showed a dangerous ignorance of what political rhetoric can do when he argued in the same minute that if responsibility for the administration of Egypt devolved on the Egyptians and if they failed in their task, then 'not even they will be able to blame us for the failure'.[204] It is not too much to say that Lindsay was utterly a defeatist in Egyptian affairs. At the start of the negotiations with Adli, the Foreign Office received a paper by Sir William Hayter, the legal adviser to the Egyptian ministry of finance and to the residency. In this paper, Hayter advocated the immediate granting of complete independence to Egypt with Britain reserving to herself the protection of foreigners, the safeguard of imperial communications and the defence of Egypt. The arrangement was not to be embodied in a formal treaty but to constitute an informal *modus vivendi* for a period of ten years. In a minute of 29 June, Lindsay described this as 'a valuable and promising' suggestion, which might have, in the end, to be adopted. He recognised that it had weak features: namely, that if the British gave away the protectorate, which was their trump card, they would have to face another negotiation ten years hence 'with our leverage *pro tanto* diminished'; also, it would create uncertainty if the *modus vivendi* was to be for a limited period, and this was undesirable. 'I admit', wrote Lindsay, 'it is like borrowing money at rather usurious terms'. but he was willing to accept this if the crisis could be postponed for ten years.[205]

Hayter's views, as expressed in the memorandum of 5 June 1921 which has been cited above, were congruent with the terms of his evidence before the Milner Mission in February 1920. He then stated that politically minded Egyptians had 'a serious grievance'. When war broke out in 1914 Egypt was developing towards a large measure of parliamentary government, and the Legislative Assembly had made a very promising start. With an optimism which the sequel proved to have been ill-judged and fanciful Hayter looked to the Legislative Assembly in an autonomous Egypt to develop a sense of responsibility in Egyptian ministers.[206]

These views found an echo among the principal British advisers who had taken office at the inception of the Allenby regime. For shortly after his arrival in Egypt Allenby had carried out a veritable purge among the senior British officials in the Egyptian government. Dunlop, the educational adviser, and Haines, the adviser to the interior, resigned.[207] The appointment of Brunyate, the judicial adviser, was terminated: 'his personality and manner', Allenby informed Curzon, 'are unsympathetic to the Egyptians, and cause friction'.[208] Allenby's purge was reported to Washington together with a possible explanation for its motive:

> The advisers of interior and public instructions [wrote the American consul] in addition to several capable subordinates have been asked to resign. A clean sweep of existing staff appears to be contemplated. There is a strong presumption that this is due to apprehension of Foreign Office with regard to commission of inquiry held by Milner which is expected to arrive in October. Inasmuch as its members are expected to be of pronounced liberal tendencies its findings may prove embarrassing to present regime. Consequently, it may be intended to confront it with a revised administrative personnel and blame for conditions placed on former occupants of the various advisory positions.[209]

It is more likely that Allenby acted not under the influence of the Foreign Office but of Sir Gilbert Clayton who, as chief political officer of the Egyptian Expeditionary Force, was very close to him, and who became acting adviser to the interior under the new regime.

Sir Reginald Patterson, who shortly afterwards became acting financial adviser, now replaced Dunlop at the ministry of education. 'It was thought', writes Humphrey Bowman in his memoirs, 'that with a new adviser at the helm, sympathetic with Egyptian aspirations, and of proved ability, discipline would return to the schools.'[210] When Patterson retired as financial adviser in 1927 he made a speech in which he 'requested Egyptians to forget what they consider bad in the old British policy . . . [and] passed some opinions to the effect that the Egyptians were ripe for self-government and able to conduct the administration of their country.'[211]

Sheldon Amos replaced Brunyate as judicial adviser. Lindsay called him in a minute 'a rather advanced Radical',[212] and a Belgian lawyer who served in the Mixed Tribunals described him as 'convinced of the value of the principles of British liberalism', a prudent application of which he now thought necessary in Egypt.[213] His views on an Egyptian settlement may be gathered from a memorandum of 27 July 1921 by Murray. This document gives the gist of a discussion at the Foreign Office in which Lindsay, Murray and Amos considered the likely situation in the event of the talks with Adli breaking down. Adli, it was thought, would then resign, and it was doubtful whether any other Egyptian would have the courage to succeed him. There would then be a risk of a revolutionary movement which would be preceded by an attempt to paralyse the administration by strikes which, as was discovered in 1919, would be difficult to combat. At this point, Murray added a marginal note to the effect that 'Mr Amos would like to paint this bogey even blacker than I have done'. Terrorism would then break out, which would be impossible to suppress. Therefore if negotiations with Adli broke down, in order to gain Egyptian sympathies the British offer must look as good as that of Milner. The British should insist only on the stationing of forces in Egypt. They should abandon all attempt at financial or judicial control, provided full publicity in the details of financial administration was secured and provided the appointment was secured of a British official to whom foreigners could appeal against abuses of power by Egyptians.[214] Amos was to play, with Clayton, a chief part in the crisis which led to the declaration of 28 February 1922.

Clayton himself, as has been seen, was in favour of a policy of concessions as early as April 1919. The British, he explained to Gertrude Bell in September 1919, had to maintain control of the Suez Canal, the Nile waters, the army and the police. Otherwise, Egyptian ministers should be left to carry on as best they could; mistakes they would no doubt make, 'but they have the right, as they claim, to a fair trial'. Such concessions, he thought, would win the majority of the country to the British side.[215] Clayton, we observe, shared with the Milner Mission the fallacy that concessions to Zaghlul and other members of the official class were demanded by 'the majority of the country', would redound to their benefit, and would thus promote among them gratitude to Great Britain. The following decades showed that, as was only natural, British unpopularity in the country at large increased in proportion to the magnitude of British concessions.

With the passage of time, Clayton seems to have favoured concessions greater than he was prepared to envisage in 1919. Commenting on Hayter's memorandum of 5 June 1921 which has been discussed above, he asked why it was necessary for the British to station an army in Egypt. For, after all, did they not have troops in the Sudan and in Palestine which could be moved to Egypt if an international crisis threatened? Again, a small British force in Egypt merely created hostility in the country. Egyptians, moreover, were not so foolish as to attack either the Canal or foreigners in the country. Why then not withdraw British troops entirely and thus both save money and disarm Egyptian hostility? And if such a policy could not be embodied in a treaty, then let it be put into force by a unilateral proclamation.[216]

The views of the British advisers were widely shared among Allenby's subordinates at the residency. One specimen of their opinions may perhaps suffice. In a letter of 1 October 1921 to Sir William Tyrrell at the Foreign Office, Walford Selby, then first secretary at the residency, declared that an agreement with Adli, if it constituted anything less than full satisfaction of Zaghlul's programme required to be imposed by the British with just as much force as they would need to impose their own desiderata. Such enforcement was not feasible, and therefore 'we should take the opportunity proffered by the negotiations with Adly Pasha to "get out" on the best terms we can'. There need be no fear that foreign troops would replace British in Egypt. British naval preponderance in the Mediterranean would prevent France or Italy from intervening on behalf of 'fat profiteers in Egypt, who are no more good to their country of origin than to that of their adoption'.[217]

Allenby himself seems to have generally accepted the policies canvassed by his subordinates at the residency, and by the advisers who, it must not be forgotten, had been selected by him. Transmitting Hayter's memorandum of 5 June 1921, mentioned above, he informed the Foreign Office that Hayter's views were worthy of serious consideration. They were in general accord with Milner's policy 'and I see no reason why the adoption of something on the lines he suggests should not be attended with ultimate success'.[218] He also approved Clayton's endorsement of Hayter's proposals: 'I am', he noted on Clayton's memorandum of 8 October, 'in general agreement with the views of Sir G. Clayton.'[219]

In the autumn of 1921, when talks with Adli were still going on but when hope of agreement was becoming dim, Allenby, who was then in London, attended a meeting of a cabinet subcommittee dealing with the situation in Egypt. He told the ministers that there was a prospect of disorders by the Zaghlulists, and Zaghlul himself would probably make some movement which would justify his arrest and banishment. If firmness were shown, Allenby declared, a moderate government could be formed and could maintain itself. Such had been the case when the rising of 1919 was suppressed, until Lord Milner resuscitated Zaghlul who at that time was moribund. He ended by saying that some form of independence would have to be conceded to Egypt and the word protectorate abandoned.[220] What is of interest here is not so much Allenby's version of what had followed the 1919 rising, but the clear indication of his ability to form and maintain in power what he called a 'moderate' government. He was equally unambiguous at a cabinet which he was invited to attend on 4 November following. Though he personally preferred more liberal terms than were being offered (and up to then, we must remember, the cabinet had not authorised Curzon to concede diplomatic representation to Egypt), Allenby affirmed that Adli could carry on with the 'firm support' of the British government.[221] He returned to Egypt shortly afterwards. In a telegram of 12 November he reported that both the sultan and Tharwat Pasha were in favour of adopting without delay a firm policy.[222] A few days later, reporting that contrary to his expectations Adli was likely to resign, he yet told Curzon that Tharwat was ready to form a Ministry and to fight Zaghlul to a finish and was confident of success.[223]

This telegram Allenby sent on 18 November. But on the previous day he had sent another telegram quite at variance in its tone and implications with the language which the high commissioner had held to ministers in London, as well as with his recent reports from Cairo. This telegram of 17 November informed the Foreign Office that the adviser to the interior, the acting financial adviser, the adviser to the ministry of education and the acting judicial adviser were 'unanimously' agreed that a decision by the cabinet which did not admit the principle of Egyptian independence and which maintained the protectorate entailed 'a serious risk of revolution' and 'complete administrative chaos rendering government impossible'. These officials warned that unless 'substantial' satisfaction were given to the expectations which Egyptians had legitimately formed on the basis of British policy in the past two years, it would be impossible to form a Ministry. The advisers, though somewhat alarmist in their language, were no doubt right to speak of expectations having been aroused among Egyptians by successive official British pronouncements. But they also went on to discuss their own state of mind and to hint that unless the British government adopted a particular policy they would refuse to carry on. They had, the telegram went on, proceeded for the past two years 'in the belief that policy of liberal concessions would be adopted and have undoubtedly given this impression to various ministers and others with whom they have been in contact'. If a contrary policy was adopted, they felt bound to warn, they could not expect 'to retain the confidence of

Egyptian ministers or be able to render useful service in the future'. It is legitimate to wonder whether in giving the impression to Egyptians that 'a policy of liberal concessions' would be adopted by the British government, these officials did not exceed their function; for, after all, they had no authority to define or expound British policy. The telegram is also surprising on other counts. As Curzon pointed out in his answer to this telegram on the following day, Allenby knew (and could have told the advisers) that in the negotiations with Adli the British government did admit the principle of Egyptian independence and was certainly not trying to maintain the protectorate which, months ago, it had declared not to be a satisfactory relationship between Egypt and Great Britain. What then prompted the dispatch of this telegram? A clue might lie in the sibylline hints which the advisers proceeded to throw out. If a 'liberal' programme were approved it could be, they said, elaborated on the spot and a Ministry formed to carry it out even if no official convention can be signed by an Egyptian minister which would admit that programme as full satisfaction of Egyptian claims.[224]

The meaning of these riddles was to appear shortly. On 5 December Allenby sent a telegram suggesting that the protectorate should be abolished and that the other British proposals which Adli had rejected should be implemented unilaterally, that is without the Egyptian *quid pro quo* which was of the essence of the whole negotiation. This then is what the advisers meant by their talk of a liberal programme which could be implemented even if no Egyptian minister would accept it as full satisfaction of the Egyptian claims. What virtue they saw in this arrangement remains obscure. At any rate, Allenby's suggestion was not well received at the Foreign Office. In a minute which totally departed from his usual views, Murray expressed his dislike of the proposal. 'Lord Allenby's proposal', he wrote, 'amounts in fact to giving away all that the cabinet were with difficulty induced to concede in the hope of concluding an agreement with Egypt, and receiving nothing in return except the formation of a government of whose stability and good faith we should have no guarantee.' The arrangement would set up a system of 'political blackmail'. Sir Eyre Crowe agreed with Murray; if such a proposal was agreed to, he minuted on 6 December, 'we should be stultifying ourselves absolutely'. Curzon also declared himself opposed to 'precipitate action', and on 8 December a telegram rejecting his proposal was sent to Allenby.[225]

Allenby returned to the charge a few days later. In a telegram of 11 December he again proposed the unilateral abrogation of the protectorate, this time producing new arguments in support. The British government, he now affirmed, could not expect treaty advantages in return for this concession, since the protectorate had taken away something which the Ottomans had conceded, 'and nothing is more resented in Egypt today than this backward step on the part of Great Britain'.

At the Foreign Office Murray, still constant in opposition, forthrightly minuted: 'I do not think that H.M.G. should be asked to provide Lord Allenby with a provisional pledge of this kind which he could then proceed to hawk round amongst potential Egyptian prime ministers.' Crowe was even more outspoken: 'It is difficult to believe', he minuted on 12 December, 'that this telegram emanated from the same Lord Allenby who when in London spoke so violently and so consistently against the Milner arrangement and claimed with such confidence that if supported by H.M.G. he would have no difficulty in giving effect to the policy of maintaining our position in Egypt.' 'I can only surmise', he went on, 'that the telegram has been drafted and submitted to him by one of the officials who have always favoured the undiluted Milner doctrine and who now want to make it impossible for H.M.G. to follow any other.

'Mr Murray is right in suggesting that the line now recommended by Lord Allenby is incompatible with the course approved, if not advocated by himself here'. Crowe then went on to suggest that Allenby should be told that 'the policy laid down and so clearly explained cannot be suddenly reversed as a result of his own complete *volte-face*', and that he was expected to take the necessary action to carry out this policy.[226]

Before an answer in these terms could be sent, two other telegrams, both dated 12 December, arrived from Allenby. They made no reference to his telegram of the previous day, but reported that Tharwat was prepared to form a Ministry, that he did not expect an immediate abolition of the protectorate, but that he hoped this to become possible in the near future. What he was proposing was a return to the conditions which had obtained before 1914, and that relations between Egyptian ministers and the British representatives should be the same as those which existed in the time of Kitchener and his predecessors. Tharwat seemed to go even further, and to agree that the director-general of the ministry of foreign affairs, who became after 1914 a British official, should continue to be British. Meanwhile, he wished to take note of the 'undertaking' of the British government to terminate the protectorate. This development seemed to make it no longer necessary to take a decision on Allenby's proposal of 11 December, but a telegram of 15 December, drafted by Curzon himself, nevertheless insisted on telling the high commissioner 'that your suggestion that H.M.G. should pledge themselves to ask Parliament for the abolition of the protectorate in the hope of obtaining an Egyptian Ministry would have been quite unacceptable. Such a course', the telegram went on, 'would have been inconsistent with the decision of which H.M.G. arrived at after consultation with Your Lordship and largely upon your advice.' To this telegram Allenby returned no answer. Indeed, for a whole month he preserved utter silence regarding his proposal of 11 December.

Tharwat, as has been seen, proposed to take note of the British 'undertaking' to abolish the protectorate. This was an attempt to commit the British government to something which neither Milner nor Curzon had conceded. The British negotiators had been prepared to give up the protectorate in exchange for a treaty. It was out of the question to acquiesce in Tharwat's language and give up what had been for two years so strenuously defended. A telegram was therefore sent to Allenby, asking him to remind Tharwat that His Majesty's Government had given no 'undertaking' to terminate the protectorate but had only offered to do so as part of a contract.[227]

Following his telegrams of 12 December Allenby remained silent for a week on the progress of his negotiations. When he broke his silence it was to report on 20 December that Tharwat had not yet been able to form a Ministry, that he was prohibiting a public meeting called by Zaghlul, and that if he made trouble the high commissioner proposed to deport him.[228] The following day Allenby announced that the Zaghlulists were fomenting trouble and that he was prohibiting Zaghlul from participating in politics.[229] Two days later, he announced the arrest and impending deportation of Zaghlul. In this telegram Allenby declared that Adli had expressed satisfaction at this step.[230] No wonder, since the removal of Zaghlul by the British conveniently removed his main and most formidable opponent, without his having to incur obloquy for it. Tharwat too, as Allenby reported in a telegram of 27 December, was 'strongly in favour' of Zaghlul's deportation, the order for which he was shown in advance.[231] It thus seems fairly clear that Zaghlul's deportation to the Seychelles was a strata-

gem concerted by Allenby with some Egyptian politicians, a strata-
gem which he sprang as much on London as on Zaghlul himself, and
that Zaghlul's mischief-making was merely its convenient pretext.[232]

Having concerted with Adli, Tharwat and their friends Zaghlul's
removal, Allenby now proceeded to concert with the same party the
coercion of the British government. In his telegram of 27 December,
just mentioned, Allenby stated that Tharwat would 'definitely' agree
to form a Ministry, but that he thought it judicious to allow a month
or so to elapse before doing so, in order that the repression of the
Zaghlulists might produce its full effect. It turned out however that
Tharwat was not as definite in his intentions as he had represented
him to be. For on 12 January 1922 Allenby abruptly recurred, after
his long silence, to his proposal of 11 December previous. He admitted
that the British government had considered unacceptable the unilateral abrogation of the protectorate, by means of which he had
hoped to obtain a Ministry. This hope however, Allenby declared,
was now a certainty, and he was therefore reverting to his proposal,
inconsistent as it was with the decision of His Majesty's Government;
it was the only course which he saw his way to pursuing. This was no
doubt the truth, since by deporting Zaghlul and eagerly pressing
Tharwat to form a Ministry, Allenby had put himself in the latter's
power. He admits as much when he declares, in the same telegram,
that his proposal was the result of 'exhaustive negotiations with
Sarwat Pasha and his immediate adherents. They, on their part', he
went on, 'have been in contact with wider circles and Adly Pasha has
been in close touch and lent valuable and disinterested assistance.'[233]
Allenby's tone, in this telegram, was extremely pressing. No other
policy, he insisted, would serve to pacify Egypt or maintain 'the
friendly disposition of those political elements in Egypt, who, through
times difficult enough for themselves have helped us and dealt
straightforwardly with us'. The alternative to his proposal was a
prospect of alternating outbreaks and repression, ending either in
complete capitulation or in the annexation and arbitrary government of a bitterly hostile country. And Allenby ended his telegram by
saying that his proposals had the 'solid and whole-hearted support
of my advisers without the least divergence', and urgently requesting
an early reply by telegram.[234]

This telegram took the Foreign Office utterly by surprise. They had
received no answer to their telegram of 15 December in which
Allenby's proposals had been declared unacceptable. Also, for a

month and more, they had been led to think that Tharwat was ready
to form a Ministry and resolutely fight Zaghlul. They had been given
not a hint that his price would be the unilateral abrogation of the
protectorate. In the lengthy and vehement apologia which Allenby
prepared when he was summoned to London at the end of January
1922, he does admit that he had been 'perhaps too sanguine' in fore-
casting, when the talks with Adli broke down, that it would be
possible to form 'a Ministry of some sort'. In this dispatch he also
tries to justify, thus implicitly admitting the fact, his complete silence
for a whole month over his negotiations with the Egyptian politicians. During that month, he writes, 'I had been engaged in preparing
from the fluid elements of wavering opinion and fluctuating passion
a momentarily stable situation. . . . I confess that the elements were
not so manageable as to render it possible for me to present my plan
gradually; nor', he adds, 'would an incomplete and tentative plan
have merited sufficiently the consideration of His Majesty's Government.' In this dispatch he also asserts that it was Zaghlul's agitation
which, in the end, prevented the formation of a Ministry, and that
his deportation created a new opportunity in which 'the use of a new
concession would produce not only a Ministry, but effects much more
far-reaching for the well-being and contentment of Egypt and for the
relief of His Majesty's Government from a harassing perplexity'.[235]
Of this, again, there is no indication in his telegrams at the time. On
the contrary, as has been seen, the impression given then was of a
move concerted with Tharwat in advance, which was welcomed by
him as a prelude to his forming a ministry: Allenby never reporting
that this would be at the price of a new concession.

Surprising as Allenby's telegram of 12 January was, yet both
Murray and Lindsay were ready to recommend acceptance of his
proposal. In a retreat from his uncharacteristic and momentary
firmness, Murray minuted on 13 January: 'Allenby's policy involves a
risk. Sarwat might try to rush a decision on reserved subjects and
resign if his wishes are not met. But I believe this risk is less great
than that involved in a rejection of Lord Allenby's policy.' Lindsay
likewise had no hesitation in preferring it to the possibility of governing Egypt without Egyptians and added that the Department could
only endorse Allenby's warning. It was left to Crowe to voice some
disquiet over Allenby's policy. 'I think', he wrote in a minute also of
13 January, 'Lord Allenby is to blame for trying to rush H.M.G.
in this way.' If his policy were followed 'we lose all right and all

power – except the actual use of military force.' He deplored this 'and would fain believe that such a surrender ought not to be necessary', but he declared himself not to be in a position to oppose 'those who speak with intimate knowledge of Egyptian conditions and the Egyptian psychosis'.[236]

It was not only Crowe who did not feel knowledgeable enough or confident enough to resist Allenby. The foreign secretary himself, who understood the question much more thoroughly than Crowe, who had himself drafted the telegram of 15 December telling Allenby that his views were unacceptable, now showed not the slightest wish to oppose the high commissioner. In fact he made himself Allenby's advocate in the cabinet. In a cabinet memorandum of 16 January, he declared that 'grave' consequences would ensue if Allenby's policy were rejected. Furthermore, he argued, the British government were not themselves taking responsibility for this policy, only for recommending it to Parliament; and he went on to praise Allenby for having successfully prevented the Egyptians from attaching as a condition to their cooperation the return of Zaghlul![237] There is nothing in the papers to explain Curzon's *volte-face*. It remains a puzzle, as difficult to account for as other erratic decisions which punctuate the last years in office of this intelligent and sagacious man.

When the cabinet met on 18 January, Curzon pressed strongly for the approval of Allenby's policy. He went as far, he told Allenby in a personal telegram, as to back it with a 'threat of personal resignation'.[238] This threat he obviously did not make good. The cabinet refused to be persuaded, taking the view that if the protectorate were abolished, there would then exist no sanction 'to compel Egyptian government to meet us in any particular way except the presence of British forces in the country, which is equally our sole effective guarantee now'.[239] They did not think the matter as urgent as Allenby and Curzon represented, and decided to ask the high commissioner to send Clayton and another official to London for consultations.[240]

Allenby rejected this suggestion categorically. The summoning of the officials to London would serve nothing and would undermine his position, he declared in a telegram of 20 January. If his proposals were rejected he could rely on the support of no Egyptian; but, on the other hand, he affirmed 'that my proposals if immediately accepted will prove basis of a lasting settlement in Egypt'. In a separate, 'most urgent' telegram, he informed Curzon that the situation brooked no delay and that if his advice were not accepted he would resign.[241] The cabinet met on 23 January to consider this threat of resignation. They did not feel disposed to give in to Allenby's threat and Curzon's urgings. They appointed a committee to consider the position created by this threat to resign. It consisted of the prime minister, the lord privy seal (Austin Chamberlain), the chancellor of the exchequer (Robert Horne), the lord chancellor (Birkenhead), the foreign secretary (Curzon), the colonial secretary (Churchill), and the president of the board of education (H. A. L. Fisher).[242]

This committee considered the draft of a telegram which was sent to Allenby the following day, 24 January. The telegram began by declaring that the government were 'most anxious ... to retain advantage of your services to which in present critical situation they attach highest value'. But it went on to say that if the cabinet accepted Allenby's proposal they might be exposed to 'the just charge of having abandoned our main position without safeguards for the future'. If the Egyptian ministers, the telegram pointed out, were agreed that Britain should have a special position in Egypt, then they should experience no difficulty in giving the explicit assurances for which the cabinet was asking.[243]

To this Allenby's prompt rejoinder, in a telegram of 25 January, was that if his advice were not taken, all hope of 'a friendly Egypt in our time' would be lost. He was still 'confident of success', but there should be no further delay. Once more he offered his resignation, and his grounds are significant and revealing. 'Though I have divulged no secrets', he wrote, 'my opinions are well-known here and if advice I have offered is rejected I cannot honourably remain.'[244] Allenby is not only saying that his views diverge from those of the government; he is also openly admitting that he had compromised himself by making his own personal policy publicly known, and encouraging certain expectations. Such behaviour on the part of Wingate, for instance, would have been censured as indiscreet and improper. In the event, the 'Bull' was able to overawe the foreign secretary and the cabinet, and he had his way. To bring them to a proper state of mind his threat to resign was swiftly followed, the next day, by a private telegram from Amos to Murray intimating that the advisers would resign if Allenby's policy were not accepted.[245]

At the outset the cabinet were not disposed to give in to the high commissioner. They held two meetings, on 26 and 27 January, and decided that Allenby should be recalled home to report, and that on his arrival the question of accepting his resignation should be considered.[246] A White Paper was even put together and actually set in type to document the government's case against him.[247] A telegram was sent to him on 28 January asking him to come home and explain the 'violent metamorphosis' in his views and the ultimatum with which he had seen fit twice to confront His Majesty's Government.[248] But this belligerence did not last long. Armed with a long, justificatory dispatch, and accompanied by Amos and Clayton, Allenby descended on London in the middle of February. His confrontation with the government took place at two crucial meetings on the morning and on the evening of 15 February. Present at the meetings were Lloyd George and Curzon attended by Sir Maurice Hankey and Sir Edward Grigg, and Allenby attended by Clayton and Amos. Allenby proved adamant and obdurate, offering his resignation on both occasions. But in the event Lloyd George shrank from accepting it, probably fearing a debate in Parliament in which Allenby – a peer – would no doubt deliver a damaging attack on the incompetence of the coalition in its handling of Egyptian affairs. Allenby's *coup d'état* had succeeded. Towards the end of the evening meeting, when Allenby was threatening yet again to resign, Lloyd George begged him to be patient and wait for five more minutes. It was in the end agreed that a committee composed of Murray, Grigg and Clayton would meet on the morrow and compose a draft declaration acceptable to Allenby and to the government.[249] The draft declaration conceded all that Allenby had demanded. A face-saving phrase was tacked at the end to the effect that pending the conclusion of agreements relating to the reserved subjects 'the *status quo* in all these matters shall remain intact'. At the cabinet held on 16 February to consider the draft, much was made of this sentence. Sir Edward Grigg, the prime minister said, had drawn his attention to the fact that the term '*status quo*' was used without further definition, and that this would give the high commissioner the widest possible powers; so much so that he could insist on maintaining every power and privilege which the British then possessed. In fact, Lloyd George assured his colleagues, this clause would retain for the British government the powers it had exercised under the Granville Declaration together with those superadded by the declaration of the protectorate.[250] Needless to say, this clause could never bear the wide construction which Lloyd George attempted to erect upon it. Nor was it ever mentioned or invoked subsequently.

Allenby got his declaration; the basis of a lasting settlement it was to be. Sultan Fu'ad became King Fu'ad, Tharwat became prime minister, and Egyptian independence was proclaimed. Zaghlul was in exile and his rivals triumphant. They would not remain so for long. For he could not be kept indefinitely in exile and whenever he returned he could always denounce Allenby's declaration and its reserved subjects as unilateral and therefore not binding on Egypt; and he would be right. In addition, another feature of Allenby's proposal was to consummate Zaghlul's triumph and eventually lead to the high commissioner's resignation. When Allenby originally sent his scheme to London it included a paragraph which said: 'As regards internal administration of Egypt. His Majesty's Government will view with favour the creation of a Parliament with right to control the policy and administration of a constitutional, responsible government.'[251] Such a sponsorship of constitutionalism and of parliamentary institutions had formed part of Milner's proposals. When Allenby was told of them in January 1921, he had immediately declared that he did not consider it a British interest to require representative institutions and ministerial responsibility in Egypt.[252] Again, reporting shortly afterwards the sultan's view that Milner's proposals would merely lead to intrigue, Allenby added: 'I think that this view is worthy of consideration.'[253] When, therefore, we see Allenby a year later recommending what he had objected to a year earlier, we may say that in this respect at least his opinions had indeed undergone a 'violent metamorphosis'. Nor is the reason in doubt. He was committed to, and compromised with Tharwat and his friends, who hankered after parliaments and constitutions, either out of conviction or in order to diminish Fu'ad's power and increase their own.

Allenby's proposal did not figure in the declaration of 28 February 1922 which contented itself with saying that the future form of government would be left for the people and the sultan to determine. The declaration was a victory for Tharwat and his friends. Much as he disliked them and their constitutional ideas, Fu'ad had no alternative but to allow them to form a government pledged to constitutionalism and parliamentary government. Fu'ad tried hard to avoid a constitution, but could not withstand Allenby who continued to press for it. After more than a year's delay Fu'ad at last granted a constitution providing for elections, a parliament and ministerial responsibility. But he was determined to punish Tharwat and his friends who were now organised in the Liberal Constitutionalist Party.

He chose to do this by allying himself to Zaghlul. After his first exile Zaghlul the girondist, the jacobin even, was on very bad terms with Fu'ad. With Tharwat in power, however, Zaghlul and Fu'ad became allies. The king's association with the Zaghlulists was, Allenby stated in a dispatch of May 1923, deliberate and undisguised. Zaghlulist newspapers were receiving large subsidies from the palace, and the king's support was responsible for the recrudescence of Zaghlulist strength in the country.[254] Here was a situation similar to that of 1918 when Fu'ad and Zaghlul each hoped to use the other as a catspaw. *Wafd* and palace now sang each other's praises. The king even took the *Wafd*'s part, and in a note to Allenby who was protesting about the continued assassination of Englishmen, his prime minister Yahya Ibrahim coolly said that this was the result of not paying heed to the desires of the majority, meaning the *Wafd*.[255] Shortly before Zaghlul's return to Egypt from his second exile, in September 1923, a palace official told an agent of the Secret Intelligence Service that Fu'ad had fully made up his mind to give his unqualified support to the Zaghlulists.[256] He also seems to have sent a message to Zaghlul through his man Hasan Nash'at to the effect that he would be glad if Zaghlul would become prime minister after the forthcoming elections.[257] In these elections which took place at the end of 1923, the palace exerted its influence on behalf of the *Wafd*[258] and Zaghlul, the hero of the people, who claimed to speak on behalf not of a party but of the whole nation, was returned with a sweeping majority. Fu'ad seems to have believed that he could, even so, impose his own nominee as prime minister.[259] He was quickly disabused. Zaghlul became prime minister and inaugurated the three decades of parliamentary misgovernment in Egypt when, as Cromer foretold, 'under the specious title of free institutions, the worst evils of personal government would reappear'.[260] As for Allenby, he had not long to wait for what Lord Lloyd has called 'the dreadful aftermath'.[261] At the end of 1924, the sirdar, Lee Stack, was murdered in cold blood in a Cairo street, and Allenby, with trumpets and proclamations, had to demolish the basis of his lasting settlement. His brusque methods, successful when practised on Lloyd George, did not now please the foreign secretary, Sir Austen Chamberlain, who thought they were 'very like the action of a little boy who puts his thumb to his nose and extends his four fingers in a vulgar expression of defiance and contempt'. He sent Nevile Henderson to Cairo to expostulate with him, and Allenby, taking offence, resigned in a huff.[262]

6

The Genesis of the Egyptian Constitution of 1923

During the last year or so of Fu'ad's life, Sir David Kelly recounts in his memoirs, the king of Egypt, old and sick, would amuse himself by giving audiences to the British diplomat who was then acting high commissioner at Cairo, in which he expressed himself with great frankness. The king, according to Kelly, showed great contempt for the intellectual qualities of the British: 'He said' – as Sir David reported him –

he understood the Italian, French and German characters thoroughly, but had given up trying to make any sense out of the actions of the British. He was especially bitter against the British for having 'imposed a constitution on the Belgian model' on the Egyptians, who were completely unsuited for parliamentary government on those lines. Our interest in Egypt, he said, was purely strategic; why had we not been content to leave him to run the country, as he well knew how to do, if we would only cease interfering, providing that as his part of the bargain he played up on all matters affecting our strategic interest and empire communications?[1]

Seven years or so before these audiences, the United States minister gave an account of Fu'ad's opinions which also reflected his bitterness towards the British, and in particular towards Allenby during whose time as high commissioner the Egyptian constitution which the king, according to Kelly, so disliked, had been promulgated. Fu'ad, so the American minister reported, found himself beset with difficulties. They were due 'first, to the passion of the small minority of politically-minded Egyptians for party-politics; second, the desire of his ministers to get rich too [sic!] quickly; and third the difficulty of having always to placate and consider the British'. The king then went on to discuss Allenby. 'Lord Allenby', he said, 'had the true soldier-mind and was lacking in comprehension'. He complained, the American minister went on, 'that even though Lord Allenby knew very little French he would never have an interpreter, the result being that he frequently left the king, who does not speak English, seeming to have understood what His Majesty had said, and only later would it transpire that he had not understood at all'.[2] Allenby, in fact, knew French quite well,[3] and Fu'ad's remarks are therefore significant in disclosing the king's reaction more to Allenby's mind and character than to his linguistic attainments.

Fu'ad, then, seemed to think that those British with whom he had to deal did not understand Egypt, and that Allenby in particular excelled in blundering obtuseness; it is also clear that the king's resentment was due to his belief that without British insistence there would have been no constitution to give their opportunity to piddling and interested politicians, and make his own life a misery. Fu'ad's lamentations should not move us overmuch, for if the constitution had been pressed on him by Allenby, it was because Allenby was high commissioner; Allenby became high commissioner because Sir Reginald Wingate had lost the confidence of his superiors in London; the loss of confidence was the consequence of agitation in Egypt; and the hidden instigator of that agitation had been Fu'ad himself.

But whatever sympathy Fu'ad's predicament arouses, it is interesting to notice that his judgment was exactly identical to that of Allenby's successor in Egypt, for it was Lord Lloyd's view that the British had 'forced' the parliamentary regime upon the country 'in the face of the King's wishes'.[4] To elucidate how this came about will throw some light on the subsequent vicissitudes of constitutional and representative government as it was attempted in Egypt between 1924 and 1952.

When Lord Allenby compelled Lloyd George and his colleagues in February 1922 to agree to his solution of the Egyptian problem, he promised them that his proposals 'if immediately accepted, will prove the basis of a lasting settlement in Egypt'.[5] They proved to be nothing of the kind, and even Allenby's three remaining years as high commissioner proved to be full of unsettlement, agitation and unrest, culminating in the Sirdar's murder and the high-handed treatment to which the high commissioner subjected the Egyptian government; a course of conduct which lost him the confidence of the foreign secretary and led to his resignation. Thus, it may be said that Allenby's solution was really no solution. We may go further and say that it was this particular solution which was the breeding-ground of later difficulties; that these later difficulties were part of the high price with which Allenby purchased the illusion of a 'lasting settlement'. The Declaration of 28 February 1922 purported to give Egypt her independence, with four reservations which generally concerned the interests of Great Britain and the British empire. The line of policy behind the Declaration is intelligible and superficially attractive. Britain, so the reasoning went, had certain interests in Egypt which were the real cause of her presence in the country. From 1882 to 1918 these interests were protected by Great Britain actually occupying Egypt and closely supervising its administration. But the events of 1919 and of the following years had shown that the Egyptian official classes at any rate had ceased to acquiesce in British control, and without their acquiescence Egypt was ungovernable. The good government of Egypt, however, was not a direct British interest; if the Egyptian official classes wished to resume the government of their country, the British could have no objection, provided Egypt was compelled to recognise and secure British interests. Hence the Declaration and its four reservations. But if this was the reasoning behind the Declaration – and only some such reasoning justified Allenby's claim that it provided the basis of a 'lasting settlement' – why then, as Fu'ad asked in his conversations with Kelly, not leave well alone and be content to see Egypt governed by a king in the same manner as it had been governed by the khedives? Or if it be argued that Egypt under British control had irrevocably changed from what it used to be under Sa'id and Isma'il, why not leave Egyptians themselves to deal with this change as best they could? Why should Allenby take it upon himself, by sponsoring a constitution, officiously to pose as the midwife of history?

The answer is that in seeking to persuade London that his policy was the only feasible one, he had had to make sure of some Egyptian support, and that this committed him in turn to support a constitution. For the Egypt which Allenby had to govern was not a crown colony, it was a protectorate with its own indigenous government, and the high commissioner could not govern unless he could find Egyptians willing to take office as ministers. By the beginning of 1922 things had come to such a pass – the consequence of combined mismanagement by Allenby, Milner and Lloyd George's government – that in order to escape from an *impasse* Allenby had to strike a bargain with some Egyptian politicians. He confesses as much when he writes to Curzon that his proposals are 'a result of exhaustive negotiations with Sarwat Pasha and his immediate adherents. They, on their part, have been in contact with a wider circle, and Adly Pasha has been in close touch, and has lent valuable and disinterested assistance'.[6] The support of these politicians was indispensable to Allenby, but he had to pay for it by supporting them in his turn with all the prestige and influence of the high commissioner. Thus he found himself compelled to identify the residency with a particular Egyptian faction, and consequently to alienate the rivals and enemies of this faction, namely Zaghlul and the king. Allenby found himself compelled to do this in order to get his Declaration. The Declaration was a voluntary unilateral abandonment of the British position in Egypt; being unilateral, it secured no concession in return; being obtained at the price of supporting one faction and alienating its enemies, it made British interests in Egypt the perpetual sport of Egyptian factions; and having foresworn control over Egyptian politics, the Declaration made it difficult and at times quite impracticable for Great Britain to neutralise the factional disputes in which her interests became a pawn. This was the ruinous cost of Allenby's policy which led his successor to write in 1927: 'We have magnitude without position: power without authority; responsibility without control'.[7] This, true as it was when it was written, became even truer as the years went by.

The Declaration of 28 February, then, committed Allenby to 'Sarwat Pasha and his immediate adherents'. What this commitment entailed may be gathered from a paragraph in the draft Declaration which Allenby sent to London. This paragraph would have had the British government 'view with favour the creation of a Parliament with right to control the policy and administration of a constitutional, responsible government'. This paragraph was amended in London, and the Declaration, as finally published, did not commit the British government to the promotion of constitutionalism in a kingdom on which, by that very instrument, they were bestowing independence. But the absence of constitutionalist manifestos from the Declaration of 28 February did not alter the fact that Tharwat and his friends were now in power, supported by the great prestige and influence of the high commissioner. They would naturally try to preserve and extend their power. In this enterprise they had to guard against two enemies: Zaghlul with his Wafdist organization and his power over the mob, and the king who, imbued with the autocratic traditions of

163

his house and coming late in life and unexpectedly to the throne was all the more rapacious for power and impatient of any who might claim to share it with him. In arguing that Tharwat and his friends were primarily concerned to enjoy the power which their collaboration with Allenby had brought them, we do not mean to imply that they had no other purpose in politics. Tharwat and his associates did, after all, stand for constitutionalism, the rule of law and limited government; among them were to be found the representatives and heirs of the pre-war *Umma* Party from which Cromer had hoped and expected so much. A sentence in the speech which Adli Yakan delivered on 30 October 1922 at the first general meeting of the Liberal Constitutionalist Party – which Tharwat founded with his friends – may be taken to express their political hopes and ideals. 'The constitutional regime', he said, 'is the only form of government worthy of a nation such as ours which is steeped in civilisation'.[8] If, however, we remember the extremely cavalier manner in which the Liberal Constitutionalists later treated the constitution, we may fairly say that they insisted on a constitution in 1922 because it was then a convenient and useful instrument for limiting Fu'ad's power, and consolidating their own.

Their cooperation with Allenby seemed at first to have all the desirable results. Allenby had taken care to exile Zaghlul and his supporters from Cairo before coercing his own government into issuing the Declaration of 28 February; and if the Declaration did not contain the constitutional manifesto which Allenby had designed, yet the very fact that Allenby was supporting Tharwat and his friends was enough, in the circumstances, to compel the king to give in to their desire for a constitution. The king, therefore, in appointing Tharwat chief minister on 1 March 1922, requested him to prepare a draft constitution, and Tharwat accepted office on the specific understanding that the constitution would ensure the responsibility of ministers to parliament. On 3 April, the council of ministers approved a memorandum by the prime minister setting up a constitutional commission composed of thirty members. The first paragraph embodies the terms on which Tharwat took office and deserves quotation:

The Royal Command to form a ministry which was addressed to me [the memorandum declares] alluded to His Majesty's wish to bring about cooperation between the nation and the government by means of a constitutional regime, and charged the Ministry with the preparation of a draft project. The answer of the ministry to the Royal Command was to the effect that it would immediately put in hand the preparation of a draft constitution in conformity with the principles of modern public law, and that such a constitution would lay down the principle of ministerial responsibility, thus affording to the representative assembly the right to supervise future political activity.[9]

The Commission of Thirty which Tharwat appointed was presided over by Husain Rushdi Pasha. It included four ex-ministers, nine members of the Legislative Assembly which was prorogued in 1914, never to meet again Shaikh Abd al-Hamid al-Bakri, head of the Sufi orders, Shaikh Muhammad Bakhit, an ex-mufti of Egypt, five Copts including the Coptic bishop of Alexandria, one Jew, representatives of the law, of commerce and of the Beduins, the governors of Cairo and Alexandria, the secretary-general of the counoil of ministers, and the permanent secretary of the ministry of finance. Of those who had played a part in recent political events, Abd al-Latif al-Mukibbati presumably represented the Nationalist Party; Muhammad Ali (Alluba) and Abd al-Aziz Fahmi had first cooperated with Zaghlul in 1919–20, had broken with him over his devious methods and dictatorial habits, and were now associated with Adli and Tharwat; whilst Ali Mahir, who had also been associated with the *Wafd*, organising a civil servants' strike in 1919, did not now seem to be identified with any group, but pursued in the commission an individual and most interesting line of argument. As for the *Wafd*, they flatly refused to have anything to do with the Constitutional Commission which Zaghlul denounced as the Malefactors' Commission (*lajnat al-ahqiya'*), alleging that a constitution was properly the business not of a commission but of a constituent assembly. Zaghlul's tactics are easily appreciated: he was on the one hand boycotting and blackening a body created by his political rivals; while on the other, the demagogical powers, which he had successfully tested on the Egyptian masses, made him confident of controlling an elected constituent assembly. The commission was ably assisted by a secretariat of legal experts and draughtsmen.[10]

The commission, then, seemed to be well balanced in affording representation to different interests and sections. Its members collectively possessed a respectable body of political wisdom and legal expertise, and most of them were traditional and conservative in their views: their attitude to constitution-making may perhaps be summed up by the remark of a member who, the American chargé d'affaires reported, 'said to me anent the difficult scholarly Arabic employed that incidentally it had the advantage that "des petits gens" [sic] . . . would not be able to understand it'.[11] But if this may be said to reflect the attitude of the majority, it certainly does not represent that of the few members who took an active and prominent part in the discussions. These included Abd al-Latif al-Mukibbati, Abd al-Aziz Fahmi, Ali Mahir and Abd al-Hamid Badawi, the secretary-general of the council of ministers. Ali Mahir, in particular, took an extreme radical, populist and anti-monarchical line, in which he was occasionally seconded – it is interesting to note – by Shaikh Muhammad Bakhit, the ex-mufti, and which was quite remarkable in its contrast to his future career as a king's man. Discussions extending over many sittings ranged over the most fundamental principles of government, and different views and opinions were defended with spirit, learning and not a little ingenuity: thus there were long debates over the right of the king to veto legislation, to dissolve the parliament and to preside over the cabinet; debates over the status of the royal household officials, over the proportion of elected and appointed senators, and whether the president of the senate should be elected by his peers or appointed by the king. There were other debates on matters equally fundamental, but the topics just mentioned have proved in retrospect to be the most significant and to have given rise to the many vicissitudes which Egyptian constitutionalism suffered in its short and chequered history.[12]

Acute controversy occurred at the very first meeting of the commission. Abd al-Latif al-Mukibbati and Abd al-Aziz Fahmi stood for a franchise embracing all Egyptians over twenty-one; Isma'il Abaza, a notable who had been a member of the Legislative Assembly, opposed this suggestion saying that he could not imagine how a peasant who merely tilled the earth and did not know how to read and write could be considered the equal of, say, Abd al-Aziz Fahmi or of himself. Those in favour of universal suffrage buttressed their contention by the argument that equality of burdens entailed equality of rights, and that since the peasant was subject to conscription, his right to vote was beyond dispute. Their opponents, however, argued that the vote was, as Haikal puts it, part of the process of government, ' 'amaliyya min 'amaliyyat al-hukm', on which depended the choice of representatives who, by their expression of confidence in the cabinet, made its continuance in power possible; it followed therefore, according to this view, that some acquaintance with

political issues and some informed interest in the operation of government was required from the voter.[13] The debate, as may be appreciated, raised issues of principle which, if not speedily resolved in
some fashion, threatened to prolong deliberations intolerably. The
chairman, Husain Rushdi, acted quickly. At the second meeting,
after prolonged debate, he succeeded in having appointed a sub-
committee of eighteen members who were charged with formulating
the basis on which the constitution ought to rest. The smaller
numbers made the sub-committee more manageable, but here too
issues of principle continued to be raised and debated with skill and
pertinacity. The main dispute within the sub-committee lay between
those who wanted to give the monarch some real powers and those
who wanted his function to be merely ceremonial. According to
Haikal, Husain Rushdi played a crucial part in these debates; Rushdi
Pasha, he writes, was 'the real motive force behind its activity'; he
got up in advance the subjects to be debated, he intervened frequently
in the debates, and used the authority of the chair to adjourn the
debate whenever it threatened to produce undesirable decisions.
Haikal describes Rushdi's attitude with some precision:

> Notwithstanding his acceptance of public liberties and indeed his warm
> defence of them [writes Haikal], Rushdi Pasha inclined to concede
> certain rights to the monarch. . . . Some people have expressed surprise
> at such an attitude in a man who had studied in France and had been
> particularly known for his courage and his preference for liberty. . . . It
> seems to me that in these discussions the man was not defending a view
> in which he believed, but rather a policy which, he was convinced, was
> the only one to ensure the realisation of the greatest part of the com-
> mission's aims. The policy depended on the fact that whatever was pro-
> duced by the commission was no more than a draft constitution which, in
> order to take effect, had to be ratified by the monarch. If, therefore,
> such a draft deprived the monarch of all power, then it would be subject
> to radical revision; but if, on the other hand, satisfaction were given to the
> monarch on some issues, while basic rights were secured to the nation
> and its representatives, then it was most probable that nothing would
> prevent the draft constitution being promulgated.[14]

Haikal goes on to say that these considerations were also very much
in the minds of those members of the commission who were most in
contact with Tharwat and his Ministry. Two other motives, Haikal
thought, further explain Rushdi's policy; the first, that, with the
constitutional issue out of the way, Egypt could begin to tackle

Great Britain on the four reserved points of the Declaration of 28 February; the second, that if it came to a contest between 'moderates' and 'extremists', as happened when Adli and Zaghlul clashed in the spring of 1921, a monarch with some effective constitutional power would exert his influence in favour of the 'moderates'. If this was really in Rushdi's mind the events which followed the promulgation of the constitution must have soon undeceived him.

The draft constitution produced by the commission was, then, a compromise between Fu'ad's desire for unfettered power and the views of those on the commission who stood for unfettered popular sovereignty. It was largely a codification and abridgement of constitutional practices and traditions which had grown up in Europe since the middle ages; which had been digested, summarised and transformed into 'principles of public law' by the academic lawyers, mainly French, from whom members of the commission derived much of their constitutional learning. The draft began by asserting (Article 23) that 'All authority derives from the nation',[15] went on to divide governmental powers into a legislative (to be exercised by a Parliament in conjunction with the king), an executive (of which the king was the head) and a judiciary. Executive power was to be exercised, under the king, by a council of ministers who were to resign from office on forfeiting the legislature's confidence. The king had a limited right of veto over legislation (Articles 33 and 34), the power to dissolve a parliament (Article 36) and the power to appoint and dismiss ministers (Article 45). The commission published a commentary to accompany the draft,[16] in which they explained that the right of dissolution was essential as a means of effecting a balance between the executive and the legislative, enabling the nation to be consulted whenever there was a deadlock between the different powers in the state. The commentary also supplied a gloss on Article 45 which gave the king power to appoint and dismiss ministers, saying that the current convention was that the king chose the prime minister and on his advice appointed and dismissed ministers.

This, then, was a model, a text-book constitution, *sage comme une image*, full of checks and of balances, an ordered and intricate toyland in which everything was calm and beauty. Its radical failing in the actual conditions of Egyptian politics was that it assumed and took for granted that elections in Egypt could possibly elicit, as they did elsewhere, the will of the electorate. As the sequel, from 1923 to 1952, showed, they did nothing of the kind; Egyptian elections, rather, proved to be ratifications by the masses of decisions taken by the king, or else by the Cairo politicians, depending on which side had, for the time being, the upper hand. Dissolutions, therefore, could not remotely help, as the commission expected, in preserving the balance of the constitution, and their judicious and elaborate considerations merely manage to look ineffective and academic. This is also the case with their gloss on Article 45 dealing with the appointment and dismissal of ministers; the commission took for granted that a prime minister would be appointed only if he had a majority in the Parliament, and fastened on the insignificant issue of the appointment and dismissal of other ministers. In fact, the clause in the draft giving the king powers to appoint and dismiss ministers – including, of course, the prime minister – was passed on the nod in the General Commission. The Commission did not consider the possibility that the king might make a literal use of his powers and appoint and dismiss his chief ministers as he liked. But this is what in fact repeatedly happened under the parliamentary regime in Egypt.

Given these conditions, the parliamentary regime which Tharwat and his friends desired and which Allenby was inclined to press on the king could not but justify Cromer's foreboding when at the end of his long rule in Egypt he affirmed that 'under the specious title of free institutions, the worst evils of personal government would reappear'.[17] Rushdi's judicious policies, and his tenacious attempts at compromise, availed nothing, for even if by some miracle he had succeeded in reconciling royal ambitions with constitutional government, he would yet have been powerless to endow an Egyptian Parliament with representativeness, or to make possible limited government in a country where unlimited power was, and continued to be, a standing temptation, easy to fall into and safe to indulge. Therefore we may say that by supporting parliamentarianism in Egypt, Allenby was engaging his credit and the credit of his government in support of a farce.

For him it was not even a profitable farce. One of the points which the Declaration of 28 February 'absolutely' reserved to the discretion of the British government was the Sudan, then administered as an Anglo-Egyptian condominium. The constitutional commission decided that the forthcoming constitution should indicate unmistakably that Fu'ad was king of both Egypt and the Sudan. Such a proposal was defended alike by those who were the king's partisans and by those who wished to challenge British power in the Nile valley. When Allenby came to hear of this proposal, he objected strenuously, but in spite of the fact that Tharwat and his friends were in office owing to British support, his protests availed him nothing and the draft constitution when it was completed and handed to Tharwat stated, in Article 29, that 'The king shall be called king of Egypt and the Sudan'.[18] The fact is that however much Rushdi, Tharwat and their friends may have disliked this provision, they had no means of opposing it without giving the king and Zaghlul a powerful pretext for attacking them as creatures of the British government. Haikal tells[19] us that Tharwat consulted Adli and his other political friends who advised him that the provision had to stand. Allenby used to complain that Adli was a broken reed, and that he much preferred to deal with Tharwat.[20] And it is true that Adli was not a fighter, but in this particular case it was Tharwat who let Allenby down, and could not do otherwise if he wanted to stay in power. The episode merely shows that the policy which Allenby thought worth coercing his government into following was of pretty little use in the defence of British interests, and that, as hitherto, British interests had to be defended by constant British intervention, which after the Declaration of 28 February could be (and was) legitimately denounced as interference.

Husain Rushdi could be as statesmanlike and moderate as he liked, but there was no disguising the fact that the draft constitution, however solicitous of the king's prerogative, represented a serious limitation of his powers. Fu'ad did not mean to be reduced to a constitutional monarch so that Tharwat and his friends might enjoy greater patronage and power. The royal palace was traditionally a power in the land, and so long as a constitution was not promulgated the king retained vast powers of initiative, intervention and patronage which Fu'ad proceeded to wield for the undoing of his chief minister. During the summer of 1922 Fu'ad made clear his disapproval of Tharwat and his policies; and the ministry's supporters within the constitutional commission tried to make haste and complete their labours; a sub-committee was appointed to produce the final draft of the constitution, and another sub-committee to produce the final draft electoral law.[21] The texts were at last agreed and six months after beginning its work the commission presented them to Tharwat on 21 October.

By then the prime minister's position was gravely weakened both by his disagreement with Allenby over the Sudan and by the king's manifest disapproval. One of Fu'ad's tactics now was to adopt a popular stance and insist that Tharwat should obtain from the British the recall of Zaghlul, the people's tribune, and of his friends, from exile – to which they had been sent in December 1921, precisely in order that Tharwat might assume office unhindered! 'There is again a coolness between Sarwat, the prime minister, and the king', reported the American chargé d'affaires on 2 October, 'due to a difference of opinion relative to the policy pursued with the Zaghlul leaders. The king is afraid of their enmity and is for leniency. This Sarwat regards as weakness and opposes'.[22] The language of this telegram indicates not so much the king's actual motives as the impression which he desired outsiders to gather. The architect of this policy would seem to have been Tawfiq Nasim, a former prime minister who since April 1922 was chief of the royal cabinet. It appears that he managed to achieve an understanding between the king and Zaghlul's party which was presumably directed against the existing ministry.[23]

The upshot of these manoeuvres was that the *Wafd* began to attack Tharwat's administration even more strongly, and to abound in fervent declarations of loyalty to the throne. In the telegram of 2 October previously cited, the American chargé d'affaires reported that Tharwat was then unpopular and that his administration could not last for long; 'it is in effect', he added, 'imposed upon the country by measures taken or supported under martial law'. The observation is correct and applies not only to the last days of Tharwat's administration, but in fact to the whole of it; it had been brought in and supported by British power, but that the truth should now be openly said about it indicated that its days were numbered. In the event, Tharwat lasted until the end of November. The *coup de grâce* was delivered with the help of another household official, Hasan Nash'at, whose role in Egyptian politics had hitherto been obscure, but who was to play a part of some importance in the following years. The king, attended by Tharwat and his other ministers, was to go to al-Azhar for Friday prayers on 1 December. Nash'at distributed money among the Azhar students and incited them to demonstrate against Tharwat on the occasion of the royal visit. Tharwat heard of this plot, and rather than be subjected to the indignity of such a contrived attack, preferred to send in his resignation the day before. Nash'at brought Fu'ad's acceptance within the hour; Allenby told the American minister how sorry he was at Tharwat's fall, and heavily remonstrated with the king for his actions, 'informing him of the displeasure of the British government at his treatment of a minister who had been appointed to implement the policy of the Declaration'![24]

Tawfiq Nasim, the new prime minister, had two assignments: to try to make the constitution as innocuous as possible, while maintaining the provision of Article 29 which assured to Fu'ad the dual monarchy of Egypt and Sudan. This latter object was, of course, impossible to achieve in the face of British objections. Allenby had protested against the offending Article when Tharwat was in power, but may have found his style cramped by his desire to support him. Such considerations now no longer inhibited Allenby, and he coerced the king into signing a declaration giving up these pretensions.[25] We do not know the exact tenor of this declaration, but Allenby's threat seems to have been to the effect that if Fu'ad persisted in his claim he would have to give up the Egyptian throne not only for himself but for his heir as well. Fu'ad signed this declaration[26] at the beginning of February 1923, and, according to Allenby, Tawfiq Nasim felt, as a result, that he could not continue in office. He resigned on 9 February, the king denouncing him as a coward.[27]

During his period of office, rumours became rife that the palace and the ministry had amended the constitution drastically, that the clause stating that the nation was the source of authority was to be omitted, that the king was to be given wide prerogatives in the distribution of honours, the dissolution of parliament (and not merely the chamber of deputies as the draft proposed), and in the control of religious endowments, that he was to have the power of issuing decree-laws even when the parliament was sitting, and that the proportion of senators appointed by the King was to be greatly increased. The Liberal Constitutionalists, and Abd al-Aziz Fahmi in particular, were loud in their protests.[28] Tawfiq Nasim resigned before any amendments were officially published, but that drastic changes had been made to conform to Fu'ad's wishes is not in doubt.

It did not prove easy to appoint a successor to Tawfiq Nasim. Adli Yakan was approached to form an administration, it would seem at Allenby's instance,[29] but the political situation which he confronted was complicated and treacherous in the extreme. Under Tawfiq Nasim's inspiration, the King's policy had been, from the summer of 1922 onwards, to encourage Zaghlul's *Wafd* to maintain popular effervescence against Tharwat and his British patrons, by means of demonstrations and terrorist outrages. These outrages continued unchecked under Tawfiq Nasim's administration. These tactics are clearly exhibited in a letter from Tawfiq Nasim in answer to a protest by Allenby against the murder of Mr Robson, a lecturer at the Law College. Tawfiq Nasim asserted that such outrages indicated that British policy did not take into account 'the sentiments of the majority', which had been further exacerbated by the understanding reached between the British and 'a minority which had no real influence over the nation.'[30] Thus Allenby – 'the bull' – was baited and ridiculed for the ill-success of his famous Declaration. When Adli was asked to form a cabinet, he realised that if he succeeded it would be in the teeth of determined and concerted opposition from the king and the Zaghlulists. He had had experience, when prime minister in 1921, of the lengths to which the Zaghlulists would go in demagogy and incitement, and had no stomach for another such experience – this is what Allenby meant when he said that Adli was a broken reed. In the manner usual to broken reeds, Adli thought to escape his difficulties by a compromise: he would take office only on condition that the *Wafd* supported him; let Zaghlul and his friends be recalled from exile and in return let the constitution as drafted by the commission be promulgated. Since Fu'ad's object was precisely to prevent this, and since the Wafdists had no desire to see their rival in power, much less support him, this compromise plan was quite useless. To help Adli see things as they really were, Wafdist incitement and terrorist outrages were stepped up. In these activities it seems that Hasan Nash'at was so implicated that the British required his departure from Egypt and refused to let him return until the constitution was finally promulgated.[31] Adli was told that he could have office with the king's approval, if he agreed to issue the amended draft as a constitution. He preferred to give up the attempt.

A cabinet was not formed until 15 March. The prime minister was Yahya Ibrahim, who was not a political personality and presumably acceptable both to Allenby and to the king. He was not of a calibre to stand up to either, but was merely the intermediary whose function was to prevent a direct clash between them. The king, we understand from Allenby's biography, had not abandoned his opposition to the draft constitution and the high commissioner 'thought it judicious' to use his influence with him and 'accordingly advised him to allow himself to be guided by his prime minister'. Allenby's constitutional tuition lasted for a month before the king allowed himself to be converted and to promulgate the constitution on 19 April. In a report quoted by his biographer, Allenby states that Fu'ad's behaviour was running counter to 'unanimous and clearly expressed public opinion' and that he intervened because it was not in accord with 'the policy of the Declaration' that the king should arrogate 'undue' powers to himself, and because he wished to avoid a constitutional struggle between king and people.[32] As regards public opinion and the possibility of a struggle between king and people, there is no evidence to support Allenby's contentions. It is true that the king's ambitions were attacked – but only by the handful of politicians and academics who dreamed of a constitutional representative government for their country. As late as 15 April, four days before the promulgation of the constitution, Abd al-Aziz Fahmi was addressing an open letter to the prime minister protesting against certain Egyptians offering the results of the anti-British struggle as a free gift to the royal house (*yahibunaha ghanima barida li-umara' al-bayt al-malik*).[33] But such protests, noble and courageous as they may have been, were not the voice of 'unanimous and clearly-expressed public opinion'. They were on the contrary the voice of a minority of politicians who – Abd al-Aziz Fahmi expected – by their later actions showed that their regard for constitutionalism speedily disappeared at the prospect of power. Again, Allenby was mistaken in thinking that an autocratic constitution would have precipitated a struggle between king and people – it might have precipitated a struggle between the king and Allenby's clients, but this is another story. As for Allenby's remaining motive, *i.e.* that the king's behaviour was contrary to 'the policy of the Declaration', it is most revealing. Allenby does not – and of course cannot – say that such behaviour was contrary to the Declaration, for there was nothing in the Declaration to show that Fu'ad had to be a constitutional figurehead, scrupulous in observing the proprieties, content merely to be consulted, to advise and to warn; 'the policy of the Declaration' is another matter altogether, and really signifies the assumptions on which Allenby had built his policy. Fu'ad was under no obligation to make these assumptions come true. Allenby as a constitutional mentor calls to mind the observation of a witty orientalist on the behaviour of the Abbasid caliph al-Ma'mun trying to force theological dogmas down the throats of his unwilling divines: *'C'était un libéral'* wrote Darmsteter of him, *'c'est-à-dire qu'il envoyait les orthodoxes à la potence'*. *Mutatis mutandis*, the description fits the methods of Allenby the constitutionalist to perfection.

The constitution promulgated on 19 April differed in many ways from the draft completed the previous October. The extent of the king's original demands may be imagined from the wide prerogatives which this document still secured to him even after a month of powerful pressure from Allenby. Article 23, which asserted that the nation was the source of authority, remained in the constitution in spite of the fears of the Liberal Constitutionalists, but it was glossed with a curious commentary from the minister of Justice, Ahmad dhu'l Faqar. 'The principle that the nation is the origin of all authority', stated his explanatory memorandum issued with the constitution, 'is not in contradiction with the origin of the Islamic monarchical and absolutist governments, because these monarchies used initially to depend on the explicit or implicit consent of the people represented by its elders and notables'.[34] The theory is not really tenable; but its effect is to substitute an autocratic interpretation for the democratic one intended by the original authors of Article 23. The modifications introduced in the constitution itself were of greater importance, however, than the merely academic dispute about the proper meaning of Article 23. The constitution[35] gave the king power to confer civil and military rank, decorations and titles at his own discretion,[36] it gave him power to appoint and dismiss military officers[37] and diplomats.[38] The constitution also increased significantly the proportion of appointed senators and made the presidency of the senate an office within the sole discretion of the monarch to bestow.[39] Again, it left religious endowments and the control of the Muslim religious institution solely within the power of the king until the parliament should legislate otherwise.[40] The draft also had specifically entrenched eight articles against amendment or abrogation, while the constitution was much more vague in stating that no proposal could be entertained which would change 'the provisions guaranteed by this constitution concerning the representative form of government, the order of succession to the throne and the principles of liberty and equality'.[41]

The king, then, got what he wanted, in part at least. But in order to get it, he had had to enlist the help of Zaghlul and his Wafdists, for which, of course, they exacted a price. The price was the king's support in gaining power. The extent to which Fu'ad was involved with Zaghlul at that time may be gathered from the fact that at his first interview as prime minister with the high commissioner, Yahya Ibrahim – who himself had no Wafdist connections – asked Allenby to allow Zaghlul and his companions to come back from their exile.[42] Egypt was at last endowed with a constitution and an electoral law.[43] Elections had therefore to be held, and when they were, at the end of 1923, the weight of administrative influence was exerted against the Liberal Constitutionalists,[44] and therefore in favour of Wafdists. Zaghlul enjoyed a crushing majority and was appointed prime minister. Later Fu'ad used to justify his behaviour in supporting Zaghlul at this juncture by claiming that it was a far-sighted scheme for breaking the 'popular idol' by burdening him with responsibility.[45] But when he held this conversation, Fu'ad was surely sighing with relief that Zaghlul's ineptitude and his failure to control the terrorist apparatus[46] had accidentally rid him of a prime minister whom his own machinations had brought to power, and who, when he unexpectedly fell, was bidding fair to overwhelm with a populist dictatorship Fu'ad's own autocracy.

7

Egypt and the Caliphate, 1915-52

It is common knowledge that religion and politics in Islam are closely related, and that in this relationship the prevalent mode has been for the man of the sword to dominate the man of the pen. This is so both in theory and practice: passive obedience to the ruler has been erected into a religious duty, while religious dignitaries, muftis, qadis and such have been usually content to play the role of

> an attendant lord, one that will do
> To swell a progress, start a scene or two,
> Advise the prince; no doubt an easy tool,
> Deferential, glad to be of use,
> Politic, cautious and meticulous;
> Full of high sentence, but a bit obtuse . . .

The men of religion were of course compelled into this long-standing acquiescence by the unremitting burden of capricious and exacting despotism, and if the burden were to be ever so slightly shifted, we might witness some stirrings, some attempt on their part to break loose from political dependence, or even – chimerical as this may sound – to assert the temporal primacy of religion over political authority. Some such spectacle confronts us when we consider the hiatus in Egyptian political history which runs from 1882 to 1952. In the first part of this period – which ended in 1919 – the British managed to establish a *rechtstaat* controlled by an efficient and upright bureaucracy, using their power to keep in check the despotic appetite of the local ruler and of his subordinates; whilst in the second part, British authority having been withdrawn and British preponderance destroyed, a confused situation ensued in which a number of contenders struggled for power, until the *coup d'état* of 23 July 1952 decided the issue and heralded a return to more habitual methods and practices. In both phases it was possible for men of religion to show initiative and enjoy unwonted freedom: in the first because the British, foreign and non-Muslim rulers, were in no position – even had they desired it – closely to control their activity, while in the second, the sharp struggle between king and politicians afforded many opportunities for manoeuvre. Thus, Cromer's support gave elbow room to Muhammad Abduh and allowed him to stand up to an imperious and ambitious khedive; while the period of constitutional monarchy, so-called, afforded some scope to Mustafa al-Maraghi to play a part in the politics of the period, and even at one stage to exert quite considerable influence. As it happens, Maraghi's later career was deeply involved in the caliphate question which in its last stages – between 1924 and 1939 – was an important issue in Egyptian internal and external politics.

Muhammad Mustafa al-Maraghi (1881–1945) was chief qadi in the Sudan from 1908 to 1919; between 1919 and 1928 he was successively chief inspector of the religious courts in Egypt, president of the religious court of first instance, member and then president of the religious high court. From August 1928 to October 1929, and again from 1935 until his death in 1945, he was rector of al-Azhar.[1] It was during this first period of tenure at al-Azhar that he came much into the public view. His appointment ended a ten-month deadlock between King Fu'ad and his Ministry in consequence of a law of 1927 which had decreed that the rector was to be appointed by the king on the advice of the prime minister. It is most probable that al-Maraghi was the nominee of the then prime minister, Muhammad Mahmud; for they both hailed from Upper Egypt, and al-Maraghi then and later had close connections with Muhammad Mahmud's party, the Liberal Constitutionalists.[2] During his first, short, tenure of the rectorship, al-Maraghi sponsored a bill which proposed many reforms in the structure and teaching of al-Azhar, but on Muhammad Mahmud's loss of office he was speedily dismissed. His successor was unmistakably the king's nominee, and Fu'ad took care to have the law amended so that the appointment should revert to being – what it had always been – solely in his gift.[3] Maraghi, having gone out under a cloud, remained in retirement for five years. In April 1935, following a long period of student strikes and disorders and as a consequence of a weakening in Fu'ad's political position, al-Zawahiri, his nominee, was compelled to resign the rectorship, and Maraghi entered on his second, much longer tenure. Faruq's accession followed shortly after. Maraghi was appointed to give the king – still a minor – lessons in religious subjects and Arabic literature and history.[4] The connection between Faruq and Maraghi became – and remained – very close, and on the Friday following the rector's death, his biographer records, the king bade the worshippers at his mosque to pray for the soul of 'my friend Shaikh al-Maraghi'.[5] It seems fair to say that if Maraghi started on his second tenure at al-Azhar as a Liberal Constitutionalist in politics, at odds with the royal palace, he ended it most definitely as a king's man. His political career in this respect exemplifies the rapid, confused, continuous change in political allegiance which is a feature of Egypt's politics under the monarchy.

Maraghi's first recorded contact with the caliphate issue occurs during the first world war, when he was chief qadi in Khartoum. In the first half of 1915 the possibility of an Anglo-Sharifian understanding was in the air, and Sir Reginald Wingate, the governor-general of the Sudan, who favoured it strongly, was canvassing Muslim opinion about the feasibility of the sharif of Mecca replacing the Ottoman sultan as caliph. The *ulama*, perhaps out of a desire to please, perhaps out of genuine conviction, indicated to Wingate that the sharif was in every way qualified for the caliphate. Maraghi wrote a note (of which there does not seem to be a copy in the *Wingate Papers*) supporting this view. But then he intervened with another brief, but skilful and subtle, contribution. He wrote a letter to Wingate which purported to set out authoritatively the Muslim doctrine about the caliphate.[6] In this letter, Maraghi manages to throw doubt on the contention – highly favourable to the sharif – that a caliph had to be descended from the Prophet's tribe, Quraish. This condition he ascribes to historical accident, and he denies that it is unanimously accepted by the jurists. 'It should not be forgotten', he says, to buttress his contention, 'that the universal acknowledgment of all Mohammedans throughout the world to the sultans of Turkey as khalifs is a sufficient proof that they respect the latter opinion, i.e. that it is not necessary for the khalifa to be a Kurashi'. Even more remarkable, he equated the caliphate with secular kingship, and divine prescriptions with man-made laws: '. . . the question of the khalifate', he writes, 'is a purely worldly one and has certain connections and relations with religion. The khalifa is in all respects a king who exercises over his subjects certain powers he derives from the Holy Books. Other kings govern their subjects by laws enacted by productive brains'. Maraghi recognised that this argument supported the legitimacy of the Ottoman caliphate: 'the appropriation by the sultans of Turkey of the title of khalifa, is in no way contrary to the principles of the faith, although they are not from the tribe of Koreish'; but this did not mean that he himself approved of or recommended loyalty to the Ottoman caliphate: 'If the Mohammedans consider, as I am inclined to hold, that their faith has reaped no good from the Ottoman khalifate, they are evidently the best judges as to whether the Ottoman khalifate should be changed or not. They can very easily find an example in the deposition by the Turks of Sultan Abdul-Hamid and the appointment of his successor. Their reason in the step they have taken was that the country made no progress in the time of Abdul-Hamid. The Mohammedans can now decide on the situation from the actual conditions of the empire under the new khalifa'.

Maraghi's letter, for all its moderate and judicious tone, for all its avoidance of open advocacy, is a remarkable example of special pleading. In his anxiety to minimise the importance of Quraishite descent, Maraghi gives the impression that this is a disputed question among the jurists. In fact, the consensus of the Muslim jurists holds that in a caliphate by election descent from Quraish is a necessary condition.[7] Admittedly, this is the case only in a caliphate by election, when conditions make it possible to conform to all the rules and stipulations laid down by the doctors of the law, and a caliphate by election was of course a strictly bookish notion, a mere jurist's dream. Yet in undertaking to instruct Wingate *ex cathedra*, so to speak, Maraghi might have been expected to give its due weight to the traditional consensus. Another feature of Maraghi's letter was the manner in which he appealed now to history, and now to jurisprudence according to the needs of his argument. He says, and it is indeed true, that obedience to the Ottoman caliphs, in spite of the fact that they were not of Quraishite descent, was lawful. But this was because, side by side with the caliph by election, the jurists had been compelled by circumstances to recognise a caliph by domination, whose claim to rule was enforced by the sword. Obedience to such a caliph was also a religious duty, on the ground that rule and religion are twins, and that civil order is a necessity. But the origins of such a caliph cannot be enquired into, his ability to rule is his sole credential, and obedience is equally due to his supplanter. Such a doctrine made due allowance for historical vicissitudes and safeguarded – by keeping it free from worldly taint – the hallowed notion of an elective caliphate. In the circumstances of 1915, there could be no question of the

British government encouraging or promoting a caliphate by domination, and yet Maraghi is found arguing that because Muslims have lawfully obeyed the Ottoman caliph, who had established his dominion by the sword, therefore descent from Quraish was not necessary in a candidate to what could be, if anything, only a caliphate by election.

The implication of Maraghi's reasoning is obvious. Having poured cold water on the necessity of descent from Quraish, and having stated that Islam has reaped no good from the Ottoman caliphate, he clearly left the door open for another candidate, who would benefit Islam and who was yet not a descendant from Quraish. Nor do we have far to go to discover whom Maraghi had in mind. Discussing with Wingate his change of views since his earlier note which had supported the claims of the sharif, he said that due consideration should be given to the claim of Egypt to the caliphate. Egypt, in his view, was far more prepared to undertake such a burden than any other state, because she took the lead in religious education and had a vast number of highly educated and intelligent Muslims who could be entrusted with the affairs of state.[8]

We have no evidence to indicate whether Maraghi was acting on his own, or at somebody's suggestion, but we do know that Husain Kamil, the sultan of Egypt, was not pleased with British encouragement of the sharif. At the start of the sharif's rebellion, Egyptian troops were sent as reinforcements to the Hijaz, and this drew a protest from Husain Kamil to Wingate, who was then in charge of military operations in the Hijaz. The dispatch of Egyptians to the Hijaz in order to fight the Ottomans, he wrote in a letter of 6 November 1916, 'could not but leave a bad impression on public opinion in the country. As the news becomes known, opinion will wonder what interest Egypt has in waging war in order to help establish an independent Arab kingdom'.[9] The sultan was not only concerned over the internal repercussions of Egyptian troops fighting Ottoman in the Hijaz, he also despised the sharif, and thought that Egypt was much more entitled than him to succeed to Turkey's primacy in the Islamic world. He hoped, so wrote Wingate to Lord Hardinge on 17 April 1917, to see Cairo, already a great centre of Islamic teaching, as one of the most, if not the most important Islamic centre in the world; he therefore disliked the sharif's movement and the generous support the British were giving it. He described the sharif's entourage in Mecca as *canaille*, and doubted whether the sharif would ever be able to control Arabian potentates such as Ibn Saʻud.[10] It may even be that the sultan actively promoted his own claims to the caliphate: we gather this from a passing reference in a letter from Fuʼad al-Khatib, the deputy foreign minister of the Hijaz to Faruqi, the sharif's agent in Cairo, which speaks of the sultan's intentions regarding the caliphate, and of his having supporters spreading his appeal;[11] also, from a memorandum by Sir Ronald Graham of 2 March 1917 in which he writes that the sultan had been recently informed that he should not aspire to the caliphate. Graham went on to say that Egyptians considered the sharif a Beduin chief, and to them Beduins were simply nomadic robbers: the prospect of the sharif as caliph was to the Egyptians what to his contemporaries would have been the prospect of Friar Tuck as archbishop of Canterbury.[12] Sultan Fuʼad held the same views and pursued the same ambitions as his predecessor, Husain Kamil. One of his motives in supporting Zaghlul was his suspicion that if Egypt were the protectorate of a Christian state, she could never hope to have the primacy in Islam. He was, said Wingate in a telegram of 26 December 1918, extremely jealous of the king of the Hijaz, and he did not hide his displeasure at the encouragement which the British lavished on Husain.[14] A year or so later Allenby reported that a new prayer for Fuʼad, originating in the Palace, had been distributed to the preachers who read it at the Friday prayers. The worshippers, it seems, howled them down because the prayer was interpreted to constitute a claim by the Sultan to the caliphate.[13]

The caliphate question became acute in 1924. In March, the Turks abolished the Ottoman caliphate and sent the last caliph into exile. Thereupon the king of the Hijaz hastened to have himself proclaimed caliph, basing himself – so he claimed – on the suffrages of the faithful in Palestine, Syria, Iraq and Trans-Jordan. But Husain's presumed election settled nothing; it was patently farcical and had no relation to the realities of the Islamic world. Fuʼad for one could not be expected to acquiesce in Husain's mock caliphate. To the United States minister who questioned him about newspaper reports which stated that he had been offered the caliphate, he said that he 'would not entertain for a moment the thought of accepting this position'. He disapproved of the abolition of the Ottoman caliphate and was bitter and contemptuous about other likely candidates. He suspected Mustafa Kemal of aspiring to the office, but was quite sure he would not obtain it. Of the king of the Hijaz, he said 'I regard him also as an impossible person for this place. He probably will have the support of his own little country and its comparatively few people' and the support of his sons, the king of Iraq and the amir of Trans-Jordan, together with that of the Arabs of Palestine.[15] It would seem that Fu'ad also more than once strenuously denied any interest in the caliphate to Zaghlul who was then prime minister.[16] But such denials were made to seem highly formal by his own and his supporters' extensive and determined activity. As soon as the Turkish action became known, letters and articles appeared in the press advocating an Egyptian caliphate.[17] At the same time, a gathering of *ulama* which took place at the house of an ex-prime minister, Muhammad Sa'id Pasha, discussed the abolition of the Ottoman caliphate and one of them said: 'Why should the caliphate not go to King Fu'ad? We have but to assemble the *ulama* of Egypt and they will elect him and give him their suffrages (*yubayi'unahu*), and the caliphate will thus come to belong to the king of Egypt'. Ahmad Shafiq Pasha, who recounts the episode, goes on to say that the suggestion was conveyed to the king, who turned it down.[18] This, however, was not the end of the matter, for on 25 March the chief religious dignitaries of Egypt (among whom Maraghi was included) issued a long statement declaring that Muslims were no longer bound to obey the deposed Ottoman caliph and that the office was vacant; they invited the Muslims to send representatives to Cairo in a year's time 'to designate the new caliph'.[19]

The speed with which these religious dignitaries acted was remarkable. It is not likely that the initiative was theirs. In a letter to Shakib Arslan dating from the latter part of 1925, Rashid Rida stated that the *ulamas* issued their official declaration 'only after having ascertained the feeling of Abdin palace on the matter'.[20] Rashid Rida can be considered well informed on this question not only because he was generally well informed on Islamic matters but also because he seems to have taken part in the propaganda which was then started in Egypt in order to advance Fu'ad's claim to the caliphate. The first number of a periodical which described itself as dedicated to the promotion of a caliphate congress in Egypt, opened with an article by Rashid Rida extolling the benefits of Islamic unity and harshly attacking King Husain – who had been proclaimed caliph in parts of the Arab world and who had subsequently had to abdicate his rule in the Hijaz in favour of his son Ali – as the despot (*taghut*) of the Hijaz who had falsely claimed to exercise kingship

over all the Arabs and the caliphate over all the Muslims and whose
designs God had defeated by stripping him of his alleged authority,
and leaving him cut off from the community, abandoned, hated and
execrated.[21] It is an interesting sign of Rashid Rida's soundness as an
Islamic scholar that even though he had a consuming hatred for
Husain, he yet did not allow himself to go against the tradition and
the consensus of the jurists and to argue that Quraishite descent is
not necessary in a caliph. The farthest he goes is to quote Ibn
Jubair, a traveller not a jurist, to the effect that people have not
seldom preferred a Kurdish sultan to a Quraishite caliph because of
the greater equity of his rule.

Rashid Rida's letter to Shakib Arslan is not the only evidence that
Fu'ad was behind the agitation to proclaim him caliph. In March 1927
the (Wafdist) minister of pious foundations, Muhammad al-Gharabli
Pasha, we asked in the Egyptian parliament to explain a payment
of £2,500 made to the rector of al-Azhar in five instalments during
1924. The minister replied that the rector had asked for the money
in order to cover a deficiency in the budget of the Religious Institutions, but that subsequently it appeared that the money was spent
on the caliphate congress.[22] The answer was probably meant to, and
did, create an uproar. The rector of al-Azhar and other shaikhs were
harshly attacked for their irregular financial proceedings. This was a
Wafdist Parliament's way of indirectly attacking King Fu'ad and his
ambitions, and to one member it appeared unfair that the rector and
his fellows should be made the vehicle for such indirect attacks. Fikri
Abaza declared that the matter was important and required frankness in its treatment: 'You all know', he said, 'that at that time the
royal *entourage* – and misfortunes always come from the *entourage* –
thought that an august will desired the caliphate. In 1924 and in
1925, sums were being spent quickly and without the proper procedure at the ministry of pious foundations. On what basis of
equity and law', he asked, 'can we justify the displeasure we are
manifesting towards the rector, whilst the heads [i.e. the principals]
are still there, and unaccountable to anyone?'[23] Stung by these
attacks, the purpose of which was all too clear, a palace-inspired
newspaper wrote:

Let us face the real facts; the present minister of Wakfs [Pious Founda-
tions] – Muhammad Gharabli Pasha – is the same minister of Wakfs who
received the chancellor's [the Azhar rector's] letter on 31 March 1924,
and ordered the money to be paid to him. He was then a member of the

Zaghlul Ministry. Why did he not ask the shaikh what he wanted the money for, if the government at that time did not know it was to be spent on the Caliphate Congress? Especially as the chancellor of the Azhar declared in his demand that the amount should not be put in the budget of the Theological Administration?[24]

The agitation against the rector of al-Azhar, however, continued; there was a demand in parliament for him to be investigated and even to be made to refund the money. The rector then visited the prime minister and, so reported the *Egyptian Gazette* of 16 May 1927, showed him a letter from the ministry of pious foundations, itself suggesting a procedure by which money could be drawn to cover the expenses of the congress, without such an object appearing openly. The agitation seems to have died down thereafter. It was no doubt equally inconvenient to both sides – though for different reasons – then to make the point that as the law stood from 1924 to 1927 the king, by virtue of Article 153 of the constitution, had control over the budget of the religious institutions. We may safely assume, therefore, that official monies were spent on the caliphate congress not only in 1924, but also in 1925 and in 1926 when the congress at last took place.

There is still further evidence of Fu'ad's interest in the caliphate. In March 1924, when the congress was first mooted, the under-secretary in the Ministry of Pious Foundations was Hasan Nash'at. Nash'at was not a Wafdist, but rather a king's man, one of those whom Zaghlul agreed to take into his Ministry, presumably in exchange for the king's support in the elections of 1923. Shortly after the abolition of the Ottoman caliphate it became clear that Nash'at was promoting an Egyptian caliphate: 'He used', writes Ahmad Shafiq Pasha, 'to take trips to Tanta and meet the *ulama* there. Then he would go to Alexandria and other cities where meetings with *ulama* could be arranged. Thereupon committees sprang up in those places known as caliphate committees'.[25] When relations between Fu'ad and Zaghlul worsened, Nash'at was used, so the Wafdists were convinced, to stir up the Azhar against the *Wafd* government. In October, Zaghlul had a showdown with Fu'ad and obtained, among other things, that Nash'at should leave his government. Nash'at then became acting head of the royal cabinet and the king's general agent and *factotum* in the country until he was dismissed in 1926 at Lord Lloyd's instance. While in this post his word was supreme, as the Liberal Constitutionalist leader, Abd al-Aziz Fahmi complained, in the ministries of pious foundations, of war and of foreign affairs, that is, precisely in those departments where the king, according to the constitution, had the final say in appointments, promotions and expenditure.[26] We may presume that such great influence was not left unused at a time when the king entertained and caressed the dream of the caliphate.

The only overt official action which indicated Fu'ad's stand on the caliphate was the manner in which Egypt fell out with the king of the Hijaz. As is well known, the rulers of Egypt have been accustomed since the thirteenth century to send to Mecca every year during the pilgrimage season 'for the sake of state' and 'as an emblem of royalty',[27] the luxurious empty litter carried by a fine camel, known as the *mahmal*. Husain objected to the *mahmal* sent in 1924 and ordered the name of Fu'ad removed from the covering on which it was embroidered. His reason was that putting on the name of the king in this manner was 'an innovation without precedent' and that the covering should be devoid of any 'political symbol or personal emblem'. The Egyptian officer commanding the escort of the *mahmal* protested and made a military demonstration in front of the royal palace in Mecca, and relations between the two countries were severed.[28] Husain seems to have been justified in considering the appearance of Fu'ad's name an innovation, for the custom apparently was, at any rate since Egypt became part of the Ottoman empire, that only the cipher of the Ottoman sultan should appear on the covering;[29] a change of this nature, in these particular circumstances, was significant and Husain could be expected to resist it.

The propaganda in favour of Fu'ad's caliphate went on throughout the year following the declaration of the *ulama* in March 1924. Such propaganda must have been extensive and effective, since we find such an experienced political operator as Zaghlul confessing in 1926 that he was afraid that public opposition to an Egyptian caliphate would harm his electoral prospects.[30] As a specimen of such propaganda we may consider the articles contributed by Shaikh Muhammad Faraj al-Minyawi to the *Review of the General Islamic Congress for the Caliphate in Egypt*. In the first number of the *Review* the shaikh enumerated the advantages of holding the Islamic congress in Egypt.

Egypt [he wrote] has a long history of learning and civilisation. It is a country where peace and tranquillity reign. It was and still is one of the greatest of Islamic states in point of progress, civilisation, riches and prosperity. Further, in some periods Egypt's place in the scale of learning was so high that it became the cynosure of learned and wise men. . . . There is no other Islamic state in the world which has done as much as Egypt in protecting the language of the *Qur'an* and in defending Islamic Law.

Egypt, again, had a central geographical position and was fortunate in possessing the Azhar. From the tone of these eulogies we may conclude that more was involved than the mere venue of a congress. In an article in the following number the shaikh discussed some suggestions, which he claimed had been made in India to the effect that Egypt and India should cover the public expenditure of the Hijaz and defend it against foreign intrigues and attacks. 'It is', said the shaikh, 'as though the Indian people wishes in this way to charge Egypt, as the nearest independent Islamic state, with responsibility for the Hijaz, in point of expenditure and protection. In fact', he continued, 'the kingdom of Egypt has been alone for a long time in providing for the sustenance of the Hijaz, out of the revenue of its pious foundations, and out of the great sums donated to the Hijazis by the occupant of the throne'.[31]

The views which the shaikh so confidently ascribed to the Indian people were somewhat off the mark. For as time went on, it became increasingly clear that Fu'ad's ambitions were arousing opposition. India, in particular, by no means showed enthusiasm for Fu'ad's cause. The Indian Muslim community was shocked and disoriented by the Turkish action; its traditional loyalty went to the Ottoman sultan, as the Khilafat agitation had shown only a year or two before. If the caliphate were now to be made the object of discussion, the Indian Muslims were sure to bring to the fore the claims of Abd al-Majid whom the Turks had so sacrilegiously deposed and expelled. As regards the Arabic-speaking countries, it is true that Husain, who had been proclaimed caliph in March 1924, found himself at the end of the year devoid of kingdom and caliphate, a pensioner of his son Abdullah and then of the British government; but there was no reason to expect that his sons and their following in Iraq and the Levant would joyfully proclaim their allegiance to an Egyptian caliph. Neither was this to be expected from Ibn Sa'ud, the supplanter of the Hashimites in the Hijaz. Whatever his original attitude, by the time he had conquered the Hijaz, Ibn Sa'ud was greatly opposed to Fu'ad's pretensions.[32] Another incident involving the *mahmal* in 1926 and resulting in bloodshed embroiled him with Egypt which, for ten years, until Fu'ad's death, refused to recognise the Sa'udi Arabian kingdom. It is possible that the conquest of the Hijaz inspired Ibn Sa'ud with the ambition to acquire the caliphate, but this is doubtful considering the known unpopularity in the Islamic world of his Wahabi creed. But there was no reason why he should acknowledge Fu'ad as his superior. We have a record of his views in 1931 which cannot have been much different from those he held in 1926. In August of that year, the Syrian notable Adil Arslan informed the American legation in Egypt that Ibn Sa'ud had told him

that he himself had no pretensions to the caliphate and that if he had had there would have been no reason for him not to have declared himself caliph when he proclaimed himself king of the Hejaz, Nejd and its dependencies. . . . On the other hand, he could not be expected to second the aspirations of other claimants, such as King Fu'ad, since the question was one which concerned the Moslem religious world as a whole, rather than any one country and he shared the prevailing opinion held by Moslem religious leaders that the reopening of the question of the caliphate was calculated to breed dissensions in the Moslem world of a character disadvantageous to the interests of Islam.[33]

So much then for Fu'ad's hopes in this quarter of the Islamic world. As for the rest, it was better to leave Turkey out of the reckoning; Persia was schismatic; the Maghrib was on the whole *terra incognita*, and Morocco's ruling dynasty, in particular, claimed Quraishite descent; and Indonesia, as we learn from a letter of Shakib Arslan's, was divided on the issue: some of the Muslims of Java, he wrote to Rashid Rida on the first day of 1925, expected nothing good to come out of the congress in Egypt, some intended to protest against an Egyptian caliphate, and most of them wanted the caliph to be in Mecca.[34] It was no doubt because opposition from so many quarters showed itself, and because they had little hope of overcoming it within the year, that the rector of al-Azhar and his colleagues (who had constituted themselves as the administrative board of the forthcoming Islamic congress) decided in January 1925 that the congress had better be deferred for a further year.[35] In the event, it was not until May 1926 that the congress assembled.

Opposition to Fu'ad showed itself not only outside, but inside Egypt as well. The nature of this opposition is described in a nutshell by Rashid Rida:

Two groups of writers and journalists [he wrote] manifested opposition to and criticism of [the call for a congress]. The first consisted of a number of heretics and atheists . . . the second, of those who believe that the partisans of the congress among the grand *ulama* and others want to establish the caliphate in Egypt. ... The newspapers of the *Wafd* or Sa'dist party are at one with *al-Siyyasa* newspaper [the Liberal Constitutionalist organ] in denouncing the holding of this congress in Egypt, and in denying the competence of the religious dignitaries to call for it; these newspapers are also agreed that the establishment of the caliphate in Egypt would harm, and would not benefit her.[36]

Opposition inside Egypt declared itself almost as soon as the Ottoman caliphate was abolished. In a newspaper article, the publicist Mahmud Azmi, who then had Liberal Constitutionalist leanings, forcefully rejected the idea of proclaiming Fu'ad caliph and declared his disapproval of the article in the Egyptian constitution which established Islam as the official religion of the state.[37] Mahmud Azmi's secularist views may put him in Rashid Rida's first category, namely the heretics and the godless. Opposition which was more clearly political was expressed by Zaghlul and his Wafdist colleagues. It seems that when the question of the caliphate was first mooted, Zaghlul went to Fu'ad and asked him whether he wanted the caliphate. Since it would have been fatal to his hopes to indicate officially that he wanted the caliphate, Fu'ad could not but express his lack of interest, and this no doubt suited Zaghlul, for he was not likely to welcome the great increase in prestige and power which Fu'ad would obtain by becoming caliph, and the king's denial would enable him to use, in seeming good faith, official influence in order to oppose and counteract the activities of the caliphate committees which Fu'ad was secretly supporting; we learn, in fact, that his minister of the interior, Fathallah Barakat, issued orders to his subordinates in the provinces forbidding them to have anything to do with caliphate committees.[38] Government and palace in 1924 were, it is clear, ranged in a secret contest against one another.

Zaghlul seems to have been even prepared to encourage other candidates in order to defeat Fu'ad's ambitions. At the beginning of 1924, when Mustafa Kemal was contemplating the abolition of the Ottoman caliphate, presumably in order to soften the blow inside and outside Turkey, he appears to have offered Turkey's support to Shaikh Ahmad al-Sanusi (d. 1933) if he were to agree to become a 'spiritual' caliph, a Muslim pope, with a seat outside Turkey. The shaikh then refused the offer, but it was renewed a year or so later, when he seems to have become tempted by it. In January 1925 he sent his private secretary to the United States high commissioner in

Constantinople to acquaint him with the new development, and he stated that the shaikh seemed assured of his election as caliph since he had the support of – among others – Ibn Sa'ud, the Imam Yahya, and Zaghlul Pasha, whilst his only opponents were Fu'ad and the ex-king of the Hijaz together with his sons.[39]

The Wafdists were not the only political party opposed to an Egyptian caliphate. The Liberal Constitutionalists were as vehement. Partly because Fu'ad's manoeuvres in internal politics during 1923 had estranged them, partly because they mistrusted his appetite for power, and partly because their intellectual leaders such as Lutfi al-Sayyid and Husain Haikal preached a doctrine of strict constitutionalism, the Liberal Constitutionalists publicly adopted towards the caliphate question the same posture as the *Wafd*. Their organ, *al-Siyyasa*, took its stand on strict constitutional propriety by arguing that since article 47 of the constitution forbade the king to acquire, without parliamentary authority, a plurality of dominions, Fu'ad could not accept the caliphate without the sanction of the Parliament.[40] The consequences of such a view, had it been put to the test, are curious, since it meant that the Egyptian Parliament, a secular, non-denominational body, had ultimate authority to institute – and depose – the caliph of all the Muslims.

But an even more radical view was to emerge from Liberal Constitutionalist ranks. In the early summer of 1925, when speculation about the caliphate was at its highest, Ali Abd al-Raziq, a divine and a judge in the religious courts, the brother of Mahmud Pasha Abd al-Raziq, one of the Liberal Constitutionalist leaders, published his famous tract on *Islam and the Foundations of Authority*,[42] in which he argued that the caliphate was not properly part of Islam, and its institution not therefore a religious duty. The argument is so novel, both theologically and historically, that it could easily and with considerable justification be denounced as a heresy. But in emptying the caliphate of its sacral quality, in approximating it to secular kingship, Ali Abd al-Raziq, it is interesting to note, was following, albeit in a more extreme fashion, the line of thought to be discerned in Maraghi's memorandum of 1915. Maraghi's memorandum, however, was written in support of an Egyptian caliphate, while Ali Abd al-Raziq's tract could not but constitute an attack on Fu'ad's ambitions. One wonders if, under a studiously academic disguise, this was not the real purpose of the book, and that which determined its timing, and also whether there would have been any official outcry if the tract, boldly controversial as it was, had furthered, instead of hindering, the designs of the king. For outcry there was: Ali Abd al-Raziq was summoned before a tribunal of *ulama*, convicted of holding unsound opinions and deprived of his status as a doctor of religion. It seems to have been generally known at the time that political considerations influenced the trial and conviction, and that Fu'ad's ambitions determined the issue. Ali Abd al-Raziq himself, at any rate, after the trial, did not hesitate to attack the propaganda for an Egyptian caliphate which he said was carried out by slaves and people who had no will of their own.[42] Ahmad Shafiq Pasha stated, in the final volume of his *Memoirs*, that one of the reasons of the harsh treatment to which Ali Abd al-Raziq was subjected was 'the appearance of this book at a time when a semi-official committee had been formed in Egypt to inquire into the caliphate and endeavour to realise it [*sic*]'. He and some of his friends drafted a petition to the king asking him to intercede on behalf of Ali Abd al-Raziq; the petition – which was not sent – was to include a reference to the caliphate and a statement to the effect that Egypt deserved the office better than any other Islamic state, and that Ali Abd al-Raziq did not intend by his book to call for a republic.[43]

When *Islam and the Foundations of Authority* appeared, Muhammad Husain Haikal reviewed it favourably in *al-Siyyasa* of which he was the editor. When the *ulama* attacked the book and announced their intention to try its author, *al-Siyyasa* vehemently took up his defence, and denied the competence and authority of the religious doctors to try and condemn the expression of opinion. The first volume of Haikal's *Memoirs*, where the episode is related, appeared in 1951 when Egypt was still a monarchy, and a certain reticence is visible in the author's treatment of these events, but he does hint that the trial took place at the instigation of the royal palace. For he says that the *ulama* derived the power to try and sentence Ali Abd al-Raziq from article 101 of the constitution which left unchanged, until further notice, the laws and regulations governing the administration of religious establishments, thus removing them from the control of Parliament: this provision, he then became convinced, was introduced into the constitution in order to preserve 'the absolute authority of the palace' over the men of religion.[44]

The cause of Ali Abd al-Raziq was thus to some extent publicly identified with the Liberal Constitutionalist cause; it became wholly so as a result of the trial. When the *ulama* sentenced Ali Abd al-Raziq to be deprived of his qualifications as a doctor of religion, they applied to the secular arm to dismiss him from his judicial office. The secular arm in question was the minister of justice, and the minister happened then to be Abd al-Aziz Pasha Fahmi, the president of the Liberal Constitutionalists who, with two other members of his party, had accepted office in a coalition with king's men (who styled themselves the Union party) in a ministry formed by Ziwar Pasha when Zaghlul resigned from office after Sir Lee Stack's murder in 1924. Abd al-Aziz Fahmi now faced an awkward dilemma. Ali Abd al-Raziq's family was one of the pillars of his Party, his cause – the cause of the freedom of expression, and that of the secular state – was one which the Liberal Constitutionalists were ostensibly dedicated to uphold. To give in to the demand of the *ulama* would have constituted for Abd al-Aziz Fahmi a grave breach of his principles, and he happened to be, what is so rare in Egyptian politics, emphatically a man of principle. Yet, there was no doubt that the palace, and the majority of his colleagues, who were obedient to the palace, expected him to dismiss Ali Abd al-Raziq forthwith. He tried to gain time by procrastinating; he formed a committee of civil servants to examine the issue and to report whether the minister was bound by a decision of the *ulama*'s tribunal. But he was urgently pressed to dismiss Ali Abd al-Raziq, and when he still delayed he himself was summarily dismissed and Ali Maher took his place, who deferred to the wishes of the palace. The episode again illustrates the close connection in Egypt under the constitutional monarchy between the internal and external aspect of what Maraghi called 'religious politics' and between so-called religious and so-called secular issues. The publicist al-Aqqad, writing of this incident in 1936, said that the Unionists, i.e. the king's men, wanted on the one hand to punish a man who obstructed the king's efforts to secure the caliphate, and on the other to embarrass the Liberal Constitutionalists and force them to leave the Ministry.[45] Whether or not the second design was as premeditated as the first, the fact remains that the Union party, organised and directed by Hasan Nash'at Pasha from the palace, thought it useful to disseminate a pamphlet containing the text of the judgment against Ali Abd al-Raziq:[46] we may presume that one purpose of such a pamphlet was to tar with the brush of heresy any supporter or defender of shaikh Ali, and since the *Wafd* did not choose to defend him, because this would have been to help their rivals the Liberal Constitutionalists, only the latter party could with a semblance of truth be denounced to the country as the source of heresy and irreligion.

The much-heralded congress to choose the caliph met in Cairo from 13 to 19 May 1926. But the reasons which had led to its postponement in 1925 had not disappeared, had, if anything, intensified. In Egypt itself, opposition to Fu'ad's ambitions appeared even among the men of religion who might have been expected to be quite obedient to royal wishes. Sympathy with Ali Abd el-Raziq in his persecution at the hands of the palace, or Wahabi leanings encouraged by supporters of Ibn Sa'ud in Egypt, may have been the cause. In any case, in January 1926 the government is found busy investigating some forty *ulama* in al-Azhar who had signed a petition to the effect that Egypt was not fit to be the centre of the caliphate. A little later, news transpires of a group calling itself the Group of the Islamic Caliphate (*Jama'at al-khilafa al-islamiyya*), led by a shaikh Muhammad Madi abu'l-'Azayim, agitating for the congress to be held in Mecca not Cairo; and Shaikh abu'l-'Azayim himself is found leading an 'unofficial' delegation to what might be called the anti-congress which met at Mecca immediately after the Cairo congress.[47]

It became therefore clear, even before the congress met, that there could be no question of electing a caliph. At a meeting of the administrative board on 25 April, Maraghi is said to have explained that those attending the congress would have no official representative capacity; this gave rise to a sharp discussion, and some *ulama* asked whether this did not mean that those attending would be merely giving their personal opinions, and whether this was the original purpose of the congress; Maraghi then said that circumstances had changed since the congress was first mooted and that the proclamation of a caliph by the congress was out of the question.[48] In his *Memoirs* Maraghi's rival, Shaikh al-Zawahiri, claims the credit for saving the congress from utter failure. When he found that it was impossible to proclaim Fu'ad caliph, he wrote, he decided that the best way to preserve both Islamic unity and the dignity of Egypt was to wind up the congress and forestall any damaging resolutions; the pretext for this was to be that not all Islamic nations were represented in the congress.[49] Whether or not al-Zawahiri may take credit for it, the remarkable fact remains that the congress, which took two years and two months to assemble, lasted barely a week, and held only four meetings. For, as Ahmad Shafiq Pasha pointed out, the *ulama* who had organised the congress found themselves in a quandary: not only was there no chance of Fu'ad being proclaimed caliph, but also each delegation wished to proclaim caliph the ruler of its country. When the Egyptian *ulama*, he continued,

found themselves members of a body deliberating over something which had no chance of being realised or executed, they had no option but to find a way out of this predicament. Three things were therefore decided, which were not the fruit of research or scrutiny or the result of examination and strict enquiry. Rather were they a bare statement of how the caliphate question at present stood. The delegations said that a caliphate was obligatory! They then pointed out the impossibility at present of establishing it among the Muslims! Finally they decided to found branches of the congress in different Islamic countries so as to prepare further successive congresses, as need be, in order to decide the issue of the caliphate! In all this there was nothing new: it was all a means whereby the honourable body might find a way out of the narrow *impasse* into which it had led itself.[50]

The deliberations of this congress[51] in which were brought together the highest religious authorities of Islam were thus from the outset distorted and denatured by the desire to avoid the consequences of a political miscalculation, and their conclusions cannot be taken to mean what, at first sight, they seem to mean. Only a laborious effort of exploration and reconstruction can restore their original political significance to these seemingly authoritative declarations, and these ostensibly academic disquisitions. Documents such as the record of the Cairo congress, or Ali Abd al-Raziq's tract arouse – and rightly so – great interest among students of contemporary Islam, and owing to the paucity and unreliability of other historical material the importance of such documents is sometimes exaggerated and their significance misunderstood. A warning is perhaps useful that just as tracts produced in the course of religious strife in early and medieval Islam may not be taken at their face value, so also may not be taken on trust much of the political and social thought of modern Islam. In fact, here, much more than in Europe, the history of ideas is an unusually treacherous and demanding discipline. The least of the difficulties besetting the student is that so many of these writings are derivative, and to establish the exact derivation and the precise channel of communication is not always easy. But an even graver difficulty is that the exact purpose and significance of a piece of writing may be expertly disguised and may not be discovered without extensive and minute knowledge of political transactions. So far from these productions providing a clue to the real state of mind of a particular individual or a particular society – which is the usual assumption underlying so many histories of modern Islamic thought – they themselves have to be painfully deciphered, and the key is usually nothing grandiose like the fate of Islam or the nature of Arabism, but only obscure intrigues and tenebrous ambitions. An excellent case in point is that of Abd al-Rahman al-Kawakibi and his writings. It has been shown that the two books he wrote *Tabai' al-Istibdad* and *Umm al-Qura*, stand heavily indebted to the writings respectively of the Italian Alfieri and of the Englishman Blunt. It has also been shown that *Umm al-Qura*, with its advocacy of an Arabian caliphate, may well have been a piece of khedivial propaganda, destined to further the ambitions of Abbas II in Arabia and the Levant.[52] We now learn that Kawakibi's political activities are even more equivocal than hitherto suspected. In a letter to George Antonius, who was gathering material for his *Arab Awakening*, Rashid Rida wrote that Kawakibi visited Somaliland 'in agreement *'bi'l ittifaq*) with Italy'. The inference that he was an Italian agent, as well as a khedivial one, seems strong, and that *Tabai' al-Istibdad* is a crib from an Italian author becomes a suggestive and significant fact. Our suspicions seem even more cogent and well-founded when we notice that Rashid Rida is very reluctant to put down in writing all that he knows of Kawakibi, for he ends his letter to Antonius by promising to give more information by word of mouth 'since not everything which is known can be spoken of, and not everything which is spoken can be written'.[53]

The fiasco of the Cairo congress removed the caliphate for a few years from the forefront of politics. The question was raised again in 1931, but it was not Fu'ad who contrived to raise it. He merely suspected that others were scheming to get hold of the coveted office: the sharpness of his reaction to such a threat – whether imaginary or not – indicates clearly enough that he was still prey to the same ambition. Following the Palestine disturbances of 1929, the mufti of Jerusalem, Hajj Muhammad Amin al-Husaini, sought to consolidate and systematically organise the widespread sympathy for the Palestine Arab cause which these events aroused in the Islamic world. As much to strengthen the Arabs in their fight against the Zionists as to enhance his own prestige and deal a powerful blow to his then uncowed Arab rivals, the mufti in October 1931 called for and began to organise an Islamic congress, to take place at Jerusalem towards the end of the year. The Egyptian government soon showed itself very hostile to this project. The mufti had announced that the congress was to consider, among other subjects, the possibility of setting up a Muslim university in Jerusalem. The Egyptian authorities took this as a threat to the primacy of al-Azhar and were not pleased. But what seems to have really agitated Fu'ad and his government was the rumour that the caliphate was to be discussed and a caliph possibly proclaimed.[54] The king seems to have taken these rumours seriously enough to invoke Italian help should the caliphate question be raised. In August 1931 Adil Arslan was telling the United States minister that Italy supported Fu'ad's claim to the caliphate,[55] while a few months later the minister himself wrote that the Italian legation had great influence with the king because Fu'ad hoped for Italian support in improving his international position and advancing his claim to the caliphate.[56] But it seems that on this occasion the king was concerned not so much to fill the office himself as to prevent others from filling it. The official Azhar Journal, *Nur al-Islam*, which may be taken to mirror palace views, published in the second half of 1931 a warning that it was not to the interest of Muslims that the question should be raised: the Cairo congress of 1926 had decided that the time was not then ripe and this was still the case. Two months later, *Nur al-Islam* returned to the charge in a more specific manner. The Indian Muslim leader, Shawkat Ali, had made a statement to the effect that the Jerusalem congress would have no reason to discuss the caliphate, since there was still a caliph living, namely Abd al-Majid, who had been expelled from Turkey and was now in Europe. *Nur al-Islam* declared that Shawkat Ali's allegation was not correct, since an assembly of *ulama* meeting in Cairo in 1924 had decided that Muslims owed no allegiance to the deposed Ottoman caliph; and to clinch its point, the journal reprinted verbatim the original statement which had served, seven years before, by calling for a congress in Cairo, to give notice of Fu'ad's claim to the caliphate.[57] One particular circumstance may have made Fu'ad especially sensitive to this renewed talk of a caliphate. The ex-khedive Abbas Hilmi was then said to be canvassing support for his candidature to a Lebanese or a Syrian throne. To further his own scheme, Abbas Hilmi might be expected to work against Fu'ad's oecumenical ambitions. Abbas Hilmi's activities were thus doubly unpleasant, and one of the aims of Sidqi Pasha, then Egyptian prime minister, in visiting the Levant shortly after the Jerusalem congress was, according to the United States minister in Cairo, to counteract and undo the ex-khedive's machinations.[58] Egyptian hostility to the congress was not in doubt. Religious dignitaries publicly attacked it[59] and official displeasure with anybody taking part in it was manifest. The Egyptian consul in Jerusalem informed Cairo that he was refusing the invitation to attend the inaugural session of the congress lest he should be taken to be officially representing his government at the function.[60] The issues involved become even clearer when we learn that Ali Al-Raziq took up his pen to attack the Azhari shaikhs who were attacking the Jerusalem congress, and that Nahhas, the leader of the *Wafd* which was on very bad terms with Fu'ad, designed to go to the congress in person; in the event, it was Abd al-Rahman Azzam, then a Wafdist, who was sent. His presence there was manifestly taken to be a demonstration against Fu'ad, and a speech of his at the inaugural session was followed by protests from some pro-Fu'ad Egyptians: a disturbance of some twenty minutes followed, and the police had to intervene.[61] The Palestine Arab opponents of the mufti took heart, and Hajj Amin, fearing for the success of his venture, had to visit Cairo in November and assure Sidqi Pasha, both verbally and in writing, that the caliphate would not be discussed at the congress.[62] After the congress, and until Fu'ad's death in 1936, the caliphate question remained dormant. But there was no question of the king giving up his claim or allowing any other claim to be entertained. In August 1933 a French newspaper suggested that the sultan of Morocco should be made caliph. The Moslem Caliphate Society in Cairo thereupon called a meeting to discuss this suggestion and drew up a manifesto pointing out that nobody in the Muslim world possessed the qualifications necessary for the office. The significance of this move, commented the United States chargé d'affaires, arose from the well-known ambition of King Fu'ad in respect of the caliphate.[63] A few weeks later, the chargé d'affaires had to report that the rector of al-Azhar, shaikh al-Zawahiri, had issued an appeal to the Muslims to avoid missionary schools; such an appeal might be considered likely to disturb the public peace, by inciting one section of the population against another, and yet the government took no action in the matter. This, the chargé d'affaires, again commented, was attributable to the influence of the king who desired to capitalise on the antimissionary agitation (which was just then loud and widespread) in order to promote his pretensions to the caliphate.[64]

A variety of circumstances contributed in 1935 to a great decline in Fu'ad's position within Egypt; a decline which the natural play of rivalry between Egyptian politicians would no doubt have soon reversed. But the king's health was failing and he died in April 1936. The prime minister who was in office during the last months of his reign was Ali Mahir who had been, in the past decade of Egyptian politics, a king's man. But the king's weakening grip over the government no doubt enabled him to follow, to some extent, a personal policy. He seems to have decided that the caliphate was dead, and that the question was not worth continuing estrangement from Ibn Sa'ud.[65] He opened negotiations with Sa'udi Arabia, which speedily issued in a Treaty of Friendship. Article one of the treaty is an eloquent commentary on the previous state of Sa'udi–Egyptian relations, for this article read: 'The Egyptian Government recognises that the kingdom of Sa'udi Arabia is a free and sovereign state, enjoying complete and absolute independence'. A contemporary comment by H. St John Philby, who was in Ibn Sa'ud's counsels, is noteworthy. 'It is a mere coincidence, of course', he wrote from Ibn Sa'ud's camp, 'that the treaty had, for all practical purposes, been negotiated and signed within a week of King Fu'ad's death. But it is for all that an interesting coincidence, for it is a matter of common knowledge that the late king of Egypt had decided views and certain ambitions in respect of Arabia'. 'Aly Maher Pasha', he continued, 'has achieved success where his predecessors have failed and he deserves the warmest congratulations of all who have the Arab cause in its widest connotation at heart'.[66] Later events have made it a moot point whether both parties – and their neighbours – would not have reaped greater benefits from Ali Mahir's failure than they did from his success.

One of those whom Philby praised for helping to negotiate the Sa'udi–Egyptian treaty was the rector of al-Azhar, Maraghi.[67] Maraghi, as has been seen, was shortly afterwards appointed tutor to King Faruq and established close personal relations with the palace.

From the start of his reign Faruq manifested certain leanings which made Maraghi his natural ally. When his minority ended and he assumed full powers, Faruq found in office a Wafdist cabinet determined to seize this golden opportunity of a young inexperienced king just ascending the throne to eliminate once and for all the royal factor in Egyptian politics, and to make henceforward impossible the kind of *coup d'état* by which twice during his reign, in 1928 and in 1930, Fu'ad dismissed a Wafdist government with a large parliamentary majority, and unjustly robbed the Wafdist politicians of the fruits of office. But the Wafdists reckoned without the shrewdness of Faruq and his advisers. For it soon became apparent that the king designed to exploit his youth and good looks, and the hopes aroused by his accession, to create for himself a popular following with which to dispute the Wafd's hold on the country. When the ceremonies of his accession were discussed, the king proposed that he should be crowned and that, since the ceremony of coronation was hitherto unknown to Egypt – and to Islam – the crown should be bought with the proceeds of a public subscription. He also proposed, in imitation of imperial Ottoman practice, that the rector of al-Azhar should gird him with the sword of his ancestor, Muhammad Ali. Finally, Faruq proposed that he should go to pray at Al-Azhar on the Friday following the ceremony of his accession. To all these proposals the prime minister, Nahhas Pasha, declared himself opposed and Faruq had to abandon them.[68] But, as is well known, in his conflict with the king, Nahhas was discomfited; he was dismissed from office, the Wafdist parliament dissolved, and Muhammad Mahmud, Maraghi's friend, installed in office. It was between 1937 and the *coup d'état* of February 1942, when the *Wafd* returned to office, that Maraghi was at the height of his power and influence. One of the means which the king and his ministers adopted in order to discredit the *Wafd* was to accuse it of being under the control of the Copts, and to allege that Nahhas, the nominal leader, was a mere puppet in the hand of his Coptic follower, Makram 'Ubaid. As an example of this anti-Coptic campaign we may take the rumours circulated in Cairo to the effect that it was Markam 'Ubaid and the Coptic element who had opposed the coronation ceremony and that Makram was against Faruq being proclaimed caliph.[69] In this anti-Coptic campaign Maraghi and the Azhar students seem to have played some part. In a radio broadcast in February 1938 Maraghi denounced the Copts as 'foxes' and declared that for Muslims to befriend them was to oppose God's law[70]. In a dispatch of 17 March, the United States minister in Cairo reported on three newspaper interviews given by the rector to the effect that Muslims should participate in Egyptian politics on a religious basis and that the entire social life of Egypt should be conducted in the light of Islamic teachings. The minister commented that these pronouncements were believed to be an attack on the Wafd and on Makram's dominant position in the Party: this was the general opinion in the country. This attack on the alleged 'Coptism' of the *Wafd* had its evident uses at a time when elections to replace the

Wafdist parliament were impending; the dispatch reported that Muhammad Husain Haikal, then minister without portfolio whose work at the ministry of the interior was connected with the electoral strategy of the government,[71] had said to journalists (his words not being intended for publication) that Maraghi was being used for political purposes, and that nothing further would be heard from the shaikh after the elections. Haikal's statement was presumably designed to allay fears of a general systematic attack on Christianity and Christian missionaries; such was also the purpose of the heir apparent, Prince Muhammad Ali, when he insisted, as the dispatch reported, that the rector's declarations were in reality anti-Coptic rather than anti-missionary. This attack on the Copts must have helped to increase tension, and worsen relations between Muslims and Copts, for the dispatch records the receipt by the legation of a letter from a copt at Damanhur complaining that Christianity was publicly defamed by a Muslim and that he himself had been summoned to the police station where the official candidate had made threats against him. The dispatch enclosed a newspaper report to the effect that Azhar students went through the streets of Shubra in a demonstration shouting: 'To Palestine with the Copts', and that a lawsuit was being instituted at Abu Tig against a Copt for having, allegedly, thrown a Quran on the ground and having said improper things about the rector of al-Azhar.[72]

But it would be a mistake to regard Maraghi's declarations as mere attacks on the Copts. They asserted also, in an extreme and uncompromising manner, the primacy of Islam in Egyptian politics. In an interview with the newspaper *al-Balagh* Maraghi stated that he did not engage in party politics, but that Islam was bound up with every facet of life. 'Neither the Koran, nor the traditions nor our theology', he said, 'can be understood without a knowledge of the politics of the nations and the history of their social lives'. 'No Moslem', he continued, 'can say that he does not engage in politics. Were he to say so, he would be ignorant of his religion. How could he make such a sweeping statement', he asked, 'since his religion has laid down the principles governing peace and war, treaties and alliances? It is indeed stipulated that the mufti should be aware of the events of his day'. The rector denied that he was engaging in anti-Coptic propaganda, but he did not hide his wish to see Egypt ruled by the dogmas and the ethics of Islam: 'I will even go a step further and say that I personally wish to see Islam rule over the social life of Egypt, because the great majority of the inhabitants of this country are Moslems, and because the official religion of Egypt is Islam and nothing else'. The rector disclaimed working for any particular party, 'but I do engage in religious politics and the politics of Islam. I do so as much for the interior as for the exterior of the country'. In another interview, with *La Bourse Egyptienne*, Maraghi added that he would like to see Islamic jurisprudence adopted in Egyptian legislation.[73] In a later dispatch, the United States minister reported that Maraghi had been giving a series of interviews in which he said that it was desirable for Muslims to participate in Egyptian politics on a religious basis.[74]

On his own admission then, Maraghi was a political divine who considered it his duty to engage in 'religious politics and the politics of Islam' both inside and outside Egypt. But what, in the context of Egyptian politics at that time, did such assertions mean? The answer is suggested in a passage of an address which the rector broadcast in February 1938 on the occasion of the Islamic festival of '*id al-adha*, which that year coincided with the birthday anniversary of King Faruq. The broadcast as a whole was a defence of Islam, an exhortation to Muslims to cherish their faith, and an attack on the 'cunning' Christian missionaries who were subverting the beliefs of the Muslims. But the rector began his broadcast by a reference to Faruq. 'The union of two holidays after His Majesty has become the ruler of the country', he said, 'is a sign that Faruq's birthday is an Islamic holiday as well as a national festival for all Egyptians whatever their different religions and creeds'. 'The Holy Azhar, professors and students', he continued, 'present their loyal and sincere congratulations upon the two events to His Majesty King Faruq. May God grant him a long and prosperous life for humanity in general and for the Islamic religion in particular'. The reference to Faruq's birthday being an Islamic holiday is curious. Birthday celebrations, in respect of living persons at any rate, are unknown to Islam. Traditional Islam, like traditional Judaism, in the words of *Ecclesiastes*, VII: 1, holds 'the day of death better than the day of one's birth'. Birthdays of Muslims are notoriously difficult to trace, and if the anniversary of the Prophet's birthday is commemorated by a festival, we must also remember that this day is also the anniversary of his death.[75] The celebration of a Muslim's birthday is clearly a modern western importation, and if a Shaikh of al-Azhar chose to describe the occasion as an Islamic holiday, we must conclude that this was nothing but a political act designed to enhance Faruq's position and his popularity. And this chimed in with the policy which the king and his palace advisers were then pursuing, namely to present Faruq as an Islamic as well as an Egyptian sovereign. All devices would be useful, whatever their provenance, provided they served to surround the king with reverence and raise his position far above that of any politician, however powerful. Hence the simultaneous demand for Faruq to be crowned and to be girded with his ancestor's sword; hence the attempt to invest his birthday with a spurious Islamic aura. Reporting on Maraghi's broadcast, the United States minister commented that Maraghi's words had weight, as coming from the rector of al-Azhar and by reason of the king's interest in Islam. The king's strict observance of ritual, he went on to say, brought the influence of al-Azhar to bear on his side in the recent conflict with the *Wafd*. The prestige of al-Azhar, the minister further said, mounted with that of the king, to whose hold on the people Al-Azhar had contributed to an important degree, and it was, in his opinion, to be expected that Muslim religious authorities should thenceforth have something to say on public affairs in Egypt.[76] 'Religious politics' then, in Maraghi's eyes, meant in effect support by al-Azhar for Faruq, in his attempt to establish his autocracy in Egypt. Other episodes confirm such a view. After France's defeat in the summer of 1940, Faruq became quite reluctant to do anything which might alienate German and Italian sympathies. This meant at the very least that the letter of the Anglo-Egyptian Treaty of Alliance, signed only four years before, should be whittled and its spirit denied. In furtherance of this policy, Maraghi in the autumn of 1940 preached a sermon in the Rifa'i mosque saying that the war was no concern of Egypt, and that she should not therefore be exposed to dangers such as air raids, which the presence of foreign troops created.[77] When Nahhas became prime minister in February 1942, agitation against Maraghi was organised in al-Azhar and Nahhas demanded his resignation, but Faruq supported Maraghi, who remained rector but ceased to attend al-Azhar for some ten months.[78] As the tide of war in the middle east receded, the king's and Maraghi's ability to oppose Nahhas became stronger, and in the autumn of 1943 and the winter of 1944 there were reports of Azhar students being aroused against the Wafdist government on a variety of pretexts, relating both to politics and to their stipends and employment prospects.[79] His biographer, quoting the unpublished memoirs of his son, Abu'l Wafa, says that a sustained attack against Maraghi was launched then by eminent writers and that he was denounced to the British ambassador.[80] But Nahhas was dismissed in October 1944 and Maraghi died in office on 21 August 1945. His successor was Mustafa Abd al-Raziq, member of the well-known Liberal Constitutionalist family, and himself an eminent member of the party. His appointment was the occasion of a show of that royal wilfulness and arbitrariness which the Liberal Constitutionalists – with whom Maraghi, as has been seen, was at the outset connected – were dedicated to combat, and again exhibits, as does Maraghi's career, the fluidity of political loyalties in Egypt. Mustafa Abd al-Raziq was not a member of the 'Areopagus of the Grand Ulema' among whom the rector had, by law, to be chosen. The king wished him, nevertheless, to be rector: a change in the law, purely *ad personam* in character, was immediately effected, and Mustafa Abd al-Raziq became rector.[81]

Maraghi, as has been seen, insisted that the 'religious politics' in which he engaged related to the exterior as well as to the interior of Egypt. Nor was there any doubt as to what he meant, for at that time he was also making public declarations expressing his scepticism towards projects of Arab unity, and exhorting the Muslims to strive for greater mutual understanding and closer union.[82] But as in the case of Egyptian politics proper, such declarations were more than general academic exercises; they must be seen in the context of a specific political ambition which the king, Maraghi's patron and pupil, nursed at the time; the ambition, namely, to obtain the caliphate for Egypt and himself. At this distance of time the ambition seems to us anachronistic, overtaken and made futile by the rise of new interests and attitudes in the Islamic world. But Maraghi had grown to manhood when the sultan-caliph still reigned in Istanbul; both he and the king were very close, through direct personal involvement or through family tradition, to the events and discussions which followed the Turkish abolition of the caliphate in 1924; and they clearly regarded the office as a great prize worth striving for. We do not know whether it was Maraghi who inspired the king with this ambition, or whether it was Faruq himself who decided to take up a line of policy traditional in his house, and required Maraghi to further it through his office and influence. Maraghi, in any case, no longer depended on the patronage of others and as rector could use his prestige to establish and extend the new king's authority. He was now a power on his own, and no doubt reasoned that 'religious politics' would be profitable to the religion, to the monarchy, and to himself. He believed, as we know, that politics and society in Egypt should be ruled by Islamic principles, and the caliphate was an essential aspect of Islam. So that notwithstanding his role in settling the caliphate issue with Ibn Sa'ud, Maraghi now worked to obtain for Faruq what in his own youth and middle age he had considered the highest office which a Muslim could attain. Rumours began to abound that Faruq was soon to be proclaimed caliph, and that Maraghi had invited Muslim notabilities to Cairo to discuss the matter. An Egyptian journalist questioned Maraghi about these rumours, and he denied them; but when the journalist asked whether this denial meant that the caliphate question would not be raised again, Maraghi said: 'No, this is another matter and depends on circumstances and what God decrees'.[83] Some three months later, it transpired that Maraghi was indeed thinking of a general Muslim assembly in Cairo; it would be a 'legislative assembly' and would examine and reinterpret the Muslim principles of private and public life.[84] The purposes to which such a 'legislative assembly' could be put are obvious. Maraghi and the palace seem to have worked to good purpose, for in the autumn of 1938 there assembled in Cairo an 'Arab and Muslim Interparliamentary congress for Palestine' – the conjunction of the epithets, Arab and Muslim, indicating well the reach of Egyptian ambition in those days – at which there was, so the United States chargé d'affaires reported, a disposition among certain of the delegates to proclaim Faruq as caliph. Cooler heads, the chargé d'affaires added, induced these to desist on the ground that the congress had been called for another purpose and that it would be best to consider the caliphate on some later occasion.[85] The congress was nonetheless made the pretext of demonstrations in favour of Faruq's caliphate. The reading of the delegates' names at the opening session ended with shouts, 'Long Live the King of Egypt Faruq I, Commander of the Faithful'. Again, in January 1939, when the Arab delegates, assembled in Cairo before proceeding to the Palestine Round Table Conference in London, accompanied the king to the mosque one Friday, the royal *entourage* prevented the imam from officiating as usual, and Faruq himself led the congregation in prayer as was the prerogative of a caliph.[86] It is significant that the Sa'udis, who had so recently thought to bury the caliphate issue, were absent from the congress. In the months following the congress propaganda for Faruq's caliphate must have continued, or even perhaps intensified. In his *Memoirs* Muhammad Husain Haikal records a conversation he had with the assistant chief of the royal cabinet, Kamil al-Bindari, who was deputising for his chief, Ali Mahir, then representing Egypt at the Round Table Conference on Palestine which took place in London in February–March 1939. At that time, Husain Haikal writes, certain notions relating to the restoration of Islamic form of government, to which Ali Maher was sympathetic, but which he had taken care not to have attributed directly to the palace, began to be propagated more than ever, and the palace was no longer reluctant to have them ascribed to it. In the course of their conversation, Husain Haikal and Bindari came to discuss this Islamic form of government:

I said to him then: 'But some of the principles of the Egyptian constitution are quite different from those of such a government'. He answered: 'No, the Egyptian constitution confirms and supports the Islamic form of government'. I said: 'How can this be, when one of the principles of the Egyptian constitution is freedom of belief? When the constitution allows a Christian to change his religion to Islam or some other creed, and the Muslim to change his to Christianity or any other creed – whilst the Islamic form of government requires the apostate from Islam to be punished with death? Further, does not the Egyptian constitution stipulate that Egypt is a hereditary kingdom, and that the family of Muhammad Ali is the ruling dynasty, whilst the Islamic caliphate is elective to the point that a ruling caliph could obtain the election of his son after his own death, and yet the doctors of religion could then say that such an election was unlawful? Again, how can this be, when the Egyptian constitution stipulates that treaties to which Egypt is a party have to be observed, and the Pact of Montreux of 1937 [which abolished the Capitulations], in order to prevent discrimination against foreigners, requires Egyptian legislation to conform to principles obtaining among the western signatories, and not all of these principles agree with those of Islam?' Al-Bindari Pasha answered me: 'All these are details which can be adjusted to the Islamic form of government; there is nothing in them which will make adjustment impossible'.[87]

The outbreak of war in August 1939 perforce arrested all these endeavours. They were the last occasion on which it proved possible, in the exceptional period stretching from 1882 to 1952, for the man of religion, if like Maraghi he had a measure of ability and personality, to manifest some independence and aspire to be not entirely subservient to the man of the sword; for the impression is strong that in his speeches, declarations and activities, Maraghi was not the mere agent of the king but was behaving as the head of an important interest in the country, who had to be pleased and conciliated, whose opposition could be formidable and whose support had to be bargained for. Very soon after Maraghi's death, the usual primacy of the sword, and the usual subservience of the pen came, once more, speedily to be the rule.

In any case, in May 1941, when Mr Eden announced British support for an Arab union, new prospects beguiled the king of Egypt, and he came to give his support to the scheme of an Arab League. In trying to make Egypt the champion of pan-Arabism Faruq was seeking to gain the same primacy which eluded him and his father in their dogged pursuit of the caliphate; and the very length and pertinacity of this earlier pursuit illuminates and makes more intelligible the later vicissitudes of Arab League politics. A document exists which sheds some light on Faruq's change of policy. Fu'ad Abaza formed in Cairo in 1942, most probably under official inspiration, a society called the Arab Union, and presented a memorandum to the king arguing the case for Arab unity. When the king received him in audience, he asked to be forgiven for having declared, in the memorandum, that the caliphate question bristled with difficulty and that it was better to cease discussing it. It was known, said Abaza, that the question had been raised during Fu'ad's reign, and there were rumours that this and Egyptian ambitions in the Hijaz had created a misunderstanding with Ibn Sa'ud. In view of all this, Abaza wondered whether he had done right in criticising a scheme which was universally known to have the backing of the palace; but Faruq said, according to Abaza: 'My late father studied fully the caliphate question and wrote in a memorandum shortly before his death that he had given up thinking of it'. Faruq added that Ibn Sa'ud was to be informed of this, so that the misunderstanding might be finally removed.[88] But the ambition of an Egyptian caliphate died a most reluctant death. In the midst of the deliberations on the scheme of Arab unity an echo of the old propaganda was still to be heard. Cairo Radio broadcasting to the middle east at the end of 1943, reported that during the celebrations of the Muslim new year, the crowds in Cairo cheered Faruq with cries of 'Long live the Commander of the Faithful' and 'Long live the Caliph'.[89] And even after the formation of the Arab League, in which Egypt was acknowledged by the other members to have the primacy, Faruq still showed a hankering for the office. In the spring of 1952, Faruq is said to have instigated Shaikh Makhluf, the shaikh of al-Azhar to issue a *fatwa* attacking the then foreign minister of Pakistan, Zafrullah Khan, for being an Ahmadi, lest silence over this sect – which was then being violently attacked by the *ulama* in Pakistan – might endanger the prospects of his caliphate.[90] At about the same time a committee was got up in the palace, which conducted researches and found that Faruq was actually a descendant of the Prophet! This was as late as May 1952. The principal authority for this statement must have been one particular member of the committee, namely Shaikh al-Biblawi, *naqib al-ashraf* of Egypt, the head, that is, of the corporation of the descendants of the Prophet in that country, one of whose traditional responsibilities was to possess a good knowledge of genealogical matters, to keep a register of descendants from the Prophet's tribe, and to examine the validity of alleged Quraishite genealogies.[91] This complaisant genealogist was assisted in his labours by two court officials and for public relations aspects by Karim Thabit, the journalist of Syrian Christian origins, whom Faruq took up and made his press adviser.[92] In this curious committee the venerable caliphate suffered its last agony, and expired hanging from a fake genealogical tree.

Appendix

Maraghi's Letter to Wingate

To his Excellency General Sir Reginald Wingate, Governor General of the Sudan.

I have the honour to submit to your Excellency the following remarks.

In the Arabic columns of the *Sudan Times* I read the translation of an article published by *The Times* newspaper on 24th April. In this article I read the following clause.

> We may now be able to say that the actual situation of the khalifate is both strange and peculiar. The ruling in this question is that the khalifa should belong to the tribe of the Prophet, i.e. the "Koreish". It is evident that the present sultans of Turkey are not in a position to claim this honour. They have, however, three reasons for the maintenance of the title. Firstly because they gained the title from the last Abbaside khalifa who lived in Cairo in the year 1517. Secondly because the sultan of Turkey is the guardian of the holy relics of the Prophet, i.e. his mantle and hairs of his beard. Thirdly, because the sultan of Turkey is the acknowledged ruler and defender of the holy places. A fourth reason may be added to this, namely that the sultan of Turkey is acknowledged as the khalifa of the Moslems because he is considered as the greatest living Mohammedan.

This is the clause which has induced me to write this explanation to you, because it is my greatest desire that the true facts of the case should be fully known to you, as I am well aware that your Excellency is always keen to know the truth and especially the sound views regarding the question of the khalifate.

The condition that the khalifs should belong to the tribe of Koreish has been maintained and supported by a party of 'Sunnites' called 'El Masha'ara' and by members of another party called 'El Mutazila'. The reason for the appearance of this condition (which seems to be inconsistent with the general spirit of the religion) is due to the following facts.

When the 'Sahaba' (friends of the Prophet) had a certain disagreement among them on the day of the 'sakifa'* after the death of the Prophet

---

* This is a well known historical event when all the friends and followers of the Prophet collected under the roof of el-Sakifa which means a thatched enclosure.

APPENDIX

the 'Ansar' told the 'Muhajirin' that an emir from each party will have to be chosen alternatively. To this Abu Bakr retorted that the idea was absurd, that the emir must be chosen from the tribe of 'Koreish'. In support of his statement, he repeated the Hadith of the Prophet, 'The imams must be from Koreish'. This brought their dispute to an end at once and the people offered their allegiance (baia) to Abu Bakr and acknowledged him as khalifa. No objection was raised as to the truthfulness or genuineness of this 'Hadith' and hence it was considered that their agreement was a sufficient proof that the khalifa must be a 'Kurashi'.

To counterbalance this opinion, there are also other opinions which have been expressed by several other Mohammedan parties, who do not consider that this should be conditional in the choice of the khalifa. It should not be forgotten that the universal acknowledgment of all Mohammedans throughout the world to the sultans of Turkey as khalifs is a sufficient proof that they respect the latter opinion, i.e. that it is not necessary for the khalifa to be a Kurashi.

This idea has been always supported by free thinkers among the Mohammedan *ulema* in all times. Besides its being logical it agrees with the fundamental teachings of Islam. It is very true that a qualified 'Kurashi' who answers all the other conditions, if found, should have the precedence to any other.

In order to prove that the mere choice of a 'Kurashi' was not in any way obligatory from a purely religious point of view, according to the great *ulema* of the faith, it may be permitted to mention a simple fact which would explain the case.

The majority of *ulema* are unanimously agreed that the rulings of the Mohammedan law are based on certain principles which make it always in agreement with the interests of the general well-being. Only matters affecting the conduct of worship are accepted as obligatory in the form they were enacted and elicit no trial and enquiry. Of these I may quote as an example the number of Kneelings that are necessary in prayers.

In the question of the khalifate there is nothing which should be included under this item, i.e. questions of worship. On the contrary the question of the khalifate is a purely worldly one and has certain connections and relations with religion. The khalifa is in all respects a king who exercises over his subjects certain powers he derives from the Holy Books. Other kings govern their subjects by laws enacted by productive brains.

Hence it may be obvious to discuss the reasons and the motives which caused the Prophet to make such restrictions about the khalifate in his 'Hadith'.

In answer to this I may say the following.

It is well known that the Arabs in the old times never had any form of government or political methods such as exist in these days. Their system

209

of government before the appearance of Islam was very peculiar and far from organisation and unity. Islam has established unity and cohesion among the various independent tribes of Arabs, who had different tribal habits, customs and traditions. It is evident that the spirit of faith alone, if not supported with sufficient power, is insufficient to ensure continued peace and tranquillity among people because the ambitions and interests of men are so different that it is not possible that religion alone could have sufficient control over them.

Religion must be supported by temporal power to ensure that its teachings are adhered to and carried out.

In those days no other Arab tribe was in a position to contest or compete with the tribe of Koreish with regard to its moral and dignified tribal position. This was the reason why the Prophet intimated that the khalifa should be from the Koreish. Besides it was considered at that time that it would be detrimental to the interests of the Arabs and the sacred cause of religion to allow the election of the khalifa to be universal and general. He was afraid that this will lead to disagreement and dissension among the Arab tribes. Under the circumstances it was exceedingly wise to confirm the khalifate in the tribe of Koreish which was then the leading and most enlightened tribe among the Arabs.

It is evident that things which depended on the special conditions and reasons obtaining at one time will only remain and continue to exist as long as these conditions and reasons existed, and will be discontinued when they vanish away.

At a certain time the Arabs became scattered and the unity of the khalifa was dissolved. At this time the Persians and others appeared on the stage of power and organisation while the Kurashis had nothing beyond the honour of the name which was devoid of the original meaning and sense.

If the Mohammedans insist on the title (Koreish), they would be showing a dangerously poor knowledge of the true principles of religion. This would mean that they depend on meaningless words. The bitter experience they had in the past and the severe lessons they can recall from their national history could prove to them that their disunion and rigid adherence to the letter of religion is dangerous and that the time has come for them to wake from their lethargy and to start to explain religious matters in a manner that agrees with logic and sound reasoning.

These are the reasons which induced many of the religious *ulema* now and in the past to say that the condition of the khalifa being a member of Koreish was not necessary.

This is not the only point which supplied a reason for discord among the Muslims, but there were many other matters which caused hot literary contests among *ulema*, and even much fighting and bloodshed. I am sure if these people could be brought back to existence in this country, they would no doubt feel ashamed of the difference and friction they created in their time.

We are now in face of events which will be recorded in history and justly decided. This is why I have chosen to give you my opinion on the matter, so that you may be able to know that the appropriation by the sultans of Turkey of the title of khalifa is in no way contrary to the principles of the faith, although they are not from the tribe of Koreish. It may, however, be admitted that some of the Ottoman khalifas might have held the title unlawfully for some other reasons which I will not endeavour at present to explain.

In this connection, I must not omit to state that my object and the only motive in writing this explanation is simply to defend an historical and religious principle. I am far from trying to defend the sultans of the Ottoman empire and proving that it is wrong and illegal to break down their khalifate. This is a totally different matter and has absolutely nothing to do with the question I am discussing now. I am simply explaining as I said before an historical and religious question.

The Mohammedans are free to measure the value of the Ottoman khalifate by the actual benefit they have obtained from its rule and the religious success they made. I am positive that things are judged by their good results. If the Mohammedans consider, as I am inclined to hold, that their faith has reaped no good from the Ottoman khalifate, they are evidently the best judges as to whether the Ottoman khalifate should be changed or not. They can very easily find an example in the deposition by the Turks of Sultan Abd-ul-Hamid and the appointment of his successor. Their reason in the step they have taken was that the country made no progress in the time of Abd-ul-Hamid. The Mohammedans can now decide on the situation from the actual conditions of the empire under the new khalifa.

It is most useful to probe this question and explain it fully and lay it before the British public opinion and the competent authorities of the British government. It is equally very beneficial to the Moslems in the presence of these great events which might result in the complete overthrow of several thrones. If the question of the choice of khalifa could be discussed and determined, it would be most important that this is opportunely declared.

The reasons mentioned by *The Times* are not correct with the exception of the fourth reason, which should depend on the agreement and acceptance of the Moslems. Such an acceptance is considered to be in a certain sense a sort of 'Bai'a' from the public in addition to the approval of special people which had to be taken on certain occasions by the sultans of Turkey. On such occasions the 'Bai'a' was taken from high personages in the kingdom and people of authority.

The possession of the holy relics, such as the mantle of the Prophet and a few hairs of his beard and the maintenance of the holy places, are not considered by the Moslem *ulema* to be a strong reason. Besides, it is not easy to believe the story about the mantle of the Prophet or the hairs of his beard.

The difficulty in the question of the khalifate is not limited to the question of his being a Koreishi or not, but the most difficult problem as far as we know is confined to the agreement of all the Mohammedans in the choice of the right man, who could be entrusted to take over the responsibility of this most dignified post, when the question of choosing a khalifa is brought under discussion.

It is not very easy to unite the various ambitions which disagree with each other. If one begins to consider these difficulties he is bound to fall into despair. In the presence of all these difficulties, if a man could be found who is well known and highly respected and honoured by Mohammedans, who could claim special qualifications and capacity, these difficulties may be surmounted.

A glance at the history of the khalifate since its existence up till the present time is sufficient to prove that this matter stands in importance far above any other question in the eyes of the Mohammedans. It is not a general question which is definitely explained by religion, nor is it a question of worship connected between man and his Creator. It is simply a worldly question which has been most intimately connected with the Mohammedan faith. Such questions have always given rise to great and serious disagreement and ambitions. I sincerely hope that the Moslems will be able, in the face of all these difficulties, to wake up and consider their interests first when the time comes for them to decide for themselves.

Please accept my heartiest respects.

(Sf.) *Mohd. Mustafa*

8

Pan-Arabism and British Policy

In the years following the first world war, pan-Arabism was the only political doctrine to make headway and to exert a powerful appeal in the Arabic-speaking lands. The nature of the war settlement itself and the political power which some of the leading votaries of this doctrine acquired in consequence of the settlement contributed alike to such a result. The situation developed suddenly, with revolutionary abruptness. Men who before the destruction of the Ottoman empire were quite obscure, emerged all at once after 1919, not only to preach a doctrine which got the Arab east into its grip, but actually to exercise political power in one of the former provinces of the empire. In 1914 such a state of affairs was impossible to imagine. It is true that there were then murmurings in Beirut, and that Syrian *émigrés* in Cairo were demanding a decrease in meddling from Istanbul and the enlargement of local initiative. But these grievances were local and specific; they related to the quality of government services or to the proper scope of local administration; and those who sought redress for such grievances were mostly men well known in their communities, able perhaps to conduct a sober constitutional opposition but not to entertain grandiose, limitless ambitions. How they would have fared under imperial rule, where their opposition would have taken them, how the Arabic-speaking provinces would have developed under their leadership, it is now impossible to say. The war made Britain and the Ottoman empire enemies; Britain fomented a revolt in the Hijaz against the Ottomans, and to this revolt gravitated a number of disaffected Ottoman officers who, when the war ended with the triumph of their patron, claimed the leadership of the Arab movement and were eventually enabled, by devious and complicated means, to obtain political control of Mesopotamia, where they set up government as the kingdom of Iraq.

The new leaders thrown up by the war were pan-Arab by nature.

They came to politics not through consideration of concrete difficulties or the grind of pressing affairs or daily responsibility, but by way of a doctrine. Their doctrine was compounded of certain European principles which made language and nationality synonymous, of a faith in sedition and violence, and of contempt for moderation. They believed that the Arabs, because they spoke Arabic, a language different from Turkish, were *ipso facto* entitled to secede from the Ottoman empire and to form a state where everybody who spoke Arabic would be included. They were not ambitious for the community they knew, or the locality where they were born and reared. The European doctrine of linguistic nationalism with which they were imbued, the oecumenical claims of the Arabian caliphate the glories of which they aspired to revive, the impetuosity of their youth, and the insignificance of their origins and their prospects alike combined to help them nurse ambitions to which only their dreams could set a bound. As one sympathiser with Arab nationalism, Professor H. A. R. Gibb, put it: 'The Arab nation . . . like all other nations, is not an entity of geographical or historical association, but the function of an act of will'.[1]

The will of these young officers willed an Arab nation, and ethnography, geography, or history were of consequence only as they offered sustenance to their imagination. When, therefore, the miraculous circumstances gave them suddenly a country to govern, it was not gratitude to fate and their patrons that they felt, but rather that they were cheated of their dream. They had desired an Arab nation and an Arab state, and they got Iraq, a specific country with specific frontiers. They denounced the imperialist dismemberment of the Arab nation, and called the boundaries drawn up at the peace settlement arbitrary and artificial. This was indeed true, for what otherwise can boundaries be when they spring up where none had existed before? These officers, of course, did not think to blame themselves for having, by their disaffection, helped the Powers they were now denouncing to defeat the Ottoman empire and thus to erect those hated boundaries. With the establishment of these men in the government of Iraq, therefore, pan-Arabism itself was endowed with a political base from which to prepare future incursions. The settlement of 1921, which created the kingdoms of Iraq, contained the seeds of its own destruction; for it gave power to men who were intent precisely on overthrowing such a settlement.

The ambitions of these men were, to start with, confined to the

Fertile Crescent, so-called – Iraq, Syria, Palestine, and the Lebanon – the stage on which, during their youth under the Ottoman empire, their dreams were accustomed to play. Between the wars, and after the outbreak of the second world war, their efforts were bent on securing a dislodgment of the French from Syria and the Lebanon, and a curtailment or, if possible, a suppression of Zionist activities in Palestine; thereafter, on putting together a unitary or a federal Arab state embracing the Fertile Crescent. This was the burden of Nuri al-Sa'id's proposal to Casey, minister of state in the middle east, in December 1942.[2] This was the original pan-Arab programme, on the realisation of which the original pan-Arabs had always set their hearts. But this was not yet to be. Instead, after negotiations lasting from 1943 to 1945, a quite different scheme of Arab unity was set afoot. In this scheme, there was no amalgamation or federation of states; it provided, rather, for an alliance of sovereign states in which, unexpectedly, Egypt figured as the leader.

Egypt had never before manifested any interest in pan-Arabism, and though we do not yet know all the negotiations which led to the formation of the Arab League, we do have a few details which throw light on Egyptian policy and which explain in some measure this new and sudden development. A pan-Arab policy for Egypt seems to have been throughout the handiwork of King Faruq and some of his entourage. The evidence for this is cumulative and convincing.

Faruq's father, King Fu'ad, nursed the ambition of becoming the Muslim caliph in succession to the dethroned Ottomans, and Faruq desired to follow his father's policy.[3] In 1939, on the occasion of a meeting in Cairo of Arab magnates to discuss Palestine, while the king, his entourage and his foreign guests were present at a mosque for the Friday prayers, the palace officials prevented the imam of the mosque from officiating as usual, and the king himself led the congregation in prayer – a traditional prerogative and attribute of the caliph – and on emerging from the mosque was proclaimed a true caliph and a pious ruler. In 1946, again, when Isma'il Sidqi was prime minister, the king, on his own initiative, assembled a meeting of Arab kings and presidents on his estate at Inshass to which neither the prime minister nor the foreign minister were invited and at which decisions on pan-Arab policy and on Palestine were taken. 'People then understood', writes Muhammad Husain Haikal, the eminent Egyptian statesman who recounts the incident in his *Memoirs*, 'that King Faruq's personal policy had for its aim the establishment of his personal leadership over the Arab states. However, the Ministry raised no protest and did not wish to make an issue of what happened.'[4] In May 1948, also, when the Egyptian troops went into Palestine to oppose the establishment of the state of Israel, they did so at the king's insistence and on his orders. Hostilities began on 15 May, and until 11 May, writes Haikal who was at the time president of the Senate, Nuqrashi, the prime minister, was quite unwilling to intervene in Palestine:

he used to say that he would not commit the Egyptian army to a position such that the British troops stationed on the Canal would be able to take them in the rear ... but from one day to the next this opinion changed. On 12 May Nuqrashi asked me to summon Parliament to a secret session to ask authority for Egyptian troops to enter Palestine. People learnt a little while later that the minister of defence, General Muhammad Haidar Pasha, the king's man and his private aide-de-camp, received an order direct from the king, and he then ordered battalions of the Egyptian army to cross the frontiers into Palestine, without the knowledge of the prime minister, and without waiting for the decision of Parliament and the decision of the cabinet.[5]

The same story, with minor variations, emerged from Muhammad Haidar's examination at the trial in October 1953, by the revolutionary court in Cairo, of Ibrahim Abd al-Hadi who was, in 1948, chief of the royal cabinet.

Faruq, of course, did not carry out his pan-Arab policies single-handed. He had coadjutors and instruments and of these the most prominent were Ali Mahir and Abd al-Rahman Azzam. Ali Mahir became chief of the royal cabinet soon after Faruq came to the throne, and acquired great influence as the king's political adviser. It was during his tenure of office that an active pan-Arab policy was initiated. In 1939 the British government convened a Round Table Conference on Palestine to which the Arab states and Egypt were invited. The Egyptian prime minister, then Muhammad Mahmud Pasha, decided to lead, himself, the Egyptian delegation to the conference. It was then suddenly announced that Ali Mahir would go instead, and would take with him Abd al-Rahman Azzam – later to become secretary-general of the Arab League. 'I do not know', writes Haikal, who was a member of Muhammad Mahmud's Ministry, 'that the cabinet ever delegated this matter to Ali Mahir Pasha, for the question never came before the cabinet'.[6] Haikal then goes on to say how, when Ali Mahir was away in London, certain notions relating to the restoration of Islamic principles of government, to the efficacy of quick dictatorial reforms, and such-like, began to get increasing publicity, and he adds: 'It is true that these notions were current before the chief of the royal cabinet's visit to England; but those who advanced them had done so somewhat shamefacedly. After his departure, however, this propaganda became more active, and the palace was not averse to such notions being attributed to it'.[7]

In August 1939, the king dismissed Muhammad Mahmud's cabinet, and appointed Ali Mahir prime minister, who included in his cabinet Azzam, as minister first of Religious Foundations, and then of Social Affairs. As soon as this government was formed, it set up a so-called 'Territorial Army', of which Azzam was put in charge. This territorial army seems to have been devised to indoctrinate youth and to prepare armed bands which could be used by the government for political purposes.[8] In this, Ali Mahir and Azzam were merely following a fashion made popular by the Nazis and the Fascists, a fashion already adopted in Iraq,[9] and in Egypt itself, where Blueshirts and Green-shirts organised by the *Wafd* and by the Young Egypt Party made the streets of Cairo hideous with riots and molestations.

The territorial army attempted, as the eminent orientalist Ettore Rossi observed at the time, to take up again 'with new regulations and new aims'[10] the traditions of these organisations which had been dissolved by Muhammad Mahmud Pasha when he took office in 1938. A writer knowledgeable in Muslim Brotherhood affairs, Dr Heyworth-Dunne, thinks that Azzam took the idea of a territorial army from Hasan al-Banna, the leader of the Brotherhood,[11] and it is worthy of note that the Brotherhood had its own private army organised in battalions and regiments, members of which had to swear to defend the faith and to obey orders unquestionably.[12] Among other members of Ali Mahir's cabinet were Salih Harb and Mustafa al-Shorbatchi, known for anti-British agitations and for their connections with the Muslim Brotherhood and similar bodies; as was the chief of staff appointed by Ali Mahir, Aziz Ali al-Misri, who 'never', says Haikal, 'at any time hid his admiration for Germany'.[13] Ali Mahir's Ministry lasted from August 1939 until June 1940. Britain was at war with Germany, which took the offensive in the spring of 1940 and soon scored a brilliant and resounding victory. Egypt was bound to Britain by an alliance, but under Ali Mahir's administration and especially in its last days, Egypt was lukewarm towards her ally, and perhaps worse. The British, comments

Haikal, 'were seeing with their own eyes what was taking place in Egypt, and hearing that Abd al-Rahman Azzam Bey, the minister of Social Affairs, and Salih Harb Pasha, the minister of War, were talking at every social gathering of German victories and British defeats . . .'[14] The British ambassador demanded the resignation of Ali Mahir; the king dismissed him, and Ali Mahir delivered a bitter speech in Parliament denouncing the British for meddling in the internal affairs of Egypt.[15]

It was these men and their party who, inspiring the king or inspired by him, invented and propagated pan-Arabism as a policy for Egypt.[16] It is true that Egypt negotiated the formation of the Arab League when they were under a cloud, the *Wafd* in power, and Mustafa al-Nahhas prime minister. We do not yet know what convinced al-Nahhas that pan-Arabism was a paying policy, but no doubt the desire to please the king, to dish his opponents by adopting their policy, the dislike of Iraq's aggrandisement should Nuri al-Sa'id's scheme be realised, the approval of the British, and visions of future grandeur had their part to play. Nahhas remained in power long enough to sign the Protocol of the Arab League preparatory conference on 7 October 1944. He was dismissed the following day. His successor, the king's appointee Ahmad Mahir fully took over without question his predecessor's pan-Arabism and actually appointed Azzam minister of state for Arab affairs. It was the king, clearly, who had set his heart on such a policy: it originated with him or with men who out of either personal ambition or doctrinaire conviction, conceived the dream of an authoritarian Muslim state in Egypt embracing gradually all the Arabs, and perhaps in the fullness of time all the Muslims. Their inspiration was not strictly the same as that of the original pan-Arabs; but this is not to say that they contradicted each other. The ideal of the pan-Arabs was authoritarian also. They desired to transform the heterogeneous, fissiparous, sceptical populations of the Fertile Crescent to the likeness of their dream, with all differences suddenly annihilated, and external unity the emblem of a deeper, still more fundamental internal unity: one state, one nation, one creed.

It is said that pan-Islamism and pan-Arabism are contradictory. Owing to an historical accident the pan-Arabs had acquired the reputation of being opposed to pan-Islamism. Pan-Islamism was used by the Ottomans to provide a support for their empire; when the pan-Arabs rose in rebellion, they necessarily had to emphasise the opposition between pan-Arabism and pan-Islamism. In Egypt, of course, there was no place and no need for such opposition: the enemy was Britain, not the Ottoman empire. Islamic sentiment and Islamic solidarity gave body and passion to the struggle against the foreigner. A remarkable illustration of this appeared in a prayer written by Hassan al-Banna, the leader of the Muslim Brothers, for the use of his followers:

O God, Lord of the Creation who giveth assurance to the insecure, who humbleth the vainglorious, and who layeth low the tyrants, accept our prayer and answer our call. Enable us to obtain our right, and give back to us our freedom and independence. O God, those British usurpers have occupied our land and made free with our rights; they have oppressed the country and spread evil in it. O God, turn their intrigues away from us, weaken their strength and disperse their hosts; annihilate them and those who have helped them to victory, or have aided them, or have made peace with them or have befriended them, in a manner worthy of an all-powerful and majestic One. O God, let their actions rebound on them, let calamities descend on them, humiliate their kingdom, release Your land from their power, and let them have no sway over any of the Believers. Amen.[17]

Here we see well exemplified the general character of Islam as at once a political and a religious creed. The pan-Arabs desired the unification of the Arab lands; they desired to expel the foreigner. These aims are acceptable to and indeed mandatory on Muslims, for the Arab world is the cradle of Islam and to expel the foreigner from it is a meritorious action. Such is the agreement in principle between pan-Islamism and pan-Arabism. It explains how the original pan-Arabs in the Fertile Crescent, though different in outlook and assumptions from Faruq and his advisers, could effect some kind of junction with them, and sign after long and difficult negotiations the Pact of the Arab League.

At this further stage in the progress of pan-Arabism, the revisionism implicit in the settlement of 1921 became explicit. To the Pact of the League two annexes were attached, one dealing with Palestine, and the other with 'Arab countries which are not members of the council of the League'. In both cases the League served notice of its right to meddle in the affairs of countries outside the jurisdiction of its members, and of its claim to advise and direct Powers ruling over or having interests in countries inhabited by Arabs, until such Powers should agree to liquidate their authority and their interests in favour of pan-Arabism. The Zionists did object to the annex on Palestine, and pointed out to the mandatory Power that it was a derogation of its authority.[18] The mandatory Power remained serene and unmoved, not thinking that a day would come when such claims as these would affect more than mere Zionists.

Such were the men and such the policies which the British government encouraged with its support and blessing. On two public occasions during the second world war, once in a speech at the Mansion House in 1941 – to which great importance seems to have been attached, for it was published as a White Paper – and once in answer to a question in the House of Commons in February 1943, the foreign secretary declared that it was 'natural and right' that cultural, economic, and political ties among the Arab countries should be strengthened: 'many Arab thinkers'[19] desired, it seemed, a greater degree of unity than was then enjoyed by the Arab peoples; 'no such appeal from our friends should go unanswered'; and the British government would give 'full support to any scheme that commands general approval'.

It is well known that in the 1930s Germany and Italy – by skilful propaganda, by judicious disbursements, by the powerful appeal of their efficiency and success – established themselves as the champions of, and set the pace for, Arab nationalism. And yet when one comes to examine what – with their freedom from local and imperial responsibilities, and their lack of scruple – they were in the end prepared to concede, one is struck with their discretion and circumspection, compared with the generous and insouciant abandon of British policy. In the summer of 1940, when Rashid Ali al-Gailani was engaged in the preliminaries of his conspiracy to take power in Iraq and range it alongside the Axis, he sent an emissary to Turkey who presented to von Papen, the German ambassador, a list of demands which included the confirmation by the Axis of the independence of all Arab countries, the abolition of the Jewish National Home, and the recognition of Arab unity.[20] But neither Germany nor Italy would be drawn so far, and after months of consideration they made a declaration in October stating that they desired to see the Arab countries prosper and occupy among the peoples of the world a position commensurate with their natural and historical importance, that they had always followed with interest the Arab struggle for independence, that in this struggle the Arabs could count on the full sympathy of the Axis.

Again, in April 1941, when Rashid Ali was in power, and before he declared war on Britain, he concluded, as the official history of the Indian army records, a secret treaty whereby in return for recognising a union – whenever effected – between Iraq and Syria the Axis would receive oil and pipeline concessions, the lease of three ports on the Syrian coast, and the right to construct naval and military bases thereon.[21] And even when Rashid Ali's movement against the British was under way in May 1941, and Hitler was persuaded to give some help, he was not ready to go beyond careful and qualified generalities. In his directive of 23 May 1941 he laid down the policy on which propaganda was to be based: 'Victory by the Axis Powers will liberate the lands of the middle east from the British yoke and give them the right of self-determination [handwritten note: except Syria]. Let those who love liberty join the anti-British front'.[22]

Exactly the same demands as were presented to the Germans were presented – albeit by different persons – to the British government. And the sympathy of the British government was full indeed, and active. To the Zionists they turned a deaf ear, and the scheme of Arab unity, realised by a fortuitous agreement between Faruq and the original pan-Arabs, they supported and blessed; and from 1941 to 1945, they constantly, pertinaciously and in the end successfully worked to elbow the French out of the Levant.

It is sometimes said that Anglo-French relations in the Levant during the second world war were so bad because Mr Churchill was frequently irritated with General de Gaulle, and because Sir Edward Spears, whose relations with the latter were also tense and difficult, happened to be head of the British mission (and later British minister) in the Levant. It is perfectly true that bad personal relations exacerbated the situation, that Churchill in particular insisted for a long time in keeping Spears in the Levant when Harold Macmillan, Duff Cooper and Lord Moyne repeatedly urged in 1943 and 1944 his recall, and that the Foreign Office complained about the way in which Spears was interpreting his instructions.[23] But we must not give undue importance to these personal quirks and quarrels. The tendency of British policy in the Levant was amply clear from the day when British troops seconded by a Free French contingent invaded the Levant in order – as they said – to deny it to the Germans. Two days before the invasion, on 6 June 1941, Churchill wrote to de Gaulle: 'I welcome your decision to promise independence to Syria and the Lebanon, and as you know, I think it essential that we should lend to this promise the full weight of our guarantee. I agree that we must not in any settlement of the Syrian question endanger the stability of the middle east. But subject to this, we must do everything possible to meet Arab aspirations and susceptibilities'. Again, a month later, on 9 July, the prime minister asked the foreign secretary to include the following points in a proposed communication to Pétain:

1. England has no interest in Syria except to win the war.
2. Arab independence is a first essential and nothing must conflict with that.
3. ... [De Gaulle] will ... keep alive the fact that, without prejudice to Arab independence, France will have the dominant privileged position in Syria among all European nations.
4. ... We are all committed to Arab independence. . . .[24]

Thus, before Churchill's relations with de Gaulle seriously deteriorated, and long before Spears had the chance to misunderstand the import of British policy, we see the British prime minister insisting that 'Arab aspirations and susceptibilities' must be fully satisfied, and that 'Arab independence' in the Levant is 'a first essential'.

When the invasion of the Levant was launched, General Catroux issued on behalf of the Free French a proclamation to the Syrians and the Lebanese: 'You are', it said, 'henceforth sovereign and independent and you can either form two states or unite in one. In either case, your sovereign and independent status will be guaranteed by a treaty, which will also define our mutual relations'.[25] The British, it would seem, wanted a British guarantee of this French promise to be included in Catroux's proclamation, but de Gaulle firmly opposed this and the British issued a separate statement.[26] In it they declared that 'they support and associate themselves with the assurance of independence given by General Catroux'. A few months afterwards, in September, Churchill, speaking in the House of Commons, professed to see in this unilateral declaration (from which de Gaulle had at the time expressly dissociated himself)[27] an unqualified pledge and a solemn obligation which the French would, in due course, be made fully to discharge.[28] And when Alamein removed the German threat to the Middle East it became less important to heed Free French susceptibilities, and the Minister of State in the Middle East could frankly avow that 'Britain's initial commitment to the Fighting French, in connection with turning over to them the administration of Syria and Lebanon, were unfortunately too broad'.[28a]

Indeed, the drift of British policy was unmistakable. Soon after the invasion, the minister of State in the middle east asked Catroux to allow Spears to be present at talks between the Free French and the Syrians concerning the grant of independence.[29] Though Catroux refused, it remained the constant aim of the British to interpose themselves between the French mandatory and the Levant mandated territories, and thus prove to the Syrians and the Lebanese that they were beholden to Britain for their independence. In the spring of 1942 the British began pressing for elections in Syria and the Lebanon. Spears informed the Lebanese president that his government which had recognised Lebanese independence 'could not very well concede that the country should go on living under a regime which was not truly democratic'.[30] Both the minister of state in the middle east and Churchill himself pressed strongly for elections. Casey, the minister of state, alleged the bizarre reason that Egypt and Iraq – those paragons of constitutionalism – were demanding elections in the Levant 'as forming the indispensable criterion' of true independence, while the prime minister later bluntly told de Gaulle that elections had to be held in the Levant 'because England had made promises to the Arabs, to Iraq, to the Wafdists of Egypt'.[31] It goes without saying that there was no demand in the Levant for elections, and that elections would themselves create turmoil and instability – the very conditions which the British government professed to wish to avoid. When Rommel reached Alamein in the summer of 1942 they were not tardy in recognising that such games were not then opportune, and elections were postponed to a more favourable moment.[32]

Elections were held a year later, and in the circumstances the local political factions became the clients either of the British or of the French. In the Lebanon, in particular, Spears took – and was known to take – a leading part in the complicated manoeuvres which led to the appointment of Bshara al-Khuri as president and Riyad al-Sulh as prime minister. These events clearly indicated that the French were no longer in unchallenged control of the politics of the Levant, and the new Lebanese government resolved speedily to exploit this situation. While Helleu, the French delegate general, was absent from Beirut, the Lebanese government on 9 November 1943 carried through the newly-elected Parliament amendments to the Lebanese constitution which deleted all reference to the mandatory and its powers. The mandate was of course still in being, and these amendments were introduced and carried through without consulting the

223

mandatory.[33] Helleu considered – it is said with de Gaulle's approval[34] – that this act of defiance merited exemplary punishment. He had the government arrested and interned. But the British, alleging that this action was a threat to military security, compelled the Free French, by means of an ultimatum, to release and reinstate the Lebanese government. The amendments remained on the statute book, and it became clear to everyone that the satisfaction of 'Arab aspirations and susceptibilities' was indeed the prime object of British policy.

The lesson was driven home by the Syrian events of May–June 1945. At the beginning of May the French were getting ready to submit proposals for treaties with the Lebanon and Syria which would formally end the mandate and secure for the French that privileged position to which Churchill, as he repeatedly declared, considered them entitled. The approach of these negotiations shortly following the creation of the Arab League in the previous March and coinciding with the end of the war in Europe created tension and effervescence in Syria which the Syrian government expertly encouraged and fed. The Syrian government no doubt knew that it could count on British – and American – support. A month before the crisis broke, for instance, Camille Chamoun, Lebanon minister in London, then on a visit to Beirut, noted in his diary on 29 April that Sir Edward Grigg, minister resident in the middle east, was expressing concern at 'French provocations' which threatened to produce a conflagration and that the United States minister, Wadsworth, was afraid that the French might be sending troops and that his advice in this case was for the Syrians and Lebanese to refuse all negotiation.[35] In the latter half of May this agitation began to increase. The pretext was the arrival at Beirut aboard two French cruisers of three battalions, two of which were replacements. This was held to mean that the French were preparing to make Syria and the Lebanon negotiate under duress. The net increase in French troops was one battalion, and it is absurd to imagine that by itself it would have sufficed to coerce the Levant. It is more probable that the arrival of these troops was taken as a convenient pretext to step up the agitation.[36] The British government, while admitting that the net increase in troops was 'very small', yet publicly warned the French that their arrival might cause 'regrettable reactions'.[37] *The Times* of Monday, 28 May reported a statement issued by the Foreign Office on the previous weekend which alleged a 'serious situation' in the Levant and regretted that 'the improved atmosphere should have been disturbed by the dispatch of certain French reinforcements'. A 'serious situation', whether provoked or not by this statement, thereupon supervened. French troops were attacked on 28 and 29 May in Damascus, Hama, Aleppo, Deir-az-Zor and elsewhere. They retaliated and in Damascus bombarded the parliament and other buildings from which they alleged they were being fired upon.[38] Promptly, on 31 May, a British ultimatum ordered the French troops to cease fire. They were confined to their barracks which were taken under the protection of British troops.[39] This British action finally ruined the French position in the Levant.

What was anticipated from such a policy? 'It is all right', declared Lord Strabolgi, in a debate in the House of Lords on the events of November 1943, 'for General Spears to be carried shoulder high by the mob in Beirut, and for us to have messages of congratulation from middle east potentates; but I am thinking of the future'.[40] Again, when Duff Cooper was urging Spears's recall from the Levant he wrote to Churchill: 'We have surely enough native problems of our own to face without stirring up native problems for others'.[41] What then of the future? We may not doubt that British diplomats and statesmen debated among themselves what policy was most likely to safeguard the substantial British interests in the middle east, and that this tender attention to 'Arab aspirations and susceptibilities' they felt to be their best protection. This policy also had another advantage. It presented no difficulty, either in theory or in practice. It assumed that the triumph of pan-Arabism was inevitable and, seeking an alliance with the inevitable, it hoped to reap the benefits of such a mighty connection. But unfortunately it was a bogus policy, since the inevitable is the ally of nobody. Having helped the triumph of the inevitable in the Levant, what stance should the British adopt when it rose to confront *them* in Iraq, and Palestine and Egypt? What rejoinder was possible to Duff Cooper's observation?

Unluckily, the starkness of this prospect seems to have been hidden by beguiling theories and false hopes. Of these theories there are many variants, official and unofficial. The Arab League, as Lord Altrincham (who was minister of state in the middle east from the assassination of Lord Moyne until 1945), said in an address at the Sorbonne in May 1947, was encouraged by Britain; but he claimed that it was an autonomous Power created by the Arabs themselves and represented their unanimous resolve to act independently in world affairs. Theirs was an ancient civilisation now being reborn, and it was possible to

capture their friendship and good will by helping them in this enterprise. Lord Altrincham buttressed his hopes by a curious argument.
If the Palestine White Paper of 1939, he explained, had not been
issued, the whole Arab world would have been against the Allies in
the most dangerous years of the war, from 1940 to 1942; hence the
way to safeguard western interests in general and British interests in
particular was to act with the Arabs, assembled in their new League.[42]
This was to confuse the wishes and anticipations of those who invented
the White Paper of 1939 with what, in fact, happened. For it was
precisely in these years between 1940 and 1942 that the Arab world
manifested great hostility to Britain. What saved the British position
in the middle east was not the White Paper, but military power,
Churchill's daring, and Hitler's obsession with the conquest of Russia.
Such arguments deserve mention to show the foundations on which
such grandiose hopes were built. Lord Altrincham's views are worthy
of notice because they provide evidence of the terms in which someone who had held high office connected with the middle east was
prepared to think of policy.

Lord Altrincham was of course not the only one to see things in this
light. Miss Stark, who served during the war as an official in the
British embassy in Baghdad, and elsewhere in the middle east, firmly
believed that pan-Arabism was beneficial both to the Arabs and to the
British. 'Their pan-Arabism', she declared in a lecture of February
1939 at Chatham House, 'we may think of as Utopia, and it may be
so: but a strong and united Arabia would be to our interest; its divisions are a source of danger, and an occasion for intrigue; and even
if the dream of federation is a dream of the future, and a misty one
at that, it is well for us to do all we can to further it'. And after war
broke out she was writing to a correspondent: 'For years I have been
unable to see why our government should not take every public
opportunity to give a blessing to the pan-Arab cry. What are they
frightened of?'[43] Towards the end of the war, at the beginning of
1945, Sir Douglas Newbold, chief secretary in the Sudan was writing:
'. . . Mustn't upset de Gaulle . . . Mustn't upset the Yanks or Weizmann . . . and then we hope to keep Arab friendship and loyalty.
Cornwallis, MacMichael, Spears, and Killearn have all told H.M.G.
of the danger of these courses, in no uncertain terms, and persuaded
Casey and Moyne of it'. 'Now', he exclaims in a frenzy of impatience,
'*now* is the time for the H.M.G. to come out with a middle east policy
and win over *effendia*, pashas, shaikhs and *fellahin* from Baghdad to

Tripoli and Khartoum.... I've met Senussi leaders, Palestine Arabs, Beirut graduates – all are waiting for Eden to implement his nebulous blessing of the Arab Commonwealth'.[44] This millennial fervour is echoed by Spears back in the House of Commons from the Levant: 'The movement towards Arab unity', he affirmed in epic language when the Arab League was inaugurated in March 1945, 'is like a great natural force, the flow of a river to the sea. It can be slowed down, diverted or impeded, but', he observed seer-like, 'in course of time it will reach its objective'.[45] And on the same occasion, *The Times* newspaper wrote with quiet satisfaction: 'To no other Power will the promise offered by these developments be more welcome than to Britain, with her long-standing record of friendship with these countries'.[46]

But to appreciate the full scope and ramifications of this theory, we must go to unofficial sources, to the writings of some British academics on middle eastern affairs, among which those of Professor Gibb are noteworthy. The theory, we find, is concerned, in the first place, with a presumed Muslim ethic, and in the second with a presumed difference within the ranks of Arab nationalists. As to the first, Gibb explains that though Muslim society has suffered from violence and lawlessness, and from corruptions introduced by non-Arabs,[47] its true principles, which had been so particularly safeguarded by Arab Muslim orthodoxy, could still be applied in the Arab Muslim east. 'Islam', for instance, 'still maintained the balance between the exaggerated opposites of *bourgeois* capitalism and communism', and 'while hostile to banking capital and unrestricted exchange it sanctioned private property and commercial capital'; Islam 'had not succumbed to the obsession with the economic side of life which was characteristic of almost all our western societies'. Gibb asserted that 'it is by these and similar ideas that the thought of the Arab nationalists is being more and more strongly influenced'.[48] After the Arab League was formed, Gibb explained that the 'duty laid upon the Arab leaders is, in its essence, closely parallel to that laid upon the leaders of the United Nations'.[49]

As to the Arab nationalists, Gibb said that there were 'two kinds of Arab nationalists: those whom I call by that name, and those whom I call pan-Arabs'. The pan-Arabs were intolerant bigots, while the nationalists, though certainly respectful of Islam, desired also to adopt western ideas in order to combat feudalism and internecine rivalries, and to collaborate with the non-Muslim minorities.

'Such there are in all the regions of the Arab east – Egypt, Palestine, Syria, Iraq, even', he asserted, 'Arabia – and it is upon them that the hopes of a revived, progressive, respected and self-respecting Arab nationhood depend'. Let, therefore, said Gibb– advocating some such plan as that being then pushed by Nuri al-Sa'id in British official quarters – let a federation of the Arab lands in Asia be constructed, and the sound Arab nationalists would be able to get on with the work which centuries of Sassanid corruption and Ottoman malpractice had left undone: 'it is a rational, reasonable, eminently practical objective'.[50]

Such were the doctrinal foundations on which a policy was based to encourage Faruq, Azzam, and the triumphant doctrinaires of the Fertile Crescent to come together and emulate the ideals of the United Nations. Many people must have felt misgivings as to how such an adventure would end, but it is safe to say that nobody of position or standing, whether British or Arab, was ready to question in public the assumptions and execution of this policy as Haikal coolly and soberly questioned it. He is reported to have declared at the time of the first formal conference on Arab unity in 1944:

> It is doubtful whether the union will be a political union; it is doubtful whether, in case one of the Arab states is attacked, the others will hurry to its aid. It is also doubtful if an effective cultural union, or a union of some other kind, could take place, because the history, the legal codes, agriculture, and industry are necessarily different in the different Arab states.[51]

Events have proved him amply right, and have shown the Arab League to be a system based on conflicting ambitions and cemented with bitter mutual suspicions. The Pact of the League proved to be a device designed not so much to bring about Arab unity, as to keep the so-called Arab states at arms length from one another. But British policy-makers came to see middle eastern questions such as the Palestine problem, or Anglo-Egyptian relations, or Anglo-Iraqi relations, as so many inseparable parts of one large and fundamental issue, that of 'Anglo–Arab' relations. This view of middle eastern policy is exemplified by an official report which Miss Stark and one of her colleagues wrote in 1941: 'Our aim', they said, 'should be to make nationalism friendly', and went on: 'We feel that it cannot be too clearly stated nor too often repeated that there is only one problem at the root of all our relations with the Arab world: this is the absence of any clear statement from H.M.G. of their intentions

228

towards Arab nationalism, the future of Syria and Arab confederation, and the still unresolved problem of Palestine'.[52] Seen in this
way, 'relations with the Arab world' were, however, amenable to no
possible negotiation or settlement. The 'Arab world' or 'Arab
nationalism' are not a known political entity, with tangible or defin-
able interests. They are slogans which various states in the middle
east, usually at loggerheads with one another, have adopted in order
to advance their own interests. As for British interests, they were lost
in the marshy wastes of this pan-Arab ideology, entangled and
smothered in pan-Arab intrigues and combinations. But it is the British
themselves who cheerfully led the way into these wastes; it was they
who eagerly sought these entanglements.[53]

The 'rational, reasonable, eminently practical objective' has failed
of its attainment, and the policy which sought to promote it is now
dust and ashes. It disintegrated on the battlefields of Palestine in
1948, three years after the foundation of the League. '*Hodie mihi*',
Bidault warned Britain when the French Consultative Assembly
debated the Syrian affair in June 1945, '*cras tibi*'. It proved a swift
reckoning. Policies are meant to succeed; if they fail, then they are
bad policies; unless, that is, new and powerful circumstances which
could not have been foreseen impinge to falsify calculations and
upset expectations. But between 1945, or indeed 1943, or 1939, and
1948 no new elements, no alien factors were introduced into the
middle eastern situation. The Zionists were there, the pan-Arabs
were there, Faruq and his men were there, and their antecedents,
capacities, ambitions were for all to see. To argue that the policy
failed because the Zionists were not docile enough, the Arabs united
enough or wise enough, is to argue either from ignorance or fanciful-
ness or sentimentality. But it does remain a curious fact that some
British policy-makers – perhaps even Mr Eden himself – entertained
the belief that the creation of the Arab League would actually facilitate a peaceful solution in Palestine. In a work published in 1944
Lord Altrincham argued that such a solution could not be found
within the confines of Palestine alone, and that hope for a settlement
lay in Arab unity: 'The Arab nations', he said, 'are ... moving
tentatively towards closer association, and within some kind of
confederation, however loose, there should be scope for a solution
of the local problems of Syria and Palestine alike'.[54] Far from the
Arab League facilitating a peaceful settlement it made – as could
have been reasonably foreseen – a violent outcome of the Palestine

dispute quite inevitable, with fatal consequences to public morality, settled society, and British interests in the middle east. Any kind of compromise solution enforced or facilitated by the mandatory became quite impossible, because the doctrine in terms of which the Arab League claimed to operate spurned and abhorred the idea of compromise, and because each of the principal states constituting the League looked on a military victory in Palestine as a quick and easy means of securing the leadership of the Arab world.

The events which preceded – and finally precipitated – the Palestine war of 1948 make this clear. As has been seen, Egypt decided to send an army to Palestine only at the last minute, and she decided to do so only when it became clear that if she were to stand aloof her primacy in the Arab League would be threatened. When, shortly after the beginning of the hostilities, the Palestine mediator, Count Bernadotte, met the Egyptian prime minister, Nuqrashi told him that Egypt had had, to start with, no intention of sending troops to Palestine but that she changed her mind 'when 8th May [1948] came and it became apparent that no settlement would be worked out'.[55] What settlement did Nuqrashi mean? It was a settlement, no doubt, which would rule out the partition of Palestine, thus preventing not only the establishment of a Zionist state, but also – which was much more important – the aggrandisement of Trans-Jordan which partition would inevitably bring about. Ever since partition was decided it was clear that the Amir Abdullah was determined to turn it, one way or another, to his profit. On the morrow of the vote at the United Nations, which took place on 29 November 1947, Abdullah proposed to the Arab League states that they should finance a Trans-Jordanian conquest of Palestine which he was ready to undertake. Trans-Jordan was not a member of the United Nations and could, therefore, defy with impunity the partition scheme.[56] The proposal was rejected, for obvious reasons, and Egypt and the others decided to put their trust in the Palestinian Arabs, organised and directed by Hajj Amin al-Husaini and in the so-called Army of Deliverance to be recruited and financed by them. Also, just before partition was resolved upon Abdullah had indicated to Mrs Golda Meyerson of the Jewish Agency that, in case of partition, he wanted to annex the area of Palestine awarded to the Arabs.[57]

In the months which followed, Abdullah actively pursued this complex and ambitious policy. He maintained his contacts with the Jewish Agency but now asked that they should better the United

Nations award to the Arabs, by conceding additional territories and thus enable him to take the credit for having obtained a better deal for the Palestinians than the United Nations. He seems also to have put pressure on the Iraqis to send a contingent in support of the Arab Legion. Internal affairs in Iraq were then quite disturbed and the Iraqi cabinet did not seem particularly eager to respond. A member of this cabinet has subsequently recounted that the students of the Law College in Baghdad proclaimed a fast to compel the government to send troops to Palestine and that the Trans-Jordanian ambassador came to the college and invited them to continue with it. Abdullah himself sent telegrams to his nephew the regent and Sadr the prime minister insisting on the dispatch of Iraqi troops.[58]

The Iraqi government was weak, divided and manifestly unable to control events in the country. Caught by its own rhetoric, and unable to resist pressure, it sent in May a force to Trans-Jordan. Abdullah therefore felt strong enough to threaten the Zionists with war unless they agreed to his demands. At an interview with Mrs Meyerson shortly before 15 May he demanded that Palestine should remain undivided – i.e. that there should be no Zionist state – and that, at the end of one year, it should amalgamate with Jordan. Two days before the outbreak of war he again repeated his demand.[59] By the beginning of May the Palestinians and the Army of Deliverance had decisively shown that they were no match for the Zionists and Abdullah seemed favourably placed to act as the saviour of Palestine, checkmating his Arab rivals and perhaps wresting from the Zionists more than the United Nations had awarded to the Arabs. When it became clear that no development at the United Nations could possibly undo partition and thus stop Abdullah, Egypt had to intervene, thus suddenly reversing a policy which Nuqrashi had consistently maintained ever since the Arab League meeting at Aley in October when he categorically refused to consider Egyptian military intervention in Palestine.[60]

What was Britain's attitude to all these developments? The question is natural since Britain was still the paramount power in the middle east, and since Trans-Jordan in particular was its client unable in the final analysis to disregard British wishes and suggestions. What was Bevin's attitude to Abdullah's adventurous policy? In his memoirs, Glubb tells us that towards the end of February 1948, an interview – at which he was present – took place in London between Bevin and the Trans-Jordan prime minister. Tawfiq abdul-Huda informed Bevin that after the British withdrawal from Palestine, Trans-Jordan proposed to occupy the areas allotted to the Arabs – bar Galilee and Gaza. Bevin is reported to have said: 'It seems the obvious thing to do, but do not go and invade the areas allotted to the Jews'.[61] On the face of it this conversation is quite peculiar. Ever since partition had been announced the constant refrain of the British government had been that since the Arabs disapproved of such a scheme, it would do nothing to further it. But in the conversation which Glubb reports, we see the foreign secretary privately approving a solution which in public the British government dismissed with heavy disapproval. Again, the informal partition which the Trans-Jordan Prime Minister proposed could not but involve risks of disorder and fighting. And on Glubb's account, Bevin seems to have preferred it to an orderly and internationally supervised operation. And further, what was to happen to Galilee and Gaza? What finally was to happen to Jerusalem? Jerusalem the United Nations had voted to be internationally administered, and the British government had obstinately refused to help in any way to set up an international administration. At the British withdrawal, then, Jerusalem would become a *res nullius* over which Abdullah and the Zionists were likely to fight, and the silence of Bevin and abul-Huda on the question of Jerusalem becomes therefore an eloquent silence. For all its mild and homely tones, this conversation on that February day, in Downing Street, is profoundly disquieting. It shows the Foreign Secretary to be, at best, dangerously ambiguous or perhaps muddled and, at worst, bent on a war in Palestine. The war at which this conversation perhaps hinted, and which it certainly entailed was, to be sure, a war between Abdullah and the Zionists; but if Abdullah was to fight then Egypt would also join – the *machine infernale* of the Arab League made this quite certain.

A sidelight on British policy is possibly provided by a letter from Fadil al-Jamali, who was Iraqi foreign minister at the time of the abortive Anglo–Iraqi Portsmouth Treaty of 1948. This letter, dated 20 September 1957, Jamali wrote in answer to a query by Sayyid Abd al-Razzaq al-Hasani, author of a well-known history of Iraqi cabinets, who published it in the third edition of volume seven of his book which appeared in 1968. Hasani had asked whether the Portsmouth Treaty had contained a secret appendix relating to Palestine. Jamali wrote of a meeting which took place in his room at Claridge's Hotel in London after the Treaty was signed, on 15 January 1948.

At this meeting there were present Bevin and his advisers, and on the Iraqi side Jamali himself, Salih Jabr the prime minister and Nuri al-Sa'id. Jamali declares that agreement was reached on the following points:

1. Speeding-up the supply of weapons and ammunition ordered from the British Government.
2. Supplying the Iraqi police with automatic weapons sufficient for fifty thousand policemen. The purpose was to arm the Palestinian fighters to enable them to participate in the liberation of Palestine.
3. It was also agreed that the Iraqi forces would enter every area evacuated by the British troops so that this would embrace the whole of Palestine, in co-operation with the Palestinian fighters so that a Jewish state would not be formed.

Jamali adds: 'This is what was agreed, and what was completely laid aside when the Portsmouth Treaty was turned down.' Another Iraqi ex-minister discusses these Anglo–Iraqi negotiations in his memoirs. The Iraqi negotiators, writes Khalil Kanna, found in Bevin a readiness to co-operate on the Palestine issue and reached an agreement with him to form two Iraqi divisions to be stationed at the Trans-Jordan frontiers ready to march on Palestine after the British withdrawal. Kanna, however, though very close to Nuri al-Sa'id, did not take part in these negotiations himself, and may have been anxious to vindicate in retrospect the Portsmouth Treaty policy by arguing that it led to tangible advantages in the Palestine question, which were lost when the Iraqis repudiated the Treaty.[62]

What possible advantage could Britain derive from war in Palestine? For even if the Zionists were defeated and humbled, the 'Arabs' could not win. It was not 'Arabs' who were fighting in Palestine, but the Arab Legion, the instrument of Trans-Jordan, and the Egyptian Army. Egypt could win, and Trans-Jordan would join the Zionists in their discomfiture; or Trans-Jordan could win, and then Egypt would be humiliated with the Zionists. In either case, the British had to choose between befriending Egypt or befriending Trans-Jordan. The Palestine war brought to the fore and made acute an issue which Eden's Arab League policy disastrously slurred over and disguised. After the mad outbreak ('arbada) over the Palestine war (as Azzam felicitously described it in retrospect[63]), the issue became inescapable and had somehow to be resolved. It fell to Eden to resolve it. By negotiating the Baghdad Pact in 1955 he made a necessary choice.

In befriending Iraq, he alienated Egypt; but to govern is to choose. It could have been argued, between 1955 and 1958, that the makers of the Baghdad Pact had at last abandoned the policy which led to the encouragement of the Arab League. If so, it was a return to common sense and prudent calculation. Friends made friendly by the persuasion of tangible interests, by a reckoning of risk and advantage, by a provident quest for military and economic security: such is a conceivable objective of foreign policy. But, in fact, it did not prove possible for the British to extricate themselves from the quicksands of a doctrinaire adventure.

Years of official pan-Arabism meant that the middle eastern political debate was securely confined within the pan-Arab groove. When the Baghdad Pact was made, its Arab enemies denounced it as a betrayal of the pan-Arab cause. To reply to them when they became most vociferous at the time of the Suez operation, Nuri al-Sa'id made a long broadcast in December 1956. The burden of his argument was that Communism, Zionism, and France were allies against whom Iraq has always fought and will always fight. Iraq, he said, was the only true servant of pan-Arabism. How can those, he asked, who maintain the frontiers created by imperialism (here alluding to Syria, and the well-known pan-Arab argument that all frontiers in the Fertile Crescent were artificial and arbitrary) be called patriots and nationalists? It may be that the Iraqi minister was trying to pay back his enemies in their own coin, but it is as probable that he was sincere in what he said: 'The call to Arab nationalism', he declared at the end of his broadcast, 'is not something new and accidental with me. It is my very being, of which I am proud, which I seek to protect and to tend, whether I am in power or not. If such has been my way in my youth, and in my middle age, it is not strange that I should remain the same in my old age'.[64] This is quite true, and to the extent that it was true and represented the terms in which, whether from habit, inclination, or necessity, the rulers of Iraq talked of politics, disengagement from the quicksand proved impossible.

Between 1955 and 1958, Britain found herself being involved by her Baghdad Pact ally in those pan-Arab complications which were the *damnosa haereditas* of earlier British policy. Iraq drawing support from Britain, and Egypt from the Soviets confronted one another in a gladiatorial posture over the middle east. The members of the Baghdad Pact had willy-nilly to support Iraqi intrigues in Syria and

234

the Lebanon[65] – intrigues stemming from Iraq's pan-Arab ambitions – lest the success of Egyptian counter-intrigues – likewise stemming from Egypt's pan-Arab ambitions – should give the Soviets – against whom the Pact was directed – a firmer footing in the middle east. The *coup d'état* of 14 July 1958 itself indirectly brought about by Iraqi ambitions in Syria, in putting an end to the monarchical regime in Baghdad at last ended, for good or evil, the British involvement with pan-Arabism.

9

The Kingdom of Iraq:
a Retrospect

I give thee a king in Mine anger
And take him away in My wrath
Hosea, XIII, 11

The events which took place in Baghdad on 14 July 1958 were
received by the world with a shock of horror and incredulity. For
years respectable journalists, enthusiastic statesmen and even sedate
academics, exhausting the vocabulary of praise and admiration, had
been expatiating on the stability of Iraq, on the wisdom and honesty
of its rulers, and their provident management of the immense wealth
which oil royalties had brought to the country. Here and there, it is
true, voices were raised to protest that Iraq under Nuri al-Sa'id was
a police state, a hot-bed of corrupt and greedy reactionaries who were
oppressing the people and betraying its national aspirations; but such
rumours were dismissed – and perhaps rightly – as the expression of
Egyptian malevolence, or as the scandal-mongering of ignorant left-
wing journalists. To foresee such a revolution would have required, of
course, divinatory powers; is it not significant, nevertheless, that
public information on Iraq was so poor, that intimations of coming
trouble should emanate only from sources which it was natural and
reasonable to discount and discredit? The unexpected character of
the revolution was not, however, the only reason for the shock it
produced. There was also the murder at dawn of the royal family, of
the king, an innocent and harmless young man of twenty-four, of his
aged grandmother, of his devoted aunt, and other inmates of the
royal palace.[1] It was not merely the indiscriminate killing which
aroused horror, but also that a king and his family were the victims.
For an obscure and tenacious instinct has always moved men to

236

consider regicide peculiarly heinous and impious: a king is the head of the state, and a state, however mean and perverted, has still something of nobility; it is an invention peculiar to man, a dyke against bestiality, and a storehouse of devotion and loyalty; to lay violent hands on it is to weaken the social fabric, to increase human insecurity, and to let loose evil and destructive passions.

But, everything considered, was there not reason to expect some such upheaval, and is there not reason, even now, to expect further, perhaps even more violent commotions? For brief as it is, the record of the kingdom of Iraq is full of bloodshed, treason and rapine, and however pitiful its end, we may now say that this was implicit in its beginning. Let us briefly examine this record. In 1933, the kingdom inaugurated its full independence by a massacre of the Assyrians carried out by the Iraqi army. At the beginning of 1935 the threat of tribal unrest in the Euphrates area forced the ministry of Ali Jawdat al-Ayyubi to resign. He was followed in March by Jamil al-Midfa'i, who after a fortnight in power also resigned under the threat of a tribal uprising. He, in turn, was followed by Yasin al-Hashimi whose Ministry lasted until October 1936. Under this ministry the tribes of Rumaitha in the Diwaniyya province rose in rebellion in May 1935; martial law was declared, and the army, helped by aerial and ground bombing, put down the revolt. At the same time the tribes of Suq-al-Shuyukh and Nasiryya in the Muntafiq province also rose and had to be put down by the army. In the summer of the same year the Kurdish tribes of Barzan showed signs of rebellion and the government had again to proclaim martial law and to send an army contingent which established order for a time. In the following October the government sent out a punitive expedition against the Yazidis of Jabal Sinjar who were objecting to army conscription, put down their opposition and hanged two Christian notables from Mosul as well as seven *mukhtars* of Yazidi villages.[2] The attempt to apply military conscription to the tribes resulted in other outbreaks, of which the most serious was at Rumaitha in April 1936, which the government, armed as it was with an air force, put down with the utmost severity: the killing, it seems, was indiscriminate, and old men, women and children were the victims of machine-gunning and bombing from the air. The Agra' tribes in Diwaniyya also objected to military conscription and revolted in June of the same year; their revolt was put down and the government hanged and imprisoned their chiefs. At the end of October 1936 General Bakr Sidqi, who had directed the operations against the

Assyrians and the Euphrates tribes, together with a fellow general Abd al-Latif Nuri, whom financial embarrassments induced to enter the conspiracy,[3] carried out a *coup d'état* against Yasin al-Hashimi, banished him, together with Rashid Ali al-Gailani, and Nuri al-Sa'id, from Iraq, having previously ordered the murder of the latter's brother-in-law, Ja'far al-'Askari. Bakr put in power a civilian confederate, Hikmat Sulaiman. Under this Ministry in May 1937 the tribes of Samawa in Diwaniyya also rose in revolt, as a result of agrarian unrest and their objections to military conscription. Their revolt was put down with the help of indiscriminate aerial bombing. In August an army corporal, instigated by his officer, shot and killed Bakr Sidqi; thereupon the commander of the Mosul garrison, Muhammad Amin al-'Umari, threatened rebellion unless Hikmat resigned office. Hikmat resigned and Jamil al Midfa'i negotiated with the officers and obtained the succession.[4] His Ministry lasted until December 1938 when five colonels in Baghdad, in a conspiracy with Nuri al-Sa'id and Taha al-Hashimi, compelled him to vacate office. Nuri became prime minister and Taha minister of Defence. Nuri remained in office until February 1940 when dissension broke out between his military supporters, who were divided into two factions. One faction attempted a *coup d'état* against Nuri, and the other a second *coup d'état* in favour of Nuri; they were victorious and Nuri remained in office until the end of March when the intrigues of Rashid Ali al-Gailani, then chief of the royal cabinet, compelled him to leave office. Nuri's supporters in the army now bestowed their protection on Rashid, who after the fall of France felt confident enough to challenge the British government by following a pro-German policy. Abd al-Ilah, the regent, who took the place of King Ghazi, killed in a motor accident in 1939, attempted to dismiss Rashid in January 1941. He was threatened by the colonels and fled to Diwaniyya. Rashid Ali, faced with the scandal, resigned and was succeeded by Taha al-Hashimi on 1 February. Exactly two months later, the colonels extorted Taha's resignation, the regent fled the country, and Rashid Ali took power again. He deposed the regent and declared war on Great Britain, but his movement collapsed at the end of May and he fled to Germany, where he spent the rest of the war. The British occupation of Iraq which followed Rashid Ali's movement froze the political situation, but no sooner was the war finished than the Kurdish tribes of Barzan rose in revolt; it took two months, from August till October 1945, to put down the rebellion; thereafter the Kurdish areas were in a constant state of effervescence, under continuous and vigilant military control, the civilian administration being frequently in the hands of the local military commander. At the beginning of 1948 the prime minister, Salih Jabr, negotiated the Portsmouth treaty with Great Britain; his enemies and rivals in Baghdad succeeded in rousing the mob which frightened the regent into disowning the prime minister. A few months later Iraq joined the other states of the Arab League in the invasion of Palestine: the enterprise proved ill-judged, futile and disastrous. After the establishment of the state of Israel the government succeeded, during 1950–1, in reducing the prosperous Jewish community, by means of intimidation, persecution and confiscatory legislation, into a horde of refugees. In 1952 riots broke out in Baghdad which compelled the government to substitute direct for indirect suffrage. And in the summer of 1958 took place the fourteenth of July of Abd al-Karim Qasim.

This bare record of twenty-six years of independent government is a grim history; and when we add that in the thirty-seven years which lie between the accession in 1921 of Faisal I to the throne of Iraq and the murder in 1958 of his grandson Faisal II, fifty-seven ministries took office, we must conclude that such a condition argues a wretched political architecture and constitutional jerry-building of the flimsiest and most dangerous kind. The kingdom of Iraq was, in its origin, an emanation of British policy. It was the ingenuity, persistence and devotion of British officials which set up this structure which has proved so shaky and so impermanent. To understand why it crashed it is therefore necessary to begin by examining the materials they chose and the methods they employed. The kingdom which British policy put together in 1921 was built round one man, Faisal, the third son of the sharif of Mecca who, at the end of the first world war, had been installed king in Damascus and from which he was evicted in the summer of 1920, by the French, who had lost patience with his intrigue and vacillation, with the anarchy which his rule promoted, and the inimical agitations of his supporters. No sooner was Faisal out of Syria than his friends in Great Britain, of whom the best known was Colonel Lawrence, attempted to instal him as king of Iraq. Faisal's character was not unknown to his partisans; in *Seven Pillars of Wisdom* Colonel Lawrence called him a weak man, while in the manuscript of his book he had added that he was an empty one as well. When, in August 1920, the British ministers asked the French government to consent to Faisal's installation in Iraq, the latter

239

made strenuous objections and Berthelot, the foreign minister, informed Lloyd George that in his view Faisal was 'a weak man, of very feeble character, of considerable prestige, but dangerous'. Lloyd George agreed with this estimate but said that Faisal was wanted by 'the sheikhs' of Mesopotamia, and that if the French consented to his candidature the British government would be able to release seventy thousand troops who were engaged in policing the country.[5] Curzon, the foreign secretary, attempted a stouter defence of Faisal's character and of British policy, but privately confessed his doubts and hesitations. 'We hinted', he wrote to Sir Herbert Samuel on 15 August 1920, 'at Feisal for Mesopotamia, but the French pronounced him a double-dyed traitor, and almost screamed with rage. The idea must probably be postponed at least for the moment. Nor am I quite sure it is sound, for he was clearly weak and was a puppet at Damascus'.[6] The doubt was not misplaced, for Faisal in Baghdad soon showed the same unreliable character and used the same devious methods which led the impatient French to rid themselves of his rule in Damascus. The same refrain is heard during the years of his rule in Baghdad. 'King Faisal', says Sir Henry Dobbs the High Commissioner to the American Consul in 1923, 'is not a masterful leader' and he therefore expects trouble after the conclusion of the Turkish Treaty.[7] In the judgment of the chairman of the League of Nations Mosul Commission Faisal was 'a poor creature';[8] 'I wish' writes Dobbs in 1929 to an official at the Colonial Office, 'King Faisal were not so chameleon-like, He is a very exhausting person to live with and I think his prime ministers all feel the same'.[9] Even Miss Bell, his warm partisan, came to confess, less than a year after his enthronement, that the king was not dependable: 'Mr Cornwallis and I', she wrote in a letter of 4 June 1922, 'had a long talk. I told him I was very unhappy over the king's indecisive attitude, his refusal to contradict the statements of the extremist papers and the backing he was giving to the most ignoble extremists. He agreed and said he had fought with him and was feeling bitterly disillusioned'.[10] 'Oh the king, the king!' she exclaims two days later, 'If only he would be more firm!' and a month later she is bitter about still more evidence of his 'double-dealing'; she confronts him with it and 'after two hours' discussion, he embraced me with great fervency and we parted on rather unsatisfactory terms of close sentimental union and political divergence!' On 31 August she is driven to write of Faisal that he is vain and feeble and timid and that his fine ideals can never come to maturity, and some two months later, reporting one of his manoeuvres she sums up admirably his usual political style as exhibited both in Syria and Mesopotamia and the lack of character which went with it: 'He wants', she wrote in a letter of 25 October, 'to get another party going composed of the extremists whom he thinks he dominates (in reality they dominate him)'.[11]

His ten years reign revealed other, baser, aspects of his character. He was a womaniser. This in a Muslim ruler is of course in itself nothing unusual or shameful, but there was a furtive underhand quality in his womanising. He was widely – and once publicly – accused of seducing the wives of his ministers and officials, and on his European jaunts he disported himself with mistresses, using the title of Prince Usama.[12] He also showed greed for money and posesssions: 'His attempts to acquire land for himself, for he had no private fortune', remarks a writer in the *Survey of International Affairs* for 1934, 'laid him open to criticism'.[13] What the writer meant may be illustrated from a case which the United States minister in Baghdad reported in a dispatch of July 1932. The case which, according to this dispatch, was widely known and talked about, concerned an extensive tract of land on the outskirts of Baghdad which an Armenian landlord had transformed into an orchard with forty thousand trees. The king coveted the land and the government started expropriation proceedings, having so changed the law that the compensation to which the proprietor was entitled became derisory.[14]

In the years following Faisal's accession it became the official British refrain that Faisal was the free choice of Mesopotamia: 'We have been accused frequently and vigorously', stated B. H. Bourdillon, a high official at the British residency in Baghdad, 'of foisting an alien king upon a people unwilling to receive him. That', he asserted, 'is sheer nonsense'.[15] The evidence, of course, absolutely contradicted this assertion. Some of it has been examined in another work.[16] It will suffice here to refer to one incident characteristic of the times. When Faisal came to Iraq the *sous-préfet* of Tauriq in the Kirkuk area one day received an order to organise a petition in favour of Faisal's candidature, but towards the evening he heard a rumour that the British had changed their minds. Having no means of discovering how things really stood he decided to prepare two petitions – signatures and all – one in favour of and one against the candidature, and in due course presented both to his British superior.[17] The words of the American consul in fact sum up the situation exactly: 'The Amir Faisal', he wrote in a dispatch of 7 July 1921, 'comes as the candidate for the throne of Mesopotamia. His candidacy is very unpopular, but he has the support of the government and will probably win. No one will dare put forward another candidate or make open propaganda against him. . . . However it is still announced that the people will be left free to choose whomever they desire'.[18] Faisal then, was brought to govern a country riven by obscure and malevolent factions, unsettled by the war and its aftermath, and confused by the sudden disappearance of a rule some four centuries old; he had now to establish his authority and impose his will on men in whom the collapse of the old order had awakened vast cupidities and revived venomous hatreds. At the best of times Mesopotamia – as its history shows – requires strong men to rule it; and Faisal, as all who had reason to know him agreed, was a weak man. In order therefore to govern his new state he had recourse to the shifts and contrivances which weak men, placed in positions of power, have to use: deceit, double-dealing, complicated intrigues, ambiguous advances and still more amgibuous retreats. Faisal owed his throne to the British; as Miss Bell put it in a private letter, 'We have carried him on our shoulders'.[19] And the British did continue faithfully to carry him on their shoulders. The high commissioner, the British advisers and inspectors, the Colonial Office in London and British · representatives in Geneva used the power and resources of the empire, to protect, uphold, shield and magnify their client. They could do little else, for if Faisal in Iraq was their creature, they by the same token were committed, were bound to him; for it became impossible, unthinkable, in spite of any doubts or misgivings to abandon a policy on which ministers and officials had publicly staked their reputations.[20]

But this British protection and support made it all the more necessary for Faisal to cultivate anti-British sentiment. He had to govern a country among whose tribes anti-British sentiments had been fanned to such an extent that civil war resulted; and he had to govern with the help of ex-Ottoman officials who had no reason to feel grateful to Britain. 'There is as yet little patriotic feeling in the country and a great deal of pro-Ottomanism', wrote Miss Bell in September 1921; 'There is a very large part of the population', wrote the American consul in the following November, 'who would welcome with open arms the return of the Turks'; and again in January 1922: 'Faisal has never been popular. He was forced upon the country and almost all the Arabs are said to harbour a resentment.'[21] And some eighteen months later the verdict is the same: 'There appears to be absolutely no enthusiasm for Faisal in any part of the country and the opposition is quite open and often very bitter.'[22] Here then was Faisal's dilemma; he could not dispense with British military support, since he was a foreigner who had neither position nor following in the country, and to create this position and this following he had to oppose his benefactors, the British, and give countenance to their enemies. The methods he adopted to resolve this dilemma well illustrate his character. He appointed as chamberlain of his court Fahmi al Mudarris, an ex-Ottoman official and a descendant of a well-known Baghdad family of divines; a man who had all reason to deplore and abominate the situation of his country and the humiliation which British arms had inflicted on Islam; he was not a friend of Faisal's patrons. On 23 August 1922, the first anniversary of Faisal's accession to the throne, the British high commissioner, Sir Percy Cox, coming to offer his congratulations, found himself received by a crowd outside the royal palace who were shouting hostile slogans; 'Evidently,' says the high commissioner in his account of the incident, 'by design on the part of the king's chamberlains, the leaders of the two extreme Nationalist parties had been given appointments just before myself, and, after offering their congratulations to the king, had prolonged their visit to the royal apartments so as to ensure that they should be present when I arrived.' And on his arrival they were stationed on the balcony of the royal palace, making anti-British speeches to the crowd below. One of these leaders was Mahdi al-Basir, a Shi'ite, one of that group of Baghdad Shi'ites who, organised in the *Haras* Party, had done much to encourage the uprising of the Euphrates tribes against British rule in the summer of 1920. On this occasion it was 'by direction or permission' of Mudarris, as the British letter of protest to Faisal put it, that he was making an inflammatory speech 'abusive of the British in Iraq'. The high commissioner demanded that the king should punish those responsible, but providentially for him, Faisal at that very moment became incapacitated by illness and it was the high commissioner himself who had to carry out, and incur unpopularity, for the measures he had demanded.[23]

Previous to this incident the king had been intriguing against his own cabinet, presided over by Abd al Rahman al-Naqib, an upright and honourable old man, and against pro-British elements in the provinces. He attempted to draw to his side the Shi'ite divines who had

243

led the anti-British rebellion two years before. 'It was then rumoured in Baghdad', writes a biographer of Muhammad al-Sadr, one of these divines, 'that His Majesty King Faisal expressed his feelings towards the Naqib's cabinet . . . and asked that something be done to destroy it. His Grace [al-Sadr] therefore assembled at his house in Kazimayn the *ulamas* and some tribal heads . . . and deliberations ended with a petition to be presented to His Majesty containing national [i.e. extreme] demands which the Naqib's cabinet would not be able to bear'.[24] An Iraqi minister who was then an administrative official tells us in his memoirs that Faisal, in order to bring about the downfall of his cabinet, incited Ali Jawdat – one of those Iraqi officers who had been with him in Syria – who was then *mutasarrif* of Hilla, to go to Najaf – a main Shi'ite centre – and rouse the Shi'ite tribes so lately pacified by his British patrons. Ali Jawdat seems also to have concerted a secret plan with the tribal leader Abd al-Wahid al-Hajj Sikar, to set up in each tribe on the mid-Euphrates a shaikh who would be the rival of the existing British-appointed shaikh, and who would refuse to obey the incumbent shaikh's orders. A similar tactic was followed in the Muntafiq, another Shi'ite area, by its *mutasarrif*, Yasin al-Hashimi, who had also been a member of Faisal's regime in Syria, but pro-British tribes were here so numerous that they attacked him and Yasin had to flee the *liwa* he was supposed to administer.[25] The king, in fact, intrigued to such good purpose that the provinces were again in turmoil, and public order in the Muntafiq, says the British official report, hung in a trembling balance. When the cabinet indicated its disquiet at these proceedings and demanded that the king should show unequivocally that it could rely on his support and assistance, he characteristically replied with an ambiguity, saying that he saw no reason to change his policy.[26] We hear the echo of these affairs in Miss Bell's letters to her parents. Miss Bell was distressed by Faisal's mischievous activities and she went to remonstrate with him and tell him how unhappy he was making her:

I began by asking him whether he believed in my personal sincerity and devotion to him. He said he could not doubt it because he knew what I had done for him last year. I said in that case I could speak with perfect freedom and that I was extremely unhappy. I had formed a beautiful and gracious snow image to which I had given allegiance and I saw it melting before my eyes. Before every noble outline had been obliterated, I preferred to go, in spite of my love for the Arab nation and my sense of responsibility for its future. I did not think I could bear to see the evaporation of the dream which had guided me day by day.

She reproached him for stirring up the Muntafiq against the British adviser, Major Yetts, who 'in the days when I had upheld the Arab cause against A. T. Wilson' has stood by her and her cause. The interview was emotional; he kissed her hands at intervals; on leaving, it was she who attempted to kiss his hand and 'he warmly embraced me'. 'I am still,' she confessed *sous le coup* of this interview.'[27] These intense sentimental encounters could not of course make Faisal more upright or more dependable. The *bouleversement* in which they plunged the oriental secretary of the British residency indicate only how sodden with emotion was her approach to oriental politics.

But it may be objected that while such behaviour merely continued the tactics which Faisal had followed in Damascus, yet as the years went by and his rule became firmer the king changed his character and shed his weaknesses; that his experience deepened and his authority increased. But such is not the case. It is, of course, true that his situation in Baghdad was vastly different from that in Damascus; the cause however lay not in him but in the circumstances he confronted. In Mesopotamia he did not have to contend with a France bent on asserting its authority; he was, on the contrary, surrounded by the solicitude and devotion of fond protectors, by British officials labouring throughout the length and breadth of the land to establish his authority and increase his influence, and by the Royal Air Force ever ready to punish tribal rebels and strike terror in the heart of his enemies.[28] Furthermore, the British government which was doing so much for Faisal seemed anxious to give in to his demands one after the other; it seemed anxious finally to be rid of responsibility, and to bestow the plenitude of power on its client. This is why Faisal's policy, which he himself succinctly and exactly defined as one of taking and demanding,[29] a policy which failed miserably with the French in Damascus, succeeded so brilliantly with the indulgent British in Baghdad. Faisal's testing-time would have come with the end of the mandate and the withdrawal of the British power which time and again so providentially solved his dilemmas for him. Fortunately perhaps for him, he died soon after Iraq became fully independent, and he did not have to negotiate unaided the murderous currents of Iraqi politics.

A decade of rule did not seem to increase his popularity. In a dispatch of February 1932 the American Chargé d'Affaires declared that when Faisal appeared on the streets no one took much notice of him. He himself has often seen the king pass along the main street but the only people who seemed to take any notice were the foreigners, who paused and lifted their hats.[30] But Faisal himself seemed to become cocky and over-confident. In a speech which he gave towards the end of 1931 he recalled his brief, inglorious rule in Damascus and told the Syrians that if they had listened to his advice they would be enjoying independence like the Iraqis.[31] He brought back from his European trips admiration for Mussolini. He wanted to emulate the Italian dictator, trying to concentrate policy in his own hands in the belief that he could govern the country with the help of a small body of advisers. A newspaper article, no doubt inspired by him, advocated a one-party system and rule by an enlightened despot, the despot in question clearly being Faisal himself.[32] A few months before he died he was, in the judgment of a high British official, in a fair way to becoming a dictator.[33] But it is extremely doubtful whether he would have been able to sustain such a role in a crisis or against determined opposition.

One episode, which took place shortly before his death, gives a clue to what might have happened had he lived on. The Assyrians, Christian hill people, who originally lived in south-eastern Turkey, were seduced by Russian promises during the first world war from their allegiance to the Ottoman state. They rose in rebellion, and finally had to flee from Ottoman territory. The end of the war found them, a miserable remnant of refugees in the care of the British government (to whom they furnished contingents of efficient and brave levies), who thought to settle them in Mosul, which the League of Nations had awarded to Iraq, one of the reasons of the award being that the Assyrians should not once again come under Turkish rule.

When Iraq became independent, relations between the Iraqi government and the Assyrians went from bad to worse. The trouble came to a head in the summer of 1933. The king was abroad and Rashid Ali al-Gailani was prime minister in Baghdad. The Shi'ites in the south were almost in open rebellion against the government. To create a diversion and unite all Muslims against non-Muslims, Gailani and his colleagues determined to hit the Assyrians hard. The government detained their patriarch in Baghdad and dispatched a force to Mosul under Bakr Sidqi which clashed with a body of armed Assyrians and then carried out an indiscriminate massacre in the Assyrian village of Simel. When the king heard of the patriarch's detention and the dispatch of the army, he repeatedly sent emphatic telegrams to his prime minister asking him to follow a policy of

246

moderation, not to push the Assyrians to desperate acts, and particularly not to insist on forcibly disarming them alone, when all the tribes of Iraq, including the Assyrians' Kurdish neighbours, disposed of weapons which the Government was not proposing to take away. The Government's measures, the king thought, were bound to leave a deplorable impression abroad. Rashid Ali was not to be deflected from his grim purpose by the king's objections; the honour of the government, he kept on saying, must be upheld; we must teach the Assyrians that they cannot rebel with impunity, firm measures must be taken. We are sorry to have displeased Your Majesty, his last telegram blandly said, but we apprehended no external danger which could threaten the country as a result of the measures we took to uphold the law.[34] The resolute Rashid Ali had his way; he brushed aside the king and his apprehensions, and was proved right, for no danger, except some League of Nations resolutions, ever did threaten the newly won independence. This incident, like the palace incident of 1922, shows that the king's character and position were still the same as in Damascus; that, as in Damascus, a crisis or an emergency would find him the plaything and the prisoner of his strong-willed and violent followers. The massacre having taken place, the king decided to return to Baghdad, where his last public act was to stand at a balcony of his palace and acknowledge the acclaim of the delirious crowd celebrating Bakr Sidqi's victory.[35] Had he publicly indicated his disapproval of the massacre, the crowd, incited by the government, would probably have turned on him and deposed him. There had indeed been rumours that he would abdicate in favour of his son and 'strong indications', as the American minister put it, that nationalists were threatening to force his abdication; and the crowd acclaiming the Assyrians' massacre shouted not only 'Long live the King' but also 'Long live the Emir Ghazi' and 'Long live King Ghazi'. When Faisal died soon afterwards, a Baghdad newspaper went so far as to allege that he had actually committed suicide.[36]

He was succeeded by his son Ghazi, who reigned until 1939 when he was killed in a car accident. The son was even less suited than the father to monarchical office. He was, as a British ambassador described him, as 'weak and unstable as water', of 'intemperate habits', choosing as his boon companions palace servants and wild young army officers.[37] The father at least had dignity and prudence, and was so charming in his manner that he seemed to have captivated and attached to himself those numerous British officials who did so much

247

to further his ambitions; he also had the good sense to trust himself to their devotion, and to allow them valiantly to fight his battles for him. Lord Keynes recounts a story which, whether true or not, is as symbolic of Faisal's pathetic incompetence as of the methods and the legends which accompanied his rise to power. 'It was about this time', writes Keynes, describing the atmosphere of Paris during the peace negotiations of 1919, 'that the Emir Faisal, so it was alleged, recited in M. Pichon's cabinet, unabashed by the naked charms of Rubens' Marie de Medicis, a chapter of the Koran, whilst Colonel Lawrence, in his capacity of the emir's interpreter, propounded an ingenious *politik* for the creation of an Arab hegemony from the Mediterranean to the Persian gulf, over Damascus and Mosul and Baghdad'.[38] Of Ghazi, such a story could not have been told. This raw youth, whose father worried about his backwardness,[39] was given to as violent courses as the wildest of his companions. One of his pranks, which de Gaury reports, was to have a servant's face painted with luminous paint.[40] This waster was, however, by no means uninterested in politics, whether internal or external. It is highly likely that he was privy to Bakr Sidqi's *coup* of 1936 against Yasin al-Hashimi's ministry, if he did not actually inspire it. Yasin, it would seem, had wished to marry his own daughter to the young monarch and this inspired in Ghazi mistrust in his chief minister and fear of his designs.[41] Yasin's brother Taha, who was dismissed as chief of staff as a result of Bakr's *coup*, recorded in his *Diaries* his conviction that the king was pleased by the *coup d'état* because Yasin's government had sought 'to preserve his honour' by preventing 'this youth who inclined to be dissolute and lewd' from mixing with 'those who had no morals'. When the *coup* took place Yasin, it would seem, asked Ghazi to sign a proclamation denouncing it, but the king was unwilling, and this led Yasin to offer his resignation without putting up any resistance. Ghazi's ex-tutor later informed Taha that the king was boasting that it was he who had organised the *coup*. Suspicion of Ghazi was strong among Yasin's colleagues who had been unseated by the *coup*, so strong indeed that Nuri al-Sa'id went so far as to propose his services to Ibn Sa'ud in securing the Iraqi throne for one of his sons.[42] Shortly before his death in 1939, Ghazi it would seem was involved in another *coup d'état*, an abortive one – against Nuri al-Sa'id who was then prime minister.[43]

In foreign politics, Ghazi seems to have had the same irredentist ambitions which are characteristic of his house. Propaganda on his behalf was rife in Syria and Palestine, and his public pronouncements reinforced this propaganda. At a military review, for instance, held on the occasion of his birthday in March 1939, his speech referred to 'our Arab brothers in whose future and welfare we are interested'. Several people reported, the American minister stated in a dispatch, that the king had actually referred by name to Syria, Palestine, and Kuwait, though the address as published did not contain these references.[44] A Syrian who was then working in Baghdad tells us that he wrote an incendiary article on Syria which was broadcast on the king's radio station and followed by Ghazi's voice exclaiming, 'I run to thine aid, I run to thine aid, O Syria (*Labbayki, labbayki ya Suriya*).[45]

A year or so before his death, he installed a private transmitter in his palace (said to be a gift from the Nazis)[46] and broadcast incitement and sedition to the population of the principality of Kuwait where, as a result, an abortive revolt broke out. One evening, shortly before his death, when the prime minister was abroad, Ghazi summoned the chief of the general staff and ordered him to arrange for the army immediately to occupy Kuwait. The order threw his entourage into a panic and they summoned the acting prime minister who persuaded the king to abandon his scheme. Ghazi was succeeded by his infant son, Faisal, who was brought up by his mother (who died when he was still an adolescent) and by her devoted sisters. A pleasant and harmless young man, he ascended the throne in 1953 and was mowed down by his army five years later. During his brief reign he lived in the shadow of his uncle Abd al-Ilah, the regent and crown prince, and of Nuri al Sa'id who, in the last years of his life, ruled pre-eminent over all the politicians of Iraq. With the murder of Faisal II the brief Sharifian period of Iraq, begun with intrigue and civil war, ended in horror and blood.

Though Lloyd George agreed with Berthelot's estimate of Faisal's character, he yet pleaded that 'the sheikhs' of Mesopotamia wanted him to be king. How far was this the case? It is of course true that when he was negotiating with the French a civil war was raging in Iraq. The Shi'ite tribes of the Euphrates, inspired by their religious leaders in Najaf, Karbala and Kadhimain, and by the incitement and help of Sharifian agents from Syria,[47] were in a state of dissidence, attacking British troops, cutting communications and besieging towns and administrative centres. But the Shi'ite divines who inspired their revolt were not exerting themselves in order that Faisal and his

Sunni ex-Ottoman officers should be installed to rule over them from Baghdad. These divines, encouraged by the departure of the Ottomans, saw in the unsettlement of Mesopotamia after 1918 an opportunity to obtain power and preponderance after so many centuries of Sunni domination. When the British government, having put down the Euphrates revolt, proceeded to instal Faisal and his followers in Baghdad, their dismay was great. So strongly did they manifest their discontent at this turn in events that Faisal's government, under British inspiration, alleging as a convenient pretext modern notions of nationality then quite unknown to the country, had them deported from Mesopotamia on the score that they were Persian subjects![48] The British official report, concerned to justify these actions, itself gives an indication of the true state of affairs and of the motives of the leaders of the revolt of 1920.

The political ambitions of the Shi'ah Religious Headquarters [we read in the report for 1922–3] have always lain in the direction of theocratic domination; they had been sedulously checked by the Turks, but it might reasonably be hoped that the Arab government in its initial stages would not offer so resolute an opposition, provided that it could be deprived of British support. The Mujtahids, who are almost without exception Persian subjects, have no motive for refraining from sacrificing the interests of Iraq to those which they conceive to be their own, nor does their attitude of obscurantist detachment from the world, and from any science save that which is based on the Moslem scripture, place them in a position to gauge the needs of a state which is striving in the path of progress and enlightened self-government.[49]

The Shi'ites remained unconvinced of these benefits and persuaded that the Baghdad government was a creature of the British and an instrument of Sunni persecution, different from its Ottoman predecessor only in that it was without benefit of long legitimate possession, and in that its rule did not derive from conquest, but was bestowed upon it by the British. A Baghdad journalist recounts how he took a trip to the Euphrates in 1927 in the company of Glubb and of a Shi'ite tribal leader who had taken part in the revolt of 1920. They were looking at one of the battlefields of the revolt and Glubb, it seems, observed that the objects of the uprising had been attained. 'You now have', the journalist reports him as saying, 'a government, a constitution, a parliament, ministers and officials, what more can you want?' Whereupon the tribal leader interrupted him, saying bitterly, 'Yes, but they speak with a foreign accent.'[50]

Another Shi'ite who took some part in the uprising of 1920 in his *Memoirs* bitterly comments on the contrast between the British treatment of those who took part in the Sharif's revolt and those who collaborated in the Iraqi revolt. In Iraq, he says, the former were overwhelmed with wealth, spoils and position so that 'having been poor, they are now men of large means and having been famished, are now satiated'.[51]

Shi'ite grievances remained alive, and led again and again to revolts and agitations in the Euphrates, engineered and exploited by the politicians of Baghdad in their unbridled quest for power. Even before the end of the mandate, the Baghdad politicians were preparing to exploit these grievances, and the Shi'ite leaders, tribal and religious, were getting ready to extract what advantages they could from the play of political rivalries in the capital. At the beginning of 1931 Yasin al-Hashimi, Rashid Ali al-Gailani and Ja'far abul-Timman, then associated in opposition to Nuri al-Sa'id's administration, visited Karbala to organise Shi'ite support; some six months later, when strikes against Nuri were being organised in Baghdad, the Shi'ite tribes were reported to have offered their assistance to Yasin who informed them that the time was not yet ripe since the British were still in control, and that they should prepare for action as soon as Iraq became an independent member of the League. When this event took place, we find the Shi'ites informing Yasin that he would not receive their support unless he was ready to offer them the majority of the cabinet posts.[52] The Baghdad politicians – Sunni ex-Ottoman officers and civil servants – who were claiming to deliver Arabism from Ottoman oppression – in exploiting and exacerbating the Shi'ite grievances were benefiting from the traditional anti-Shi'ite policy of the Ottomans. This anti-Shi'ite policy had its roots in the traditional enmity and mistrust obtaining between the Persians and the Ottomans since the sixteenth century. In fomenting an anti-British rising in 1920 the Shi'ite divines no doubt hoped to gain and establish ascendancy for their community in a country where the Shi'ites were a majority, albeit hitherto a powerless one. It is difficult to say whether the failure of the uprising or the importation of Faisal and his men which followed it was to them more galling. A Sharifian regime in Baghdad, at all events, spelt renewed Sunni dominance. Bazirgan, who was in Faisal's entourage when he arrived in Mesopotamia, reports as a kind of premonitory symptom the fact that Faisal's followers were already asking how many Shi'ites had been in government employment in Ottoman times.[53] Sunni–Shi'ite antagonism was a constant of Iraqi politics under the mandate. The government, the Shi'ites complained, was the privilege of Sunnis, against whose fanaticism nobody would now protect them. These Shi'ite grievances we find expressed in a document which appeared early in 1932 when the mandate was nearing its end. Issued by the 'Executive Committee of the Shiahs in Iraq', the document is no doubt in some respects a partisan exaggeration; but it is on the whole valuable, not only because many of its complaints were well-founded, but because it gives us some idea of Shi'ite disaffection towards the political institutions of Faisal's kingdom: 'Since the House of Parliament has been formed we have never heard of one Shiah Moslem having been elected from the northern [i.e. Sunni] district; whereas from our districts only one or two [Shi'ites] are elected and the rest are from the other faction'; no Shi'ite had been given the ministry of the interior 'or other such important post'; the government's land policy 'has created all kinds of enmities and feuds between the shaikhs of our tribes'; government teachers 'imbue the students with all kinds of religious beliefs'; Shi'ite officials were few in number and inferior in position, and the document ended by calling on Great Britain to 'take effective measures and relieve us from the disgraceful rule of this faction and the religious fanaticism it exerts to satisfy its personal ambitions'.[54]

The end of the mandate provided no abatement of Sunni–Shi'ite friction. On the contrary, As Yasin al-Hashimi predicted in 1931, the total disappearance of British control enabled the Baghdad politicians to exploit intensively Shi'ite grievances, and the mid-1930s saw the outbreak of one revolt after another, encouraged and abetted by one faction or another in Baghdad, and feeding upon Shi'ite grievances. One such revolt was prefaced in March 1935 by a Shi'ite manifesto, the first article of which stated:

Since independence until today the Iraqi government has followed a foolish policy inconsistent with the interests of the people. It has adopted the policy of sectarian discrimination as a basis for rule, usually having only one or two acquiescent ministers in the cabinet to represent the [Shi'ite] majority. It has followed the same policy in the appointment of officials, and its partiality in the selection of civil servants and members of Parliament has become obvious. . . . In order to infuse once more confidence and a sense of security in the people, and to do away with discrimination, all must participate in the cabinet, in Parliament and in all public employments, as they share in the payment of taxes and military service.[55]

Faisal himself, towards the end of his reign, showed that he was quite aware of the Shi'ites' attitude to the regime. In a memorandum which he wrote and circulated among his intimates in 1932 he said that the Shi'ites believed that death and taxes were their lot, while official positions went to the Sunnis, and that even the holy days of the Shi'ites were not respected by the government.[56] Nor were the Shi'ites mistaken in their grievances. In the Parliament of 1933, for instance – and in this it was typical of other Parliaments that preceded or succeeded it – a country predominantly composed of Kurds and Shi'ites returned a Chamber of Deputies in which there were twenty-eight Shi'ites, sixteen Kurds, and thirty-six members drawn from the small Arab minority which the British Government had installed in power in 1921.[57] The Shi'ites had other grievances. One, which they shared with the Kurds, the Yazidis and the other minorities, was that the government, which entertained grandiose pan-Arab ambitions, was intent on making Iraq into a great middle-eastern military power; for this universal military conscription was necessary. So long as the mandate lasted, in alliance with the Kurds they had successfully opposed its introduction, since the British government was also unwilling to agree to it.[58] With the disappearance of British control, the government was able to push through its parliament the necessary legislation. But the attempt to apply the law caused resistance not only among the Yazidis but among the tribes of the south, who revolted in September 1935 and in February and April 1936. As they said in a letter written before the April 1936 revolt, they found it incredible that the government should impose such a burden on them. Government, they wrote, had a right to their taxes and their obedience and had never demanded more.[59] The pan-Arabism of the regime sometimes also took a form offensive to Shi'ite religious beliefs. The pan-Arabs wished to revive the glories of Arab empire, and to the more fervent among them this meant exalting the purely Arab Umayyads, depreciating the Persianised Abbasids, and denouncing Shi'ism as a foreign, subversive heresy. In 1927 a Syrian Muslim teaching in a government college published a book in which the Umayyads, who had persecuted the caliph Ali and his house, were glorified. The Shi'ites took great offence at this insult to their religion and organised demonstrations in Baghdad to which the Sunnis replied. The demonstrations turned

253

into riots in which many students and policemen were killed.[60] The Shi'ites were again insulted in 1933 by a Sunni polemist who denounced them as anti-Arab in belief and tendency.[61] The scandal caused by his pamphlet led to those disturbances to alleviate which perhaps the repression of the Assyrians was decided upon.

If, despite Lloyd George, 'the sheikhs' neither wanted nor were ever reconciled to Faisal's regime, who then was in its favour? In a Muslim country the cities are traditionally pre-eminent in politics. What did the cities think of Faisal? When the news of his impending arrival in Mesopotamia reached Basra, four thousand, five hundred notables, as the British official report indicates, signed a petition which an 'influential deputation' presented to the high commissioner, requesting that they should not come under Faisal's control.[62] Sulaimaniyya was a purely Kurdish town and the Kurds, as will be seen, would have no part or lot with an Arab government. Kirkuk, as the League of Nations Commission on Mosul reported in 1925, was Turkish; Arbil, the commission also wrote, was divided into seven boroughs. 'We interviewed the *mukhtars* of these boroughs. When asked what was their nationality five replied that they were Turks, one that he was as much a Turk as a Kurd, and the seventh stated that he was a Jew'.[63] Of these towns and cities, only Mosul, a Sunni Arab city on the fringe of a Kurdish and Turkish area, could perhaps be said to favour an Arab Sunni government for Mesopotamia. Even so, it proved by no means easy to elicit unequivocal support for the kingdom. The residency had to exert its influence, and as Abdullah al-Qassab, who was then Iraqi *mutasarif* of Mosul, tells us in his memoirs, it proved necessary for him to take in hand the witnesses appearing before the commission; and since the notables were reluctant to declare for Iraq and Arabism, he also found it necessary to organise and encourage popular and student demonstrations. Though he is rather discreet on the subject, we may suspect that he also winked at even more forcible methods by which Turkish sympathisers – who seem to have been numerous – were persuaded of the error of their ways.[64] Baghdad itself, the capital and most important city of Mesopotamia, could hardly be considered an Arab Sunni centre. It was the administrative and commercial centre of the area, a city with an illustrious Muslim past, and with a population mixed in the extreme; in it lived Shi'ites, Kurds, Persians, and the official and religious classes who supplied the personnel of the local Ottoman administration; in it the Jews were actually the largest single group in the population.[65] The Jews declared that they did not want Faisal, and the Shi'ites, as has been seen, were playing a tortuous game which they lost when Faisal was imposed on them. As for the official classes, they had remained loyal until the end of the Ottoman state and were now smarting under the humiliation of defeat at the hands of a Christian Power, a defeat to which they might yet learn to be resigned but which in 1920 was still too near not to arouse bitterness and hatred. They were certainly anti-British but this did not mean that they were ready to welcome or even to acknowledge the leadership of Faisal and his followers, who had deserted the Ottoman state in the hour of its need and collaborated with the enemy. The older and wiser among them, such as the principal Sunni notable in Baghdad, Sayyid Abd al-Rahman al-Naqib, who accepted defeat and cooperated loyally and honourably with the British, indicated in no uncertain terms their distaste for, and poor opinion of Faisal. For these official classes had never taken seriously the plots and agitations of the nationalist officers who went over to the British after 1914, and had never shown the slightest inclination to secede from the Ottoman empire. The chroniclers, it is true, record the brief appearance, before 1914, of so-called nationalist secret societies in Basra, Baghdad and Mosul, but these, it would seem, were inspired by the Basra magnate Sayyid Talib, the better to prosecute a private quarrel with Constantinople, and were no more heard of when the Sayyid and the state were reconciled. Indeed, when war broke out the British government made overtures to Sayyid Talib which he refused. He was caught by the British on a mission to incite Ibn Sa'ud to join the Ottomans; he was deported to India where he remained until 1917. This episode, it may be said in passing, can perhaps throw light on a period in the life of Nuri al Sa'id which he always kept obscure. Before joining the sharif's rebellion in 1916 Nuri was confined in a prisoner-of-war camp in India. He had not been taken prisoner in battle as an officer in the Ottoman army, for he had deserted from that army a few months before the outbreak of war and had taken refuge in Basra with Sayyid Talib. It was there that the British found him when they occupied Basra, and deported him to India. Why, it may be asked, was a man with such a record, a deserter from an enemy army, treated in such a way? Can the explanation be that he fell under suspicion because he was a retainer of Sayyid Talib's, and thus he was anxious to disown the connection when the Sayyid became later Faisal's rival? Sulaiman Faidi, Sayyid Talib's principal political lieutenant at that period, whose *Memoirs* shed so much light on these obscure events, has recorded that when T. E. Lawrence, who visited Basra in 1915, tried to persuade him to undertake an anti-Turkish movement in Mesopotamia, he refused and informed Lawrence that if the Turks were the enemies of the British, it did not follow that they were also the enemies of the Arabs.[66] Neither the towns then, nor the Shi'ite tribes could be said to have wanted Faisal; some, as has been seen, were actively opposed to him and his party. Exactly the same is true of the Kurdish tribes of the north. They vehemently declared that they had no desire to be ruled from Baghdad. Immediately after the war the British authorities had officially informed the Kurdish tribal chiefs that there was 'no intention of imposing upon them an administration foreign to their habits and desires'.[67] When Faisal was imported into Iraq, the north as a whole had first to be coerced by the Royal Air Force and then gradually coaxed by British officials, using their influence and good repute, into casting their lot with the Baghdad regime.[68] As Bourdillon publicly admitted as late as 1924 it was absurd to say that the Kurds wanted to merge with the Arabs.[69] It is clear that when the League commission investigated the Mosul territory in 1925, the Kurds, as well as other sections of the population, would have emphatically desired to join Turkey had they not been given the impression that British officials would remain for a long time to guide and control the actions and policies of the Faisal regime; and the commission itself recommended that the territory be attached to Baghdad only on condition that the British mandate would last for at least twenty-five years.

But we may doubt whether the mandatory ever intended the mandate to last for anything like a quarter of a century. In 1922 the text of the Anglo–Iraqi treaty had originally set for the mandate a term of twenty years. Owing to agitation in parliament and the press about the cost of holding Mesopotamia, the Conservative government which succeeded Lloyd George's administration reduced this term to four years. The amended treaty was ratified in 1924 after strong British pressure, and the Mosul issue figured a great deal in the debates preceding ratification. To overcome the powerful resistance to the treaty which was organised in the constituent assembly and on the Baghdad streets, the British authorities carried on a press campaign in *The Baghdad Times* – their official mouthpiece – which threatened that unless the treaty was ratified Mosul would be lost to the Turks. On 2 June 1924 the newspaper wrote that the deputies 'ought also to know . . . that if they do not ratify the treaty they will probably lose Mosul. If the treaty is ratified, Britain intends to do all that lies in her power to keep the old Mosul Vilayet as part of Iraq'. Again on 6 June: 'Rather than have Sir Percy Cox and the full might of Britain to defend Mosul, the Assembly prefers to trust Shaikh Ahmad al Shaikh Daoud [a prominent opponent of ratification] to defend Mosul against the Turks!' Two days later an editorial proclaimed with liberal use of italics: 'Britain, the country with the noblest record in Europe, has offered to help Iraq to become free and independent in *four years at most, perhaps in less.*' Finally on 10 June – the climax of the campaign – again making heavy use of italics, the leader suggested: '*We think the government would do well to ask each member of today's session publicly to state whether he wishes to restore Mosul to the Turks or to keep it for Iraq.*'[70] When that day, in the late hours, enough deputies were finally got together to provide a majority for ratification, the motion ratifying the treaty which they approved stipulated that this instrument would have no force if the British government did not safeguard the rights of Iraq in the whole of the Mosul vilayet.[71] And, as is well known, the British did their best to secure this province for their client.[72] But when the Mosul commission recommended that Iraq could have the vilayet only on condition that Britain continue to be the mandatory for twenty-five years, a situation arose which neither the Anglo–Iraqi treaty nor the debates which preceded it had contemplated. It is instructive to note Miss Bell's reaction to the recommendation of the Mosul commission. As early as March 1925, when the commission was still in the country, she gathered unofficially from the Italian secretary to the commission who was her informant that such a recommendation was likely; writing to her step-mother she remarked how silly such a stipulation was since in the last resort, the League of Nations was quite powerless to enforce it, and she added: 'I don't think it will matter.'[73] She was, of course, right. When the report was laid before the League the British government abounded in promises and assurances, and Mosul passed to Iraq. Barely a year later we find the ending of the Iraq mandate being already actively discussed. 'I do not think', remarked Amery to Austen Chamberlain in a letter of 4 April 1927, 'that anyone at Geneva fifteen months ago dreamt that we should propose Iraq for membership of the League in 1928, and at first sight I am inclined to think that we might have trouble from Turkey, as well as from the League, on the ground that we had secured the Mosul frontier by a trick'.[74] In the event, the mandate lasted barely six more years, which saw the British government rapidly abandon one after another of the responsibilities it had solemnly accepted.

The Kurds and the Turks – whom with misplaced ethnological zeal the British officials and the Iraqis after them have insisted on calling Turkomans – of Kirkuk, Sulaymanieh, Arbil and Mosul, together with their rich oil fields, were given over to an Arab regime which came to dispose of the vast oil revenues how and where it liked. The Kurds in particular could with justice complain that left to its own devices the Iraqi government would have never been able to bring them into subjection; that pressure exerted by British officials and bombing carried out by the Royal Air Force until the very eve of independence alone subdued them, delivering them to the alien, heavy-handed, but precarious rule of Baghdad.[75] It is, of course, not unusual in the middle east for government to be exercised by one group over other alien groups. Such exactly was the situation of the Ottomans before the destruction of their empire. But the Ottomans had exercised rule not by false pretences but on the strength of their military and administrative ability. Again, the Ottoman government was not given to doctrinaire adventures, while the Baghdad government was a government of pan-Arabs, perpetually looking beyond the frontiers of Iraq to other Arab territories, and dreaming to be the Prussia or the Piedmont of a new Arab empire. The Kurds had no use for such dreams; they might say, and they did, that the state of which they formed part was Iraqi, not Arab. These things it was possible to say before the British finally relinquished their mandate;[76] after 1932, with the Baghdad government enjoying the utmost plenitude of power, talk of this kind became disloyalty and treason.

British action then, from 1920 until the end of the mandate in 1932, worked powerfully to create in Baghdad a centralised government ruling over a population disparate and heterogeneous in the extreme, whom no ties of affection, loyalty or custom bound to its rulers. To establish the authority of these rulers, therefore, the British, following the logic of their choice, had to exert their power and their influence and eliminate all potential and actual resistance to them; and the fortunate Baghdad government found at its disposal the Royal Air Force to coerce and to inhibit all opposition, and devoted British officials who used their prestige, ability and good name in its favour. Seldom did a government of Mesopotamia have, in the past, the benefit of such assets. The British tamed the Shi'ites and Kurds and made it clear to the Jews, the Assyrians and the other groups that they had to look to Faisal and his men for their protection and welfare. Under their auspices a constitution was promulgated which concentrated all authority in a cabinet responsible to a legislature. This constitution, moreover, deliberately denied in all its provisions any safeguards for the various large and important communities who found themselves, willy-nilly, subjects of the Baghdad government. Many attempts were made to secure and entrench some safeguards for them, but they came to nothing. The Baghdad politicians, with the centralising instincts of ex-Ottoman officials set their faces against it, and it does not seem that the British officials who then guided and supervised them expressed any misgivings about the working of a constitution on the Westminster model in the peculiar conditions of Mesopotamia. The arguments against separate representation as expressed in the Constituent Assembly is exemplified by the words of Da'ud al-Chalabi of Mosul, in the debate of 31 July 1924.

It has been said [he declared] that minorities should be given a fixed number of seats in the Assembly regardless of their proportion among the inhabitants. What is the reason for this demand? When we were considering the matter in committee we summoned the representatives of the minorities to inform ourselves of their allegations and we asked them, Why do you want deputies out of proportion to your numbers? Their answer was silence. If they believe in our brotherliness and rely on our patriotism why do they demand more than their due? The population of Iraq is known, and for every twenty thousand inhabitants there is a deputy. If we allot extra deputies to them, we will be doing an injustice to the majority, but justice should apply to all. Is it right to apply the rules of the constitution to one group and not to another?

The speaker went on to say that the example of the Ottoman empire had shown that minorities should not be given privileges which in the end would harm both majority and minority. The sultans had ceded such privileges as an act of grace, but in the end they had come to be considered a standing right and had threatened the very existence of the state.[77]

In the conditions of Iraq then, such a government was bound to be a centralised despotism. The constitution contained no such checks and balances of the kind made familiar by that of the United States;

259

nor did the country, after the levelling action undertaken by the British government from 1921 to 1932, contain independent centres of power able to check, short of rebellion, the actions of the Baghdad government. The cabinet, it is true, was supposed to be responsible to the legislature. But even before the mandate ended it had become clear, as the Report on the Administration of Iraq for 1928 admitted, that elections and representative government were, in Iraq, a mockery.[78] The writer of the Report consoled himself with the thought that if the Iraqi chamber of deputies was not what is normally meant by a representative assembly, yet elections 'produce a body of men capable of criticising the proposals of the executive and of effectively resisting unwise legislation which might otherwise be put through by a small executive not too closely in touch with rural feeling'. It did not seem to occur to this writer that an assembly which consisted of creatures of the government, nominated by the minister of the interior, and elected on the instructions of his officials in the provinces, was not best calculated to oppose a policy of resistance to the government. What was already apparent during the mandate became unmistakable during independence, namely that the legislature could not control the cabinet, but that on the contrary, elections to the chamber of deputies and appointments to the senate were an additional weapon in the hands of the government wherewith the better to control the country.[79] A curious and revealing incident which took place in the last years of the monarchy shows that it had come to be universally accepted that election was exactly equivalent to appointment. In 1953, the People's Socialist party – i.e. Salih Jabr's faction[80] – decided to boycott the elections. One of its members, a tribal leader from the Euphrates, sure of being returned, disagreed with this decision. He himself, he said, was not prepared to withdraw his candidature unless the party's members who were senators – and membership of the senate was by appointment – also resigned, since, as he claimed, both deputies and senators were equally appointed and there was no difference between them.[81]

Iraq under the monarchy faced two bare alternatives: either the country would be plunged into chaos or its population should become universally the clients and dependents of an omnipotent but capricious and unstable government. To these two alternatives the overthrow of the monarchy has not added a third. The quality of government in Iraq and the outlook it had bred in subject and servant alike, has been sensitively described by an officer of the royal airforce who spent some years in the Euphrates towards the end of the Mandate.

Here [he wrote], the structure of government is shaky and impermanent. Moreover, such control as government exerts over one's affairs is a terribly personal one. Government is not, as with us, a machine which grinds out laws; takes money out of one's pocket or puts money into it; forbids one to do this and permits one to do that with dispassionate implacability. It enters into the house here. It knows that you have four sons and that one of them is a post office official in Mosul. It knows that you have Turkish leanings, and that, as a natural consequence of such, you are not to be trusted. It knows that you were friends with Hamid Khuluf before his exile, that you are therefore probably sending information to Persia, and that it must on that account consider in a fresh light what to do with your claim for water-rights against Muhamed Derwish. It makes a vital difference to the issue of this or that land case whether Abdul Qadir happens to be Mutesarif at the time of its coming before the courts or whether he has been transferred to another district and someone else is sitting in his place. . . . It is this grossly personal element in the all-pervading activities of Government which evokes from the uneducated people that quality which we are all too apt to dismiss as insincerity, but which is, in reality, nothing but the inevitable compromise of any simple man chased by the bogey of insecurity. For an Englishman with a clear conscience there are few occasions when, in facing an acquaintance, he is tempted to express views at variance with his true ones. But the Iraqi before an official, or even before another of his own kind, is in doubt. He must propitiate, and speak fair words. His position is unstable. There is no permanence. He knows that the fact as to whether the official has a good or bad opinion of him will affect his private life vitally. He feels the ground shifting beneath his feet. It is the same with the official himself when he addresses a superior. He too feels the ground quaking beneath him, feels his confidence welling out. He may be sacked because his enemies have spoken ill of him. There will be no redress for him, no rehabilitation, unless he has influence in high places. . . .[82]

The attitude of the ruling classes to the population they ruled was one of disdain and distaste: they were townsmen ruling over a population of primitive countrymen; they were Sunnis ruling over Shi'ites, Jews, Christians and other outlandish sects; they were the government in its exalted majesty and boundless power, the others were the subjects who must be prostrate in obedience. The texts of proclamations to the tribes in revolt are characteristic and revealing: The government desires to spare you, come therefore with all speed to the offices of the government and offer your obedience; otherwise the government will punish you, and yours will be the responsibility.

261

When we consider the long experience of Britain in the government of eastern countries, and set beside it the miserable polity which she bestowed on the populations of Mesopotamia, we are seized with rueful wonder. It is as though India and Egypt had never existed, as though Lord Cornwallis, Munro and Metcalf, John and Henry Lawrence, Milner and Cromer had attempted in vain to bring order, justice and security to the east, as though Burke and Macaulay, Bentham and James Mill had never addressed their intelligence to the problems and prospects of oriental government. We can never cease to marvel how, in the end, all this was discarded, and Mesopotamia, conquered by British arms, was buffeted to and fro between the fluent salesmanship of Lloyd George, the intermittent, orotund and futile declamations of Lord Curzon,[83] the hysterical mendacity of Colonel Lawrence, the brittle cleverness and sentimental enthusiasm of Miss Bell, and the resigned acquiescence of Sir Percy Cox. What are we to say when we find a State Paper presented by a secretary of state to Parliament in 1929, declaring without the suspicion of a doubt or the shadow of a qualification that 'it seemed evident ... that Iraq, judged by the criteria of internal security, sound public finance, and enlightened administration, would be in every way fit for admission to the League of Nations by 1932',[84] and fit, therefore, to exercise the unfettered sovereignty which independent states possess? What, save that the style of State Papers, like so much else, suffered during the first world war irremediable degradation?

But were the wages of degradation, we may ask, at least substantial? Let us look briefly at the record. The British imposed Faisal on Mesopotamia. But Faisal had been earlier imposed by the British on Syria and his followers had used it as a base from which to foment rebellion in Mesopotamia. Faisal's imposition on Mesopotamia therefore looked, paradoxically, like an act of weakness. Miss Bell, coming back from the Cairo conference where Faisal's appointment was decided, admitted as much in a letter to Engert: 'The tribes of the Euphrates,' she wrote, 'discouraged by the failure of the rising which they now regard as a relapse into madness, are also bewildered to find that the sharif's house which last year (so they were told) was anxious to turn us out, is now regarded by us as a suitable source from which an amir might spring'. Miss Bell went on to deny that Faisal had a hand in stirring up the country; but since this assertion is flatly contrary to the evidence we may regard it as expressing not the historical truth but her emotional commitment to Faisal, whom in the same letter she describes as 'a man of high principles and high ideals'. But in any case, whether or not the Sharifians were responsible for sedition in Mesopotamia this, as she wrote, was what the propagandists said and, she added, 'it was believed'.[85] The subtleties of British policy after Faisal's establishment were not calculated to diminish bewilderment and perplexity in the country. Reviewing P. W. Ireland's *Iraq* in 1938, a British official who knew Mesopotamia under the mandate, wrote: 'Sir Percy Cox, Sir Henry Dobbs, Sir Bernard Bourdillon, and above all Sir Kinahan Cornwallis kept on insisting: "Let Mutasarrifs [*préfets*] make mistakes if they want to, don't hamper their initiative. The best way to learn and appreciate the task of administration is by being free to act on one's responsibility".'[86] This confusion between the activity of governing and the activity of educating is in itself and at all times fatal. Its consequences for the people of Mesopotamia were always unpleasant and sometimes disastrous. As for the British, it eroded their prestige and gave them a bad name for unreliability and deviousness; for who in their senses could believe that British advisers, in shielding and supporting native officials who were incompetent, tyrannous and corrupt, were only applying the educational theories of Sir Percy Cox, Sir Henry Dobbs, Sir Bernard Bourdillon, and 'above all' Sir Kinahan Cornwallis? No wonder that, as a writer put it in the early days of Faisal's reign, the mass of the people neither understood nor knew how to deal with the Iraqi government:

In Turkish days [he continued] they knew their position, and knew that they could usually get what they wanted for cash, while in the days of the British government they knew equally well that bribery was useless. They now see the same officials of the old Turkish days back in office again, but with British advisers somewhere in the offing, and they are mystified. They know the official can be bribed; they have bribed him before, but neither the official nor the Arab knows quite how much the adviser sees or what will happen if he does see. . . . It is this [the writer concluded] which makes many of them think that the days of the Turks were the best after all, and might be the best thing for the future.[87]

British advisers and inspectors in the decade between Faisal's accession and the end of the mandate found themselves, it is true, in an impossible position. The executive power lay in the hands of the Iraqi government and its agents and they were merely supposed to advise and supervise. Such advice and supervision was, on the one hand, deeply (and naturally) resented, and was, on the other, quite

ineffective. This ineffectiveness had a simple origin: the British govern-
(which alone could have made the advice of British advisers effective)
was interested not so much in the good government of Mesopotamia
as in speedily shedding all responsibility for it. British advice and
inspection became therefore a make-believe and a rigmarole and it
became profitless to cultivate their friendship or be loyal to them.
This uneasy and equivocal situation is acutely observed by a British
official (whom we have already quoted) who was stationed in the
Euphrates in the late 1920s. *A propos* British officials serving with the
Iraq government, A. D. MacDonald wrote

> The independence which comes from security and the confidence
> which is the fruit of loyal cooperation towards a common goal, are
> lacking. The pressure of material circumstances weighs on this decent
> little group of Englishmen, and robs them of their liberty of thought and
> action. They turn aside to compromise, chafe at the necessity of doing
> so, and begin to hate their masters for forcing them into hating themselves.
> The spirit of enslavement galls and produces in the masters something
> akin to contempt. These shadows of hatred and contempt are discreetly
> cloaked over by good manners, but the percipient observe that they are,
> for all that, present. British prestige declines.[88]

To illustrate the make-believe which British policy encouraged
in Mesopotamia, and to contrast it with the reality, we may set side
by side two documents emanating from the same official, Sir Henry
Dobbs, who succeeded Sir Percy Cox and preceded Sir Gilbert Clayton
as high commissioner in Baghdad. The first is a draft dispatch –
meant for eventual publication – which Dobbs sent to the Colonial
Office early in 1927 for their observations and emendations. The
draft dispatch tries to make out a case for the British laying down the
mandate, and in doing so, makes use of the rhetoric by which such a
policy had been advocated and defended: 'The more we show ourselves disposed to withdraw from Iraq and to foster her advance to
real independence', lays down the dispatch with assurance, 'the
greater and more permanent will be our influence in that country';
and pressing into use the cadences of the English Bible it affirms with
self-satisfied virtue: 'So true is it that whosoever will save his political
influence shall lose it, but whosoever will lose his political influence
for the sake of right dealing the same shall save it.'[89] These were the
public and official sentiments, maintained against all objections and
in the face of the evidence. It is instructive to compare this dispatch
with another from Sir Henry Dobbs to the colonial secretary written

at the end of 1928. In this later dispatch – which was not meant for publication – the high commissioner explains that Faisal was imported by the British and had had no time to strike roots, that there was little affection for or awe of the crown, that there was no national consciousness outside the schools of Baghdad and Mosul (where, as will be seen, the ministry of education subjected pupils to intensive indoctrination) and no respect for courtiers and politicians. Dobbs went on to affirm that the strength of the Iraq government rested overwhelmingly on British support and on the fear inspired by British aeroplanes and armoured cars.[90] It was not only the high commissioner and other British officials who were aware of this gulf between things as they really were and their official and public disguise. The country's official classes therefore concluded that the British in affirming that the emperor was most splendidly clothed, were either gullible or hypocritical. And in both cases it was useless and dangerous to trust and rely on them.

The very bringing of Faisal to Baghdad, then, inevitably entailed for the British consequences ruinous to their prestige. The character of the Iraqi state which they proceeded to set up also involved them in a difficult and unprofitable situation. Iraq was to be a kingdom run on constitutional lines with cabinet and parliament; it was also for the time being a British mandate. A constitution had to be agreed and the mandatory relationship to be defined by treaty. It therefore became necessary for a constituent assembly to be elected which would promulgate a constitution and ratify the Anglo–Iraqi treaty. Having by a *coup de force* made the Shi'ite divines leave the country in 1923, the British thought that all opposition to their schemes was now ended; as Dobbs put it, 'the completion of the registration of primary electors, which had before been found impracticable, was everywhere carried through with success, the most distant tribesmen of the Euphrates and of the Kurdish hills enrolling themselves with astonishing alacrity'.[91] This reaction by 'the most distant tribesmen of the Euphrates and of the Kurdish hills' was perhaps a gratifying but hardly an astonishing reaction to a show of British power. The ensuing elections, such as they were, went smoothly and in the spring of 1924 a Constituent Assembly was in being which seemed quite docile and amenable. This proved an illusion. A number of deputies led by Yasin al-Hashimi organised opposition to the ratification of the Anglo–Iraqi treaty and succeeded so well in terrorising their fellow-deputies[92] that by the beginning of June the docile pro-British majority had quite evaporated. On 4 June, street demonstrations brought the assembly to a stop. 'Ken [Cornwallis] and I,' Miss Bell wrote that day, 'agreed that we have made a mistake. It is, we now see, useless to ask a people entirely unversed in politics to take, through its representatives, a vital decision as to its own future.'[93] But such a mistake the British still had the power to rectify. The high commissioner informed the king that if the treaty was not immediately approved, the assembly would have to be dissolved the following day. The treaty was approved. The episode may be considered the first *coup d'état* to be suffered by the parliamentary system in Iraq.[94] No doubt, the lesson – if they needed to learn it – was not lost on Nuri, Yasin and their fellows. But this was not the only lesson – superfluous as it may have been – which could be learnt, for the British found themselves compelled not only to resort to ultimatums against the parliament they had called into being, but occasionally to help in the rigging of elections. Thus the British officials at the ministry of the interior worked hard in the elections of 1928 to return a pro-government majority.[95] To rig elections, to coerce a parliament, to acquiesce in corruption: the British were driven to such shifts by their very decision to transform Mesopotamia into Iraq and to make Faisal its constitutional king. Not only did the policy they adopted not safeguard their interests – as became clear in 1941 and afterwards – but its very carrying out ruined their prestige and made them widely mistrusted or hated. And those for whose sake they incurred all this, neither then nor later, were able or willing to stand by their benefactors.

Nothing better illustrates the gap between the needs of Mesopotamia and the capacity of its government under the monarchy than the land problem of the south and the manner in which it was tackled. 'Not less than three-fifths of cultivated, and perhaps nine-tenths of ultimately cultivable land in Iraq,' states an official British Report,[96] 'belongs nominally and legally to the state.' Such of this land as was cultivated was occupied, sometimes communally, by tribes in various stages of detribalisation. Their title to the land was imperfectly defined; it had no legal sanction and there existed no land register in which ownership was recorded and boundaries accurately determined. And there was potential divergence and conflict between the customary norms of the tribes and the legal norms of the state. In other words, private property, the foundation of modern constitutional government and the indispensable safeguard against despotism, was in a fluctuating state, imperfectly established and easily disputed. The responsibility and power of the Iraqi state in deciding disputes and conferring legal title was enormous; and only a stable, impartial, benevolent and far-seeing government, or, alternatively, government so constituted as to be responsive to the legitimate demands of all sections of the population, could successfully tackle this vital problem. Either a Cromer or a well-articulated democracy was required; the Faisal regime was neither. To make a satisfactory land settlement one of two policies seemed possible. The government could try to make use of tribal organisation which existed on the margin of the state, and out of the tribal shaikhs make an independent landed gentry, drawing their strength from tribal traditions and practices, which would gradually create a new kind of political life in Mesopotamia free from the centralising bureaucratic tendencies of the Ottoman regime. This was Miss Bell's vision before she succumbed to the charms of Faisal. 'The power of the shaikhs or headmen,' she wrote in a wartime paper, 'was derived neither from the sultans nor from the constitution, nor can it fall with them. It is deeply rooted in the life of the people and with wise supervision will form for several generations to come the staple law and order.'[97] But it is doubtful whether such a scheme would have succeeded. Aristocracies are not made by statute: some such settlement Lord Cornwallis had attempted in Bengal towards the end of the eighteenth century and the result had been the creation of a class of *zamindars* who exemplified all the vices of absent and irresponsible landlordism. There remained the other alternative, namely that the state should accelerate the process of detribalisation, suppress the powers of the shaikhs, and endeavour to create a small settled peasantry with defined rights and duties which would have a visible and permanent stake in the land. Such a policy was more consonant with the traditions of the Ottoman officials and with the aims of the Ottoman state since the initiation of the *Tanzimat*. In the event neither policy was followed. Nothing was done for the cultivator and the shaikhs became a weapon in the hands of Baghdad politicians, to be rewarded or punished according as they supported the winner or loser in Baghdad.[98] When the British occupied the country, in order to facilitate administration and keep control of the tribes, they promoted some sectional heads of tribes to paramount rank. 'The remaining sections', states the official Report for the year 1922–3, 'jealous of the position of their quondam rival and fearing, not without reason, that he might use it unfairly, united to oust him, seeking support from any quarter which was thought to be unfriendly to him'.[99] The pattern thus established subsisted and became ever more permanent as the years went by. The government, able through its monopoly of modern arms to control the tribes as they had not been controlled for centuries, made use of tribal rivalries and established, not an independent landed aristocracy but a servile *clientèle* of tribal shaikhs who were increasingly compelled to look to the politicians in Baghdad for aggrandisement and enrichment, who in turn found them useful weapons in the struggle for power. The Report for 1922–3 already gave an inkling of what was to come. Speaking of the agrarian problems of the Muntafiq province, it said: 'While holding to the principle laid down by officials who have recently been in supreme charge of the division, namely, that good citizens must be judged by their willingness to perform their duty towards the administration, the time is ripe for Arab statesmen to see that rights and duties are apportioned with justice'.[100] A few years later, Sir Ernest Dowson, investigating the problems of land tenure in Iraq, noted how administrative caprice over-rode the best-established prescriptive rights. 'Possession,' he wrote in 1931, 'is ordinarily nine points of the law, but neither long possession nor any other mode of acquisition confers security. Personal influence with the most effective arbiter is commonly the decisive factor at any moment in any particular land dispute: and anyone may find the most convincing claims set aside.'[101] And as late as 1952 we find a law passed for the land settlement of Amara which, continuing the tradition of absolute administrative discretion in matters of landed property, again vested in the minister of finance the ultimate power to determine and assign ownership.[102] Such a development was but taking to its ultimate conclusion the logic of the Ottoman reforms which tried to found an efficient state on the model of the enlightened absolutisms of Europe, and which ended in eliminating all local centres of influence, religious, economic, or tribal, and in making them subordinate to the state. And as is usual in despotism, political power became an avenue to wealth. The ex-Ottoman officers who came with Faisal were obscure upstarts; by the end of the monarchy they and their descendants had become men of substance. Yasin al-Hashimi's methods to this end, having to do with land, are an apposite instance to cite here. When he was a minister of finance from the end of 1926 to the beginning of 1928, a law was passed providing for the distribution

268

of government land to persons undertaking to instal irrigation pumps on them. 'Large estates', declares a dispatch from the United States consul 'were distributed among government officials and their friends'.[103] When Yasin died in 1937, he was a large landowner and was said to have acquired sixteen estates by means of this law. When the same Hashimi was minister of finance in 1933, he had enacted the notorious Rights and Duties of Cultivators Act which deprived the *fellah* of all rights, and made him into a serf. Under this law, the landowner could evict the *fellah* for any activities deemed 'harmful to agriculture'. On the other hand, the agricultural worker was virtually tied to the land: so long as he was in debt to the landowner, it was laid down in the law, he could not be employed by another landowner; and should he be dismissed or evicted, his debts were recoverable from his personal property. This law thus transformed a large – perhaps the largest – number of Iraqis from free persons into mere *adscripti glebae*.

The utter defencelessness of property in the face of official greed and wilfulness appears even more clearly from the sweeping confiscation of Jewish property which, barely constitutional in form, but certainly unconstitutional in substance, was hustled through a secret sitting of the parliament in one single day in March 1951. The cabinet which prepared this measure – headed by Nuri al-Sa'id – included as minister of justice one eminent jurist, Hasan Sami Tatar. He, in common with other ministers, put his name to the law, and no protest at this despotic subversion of what the state existed to safeguard was made by him, or by any other jurist or legislator. This episode presents us with the even more lurid spectacle of the Baghdad Chamber of Commerce – which might have been expected to act as the defender of property – itself co-operating with government in order to facilitate its confiscatory operations.[104] In this, as in so many other respects, the traditions established by the monarchy were merely taken over and extended by its successors.

Baghdad reigned supreme over the country. It disposed of a Parliament which turned out laws at the bidding of ministers, it had an army which, rudimentary as it was, could yet easily over-awe the tribes with their even more primitive rifles, and its civil agents were everywhere, *mutasarrifs* doing the bidding of the minister, *qaimmaqams* doing the bidding of *mutasarrifs*, and *mudirs* doing the bidding of *qaimmaqams*. With its monopoly of law-making and the modern instruments of coercion at its disposal, the state engaged in a whirl of legislation and administration, laying down rights and duties, and as oil royalties came to swell its purse becoming well-nigh the universal provider of livelihood and prosperity for the populations on whom its rule had been imposed in the name of democracy and self-determination.

As the years went by, the state machine expanded and became top heavy, while its control was more severely centralised. The regent, Abd al-Ilah, was determined that his house should no more be exposed to the dangers of army interference of which it had so recently been the victim. Therefore, he who owed his position to the threat of a *coup d'état*,[105] in order to tame the army set out to pursue and punish those officers who had been ready to mutiny on his behalf but who had subsequently mutinied against him. They were, one by one, caught and executed. The last one was Salah al-Din al-Sabbagh, who had taken refuge in Turkey and whom the Turks, when the issue of the war was no longer in doubt, handed over to the British, who delivered him up to Iraq. He was hanged publicly at the gates of the Ministry of Defence. This policy, which the army took to be Abd al-Ilah's own, created fear but also great hatred for the regent, a hatred which was at last satiated when the regent's mutilated body was in turn hung up in the very same place where Sabbagh had been displayed.

Also to ensure that there would be no repetition of Rashid Ali's attempt, the constitution was amended to give power to the king to dismiss cabinets at his discretion. This increased enormously the influence of the royal court and made Abd al-Ilah's will the last word in the state. He disliked opposition and did not scruple to put down the slightest manifestation of it. In 1950, Muzahim al-Pachachi, a senator and ex-prime minister, complained in a speech in the Senate that ministers nowadays were so may Teymourtaches – an allusion to Reza Shah's slavish minister – and continued, 'We are afraid to say the truth, which is that there is a limited number of people in Iraq who direct state affairs according to their own wishes'. This was taken to be an attack on the regent, and Pachachi was shortly afterwards deprived of his seat in the senate on a technicality.[106] At a meeting of ministers and political leaders in the royal court in November 1952 an ex-prime minister, Taha al-Hashimi, defied those present to say that a prime minister was free to choose his colleagues; the regent became angry and started shouting at Hashimi, denying all responsibility for the distempers of the state which he put squarely on the political leaders present. 'You are all responsible for the situation, you are all liars', he exclaimed.[107]

Such then was the state, or, to use a term applied to the Ottoman empire but no less apt in the conditions of Iraq since 1918, such were the members of the state institution. From the nature and origin of the Iraqi kingdom it is clear that they could not be men who represented the principal interests of the country, the Shi'ites, the Kurds, the Jews, the Christians, the commercial interest or the agrarian interest. The state institution was in fact run, to a large extent, by members of the same official classes from whom the Ottoman state recruited its officers and civil servants; and the first generation of ministers, politicians and high administrators were themselves ex-Ottoman soldiers and administrators. It was they who established the political and administrative traditions of the new state and set the pattern to which their successors conformed. These men were not used to the game of politics in a constitutional state. When they had served the Ottoman empire they had not been expected to show initiative or accept responsibility; they had been cogs in an administrative and military machine required to perform as their superiors dictated. When the crust of loyalty to the Ottoman state broke after 1918, they found themselves in an explosive and fluid situation with which they were quite unable to cope. They were also disoriented by the sudden disappearance of the authority to which they had been so long accustomed and by the fact that Faisal and his followers, who had rebelled against the Ottoman state, now occupied all the highest positions in the kingdom. One gets the impression that the senior officers in particular, who had fought until the end in the Ottoman army and who had then been recruited into the Iraqi army, found it easy to stage *coups d'état* and to regard military discipline with scant respect because they could not bring themselves to consider the Iraqi army to be as real as the Ottoman army in which they had been brought up, and because they had before their very eyes the lucrative results which had rewarded the indiscipline of their brother officers who had deserted to the sharif.

The men of the ruling institution who came with Faisal were the pan-Arab doctrinaires whose programme and ambitions became the foundation of Iraq's foreign policy. These ambitions chimed in perfectly with the dynastic views of Faisal and his house who were always looking beyond the frontiers of Iraq, seeking to rule over a Greater Syria or a Fertile Crescent. Iraq's foreign policy was therefore a restless quest for prestige and position in the middle eastern cockpit. Baghdad became a meeting ground of malcontents from Syria and Palestine and further west; and Iraq subsidised pan-Arab propaganda in the Arabic press of Palestine, Syria and the Lebanon; it offered refuge to men like Abd al-Aziz al-Tha'alibi, at odds with the French in Tunisia, to Abd al-Rahman al-Shabandar, fleeing from Syria after the 1925 uprising, to Fawzi al-Qawuqji, the guerilla leader from Palestine, and to the mufti of Jerusalem who was in Baghdad from 1939 to 1941; he was voted £18,000 by the Iraqi Parliament, the Iraqi government paid him £1,000 a month from secret funds and he received two per cent of the salaries of government employees;[108] his men were everywhere, and he became a power in the land; Iraqi officers also, with the knowledge and connivance of the Defence minister and the chief of staff sent arms to the Palestinian guerillas when they rose in 1936-9.[109] Ghazi, as had been seen, coveted Kuwait and sought to create a following in Syria. When he died in 1939, his cousin Abd al-Ilah was imposed as regent by Nuri al-Sa'id, then prime minister. Abd al-Ilah was the only son of Ali, the eldest son of Sharif Husain, who very briefly became king of the Hijaz when his father abdicated in 1924. After his abdication Ali had at various times hoped to be installed by the French as king of Syria.[110] The son considered himself the heir of his father's throne in the Hijaz, and up to his appointment as regent claimed Hijazi nationality.[111] Thereafter, the Hijaz remained a focus of his ambition, to the detriment of Iraqi–Sa'udi relations. As late as the mid-1950s we find him still yearning for the restoration of his house in the Hijaz and instructing the Iraqi ambassador to Saudi Arabia to look out for Sharifian supporters in the country.[112] Abd al-Ilah's ambition also extended to Jordan and Syria. After King Abdulla's murder in 1951 he tried to prevent Abdulla's heirs from ascending the throne so that Jordan might be joined to Iraq.[113] As for Syria, from the end of the second world war to the day of his murder, Abd al-Ilah may be said to have been obsessed by it. He inspired and instigated active Iraqi intervention in Syrian politics which in its mischief and danger was paralleled only by the policies which the Egyptians and the Sa'udis adopted in retaliation.[114] The long duel between Iraq on the one hand and Egypt and Saudi Arabia on the other ended with a decisive defeat for Abd al-Ilah when Egypt and Syria declared a union in February 1958. On that day, Khalil Kanna – who was a minister under the monarchy – tells us one of Abd al-Ilah's eyes burst (*infajarat*) from emotion and vexation.[115] The obsession with Syria may even be said to have directly occasioned the monarchy's downfall, for the Syrio–Egyptian union led to pro-Egyptian disorders in the Lebanon, which in turn led the Iraqi government to send an armed force to the Syrian and Jordanian frontier. This force, led by Qasim, took the opportunity of its passage through Baghdad to carry out the massacre of 14 July.

This dynastic and doctrinaire pan-Arabism also had its great effects on the educational policy of the kingdom. Schools early became seminaries for political indoctrination; men like Sati' al Husri, who was later to sing the virtues of Nazi discipline in a public lecture in Baghdad, were placed by Faisal in charge of the country's youth, who were early taught how to meddle in politics. Husri's role in the schools was crucial. This ex-Ottoman official combined the cold centralising passion of the Ottoman bureaucracy after the Tanzimat with a rigid and humourless pan-Arabism. This pedagogue may literally be called the recruiting-sergeant of pan-Arab ideology, for as he himself said in an address to the Teachers' Club in Baghdad in 1934, universal compulsory military training in Iraq (which had been instituted that year) was the most important event to happen in the Arab east, since compulsory education and compulsory military training complemented each other.[116] With Faisal's support, he early became the dominant power in the Ministry of Education in imposing in educational matters a centralised uniformity on this heterogeneous country and its variegated communities. As he himself tells us in his *Memoirs*, he successfully opposed schemes for opening teachers' training colleges in Mosul and Hilla where he thought that the majority of students would be respectively Christian and Shi'ite; this, he feared would lead to the consolidation of a communal spirit among the teachers.[117] He also opposed *per capita* subsidies to schools established and run by the Jewish or Christian communities because these proposed subsidies – which Jewish or Christian taxpayers might claim as of right – were not conditional, and would therefore not give him the power to impose his views and doctrines on these schools.[118] Husri's aim as a pedagogue was, he tells us 'to spread faith in the unity of the Arab nation and to disseminate consciousness of its past glories'.[119] This was the purpose of his centralising policy, of the curricula he devised, the appointments he made, the frequent addresses and circulars by which he attempted to indoctrinate the school-teachers. In his *Memoirs* he gives us the text of a circular he sent to school-teachers when he was director general of education in 1925. In this circular he points out – which was in fact the case – that people used the word 'Arab' to mean *fellah* or bedouin and that it is associated in their minds with contempt and mockery. Teachers, Husri lays down, must discourage such usage; they must avoid making such a mistake and using the name of this great nation, 'in belonging to which we ought to glory', in this vulgar manner. Teachers have the duty 'particularly to strengthen patriotic and national feeling', and must not use the word 'Arab' in this derogatory sense 'either in their lessons or in their conversation'.[120] Husri's doctrine was spread in the 1920s and 1930s zealously and effectively, the more so that behind it were arrayed the resources and the power of a state. The popularity and influence of the doctrine just before the outbreak of the second world war was such that an Egyptian writer could refer to 'the extreme "Husrism" [*al-husriyya*] which we see rampant in Iraq'. This writer went on to describe the doctrine and its implications:

> We mean by 'Husrism' [he wrote[the feeling that to labour for the sake of Arabism requires the adoption of an inimical stance towards non-Arab elements whether these elements are found within the Arab environment or outside it. This Husrism which we have seen in Iraq weakens the Iraqi entity itself since it looks upon the Kurds with some hatred, and does not desire closer relations with the Iranians or other Muslims who neighbour the territories of the Arabic-speaking peoples. . . . And this cannot but create problems for the Arab front.[121]

In his *Memoirs* Husri also gives details of a history syllabus which he composed for primary schools. The main purpose of the teaching of history in primary schools, he begins by saying, is to impart knowledge of the history of the fatherland and of the nation's past, the aim being to strengthen patriotic and nationalist feeling (*al-shu'ur al-watani wa'l qawmi*) in the pupil's heart. The syllabus culminated in a study of: Italian unity (Cavour and Garibaldi), and German unity, the Hohenzollerns, Bismarck.[122] The purpose of such a curriculum is transparent: Italian unity and German unity were the analogues and prefigurations of the coming Arab unity. Tantawi, a Damascene school-teacher, one of the numerous Syrians and Palestinians whom the Ministry of Education began to import in the 1920s in order to preach pan-Arabism to the less sophisticated Iraqis, tells us that one of the most fervent wishes of the secondary schoolboys whom he taught in Baghdad in the 1930s, while reading the story of Italian unity and German unity, was that Iraq should become a Piedmont or a Prussia and 'thus realise unity with both hands, the hand of the people with its emotions and desires, and the hand of the government with its policy and its weapons'.[123]

The corollary of this indoctrination was that the schools became – and were encouraged to become – political seminaries. Thus those responsible for the riots against the Shi'as in 1927, when the pro-Umayyad book was published, were treated leniently:

The punishments inflicted by the Ministry [the official British Report informs us] were eventually all remitted, even to the extent of recalling three Syrian teachers who were dismissed for publishing in the newspapers a gross insult both to the minister of Education who was a Shi'a, and to the government. ... The incident and its sequel [the Report continued] are ominous. Political and religious agitators have learnt thereby that schools can be stirred up, even on the most childish pretexts, into action which may well result in a breach of the peace. The Ministry of Education must apparently reconcile itself to the fact that in a crisis it cannot trust either the commonsense or the loyalty of teachers.[124]

Similar incidents with similar consequences occurred in 1928 when Sir Alfred Mond visited Baghdad. Then, an anti-Zionist riot took place of which the nucleus was formed by students of the Teachers' Training college and of secondary schools. 'In meting out punishment for this breach of discipline and good order', observed the British Report, 'the authorities perhaps erred on the side of leniency'. It would seem that we may date from this incident the first organisation in Iraq of political extremism which drew its strength from the schools and colleges as well as from the army officers. It was then that a number of young men, including Sab'awi, Fa'iq al-Samarra'i, Husain Jamil, Abd al-Qadir Isma'il, Aziz Sharif and Khalil Kanna, got together in order to organise demonstrations against the mandate and against Zionism in Palestine.[125] The situation became much more serious in the 1930s when the attractions of the Hitler Youth and the activities of the Nazi propagandists in Iraq combined to create in students and teachers a heady nationalist intoxication which reached its paroxism in the Rashid Ali movement. But it is not merely the case that student extremism was the indirect corollary of the politicisation of schools and curricula. On occasion the government itself directly encouraged students to demonstrate and riot. Thus Tantawi tells us that when Ghazi was pursuing an active pan-Arab policy, one morning he and his fellow teachers were assembled by the principal of the Central Secondary School and secretly informed that the

275

government desired a demonstration against French rule in Syria and that the teachers were to organise it. A teacher was detailed to each of the ten secondary schools in the capital and made responsible for bringing the students out.[126] When the British occupied Iraq in 1941 they had to instal their own men in the ministry of education and attempt – of course, in vain – to clean it out. The regent himself, in a speech from the throne delivered in 1941, recognised that education in Iraq had been exploited for political purposes and that the youth had been perverted and led astray.[127] But it was the state itself which had been responsible for perverting and leading the younger generations astray. At the time of the Suez affair the well-known ideologue Abd al-Rahman al-Bazzaz – himself a product of the regime – was the dean of the Law College and he was taken to task by Nuri al-Sa'id's government for not curbing student demonstrations in favour of Egypt; his answer to a police official investigating student activities against Nuri and the Hashemite regime has in it something of poetic justice. 'How', Bazzaz asked, 'can I oppose student strikes in favour of national issues concerning which I entirely share their feelings?' 'Any attempt to prevent students from expressing their sincere and well-behaved [*muhadhdhaba*] feelings in this respect', he affirmed, 'is vain. It only proves how ignorant the authorities are of the spirit of the age and of the public feelings current in student circles.'[128]

The culmination of Iraq's pan-Arab policy came in the middle of the second world war when Nuri al Sa'id, then prime minister, succeeded with British encouragement and support in setting up, with Egypt as principal partner, the Arab League. This enterprise proved a source of endless troubles and intrigues between Egypt and Iraq who sought, each of them, to establish their sole dominance over the other Arab states. In pan-Arab intrigues and combinations were lost not only the Palestine Arabs, but the British position in the middle east as well. We may therefore say that for Britain, which became involved in a pan-Arab policy as a result of his pressure and persuasion, Nuri was one of those friends from whom one prays to be protected.

The Sharifian officers whom Faisal brought with him were, of course, too few to govern the country on their own. As has been seen, they had to share power with the ex-Ottoman officials, who had neither taken part in the sharif's rebellion nor had desired secession from the Ottoman state. For these officials, who had themselves

276

formed part of the state, the condition of Iraq after 1918 was most unsatisfactory. Once they had helped to rule a state which was the one Muslim Great Power in the world, now they were confined to a petty kingdom which a Christian power occupied and controlled. This power had, furthermore, brought in a number of obscure men and put them in positions of authority; and these men were claiming that they were the only genuine Arab nationalists, that their uprising had inaugurated a new Arab renaissance, when in fact they had merely been accessories to the humiliation of Islam. The sardonic bitterness of these official classes, without whom Iraq could not be governed, knew no bounds. The clients of the British, Arab nationalists? They would show them who were the true nationalists. When Nuri al-Sa'id negotiated a treaty with Britain in 1931, his opponents set up a great agitation, claiming that the treaty did not give Iraq true independence but was merely a diabolic device to subject the country more firmly than ever to British control. In the controversies which ensued, the supporters of Nuri and Ja'far al 'Askari taunted Yasin al-Hashimi, who was opposed to the treaty, with having done nothing for Arab nationalism: he had not abandoned the Ottomans in mid-war as the Sharifian officers had done, but had fought by their side until the end, and had only changed sides when Faisal was already in Damascus. One of Yasin's partisans, Fahmi al-Mudarris, was moved to reply in these terms:

It is not wise [he wrote] to blame His Excellency al-Hashimi for having stood firm with the Ottoman army until the last shot had been fired; for his behaviour can be justified on two counts. In the first place, he had the duty, as a faithful commander, to preserve the army and his own honour; in the second, he believed that the destruction of the Turkish army would lead the Arabs to be delivered over and to submit to the Allies who would divide up their country into zones of influence, which is in fact what happened. ... Seeing what it means to keep faith, and what military regulations are, had al-Hashimi abandoned the Turks he would have included himself in the category of traitors.

Again, how dare Faisal and his family claim to be the leaders of the Arabs, and to have saved them from Ottoman despotism? In Ottoman times people were not used to hear of titles such as King of the Hijaz – a title which the Sharif Faisal's father had taken to himself; on the contrary, the proudest title of the Ottoman sultan on the ruins of whose empire Iraq and so many other countries were built, exclaimed al-Mudarris, was that of *Khadim al-haramain al-sharifain,* the Servant of the Two Holy Places (of Mecca and Medina); the highest rank in which the sultans gloried was that of Sweepers of the Holy Places; did they not use the broom as a symbol of their rule? Al-Mudarris has a passage in which he expresses to perfection an attitude which is encountered again and again among the official classes of Iraq whose Ottoman careers had been ended by the British Occupation:

Iraq [al-Mudarris wrote] never was a Turkish colony; it was part of the Ottoman empire which had been independent and autonomous for more than six centuries. Neither was the state Turkish, but Ottoman. This meant that it gathered under its banner different races in the same manner as the Iraqi state would today, had it been independent. The Iraqis were not under the yoke of Turkish rule, as they are today under the yoke of the British mandate. They shared, rather, in the rule together with the Turks and the other races, in all the departments of the state: there was no discrimination in rights or duties between the Turks and the Iraqis; and they shared offices, high positions, and the good and the bad equally. The Iraqi exercised rule, justice, administration and politics for succeeding centuries, not only in Iraq, but in all parts of the Ottoman empire, which extended to Europe, Asia and Africa.[129]

From the very foundation, then, of the Iraqi kingdom, there was this nagging feeling that it was a make-believe kingdom, built on false pretences and kept going by a British design and for a British purpose. This is the origin and explanation of the rabid anti-British feelings of large sections of the ruling classes of Iraq, a feeling which persisted until the end, and which occasionally exploded in bursts of hatred and violence. The British indeed had few friends in the kingdom they founded. The king and the Sharifian officers who came with him did not dare show gratitude to their patrons, but must always be pressing them for further concessions to make secure their own position and prestige; the Shi'ites and the Kurds felt that they had been betrayed for no good reasons; and further, why should anybody befriend the British when they themselves were so unreliable? Did not the Sharifians, operating from Syria, raise a sedition against them in Iraq, and were they not royally rewarded for their behaviour? Further, though the British had imposed Faisal on Mesopotamia, yet in their public professions they kept on insisting that they had brought him to rule Iraq in response to popular demand, so that they could not even exploit the prestige which comes to governments when they successfully assert their views and impose their authority. As for the non-Muslim minorities, delivered as they were to the Baghdad government, was not the spectacle of the Assyrians enough to frighten them off? The institutions of the mandate, again, were calculated to arouse suspicion in the minds of the Muslim politicians and administrators. Their blunt, uncomplicated minds saw in politics nothing but the exercise of power, and when they found themselves flanked by British advisers who were supposed to guide their steps and instruct them in League-of-Nations virtues, they were convinced that this was but an underhand manner of undermining their authority and diminishing their power; they were also indignant that Christians and foreigners should presume to teach them, who had ruled the country in Ottoman times, how to govern.

Such was the kingdom which met its doom on the fourteenth of July of Abd al-Karim al-Qasim. While the going was good, rulers of Iraq drank from it to satiety as from a bowl of soup, or else used it as a pawn in their dreadful game. The politicians intrigued with the tribes, as in the Euphrates uprisings of the mid-1930s when Yasin al-Hashmi, Hikmat Sulaiman and Rashid Ali al-Gailani secretly suborned tribal chiefs and touched off a long period of tribal unrest, or again they debauched the army officers and incited them to mutinies, as when Hikmat conspired with Bakr Sidqi, or when Nuri al-Sa'id with those whom he was later to execute for their rebellion in 1941. The world was shocked at Nuri's end, at the demonic hatred which his enemies manifested for him. For Nuri had come to seem in the second world war and after the supreme master of Iraqi politics, strong, adroit and straightforward. But Nuri, it must not be forgotten, was, before his ascent to this respectable eminence, but one of the many politicians in Baghdad scrabbling and plotting for power. 'In the early days of the kingdom,' Mr de Gaury tells us, 'as an extreme Arab nationalist, he went through a picaresque period, when he was guarded day and night by a selected gang of toughs, some in the uniform of the Iraqi military police;'[130] '. . . except for Col. Joyce, Capt Clayton and me,' writes Miss Bell in a letter of 8 August 1922, 'everyone holds Nuri to be an imp of mischief.' As for herself, she confessed that 'of all the people from the king downwards, there is no one I really love as I love Nuri'. It is she who presents the bizarre spectacle of Nuri, during the tumultuous debates in the constituent assembly on the Anglo-Iraqi treaty of 1924, going about with a bomb in his pocket designed to encourage supporters of the treaty and no doubt discourage its enemies.[131] In

February 1924, Taufiq al-Khalidi, a senator, ex-governor of Baghdad and ex-minister of the interior and of justice, was murdered in the street in Baghdad. He had been suspected of republican, perhaps Turkish sympathies, and his murderers were never caught. They are now identified for us as Abdullah Sariyya and Shakir al-Qaraghuli, clients of Nuri and his brother-in-law Ja'far al-Askari.[132] It is commonly accepted that the instigators were either or both, and that the aim was to terrorise Faisal's opponents. But this champion of the Sharifian house was also capable of making overtures to its Sa'udi enemy. After Bakr Sidqi's *coup d'état*, while in exile in Cairo in 1937, as has been seen, he seemed to have offered his services to Ibn Sa'ud to secure for a son of his the Iraqi throne. And this steadfast upholder of the British connection was prudent enough to keep a line open to the Axis. In September 1940 we see him instructing the Iraqi minister in Ankara 'to seize every opportunity' to get in touch with Axis representatives, 'directly or indirectly', to exhort them to persuade their governments of the utility and necessity of proclaiming their support for the independence of Syria, Palestine and other Arab countries, and to instigate Syrians who might be in touch with the minister themselves to make these approaches and even to visit the Axis capitals.[133] Men who after 1941 were condemned as Nazi agents had earlier been his friends and coadjutors. The *coup d'état* which he engineered in 1938 succeeded with the help of, among others, the four colonels known as the Golden Square, whom he later executed for their part in the Rashid Ali *coup*. Rashid had been exiled from Baghdad by the cabinet of Jamil al-Midfa'i, and when Nuri became prime minister he recalled him and appointed him head of the royal cabinet. Salah al-Din al-Sabbagh, one of the colonels executed in consequence of Rashid Ali's movement, was surely justified in saying that it was Nuri – among other politicians – who encouraged the soldiers to assume control over successive Ministries.[134] Apart from promoting military disaffection, Nuri helped further to debauch the public institutions of the state. It was he who, when he became prime minister in 1930, for the first time in the history of the kingdom enacted a law which enabled ministers to dismiss civil servants arbitrarily and at their discretion;[135] it may be imagined to what use such a weapon was put by successive Iraqi governments. Again, it was during his Ministry that the *Futuwwa*, a semi-military formation of schoolboys modelled on Nazi and Fascist patterns, was formed in 1939; also it was he who gave ministerial office in 1940 to Sami

Shawkat, one of the high officials of the Ministry of Education most responsible for introducing political fanaticism in the state schools.[136] Again, seeking to avenge the murder of his brother-in-law, Ja'far al-'Askari, he arrested Hikmat Sulaiman and an officer suspected of having taken part in the murder, tried them on a trumped-up charge of conspiracy against the state, and had them condemned to death; the British ambassador intervened to prevent the death sentences being carried out.[137] The British occupation of the country in 1941 enabled him to discredit his enemies, weaken his rivals, and reign supreme for nearly two decades, presenting to the world the picture of an old statesman full of wisdom and uprightness, dedicated to progress and reform. This is not at all how the matter looked to his opponents, who considered him a cunning and dangerous enemy, an autocrat in power and an intriguer out of it; and his very skill in manipulating power, unmatched by any other politicians of his day in Iraq, served but to increase the hate and envy to which, in the end, he fell victim. For this man who rose from obscure beginnings to such a position of power exemplifies perfectly Machiavelli's man of *virtù*. Fate presented him with two golden opportunities, which he dared to grasp stoutly and to exploit fully, once when he deserted from the Ottoman army and threw in his lot with the sharif, and again when he ranged himself by the side of Britain in 1941. His bloody end was a fitting conclusion to a life lived dangerously. He was caught in a Baghdad street disguised as a woman and killed on the spot. His body was reduced immediately to a pulp by the wheels of innumerable motor-cars joyously driven over it. Is this horrible death the fated re-enactment of a rite which Baghdad's sombre and unappeasable genius seems now and again to exact? It is, in any case, the uncanny echo of another such death which took place in 1763. In that year also the Janissaries rose against the vali; he also tried to flee disguised as a woman, was recognised at one of the city's gates, and immediately executed.[138]

Over a century ago, an unknown citizen of Baghdad kept a diary in which he recorded, with a sceptical and jaundiced pen, the misdeeds, the peculations, the intrigues and the murders of the rulers of his day. In this grisly spectacle, which seems to repeat itself in Baghdad every decade and every century – and to have seen which is itself a kind of bruised and forlorn glory – one actor who had his brief moment of power, may stand as a symbol for the rulers of this wretched country. This man who flourished when Ali Riza al-Laz was vali from 1831 to 1842. started as a small clerk in a village, al-Khalis, and grew to become one of the most powerful men in Baghdad. His greed and cruelty, says the chronicler, knew no bounds, to retail them would fill many volumes, and the compiler would be accused of lying and exaggeration; the notables of Baghdad, among whom were numerous men of learning and piety, were terrified of him and did not dare complain to the vali. Yet who, but for this chronicler, would have remembered this terrible man? The diarist knew him as Mulla Ali al-Khasi, Mulla Ali the Eunuch, and adds that it was not even known whether he was a eunuch or not.[139] Of his circumstances we know nothing, neither his father's name nor his mother's, whence he came or whither he went; only this, that he had power for twelve years and then fell. It is a consoling thought that perhaps today, in circumstances no less sombre than those of previous centuries, there may still be in Baghdad a private person, uncorrupted by ministers of guidance and ministers of education, to chronicle in secret with an unlettered and literal pen, the doings of the Mulla Alis of his day.

Appendix

A Shi'ite Proclamation

THE VOICE OF IRAQ

PROCLAMATION BY THE EXECUTIVE COMMITTEE OF THE SHIAHS IN IRAQ*

The greater portion of Iraq is inhabited by the Shia sect of Islam which represents 70 per cent of the total population according to the census made by both the British government and the government of Iraq. Throughout the world the majority rules if the government is a national government. It is of course otherwise in exceptional cases, i.e., during the occupation of a country or during a time when the status of the country is not in its usual form.

For more than ten years since the formation of the government of Iraq the administration of the country has been in the hands of a certain faction of the population. This faction is sharing among itself the revenues and benefits of the country and is depriving us of our share although foreign powers consider us as representing the majority of people. We have lived in this country for centuries and so did our forefathers, and to our regret we possess practically nothing, having been deprived of our lands. This faction has appointed savages from the desert who are handling us as they wish. Intrigues have always been their object and that is how they have been able to hold the administration of the country in their own hands.

We have been very badly treated and our position at the present time is worse than it was during the Turkish regime. We are tired of this sort of life. Our endowments have been taken away, our lands confiscated, our trade depressed, and even our cemeteries have come under their control. Furthermore, our lives are threatened and the districts where the majority of the population is Shiah have been altogether neglected. These districts have been deprived of proper educational advantages, of efficient health service and are left undeveloped. However, they do not fail to look after the sections of the country inhabited by their sect and make their improvements by means of taxes collected from us. If one compares the number of schools in the northern district with the number in the southern district he will find a difference existing between these two sections. It is the same with sanitation, development, commerce, *et cetera*.

If we ever ask that state domain lands be granted us for cultivation our request is not acceded to; however, such lands have been distributed to

* Enclosure with dispatch from Sloan, Baghdad, 11 February 1932; 890g.00/179

their *effendis* and officials in order that they may obtain the majority during parliamentary elections. Since the House of Parliament has been formed we have never heard of the Shiah Moslems having been elected from the northern district. Whereas from our districts only one or two are elected and the rest are from the other faction. Similar instances are many. Among the cabinet members only one is a Shiah and even this member is not actually a minister, only a diplomatic attaché with no influence. A Shiah has never been given the portfolio of minister of the Interior or other such important post. He has always been assigned to the post of minister of Education and this portfolio carries little, if any, power or prestige.

We have been imprisoned without cause. We have been deported without reason. Our chief and prominent men have been offended without justification. Many taxes have been collected from us and we are rendered so poor that it seems to us that we were better treated during the old regime. They blame the British policy in order to camouflage their evil desire. They enact legislation to our hurt, their object being to deprive us of our freedom and our legal rights. Among us they have even deported our *ulamas* and by stirring up religious dissensions have put into practice the policy of divide and rule. They have created all kinds of enmities and feuds between the shaikhs of our tribes in their distribution of land, taking from one and giving to the other. Their teachers imbue the students with all kinds of religious beliefs. Such action has rendered us very suspicious as to their object. If we should go through every page of their history, such as the unfortunate events which have taken place at Kerbela, Kadhimain and Najaf, or other holy places, it would take large volumes to record them. The Shiahs have very few men in the different government posts. The number of officials we have does not exceed the number of fingers on one hand. This small number is bound by all kinds of fetters and is always threatened. They have no high posts and have no permanent jobs in spite of the intelligence and efficiency they possess to hold government positions. It is to our regret that the Shiah officials are treated as though they were not sons of the country and as if they had no right to claim any part in the administration of the government. We have never before experienced such treatment not even during the dark ages. They want to milk us.

They are benefiting from the taxes collected from us. We do the hard labour and they reap the harvest. They spend lavishly for their personal ambitions and were it not for these heavy expenses our Shiah communities would not be so heavily taxed. Their officials are very highly paid. The wages they receive are higher than those of any other civilised and rich country. In addition to this they misappropriate funds from the national treasury. They have enacted a pension law to ensure for themselves a perpetual income and the Shiahs were deprived of this.

One-third of the revenue of the state is distributed among this faction and each one has become wealthy.

Now that the tide has reached its peak, that the fate of Iraq is dependent upon the League of Nations, our case has become a vital point which can not be neglected any longer in view of the fact that it has reference to our interests, our living, and our future; and in order to give protection to our lives, our properties, and our honour and to further protect us from being attacked by their evil deliberations we have summarised our demands as follows:

1. The Shiah sect shall take charge of the administration of the country and the other sects will have the posts and power to which their numbers entitle them.
2. The revenues of Moslem *awqafs* shall be distributed equally among all the religious Moslem institutions in the holy places and elsewhere and the past *awqaf* accounts shall be audited.
3. Government jobs should be given to Shiahs in numbers proportionate to their population in the state.
4. Likewise Shiah farmers shall be granted lands from the public domain in proportion to their population in the state.
5. Roads in the Shiah districts shall be repaired and an efficient health service established there.
6. Roads in the different Shiah *liwas* shall be constructed, and more attention shall be paid to the education of Shiahs.
7. The majority of educational missions sent abroad each year shall be composed of Shiahs.
8. Every person shall have complete freedom to express his views. Rights usurped shall be given back, whether in lands or otherwise and shall be protected from future transgressions.
9. A general plebiscite shall be held under the supervision of the League of Nations and without interference from the present administrative officials, to vote on these demands.

Our demands are the aspiration of every Shiah who lives in this country and enjoyed prosperity before this era. In the name of justice and international right we ask the British government which has the mandate to consider our demands lest the tear is made larger and lest the occurrence of 1920 [the revolution] upon which this government was constructed and from the results of which we hoped to gain our freedom, be repeated in a more dreadful manner as the next revolution will be of larger scope.

We await the decision of Great Britain in this matter. In its capacity as the mandatory power it should take effective measures and relieve us from the disgraceful rule of this faction and the religious fanaticism it exerts to satisfy its personal ambitions before the situation leads to more serious and deplorable results and before the country is given up to anarchy.

285

10

'Minorities'

> We had fed the heart on fantasies
> The heart's grown brutal from the fare
> w. b. yeats, *Meditations in Time of Civil War*

It is the common fashion today to denounce the imperialism of western powers in Asia and Africa. Charges of economic exploitation are made and the tyranny and arrogance of the European are arraigned. Yet it is a simple and obvious fact that these areas which are said to suffer from imperialism today have known nothing but alien rule throughout most of their history and that, until the coming of the western powers, their experience of government was the insolence and greed of unchecked arbitrary rule. It is not on these grounds, therefore, that the appearance of the west in Asia and Africa is to be deplored. A curse the west has indeed brought to the east, but – and here lies the tragedy – not intentionally; indeed the curse was considered – and still is by many – a precious boon, the most precious that the west could confer on the east in expiation of its supposed sins; and the curse itself is as potent in its maleficence in the west as it is in the east. A rash, a malady, an infection spreading from western Europe through the Balkans, the Ottoman empire, India, the far east and Africa, eating up the fabric of settled society to leave it weakened and defenceless before ignorant and unscrupulous adventurers, for further horror and atrocity: such are the terms to describe what the west has done to the rest of the world, not wilfully, not knowingly, but mostly out of excellent intentions and by example of its prestige and prosperity. At the stage where we are it becomes possible to follow, in certain cases, the course of the malady, to trace the first treacherous symptoms and link them through a long agony to the last spasm of resistance, to recount the complications, the attempted remedies and to record the final irrevocable relapses. And of the decomposing matter that is left what shall we say? That those who are sanguine enough may hope that out of it, one day, the tissue of a living society will, once more, grow.

Of these cases the purest, perhaps the most classical, are to be found in the communities which not so long ago constituted the Ottoman empire. And the most pitiful among them is perhaps that of the Armenian community. The Armenians are a very ancient people whose history, owing to their geographical position, has at all times been grim and difficult; the history of a small group bruised and crushed in the eternal rivalry and contention of powerful empires. With the advent of the Ottoman supremacy the Armenian community, like the other religious groups in the Ottoman territory, was established with a certain measure of internal self-government, and its members took their place in the delicate balance of Ottoman society. Such was still the situation at the beginning of the nineteenth century, when the west suddenly impinged on the Ottoman dominions, setting the Armenians and the other elements of this eastern society new problems and dangling before them new temptations, with which their experience had hardly taught them how to deal. It is to be observed that these problems and temptations were, at the outset, not political, and that the challenge would not have been so serious had they been merely political. For with politics the Armenians were well acquainted, and how to protect themselves in the clash of Great Powers was something not alien to their tradition. The problem and the temptation was not that of western political ambitions but that of western philosophy.

The religion of the Armenians was their distinctive badge in an Ottoman society regulated and governed according to denominational distinctions. This religion was not only a matter for the individual conscience, for personal and private devotions; it was a rule of life regulating all social activities and all relations with the suzerain power, itself suzerain by virtue of professing the dominant religion. And the internal government of the community was similarly the prerogative of the religious hierarchy, which drew its civil power from the fact of its ecclesiastical authority.

Into these long-standing and well-understood arrangements the west, round about 1830, suddenly intruded. It came in the shape of American Protestant missionaries. They arrived with arguments and tracts and funds. Their purpose, they said, was to infuse vitality and spirit into the unprogressive and dormant eastern Christian communities. They proceeded to make converts and to propagate their tenets by founding schools on the Lancastrian system. The established hierarchy resisted these encroachments. It exiled and imprisoned Armenian converts to Protestantism. It approached the Ottoman Government with a request to forbid the activities of these missionaries. In 1839, Hagopos, the patriarch adjunct, issued a bull forbidding the reading of all books printed or circulated by them.[1] The objections of the hierarchy to missionary activity were deep-seated and violent, but they were not very articulate. Dwight, the chronicler of the missionaries, gives an indication of these objections: 'The words Framason (Freemason)', he says, 'Lutran (Lutheran), Volter (Voltaire) and Protestan (Protestant) were freely and indiscriminately applied to us, all of them being considered by the common people as synonyms, and the meaning being rather indefinite, but yet implying an atheist of the most wicked and dangerous description'.[2] Horatio Southgate, an American Episcopalian bishop and a traveller in the east, shared, it seemed, these prejudices; in an English religious periodical he described the converts as 'infidels and radicals'.[3] And nearly half a century later, at the beginning of the Armenian troubles, the Ottoman government also gave expression to the same view. In 1894, it issued instructions affecting the free attendance of Armenian children at American schools. 'As far as I have been able to learn,' wrote Consul Cumberbatch from Angora to Sir Philip Currie at Constantinople, on 5 October 1894, 'these new measures are to the effect that Armenian parents must become sureties for their children's conduct as loyal subjects both during and after their attendance at American schools.'[4] What actually were the doctrines that the missionaries, arousing so much opposition and anger from so many different quarters, were teaching? Dwight defines them for us: 'The standard doctrine of the Reformation – salvation by grace alone, without the deeds of the law – was usually the great central truth, first apprehended by their awakened and inquiring minds, and made the ground of satisfactory repose.'[5] The 'standard doctrine of the Reformation' had meant in Europe, its native breeding ground, a great and prolonged upheaval. And it would be surprising if its sudden introduction into a society totally unprepared for it were not to result in even greater upheavals and in dislocations even more fundamental.

288

Salvation by grace alone, without the deeds of the law: the implications of the doctrine are as exhilarating as they are dangerous. As a principle governing the religious life, its application is limited and its practice exacting. It cannot, obviously, offer guidance to the majority of those who profess any creed; it demands a severe mystical discipline of which only a few, after long preparation, are capable. Even then the pitfalls are so numerous and so subtle that there is a mere hair's breadth, on this particular path, between salvation and damnation. It seems then inevitable that the general introduction of such a doctrine into a society should act as a solvent of the long-standing restraints which more pedestrian rules had enjoined. This, if only because the doctrine presupposes the independence of individual judgment and the primacy of individual will. Nor is this the end of the matter. The individual is set free, and his judgment is declared, under God, supreme. Suppose then the individual takes a further step and affirms that he is indeed free and that his judgment is, without any qualification, supreme. The inevitable happens: Secularism and Protestantism merge into one another; and the doctrine of salvation by grace, which was a means of attaining the Life Eternal, becomes an alluring instrument for the building of Heaven on Earth; Nationalism is begotten. Thus a later American missionary, in his horror at the Armenian massacres of 1895 and at the responsibility of Armenians for them, tries to explain the situation to himself by ascribing the disaster to those Armenians who 'having imbibed the free thought ideas developed in the French Revolution, and fired by the experience of 1848, were utterly impatient of the slower process of education'.[6] He is right, but he does not consider that there is a path which *may* lead from salvation by grace to 'the free thought ideas developed in the French Revolution'.

The introduction of these ideas, then, could not fail to affect the internal affairs of the Armenian community, as well as its relations with the Ottoman Power. To start with, a schism, encouraged by the missionaries,[7] took place between the Orthodox majority and the converts to Protestantism, and a new Protestant Armenian community was formed. Then, within the Orthodox community itself, parties of 'Enlightened' and 'Reactionaries' were formed. After a while, the 'Enlightened', as is proper, won and reorganised the government of the Armenian community. Extensive powers were taken away from the ecclesiastical hierarchy and vested in a new elective Communal Council of Deputies. In 1860, the Ottoman government, which was then looking on reforms in general with a benevolent eye, gave its approval.[8] The Ottoman government no doubt thought that reform of the millets went hand in hand with reform of the army and the administration, and like the latter would strengthen the state. This, of course, did not prove to be exactly true of the *Tanzimat*, and proved to be even less true of millet reforms. By their very nature the reforms favoured the 'Enlightened' and weakened the ecclesiastics and the old-fashioned notables who had between them for so long governed these communities. The 'Enlightened' were men who read books and believed what they found in them; they were prone to be impatient, querulous, and ready at whatever cost to 'pursue their principles' wherever they led. And their 'principles' necessarily led them much farther than the Ottoman patrons of reform had imagined. If rebellion against the hierarchy was to be proclaimed, then, logically, rebellion against the master of the hierarchy, the Ottoman state, had also to be proclaimed. In 1872 an Armenian was writing in a new patriotic paper in Tiflis: 'Yesterday, we were an ecclesiastical community; tomorrow, we shall be a nation of workers and thinkers.'[9]

How then should the Armenians become a nation? Till now, what distinguished them from others were a religion and a language; they had no cohesion, no sense of political unity and they were geographically scattered. There were important groups of them in eastern Anatolia, in Cilicia and in the Russian Caucasus. These were the principal groups, but there were others, not negligible, scattered across the length and breadth of the Ottoman empire. Nowhere were they in a decisive majority; the Kurds, in Anatolia, notably, were an important and uncontrollable element of the population. More important still, the Armenian community was intimately intertwined with the other elements of Ottoman society. And in any case, they had no classes accustomed to the exercise and responsibility of power, and the population at large was not likely, in any forseeable future, to become a body of independent and knowledgeable citizenry, which is the first requisite in a 'nation'. Such were the internal difficulties. There were external ones, no less formidable. Was, for instance, the Ottoman state to acquiesce in another amputation of its dominions? And if, *per impossibile*, it did acquiesce, what would Russia have to say to a small irredentist nation on a sensitive and difficult border area?[10] And if Russia favoured the Armenians, would not this make the resistance of the Ottomans even more implacable?

And what would be the attitude of the other Great Powers to this further complication of the eastern question?[11] But this was to talk sweet reasonableness to men exalted with the promise of salvation. And those among the Armenians who ventured to speak this language were murdered for their pains.

The thing, then, was to act. The obvious plan was to get, first of all, the support of a Great Power, like all the other nationalities which had seceded from the Ottoman state. Great Britain was then unlikely to encourage projects tending to the disruption of the Ottoman empire. There remained Russia, with whom the Armenians had many connections and which ruled over an important section of the Caucasus. Russia might be prepared to listen and to extend a benevolent support to the Armenian cause in the interest of her own Ottoman policy; but Russia, on the other hand, would always have reasons to discourage an Armenian national movement, and presumably the Armenian leaders reasoned that they would cross this bridge when they came to it.[12] The opportunity soon came in the crisis of 1877. The victorious Russians at the gates of Constantinople were dictating the Peace of San Stefano. The Armenians approached the British and the Russians to ask their support for a scheme of an autonomous Armenia under a Christian governor. Before and immediately after the Congress of Berlin, encouraged by the Bulgarian example, Armenian notables approached the British Embassy to demand autonomy for an Armenia which was to include the provinces of Van and Sivas, the greater part of the province of Diarbekir, and the territories comprising the ancient Armenian kingdom of Cilicia.[13] But at the Congress of Berlin 'autonomy' was whittled down to 'reforms and improvements' which the Great Powers, and especially Great Britain, pledged themselves to see accomplished. From that date autonomy became an obsession with the Armenian leaders. It constituted at once the maximum and the minimum of their demands. The minimum since it was doubtless argued that once autonomy under a Christian governor was gained, the rest would come easily, as they had only to look at Rumania and Bulgaria to realise; the maximum: since they argued that 'they would get in proportion as they asked; hence they asked for the greatest that could be given with the expectation . . . of securing not that but something less which should be, after all, a great advance . . .'.[14] Thirty-five years later, in 1913, after the massacres and the disasters and the setbacks, under a more centralising and even more intransigent Young Turk government they were still asking for autonomy.

In September 1913, the Armenian community addressed a circular to the Powers in this sense, but when the French ambassador asked what the Armenians really expected he was told that it was for the Powers to see whether the desires of the Armenians could be satisfied.[15] It was an artless, a pitiful policy, since the Ottomans were not prepared to accord autonomy nor would the Russians really favour it; the Russians were always ready to use the Armenian agitation as a convenient pretext to achieve their end, which was to annex the Armenian provinces. On two occasions Great Britain proposed to Russia to take drastic measures to solve the Armenian question, once in 1895 and again in 1913; and on both occasions the Russians first equivocated, and then refused: with the Armenian questions the Russians would deal strictly on their own terms.[16] With neither the Russians nor the Ottomans willing, what chance did autonomy stand? As Salisbury told Canon MacColl, a turbulent leader of the Armenian agitation in Great Britain, in 1896: 'You might turn this government out, and ten other governments after it, but you would not be able to accomplish a result which Austria, Russia, Germany, France and Turkey are determined to prevent'.[17] This persistent and obstinate pursuit of a fantasy is an indication of how little the Armenians were ready to deal with the world as they found it – and the world broke them.

There remained the 'reforms and improvements'. The aim of these in the Armenian provinces, as elsewhere in the Ottoman empire, was twofold: to procure security for the subject by protecting him from arbitrary impositions, and to create machinery whereby the business of government could be efficiently and expeditiously dispatched. For these to be attained or even approximated, two conditions were essential. These were indicated by Sir Edward Grey in 1913, after nearly three-quarters of a century of experiments in 'reform' with which Great Britain had been intimately associated. 'As to reform', he wrote to the British ambassador at St Petersburg, 'Your Excellency should impress upon Mr Sazonow that two conditions are essential to success: (1) Unanimity amongst the Powers; (2) Acceptance of their scheme by Turkey, without coercion'.[18]

From the circumstances of the case the first condition could never be attained. Till the emergence of the German empire on the European scene, Great Britain and Russia could never reach agreement on the eastern question. Germany only made the situation infinitely more complicated.

As to the second condition, some Ottomans had at times, it is true, been themselves zealous exponents of reform. But there were always many who objected to it, not, it would seem, from obscurantism, but from a correct understanding of the nature of the Ottoman state and of the sources of Ottoman power. The Ottoman state was a vast conglomeration of groups held together by the might and prestige of the house of Osman; the Ottoman state and the Ottoman house were bound up each with the other. This the Ottomans understood very well. They also understood another thing: that Ottoman power meant Muslim supremacy. It was that 'domineering Mahometan sentiment, which has determined the relations of Islam and non-Islam in daily life' of which Gladstone speaks,[19] which gave strength and loyalty to those on whom the security of the Ottoman state depended. The realisation of this was very vivid in Europe till this century when it seems to have been strangely forgotten. Now, since reforms would do away both with the personal power of the Ottoman rulers and with Muslim supremacy, the Ottomans could hardly be expected to acquiesce in them: hence the failure of reform. As Sir Charles Eliot made his pasha say:

> This country is a dish of soup, and no one has any real intention except to eat it. We eat it in the good old-fashioned way with a big spoon. You bore little holes in the bottom of the soup bowl and draw it off with pipes. Then you propose that the practice of eating soup with spoons should be abolished as uncivilised, because you know we have no gimlets and don't understand this trick of drinking through pipes.[20]

There was also another reason for this failure. Before the advent of European Powers, Ottoman administration was certainly corrupt and arbitrary, but it was ramshackle and inefficient and left many interstices by which the subject could hope to escape its terrors, and bribery was a traditional and recognised method of mitigating severities and easing difficulties.[21] The reforms sought to introduce European methods into this completely alien tradition. In the absence of the honesty and public spirit which make them tolerable in Europe, such novelties tend rather to make matters worse: they teach the corrupt and unscrupulous administrator new ways of extorting bribes and perquisites, they make it more difficult to escape the eye of malevolent authority, and easier for adventurers and desperadoes to establish themselves securely in office. Railways, telegraphs, filing cabinets, etc. become instruments of a monstrous and inescapable control. In the case of the Armenians, for instance, the telegraph enabled Abdul Hamid to concert and supervise those outbreaks of savagery which were his remedy for the Armenian difficulty.[22] In truth, it was well recognised by liberal opinion in England in the nineteenth century – and it was liberal opinion which was convinced of the necessity of reforms in the east – that the only way to make reforms work was for a European government to administer them directly.[23] The change from a belief in reforms supervised by Europe to one in national self-determination constitutes a significant moment in the degradation of liberal dogma.

'Reform and improvements' were, then, of little help and they were not wanted by the Ottomans. But neither were they wanted by those Armenians who now took hold of the Armenian community and imposed on it their leadership. Thus we find the leader of the Hintchak Revolutionary Party rejecting the idea of reforms:

> This plan of ours which can be summed up in the words 'autonomous Armenia for the Armenians' . . . cannot be considered extravagant. But there is a very wide gulf between this moderate practical plan of ours, which is that of the whole of Armenia, and the plan of reforms proposed in the collective notes of the ambassadors, and to bridge that gulf no means are left to the Armenians but insurrection, which would once again bring to the front the Armenian Question . . .'.[24]

No means but insurrection: this was clear and it was meant seriously. The leaders of the Armenian nationalist movement had already decided that autonomy was their goal and they thought they had a strategy to achieve it. And these leaders took care that Armenians would not be found to help with the reforms.[25] For it was not in vain that they surveyed the history of Europe from the French Revolution, and not in vain that they meditated on the liberation of Greece, Serbia, Rumania and Bulgaria from the Ottoman yoke. They would make insurrection and they would bring the Armenian Question 'to the front'. Then the Powers would have to deal with it, and if they failed to deal with it according to the desires of the nationalists, why, there were always other means of keeping the Armenian Question 'to the front'.

It might seem, however, that the decision to resort to rebellion came with the failure of reform. But this is not so. As early as 1882, four years after the Congress of Berlin, action committees were being formed by the Armenians in Erzerum and arms were being procured.[26] Secret societies were set up, notably the Hintchaks in 1886 in Switzerland and the Troshaks in the Caucasus which, combining with other revolutionaries became in 1890 the well-known Dashnakzoution, or Armenian Revolutionary Federation.[27] Agents were sent from the Caucasus to Ottoman Armenia in order to spread the creed and to collect money for the cause from rich Armenians. These agents, being outsiders who had moreover learnt from the Russian nihilists the methods and doctrines of revolutionary activism,[28] were not particularly concerned at the effect which their activities might have on the objects of their proselytism.[29] The Ottoman authorities took alarm and began to persecute, and the vicious circle was created that was to lead, at last, to the extermination and dispersal of the Armenian communities of Turkey. Thus, in 1889, Colonel Chermside reports from Trebizond: 'The petty, harassing persecutions of Armenians in the Van district are a matter of regret. I consider the Armenian populations in those districts restless and disaffected . . .'.[30] In 1893, a few years before the massacres were to be unleashed by Abdul Hamid, Vice-Consul Newton writes from Angora:

Last autumn the movement in a modified form extended to this province, first showing itself in the district of Caesarea and afterwards at Yuzgat, by meetings held by the Armenians in the gardens and fields outside the towns. Finding the authorities did not appear to take any notice, they began to hold meetings in their houses, in the towns, which excited the suspicions of the government. Consequently spies were set to watch them, and sufficient evidence was thus procured showing a revolutionary feeling, which evidently justified the authority in arresting many of those who attended these meetings.[31]

The aim of nationalists is clear. It was to create 'incidents', provoke the Turks to excesses, and thereby bring about the intervention of the Powers. The British Blue Books of the period before the massacres are full of reports of attacks by Armenian agents or bands on Turks and Kurds, of the distribution of seditious prints, of the discoveries by Ottoman authorities of caches of bombs and arms, of demonstrations organised by Armenians in Constantinople and the provinces. In most cases, the incidents would have no immediate far-reaching consequences, but some of them, either owing to circumstances or to the ill-will of Ottoman officials, led to serious results. In Sasun in 1894, in Zeitun in 1895, the incidents led to armed risings by the Armenians of these localities which were, of course, bloodily suppressed. An outcry was the result, consular commissions were appointed to investigate, and the Armenian leaders had the consolation

295

of knowing that another blow had been struck in the cause of Armenian independence.

The Blue Books also record another class of incident, quite as large as the first, created by the nationalists, but this much more sinister. It seems that the nationalists had to convince not only the Ottoman government and the Powers of the wisdom of satisfying their desires, they had to convince the generality of the Armenian people as well. This must be the explanation of the attack organised by them on the patriarch as he was officiating in the cathedral of Koum Kapou at Constantinople in July 1890, as a result of which he had to resign his office;[32] of a subsequent attempt to assassinate another patriarch in 1894;[33] of the recurrent reports of Armenians executed for being 'informers', for refusing to contribute to nationalist funds, for 'collaborating' with the Ottoman government. Nor did the nationalists try to hide or excuse these activities. Here is a passage from a revolutionary placard posted in Sivas in December 1893:

Osmanlis! . . . The examples are before your eyes. How many hundreds of rascals in Constantinople, Van, Erzerum, Alashkert, Harpout, Cesarea, Marsovan, Amassia and other towns have been killed by the Armenian revolutionaries? What were these rascals? Armenians! and again Armenians! If our aim was against the Mohamedans or Mohamedanism, as the government tries to make you think, why should we kill the Armenians?[34]

The Armenians were forced to be free.

What did the Ottoman government have to say to all this? Its attitude was as clear as that of the nationalists: this agitation would have only one result, to invite Europe to meddle again in the affairs of the Ottoman empire. This was not to be tolerated; the Armenians had to desist or they would take the consequences. As early as September 1878, at the very beginning of the Armenian Question, Layard reported a significant discussion he had with the Grand Vizier on the subject of agitation by Russian agents among the Armenians. An Armenian exodus from the Empire, remarked the Grand Vizier, might be thought by some to be rather to the advantage than otherwise of Turkey, for she would thereby be relieved from a Christian population which might become thereafter a source of danger and trouble by inviting foreign interference. On such a view, the Porte would do well, the Grand Vizier added, to imitate the example set to it by Russia in Bulgaria, where large Muslim populations had been expelled from their ancestral homes.[34a] It is worth while also to reproduce an address made by the mutassarif of Amasia in 1893 to Armenians in his district, which expresses eloquently and concisely the Ottoman view of the situation:

> You are hoping to get help from Europeans [he told them] and you kneel down before them. You do not remark that they are playing a joke on your backs. Europeans have been trying for a long time to destroy the Turkish empire, and they put you forward now to create new troubles. If even their plans would succeed would you be any better off than now? You pay little tax; you are free from military service; you keep your religion, your language and your customs. Would the Power coming in our place give you the same liberties? Look at Russia, where the government has shut up all your schools and is now considering the question of shutting up your principal church at Etchmiadzin. Why do you send your children to the schools of the Europeans where their spirit is corrupted by new and foolish ideas?[35]

So, if the Armenians needed a lesson, Abdul Hamid felt he was quite able to give them one. His policy was that amalgam of massive brutality and of primitive cunning which constitutes traditional oriental statecraft. The Armenians wanted autonomy, did they? They created incidents? They threatened the intervention of the Powers? He would show them what his loyal Kurdish tribes would have to say to Armenian autonomy in *their* Kurdistan, and what their way was of dealing with incidents. A massacre or two would show the Armenians what he meant.[36] And as for the Powers, he could easily settle them. Did Russia propose intervention? He would whisper in her ear that Britain wanted a foothold on the Caucasus. Did Lord Salisbury threaten action? *He* would threaten Lord Salisbury with placing the Ottoman empire in the hands of Russia. Abdul Hamid's reaction then was straightforward and elementary. The Armenians were rebelling against their lord: punishment should be meted out to them. They wanted reforms and constitutions and such like Frankish abominations: they would not be permitted to indulge their perverse desires. They threatened to diminish the Ottoman estate and to introduce into it the meddlesome foreigner; they would see retribution. As for the indignation of the Europeans and their outcries, all that was part of a hypocritical conspiracy to defraud him and the house of Osman of another province. He would not give way, he would resist, he would massacre. It was perhaps the last powerful manifestation of the pride of family and of religion as a motive for the policy of an empire. After that, the Ottomans became Young Turks.

The nationalists were checkmated but did not confess defeat. 'A l'organisation militaire de l'Empire Ottoman, nous opposons des bandes volantes et bien armées d'intrépides révolutionnaires qui ont infligé maintes pertes aux troupes régulières et aux hordes de "Bachi-bousouks" . . . aux délations judaiques de la police secrète nous opposons la terreur rouge . . .'. Thus the Armenian Revolutionary Federation on 1896. And the incidents continued to be organised. In 1897, just after the massacres of 1895–6, and in 1905, there are records of minor insurrections also leading to massacres.[37] And on the eve of the Young Turk *coup d'état* of 1908, there was still the same tension in Ottoman Armenia fed and tended by the revolutionaries. Thus the American ambassador in a dispatch of 5 August 1907 speaks of 'a considerable degree of disaffection and revolutionary movement on the part of a portion of the Armenian population in the district of Van. Several cold-blooded murders have been committed even in the streets of that city and a certain feeling of apprehension and unrest appears generally to prevail'; and in another dispatch of 10 February 1908 he reports more disturbances in Van, revolutionaries killing and wounding seventeen Ottoman soldiers, executing a 'traitor', and a considerable store of rifles, cartridges and dynamite seized.[38] Later, when the catastrophe was final, complete, irredeemable, the nationalists were still indignant that their methods had had such untoward consequences. They could not understand why salvation was so recalcitrant in coming, why the easy path which the example of so many European revolutions had promised should have proved full of vipers and of nettles. The desolate wind of futility blows through the report the Dashnaks presented to the International Socialist Congress in Hamburg in 1923.

Every time that, through the irresistible force of things, the movement of Armenian emancipation expressed itself in revolutionary action, every time that the party of the Armenian Risorgimento tried, at the head of the conscious elements of the country, to draw the attention of the world, by armed insurrections or peaceful demonstrations, to the intolerable fate of the Armenian people, the Turkish government threw the Armenian masses, peaceful and disarmed, to the mercy of its troops, its bachi-bazouks and of the Turkish and Kurdish mob.[39]

There is a surprised air about the statement.

But the Hamidian massacres were not the end of the story. When the Young Turks deposed Abdul Hamid and took over the government of the Ottoman empire, the Dashnaks, who had had some kind of understanding with the Paris group of Young Turks, permitted themselves for a time to hope that their aspirations would be fulfilled. They soon found out that it was not to be so. The Young Turks were nationalists, just as the Armenian leaders were, and therefore even less prepared than Abdul Hamid to concede autonomy – which was what the Armenians still wanted. According to Young Turk theory, the Armenians were not really Armenians but Ottomans who happened to speak Armenian and to profess the Christian religion; they were part of the Ottoman nation like their brothers the Muslims, the Greek Orthodox, the Kurds and the Macedonians. This absurdity could, of course, take in nobody for long, least of all the Armenian nationalists, whose creed was that an Armenian nation existed on its own. Very well then, said the Young Turks, if they refuse to be part of the Ottoman nation they shall be cut off from the body of that nation. It is to be observed that the Young Turk theory of persecution differed sensibly from the Hamidian theory.

And cut off the Armenians were. Just before the war of 1914 the Russians were again in contact with the nationalists, holding out hopes and stirring them up.[40] At the outbreak of the war the attitude of the Armenian nationalists in Turkey was ambiguous and the Young Turks must have been, from the start, suspicious. Then occurred the final folly which gave the Turks the pretext for the ultimate liquidation. In December 1914 an Armenian volunteer division, wearing Russian uniforms, invaded the plain of Passinlar, north of Erzerum. In 1915 the town of Van, predominantly Armenian, was seized by the population and a local Armenian government instituted.[41] The deportations started. Everywhere the Armenians were assembled and sent off suddenly on foot, without notice, without any baggage, to perish from famine, cold, maltreatment and hard labour in the wildernesses of Anatolia, the mountains of Cilicia and the deserts of Syria. A law was passed concerning 'the properties of persons who have been transported elsewhere' to regularise the distribution of Armenian goods to the populace and the soldiery. The largesse of the progressive Young Turks was as generous as that of any primitive sultan. Then there was the short, miserable episode of the republic of Armenia in 1919–20. That was the end. But is not Armenian autonomy now to be at last enjoyed in the benign shadow of the Soviet Union? and has not the labour of the reformers at last come to fruition in a Turkey the very image of Europe? And is not the ramshackle, tyrannous, inefficient, blasting and withering rule of the Ottomans destroyed for ever? Thus we may rejoice that all things in the end are well.

The Armenians had nearly a century to deal, as well as they could, with the disturbance introduced by the west in their midst. They failed utterly; but the struggle they waged – such as it was – was long and desperate. The Jews of Iraq did not have even this measure of luck. A bare thirty years sufficed to destroy their community and achieve their ruin, and the resistance they could offer was derisory and from the start ineffective. When the British troops occupied Baghdad in 1917, the Jews were the most important single element in the town[42] – by their numbers, their wealth, their relations with those among them who had established themselves overseas (notably in Bombay and Manchester), and by their acknowledged superior position in the Mesopotamian economy. In November 1918, when it looked as though the Ottomans were finally repulsed and that the British would remain in occupation, they decided to try to define their relation to the new rulers of the land; they were also moved by rumours and allegations – following the publication of an Anglo–French Declaration which promised 'to encourage and assist in the establishment of indigenous governments and administrations in Syria and Mesopotamia' – that the country was to be given over to the 'Arabs' to rule. They petitioned the civil commissioner in Baghdad and asked to be allowed to become British subjects. They said that they did not like the prospect of an indigenous government to rule over them, and gave three reasons in support of their position: the Arabs were politically irresponsible, they had no administrative experience, and they could be fanatical and intolerant. In 1919 they returned to the charge with another petition, and it is interesting to reproduce it, to show the pathetic caution with which they proceeded and their anxiety to pay lip-service to the shibboleths of the age. They said:

The proclaimed aim of the Great Allied Powers in the most tremendous world war is the complete liberation of oppressed nationalities with the object of assuring their legitimate political aspirations as well as their economical and social development.

The full development of peoples whom several centuries of national lethargy plunged into a state of utter unpreparedness for self-administration is only obtainable through the material and moral cooperation of a great European Power. We are therefore of opinion:

That the nomination of an amir for Mesopotamia is inadmissible.

That a direct British government is indispensable for the future administration of this country.

The petition was not granted. It could not, by any conceivable means, have been granted in 1919. The Jews of Baghdad were defeated from the start; but they did not know it and would not know it for a long time to come. The situation was completely beyond their understanding. For how could they have discerned the prodigious spectacle that then appeared, of deliquescent Liberals and *Tancred* Tories, banding together in London to utilise the might and authority of a victorious empire in order to bring about in the middle east, consciously and willingly, such conditions as had hitherto been seen only with the decay of authority and the decline of empire? Power the Jews of Baghdad could understand, certainly, and the coarse, capricious exercise of power. The right of conquest they could cheerfully acknowledge, for all their history had taught them that there lay safety. These things and these things alone lay within their experience, and how pitifully inadequate they were going to prove! It was not by the help of this experience that they would understand the strange, exquisite perversions of the western conscience: the genial eccentricity of Mr Philby, proposing to make a thug who took his fancy the president of an Iraqi republic; or the fond foolishness of Miss Bell, thinking to stand godmother to a new Abbassid empire; or the disoriented fanaticism of Colonel Lawrence, proclaiming that he would be dishonoured if the progeny of the sharif of Mecca was not forthwith provided with thrones. Yet it was with such people that their fate rested.

So Faisal, the son of the sharif, was brought from Mecca to govern his new kingdom of Iraq. The Jews decided on a last attempt. In 1921 they went to see Sir Percy Cox, the high commissioner, and again asked for the privilege of becoming British subjects.

They based their claim on the fact that their country had been conquered by British troops, and that they were actually at the moment Turkish subjects under British control; and that therefore the British had no moral right to force them to accept a change of nationality unless they so desired it. They were eventually appeased by the personal influence of the high commissioner, and by his assurance that ample guarantees would be afforded them by the British government against any form of local tyranny . . .'.[43]

There was plainly little prospect of anything but Faisal and his Iraqi government. To this they would have to resign themselves.

Many who were experienced and wise, of whom perhaps the most eloquent was Sir Arnold Wilson, have expressed their misgivings over the policy of setting up ramshackle national sovereignties in the middle east. But the most moving protest is that of a young British officer, straight and upstanding and true, one of those whom the genius of England knew so well how to nurture and rear. The fortunes of war had taken him to Mesopotamia, and he found himself in 1918 – he who was nothing to Mesopotamia and to whom Mesopotamia was nothing – in charge of a district in the Middle Euphrates, where he was to be killed in the rising of 1920. Prior to that rising, the *Nation*, in common with many other newspapers in Britain, was waging a campaign in favour of self-determination. From the depth of the Mesopotamian countryside he was moved to write to the editor, his qualification being that, as he put it, 'a year ago I was writing college essays upon the Will of the People and Natural Law'.

> You, Sir, and your correspondents [he told the editor] want to see 'national aspirations gratified', the recognition of the 'unity of the Arab race', the establishment of responsible Arab government, and the absolute prevention of any further additions to the already over-weighted British empire. So do I, and it is just for this reason that I want you not to allow this slipshod thinking, and to make it clear, as it has never (to my knowledge) been made clear, that progress on such lines is a matter of extraordinary difficulty and that theory, alike with history, gives no help in solving a problem which has never yet been attempted. The problem is, of course, how to provide a native government with the force required to govern a wild and very mixed race divided by the bitterest religious hostilities and tribal feuds, and containing in its midst also colonies of fiercely hated Jews and Christians. Once stated, the problem needs no enlargement from me: that you allow your correspondents to proceed airily in the assumption . . . that, if left alone, these people could govern themselves and freely employ European advisers, is almost Tolstoyan in its view of human nature.

He went on to make these points:

1. We are dealing with people who have lost all consciousness of nationality in the political sense, who have from time immemorial been governed by foreigners, and among whom indeed the very word 'Arab' is used scornfully.
2. These people are utterly unvocal, like all uneducated masses, and it

is impossible to find out at all what they think about government. We deal with them largely in the mass, through their shaikhs, and the shaikh's view of government is an objectionable means of extracting money. . . .[44]

So, the unvocal masses and the colonies of Jews and Christians in their midst were handed over the next year to a band of men who were, to start with, for the most part, minor bureaucrats or little officers in the Ottoman service, and who were moved with certain crude and virulent notions, spreading from Europe and picked up second-hand in Constantinople, Cairo and the ports of the Levant; men narrow and ignorant, devoid of loyalty and piety, of violent and ungovernable impulses.[45]

It may clarify the situation in which the Jews of Iraq found themselves, as a result of this policy, if we consider the situation of another minority which found itself very early *in extremis* under the Iraqi government. The Assyrians (as they came to be known in Britain and America in the nineteenth century) were Christians long established in the Hakkiari range in southern Anatolia. During the war, at the instigation of the Russians, they rose against the Ottomans. Unlike the Sharifians their move was a disaster. They had to fight their way under very difficult conditions through the mountains between Persia and Anatolia. They at last got through to Mesopotamia and were safe under the protection of the British army. After the war they were concentrated in Mosul, just to the south of their former dwelling places but on the other side of the mountain. They were landless, destitute, and their resettlement would require patience, skill and goodwill. In the 1920s the British recruited them into levies. They showed themselves to be good fighters and took part in the various expeditions by which the British quelled the Kurds and compelled them to submit to the Baghdad government. When, in 1929, the British government announced that it was giving up the mandate for Iraq and recommending its admission to the League, the Assyrians were alarmed. Were they, then, to be left to the mercies of Muslim savages and that by the action of a Christian Power? They would not believe it, it was too absurd, a sinister joke which somebody was playing at their expense. They approached the British high commissioner and were told, Yes, it was true, they were going to be under the Iraqi government. Could they then have some safeguards, at least the same communal rights, as they were accustomed to under the Ottomans, and as the Mosul commission had recommended in 1925 that they should continue to have in Iraq?[46] No, they could not, and the high commissioner impatiently told them 'to make the best of the inevitable and have nothing to do with such impracticable separatist pretensions'. Petitions were sent on their behalf to the League of Nations. On these petitions the comment of the British government was:

> They are satisfied that, upon the establishment of Iraq as an independent state, member of the League of Nations, there will be no need for any special discrimination in favour of racial and religious minorities beyond such general guarantees as have been taken in the past from other candidates for admission to membership of the League.

As the high commissioner, Sir Francis Humphrys, told the Permanent Mandates Commission, such special discrimination

> might have a tendency to prevent the minorities concerned from regarding themselves, or being themselves regarded . . . as true citizens of their native state, in which lies the only certain hope of their future welfare.[47]

And indeed, the whole business was being taken altogether too seriously:

> Too much importance [he said] should not be attached to local sectarian dissensions, the explanation for which was often to be found in some purely trivial matter or incident.[48]

The colonial secretary, for his part, firmly closed his ears to representations made on behalf of the Assyrians.

> In his Lordship's opinion [read a letter sent on behalf of Lord Passfield at the end of 1930 to someone who had ventured on such representations] the dissemination of these misleading reports can only serve to excite religious animosities, to estrange the Iraq government, and to unsettle the Assyrians themselves, whose hopes of future welfare depend on their becoming merged in the body politic of Iraq, being accepted as loyal subjects of King Faisal and living in peace with their neighbours. . . . His Lordship [the letter sternly continued] can imagine no greater disservice to the communities whose welfare you claim to have at heart, than to encourage them in agitation against the government of the country in which they have to live.[49]

The Assyrians and the Iraqi government were face to face, and the essence of their respective positions is to be found in a letter of the Assyrian patriarch and an address of the Iraqi mutassarif of Mosul. The Assyrian patriarch pursued with the Iraqi government his request that the Assyrian community should be grated a measure of self-government under his direction. It is a symptom of the confusion which the arrival of the west introduced that he has to borrow its inadequate political idiom in order to describe something for which this idiom was never meant. He thus has to describe the communal government of the Ottoman system as a 'temporal power' exercised by the head of a community. The implication of this, of course, was that 'temporal power' is distinct from 'spiritual power' – a commonplace in western thought but unknown, till quite recently, in the east, where temporal and spiritual power were always one, and their separation a nonsensical notion corresponding to no known reality. The patriarch, therefore, put his case in these terms:

> The temporal power has not been assumed by me, but it has descended to me from centuries past as a legalised delegation of the people to the patriarch. It was not only tolerated, but also officially recognised in the past by the old Sasanid kings, Islamic caliphs, Moghul khans and Ottoman sultans.[50]

To speak of 'temporal power' was to concede half the game; and the mutassarif was quick with his rejoinder, improving the occasion too, with an original theory of Ottoman history:

> The government do not agree to grant to Mar Shimun [the Patriarch] temporal rule, for she is not in the habit of granting such rule to any religious heads of Iraq, and there is no reason why we should make any exception for Mar Shimun. Before the world war he was recognised as spiritual and temporal head of the Assyrians. This was due to the lax (sic) of the Turkish regime. . . . But by the declining of the Turkish regime this rule was abolished. . . . Any individual will be treated distinctly by the government and not through the heads who consider the peasants as their slaves, and master the results of their toil, to live easy lives.[51]

And the argument was reinforced by the British administrative inspector:

> Either the Assyrians should admit that they are Iraqi subjects, enjoying the same rights and subjected to the same laws as the other natives of the country, whether Kurds, Arabs, Mohammedans, Christians or Jews, or they should be prepared to leave the country.[52]

No, the Iraqi government was not a Sasanid king, as Islamic caliph, a Moghul khan or an Ottoman sultan. It was a modern state with all the latest western improvements. The Assyrians were at its mercy:

but they could never grasp this. In the summer of 1933 they were involved in a fracas on the Iraqi–Syrian frontier, which was the pretext for a massacre carried out by the new army of the Iraqi government, which, in raping Assyrian woman and killing Assyrian men felt that they were inflicting a defeat on the British whose clients and auxiliaries they considered the Assyrians to be.[53] The account of the Assyrians was well and truly settled. The British did not even protest, the embassy believing that the best policy at that juncture was delicately to advise without making 'irritating' demands and holding that, in any event, proof of a massacre was difficult legally to establish.[54]

Such was the situation with which the Jews – and the other 'minorities' had to cope. They failed to master it, because they did not know how to. They were considered Iraqis first and Jews second – that is, as far as their duties went. When it came to their rights, they were still the second-class subject of Ottoman times – but they had, in the meanwhile, lost all the advantages of the Ottoman arrangement: communal standing and self-government; now, as the mutassarif of Mosul put it, 'any individual will be treated distinctly by the government'. Leviathan was hungry. He was also ferocious. For the other great advantage of the Ottoman regime, its imperviousness to ideology and doctrinaire adventure, had also disappeared. The Iraqi government was out to create, with the heterogeneous and unwilling elements under its control, a 'nation'. And here, Jews would suffer from additional disadvantages. They were conspicuous: the majority of them lived in Baghdad, the capital, where their position was prominent. They were utterly without interest in this absurd attempt to form a nation; they had tried to regulate their position with the British overlord in the only way they understood. Their attempt had misfired, so they withdrew into their own affairs, and looked on with superior amusement at the childish and dishonest ways of these upstarts who pretended to be a government. So that any young nationalist worth his salt would – and did – reason that the Jews, by their very prominence, were a danger to the unity of the Iraqi nation. The young nationalists found encouragement in this train of thought from the Nazis who, about 1936, began to pay attention to the middle east. On the pretext of making gestures against Zionism – with which the Iraqi Jews had no connection – demonstrations were organised in which Jewish shops were wrecked and looted, bombs were thrown at Jewish clubs, and individual Jews were murdered in the streets. These activities occurred in 1935–6 during the administration of Yasin al-Hashimi whose dictatorial proclivities and pan-Arab ambitions no doubt led him to tolerate, if not to instigate them. This terrorism created such fear in the Jewish community that they organised a one-day strike during which all Jewish shops and businesses were closed. The terror ceased when Yasin was toppled from power by Bakr Sidqi's *coup d'état*.

Then, in 1941, occurred an event which must remain a landmark in the modern history of Iraqi Jewry. In April of that year some politicians and army officers with Nazi connections staged a *coup d'état*, and soon afterwards declared war against Great Britain. By the swiftness and decision of Mr Churchill the movement – which could have had very serious results – was promptly snuffed out. On 1 June, its leaders were in flight and Baghdad had fallen to the British. On the following two days, a massacre broke out, carried out by soldiers and policemen who had been fanaticised by the collapsed regime and were now enraged by its failure. The responsible officials in Baghdad – the mutassarif, the director-general of police and the mayor – proved feckless and cowardly. They refused to take any action to check the disorders; hordes of tribesmen, therefore, attracted by the prospect of loot, poured into the city and joined the soldiers and the police in their work. The victims of the outbreak were the Jews. It is thought that some six hundred were murdered, and a very large number wounded. The damage to property was extensive.[55] The British army, standing on the outskirts of Baghdad, did not interfere in any way. Mr Somerset de Chair, who was intelligence officer of the force, tells the story well:

Reading came to me. 'Why do our troops not go into Baghdad?' he asked. 'Already they may be looting, I know there will be many people killed if our troops do not enter.'
This was my own view and the ways of the Foreign Office were beyond my comprehension. From the hour of the Cease Fire their word had prevailed. Having fought our way, step by step, to the threshold of the city, we must now cool our heels outside. It would, apparently, be lowering to the dignity of our ally, the regent [who had fled to Palestine at the *coup d'état*], if he were seen to be supported on arrival by British bayonets.[56]

This could not be allowed. As the British ambassador, Sir Kinahan Cornwallis ('whose word', Miss Stark says, 'was the deciding factor in immediate policy') solicitously informed the Iraqi armistice delegates: 'Many years ago I fought, together with King Faisal the lamented who was my friend for the freeing of the Arabs, and together we built up the kingdom of Iraq. And do you think I would willingly see destroyed what I myself have helped to build?'[57] It was not only Cornwallis who entertained and expressed such elevated and fervent sentiments. Behind him stood Wavell, the commander-in-chief, middle east. Whether following his own judgment or that of his advisers in Cairo, all through the month of May he had engaged in a polemic with Delhi and London, accusing the former of wanting a military occupation of Iraq and impressing on the latter the necessity of securing the good graces of the Iraqi government, failing which the whole Arab world would go up in flames. In the course of this polemic, he had declared, in a telegram of 10 May, that Baghdad should not be occupied 'except temporarily to secure favourable government or at request Iraqi government'. We may here have the explanation why the British troops were allowed to look on while a city lying in their power was given over to murder and rapine.[58] We may contrast what happened in 1941 with an earlier British occupation of Baghdad. When the city fell to the British arms in March 1917, looting and disorder also broke out, but, as honour required, they were speedily repressed and the commander, General Maude, noted at the time: 'The city was rather in a turmoil, for directly the Turks went out at ten o'clock in the morning, Kurds and Arabs began looting everywhere, and although we got into the city by about 6.00 a.m., there was time for them to do a considerable amount of damage. Still we soon reduced them to order'.[59] Such, then, was the ultimate degradation of a policy which, in the days of its arrogant youth, gloried in branding every other policy for the middle east as sordid and degrading. It has already been remarked by students of the period how many of the same men who were prominent in the middle east in the first world war came back to the scene of their activities in the second.[60] It remains, perhaps, to be added that the massacres also had their parallels: for in Damascus, too, in October 1918, where Lawrence had contrived to install the Arab 'army' in sole occupation, massacres broke out after their entry;[61] and the Jews of Baghdad, in June 1941, stood exactly in the same relation to the Arabs and the British as the Armenians did in Aleppo, in the massacre of February 1919.[62] The Jews were terrorised and demoralised completely. They had been slaughtered and looted, and nobody had come forward to protect them. Their sense of security experienced a shock from which it was never to revive. The governors of Iraq, no doubt, also realised how completely they had the Jews in their power, to do with them what they chose.

It was then that a saviour declared his presence to the Jews of Baghdad. The Zionists came to offer their help. Palestinian Jews were enrolled in, or employed by, the British army and the Zionists made some of these their emissaries to the Jews of Baghdad, whom otherwise they could not have hoped to reach.[63] These emissaries argued eloquently and forcefully the Zionist thesis: that Jewish life in the Diaspora was poisonous and impossible, that the only salvation was to become pioneers on the land, in the collectives of Eretz Israel. Zionism is a doctrine that had no appeal to oriental Jewries. Their historical experience is profoundly different from that of the east European Jewries, where Zionism was invented. From the start, when the Balfour Declaration was issued, the reaction of the Jews of Baghdad to Zionism was tepid, not to say unfriendly,[64] and they kept aloof from it. As it was, the Zionists had to force themselves on their attention, when they got the opportunity after 1941. Two factors favoured the Zionists, one immediate and obvious, the other hidden and long in elaboration. In the first place there was the recent massacre, a proof of the precarious position of the community. In the second, a long preparation had been going on, tending to favour the reception of the kind of ideas of which the Zionists were the carriers. The western Jewries, the French one in particular, had long taken an interest in the welfare of oriental Jewries and had established through the *Alliance Israelite Universelle* numerous schools in North Africa, Persia and the Ottoman empire. The personnel of these schools, unlike the American missionaries working among the Armenians, did not conceive it their duty to propagate novel theological doctrines; but inevitably, they were the agency through which 'modern', 'progressive' and so-called liberal ideas spread among the communities where they worked. They were at first opposed bitterly by the religious hierarchy, and in some cases, as in Baghdad in the 1860s, actually excommunicated and the Jewish population forbidden contact with them.[65] Gradually however the resistance to them diminished, and they came to be considered as the leaders of thought in these communities. A good example of the attitude of mind they brought to their work may be found in the annual Report for 1909 of the headmaster of the *Alliance* school in Baghdad. This is the year when the Young Turk regime, the precursor of these modern 'national' states in the east, was consolidated. The Report records the headmaster's reaction to the events.

The Jews [he says] were of the most enthusiastic over the triumph of liberty in this country. Well understanding the importance of the new duties which they now have to shoulder, desirous of preparing themselves for the tasks of citizenship, wishing to have a share in the economic revival which is taking place in the empire, their first thoughts turned, as they should, to the active promotion of the official language in their schools. The study of Turkish was neglected in the past by the Jews of Baghdad. They did not use it in business, and they did not aspire to governmental posts. But now, since the coming of the liberal regime, they are zealous in the study of this hitherto neglected language.

In the 1920s and the 1930s, this was exactly the talk that the Jews of Baghdad were to hear from the Arab nationalists, in connection with the revival of classical Arabic; they are now, doubtless, hearing the same strains from the Zionists in Israel about neo-Hebrew. There was also another thing which elicited the headmaster's approval: conscription, made universal by the Young Turks.

Military service will help the bodily regeneration of this enfeebled race. It will also have other notable results. The rough life of the soldier will not only season their weakened bodies, it will also fortify their courage and give them a heightened conscience of their dignity as men and citizens.

Life in common under the tent or in the dormitory, the fact of undergoing the same trials and privations, of being exposed to the same dangers, of feeling the same anxieties or the same enthusiasms, will create links of solidarity and of mutual respect and esteem between the members of different sects. The Jews, morally raised in their own eyes and in the eyes of their compatriots, will know how to defend, if need be, their dignity and their honour.[66]

All the prestige of Europe lay behind these plausible sentiments. If, when they were preached later by the Muslim professors of 'history', which the Iraqi government insisted on planting in Jewish schools, Jewish students were not altogether convinced, these same sentiments did have a receptive audience when expounded, with reference to the National Home, by Zionists missionaries at clandestine meetings in the years after 1941. The Zionists, of course, knew nothing about oriental Jewries, neither their history nor their condition nor their future. All they knew was that these Jewries were in the past the object of philanthropy and were now to become the object of proselytism. They had nothing but contempt for the way of life of these Jewries which according to them was primitive, feudal and unprogressive.[67] They, the Zionists, knew how to remedy these evils. They offered trade unions and sanitation and collectives – all the things that to their surprise still did not make the population among whom they themselves dwelt, take kindly to them. All the problems then of the Jews of Baghdad had one source, the fact of the Exile, and would all be automatically solved by migration to the Holy Land. It was this that their envoys pursued, this, and whatever possibilities there were of obtaining information to help them in their struggle against the Arabs. So they organised 'cells' of young men attracted to these ideas, taught them Hebrew, and sometimes the use of arms.[68] The Iraqi police, larger and somewhat less inefficient than the ordinary run of government departments, could not remain ignorant of these activities. When the Palestine war began in 1948 they made many arrests of persons more or less or not at all involved in Zionist activities, and in the process (as happens in these cases in countries like Iraq) proceeded to terrorise the Jewish population wholesale, terror being itself an ordinary method of government in the east and a convenient means of extracting large bribes. The organisation which the Zionists had been building began, at last, to show its uses. They started to agitate and to distribute clandestine tracts, inciting the Jews to an active opposition to the rough proceedings of the Iraqi authorities; they offered facilities – though at high prices – for the smuggling of persecuted Jews to Israel; and obtained, at last, their first success by organising a Jewish demonstration which unseated by violence the chief rabbi and head of the community, who was opposed to Zionism. A scheme of so-called exchange of population then began to be mooted in many quarters. The idea was, it seems, to exchange the Jews of the Arab countries against the Arab refugees from Palestine. The Zionists were, a priori, in favour of such a scheme. It tallied very well with their doctrines,[69] and indeed we find an Israeli foreign minister speaking of a 'sorting out' of populations in the middle east as leading to 'greater stability and contentment for all concerned'.[70] It is also said that the Powers were in favour of an exchange of population.[71] There is nothing implausible in this, for is it not a pendant of the national self-determination invented by them? To the Iraqi government the idea would also have its attractions for exactly the same reasons as it appealed to the Israeli minister – it would do away with an element which was a hindrance to national unity. In April 1950 the Iraqi government passed a law allowing those Jews who desired it the option to abandon their Iraqi nationality within a year from the passage of the law and to migrate to Israel. This gave the Zionists their big opportunity. They desired to liquidate the Jewish community in Iraq and to transport it to Palestine on the general theoretical ground that a 'sorting out' was the answer; they also wanted to make Israel as much of a *fait accompli* as they could by concentrating as many Jews in their territory as possible. There was, of course, also the loss of lives in the recent war with the Arabs to be made good. So they set out to help the Iraqi government to achieve its national unity; it was one of these tacit, monstrous complicities not entirely unknown to history. The Zionists, then, began to encourage and incite the Jews to emigrate to Israel. They pointed out to them their present miserable condition and painted in glowing colours the wonderful prospects that awaited them in Israel, where a paternal and provident government would enfold them in its all-seeing care. They were at an advantage in this work because they seem to have captured the communal machinery set up to organise the emigration, a fact which gave them contacts, position and authority. The number of Jews who desired to emigrate was, to start with, very small; but the Zionists were persistent, and as the number of Jews registering for emigration increased a vicious circle was created and those Jews who had no wish to emigrate found it harder to remain. It happened at that time that several bombs were thrown at Jewish places of business, at a coffee-shop where Jews used to congregate, and at a synagogue where the intending emigrants were assembled. It is alleged by the Iraqi government that it was Zionist agents who threw these bombs.[72] This may be so, for the Zionists were capable of using such tactics.[73] Be this as it may, the Zionists did profit from the incidents, distributing immediately afterwards warnings to the Jews to hasten the emigration; and in fact, after these incidents, Jews in their thousands did register for emigration.

By March 1951 then, the great majority of the Iraqi Jews had, obeying a variety of powerful pressures, registered for emigration. A few thousand who felt able to disregard the repressive and discriminatory treatment to which they were subjected and the agitation of the Zionists, had decided to remain. It was then that the prime minister, Nuri al Saʻid, convoked Parliament in secret session and had two laws passed. The first decreed that the possessions of the emigrating Jews were to be confiscated to the profit of the government and to be administered by a secretariat-general of frozen property. The possessions of the Jews of Iraq became a welcome addition to the Treasury, and yet another lucrative government department for the employment and enrichment of yet more functionaries was created. A newspaper under Nuri's control declared that the Iraqi people had received this law with 'appreciation and satisfaction' and that Nuri had realised a great aim. The newspaper also praised the particular timing adopted by the statesman, for if his intentions had been divulged earlier many Jews would have hesitated to relinquish their nationality.[74] The government of Israel protested against this legislation. It declared that, such being the proceeding of Iraq, it could not but retaliate: it would be obliged to confiscate property in Israel belonging to Arab refugees. But this property the government of Israel did not use to repay the dispossessed Iraqi Jews. The Arab refugees are still in their camps; the Iraqi government is always ready to air their grievances in the United Nations but not to provide for them out of the money of the dispossessed Jews.[75] And still another pool of misery and discontent was created: the Iraqi Jews in the Israeli immigrant camps, tricked and dissatisfied, their livelihood and homes taken away from them, their coherent community destroyed, and themselves forcibly brought to the service of an ideal which they neither understood nor shared. The second edict proclaimed by Iraq concerned those Iraqi Jews who had not given up their Iraqi nationality and who were abroad, but not in Israel. It decreed that if these Jews did not return to Iraq within a specified time they would lose their nationality and their goods would be forfeit to the Iraqi government. The Iraqi Jews who went abroad also faced the same penalty. These laws, and particularly the second, were clearly unconstitutional, since the Iraq constitution prohibited discrimination and declared confiscation illegal.[76] But a remedy lay nowhere. Not in the Iraqi courts, and not anywhere else. Israel was, of course, indifferent, since the state of these Jews was but a welcome proof of the Zionist contention that Jewish life in the Diaspora was impossible. And none of the Great Powers felt any interest of theirs threatened by such a situation. When the subject of these laws was brought up in the British parliament, the minister of state for foreign affairs replied in tortured and involved language as follows: '. . . . His Majesty's government have drawn the attention of the Iraqi government to the unfortunate consequences which might ensue if any ground was given for a charge that those who are involved by these laws were being subjected to any form of persecution.'[77] In 1931, a representative of Great Britain stood before the League of Nations and, proposing to bestow the dangerous device of sovereignty on the handful of those politicians who for some thirty years were to bind and loose in Baghdad, uttered these urgently persuasive words: 'His Majesty's Government fully realised its responsibility in recommending that Iraq should be admitted to the League ... Should Iraq prove herself unworthy of the confidence which had been placed in her, the moral responsibility must rest with His Majesty's Government ...'.[78] This Iraqi legislation will inevitably remind one of so much familiar central and east European discriminatory legislation, usually directed against the Jews. Such legislation, however, was inspired by anti-semitic doctrine and found its logical culmination in the gas chambers. We must, therefore, guard all the more against attributing the same motives to the rulers of Iraq. Anti-semitism is generally unknown in the east, though it may yet spread there.[79] What we see here rather is a manifestation of the same old, deep-seated instinct for rapine which has been inseparable from eastern government. But this instinct has now at its service the techniques of administration introduced by the west. Thus we find the Iraqi government using administrative and financial controls, usually first introduced by British advisers and experts, for quite different ends, in order to prosecute a policy of exaction and plunder such as the east has indeed always known, but the effects of which were in the past largely nullified through the primitiveness of the means available to the rulers. A horrible fascination lies today in the prim and proper prose of the Colonial Office reports of the 1920s, recording the organisation of this or that department of the police in Iraq, the satisfactory progress of this or that financial department.

The operation, it may be said in conclusion, was elegantly executed with the very least of fuss. The Jews of Iraq were uprooted, dispossessed and scattered in the space of a year. It was a remarkable achievement.

In 1918, when the Arab nationalists were agitating for a state in Iraq, one of them addressed the Jews of Baghdad as follows: 'Did not the prophet Moses lead you for forty years through the wilderness to order to effect your purification? We, following his example, bring for your regeneration a pure Khalif from the wilderness.'[80] Yes, they did effect the purification of the Jews of Baghdad, and they

314

did make them, with the help of their brethren from over the Jordan, enter the Holy Land. Thus is manifested in a practical manner that Arab–Zionist cooperation on which such store was set in 1919. Is it not at last satisfied, that profound *nostalgie de la boue* which so moved the European Jewries at the hour of their supreme catastrophe, and do they not have now their own postage stamps and their own ministers, their own passports and their own secret agents? Are they not now like all the nations? So is the dream at last realised, and the design in the end accomplished.

One's first impulse in the face of all this is to say, No good can come out of it. But this is in the lap of the future, and we are not diviners. Be it sufficient for the present to record that these things are evil. That persecutors and persecuted, hunters and hunted are in the grip of the powers of darkness. It is enough to elucidate how this came to pass, for the story can at least have this moral, that the consequences of action are incalculable, and that out of the desire to do good, good may not in fact ensue. The reforms proposed for the Ottoman empire were not really reforms, but crude, ill-considered, half-hearted measures to shift power from one group to another and to distribute it differently within the empire. This was in itself a formidable undertaking for foreigners to attempt, their first consideration being in any case not this but the protection of the interests of their countries. It was therefore mischievous and misleading to call these measures 'reforms', as this only served to hide the nature and the extent of the problem, and to make the inevitable explosions as unexpected as they were disastrous. The process of change from one arrangement to another in the middle east could not be easy, and the manner in which it was initiated ensured that this process bore with extreme harshness on the populations affected. The improvement of conditions in the east needed knowledge, good-will and patience; the statesmen and diplomats who undertook the task were, for the most part, ignorant, indifferent and in a hurry; or if not indifferent then seized with unwholesome passions for Ottoman or Armenian, Arab or Zionist. Hence the atrocities incident to national self-determination, the destruction of these small frail communities with very limited political experience, who were unable to deal with such new and terrifying manifestations, and the origin of these perverted commonwealths of the east to which no good man can give his loyalty. The measure of the failure is that today the west should be exhorted to build in the east nations where 'Moslems, Christians and Jews can and will live in harmony'.[81] The Ottoman state was organised in such a way as to fulfil precisely this requirement.

The Ottoman system was far from perfect. It was narrow and hidebound. It knew nothing of the richness, the flexibility and the opportunities existing in the western tradition. But its conventions were well established and its modalities well understood. In due course, the habits perhaps would be capable of being fostered,

> that made old wrong
> Melt down as it were wax in the sun's rays.

If reforms were needed or were practicable, there is nothing clearer than that they could succeed only if they proceeded from native traditions and were accomplished with native means. The pressure, the example and the inevitable influence of Europe put this out of the question. But even if European ways had not been alien and confusing, the fact that reforms were inextricably mixed with the interests of the Powers was enough to bedevil everything. If there had to be European reforms, if 'nations' were going to be built up, there was only one way by which these operations could prove beneficial and not catastrophic. It was for Europe itself to administer them and carry them through. This proved impossible, either because of the rivalries of the Powers or because such a course was rejected by Europeans as imperialistic and immoral, or, finally, because of that failure of nerve and morality which made attractive the exercise of power and influence without responsibility.

The fate of minorities such as the Armenians or the Jews of Iraq is merely an extreme result of the turmoil introduced by the west in the east. But even where the results are not so extreme and final, the condition of the east is today pitiful enough. From the west there can be no escape: the Armenians tried to emulate its political ways, the Jews of Iraq tried to ignore them. For both disaster lay in wait. What can be said of these, can also be said of other groups and of the other western innovations, economic or cultural, to which they must submit. They are all delivered over into the power of the legions of ill-will abroad in the world. The dangers are manifold; the remedies scant and impotent.

11

Religion and Politics

It is a well-known feature of Palestinian politics during the mandate that the Christians – of whom the great majority were Orthodox – seemed to make common cause with the Muslims in the struggle against Zionism. They, or at least the leaders who claimed to speak in their name, asserted that both Muslims and Christians were part of the Arab nation, and that this fact made their solidarity natural and inevitable.

The circumstances of Palestine under the mandate were, of course, exceptional, placing a small religious minority, anxious to survive unscathed, in quite a difficult position; and it is possible to argue that expediency and prudence made identification with the majority attractive. But it was quite late in the history of the mandate before it became finally apparent that the mandatory had decided no longer to advance Zionist interests at the price of Arab antagonism. Until 1939 or thereabouts expediency might also have counselled a measure, at least, of acquiescence in British policy, and in Zionist expansion, seeing that the British were the masters in Palestine and that the prudent have a lively respect for their masters. But the articulate leaders of the Orthodox Christian community never deviated in the least from the Muslim line in Palestine. Their policy did not seem dictated by expediency. On the contrary, shrewd and experienced observers remarked more than once on the fervent commitment of Orthodox Christians to the ideals of Arab nationalism, and their whole-hearted involvement in the nationalist struggle. Thus, in 1926, Bertram and Young, reporting on the controversies opposing the patriarchate and the Orthodox laity, said with accents of conviction:

National consciousness is not a matter of what ought to be felt, but of what actually is felt. No amount of eloquent reasoning could persuade the inhabitants of Alsace–Lorraine that their true national consciousness is German. Similarly no amount of such reasoning would persuade the

317

Orthodox congregation of Palestine that they are not Arabs ... The dearest thought of every young local Orthodox Christian is that he is an Arab, and his most cherished aspirations are those of Arab nationalism, which he shares with his Moslem fellow-countrymen.[1]

Some ten years later Professor Hancock, visiting Palestine, was also struck by the seeming solidarity of Muslim and Christian.

The British government [he writes] had taken over the Turkish tradition of classifying the population of Palestine by confessional allegiance; The categories under which the census officials grouped their figures of births and deaths, immigration and emigration, employment, education and the rest were: Jews, Moslems, Christians, Others. This classification fitted the facts of Jewish solidarity and on the Zionist side was in effect a classification by nationality; but it completely ignored the national solidarity which on the Arab side was transcending the old distinction between Moslem and Christian.[2]

To the outside world this solidarity was illustrated by the career of George Antonius, an Orthodox Christian, who resigned from a high post in the mandatory administration in protest against British policies, and then wrote *The Arab Awakening*, the most eloquent, able and influential exposition of Arab nationalist claims that has so far been written. And there were other Orthodox Christians, less well known outside Syria and Palestine but quite prominent in their own community and in the nationalist movement, men such as Rafiq Rizq Sallum, the Orthodox lawyer from Homs who had been intended for the priesthood but who deserted the Orthodox seminary at Belmont for the Syrian Protestant College at Beirut and the Imperial Law College at Istanbul, became an Arab nationalist and was hanged by Jamal Pasha at Damascus in 1915;[3] men also such as 'Issa al-'Issa, editor of the Jaffa newspaper *Filastin*, and a member of the Nashashibi faction which went under the title of *The National Defence Party*; Ya'qub Faraj, president of the Arab Orthodox Executive Committee, a prominent member of *The Muslim–Christian Society* which operated in the early days of British administration, and later one of the nine members of the Arab Higher Executive Committee set up in 1936 under the mufti's chairmanship; or his cousin Khalil Sakakini, at one time secretary of the executive committee of the *Arab Congress of Palestine* which functioned in the 1920s, and for many years a high official in the Palestine Education Department, whose diary, published posthumously a few years ago, affords striking evidence of the state of mind of the educated class of his community and generation.[4]

And yet, the unanimous witnesses, the emphatic declarations, the clear commitment are not enough to banish all puzzlement. These Orthodox Christians, living for centuries under the dominance and on the fringes of Muslim society, are suddenly found asserting that they are no mere political minority but part and parcel of the Arab nation, equally entitled with the Muslims, should this nation achieve sovereignty, to the exercise of political power. The reactions of the Muslims to such claims, should it be attempted seriously to make them good, we may leave on one side, for the habit of power stoutly held for centuries would enable them to deal with these easily and confidently. The situation of the Orthodox themselves is more diffi-cult and more interesting. In order to convince themselves – if not others – that they formed part of the Arab nation they would have to reject what had governed the social arrangements of their com-munity for countless generations and provided a sense of identity with their fathers and fathers' fathers. In the past they had been members of a religious community, and this membership at once defined their status and set the bounds of their public as of their private activity. Loyalty did not extend beyond the community, and traffic between communities was confined to an inescapable minimum of externals. But now this religion suddenly seemed a badge of servitude. Membership of the Arab nation had a price – which Muslims, being the majority and the rulers, did not have to pay. It meant the abandonment of communal organisation and the defiant assertion that religion was a strictly private affair, that it could not be the constitutive principle of a society, that it had no political and little social significance. This radical change of view in a matter so intimate and so fundamental came abruptly, and if only because abrupt, it must also have been violent, creating schism and discord within the community. When, therefore, outside observers reported the solidarity of Christians with Muslims, were they not perhaps un-wittingly echoing the claims and professions of the victorious party in a species of civil war which had raged inside the Orthodox Christian community?

Such a view is supported by the experience which similar com-munities underwent as a result of the sudden impact of new theo-logical and political ideas imported from outside. The Armenian nationalists, for instance, seeking to transform the Armenian community of the Ottoman empire into a European nation state, succeeded in establishing hegemony among their people only after a sanguinary struggle with other Armenians who opposed these ambitions, and who were inclined to achieve some compromise with the Ottoman authorities. And before the Zionists could become a powerful party among the eastern European Jews they had to surmount the formidable and relentless opposition of the religious and secular leaders of their communities. Strife was undoubtedly embittered by the intrusive character of the new ideas. They did not arise within the communities they affected so profoundly but were brought in from the outside with superior airs. The supporters of the old order, considering these notions the invention of misguided unbelievers or diabolical persecutors, rejected them with horror and never attempted to discriminate between innovations which they could accept and those which they had to reject. Those who were attracted to them therefore became easily disaffected and were forced into radical attitudes and uncompromising postures.

It is interesting to notice that such strife, and the extremism it engendered, never seriously affected the Maronite community. Can the cause be the Maronite connection with the Roman Catholic Church, so alive to European intellectual currents and so skilled and experienced in shielding its charges from disruptive influences? For outsiders were not left alone to introduce the Maronites to European ideas and methods; these were mediated through the educational enterprise of Roman Catholic orders, who would naturally exert all their efforts to combat the notion that modernity and religion were hopelessly opposed, and that modernity was necessarily superior.

But even among the Maronites things could easily have been quite different. In 1825 American Protestant missionaries came to Beirut and attempted to gain converts among the local Christian population. The Maronite patriarch reacted strongly to their activities and issued two manifestos, first in 1824 and again in 1829, ordering the members of his community to avoid all contact with them, whether in religious or temporal matters. Nobody was to handle their publications or attend their prayer meetings or frequent their schools or take service or have financial relations with them. 'Let them hereby,' said the patriarch in his second manifesto, 'be excluded from all Christian society; let the curse cover them as a garment and sink into their members as an oil and make them wither as the fig-tree which the mouth of the Lord has cursed; the evil spirit shall also take possession of them, torturing them day and night; no one shall visit or greet them.' Disobedience led to excommunication.[5] A young Maronite, As'ad al-Shidiaq, publicly embraced the teachings of the missionaries. He now declared that he had never before been 'a believer, according to the living true faith', that 'it would be but a lie if I should say I believed as the Romish Church does' and that 'by reason, and learning, and prayer to God, with purity of motive, we may know from the holy Scripture everything necessary to our salvation'. The religion in which he had been brought up, he now became persuaded, was hopelessly sunk in superstition and corruption.[6] Eventually, the patriarch had As'ad imprisoned at his seat where he died shortly afterwards. His youngest brother, Faris, was also attracted to the missionaries' doctrine and became fond, as the Maronite bishop of Beirut put it, of reasoning on the subject of religion. His family disapproved greatly of his behaviour, the more so that they feared it might influence his brother As'ad's fate for the worse, and he clashed with his eldest brother, Mansur. He fled to the missionaries, declaring that 'I will either go to a place in this country where I can enjoy my liberty, or I will take ship and leave the country altogether'. The missionaries put Faris aboard a ship for Malta and employed him at their printing press there.[7] He became a famous Arabic writer, ended by embracing Islam, and died a pensioner of the sultan and a notable advocate of his pan-Islamic pretensions. His best-known work, a curious autobiography, contains a sustained diatribe descending at times to obscenity and foul language, against the hypocrisy and cupidity of the Maronite clergy. In a passage bemoaning the misfortune of his brother, he says to the Maronite hierarchy: 'And even if my brother discussed religion controversially, and said that you were mistaken, you had no right to kill him for this.'[8]

Among the Maronites, Faris al-Shidiaq was not the only one to rebel against his religion and community. There was also the writer Adib Ishaq (1856–85) who, when he died in Beirut, was refused a Catholic burial. He was outspoken and intemperate in denouncing the clerical power in the east, but seemed to attribute its corruption to western example.[9] Towards the end of the nineteenth century and the beginning of the twentieth anti-clericalism (allied with freemasonry) in fact knew some vogue among educated Maronites in Lebanon and in America.[10] The most famous example of this anti-clericalism was that of the writer Amin al-Rayhani (1876–1940).

Rayhani went to the United States as a boy of thirteen, and it was there in fact that he began his literary career, with an onslaught on religious dogma and institutions. In 1903 he published a satire, *al-Muhalafa al-thulathiyya fi'l mamlaka al-hayawaniyya* (*The Triple Alliance in the Animal Kingdom*). which he followed a year later by another diatribe *al-Makari wa'l kahin* (*The Muleteer and the Priest*). In the first of these works he pictures the clergy in the guise of an ass, a mule and a horse. These three animals are challenged by a fox who denounces the superstitions which they purvey in order to resist the march of progress and preserve their power over their followers: 'I do not believe in your God,' he exclaims, 'I hate your Jehovah, I recognise no authority, and I absolutely deny your allegation that God Almighty has given you authority over us.' The three animals, thus challenged, kill the fox, who becomes a martyr to his beliefs; but shortly afterwards they themselves are overtaken and run over by a railway train, that symbol of progress.[11] *The Muleteer and the Priest* takes up the theme with virulence. A muleteer of the Lebanese mountains is made anti-clerical by his experience of oppression and deceit at the hands of the clergy. While on a journey in a carriage from Beirut to the mountain, he meets a Maronite priest as a fellow-passenger and he proceeds to harangue him: 'You vow,' he tells him, 'the three vows of obedience, chastity, and poverty. These are the vows which are known to the people. But you also take a fourth vow, and you take it in secret. You then take the vow that you will not be bound by your vows.' The priest is converted by the muleteer's cogency and eloquence; he writes to his son, who is studying theology at Rome, to give up the priesthood which God's book does not sanction, and that the church is an invention by means of which its heads are able to accumulate wealth. He abandons his parish and takes up an itinerant life, preaching the new tidings in company with the muleteer. In a final episode recalling As'ad al-Shidiaq's fate, the patriarch has him imprisoned in a monastery on the pretext that he is a madman, where he is beaten by the monks and finally dies.[12]

In a letter to a friend from this period, Amin Rayhani declares that 'the Syrian people had hitherto been the anvil silently receiving the blows of the clerical hammer'.[13] It was to deliver them at last from this fate that the young Amin embarked on this campaign which exposed him to the bitter hostility of the Maronite and Catholic clergy.[14] But what did he have to offer in place of this superstition? He offered a syncretism or perhaps a natural religion which men should recognise as common to them all, a belief free of dogma and unencumbered with the specific and the positive. He wanted his fellow Syrians to become what he himself claimed to be, Christian with the Gospels and Muslim with the Koran. Fanaticism would then disappear and the Syrians would be launched on the road of progress and prosperity. As he wrote to a correspondent:

I have no doubt that the Muslim who loves a Christian and would marry her, or the Christian who loves a Muslim and would marry her, is so elevated in his morals, his intellect and his behaviour that he may neglect some – or many – of the traditions of his kin and people. . . . I consider [he went on] that inter-marriage today between the two groups is one of the most important conditions for our reform and progress. The social and religious toleration which will grow in a home composed of these two elements is the only remedy for all our religious and social ills; nay, it is the elixir of our new life.

As for the children who will be the fruit of this marriage, the question of teaching them religious principles is simple. Let them read something from the Gospel and the Koran . . . and let them sometimes go to this and sometimes to that place of worship until they reach their majority. They will then have the freedom of worshipping as they choose and may pray wherever their reason and their conscience directs.[15]

His fellow Maronite, the writer Marun Abbud (1886–1962), subscribed to something like these beliefs and called one of his sons Muhammad. Amin al-Rayhani congratulates him on this gesture and writes that if the Muslims, the Druzes and the Jews were to follow his example a new generation of brethren – of true brethren – would arise in the country who outside their places of worship would not be able to distinguish between Christian and Muslim and Jew.[16]

But this natural and universal religion was not as easy and rational as it seemed on the surface. Consider Marun Abbud who, in the cause of religious amity, had named one of his sons Muhammad. His friendly feelings towards Islam had also, and characteristically, been preceded by a clash with his own religious authorities.[17] In 1934 he published a poem in celebration of the Prophet Muhammad in which he is praised for unifying a nation divided by religious fanaticism. The poet deplores religious divisions, for what difference can there be between Marun (a Christian name) and Marwan (a Muslim name)? And he goes on to declaim: 'Let the generations bow in reverence whenever the Most Pure Prophet from Adnan is mentioned, who has filled the world with the name of God and has called the people of the earth to

323

unity. Let the fanatics go on croaking; the bird of paradise is not harmed by the mouthings of the crows.'[18] It would seem, then, that in this new universal religion a privileged place is accorded to Islam and its Prophet. The reason, we may suspect, is that in abjuring the tradition of their community as superstitious and divisive, in refusing to be identified as Maronites, men like Marun Abbud and Amin al-Rayhani find that they have to seek a new identity for themselves, and that the syncretistic universalism which they preach cannot readily supply this identity. If their syncretism had not precluded them from it they would have perhaps gladly identified themselves as Muslims and taken their place within a dominant, self-confident group. For them, not so much Islam as a system of belief, but the Muslim community as a powerful and cohesive group, exercised a tremendous fascination. It is this fascination which may explain Marun Abbud's poem in praise of the Prophet, and a statement such as this by Rayhani:

> The Muslims are more devoted in their patriotism and have a sounder view of it than the Christians. They demand complete independence without a mandate or similar pretexts. This is absolutely clear. The Christians, on the other hand, invoke patriotism but ask for an incomplete independence which is supervised by this or that Power. The Christian minority will, it seems, remain a minority and will diminish daily owing to emigration, while the Muslim majority will remain a majority. The Christians, therefore, will remain in need of protection, and permanent protection is imperialism.[19]

Christianity, then, is not only superstition and corruption, it is also an instrument of imperialism. Were it possible to find an Islam without dogmas it would surely provide an escape from it. And providentially, after the first world war such an Islam came to hand. For Rayhani and those who thought like him it was known as Arabism, and it was Arabism which came to provide for them a new identity in place of the traditional one which they had discarded. Characteristically, just as the rejection of the Maronite tradition was the outcome of exposure to western thought, so Arabism also was drawn from western literature. Rayhani tells us that when he left the Lebanon as a boy, in his breast was fear of those whose language he spoke and hatred for them some of whose blood flowed in his veins. In the New World he came across Carlyle's essay on Muhammad in *Heroes and Hero-Worship* 'and I felt for the first time some love for the Arabs and became inclined to seek out more of their history'.

He then discovered Washington Irving's book on the Alhambra and began to dream of the ancient Arab glories. He sought out orientalist works in the New York Public Library and found in them 'poetry, prophecy; the desert oases in oceans of sands, and the date-trees in the oases, through the branches of which whispers the breeze and the trunks of which are shaken by the hot desert wind'. He also finds in them 'the voice of the *sāqiya*[20] singing to the blessed earth under the shade of the date-trees and the Beduin girl singing to the camel of the *sāqiya*'. This he finds in the books in the New York Public Library – an enchantment which removes him utterly from the drabness of this bustling and crowded city where he had to earn his keep by balancing the books of his uncle's export-import business.[21] It was this western exoticism which at length provided a new identity for Rayhani and made of him an Arab nationalist preaching that the Maronite, the Druze, the Shi'ite and the Sunni had to forget that they were Maronite, Druze, Shi'ite or Sunni and to remember only that they were Arab: 'Arabism brings us together', he exclaims, 'Arabism unites us'. Arabism it is which creates that strength which the Europeans respect, a strength which can never be defeated or brought low.[22] They all had to forget their particular identity but, we may suspect, not all equally. It is the Maronite and other non-Muslims who had to forget most, who had, as Rayhani put it in his political testament written in 1931, so to unite with the Arabs, so to coalesce with them intellectually, morally and spiritually that no majority or minority would subsist.[33] On a visit to Ibn Sa'ud he proclaimed that if the Arab cause required him to become a Wahabi, he would become one; it is quite inconceivable that he should demand reciprocity, that if the necessities of the Arab cause required Ibn Sa'ud to become a Christian, then he should become one. He is terribly flattered that Ibn Sa'ud should describe him as a 'true Arab' and seems unconscious of the king's patronising attitude when he continued: 'He is more devoted to the Arabs than the Arabs themselves, and nobler than many Muslims.'[24]

In rebelling against his community and religion and finally becoming a Muslim and an advocate of pan-Islam, Faris al-Shidiaq was very much the exception in his generation. So on the whole were Adib Ishaq, Amin al-Rayhani and Marun Abbud in their rebellions and in the cause which they chose in substitution for their ancestral faith.[25] Different circumstances made this kind of rebellion in other communities more common and more effective. This was the case in the Orthodox Christian community in Palestine. Its situation was peculiar enough. The patriarchate of Jerusalem, like its neighbour to the north, the patriarchate of Antioch, was composed mainly of an Arabic-speaking laity. But in both patriarchates the clergy, with the exception of the village priests, was Greek. In Jerusalem, the patriarch – holding, as usual in the Ottoman empire, both temporal and spiritual power – together with the metropolitan, bishops and archimandrites, was always recruited from the Brotherhood of the Holy Sepulchre, an old monastic order but which under its modern constitution dates from 1662.[26] The order was a closed corporation. The patriarch was *ex officio* president of the Brotherhood and it admitted none but Greeks to its membership. On entering the order the members took the vows of obedience and chastity but not the vow of poverty. They were paid salaries and they could hold property which, however, if immovable, reverted on their death to the Brotherhood.[27] The Brotherhood was rich and disposed of important revenues derived from bequests left by the pious in Russia, the Balkans and the Ottoman empire, and from the donations of Orthodox pilgrims to the Holy Places. As for the parish priests, their position was quite wretched. They were drawn from the Arabic-speaking laity, they had little education and received very little pay. An observer writing before the first world war remarked that though there existed an Orthodox theological college in Jerusalem, the natives, with one or two exceptions, were excluded from it. The parish priests, he reported, were paid for Sunday Masses from church funds at a rate varying from 20 to 82 cents, and received similar fees from the faithful for baptisms, marriages and funerals. These priests were not properly recruited, their position in many cases being quasi-hereditary, and it was not unusual to see different clans in the village using the services of different priests.[28] This situation seems to have continued much the same after the war, for a subsequent writer also remarked on the paucity of their knowledge as of their income.[29]

The patriarch was not only the spiritual head of his community. On him also devolved – or should have devolved – responsibility for its temporal welfare, for the Ottoman government provided neither education nor medical services nor care for the old. Such services were a communal responsibility and in Jerusalem their provision was elementary; here again, the patriarch and the Brotherhood of the Holy Sepulchre could with justice be convicted of neglecting their pastoral duties. When these shortcomings were later brought vehemently to their notice, they argued that the patriarchate of Jerusalem was not like other sees; in Jerusalem, they said, their first duty was to guard and maintain the Holy Places, for which they were responsible to the whole of Orthodoxy. Pastoral care took second place, and in any case the Greek Orthodox population of Palestine contributed nothing to the upkeep of the see; whatever the patriarchate spent on them came from the bounty of the Orthodox world, and they had no right to question the actions of the patriarch or to demand accounts.

This situation, potential in estrangements and conflicts, began to be exploited by Russia in the nineteenth century. Ever since the treaty of Kutchuk Kainardja of 1774 Russia had been trying to penetrate the Ottoman empire and establish therein a position of influence and dominance; and she found the Orthodox populations of the empire useful in furthering these designs. In 1842 a Russian archimandrite, Porphyr Uspensky, whom Bertram and Young describe as an 'ecclesiastic of peculiar propensities',[30] was established in Jerusalem and continued there a number of years, ostensibly to look after the needs of Russian pilgrims. But it is clear that he also worked to advance Russian political interests,[31] and to this end strove to establish a following among the local population. He set himself up as their champion and espoused their grievances against the patriarchate. His reputation in this respect became legendary. Witness the stand he is made to take against the Greeks, in an anti-Greek pamphlet published in Arabic in 1893:

'Your priests', says Uspensky to the patriarchal delegate, 'your priests are ignorant of their duties. . . . Instead of instructing and training them when they come to see you, you spurn them like vile slaves. When they knock at the gates of the patriarchate, imploring you in the name of our holy ancestors, your answer is "Get out of here, take yourselves off".'

The Greek is made to say: 'We do not allow Arab priests to approach Us because this would derogate from Our episcopal dignity. As for their requests, the dragoman acquaints Us with them.'

Uspensky: 'This is the first time in my life that I hear it said that the approach of a priest is derogatory to episcopal dignity. My lord, what mean these words?'

Greek: 'We do not understand their language.'

Uspensky: 'Why not learn it? But let it be! Your age may no longer make it possible for you to study the language of the country. But why not allow the dragoman to set out the requests of the native priests in their own presence?'

Greek: 'This is impossible! We cannot introduce new customs.'[32]

With Russian help, then, the grievances of the laity and the lower clergy against the patriarchate became crystallised as the grievances of Arabs against Greeks. In 1873, after Uspensky's departure from Jerusalem, the patriarch Cyril was deposed by the Jerusalem synod for siding with Russia against the patriarchate of Constantinople on the issue of the autocephaly of the Bulgarian Church. Russia was able to get up an agitation among the local people against his dismissal. Bertram and Young quote a pamphlet published on that occasion 'under Russian influences' which accuses the 'Greek element', lazy and turbulent priests, of monopolising the riches of the see of Jerusalem, which really belong to the whole of Orthodoxy; 'as for the natives', the pamphlet adds, 'they may well be compared to that poor Lazarus of the Gospels, who was laid at the rich man's gate and who desired to be fed with the crumbs which fell from his table (St. Luke, XVI, 19–21).'[33] Russia's championship of the native laity became most manifest in the see of Antioch in the 1890s when, with her pressure and diplomatic support, the Greek clergy were finally ousted from the see by a *coup d'état* and Arab clergy replaced them.[34]

As time went on, Russia worked powerfully and methodically to strengthen her influence in the Levant. After the Crimean war a consul-general in Jerusalem seconded with his authority the efforts of the resident archimandrite; and in 1882 the Imperial Orthodox Palestine Society began its operations. This society, whose patron was the tsar himself and whose president was a grand duke, was founded to look after the needs of the Russian pilgrims in the Holy Land and to set up hostels and hospitals for them. But it soon acquired other functions. It began to open schools and to train locally teachers for the native Orthodox population. In 1886 a women's teachers' training college was opened at Beit-Jala, in 1889 a men's college at Nazareth. By 1898 over six thousand five hundred pupils were in attendance at the society's schools; by 1912 there were eleven thousand of them in more than a hundred schools and the society's expenditure amounted to 336,000 roubles.[35]

It is difficult to imagine nowadays the effect which such attentive solicitude had on the local Orthodox communities; what feelings of security and of pride were evoked in them by this tangible evidence of Russian care and protection, what vast horizons these schools opened and what new possibilities they conjured up in these hitherto neglected and almost forgotten communities. In his notable autobiography, *Seventy Years*, the well-known Lebanese writer Mikha'il

Nu'ayma describes for us his education as it began in a primary school founded and maintained in his village of Baskinta by the Imperial Orthodox Palestine Society, how it continued in the college of Nazareth, also at the expense of the society, and how excellence in his studies there took him on a scholarship awarded by the society to the seminary at Poltava. As he begins his chapter on the Baskinta school which opened in 1899,

'Muscovy' became in our vernacular 'Maskoby' and Russia came to be known among us as the 'country of the Miskub'.

'The Miskub is coming to open a school in Baskinta! May God give him victory!'

The news spread in the village as light spreads at dawn. The Orthodox community received it with songs of praise and glorification. And no wonder! It was something taken for granted among the inhabitants of the Lebanon in the era of the *Mutasarrifiyya* that Russia was the traditional protector of the Rum, France of the Maronites, Britain of the Protestants and the Druzes and Turkey of the Muslims. But Russia pushed her rivalry so far that she began opening free schools for the Rum in Palestine, Syria and the Lebanon, schools the curricula and administration of which were of the latest model. It made no condition on any Orthodox community which desired to have a school except it should provide a suitable building. As for the teachers, the books, the exercise books, the ink, the pencils, the furniture, the salaries and the administrative expenses, they were all free. ... For the first time in its history Baskinta knew what may be called a model school. For the first time in its history its girls began to study on an equality with the boys. The school had five school-masters and three school-mistresses presided over by a headmaster who had graduated from the Russian teachers' training college in Nazareth and studied pedagogy and educational administration. For the first time we felt we were in a school which had a curriculum and which was orderly.[36]

Of course it was not the aim of the Russians to estrange the Orthodox of Palestine from their religion. They desired merely to estrange them from their religious superiors. But there was no way of circumscribing disaffection or of attacking persons without undermining institutions. We may illustrate this by an example from Nu'ayma's autobiography. Nu'ayma dwells at length on the official adulation of the Ottoman sultan and the Russian tsar which was inculcated in the establishments of the Imperial Orthodox Palestine Society – the first surely a matter of prudence and policy, while the second was clearly the expression of affection and loyalty. Yet he also recounts

329

that in the college at Nazareth, one of the teachers he most admired,
Antun Ballan from Homs who had studied in Russia

was the first who wakened patriotic feeling in us. Whenever the opportunity offered, he used to tell us of the misery of our country under the
Turkish yoke, of Abd al-Hamid's despotism, the crimes of the Bosphorus,
the corruption rampant in the departments of the state from the sultan
down to the lowest *mukhtar* in the most insignificant village. If therefore
the Arabs desired a life of some honour and independence, they had to
regain possession of their lands and their stolen liberties; and the Muslims
among them had to take back the usurped caliphate, since the caliphate
belongs exclusively to the Arabs.[37]

It may be true that what came at the hands of the Russians was
anyway inevitable, and would have been accomplished at others'
hands; that the unbending obscurantism of the hierarchy and their
foolish contempt for their pastoral charges would sooner or later
have led to an explosion. But the fact remains that it was principally
Russian action on a young generation of Palestinian Orthodox which
led the way to further developments, and that it was Russian efforts
which made the quarrel between laity and clergy a definite and
inevitable quarrel between Arabs and Greeks. A new generation grew
up, bitter at the pitiful spectacle of their community, resentful of the
corrupt hierarchy which ruled them, contemptuous of their spiritual
directors and convinced that only a radical parting with tradition
would ameliorate their condition. Tradition was mute or gave a
hateful sound; and therefore abstract principles, brought to them by
missionaries and educators, had to replace and do the work of tradition. The younger generation were men of principles, and that they
were young and in revolt against the old only made their radicalism
more radical. Finally, this radicalism became a built-in political
attitude because these men of principles had nothing but principles.
They did not claim authority on behalf of classes and interests, but
because they were educated men and knew the right answers. They
were lawyers or school-teachers in a society where such occupations
were meagrely and precariously rewarded and those who followed
them little respected. For instance, again and again in his *Diary*
Khalil Sakakini complains of financial insecurity and the low standing of his profession. 'Shall I', he writes while on a visit to America,
'go back to my native land, go back to teaching in schools and private
houses, to witness every day such painful sights that my life becomes
a hell?'[38] He decides to go back, and a few months later we find him

in Jerusalem complaining: 'I wish I could find work in Jerusalem, but how is this to be done since I am Orthodox? The English bishop wants me to put on clerical dress, to accompany the pupils to Church and read the Bible: the Church Missionary Society wants me to become a missionary, and I can do neither.'[39] The passage of the years does not seem to improve his condition. In 1919 his finances are as precarious as ever. 'It is a long time now', he writes in April 1919, 'that my pocket is empty and I possess nothing. We live on our provisions at home. I borrowed a quarter of a lira today . . .'[40]. He gives Arabic lessons to British officers, and one day earns twenty-five shillings from these lessons: 'This', he writes, 'is the highest income per day I have earned in twenty-five years of teaching'.[41] And all the while, whether under the Ottoman or the British regime, he is at the forefront of radical agitation.

The ferment created by the Young Turk Revolution gave the new men their opportunity. Article III of the Ottoman constitution, restored in July 1908, made provision for the setting up of local communal councils to supervise the administration of communal property and the use of revenue therefrom. In September 1908 a delegation of priests and laymen, basing itself on this Article, announced to the patriarch that a communal council had been formed to control the finances of the patriarchate. The Brotherhood of the Holy Sepulchre vehemently rejected this, whereupon meetings, demonstrations and riots against the Greeks took place in Jerusalem and elsewhere and Greek monks were ousted from monasteries.[42]

The Ottoman government had to interpose itself between the contending parties. It appointed a commission to investigate the dispute and engaged in patient negotiation, inducing the parties to accept the compromise of a mixed council, composed half of laymen and half of clergymen, to supervise certain departments of patriarchal activity.[43]

The outlook of the leaders of the revolt against the patriarchate is illustrated by Sakakini's *Diary*. When the Young Turks came to power, Sakakini returned to Jerusalem from America, whither he had gone to engage in business, to earn a living less precarious than school-teaching offered. The journey was not a success, and he came back confirmed in the moral superiority of education over mere practical skills. 'Commerce,' he wrote, 'requires capital, and nobody will succeed in it unless he relies on deceit, trickery and similar practices to which I would sooner prefer death by hunger.'[44] He was

331

indeed prepared to concede that in western countries wealth might be the reward of competence and poverty the sign of incapacity, but in Palestine poverty was almost a badge of honour, a cause for pride, a token of dignity and self-respect.[45] In his eyes, then, and in the eyes of those like him, the Young Turk Revolution appeared as a great deliverance from the small, mean, constricted world in which their education and their ideals were mocked and misunderstood. 'Now,' he exclaimed when the constitution was announced, 'now I can serve my country. Now I can found a school, a newspaper, and societies for Youth. Now we can lift up our voices without impediment.'[46] These voices were soon raised against the patriarchate. 'We are rid of the tyranny of the government,' proclaimed Sakakini, 'but that of the spiritual authority still remains.'[47] He became a leader in the struggle; he organised meetings and processions, sent emissaries to other communities in Palestine, drafted petitions to the Government, and argued with the patriarchate. When the patriarch Damianos, who had shown himself somewhat conciliatory towards the native community, was deposed by the Brotherhood, Sakakini was elected as a member of a delegation which went to Istanbul in January 1909 to protest against the deposition.[48] He even imagined, rightly or wrongly, that he was being personally persecuted for his activities. When, a few years afterwards, in 1912, he wanted to marry, no priest in Jerusalem was willing to officiate, all alleging that the proposed marriage was within the prohibited degrees. Sakakini attributed this to the malice of the patriarchate and went off to Jaffa where a priest was found to perform the ceremony.[49] His attitude to the struggle was characteristic: its object was not to obtain concessions but to vindicate principles. From the very beginning he was afraid that his associates might be tempted and corrupted by concessions regarding schools, hospitals, the training of priests, and similar matters, which after all constituted the substance of the community's grievance against the hierarchy. 'I noticed,' he wrote in September 1908, 'that ... members of the committee preferred to give their attention to questions affecting schools, hospitals, the Church (and other financial matters), and I became afraid that this might distract the community from pursuing its other rights.'[50] When, a few years later, the excitement died down and the contestants settled down again to a kind of acrimonious and suspicious intercourse. Sakakini decided to announce his abandonment of the reform movement and his secession from the Church: 'My soul

revolted', he records, 'and I saw that I could not stay any longer in
the Orthodox community. I cannot stay under the authority of these
corrupt and degenerate priests; I cannot be a member of this degenerate community. I cannot . . . I am not Orthodox! I am not
Orthodox!'[51] He had decided that the case of the Church was hopeless, that it was not to be reformed, that secession was the only step
practicable. Hatred and contempt manifest themselves not only for
the Greek hierarchy, but for the rites, traditions and religious life of
the Orthodox community.

Anyone who stands at the gates of a church [reads an entry in 1918]
will not think himself standing at a place of worship. He will see children
playing gaily in the churchyard; he will see bands of young men here
and there exchanging jokes and pleasantries as though at a party or a
circus or a dance-hall. . . . The candles, the incense, the chanting, the
beauty of the vestments merely awaken feelings of joy and approbation,
nay, feelings of love and desire. This is perhaps a survival in the Orthodox
Church of traces of ancient Greek religion, of the worship of Bacchus, the
God of Wine. I wrote on this subject at the time of the Orthodox awakening, which greatly agitated the priests of the Jerusalem patriarchate, and
impelled the patriarch to publish an official notice excommunicating me
and warning the community against frequenting me and listening to my
opinions.[52]

The dislocation, as may be seen, is radical. Sakakini broke violently
loose from the beliefs of his community, repudiated its manner of
life and rejected what practical wisdom it had accumulated in its
long history as a minority under Islam. No doubt the heritage was
poor, and to have seen what western civilisation could offer was
enough to justify intellectual rebellion. But in Sakakini's case, as in
that of his friends and contemporaries, the rebellion itself was a poor
affair, fervent no doubt, but disoriented and undiscriminating. These
men of principles who claimed the leadership of their community,
clutched now at this, now at that principle, and ended by involving
themselves in a style of politics as devoid of charity as of principle.
'I am,' exclaims Sakakini, 'neither a Christian, nor a Buddhist, nor a
Muslim, nor a Jew. I am neither an Arab, nor a Frenchman, nor a
German, nor a Turk. I am a member of humanity . . . .'[53] 'You,' he
tells a missionary, 'derive your principles from Revelation, accepting
them without scrutiny, while I derive them from myself, my mind,
and my daily life and experience.'[54] These principles fluctuated
alarmingly. One day he advises his son to be a pacifist, and three days

later he exclaims, 'Power! Power! This is the new gospel which we must spread. He who is stronger in body, mind and spirit has a greater right to exist than he who is weak. . . . The strong shall inherit the earth'. And he again advises his son to adopt this 'philosophy'.[55] Traditional lore and learning is thus rejected, and an eager, incoherent grasping at the latest novelty takes its place.

This is best illustrated by Sakakini's attitude to Judaism. Estrangement and mistrust are of course the traditional attitudes of the different religious communities in the middle east towards one another. But these traditional attitudes were never complicated by the kind of doctrinaire refinements which accompany modern European anti-semitism. And much of these traditional attitudes have survived in and may be illustrated in Muslim writings about Zionism. These writings provide an ambiguous picture of admiration and contempt, of attraction and repulsion. Jews are cowardly, yet an example of courage; they are the scum of the earth, yet worthy of imitation in their social arrangements; Jewesses, with uncovered faces, arms and legs, are infinitely attractive, yet an unholy temptation to believers. Take a book on Zionism written by two Muslim journalists for a popular audience and choose almost at random one of the many luscious descriptions of Jewish girls:

Here is a girl from Hungary, her face radiant with fascination and allurement, that sex appeal, which the male sex dreams of, flowing from her body. She is in conversation with two companions, legs crossed, slightly leaning back, so that her skirt gives a glimpse of glittering lights and cool, firm flesh . . . And here is a gazelle . . . langorously lying on the rocks . . . intimating the softness and the yielding firmness of the flesh of the daughters of Eve.

And yet their admiration for the modesty, neatness and discretion of women going about the streets is also unbounded. They contrast them to the lazy, useless, heavily-made-up wives of Damascus. They present an idyllic picture of family life among the Jews:

Outside the house there was a white cot, covered with a white, clean, billowing mosquito-net. Inside was the baby daughter of our host, there in the open air, in sunlight, in the midst of nature. . . . [The wife] was a German blonde, mature and pretty. . . . The couple appeared from the first glimpse to be completely fitted for each other; he was calm and good-tempered, she was orderly and obedient. By God, if one of us had this young woman, distinguished by her good looks and her smartness, she would have been a tyrant to her elderly husband,[56] and made his life unbearable hell.[57]

The lurid charms of the Jewesses seem in fact to have become a stock-in-trade of Arab publicists writing on the state of Israel. An Egyptian journalist for instance who visited Israel regales his readers with a report about the easy and uninhibited ways of Israeli women. All of them, he says, go about in very brief shorts which 'disclose the articulation between the thigh and the trunk, and in the evenings I used to see young men and women on the two sides of the street behaving as if they were in a bedroom'. Israeli beauties sit waiting in the hall of the Dan Hotel in Tel-Aviv, and if you should pull one of them by the hand she would get up and go with you anywhere.[58] An anti-Nasser pamphlet, again, disseminated by the Muslim Brethren after the June 1967 war taunts the Egyptian president with having so mismanaged things that 'the fighting daughters of Israel can now swim naked in the Suez Canal in your sight and hearing'.[59] Or take quite a different book, a polemic against non-Muslims written by a well-known leader of the Muslim Brethren, Muhammad al-Ghazali. He attacks the view that the Bible is all divinely inspired: 'Have you heard these inspired verses from the Holy Book? I fear that you may be a young man with burning desires, and these lurid pictures might wreak havoc on your conscience. . . . How strange, these sacred verses through which glides the snake of sexual love, agitated and excited, as though dancing to the rhythm of a tainted music!', and to clinch his point – and gratify his readers – al-Ghazali proceeds to quote several verses from the *Song of Songs*. And yet he also holds up as an example to the divided and incompetent Arabs the energy and resourcefulness of the Jews. 'In spite of [this contrast] there are mouths which open – Oh! how I wish they would have been stuffed with actions – and say: We are the descendents of noble-born heroes . . . and these are the rejects of the world. . . . What is this blindness?'[60] These attitudes, ambiguous as they are, seem yet innocent of European anti-semitic doctrines. They derive from Muslim conditions, from the inaccessibility of Muslim women, and the shock administered by the victory of an inferior group hitherto held in contempt.

As for anti-semitism, there is no doubt that in its traditional theological variety so well known in Europe it was increasingly propagated in the middle east through the nineteenth century by the indigenous Christian communities who were in many cases confirmed

335

in their prejudices by European indoctrination. No doubt the increasing prosperity and assertiveness of the Greeks in the Ottoman empire, their rivalry with the Jews in economic affairs, the greater ease of travel, the greater availability of cheap books and newspapers, all contributed to an increase in tension between Jews and Christians in the nineteenth century. By 1800, a contemporary observer noted, Jews hardly dared to enter, much less live in, those towns of the Bosporus which had a heavy Greek Orthodox population, who believed that they acquired merit by inflicting whatever injury they could upon the Jews. Holy week was particularly dangerous and on Good Friday the effigy of a Jew was paraded and burnt publicly in order to atone for the original sin of the Hebrew nation.[61] The century is punctuated with reports of Christian, frequently Greek Orthodox, anti-Jewish outbreaks in Rumelia, Anatolia, Syria and Egypt, most frequently occasioned by the blood libel.[62] An Orthodox from Beirut describes for us the anti-Jewish legends current in his community:

> I was not to stray away from my guardians – not even a few yards – because the cursed Jews might steal me and murder me. I was told that the sons of Abraham feasted on the blood of Christian children. Several instances were mentioned to me when Christian children known to my kindred had been captured in the Jewish quarter in Beyrout and bled to death by those enemies of Christ. My flesh crept and crawled when the process of 'bleeding' was described to me.

The traditional beliefs acquired a new lease of life with the increase in literacy, and the propagation of European books which seemed to confer on these beliefs all the authority and prestige of Europe. Thus we find the erudite Cheikho commending in the learned journal which he edited a French work rehearsing the familiar blood libel of 1840 in Damascus (in which the French consul took so sinister and murderous a part). The book, writes the Reverend Cheikho, sets out 'the horrible crime of the Jews in seeking time and again to bleed once a year a Christian in order to mix his blood with their Passover cakes. The true reports concerning this are countless'.[64]

By this century, then, the traditional anti-Jewish themes of Christian theology became widespread and popular in a way in which they had never been in the middle east ever since Byzantium and St John Chrysostom's incendiary sermons in Antioch. But they now also became jazzed up by the introduction of a modern European theme, that of 'scientific' anti-semitism. Anti-judaism and anti-semitism now fed on each other and provided arguments for anti-

Zionism. Marun Abbud explaining how natural anti-Zionism is to him, says: 'Do not forget that our hatred for "God's chosen People" flows in our veins. We curse them in our churches and always we abuse them in our prayers and masses'.[65] Another Lebanese writer, the Orthodox George Hanna, exemplifies the transition from anti-Judaism to anti-semitism when he tells us in his *Autobiography* that the 'terroristic' (*al-irhabiyya*) teachings of the Old Testament used to capture his imagination as a school-boy before it began to be subjected to the 'tolerant' teachings of the New: and he adds that it is part of the Zionist conspiracy to spread knowledge of the Bible in order to gain the sympathies of non-Jews. However virulent, ecclesiastical anti-Judaism would never have described any part of the Bible as terroristic in its teachings;[66] and it is clear that George Hanna is superimposing on the anti-Judaism which he no doubt imbibed in his boyhood a later and quite different doctrine.

There is little doubt that this modern doctrine of anti-semitism was propagated in the middle east, before the Palestine war of 1948, from European and western sources, frequently through the intermediary of native Christians who themselves in many cases were already predisposed to its acceptance by the anti-Judaism with which they were already acquainted.[67] An interesting and apposite example lies to hand. The American millionaire Charles Crane who was George Antonius' patron was a votary of the fashionable anti-semitism according to which the Jews were ruining the world with their atheistic communism, and therefore an admirer of Hitler and Nazism. We see him diligently endeavouring to propagate this belief among Muslims, employing Antonius to arrange meetings with such Muslim notabilities as Hajj Amin al-Husaini, Rashid Rida, Ahmad Shafiq Pasha, Mustafa and Ali Abd al-Raziq, and Mustafa al-Maraghi, where he endeavoured to awaken them to the dangerous Jewish campaign against religion and private property, and to convince them that the arrival of Jews in Palestine was only another move in the anti-God campaign which they had started in Russia and elsewhere and by which they hoped to accomplish their programme of annihilation.[68]

In Sakakini's case too the traditional anti-Judaism based on religious grounds is certainly present: 'It seems to me that you Jews,' he says to a Zionist, 'are most in need of divine scriptures, but I fear that the prophet among you today will suffer the fate of his predecessors whom you killed and burned. . . . The prophets and Holy

Scripture have come from you, but they are not for you.'[69] But this anti-Judaism is yet laced with more novel doctrines borrowed from Europe, as usual in an incoherent and contradictory fashion. Thus, Sakakini considers that Judaism makes its followers soft and un-manly: 'The Jews in their festivals lament and weep. . . . Muslim festivals, on the contrary, are rousing events. . . . If the nation is to have festivals, let them be like the Muslim ones . . . let us have nothing but rousing songs and let us dance with swords.'[70]

And yet, far from encouraging 'spirituality', the God of the Jews is a nature deity: 'If you compare Judaism and Christianity you will find that the God of the Old Testament is the God of Nature, while the God of the New is the God of Reason. The God of the Old Testa-ment says: Multiply and fill the earth and may your progeny be like the stars of heaven or the sands of the sea. In other words, the God of the Old Testament is the God of procreation.'[71] This doctrinaire anti-semitism, difficult to reconcile with traditional Islam, as has been said, seems to have been introduced to the middle east mainly by eastern Christians who had easier access to western literature but not enough judgment to exercise critical and discriminating choice. The point may be illustrated by a lecture in the Department of Public Administration of the University of Beirut by a director-general of the Lebanese Ministry for Foreign Affairs, Fu'ad Ammun, a Maronite. Warning America against the Jewish Peril, the speaker quoted an alleged speech of Benjamin Franklin's at the Constitutional Conven-tion of 1787, warning the convention against the admission of Jews to America. If they did not take the necessary measures, Franklin is said to have warned his colleagues, they would be cursed by their children and grand-children. But this speech is not by Franklin. It is a forgery widely circulated by Nazi propaganda in the United States during the 1930s.[72]

The disorientation was not only intellectual but also practical. Political action, which to their ancestors was an unprofitable and evil necessity, began to seem to the new men an exciting game in which no stakes were adventured or hostages risked, but the rewards of which were ample and sure. After the Young Turk Revolution, Sakakini was asked by the local committee of Union and Progress to join this secret society. He agreed, and with melodramatic ceremony involving masked men, revolvers, etc. was made a member. He swore on oath to defend the Fatherland and the constitution with his life, if need be. He remarked to his sponsor that he had really taken this oath at birth, and on this night was merely renewing it.[73] A few weeks later he was asked to join another secret society, that of Arab Brotherhood, which was directed against the committee of Union and Progress, and again Sakakini enthusiastically agreed to join.[74] He had, it is true, occasional qualms about the new model politics which his public actions and utterances recommended to his co-religionists and pupils. He was taken aback by the announcement of jihad when the Ottoman empire entered the war, and feared that an old spirit of fanaticism would be resuscitated.[75] He confided to his diary that the Muslims were incapable of civic spirit, that they were riven by family factions and would promote only family interests.[76] He refused the post of director of Arabic Broadcasting in 1935 because, as he told George Antonius, a Muslim would be preferable in this post.[77] This on the part of an Arab nationalist – votary of a doctrine which, if it meant anything at all, meant that among Arabs religious differences were utterly of no account – is paradoxical, and in one who is himself not a Muslim, somewhat pitiful. Antonius, we are interested to see, shared the belief that Islam and the Muslims ought to have the primacy in Arab nationalism; in a letter of 1935 about Kawakibi to Muhammad Rashid Rida he makes a curious – and revealing – statement. Kawakibi, he told his eminent Muslim correspondent, was working towards the two fundamental and related aims, 'I mean the revival of Arab nationality through the revival of Islam – without which revival the Arabs can have no life.'[78] This attitude finds its paradigm in another Arabic-speaking Orthodox, Khalil Iskandar Qubrusi, who published before the second world war a series of articles in a Muslim religious periodical in which he called upon his co-religionists to embrace Islam because it was the true Arab religion and if they adopted it then all the Arabs would be Muslim and only the foreigners Christian.[79] There is a letter from Sakakini to his son which gives us a glimpse of the inner insecurity and bitterness which these expressions of solidarity with, these glorifications of, Islam, all too often masked. The letter was sent in 1932, and the son who was then studying in the United States thought so highly of it that he translated it and distributed it among his friends, providing it with a preface in which, among other things, he explained that his father never went to church because he feared to come out of there rebellious and because he feared to disturb the calm of his soul and the stability of his mind. Sakakini writes about a lecture he had given which seems not to have been properly appreciated; he burst out: 'No matter how high my standing may be in science and literature, no matter how sincere my patriotism is, no matter how much I do to revive this nation, even if I burn my fingers before its sight, as long as I am not a Moslem I am nought. If you desire to amount to anything, then be a Moslem and that will be peace.' He tells his son that if the Muslims respect him, it is only because they think him more sympathetic to Islam than to Christianity and Europe and because he has an erudite knowledge of Arabic and its literature; but 'if I were to struggle with a Moslem who is less founded in knowledge and heritage than I, I would not doubt that they would prefer him to survive'. He confesses that 'whenever I think of you and your sister's future, I am alarmed for you' and concludes by wishing that his son's generation will be better than his own and 'that you will not return to this country until it has changed land for land and people for people, and when a man will be estimated by what he achieves and not according to how he preserves these outworn customs'.[80]

But these forlorn and despairing accents are not heard in his public doctrine, which is clear and categorical. Religion is reactionary and divisive. A Muslim–Christian union and the advocacy of pan-Arabism ought to be the only policies of the Orthodox. A delegation of Orthodox from Jaffa came to Jerusalem in March 1914, to propose the formation of a party for the defence of Christian interests. He opposed this and told them: 'If your aim is political, then I do not approve it, because I am an Arab first of all, and I think it preferable that we should form a national party, to unite all the sons of the fatherland regardless of religion and sects, to awaken the national feeling and infuse a new spirit . . .'.[81] 'As for temples', he wrote at the same time, 'they will be transformed in time into societies or national schools, and instead of preaching on religious matters, there will be preaching on national matters'.[82] He gave refuge to a man wanted by the Ottoman police and wrote that he was only emulating his Bedouin ancestors for whom hospitality was a law: the man had not taken refuge with Khalil Sakakini, but with the Arab nation itself represented by one of its members.[83]

After the war as a correspondent of the Egyptian newspaper *al-Siyyasa*, he wrote a series of articles on Palestine and Zionism which he later collected and published in a booklet. These articles also exhibit the extravagant and bombastic lengths to which he went in identifying himself with Muslim and Arab history. Apostrophising the Jews, he says: 'We conquered the world, founded illustrious

kingdoms, actively built the foundations of learning, carrying high in
our turn the banner of civilisation. How can your history be compared to ours?' The Arab nation was and still is warlike, 'if it finds
nobody to fight, it will create an enemy in order to fight him'; on
'our' festivals 'we dance with swords as though marching to war or
victoriously returning from it. As for you, your festivals – this is not
said to taunt you – are festivals of mourning and lamentations from
which you emerge with dulled senses and drooping spirits. How can
the nation which knows naught but weeping stand fast in the swamps
of death?'[84]

In 1919 he became a leading advocate of pan-Arabism, agitation
for which was then being directed by the Sharifians in Damascus.[85]
In 1920 he resigned from the Education Department because the
high commissioner, Sir Herbert Samuel, was a Jew.[86] In 1935 he
built a house in Jerusalem, and gave each room the name of an Arab
capital: 'This is San'a, this is Damascus, this is Cordova, this is
Baghdad, this is Cairo'.[87]

In the end, of course, all this fervour, which made the Orthodox an
appendix to the pan-Arab campaign against Zionism, availed little.
With it, as without it, the Orthodox could have had little say in the
direction of events, which, for a sizeable portion of their community,
ended in disaster. It may be argued that had they remained aloof
from the Zionist–Arab quarrel and from the incompetent Muslim
leaders they might not have become quite so involved in the catastrophe; but this is mere speculation. Something else may be said with
more certainty. Sakakini was a teacher, an educationist. His doctrine
as well as his practice introduced political fanaticism into the class-
room. Literature for him was a means for rousing national fervour
among the young.[88] Practice reinforced theory, for while a lecturer
in the Teachers' Training College he had led his students in a political
demonstration against the government.[89] At the summit of his
official career, as an inspector of education, a few years before his
retirement, he gave a lecture to the school-teachers of Nazareth
entitled: What is national teaching and what is wholesome teaching.
He referred to a poem by Shawqi in which the sentence, Nothing
equals the Fatherland, occurs. This sentence, the teachers said in
answer to his enquiry, ought to be the title of the whole poem. And
he told them: 'The teacher ought to tell his pupils: Repeat this title
five times, and then he ought to tell them: Come let us shout with all
our might: Long live the Fatherland!'[90] Of Sakakini this, therefore,

can be said with certainty, that like other pedagogues of his time and place he was a recruiting sergeant for the ignorant armies whose endless brawls now have the middle east for a stage.[91] So poor, so arid, so common a vocation hardly arouses interest. But things are not what they seem. The frenzy, the assurance, the dogmatism did not spring fully armed from the brow of some fateful deity, nor were they the outcome of mere intellectual conviction. Obscure conflicts and dim torments fashioned them; and it is these, rather than what they fashioned, which deserve our attention and justify our curiosity.

Appendix

A Call to the Arab Christians to join Islam*
by Khalil Iskandar Qubrusi

> Summon them to the way of thy Lord
> with wisdom and with kindly warning;
> dispute with them in the kindest manner.
>
> *Qur'an*

> The Arabs were the first to teach the
> world how to reconcile freedom of thought
> with true religion.
>
> GUSTAVE LEBON

My call is not to a recent innovation nor to a contemptible heresy but to a true Arab religion which God revealed to his messenger Muhammad, may God's prayer be upon him. He was faithful to his message and spread it conscientiously among nomadic tribes who were busy worshipping stones and statues, and who found pleasure in the trivialities of the *jahiliyya*. He united them when they had been disunited, he established unanimity among them where there had been only dissension, and he directed them to the worship of the Creator. He was undoubtedly the best of the creation by virtue alike of his descent, parentage, leadership and prophetic office.

Such is the Prophet whose religion has been embraced by four hundred million Muslims scattered all over the inhabited world who recite a clear Arabic Qur'an. He is the glory of the Arabs and the founder of their power, of their renown, of their conquests and of their civilisation. He it is whose apostolic successors reached out to the extreme limits of Europe and lightened its darkness with their justice, their righteousness, their piety and who, with the light of their Qur'an, dispelled the depths of its ignorance.

A prophet such as this one is indeed worthy to be followed. It is incumbent on us to embrace his message and adopt his call; for it is an honourable call based on the acknowledgment of the Creator, the encouragement of good actions and the prohibition of evil. Everything in it, indeed, aims at righteousness and righteousness is the goal of the believer. This is the religion to which I call all Arab Christians without exception

---

* *Da'wa nasara al-arab ila'l-dukhul fi'l-Islam*, Cairo, n.d.

343

in order to free them from the trivialities of the foreigners and to rid them of their corruption. If religion can only come to us at the hand of the foreigner, and is efficacious only by means of a foreign sounding prayer, then let such a religion not live or be; for it hurls us to the depths of corruption and anarchy. Our religion now is more like a childish toy with which we are distracted from the true worship of the Creator and led to the worship of various nationalities. It is a vehicle for mean and base designs; it is a means of destruction, a tool of death and ruin. Tell me O Arab Christians: Is there a priest who praises to you your own nationality and encourages you to its service? Is there a religious leader who wishes you to establish amity with your Arab Muslim brother? Has the Lord Jesus – peace be upon Him – decreed such a thing?

The teaching of the Gospel does not tally with their teachings. They say: Hate, avoid, beware, detest, abhor, while the Gospel says: Love your enemies and bless those who curse you; how then much more deserving of love are your brothers in nationality especially seeing that the Arabs – Muslim be they or Christian – have ever lived brothers in spite of those who have tried to divide them. There now come creatures in the shape of man to sow dissension among us. The religious head who says 'The Arabic language is a language of dogs' humiliates me by despising my language and my nationality, and he is himself worthy of scorn and rejection. The religious head who inculcates hate in the heart of his pupils, hate by asking 'Should we help the Muslims?' and by replying 'Hell for the Muslims is preferable to paradise for you' is worthy of scorn. Are these the teachings of Christ? Did the Lord Jesus ordain that school children should support foreign flags at official ceremonies?

There are now in Jerusalem many societies – or if you prefer, brotherhoods – each under the patronage of a foreign mission and every one of them a tool in their hands for the purpose of a vast nationalist propaganda. Strange to say, each one of those societies is loath to mention the name of any of the others and seeks to destroy them. Does 'brotherhood' mean anarchy, then? How I have tried to save these societies from those ruinous depths and how I have tried to secure their independence and freedom from the yoke of their tyrannical masters, but I have failed because, according to religion as they know it, they must have a guide, and the guide must be a foreigner; in this way, independence is ever out of the question. They have misled our children, trampled on our feelings and destroyed us utterly. Is it still worthy of us to follow them? Does a man follow the guidance of his executioner?

What harm would it do the Arab Christians if they should guide themselves by the light of Islam, which is a true Arab religion recognised even by European thinkers? If I call to it it is because I bring tidings of a blessed union which is the foundation of strength, assuming, that is, that we intend to free ourselves completely from the yoke of the British –

from British, Zionist and foreign imperialism, so that there should be only Muslim Arabs and Christian foreigners.

The Qualities of Islam

Those who listen to the word, then follow the best of it; those are they whom Allah has guided, and those it is who are men of understanding.

Qur'an

I promised the reader to discuss the qualities of Islam, and when I took up my pen to fulfil my promise, I found myself in a difficulty from which it is hard to extricate oneself. I found that the qualities of Islam were not of those things which can be counted, or from which a choice could be made. These qualities are rather like the sea without a shore to be reached by the sailor, and a depth which no diver could plumb. I therefore decided not to embark on such an ocean but rather to leave it to its owners, those whose righteousness in the eyes of God is of more ancient date, and who have excelled in extracting its pearls and benefited thereby themselves and others. But if I thought of giving up the enterprise, I remembered the word of God 'Fulfil the promise of God if you do give a promise'; I therefore found it imperative to return to the subject, not in the hope of doing it justice, for I am convinced of my inability to do this, but in order to keep faith and to obey an honoured and august command. I then say:

It is enough for you, O fair-minded Arab Christian to understand what you may of the secrets of the verse with which I have prefaced this chapter. In spite of the intelligence with which man has been endowed, his mind still remains dark and its light dim, and it is this verse alone which proclaims the freedom of Islam and the freedom of its votaries; it gives them full freedom to meditate on the Creation in all its aspects and allows them to listen to all advocates irrespective of the diversity of their aims and their species, for it is assumed that sensible people will listen to what is said and follow the best of it; and if there had been anything better than the Qur'an, the honoured speech of God, he would not have urged people to listen to something else, for then they would have given it up for its opposite. This is the case with clerical bodies who prohibit the reading of religious books other than theirs and forbid their flock to listen to them for fear of comparisons. Such a comparison would show that there is a speech better than theirs and it would be followed. Such a prohibition then results in the suppression of the freedom of thought and compulsion in religion and belief, preventing the believer from reflecting about his creed in order to discriminate between right and wrong.

Islam then is the religion of freedom and the Christian religion in its

345

Frankish dress has become the religion of slavery. How foolish is the man to whom God has granted freedom who sells it for nothing and consents to live humiliated and oppressed in all his activities and even in his thinking, whilst his Creator calls out to him from the heavens 'I myself am the Lord and there is no God beside me, Worship me', that is, Do not worship another beside Me and do not bow down to any man by allowing him to dispose of your mind, of your spiritual gifts which I have given you. From this Omar has drawn his memorable saying 'Since when have you enslaved men and their mothers have brought them forth free into this world?'

(There follows a passage concerning the proverbial justice and equity of the caliph Umar, his humility and love of equality. The author then continues:)

You may be surprised O Christian when I tell you that the leading place in a mosque is reserved to the first comer no matter how low his station; the prince has no precedence over the beggar should he arrive after him. What may surprise you in this respect is that this arrangement *wherein oppression is forbidden has no equivalent in the churches where the masses are not allowed to sit in the seats of the classes.* This is because the clergy have blasphemously transgressed the saying of God: 'The most worthy among you in the sight of God is the most pious'.

Thanks to this equality pride took its root in the souls of the Muslims; it was nourished by the proclamation of God's name in the daily and in the Friday prayers and by constant obedience to God. This is all contained in this great saying 'God is most Great', meaning that whoever is inferior to him is of no account and no heed is paid to him however high and exalted he be. 'Glory be to God, to his Messenger and to the believers'.

That they all pray towards Mecca results in their union, that they give alms engenders pity for the weak among them, their fasting is exercise for their body and purification for their souls, their pilgrimage is a reminder of their life hereafter, for it is a symbol of the Last Judgment, and the land of their pilgrimage is the country best suited for their congresses which fully represent their different nations and classes 'in order that they may witness what is profitable to them and that they may mention the name of God on fixed days'.

In Islam then is to be found that which is best both for this world and for the next, and to embrace it is to find eternal everlasting happiness. (Then follow exhortatory verses from the Qur'an.)

A Word from a Christian Arab to his Brethren The Christian Arabs

'Summon thou to the way of the Lord with wisdom and with kindly warning; dispute with them in the kindest manner; thy Lord best knoweth those who stray from His way, and He best knoweth those who have yielded to his guidance'.

Qur'an

'If the Christian religion is nothing more than Catholicism in need of reform (the Roman creed) or Catholicism which is reformed (the Protestant creed), then the century which is leading up to the twentieth (the present century) cannot be Christian at all'.

A Protestant scholar

The meaning of this is that the religion which needs reform is an incomplete religion, and that which is incomplete cannot be divine. Therefore Catholicism is not a divine religion since a reformed religion is far removed from inviolable perfection because this reform is human and man is not infallible. Therefore the man of the twentieth century has to be guided by another religion, and perhaps the Protestant scholar has Islam in mind. When he was writing this he was ignorant of the disasters which have befallen us Arab Christians, and without being aware of our suffering and tribulations, but nonetheless his meaning applies to what I intend in this article. After the *jahiliyya* the Arabs practised two great religions, Christianity and Islam. The birthplace of these two religions was the east – the east alone, at a time when the west was wandering in the errors of pagan ignorance. Christ appeared like a brilliant meteor in the Palestinian sky and pierced with the light of his goodness the dark and with the light of his teaching dispersed the murk of error. The apostles came after him; they too were orientals and they completed what he had planned for them. They spread over all the inhabited globe preaching and proselytising and those of the Arabs who heard their teachings followed them, just as the west was guided by the light of the teaching of their first teacher – the west which was and still is the source of our misery and the origin of our distress and our trial. Some of their men pretended that they were the messengers of Christ, the messenger of love and peace. And they committed in the name of this love and this peace shameful and corrupt actions which have stained the brow of humanity – not of Christianity alone – with a stain of shame which cannot be erased. They inflicted tremendous and savage oppressions which even savages now extinct would not commit: they killed the innocent, they tortured the pious, they desecrated the sanctuaries as is

347

happening now in North Africa for the sake of national and religious fanaticisms. They committed all this in the name of religion but, in truth, religion is innocent of their slanders. Thus religion became a plaything with which to distract the masses and to guide them according to their own whims. I do not think that there is a Christian who has not yet heard of the Inquisition (The Council of Ten) in the Middle Ages. This evil then burst open and its volcano erupted its lava upon us. The devils of hell – or, as they call themselves, the heads of religion – came to us to this east – the lustre of their light and the sunrise of their learning. They started to teach – in the name of the religion which we originated – tenets that used to be true but which they have disfigured, and truths with which we lift the darkness of their skies but which they have enveloped in the darkness of their errors. They swooped on us as vultures on their prey; they hurried to us as the thirsty hurry to the source; they stretched their hands towards our national unity and tore it asunder, and to the source of our tranquillity which they muddied. They administered to us the poison of anarchy as though we were a booty given over to them or cattle without owners. Instead of carrying on with their religious duties, they carried out a racial propaganda. They made the land of the Arabs a base for their propaganda and used it as a seat to exercise their seduction. There are Catholics who call for loyalty to the French, Protestants singing the praises of the British, and Italians doing their national duty towards Italy. In short, they appear as the mild lamb but they are in reality nothing but dogs barking at each other and devils deceiving one another. They have become devouring lions, and famished dogs. They have swooped down calling in their assistants, fought battles and created factions. And they were more ready in support of their obvious false claims than we were in support of our obvious right; and in their manifest error more clear-sighted than us with our straight guidance. They forgot that the good leader exposes himself to dangers and perils in order to benefit his people. What is worse, they give the lie to God and to us by saying that the Christians of this country are not Arabs but the remnant of the Crusaders; this only to weaken us and to kill our nationhood and to transform us into a nameless nonentity. . . . Because they despise our glorious Arabic language, the language of the exalted Qur'an, they scorned to use it as the language of their ritual, compelling us to pray in their languages. Is it not right after all this for us to hate them; to detest and to despise them and to seek for a religion to deliver us from the yoke of this slavery?

Since the religion of God has always been one among the ancients and the moderns, and has differed in nothing but in its outward form, while its essence and truth are always one, namely what the whole world is commanded to do throughout the intermediary of the prophets and the messengers, and since the highest aim in religion is belief in God alone

348

and his steadfast worship, as well as mutual aid and forebearance, and since the good is worthy to be loved wherever it is found, what harm would it do the Christian Arabs if they united in religion as they are united in race [with the Muslims], and we may then get away from this misleading faction in fulfilment of His saying, glory be to Him: 'I have not taken as a support those who lead into error'.

Of Priests and Monks

O you who believe; most surely many of the doctors of law and the monks eat away the property of men falsely, and turn them from Allah's way; and as for those who hoard up gold and silver and do not spend it in Allah's way, announce to them a painful chastisment. On the day when it shall be heated in the fire of hell, then their foreheads and their sides and their backs shall be branded with it. This is what you hoarded up for your selves therefore taste what you hoarded.

Qur'an

(This chapter begins with a vehement repetition of the concluding paragraph of the previous chapter.)

Religious men have come from Europe, dressed in black not as a sign of piety and humility but as a symbol of the blackness of their heart and the darkness of their souls. In the name of Christianity they spread a racialist propaganda in order to sow dissension between the Muslims and the Christians of Palestine, the better to enslave them. Their latest intrigue as the newspaper *Filastin* has recounted is to attempt to filch King David's tomb from 'our brethren the Muslims' in order to increase the hatred of the Muslims for the native Christians. . . .

If we consider how they have trampled our rights and desecrated our sanctities, we would find no explanation for this except that they are westerners and sons of god, and that we are easterners and therefore sons of men. Here are some instances of their iniquities:

1. Holiness is a preserve of the westerners alone! Not a single Arab has been proclaimed a saint. Does this mean that we are all evil men, while some of them are saintly men?

2. Their monopoly of high religious office from cardinal to bishop. The sons of gods, no matter what their nationality, occupy these offices but not the Arabs.

3. The sway exercised by foreign religious missions and missionary institutions over our own people and their trampling over the right of the Arab clergy and the denial to these of administrative independence which obtains in other countries.

349

4. The fact that no Arab sits in the religious courts and the communal council while many foreigners are members.

5. Their begging for alms in the name of the Arab Christians in order to lower their dignity, not for love of benevolence. They rejoice in this falsehood in order to have an excuse for begging, to expose the infirmities of the Arabs and their shame, and to swell up with pride.

(The author then goes on to say that words cannot exhaust the misdeeds of this foreign priesthood. They have become so unbearable that the people of Nazareth have preferred to secede from them and to set up a separate community with an Arab religious head. Others have gone so far as to renounce any contact with them preferring to lead an honourable life rather than to burn in the fire of their hell. The author reminds his readers that he is not a stranger to them but has endured the oppression of their priesthood and experienced their arrogance. He has therefore come to the conclusion which he presses on his compatriots:)

I have therefore called you to Islam, your Arabian religion, which God has sent down in your noble language. Be not therefore like a child whose sleep deepens as you try to wake him up, or like those who have become careless through procrastination. I am not calling you to give in to a passing whim or to a novel opinion but to the exemplary path in which is to be found the best both of eternity and of this world. Let souls be one, let all the hands cooperate and let all dispositions be cordial and all purposes be in harmony and concord, and peace be with you.

(There follows a chapter entitled *The foreign clergy yesterday and today* where the author recurs at some length to the cruelties perpetrated by the Christian Church and to its hatred for Islam. He reminds his reader of the callous way in which the Muslims were at last expelled from Spain; of the Inquisition which from 1481 to 1499 burnt at the stake 10,220 people, hanged 67,860 and condemned 97,023 more to other punishments. He gives instances of recent sayings attributed to Roman Catholic ecclesiastical dignitaries and missionaries in which they state that their aim is to undermine and destroy Islam. He contrasts these proceedings with the humility and forebearance of the legendary and proverbial Umar, the second caliph. It may be said in passing that in Arab nationalist literature Umar stands second only to Muhammad as an exemplar of the virtues of Arabism; his role as a culture hero may be worth investigating. This is followed by a last chapter on *Missionaries and Missions*, in which he exhorts the missionaries to go and labour among the idolaters for the Palestinians have no need for them. 'You are a danger to yourselves', he tells them, 'and to us'. As a Christian he expresses his indignation at their activities and calls on the newspapers to investigate the problem again and to draw the attention of the government to the evil consequences of these activities.)

12

The Chatham House Version

I

Between 1918 and 1945 the British empire was the dominant power in the middle east. It was precisely during this period that a particular version of the recent history of the middle east was put forward in Britain which gained – and perhaps to this day retains – great credence both among the public and in official circles. This version may be called the Chatham House Version. Publications of Chatham House – the Royal Institute of International Affairs – used regularly to carry a statement to the effect that 'the Institute, as such, is precluded by the terms of its Royal Charter from expressing an opinion on any aspect of international affairs. Any opinions expressed in this publication', the statement concluded, 'are not therefore those of the Institute'. The disclaimer is neither to be dismissed, nor even to be taken lightly; but the books and other publications dealing with the middle east which, for some three decades, came out under the auspices of the Institute, are seen on examination to have in common not only a publisher's imprint, but also assumptions, attitudes, and a whole intellectual style which make it possible to speak of the Chatham House Version.

That this version of recent middle eastern history was widely influential and authoritative cannot be doubted. Chatham House was during this period perhaps the only centre in the English-speaking world to devote attention, steadily and systematically, to the affairs of the middle east. Again, unlike the usual kind of learned body, it was a place where journalists, men of affairs, officials and politicians rubbed shoulders and exchanged views with academics. This was the intention from the start. The statement just quoted also told us that the Institute was 'an unofficial and non-political body, founded in 1920 to encourage and facilitate the scientific study of international questions'. This brief statement is also no doubt accurate, but its very brevity tends perhaps to obscure an ambiguity or complexity of intention on the part of its founders. For, as we discover, the 'scientific study of international questions' was not an activity to be pursued for its own sake. The founders of the Institute rather entertained the view that such study would serve to enlighten public opinion, and by enlightening it to prevent catastrophes similar to that of August 1914. 'The passions which embroil nations against each other and wreck civilisation' declared the Provisional Committee of the Institute in its report to the inaugural meeting which took place on 15 July 1920, 'all have their roots in the ignorance born of isolation'. The League of Nations enabled and encouraged the peoples of the world to subordinate their narrow and parochial interests to those of humanity, and the committee regarded the Institute as 'the natural correlative' of the League, in the belief 'that that project will succeed by virtue of such measures to promote international thought and feeling as are here recommended'. This high-minded aspiration rested on the equally high-minded assumption that the pursuit of selfish interests and the conflict which this occasioned, was merely the result of misinformation and ignorance. This comes out clearly in the statement of the Provisional Committee to the effect that the 'inadequate' postwar settlements were the consequence of the 'discordant opinions' which had been propagated in the past.[1] It was therefore not only by reason of its work and publications that the Institute became influential. Rather, we may say that proceeding on this hopeful theory about the relation between knowledge and action, the founders and directors of the Institute actively sought to create for it a position of influence in public affairs.

With the outbreak of war in September 1939, it became abundantly clear that sweetness and light in international affairs were not the outcome of surveys, study groups and information papers. As a contribution to the war effort Chatham House established the Foreign Research and Press Service which was housed at Balliol College, Oxford, and which consisted of 'a group of leading authorities in this country on the whole range of world affairs, under the direction of Professor Arnold Toynbee'.[2] In April 1943 the Foreign Research and Press Service was taken over by the Foreign Office. 'The work in the new Department', the Annual Report for 1942–3 tells us, 'continues under the direction of Dr A. Toynbee, the Director of Studies of Chatham House, and the staff consists of certain members of the regular staff of the Institute who have been seconded to the Foreign Service . . . with reinforcements from the former Political Intelligence

Department of the Foreign Office, which has been amalgamated with the Foreign Research and Press Service in the new Research Department.'[3] Of this Research Department of the Foreign Office, Dr Toynbee remained the director until 1946. Thus, in a manner perhaps not envisaged by its founders, Chatham House continued to maintain a strong connection with practical affairs, and this ensured for the views of its writers and research staff a privileged access to the official world.

In middle eastern affairs, particularly, this official connection was perhaps even closer and more intimate by reason of the formation of the Cairo Group. The report for 1942–3 states that members of Chatham House and others then in Cairo had suggested the formation of a discussion group, which was approved by the Council of Chatham House. The group, the chairman of which was H. S. Deighton, 'has', the report goes on to say, 'good relations with the British embassy, the military authorities and the minister of state's office, as well as with the British Council and the Middle East Bureau'.[4] We learn from the report for 1944–5 that the Council of Chatham House, anxious to place the Cairo Group on a more permanent basis, had discussed its future with Brigadier I. N. Clayton, adviser on Arab affairs to the minister of state in Cairo, who was on a visit to London in the spring of 1945;[5] and the report for 1945–6 tells us that Brigadier Clayton was now the chairman of the group.[6]

The belief then, that there is a tight connection between the study of policy and the making of it, the assumption of the unity of theory and practice, has deeply marked the character and the activities of Chatham House. This is no doubt what its founders aimed at and desired. It is also the outcome of the long connection with the Institute of Arnold J. Toynbee. He was appointed Director of Studies at Chatham House in 1925, and retired from this post only in 1955. During thirty years he was the dominant intellectual influence at Chatham House, and the Chatham House Version is very much his handiwork.

II

During the thirty years of his tenure at Chatham House Toynbee wrote or edited the numerous annual volumes of the *Survey of International Affairs* which chronicled world politics from the morrow

353

of the first world war to the morrow of the second; during this period he also began and finished the ten volumes of *A Study of History*; and, as has been seen, from 1939 to 1946 he presided over the Foreign Research and Press Service and the Research Department of the Foreign Office. All through these three decades therefore Toynbee's practical and historiographical preoccupations are seen to be intimately intertwined. But, for him, this was more than mere accident, the outcome of his particular circumstances, of his prodigious industry, his devouring curiosity, and his wide-ranging imagination. Rather he believed that what happened a thousand years ago has its analogy with and its bearing on what happened only yesterday, and on what should be done here and now. There is a remarkable passage in what is perhaps the most interesting and eloquent section of *A Study of History*, the section entitled 'The Quest for a Meaning behind the Facts of History', in which Toynbee tells us of a mystic vision which he had and in which all difference between past, present and future was at that instant utterly annihilated. He says: 'In London in the southern section of the Buckingham Palace Road, walking southward along the pavement skirting the west wall of Victoria Station, the writer, once, one afternoon not long after the end of the first world war – he had failed to record the exact date – had found himself in communion, not just with this or that episode in History, but with all that had been, and was, and was to come. In that instant he was directly aware of the passage of History gently flowing through him in a mighty current, and of his own life welling like a wave in the flow of this vast tide.'[7]

All that had been, and was, and was to come: this clearly is the scope of Toynbee's enterprise. Readers of *A Study of History* know that it is a history not only of the past, but also of the future. Part 12 discusses, *inter alia*, 'Possible Constituent Elements of a Future World Order', 'Probable Functions of a Future World Order', and 'Probable Employments in a Future Oecumenical Society'. In this vast panorama, current affairs take their allotted place and, as Toynbee has himself insisted, the *Survey of International Affairs* and *A Study of History* have exercised a mutual influence upon each other. 'A survey of current affairs on a world-wide scale', he has written, 'can be made only against a background of world-history, and a study of world-history would have no life in it if it left out the history of the writer's own lifetime, for one's contemporaries are the only people whom one can ever catch alive. An historian in our generation must study Gandhi and Lenin and Atatürk and F. D. Roosevelt if he is to have any hope of bringing Hammurabi and Ikhnaton and Amos and the Buddha back to life for himself and for his readers.'[8]

But it is not only that the historian of Ikhnaton has to concern himself with 'Gandhi and Lenin and Atatürk and F. D. Roosevelt', thus giving a peculiar twist to Croce's dictum that all history is contemporary history. It is also that for such a historian, history is morality teaching by example and by analogy, is the illustration of certain eternal and inflexible rules of conduct, to break which must lead to unhappiness and catastrophe. The historian, therefore, by virtue of his calling, must be deeply immersed in the problems and dilemmas of the practical life. Toynbee quotes with approval Polybius' statement that either men of action should write history, or historians 'should take the view that history cannot be written effectively unless the writer has acquired an outlook that can be given only by actual experience of practical life'.[9] He also believes that the accumulation of historical knowledge will promote a better world: 'In order to save mankind', he declares, 'we have to learn to live together in concord in spite of traditional differences of religion, civilisation, nationality, class, and race. In order to live together in concord successfully, we have to know each other, and knowing each other includes knowing each other's past.'[10] It is in this way that Toynbee's work has chimed in so well with the preoccupations of the founders of Chatham House, and perhaps satisfied their eagerness to influence – of course for the better – the practice of international politics.

What then is the historian Toynbee's political doctrine? To elucidate this, we must remember that he is primarily concerned not with the study of politics, but with the study of civilisation. Civilisations are not states or political structures; rather they are a cluster of art, architecture, language, technique and, above all, religion.[11] Toynbee is concerned to enquire how they came to be, what holds them together, when and how they disappear. He wishes to find out why people cease to greet one another in Akkadian or Latin, how one style of architecture begins to replace another, and the way in which one religion ceases to provide solace to a particular society and another begins to attract its allegiance. He is above all oppressed by the transitoriness and mortality of all human artifacts. It may even be that his earliest and most powerful impulse to historical enquiry was such a vision of decay and death. This vision which he had in 1912 when he was a very young man must have touched him deeply, for

355

he recurs to it three times in *A Study of History*. He also mentions it in an early substantial work, *The Western Question in Greece and Turkey*, which came out in 1922. We may quote his account of this early intimation of mortality as it appears in volume 4 of *A Study of History*, published in 1939:

> The truth that Venice is 'dead and done with' and the moral that others, besides 'Venice and its people', may be 'merely born to bloom and drop' [he writes], have also been impressed upon the present writer's imagination by another visual image which remains as sharply printed on his mind today as at the instant when he received it more than twenty-five years ago. Turning the corner of a mountain in a lonely district at the eastern end of Crete, he once suddenly stumbled upon the ruins of a baroque villa which must have been built for the pleasure of a Venetian grandee in the last days of Venetian rule in the island before the 'Osmanlis came to reign there in the Venetians' stead. It was a house which might have been built for a contemporary nobleman in England, and have been lived in – had it stood on English ground – by its builder's descendants down to the tenth generation in the writer's own day; but, having been built, as it happened, by Venetian hands in Crete, this piece of modern western architecture was as utterly 'dead and done with' – as veritably 'a museum piece' – in AD 1912 as the Minoan palaces at Knossos and Phaestus which the traveller had been looking at a few days before. In the common mortality which had overtaken each of them in turn, at moments more than three thousand years apart, these desolate habitations of vanished thalassocrats bore witness, against their makers, that
>
> > in due time, one by one
> > Some with lives that came to nothing, some with deeds as well undone,
> > Death came tacitly and took them where they never see the sun.
>
> As the English traveller recalled the English poet's lines, he reflected that the four and a half centuries for which Venice had been mistress of Crete were a longer span of time than the present age of his own country's rule over the earliest acquired of her overseas dominions. ... That baroque ruin in Crete, as it stood in AD 1912, was a *memento mori* for an England that was then still alive, as well as for a Venice that was then already dead.

It is when Toynbee's tone is at its most melancholy, when he is prophesying the sure doom of worldly ambition and the utter vanity of mundane enterprise, that the voice of this classical scholar turned polyhistor reaches furthest and carries most conviction.

356

Civilisations die. But why do they die? We are almost tempted to say, because they had the misfortune to be born. Civilisations are always the offspring, the creation of creative minorities. These creative minorities are creative because they enjoy a high degree of self-determination. But civilisation to be civilisation cannot remain confined to the creative minority. Civilisation spreads to the mass, and in so spreading become mortally stricken. In the mass creativity ceases, self-determination fails, and a mechanical mimesis becomes its substitute. Volumes 4, 5 and 6 of *A Study of History* which treat of the disintegrations of civilisations are the memorial of our condition, and their tables of contents themselves a *miserere*, a litany of lamentations: The Mechanicalness of Mimesis, the Intractability of Institutions, the Nemesis of Creativity, the Idolisation of an Ephemeral Self, the Idolisation of an Ephemeral Institution, the Suicidalness of Militarism, the Intoxication of Victory, Schism in the Body Social, Schism in the Soul, *Pammixia* and Proletarianisation. So emphatic and insistent is Toynbee on active and continuing self-determination as the – unattainable – preservative of civilisation that at one point in his argument he is led to sketch out a theology *à rebours* in which, reversing, somewhat like the ancient Ophites, the hierarchy of the Book of Genesis – or the Syriac legend of the Creation of the Physical Universe as he calls it – he makes the Serpent, not God, the creative principle in the universe. According to this legend, then:

when 'God saw everything that He had made, and, behold, it was very good; and the evening and the morning were the sixth day ... and on the seventh day God ended His work which He had made; and He rested on the seventh day from all the work which he had made; and God blessed the seventh day and sanctified it, because that in it He had rested from all His work which God has created and made' – the immediate result was a static paradise, and it needed the Serpent's undesignedly beneficent intervention to liberate God's energies for performing a fresh act of creation in spite of Himself.[13]

The more self-determination there is, the more one acts in response to an internal call rather than to an external challenge, the more growth and progress there is: 'In other words the criterion of growth is progress towards self-determination; and progress towards self-determination is a prosaic formula for describing the miracle by which Life enters into its Kingdom.'[14] To describe this miracle which is or ought to be the goal of all human endeavour, Toynbee uses another term: etherialisation. This is the 'conversion of the soul from the World, the Flesh, and the Devil to the Kingdom of Heaven' and the transfiguration 'of a precarious Brotherhood of Man into a Communion of Saints'.[15] This universal sainthood entails nothing less than the elimination of mimesis from society, and no civilisation, Toynbee observes, has even distantly succeeded in this.[16] Hence their successive and fatal disintegrations.

The communion of saints, a civilisation utterly ethereal, has no need of states or of politics. It is no surprise, therefore, to find that Toynbee is profoundly hostile to them and considers them carriers of corruption and harbingers of decline. His distinction between what he calls culture and what he calls politics is sharp and categorical: 'the cultural element in a civilisation is its soul and life-blood and marrow and pith and essence and epitome, while the political and, *a fortiori*, the economic element are, by comparison, superficial and non-essential and trivial manifestations of a civilisation's nature and vehicles of its activity.'[17] But superficial, non-essential and trivial as they are, yet these manifestations are also demonic. Institutions, in contrast to personal relations, Toynbee says, oblivious of Freud and Dostoevski, are 'slums'.[18] 'It is not easy', he also says, 'to draft a definition of the state that distinguishes it from another ancient institution: slavery.'[19] In speaking of it, he adopts the language and imagery of Augustine of Hippo: 'Human Life on Earth', he declares, 'is lived in two societies simultaneously – the Ergastulum of Leviathan and the Commonwealth of God.'[20] But unlike Augustine, he does not allow that the state could be a remedy, as well as a punishment, for sin. On the contrary, his language leads one to believe that human beings can live a life of ethereal 'culture' and utterly avoid the evil of 'politics'. His Augustinian simile is therefore something of a paradox, used as it is to support a Manichaean view. His categorical separation of the ethereal from the material, his uncompromising demand that 'love' take the place of 'politics', his refusal to allow that (as Crazy Jane tells the Bishop in Yeats's poem)

> love has pitched his mansion in
> The place of excrement

lead Toynbee to that rigid and narrow moralism which is so striking a feature of his system. As is well known, Toynbee insists that all the civilisations he has studied – with one or two exceptions – died by their own hand. They committed suicide by their unwillingness to become ethereal. They are guilty, and their blood is upon their heads.

358

As one of Toynbee's profoundest critics has written: 'We have here an historian whose moralistic ideas of immanent justice, which make history a succession of guilts and punishments, goodness and reward, clash with the Jewish revelation of God's dealings in history, which are beyond human standards and responsibility.' And as Toynbee, the same writer acutely adds, 'deliberately ranges himself on the side of the believers, his views on the collapse of civilisations amounts to carrying unholy fire to the altar.'[21]

This dogmatic and insistent moralism clearly ends by seriously impairing Toynbee's judgment. He refuses to concede what common experience teaches, namely that the wicked do quite often flourish like the green bay tree, that in human affairs force and violence are occasionally decisive, or that love and gentleness are sometimes productive of evil. He insists that the only fruitful human encounters are the works of peace,[22] that 'it is the gentle and not the violent vein which is apt to be fruitful in the religious field'.[23] Since religion holds such an important place in Toynbee's system, such a statement constitutes a crux in his argument, and we are curious to see with what evidence he buttresses it. He contrasts the 'gentle êthos' of Christianity and Manichaeism with the 'violent êthos' of Maccabean Judaism and Sasanian Zoroastrianism. The contrast is perhaps forced and questionable, but such as it is, it serves to account, in Toynbee's scheme for Christianity's success and the failure of Judaism. What then are we to say of a similar contrast which he makes? For Toynbee opposes the Baha'is and the Ahmadis who are said to be 'alike distinguished by a spirit and cult and practice of gentleness' to the 'militancy' of the Islam from which they are both derived; and lest we mistake his meaning he insists in a footnote that 'The Sunna has been militant from first to last'.[24] The historical value of such a contrast is again not at issue here, but if Islam has been militant – and its major section militant 'from first to last' – how then to explain its great success and the comparative lack of success of its Baha'i and Ahmadi offshoots?

It is not only in religious history that Toynbee's moralism leads to failure of judgment. The same failure is even more manifest when he discusses politics. The figures in modern history whom he admires themselves tend to the same arid, ineffectual and dogmatic moralism: Gandhi, Tolstoy, Lansbury, Sheppard;[25] and his partiality to their style of thought and action leads him to some such statement as that 'it can already be forecast with some confidence that Gandhi's effect

359

on human history is going to be greater and more lasting than either Stalin's or Hitler's'.[26]

Toynbee's dislike and depreciation of politics leads him to dismiss political arrangements and devices as tainted with cynicism. Thus religious toleration as it began to be practised in modern Europe after the Wars of Religion is 'unedifying' and expresses 'nothing more noble or more constructive than a cynical disillusionment with the fruitlessness of a violence which has been previously practised *ad nauseum*'.[27] Again, so impatient is he of all politics, and so ready to smother it in heavy moral condemnation, that he comes to consider all political activity as a homogeneous whole in which accident, circumstance, intuition and character are quite unimportant, and to look upon every political act as, by definition, morally equivalent to every other political act, equally heinous and equally pernicious. In a discussion of papal policy in the thirteenth century, Toynbee condemns Innocent IV for his 'moral aberration' in refusing to make peace with Manfred, the son of Frederick II Hohenstaufen 'who had abandoned his father's aggressive ambitions and who was only anxious to be left in peace'. Toynbee tells us, in a footnote, that the historian Barraclough considered this description of Manfred's attitude and intentions 'beside the point from Innocent's point of view, just as Hitlerian protestations of goodwill and peacefulness are beside the point for France today'. To this comment Toynbee's rejoinder is that this 'striking parallel damns Poincaré-la-Guerre without exculpating Sinibaldo Fieschi'.[28] Hitler and Poincaré are thus judged morally equal. Morally equal also are Zionists and Nazis. Toynbee is able to make such an analogy by describing the Jews murdered by the Nazis as 'the vicarious victims of the Germans' resentment over their military defeat at the hands of their western fellow Gentiles in the war of AD 1914–18', and by describing the Palestinians made homeless in consequence of a war which they lost to the Zionists as, similarly, 'the vicarious victims of the European Jews' indignation over the "genocide" committed upon them by their Gentile fellow westerners in AD 1933–45.'[29] To distinguish and to specify is required not only of the historian, but also of the judge – unless he is a hanging judge. But eagerness to deliver a moral verdict has resulted here in a failure to distinguish and to specify, to the detriment both of moral and of historical judgment.

The state is an *ergastulum* and all politics is pernicious. But in Toynbee's scheme, one particular kind of state surpasses all others in oppressiveness. This is what he calls the universal state. When civilisations disintegrate through failure to maintain creativity and self-determination, there comes upon them a 'time of troubles' from which they seek relief and a measure of security in a universal state. Such a state is established by saviours with a sword. But salvation by the sword is illusory; violence begets greater violence, and in the end those who wield the sword – or their descendants – find that they have wielded it in vain: 'though their fair-seeming *Pax Oecumenica* may stand steady on its grim foundations of buried sword-blades for thirty or a hundred or two hundred years, time sooner or later will bring their work to naught.

'Time is, indeed, working against these happy empire builders from the outset; for sword-blades are foundations that never settle.'[30] A universal state, again, is a dead weight and a dead hand which stifles all creative impulses. It is 'passive, conservative, archaistic, and in fact negative in every respect'; it is an 'incubus' and a 'vampire state'.[31]

One such universal state was the Ottoman empire. It was called into being by the disintegration of the Orthodox Christian Society, and in fact constituted the universal state of that society. It is true that at one point in Toynbee's discussion, the Ottoman empire escapes harsh strictures which, in his eyes, universal states always deserve. In volume 8 he laments that 'in the name of an alien ideal which had thus been imported in an evil hour [i.e. Nationalism], the shot-silk fabric of a seamless Ottoman robe was remorselessly plucked to pieces by cruel hands, and the broken threads of each diverse national hue were then roughly rewoven into so many separate rags to make a patchwork coat of many colours, in which the only note of uniformity was a monotonously pervasive stain of blood.'[32] This encomium is not easy to reconcile with what Toynbee usually has to say about the Ottoman empire, and we may suspect that it was called forth by his even greater dislike for what he calls Late Modern Western Society in which Nationalism originated.

Everywhere else in his work Toynbee's judgment of the Ottoman empire is as unfavourable as that of other universal states. The empire has been an 'incubus', at any rate since the close of the seventeenth century. Before then, it had been an institution whereby 'human watch-dogs' controlled and exploited masses of 'human cattle'.[33] Readers of *A Study of History* know how taken the author is, how obsessed almost, with analogical argument, and what weight it is made to bear in his complex and baroque structure. It is always interesting, and occasionally rewarding, to follow the convolutions and meanderings of Toynbee's analogies. Why, we wonder, this likening of Ottoman rulers to watchdogs and of Ottoman subjects to cattle? At first sight, the answer seems to be that the Ottomans were originally nomads, and that therefore the political institutions of the empire ever after bore the indelible mark of the conqueror's simple pastoral past. A shepherd boy in central Asia mustering his sheep with the help of a faithful sheepdog, and the padishah keeping order in his far-flung realms by means of janissaries, are they not exactly alike? The comparison seems perfectly obvious and utterly illuminating until we remember that Ottoman military organisation had, at its origin, no place for a corps of slave soldiers, and that the janissaries, as their name implies, constituted a deliberate innovation quite some time after the simple shepherds of central Asia had become a formidable power in Anatolia. The analogy, we begin to suspect, does not originate in the remote uplands of central Asia, but, ironically enough, in the prejudice and misunderstanding with which Europeans have long viewed Islam and the Ottoman empire. This prejudice and misunderstanding Toynbee had begun by sharing, but with *The Western Question* and subsequent writings did his best to shake it off, sometimes with startling results. Thus, in the syncretistic prayer which concludes *A Study of History*, he invokes Muhammad's intercession in these terms: 'Tender-hearted Muhammad, who art also one of the weaker vessels of God's grace, pray that His grace may inspire us, like thee, to rise above our infirmity in our zeal for His service.'[34] It is difficult to say which is more out of place, the epithet, 'tender-hearted', or the nice judiciousness with which the Prophet is patronised as 'one of the weaker vessels of God's grace'.

The clue, then, to Toynbee's view of the Ottoman empire lies in a common European misunderstanding of the relation between ruler and subject in the empire. What the misunderstanding is we may gather from a statement which is crucial to his argument: 'The Ottoman Pādishāh', writes Toynbee, 'himself is a shepherd of men; his trained human slaves (*qūllar*) correspond to his Nomadic forefathers' auxiliary animals; while the function of the rest of the Pādishāh's subjects in the Ottoman social system is plainly indicated by their official designation as human cattle (ra'iyeh).'[35] Familiar as is the European translation of *ra'īyya* or *ra'āya* as human cattle, it is none the less erroneous, and erroneously pejorative. The word derives from the Arabic root, *ra'ā*, to tend a flock, and means the subjects for whom the ruler is responsible, as a shepherd (*rā'ī*) is responsible for his flock. The word therefore has none of the undesirable associations which the expression 'human cattle' conjures up. On the contrary, it implies rather that the ruled, the *ra'īyya*, are the object of the ruler's benevolent concern. As any one acquainted with the Psalm which begins 'The Lord is my shepherd' will appreciate, there is nothing particularly Ottoman or central Asian about this idea. It is on the contrary a very old notion, bound up perhaps with primitive ideas of kingship, and of the king's function in protecting his community and in shielding it from natural or supernatural harm. In classical Arabic usage the word applied indiscriminately to all subjects, whether Muslim or non-Muslim. This seems to have been also the case in Ottoman usage except that by the beginning of the nineteenth century – when Toynbee's 'human watchdogs' had long ceased either to bark or to bite – the word, while continuing to be applicable to Muslims as well as non-Muslims, came popularly to denote specially the non-Muslim subjects of the sultan.[36] This popular usage was picked up by European travellers in the east. In their prejudice and ignorance, these hastened to translate *ra'īyya* as cattle, and thus to denounce the callous oppression of Christians by Muslims. And it is on this blind and probably wilful misunderstanding that Toynbee rests his imposing analogical edifice.[37]

His view of the Ottoman empire as composed of watchdogs and cattle leads Toynbee in turn to yet another analogy even more complicated, and more misleading. He compares the Ottoman empire to Sparta; the slave janissaries to the free-born *homoioi* and the free subjects of the Ottoman sultan to the enslaved helots and the servile *periokoi*. What to us seems a crying contrast, to him seems, by a perverse paradox, a perfect similarity: the Ottoman empire was composed of human watchdogs and human cattle; Sparta was likewise; therefore Sparta and the Ottoman empire become two instances of a law which describes the character of nomad rule over a settled population. Toynbee carries this notion to extreme and ludicrous lengths, devoting a whole appendix in volume three to complicated and abstruse calculations which prove that the numerical ratio of 'human cattle' to 'human watchdogs' was as high in Laconia as in the Ottoman empire.[38] And to emphasise this parallel between Sparta and the Ottomans Toynbee draws upon his powerful topographical imagination – which is usually one of his strong points as a historian –

to show how akin and alike were these two incubi. He compares the conspiracy of the helots against the Spartans with the Greek revolt against the Ottomans. 'The Christian *ra'īyeh* of the 'Osmanlis' he says, no doubt wishing by this choice of words to remind us that the Greeks in 1821 were mere cattle, succeeded 'in wiping out the local representatives of the Ottoman ruling class – men, women, and children – in their Laconian citadel of Mistrà and throughout the Morea. The ruins of Mistrà, which remain down to this day as they were left on the morrow of the sack of the city in 1821, bear grim witness, for any visitor who seeks ocular testimony', concludes Toynbee with a clinching argument, 'to the virulence with which the 'Osmanlis were hated by their *ra'īyeh* – and the Spartans, before them, by their helots'.[39] All this vast structure of analogy and comparison, in itself extremely shaky and doubtful, is erected, as we remember, on the mistaken translation of the word *ra'īyeh* to mean human cattle.

But the Ottoman empire, in Toynbee's view, has a peculiarity of its own, which serves to set it apart from other universal states. The justification of the Ottoman empire as a universal state was that it provided protection and security – however illusory, and however ruinous its price – to the disintegrated Christian Orthodox Society. But in the sixteenth century the empire went beyond, or rather transgressed 'the precise and limited programme' which history had assigned to it. And this was the manner of the transgression: the Ottomans themselves, though acting as the universal state of the Orthodox Christian Society, were themselves members of an Iranic Society which, together with an Arabic Society, emerged, by the mediation of Islam, from the disintegrated Syriac Society of which the caliphate had been the universal state. In his volume of *Reconsiderations* Toynbee was to describe the – admittedly peculiar – notion of a Syriac Society as a 'hypothetical construction' which he thought up in order to solve problems posed by his system; he also admitted that the notion of an Iranic and an Arabic Society sired by Syriac Society was also rather difficult to entertain.[40] But the argument in the main body of his work depends rather heavily on these constructions.

It so happened, then, that in the sixteenth century, one branch of the Iranic Society – the Ottoman – prosecuting a quarrel with another branch of the Iranic Society – the Persian – set upon and assassinated its sister Society, the Arabian. The occupation of Cairo by Sultan Selim in 1517, Toynbee tells us, was the analogue of the conquest of Constantinople by the Crusaders in 1204. Down to about 1500, we are further told, the Arabic and Iranic worlds were more or less isolated from one another, and each world a unity itself. The Arabic Muslim Society, which had been defended by the Ayyubids and the Mamlukes – and how utterly surprised, like M. Jourdain, they would have been to know what they had been so long and so unconsciously doing – was by 'an apparently wanton attack upon inoffensive neighbours' – how offended the Mamlukes would have been to be called inoffensive! – 'forcibly incorporated' into Iranic Society in order to be merged in the 'united Sunni Islamic World'.[41]

Arabic Society, we thus see, also has a peculiar place in Toynbee's system. It is not, like other societies, guilty of *felo de se*. It is purely a victim of the Ottoman assassin. The Arabs, Toynbee is emphatic, had not 'prepared the way for the Ottoman aggressor by doing themselves any fatal injury with their own hands'. The 'indigenous Arabic Society of Egypt', for instance, 'still continued to lead its separate and self-sufficient life, in which the peasantry and the '*ulama* and the urban guilds of merchants and artisans each played their interdependent parts, and all recognised one another's respective functions in the corporate life of their common body social. Indeed', he goes on to say, 'the forcible unification of the Arabic Society with the Sunni fraction of the sister Iranic Society through the external act of the Ottoman conquest did not ever pass over into an inward social fusion; and the unitary Islamic Society which has confronted the modern Western World, and which has made such an imposing impression of unity on our Western minds, has always been something of an illusion.'[42] The Islamic world, he also says, is 'really not an organic unity but a pile of wreckage', in which the Osmanlis have lived a 'cultural life-in-death' and in which the murdered Arabic Society has taken vengeance on its assassins by raising the 'ghosts of a Primitive Muslim puritanism in the successive explosions of Wahābī, Sanūsī, Mahdist, and Idrīsī zealots'.[43] Religious movements such as Wahabism, it is notorious, are extremely difficult, especially for outsiders, to understand and interpret, and to assert that they arose as a reaction to Ottoman conquest seems blithely and cavalierly to go beyond the known evidence. That they are the reactions of an Arabic Society to such a conquest is even more doubtful. For even on Toynbee's own criteria, the generation of the Arabic Society remains obscure, and its existence shadowy. The interest of his peculiar treatment of recent Islamic history (with its populist and romantic picture of an autonomous Arabic Society led by its notables and divines, and carrying on an existence separate from that of its Ottoman overlords) resembles nothing so much as the apologetic historiography of pan-Arabism. In this historiography, as in Toynbee's, the 'Arabs', long oppressed by Ottoman imperialism, have now at last emerged to claim their rightful place as an autonomous nation. This, of course, is a very recent interpretation, made possible by the diffusion in the middle east of the European doctrine of Nationalism. One can see its role as a myth contributing to that transvaluation of values in the throes of which the Arabic-speaking world finds itself. Its presence in Toynbee's work shows that it is still infected with the categories of Nationalism which he has emphatically repudiated and denounced, after having enthsuiastically embraced it, in common with other liberals and radicals of his generation.[44]

The Ottoman empire has always occupied a special place in Toynbee's historical imagination. As has been seen, it was in Crete in 1912 when the island was nominally still part of the empire, that he had his crucial vision of the decay and death to which every civilisation, every domination is doomed in turn. Again, it was to a situation arising out of the destruction of the empire that he devoted what remains perhaps the best book he has ever written, *The Western Question in Greece and Turkey*. The book admirably shows Toynbee's virtues as a historian: the breadth of his learning, the fecundity of his imagination, his ability to connect the political, the economic, the social and the spiritual, and his topographical eye.

In *The Western Question* the reader will find briefly and lightly stated many of the themes which Toynbee was later to develop, with such a profusion of extravagant and wearisome detail, in *A Study of History*. One major theme of the latter work constitutes in fact the main theme of *The Western Question*. The subtitle of this work is, *A Study in the Contact of Civilisations*. Toynbee's contention here is that the conflict between the Greeks (who were allowed by the Allies in April 1919 to invade Smyrna and its hinterland) and the Turks (who under Mustafa Kemal successfully resisted the invasion) was the outcome of the spread in the middle east of European political ideas which were particularly ill-suited to the area, and hence profoundly destructive. The theme is magisterially stated in the opening paragraphs of the first chapter which is entitled: 'The Shadow of the West':

Savages [writes Toynbee] are distressed at the waning of the moon and attempt to counteract it by magical remedies. They do not realise that the shadow which creeps forward till it blots out all but a fragment of the shining disc, is cast by their world. In much the same way we civilised people of the west glance with pity or contempt at our non-western contemporaries lying under the shadow of some stronger power, which seems to paralyse their energies by depriving them of light. Generally we are too deeply engrossed in our own business to look closer, and we pass by on the other side – conjecturing (if our curiosity is sufficiently aroused to demand an explanation) that the shadow which oppresses these sickly forms is the ghost of their own past. Yet if we paused to examine that dim gigantic overshadowing figure standing, apparently unconscious, with its back to its victims, we should be startled to find that its features are ours.

'The shadow upon the rest of humanity', Toynbee declares, 'is cast by western civilisation', but westerners are quite unaware of the havoc they unconsciously wreak in the rest of the world, and their very ignorance constitutes the tragedy of this particular contact between civilisations: 'This conjunction of great effect on other peoples' lives with little interest in or intention with regard to them', Toynbee points out, 'though it is common enough in human life, is also one of the principal causes of human misfortunes; and the relationship described in my allegory cannot permanently continue. Either the overshadowing figure must turn its head, perceive the harm that unintentionally it has been doing, and move out of the light; or its victims, after vain attempts to arouse its attention and request it to change its posture, must stagger to their feet and stab it in the back.'[45]

In *The Western Question* contact between western and middle eastern civilisations was strikingly invoked to explain the character and the virulence of the conflict between the Greeks and the Turks. In *A Study of History*, the first three volumes of which were published twelve years later, such contact itself became the subject of a complex and far-reaching theory. According to this theory, the diffusion of artifacts and ideas from one society to another assumed a sinister aspect. Toynbee has recourse to an analogy, and describes this diffusion as 'social radiation'. 'For our present purpose', argues Toynbee, 'we may confine ourselves to noting the fact that in social, as in physical, radiation a ray is a composite affair which requires to be diffracted into its elements in order to penetrate a foreign body.' The rays emitted by a civilisation in a process of growth, Toynbee further declares, are undiffracted and hence do not penetrate an alien social body. They are undiffracted, it would seem, because 'one of the characteristics of civilisations in process of growth is that all the aspects and activities of their social life are co-ordinated into a single social whole, in which the economic, political, and cultural elements are kept in a nice adjustment with one another by an inner harmony of the growing body social.' In a disintegrating society – which is a sick society – this harmony is no more, and the 'discord in the fabric of the radiating body is reproduced, in the form of diffraction, in the rays which the body now emits; and these diffracted rays of the disintegrating civilisation have greater power to penetrate the tissues of alien social bodies than the undiffracted rays which the same civilisation used to emit in the time before the breakdown, when it was still in the growth stage.'[46]

The analogy may seem both fanciful and obscure. But at any rate we are to understand from it that the diffusion, say, of the idea of nationalism in the middle east, which in *The Western Question* was ascribed to a mere contact between civilisation,[47] must now be laid at the door of western society itself which, sick and disintegrating, emits its cancerous rays to infect and destroy other societies. To leave the analogical for the literal, Toynbee believes that the 'westernisation' of the world and the geographical expansion of western civilisation indicates the breakdown of this civilisation. We are 'almost warranted', asserts Toynbee, in regarding geographical expansion which is 'an index of the encroachment of one society upon the domain of another' as 'a social disease: an elephantiasis or fatty growth; a running to stalk or a running to seed; the malady of the Reptiles who turned huge on the eve of being surpassed by the Mammals; or the malady of Goliath who grew to gigantic stature in order to succumb to David; or the malady of the ponderous Spanish galleons which were routed by the English mosquito-fleet.'[48] This, for Toynbee, is a law. It is a law because geographical expansion is associated with military power; military power is the practice of violence; and violence is the concomitant of disintegration.[49] Many critics have pointed out that violence is not peculiar to a disintegrating civilisation, that a civilisation in the growth stage is also apt to be violent. If this criticism has any substance (and Toynbee seems to accept its force),[50] then its consequences for his system are devastating. Growth and disintegration become tinged alike with violence, and it is no longer possible to set up these striking and crucial contrasts between self-determination and mimesis, between the glorious freedom of creative epochs, and the remorseless oppression exercised by mere mechanical institutions.[51]

It is, in any case, quite doubtful whether Toynbee can sustain his thesis that the Greco-Turkish conflict in all its violence and atrocity is a consequence of the contact of civilisations. The Greco-Turkish conflict was the outcome of territorial ambitions familiar in every period and under every clime. It is true that it was exacerbated by pan-Hellenic nationalism which was clearly a western importation. But the virulence of pan-Hellenism did not derive from the fact that it was an importation. Rather it derived from the fact that it was a species of that ideological politics which had wreaked as great – or a greater – havoc in Europe, where it originated, as in the near east whither it was imported. Auschwitz and the French Terror did not happen as a result of contact between civilisations.

As has been seen, in spite of his vehement opposition to nationalist doctrine, Toynbee's system seems here and there infected by it. A case in point was his treatment of the Arabic Society. It is interesting to note that the distinguishing mark of this Society, if the name given to it is any indication, must be language. Language, as is well-known, is the very criterion by which nationalist doctrine defines a nation and recognises its existence. According to this doctrine, the purity of a language, the absence from it of foreign accretions indicate the vitality and well-being of a nation. We are interested to see Toynbee holding such a view. For, according to him, expansion of a civilisation – which is a sign of its disintegration – is accompanied by promiscuity, *pammixia*, and the vulgarisation and barbarisation of the dominant minority. One of the signs of this promiscuity is the transformation of the language of the expanding civilisation into a *lingua franca*. This happens because a *lingua franca* 'owes its success to the social advantage of having served, in an age of social disintegration, as the tool of some community which has been potent in war or else in commerce'. A *lingua franca* loses its native subtleties and niceties: 'for it is only on lips that have learnt it in infancy that any language is spoken with that effortless perfection which is the dower of Nature and the despair of Art. In fact', Toynbee asserts, 'a language – even a natural language – cannot gain an artificial currency without a risk of becoming vulgarised.' '*Lingue franche*', he therefore concludes, 'are rare in primitive societies and also rare in civilisations while these are still in growth. *Lingue franche* only flourish on a spiritual soil that has been coarsened by that loss of sensitiveness and that appetite for promiscuity which are symptoms of the process of social disintegration'.[52] This nativism, which also makes of a literary – or an artistic, or a musical – style the index of social disintegration, is in no way convincing. Judgments whether a style is vigorous or effete, pure or impure, lofty or degraded, are apt to change from time to time. Again changes in the style of a particular activity – say painting or sculpture, or musical, or literary composition – may have an autonomous character, and no significant relation with social or economic or political events. Is there anything in English or French or German history to explain why Shakespeare or Racine or Bach or Hegel appeared when they did? Finally, this nativism cannot possibly account for the rise of such languages as Arabic or English to the status of world languages. Innumerable people received these languages as a result of conquest or commerce or migrations and have learnt to speak and to write them with ease and elegance, and to express, through their medium, the most difficult and elusive ideas, and the most complex and evanescent feelings.

However different their formal arguments, both Toynbee and the doctrinaires of nationalism look upon cultural diffusion as deeply harmful and pernicious. Herder and Fichte would not have dissented from Toynbee when he speaks of an 'assaulted body social' undergoing 'cultural radiation' by an 'assailant' society. As has been said, the 'assailant' society itself is an assailant precisely because it is in disintegration, because its creative minority has ceased to be creative and, resorting to violence, has become a mere dominant minority. The price which such a society pays for its dominance is the further degradation which becomes its lot when it has to admit within its bosom an imperfectly assimilated 'external proletariat'. Toynbee thus fully shares Juvenal's aversion for the squalid spectacle of the Orontes discharging into the Tiber: 'In a Modern Western World that had made itself literally world-wide by radiating its influence over the whole habitable surface of the Earth, not only the Orontes', he distastefully comments on these affluents, 'but the Ganges and the Yangtse had discharged into the Thames and the Hudson, while the Danube had performed the more sensational miracle of reversing the direction of its flow in order to deposit a cultural alluvium of Roman and Serb and Bulgar and Greek proselytes up-stream in a Viennese melting-pot. *Si testimonium requiris*', Toynbee fastidiously points out 'was not the evidence printed *in extenso* and made public in the telephone directories of Vienna and Paris and London and New York and Chicago and a host of lesser cities in the European and American provinces of a Western Society's homeland?' And what did 'these endless columns of close print, bristling with outlandish non-Western surnames' portend? They attest this, namely 'the advent, in a twentieth century Westernising world, of the blight of promiscuity that had been demoralising a Hellenising world in Juvenal's day'. 'The social price that a successfully aggressive civilisation has to pay', we are invited to conclude 'is a seepage of its alien victims' exotic culture into the lifestream of the aggressor society's internal proletariat and a proportionate widening of the moral gulf that already yawns between this alienated proletariat and a would-be dominant minority.'[53] While it is not evident why the 'seepage' of an exotic culture should necessarily increase the gulf between the proletariat and the dominant minority, yet it is clear that for Toynbee such 'seepage' is a squalid affair which increases the degeneracy of the 'assailant' society.

Late Modern Western Society, thus, is and has been the aggressor for a very long time and is now, in its degradation, reaping the wages of sin. This is perhaps the best and most widely known of Toynbee's views. Thanks to the British Broadcasting Corporation, who commissioned Toynbee to deliver the Reith Lectures subsequently published as *The World and the West*, these views have reached a wide and respectful popular audience. The west, Professor Toynbee informed his fellow-westerners, is universally condemned for its aggressions. The Russians, the Muslims, the Hindus, the Chinese, the Japanese and all the rest will all say that the west has been 'the archaggressor of modern times':

The Russians will remind him [the westerner] that their country has been invaded by western armies overland in 1941, 1915, 1812, 1709 and 1610; the peoples of Africa and Asia will remind him that western missionaries, traders, and soldiers from across the sea have been pushing into their countries from the coasts since the fifteenth century. The Asians will also remind him that, within the same period, the westerners have occupied the lion's share of the world's last vacant lands in the Americas, Australia, New Zealand, and South and East Africa. The Africans will remind him that they were enslaved and deported across the Atlantic in order to serve the European colonisers of the Americas as living tools to minister to their western masters' greed for wealth. The descendants of the aboriginal population of North America will remind him that their ancestors were swept aside to make room for the west European intruders and for their African slaves.[54]

371

In making this abject public confession for and on behalf of the west, Toynbee speaks as though all the rest of the world were innocent of all violence and all misdoing. He had not always been so extreme and so highly-strung; he did use to recognise that to do and suffer evil is the universal human condition. Discussing the policies of the Great Powers in the middle east in the last two hundred and fifty years, he remarked in *The Western Question*: 'It has been wrong headed and disastrous behaviour. The mere description of it is an indictment, but it is an exposure of the little wisdom in the government of human affairs rather than of any special depravity in western civilisation.'[55]

This sensible recognition that depravity is not to be imputed to one section only of humanity steadily gave way, as *A Study of History* was being written, to a mounting passion of self-accusation, and to ever more determined self-flagellation. Toynbee seems to have started out by sharing the Hobsonian 'anti-imperialism' prevalent among English radicals before and during the first world war, and to have believed that empires were acquired and maintained by European states for the sake of their economic benefits.[56] He seems to have become, with the years, more anchored in this belief, and more extreme and uncompromising in expressing his hatred for western greed and oppression. In the first volume of *A Study of History*, published in 1934, he chides his fellow-westerners for complacently assuming the superiority of their own civilisation,[57] and convicts them of oppressing the coloured peoples whom they have subjugated; they have 'almost everywhere abused their power in some way and in some degree'.[58] In volume 2, also published in 1934, he denounces western economic activity overseas: in Ceylon, he contrasts the ancient Sinhalese bund-builders with modern western planters 'who have interested themselves in Ceylon not in order to propagate a civilisation but in order to get rich quick'. It does not occur to him that the ancient bund-builders might have been as interested, and perhaps more efficient than western planters, in exploiting the Ceylonese peasantry. Again, he remarks: 'Nanking is only one short night's railway-journey distant from Shanghai: the den – and school – of thieves which western enterprise has planted at China's eastern door.'[60] In the next batch of volumes, published in 1939, his denunciation of modern western economic enterprise becomes even more emphatic. He remarks that in fifth-century Greek usage, *idiotes* denoted a superior personality who committed the social offence of 'living to himself' instead of putting his gifts at the service of society, and goes on ironically:

> It is amusing to reflect that, if we had managed to forget the original connotation and to carry the original meaning over into the un-Hellenic moral environment of our own code of social ethics, then the English word 'idiot' would presumably be used today as a laudatory term; for it would then still signify a man of parts who has devoted his abilities to the acquisition of a personal fortune through private business; and this classical Hellenic *bête noire* is our latter-day western hero.[61]

He finds the exact analogue of such military 'wastrels' as the Mamlukes and pre-Tokugawa warlords to be in modern times 'the more discreetly predatory plutocrats of the nineteenth and twentieth centuries, who have put the princes in irons in order to usurp for their own bourgeois profit the adventurer's self-confessed privilege of playing the game of *Raubwirtschaft* with the whole world for their oyster.'[62] Western economic enterprise is an enterprise of plunder. Western civilisation is based on, and sapped by, 'social injustice'. It is 'branded with the mark of Cain', namely economic inequality, in protesting against which 'Communism was proclaiming in a challengingly loud un-Christian voice a commandment of Christ's which, on the Christian Church's lip, had sunk to a discreetly inaudible whisper repeated by churchmen.'[63]

This appraisal of the west has remained Toynbee's considered judgment. 'In my eyes', he states in the last volume of *A Study of History*, published in 1961, 'the west is a perpetual aggressor'. The guilt is clear beyond any doubt. But Toynbee is ready to entertain a plea of diminished responsibility, for he immediately adds: 'I trace the west's arrogance back to the Jewish notion of a "Chosen People".'[64] This theme is constant in his writings. As he himself has stated, he has seen Judaism through the eyes of the Christian Church supplemented by Eduard Meyer's. It has been, for him 'a prelude to Christianity and one which rejected its manifest destiny when it repudiated the new religious insight or revelation to which it had been leading up.'[65] This traditional Christian anti-Judaism – which is incongruous in someone as religiously eclectic as Toynbee – was laced with something else, which is a by-product of his system. As is notorious, for Toynbee the Jews, who have seen the light and rejected it, are also a fossil. How he came to this judgment provides yet another instance of his tendency progressively to build up initially simple and perhaps useful metaphors into doctrinal edifices, neo-Gothic in the luxuriance of their complicated fancies. Originally, it was only a specific community of Jews whom Toynbee considered to be a fossil. This was the community of the Ashkenazi Jews in Jerusalem whom he coupled with the Samaritans, the Druzes, the Maronites and the Alawis as 'fossils of ancient faiths'.[66] His meaning here is quite clear. To the progressive liberal that he was, these traditional communities out of touch with modern realities were, so to speak, fossils surviving from another age. With *A Study of History* this analogy became petrified into a rigid theory. The needs of his system required Toynbee to postulate the existence of a 'Syriac Civilisation' in which the Jews willy-nilly had to accommodate themselves, the Bible, for instance, becoming an example of Syriac mythology. Since the system further required that Syriac Society should be dead, the Jews, who were manifestly still alive, had to be 'the "fossil" remnant of a society that is extinct'.[67] Of Judaism as a living faith practised by successive generations of Jews since the Roman destruction of the Temple Toynbee was utterly ignorant. Pharisee, for instance, remained for him a term of abuse, and it is only very late in his career that he seems to have discovered such authorities on rabbinical Judaism as G. F. Moore and R. T. Herford.[68] The epithet Judaic has thus served, throughout *A Study of History*, to denote all that was most evil in the modern world. 'Fanaticism and race-feeling' among Protestants derives from the Old Testament; Marxism 'has caught its spirit of violence from an archaic strain in Judaism'; 'post-Christian western rationalism' has inherited from Christianity 'a Judaic fanaticism and intolerance'; Christianity took the wrong turning when it refused to heed 'Marcion's prophetically warning voice [that the God of Abraham was really a maleficent demiurge]'; the west since the seventeenth century has been trying to purge itself of 'its ancestral Judaic fanaticism and intolerance', but this has erupted again 'in such ideologies as Communism, Fascism and National Socialism'.[69]

In brief the west is a disintegrating society which, owing to its Judaic heritage, has shown itself to be murderously aggressive. Its victims, by Toynbee's count, amount to no less than eight societies,[70] who have been assaulted militarily, economically and culturally.

III

This, then, in all its labyrinthine complexity, is Toynbee's doctrine concerning the west and its relation to the world. But for all its analogical outworks and its learned incrustations, the doctrine is essentially simple and familiar. Listening to the far-fetched analogies, the obscure references, the succession of latinate, polysyllabic words, and one involved period following another, we begin to discern the shrill and clamant voice of English radicalism, thrilling with self-accusatory and joyful lamentation. *Nostra culpa, nostra maxima culpa*: we have invaded, we have conquered, we have dominated, we have exploited.

Nowhere is this feeling of guilt more pronounced than in respect of the Arabs and of Britain's dealings with them. This is an abiding theme in Toynbee's writings and in the Chatham House Version. Toynbee's conviction that British (and French) dealings with the Arabs were neither straightforward nor just, was acquired fairly early in his career. While working in the Political Intelligence Department of the Foreign Office, he was asked at the beginning of October 1918 to prepare a paper setting out British commitments in the middle east, and to indicate whether, in his opinion, these commitments were compatible with each other.[71] His examination of the correspondence led Toynbee to believe that large tracts of land, including Syria and Palestine, had been unconditionally promised to the sharif of Mecca, and that therefore the Balfour Declaration, for instance, was incompatible with this promise. In reaching this conclusion, Toynbee seems to have overlooked the fact that the British had expressly informed Husayn that all their promises to him were subordinate to their commitments to France and Russia, and that Husain (as shown for instance in his remarks to D. G. Hogarth who was sent at the time to inform him of the tenor of the Balfour Declaration) was quite aware of these reservations. His misunderstanding of the Husain–McMahon correspondence comes out clearly in a contemporary minute. When his memorandum was circulated Colonel L. Storrs of the War Cabinet offices wrote to ask what ground Toynbee had for including Palestine in the area committed to Husain. 'I think', Toynbee minuted on 26 November 1918, 'our territorial commitments to King Husein depend on his (undated) letter of July 1915 to Sir H. McMahon, the terms of which Sir H. McMahon, acting on instructions from the F.O., accepted, with certain reservations in his letter of October 24, 1915.' 'I think,' he went on, 'a comparison of these two quotations indicates that we are pledged to King Husein that Palestine shall be "Arab" and "independent" .'[72] As a later Foreign Office memorandum put it, Toynbee's 'well-known' paper, which 'had a wide circulation' contained 'no hint of an attempt to examine [McMahon's] pledge critically.'[73] But Toynbee has never given up his belief that in their negotiations with Husain, the British were guilty of double-dealing. He has occasionally stated that British commitments to Husain and British commitments to other parties were incompatible only 'in spirit';[74] but on the whole he has continued to believe that the British were the villains of the piece, that during the first world war they sold twice over a pup which wasn't theirs to sell.[75]

Along with this view of the wartime transactions, Toynbee took for granted the idea that political unity was desired by the inhabitants of Arabia, which in an article of 1931 he defined as 'bounded by the Mediterranean and by the rivers of Mesopotamia as well as by the Red Sea and the Persian Gulf ... up to the foot of the mountain ranges which form the southern boundary of Turkey and the Western boundary of Persia'. Before the first world war, this 'Arab domain' was politically united; but the French and the British had, after 1918, established 'artificial and arbitrary frontiers' in a manner reminiscent of the iniquitous partition of Poland in the eighteenth century. This partition, he affirmed, 'has been imposed on them against their will ... and they have so far refused to recognise the justice or legitimacy of the arrangement. They have had no voice in it; they regard it as contrary to their welfare; and they would wipe it out at any moment if they had the chance.'[76] This, of course, was to accept at their face value the claims and pretensions of a very small and unrepresentative minority in the Arabic-speaking world. This polemical version of recent middle eastern history with its guilt-sodden moralism obscures, indeed makes quite unintelligible, the acute political and social crisis which has this area in its grip, and of which the short-lived European rule, the failure of pan-Arabism, or even the Palestine dispute are by no means the most important aspects. Toynbee seems to have accepted and taken up the successive claims of the pan-Arab ideologies as these have changed and grown over the years. Thus in 1931, as has been seen, 'Arabia' for him was wholly contained in western Asia. But, as is well known, in the late

1930s and the early 1940s, pan-Arab ideologues began to claim that Egypt was part of the Arab nation. We find this claim implicitly accepted by Toynbee who, with a fine disregard for the historical context, in *A Study of History* describes the 'Urabi revolt as having been initiated by 'Arab officers' of the Egyptian army.[77] Again, in an article of 1964 published in *International Affairs* (and subsequently distributed as a pamphlet by the Arab Information Centre in London) Toynbee declared: 'The Arabs' grievance against Britain for her treatment of Egypt from 1882 to 1956 has been surpassed, in intensity and in justification, only by their grievance against us for our treatment of Palestine since 1917.'[78] It is therefore no wonder that, as he himself has acknowledged, Toynbee should become 'known as a western spokesman for the Arab cause.'[79] The reputation does not seem to have caused him discomfort for, as has been seen, Toynbee is a believer in the practical uses of historical authorship.

The picture of the middle east between the wars which emerges from the *Survey of International Affairs* and other writings of Toynbee's is in keeping with the radical, so-called anti-imperialist doctrines which have been instanced above. Thus he defines for the readers of the *Survey* for 1930 the goal of middle eastern politics:

The relations [he says] between the middle eastern countries and extraneous powers during the years 1929–30 were developing, for the most part, towards an identical goal: the replacement of an unequal relation, resting ultimately on force, in which the middle eastern country was subject to the extraneous power's control by an equal relation resting on a treaty negotiated freely between the two parties.[80]

Such a statement shows little political judgment. There was, in the first place, no indication in 1930 that the fortunes of the middle east were ceasing to be affected – and sometimes actually determined by the decisions and policies of the European great powers. There is again the assumption that the world and its ways – the existence of unequal relations 'resting ultimately on force' – may be conjured away with high-minded covenants and pious, elevated declarations. And there is the implicit assumption that relations between middle eastern states are not just as much based on force as the relation between outside powers and the middle east, or that the force exerted by one middle eastern state over another would be somehow less evil than force exerted by a European state over a middle eastern one.

This line of thought went along with the belief that the mandatory system instituted at the end of the first world war was superior to annexations or to protectorates which merely clothed 'the nakedness of the rapacity with which western lions and bears and eagles were seizing and devouring their prey'. Mandates 'marked a notable step forward in the advance from the Machiavellian regime of parochial sovereignty towards a new oecumenical order of society.'[81] Toynbee did not consider whether mandates, with their temporary and make-shift air, were not actually a grave disservice to regions where stable and steady rule was a crying necessity. Mandates, as is well known, were meant to prepare the mandated areas for constitutional and representative self-government. Toynbee believed that in Iraq the British mandatory had completed its task by the end of the 1920s and that Iraq should now speedily assume complete sovereignty. Iraq, he reported on a visit to the country in 1929, 'is a going concern' and the Iraqis are 'living in the future'. Relations between Englishmen and Iraqis are excellent; but if they are to continue so, Britain must shortly sponsor Iraq for admission to the League of Nations, and in this case 'what state member of the League will have the effrontery to oppose her candidature?'[82] Toynbee clearly approved of British policy in Iraq because he believed that it recognised 'the force of Arab national aspirations',[83] and that the Iraqi government as set up and supported by British force represented and expressed these aspirations. Nowhere in his writings does he indicate that this government was a narrow unrepresentative clique whose ideology was shared by a few in the country which they had been given to rule, and which they made the stage of their sanguinary intrigues and ruthless ambitions. Commenting in the *Survey* for 1934 on the Iraqi clash with the Assyrians which took place in 1933, and which resulted in the massacre of Simel carried out by the Iraqi army, Toynbee stated that 'apart from the Assyrian tragedy, there was no suggestion that Iraq had either failed to carry out her undertakings to the League Council or proved not to pass muster under the test of the five conditions for sovereign independence which the Mandates Commission had laid down.' In fact, of the three parties in the Assyrian tragedy, the Assyrians, the British, and the Iraqi government, the last, Toynbee declared, was least to blame: the Assyrians had behaved in a headstrong fashion, and the British had compromised them and then withdrawn.[84]

If Toynbee approved of British policy in Iraq and of its recognition of the 'force of Arab national aspirations', he was correspondingly heavy in his disapproval of French policy in the Levant. Indeed in *A Study of History* where, as is well known, he compared the Nazi murder of the Jews to the Zionist treatment of the Palestinians in 1948, he also compared to these two episodes the French occupation of Syria in 1920. He reasons thus: the Nazis murdered the Jews to take revenge for the German defeat in 1918; the Zionists evicted the Palestinians from their country in order to take revenge for the Nazi murders. Similarly, Toynbee argues, in invading Syria in 1920, 'the French were taking their revenge for an occupation of French soil in AD 1914 in which the invaders had been not the Syrians but the Germans.'[85] Leaving aside the exact relationship between Nazi and Zionist actions, we may affirm that no evidence exists to show that the French occupied Syria in 1920 because the Germans occupied France in 1914. The French, it is more accurate to say, occupied Syria in 1920 in order to put an end to the sharifian regime. They considered this regime the outcome of a British intrigue to do them out of their rights under the Sykes–Picot Agreement. This agreement was, of course, disreputable in Toynbee's sight, and the French pretensions equally so; but he betrays no suspicion that 'Syria' and the sharifians were not necessarily synonymous, or that the ambitions of this ramshackle and disorderly regime were possibly just as disreputable as those of the French.

French policy in Syria, Toynbee wrote in a magazine article in 1922, was anachronistic, unintelligent, pig-headed and a nuisance to Britain. France had to amend her ways, recognize the 'legitimacy of the Arab national movement', and follow the same policy which Britain was pursuing in Mesopotamia. But France did not follow this advice, and on his visit in 1929, Toynbee found Syria 'a sad country', in contrast to Iraq which was 'a going concern': 'The mischief was done by the political map-makers at the Peace Conference of Paris – or, rather, by the authors of the "secret agreements" that were negotiated between the Principal Allied Powers during the war. . . . The territory mandated to France', he asserts, 'is a torso without the limbs. . . . Syria is being strangled.'[87] More particularly, Toynbee held France guilty of fostering Christian and generally non-Sunni separatism in the Levant. This, in his eyes, was reactionary, at a time when 'in Islamic countries that were left to themselves, the minorities were being either eliminated or assimilated in the evolution of homogeneous national states on the western pattern.'[88] Toynbee does not explain why Sunni Arab nationalism is preferable to Maronite or Kurdish or Alawite separatism, but he clearly takes it for granted that the British policy in Iraq which imposed Sunni Arab dominance over this extremely heterogeneous country was more virtuous, more in keeping with mandatory responsibilities than the contemporary French policy in the Levant. But his preference for British over French policy clearly derives from his belief that here were societies fast becoming homogeneous national entities in which traditional religious antagonisms were no longer of much account. In the *Survey* for 1928 he declares, with no shadow of doubt to cloud his conclusions that:

the facts reviewed in this chapter indicate that at this time religious fanaticism was either extinct or in abeyance in the greater part of the Islamic World – at any rate in the leading countries of 'the solid core'. In Turkey, there was no overt opposition at all to a westernising movement which had committed itself unreservedly to the policy of secularism.

In Egypt, Palestine, Syria and Iraq, there was a marked tendency for the old alignments of Christian against Muslim and Sunni against Shi'i to give place to new alignments on lines of nationality and for the pursuit of secular ends.[89]

Anyone acquainted with the character of middle eastern society, in 1928 or today, will recognise how wide of the mark is Toynbee's judgment. But even if it were not superficial and erroneous to believe that religion has lost its tenacious hold over middle eastern society, is it not mere radical rhetoric to assume that 'new alignments on lines of nationality and for the pursuit of secular ends' are not productive of fanaticism?

We see this radical rhetoric also manifest in Toynbee's assumption that middle eastern representative institutions were actually representative of the people. Thus he refers in the *Survey* for 1928 to 'the long struggle between the Egyptian crown and the Egyptian champions of parliamentarism', and in the *Survey* for 1930 declares that with the prorogation of the Syrian Assembly in 1929 'the relations between the people of Syria and the mandatory power' relapsed into an *impasse*.[90] In *The Western Question* he had derided the idea that Zaghlul, for instance, did not represent a coherent national movement. 'Opponents of political movements claiming to be national should', he solemnly tells us, 'take to heart Gamaliel's advice to the Sanhedrin: "Refrain from these men and let them alone, for if this counsel or this work be of men, it will come to naught; but if it be of God, ye cannot overthrow it – lest haply ye be found even to fight against God." ' Firm in the belief that Zaghlul and leaders like him are 'of God', Toynbee proceeds sorrowfully to remark of 'imperial peoples' that it is hard for them 'to avoid the paths of destruction. Their prophets prophesy falsely, and their people love to have it so.'[91]

The castigation would have been well deserved if middle eastern politics were as Toynbee implies. But in fact representative institutions in this area have generally been the exclusive apanage of an official class which, because of its westernisation, has ceased to share the same universe of discourse with society at large. The gap, in modern times, between ruler and ruled has grown larger than ever, and modern representative institutions usually have betokened a decrease rather than an enhancement in the representativeness and the responsiveness of the rulers. It is therefore absurd – as later events have amply shown – to imagine that a Syrian assembly prorogued meant a breakdown in communication between the French mandatory and the people in Syria. More, it is perfectly possible to argue that it was in 1936, when they decided to make a deal with the Syrian official classes, that the French foresook their duty and abandoned the Syrians – for whom they had accepted a responsibility – to cruel and hazardous experiments. Similarly, it is hardly the case that Zaghlul was the representative and spokesman of twelve million Egyptians. What Zaghlul portends is the appearance in the modern middle east of the demagogue appealing to a mass perplexed and discomforted by the destruction of its traditional way of life, and bewitching it with unfamiliar slogans drawn from an alien political tradition. It is therefore not the case that Zaghlul's *Wafd* was a parliamentary and constitutional party while its opponents, like Muhammad Mahmud and Isma'il Sidqi, were arbitrary dictators. Rather, all politicians in Egypt under the monarchy exercised power quite unchecked by elections or parliaments. The record of Zaghlul and Nahhas who claimed to speak for the people is little different from that of Muhammad Mahmud who claimed to uphold constitutionalism and limited government, or of Isma'il Sidqi who exercised power as a king's man. They came and went not in response to popular wishes, but in consequence of manoeuvrings, sometimes obscure and sometimes blatant, between them, the king and the British. The difference between the *Wafd* and the others is simply that the *Wafd* inherited and successfully exploited Zaghlul's populist rhetoric. There is no more striking evidence of the essentially unrepresentative character of these factions and movements in Egypt – and elsewhere in the Arabic-speaking world – than the fact that when the military swept aside the civilians, the *Wafd* and other so-called political parties disappeared in a day, without a trace.

This cursory review of some aspects of Toynbee's writing on current affairs shows that he is right to insist on the intimate connection between *A Study of History* and the *Survey of International Affairs*. The 'anti-imperialism' of the one echoes the censorious condemnation of the west which runs through the other. We may see them both as serving to instil in their western readers a feeling of unease and guilt, and by so chastening them to diminish their greed and aggressiveness, and thus promote what the founders of Chatham House desired, namely a just and peaceful international order. We may go further and say that this practical aim, belief in the importance of which was no doubt sincere, did actually get in the way of that 'scientific study of international questions' to promote which was also the stated purpose of the founders of Chatham House. For this eagerness to preach repentance to the west clearly promoted, so far as the middle east at least was concerned, a superficial and eccentric view of its society and politics. Absorption in the sterile polemics of 'imperialism' and 'anti-imperialism', of Zionism and Arabism, eagerness to award good or bad marks to this or that action or policy clouded the understanding and made it the captive of current political slogans. The *Survey of International Affairs* particularly suffered from these shortcomings. As an annual survey, it was chained to the chariot of current affairs, endeavouring breathlessly to keep up with them. But this was a vain endeavour since history cannot be written from newspaper cuttings. The attempt to do so only meant that partiality to fashionable political rhetoric was not checked, but rather reinforced by the uncritical assertions of restless 'newsmen' avidly questing for 'stories'. Instances of the resulting superficiality and eccentricity abound. One may perhaps suffice. In 1936 a treaty was concluded between Iraq and Saudi Arabia which was supposed to promote Arab friendship and brotherhood. The treaty is now as forgotten as the spring fashions of that year, and was in fact of no visible consequence in middle eastern politics. In the same year Saudi Arabia also made a treaty with Egypt which provided for Egyptian diplomatic recognition of Saudi Arabia, and attempted to mitigate the state of touchy suspicion which had obtained between the two kingdoms ever since Ibn Saud had conquered the Hijaz and Fu'ad had tried to become caliph. The *Survey* for 1936 had to take notice of these two novelties. Because they occurred in the same year, the *Survey* saw them as manifestations of some deep underlying trend in Arab affairs. They were 'effective and lasting', indeed they were so many links in the 'chain-mail of Arab solidarity'.[92] It is easy to see how a doctrinaire view of middle eastern politics, reinforced by a belief in the significance of the latest newspaper headline, has resulted here in utter lack of judgment.

Toynbee, then, we may fairly say, is the principal author of the Chatham House Version. But he was not the only one. His assumptions and attitudes are found more or less mirrored in the flow of surveys, information papers, monographs and comments which issued from Chatham House or under its auspices during his tenure. This is not to say that they were inspired by him. It was of course natural that as Director of Studies he should attract and encourage the expression of views and attitudes of the soundness of which he approved. But such views and attitudes, we must remember, were in any case widely shared among the intellectual and official classes in Britain. The Chatham House Version provided for them imposing scholarly buttresses and incorporated them in a philosophy of history which satisfied by its comprehensiveness and finality.

All this literature, then, shared much with Toynbee's own writings in large as in small things. There was thus the same – somewhat unsuccessful – pursuit of exactitude in the transliteration of oriental names, the same recourse to analogical argument, at times gratuitous and at others misleading. Thus the anonymous author of an information paper on *Great Britain and Egypt* writes: 'The result of this attempt to combine the Egyptian and British theses on the Sudan in a single compromise formula was no more successful than the attempt (which it so closely resembled) of the Oecumenical Council of Chalcedon in AD 451 to reconcile the Orthodox and the (Egyptian and Syrian) Monophysite views on the Incarnation.'[93] The analogy is strictly pointless, an example of sterile academicism, and in its reference to Monophysitism as being Egyptian and Syrian anachronistic and hence misleading. Another analogy, more seriously misleading, occurs in the same publication. Discussing corruption by *Wafd* and other governments in Egypt, the author is moved to comment: 'Analogies, *mutatis mutandis*, in countries nearer home will come readily to mind, e.g. the *Report of the Tribunal appointed to inquire into allegations reflecting on the Official Conduct of Ministers and other Public Servants* (The 'Lynskey Tribunal'), Cmd. 7616 of 1949, and cf. the Marconi Scandal of 1912–13.'[94] The extent and character of official corruption in Egypt, as is well known, is so widely different from what obtains in Britain, that one is left wondering whether the purpose of this analogy here is less to provide enlightenment than to insinuate an obscure innuendo.

But similarities between Toynbee and other Chatham House authors extend beyond matters of style and form, to issues of substance. There is, for instance, the pervasive notion that government and society in the middle east are to be understood with the same categories which serve to explain western political and social arrangements. H. A. R. Gibb, author of a section on 'The Islamic Congress at Jerusalem in December 1931' in the *Survey* for 1934 remarks that the organisers of this Congress had sent invitations 'to all the Muslim Associations which had sprung up throughout Egypt and the Arabic-speaking countries during the immediately preceding years, and also to the various corps of Shī'ite *'ulamā* in Syria and Irāq. The significance of the invitations issued to the former', Gibb proceeds to argue, 'lay in the perception of the organisers of the Congress that these associations formed a new and important element in the structure of Muslim Society, by which, for the first time, the lay and middle classes were organised for the furtherance of Muslim objects.' It is quite safe to say that the organisers of the congress (i.e. the mufti of Jerusalem, whose object in the congress was to aggrandise himself and diminish his Palestinian Muslim rivals) were far indeed from perceiving any such thing. Indeed, even today (or perhaps today more than ever), such a perception is still premature, and these associations far from forming 'a new and important element in the structure of Muslim society' – as voluntary associations do in European society – have in fact been quite insignificant, and have since become even more insignificant with the spread and perfection of centralised absolutism. Similarly Europocentric is the reference to the 'middle classes' of Muslim society. Middle class in European society is an intelligible notion; in the middle east however, with its tradition of oriental despotism reinforced by modern centralised absolutism, there are only two classes: the official class, and the non-official class; those who are at the centre, and those who are at the margin of power; those who belong, and those who do not belong to the ruling institution. Again, fanciful and premature was Gibb's observation that the 'invitation to the Shī'ah divines to participate in the congress was an even more striking innovation, inasmuch as it was the first outward manifestation of a new spirit of cooperation'.[95] Such eagerness to find great significance in public professions argued a dangerous tendency simple-mindedly to assume that, as in Europe, there is some direct and not so remote connection between what is said and what is done, between what is stated in public and what is divulged in private. For, needless to say, this spirit of cooperation between Shi'ites and Sunnis was visible neither then nor since.

Implicit reference to the same western model is found in other Chatham House authors. Thus G. E. Kirk in a chapter on the middle east in *The World of March 1939* (part of the *Survey* for 1939–46) refers to 'a nationalist alliance of upper and middle classes', describes government in Iraq as being dominated by 'a few score members of the landowning and mercantile oligarchy', and asserts that in Egypt the *Wafd* 'in normal circumstances commanded the votes of . . . the Egyptian "common man".' In contrast, he proceeds to observe 'the other parties were fragmentary groupings round some upper-class notable, representing privileged interests with no roots in the people'.[96] The assumption here clearly is that as in modern industrial Europe society can be usefully divided into 'upper', 'middle' and 'lower' classes according to some economic yardstick, and that it is economic power – that, say, of some 'landowning and mercantile oligarchy' – which somehow determines political power. In fact, Iraq under the monarchy, to which Kirk applies this analysis, is a clear example of the well-known condition of oriental despotism whereby it is political power which bestows wealth and not the other way round. Again, there is nothing to justify the derogatory description of the opponents of the *Wafd* as 'representing privileged interests with no roots in the people', as though Nahhas, Sarraj al-Din and Salah al-Din and the other *Wafdist* leaders were so many Gracchi, F. D. Roosevelts and J. F. Kennedys. Similar European assumptions lead another Chatham House writer to a rather bizarre conclusion. Discussing Palestine in the *Survey* for 1938, H. Beeley writes thus of Hajj Amin al-Husaini: 'Only the exiled mufti, from his residence at Zuq in Lebanon, contrived to express a preference for the western democracies in the European conflict without appearing to compromise on any of the questions at issue between the Arab Higher Committee and the mandatory power.'[97]

M. Khadduri's *Independent Iraq*, the principal object of which is to explain Iraqi politics under the monarchy, suffers from the same misconception. The author begins by stating that 'When the mandate came to an end there were grounds for confidence that the progress of the Iraqi government was ensured. Judged by relative standards, Iraq possessed a modern form of government, a well-guided public opinion, and civil servants learning by experience and growing in efficiency. Above all there was', the author tells us, 'the wise leadership of Faysal who inspired public spirit in every department of government.'[98] If this were in any way true, there would be no accounting for the degraded and murderous politics of Iraq from the end of the mandate to the end of the monarchy. The fact is, of course, that this kind of language is most inappropriate to Iraq under the monarchy or afterwards. Equally out of place are this author's attempts to describe the sanguinary in-fighting of the Baghdad politicians, the southern shaikhs and the officers as 'Trial and Error in Self-Government',[99] or to divide them into 'liberals', 'reformists', or 'conservatives', 'moderates', or 'extremists'. Lack of scruple greater or lesser, cupidity more or less unrestrained, ability to plot more or less consummate, blood-lust more or less obsessive: these rather are the terms which the historian must use who surveys this unfortunate polity, and those in whose power it was delivered.

Yet another misleading notion is that these middle eastern societies are as politically homogeneous as western nation-states: 'To the Arabic-speaking peoples', asserts Kirk, 'the frontiers drawn in the middle east after 1918 could not appear as anything but artificial, quite apart from their political objectionableness.'[100] This is to assume that the Arabic-speaking world had been, except in a very remote past, a political unity, that the Arabic-speaking peoples are politically conscious in a manner such that it could be said of them that they desired or did not desire unity; it is to take for granted the romantic European notion that frontiers exist which are not artificial. Another Chatham House author, S. H. Longrigg, as uncritically accepts the anachronistic slogans of Arab nationalist ideology when he writes of Syria in 1914 that 'like its sister-countries, [it] had been, in respect of at least nine-tenths of its people, self-consciously an Arab country for a thousand years', that all Syrians 'shared a deep background of Arabism' and that 'all were at one in enduring a foreign government'.[101] If 'self-consciousness' is in question, and if we are to use historical and not ideological categories, what we have to say of 'Syria' and its 'sister-countries' is that its inhabitants for a thousand years considered themselves either Sunnis or Shi'ites or Druzes or

Maronites or Greek Orthodox or Jews. Of course, they spoke Arabic, but this fact until very recent times was of no political consequence and the majority of the population, namely the Sunnis, by no means felt that they were 'enduring a foreign government'. Shi'ites and others of course did, but in this feeling the Sunnis were certainly not 'at one' with them. This view of what Syria 'self-consciously' was leads this writer to accept without question that in 1918–20 all the 'Syrians' knew what they wanted, wanted one thing, and took organised action in order to achieve their desire. He thus contemptuously rejects the idea that Faisal's government in Damascus may have been looked upon as a government by outsiders. 'From the first . . .,' he asserts, 'the administration was Syrian; it continued to be called "Sharifian" only through habit, ignorance, or the pejorative malice of its critics.' He would have his readers believe that the delegates to the Arab Congress organised by Faisal in order to impress the King–Crane Commission 'were no doubt effectively representative of the great majority of Syrians' – which would have been a remarkable and noteworthy exception to the record of representative assemblies in the middle east – and he solemnly affirms, without a hint of irony, that the 'heads of the Christian communities were prominent among the swearers of allegiance' to Faisal. Similarly, Beeley finds that the presence of an Orthodox Metropolitan of the Bludan pan-Arab Congress of 1937 'emphasised the growing unity of Arab national feeling.'[102]

We find Longrigg also taking for granted the notion – for which, as has been said, there is no warrant – that before 1914 there had been a 'Syria' much larger than the Syria of the French mandate; that this larger pre-war 'Syria' 'had been truncated by the loss of Palestine and Transjordan' and, he implies elsewhere, by the setting up of a separate mandate for Lebanon. He speaks of 'the Syria of geography, of natural economics . . . of national claims' and complains that the frontiers of the postwar settlement did not correspond 'to logical or natural units of area'.[103] But before 1914 it was not Syria which had constituted a unity, it was the whole Ottoman empire. When that empire was destroyed, all its territories were subject to 'truncation'. The fate of these territories could be settled only by negotiation between the various interests, more or less powerful, who could claim to a say in the settlement. This settlement (like any other) would of necessity be in the nature of a compromise. It is inappropriate to demand that political settlements should be 'natural' or 'logical'. Politics is neither like a geometrical theorem, nor like the mating instinct.

Starting from these assumptions, therefore, this author could not but repeat the particular theme of the Chatham House Version to the effect that French mandatory policy in the Levant was both impolitic and unjust: 'no overriding necessity existed in 1920', he confidently asserts, 'to create, small weak non-viable states [in the Levant]. . . . Even in the case of Mount Lebanon . . . it might well have seemed desirable to limit rather than to expand its necessarily invidious privileges . . .'. This, he believed, emphasised the 'evident differences' between communities and ignored their 'greater fundamental similarity'. The policy was 'deficient in broad wisdom and vision, it ignored the basic facts of Syrian ethnography and culture, and the strength and convictions of the majority community'. Writing in 1958, he still believed that Lebanon should have been incorporated in a Syria dominated by a Sunni majority: 'friends of Lebanon', he wrote in sorrowful reproof, 'may well regret the bestowal on that fragment of Syria a never justifiable national status, and may believe that it would today be more advantageously placed as part of a united country, to which it could have made a valuable stabilising contribution.'[104] Syrian politics in the last two decades are sufficient comment on this judgment. But neither on this aspect nor on any other is it necessary to have recourse to hindsight in order to exhibit the systematic unsoundness of the Chatham House Version. For this unsoundness stems from a fanciful and doctrinaire view of middle eastern politics and middle eastern relations to the Great Powers. In the case of the Levant, it is mere question-begging rhetoric to insist that similarities are more fundamental or essential than differences. For who is to say, where human groups and their interests are in question, what is fundamental and what is secondary, what is essential and what is accidental? And even if the answers were clear, they could not by themselves determine a political decision. Political decisions are not scientific conclusions; they are rather the promptings of the practical judgment, in which play their part inclination and duty, circumstance and foresight. So that Longrigg's argument about what is fundamental and what is merely accessory in the Levant can tell us nothing about the character and motives of French policy. It only shows that the author is, for some reason, much in favour of Sunni Arab dominance in this area: they are the majority and therefore should have the primacy.

This also is an abiding theme in the Chatham House Version. A most curious and arresting expression of it occurs in a review by Gibb of R. S. Stafford's *Tragedy of the Assyrians*. The book is an account of the Assyrian massacre carried out by the Iraqi Army in 1933, and of its antecedents. Gibb finds in the book sufficient evidence of 'the goodwill of the Iraqi administration down to the last' and of the Assyrians' fractious obstinacy. The Assyrians were standing out for terms 'which, though ideally justifiable, would in practice have made any coherent Iraqi state impossible'. The author, Gibb says, goes no further than this, and perhaps not even quite so far. 'But one reader at least', he continues, 'finds himself forced to the conclusion that the final outbreak, however morally inexcusable, was in effect a violent assertion that in an Arab Muslim state non-Arab and non-Muslim minorities have rights only in so far as they recognise that fundamental fact. The fate of the Assyrians was directly due to their refusal to accept that position, and it is difficult', adds Gibb, 'to see that any prolongation of the mandate and its equivalent could have affected the ultimate issue.'[105] Original as it is, the argument that the Assyrians were really responsible for their own massacre sheds light on an attitude and a state of mind, rather than on Iraq in 1933. For what Gibb calls 'a coherent Iraqi state' was no necessary part of the natural order of things; the mandate did not have to end when it did and as it did, and if matters had been managed differently this would have certainly affected 'the ultimate issue'. It is Iraq where Arab Sunni supremacy was established and entrenched by the British mandatory which Longrigg holds up as the proper example for the French to have followed in Syria: 'The temptation to apply a separatist policy – to govern by dividing', he admonishes the French, 'could have been no less considerable in Iraq, with its well-marked Kurdish Shi'i, Yazidi and Assyrian minorities, and its regionalism as between north and south. Such a policy', he observes, his language here hinting at a powerful temptation virtuously withstood, 'was resisted by British as well as Iraqi authorities, with a broad wisdom which even the tragic Assyrian episode of 1933 . . . does not discredit.'[106] The bloodstained record of Iraqi politics after the mandate is hardly the example to hold up to the French in the Levant. The irony of this sermonising is enhanced by the fact that the Arab Sunnis in Iraq are a clear minority in the population, and that it is a minority of this minority – an exceedingly small one of officials and officers – which had bestowed upon it the plenitude of power.

If the Assyrians were ultimately responsible for their own woes, there could be no doubt, on the other hand, that the 'Arabs' were rather victims of injustice on the part of the Great Powers. Victims of France, but also of Britain. It was one of the most important themes of the Chatham House Version that the Balfour Declaration was both impolitic and immoral, and that the Palestine problem was the key issue in the middle east. Toynbee's own writings, reviewed above, amply illustrate this outlook. But he was by no means the only one heavily to disapprove of British encouragement of Zionism. Had it not been for the Jews, declared Gibb in a comment on Toynbee's address on 'The Present Situation in Palestine' delivered at Chatham House, Palestine would have been only a district in some larger state, and such a development was indeed only a matter of time, for an independent Palestine was 'an anachronism'. On the same occasion Gibb added that if the British had 'encouraged Zionist aspirations in Palestine in order to form a buffer state for their own selfish aims, and had hidden those aims behind a mask of altruism, then the blood of the Jews be on the head of those who had done this thing'.[107] The British, then, were guilty. They were guilty not only collectively, but also individually. As Gibb put it on a later occasion: 'each one of us who lives in a democratic country is, in a sense, individually responsible for it [the near eastern problem]', and: 'The near east is not only on our hands but on our hearts'.[108] British guilt is clear, and it admits no extenuation: 'What is much worse . . . and genuinely perplexing', declared Gibb, 'is that a government which professes the principles of democracy should deceive, and keep on deceiving, its people, firstly by concealing its imperial objects behind a mask of idealism, and subsequently by refusing to disclose both its original commitments to the Arabs and the fact that it has been forced in consequence into a policy which is abhorrent to the traditions of its people and furnishes ammunition to its enemies.'[109] Moral indignation is a bad counsellor, else the suspicion that the British government was out to deceive the sharif Husain might have been more carefully scrutinised.

But, in any case, if one is to set up as moral censor, one might bear in mind that the guilt of governments and peoples cannot be ascertained with the summary methods of a drum-head court-martial. Consider: the British government is declared guilty of encouraging, for its own selfish reasons, Zionism, an alien creed and a harmful movement; but yet, at the same time the British government clearly encouraged Arabism, also for its own selfish reasons. Can we not say that this also was a crime, which foisted an alien creed and a harmful movement on a middle eastern society much too diverse and complicated and delicate for such crude simplifications? If the British are adjudged guilty of promoting Zionism, they must likewise be adjudged guilty of promoting Arabism. Equity demands no less.

But such perplexities and ambiguities do not sit well with the simple certainties and the draconian verdicts of the Chatham House Version. British bad faith and deception are clear and not to be gainsaid. A plea, however, of diminished responsibility can be entertained. Gibb remarks that Antonius is 'justified in stressing the virtual control of public opinion in Britain and the west by the all-pervading Zionist propaganda'.[110] This Zionist propaganda had clearly acted to lead astray governments and peoples from the first world war onwards. Thus Longrigg declares that the recommendation of the Bunsen Committee in 1915 that Palestine should be internationalised – a decision which the Zionists greatly disliked and opposed – was one 'in which a considerable element was, no doubt, the pressure of Zionist spokesmen on British ministers'. This author goes even further and states quite flatly that 'The immediate background to the issue of the Balfour Declaration was one of pressure on the British cabinet from British and American Jewry' and that 'the pressure of Jewry on successive British governments was sufficient fatally to preclude the adequate acknowledgment of Arab rights'.[111] Such an account, of course, woefully misconceives the situation; for it was not 'Jewish' or even 'Zionist' pressure which had led to the issue of the Balfour Declaration; Jews and still less, Zionists, were not as powerful as all that. It was, among other things, eagerness by the British government to use Zionism in order to do away with the rights which they had themselves shortly before conceded to the French in Palestine. Arabism was used to the same purpose in the Levant, and we may therefore say that, far from being considered rivals or enemies, Zionism and Arabism were, in British eyes, movements which complemented and reinforced one another.[112]

The Chatham House Version relating to Palestine has yet another characteristic. It takes for granted that the Palestine problem was the most important, indeed the key issue, in middle eastern politics. Kirk's way of putting the matter is representative. 'They [the Zionists]', he wrote, 'studiously refrained from allowing themselves to consider to what extent, in default of the White Paper policy, Arab political agitation, strikes, sabotage, etc., might have interfered with the British middle east war-effort in 1940-2 and consequently with the Persian supply-route to the USSR – and what the ultimate consequences might then have been, for the National Home, for world-Jewry, and for all mankind.' And again: 'Rashid 'Ali's pro-Axis *putsch* in Iraq in 1941 . . . might have found much greater support in other Arab countries had it not been for the appeasing effect of the White Paper on moderate Arab nationalism'.[13] The assumption here is that British policy in Palestine vitally affected all other developments in the Arabic-speaking world. It is no doubt true that in 1938-9 the British government thought it prudent to discourage the Zionists and encourage their opponents; but to argue retrospectively that it was this policy which prevented anti-British and pro-Nazi movements in the middle east is clearly untenable. For, in the first place, such movements did manifest themselves; if they were inefficacious this was not thanks to the Palestine White Paper of 1939, but to swift military action by the British which, owing to their remoteness and preoccupation elsewhere, the Axis powers could not checkmate. It was, further, an illusion to suppose that all British problems in the middle east stemmed from the Balfour Declaration. British relations with Iraq, Egypt or Iran, say, were bedevilled by purely local issues; and again, Balfour Declaration or no Balfour Declaration, an activist and initially successful Germany was bound to – and did – attract, for a time, a large and influential following.

Toynbee, as has been shown, believed in the practical uses of history and had no compunction in exhorting and advising. The Chatham House Version, too, purported not only to give an account of middle eastern history, but to show what lessons for future policy this history disclosed. This didactic function reached its apogee during the second world war. In an address on 'Middle Eastern Perplexities' given at Chatham House in July 1944 Gibb declared: 'In the middle east, at least, we have only one alternative before us: either to do the big thing, or to crash. But my heart sinks when I think of some of our political leaders and their followers, of the strategists and the vested interests, and the difficulty of getting public opinion in Great Britain to understand the problems of the middle east.' Britain had to assist in the reconstruction of the middle east, and her 'only chance' to do so would be for her to work with and through 'the progressive intelligentzia' and 'to by-pass the attempts of the local governments to stir up trouble'. In this task 'we should', he said, 'be well-advised

in every way to invite Russian co-operation from the beginning.
. . . I have long held', he went on, 'that the USSR has an invaluable
contribution to make towards the solution of some difficult political
and social questions in Asia, in which we have no experience to guide
us, while the Russians have.' But he was prepared to go farther. The
'progressive elements' in the middle east would prefer that the initiative in reconstruction should come from Britain: 'But if we fail them,
there is still an alternative. That alternative', he affirmed, 'is Russian
leadership; and I have no doubt whatsoever that if we are content
to go on muddling along as we have done in the last twenty-five years,
then it will be in the real and best interests of the middle east and
of the world that the Russians should step in and take from out hands
a task which we shall no longer be fit to execute.'[114]

Also towards the end of the war, the Chatham House Cairo Group
produced a paper on *Great Britain and the Middle East* which, like
Gibb's address, made recommendations for a postwar policy. The
paper listed various possible policies and discussed their advantages
and disadvantages. Britain could either rule the area directly – which
was unlikely – or indirectly by means of puppet states – which was
also improbable. It could also attempt to safeguard its interests by
means of 'disintegrative alliances, i.e. by alliances with one or more
local states or groups which would most likely represent minorities
so far as the whole middle east was concerned, on the principle of
Divide et Impera'. This, which is the classic policy of a power with
Britain's position in the middle east 'would mean placing reliance
upon a close association with the non-Arab peoples of the area and
emphasising the differences between the Arabic-speaking group.
Such a policy might, for example, seek to continue to treat Egypt and
Iraq as individual nation-states whose connection with their Arabic-
speaking neighbours was sentimental rather than actual, and to
depend upon alliance with them and with Turkey and an expanded
Jewish State in Palestine. This policy', the paper declared, 'might
commend itself to those who do not know the middle east because of
the continued existence of the tendency not to take the Arabs
seriously.' This policy clearly did not commend itself to the group.
What they favoured rather was an alliance with 'the majority group
of the area, i.e. with the Arabs'. It is, said the paper 'based on the
fact . . . that the core of the middle eastern area is Arabic-speaking
and that there is a great and growing desire for unity on the part of
its peoples.' This in fact was the actual British policy, and it had

been quite successful: 'It is not too much to say that it would not have been possible to have defended Egypt successfully against the Axis if the Egyptians had been hostile and, in spite of the Rashid Ali episode, in 1941, the situation in Iraq during the present war has been surprisingly favourable to British interests.' The policy, the paper affirmed 'has stood the test of war extremely well', and was clearly the policy to adopt after it. Some two years after the end of the war, H. S. Deighton, chairman of the Cairo Group from 1943 to 1946 was still maintaining that this was the only possible policy for Britain. 'It is clear', he wrote in an article, that the policy of supporting the Arab League is the only alternative to the complete abandonment of the middle east . . . and given the fact that the British government has decided to maintain itself in the middle east, the only possible policy – the only defensible policy perhaps – is that of friendship with the majority.'[116] The events which followed and the ruin of the British position in the middle east are sufficient commentary on this prescription.

The prophets thus, to borrow Toynbee's expression, did prophesy falsely. The issues on which they prophesied are now dead and gone, and do not matter any more. The desire to prescribe and prophesy was however clearly one main reason why the Chatham House Version, as has been shown, also failed as history. And this is perhaps the more serious matter. As for prophecy it may be that, as the poet wryly observed,

> We are only undeceived
> of that which, deceiving, could no longer harm.[117]

Notes

1 The Middle East and the Powers

1 In the Foreword to *The Proceedings of the First Muslim-Christian Convocation*, n.p., n.d. (1955?). See also E. Kedourie. The American University of Beirut' in *Middle Eastern Studies*, vol. III (1966–7).

2 Cairo and Khartoum on the Arab Question, 1915–18

1 *Wingate Papers*, School of Oriental Studies, Durham University (hereafter referred to as *W.P.*), file 141/4.
2 *W.P.*, file 134/5.
3 Curzon to Cromer, 9 June 1915, *W.P.*, file 134/7.
4 The other members of the committee were Mr G. R. Clerk of the Foreign Office, Sir T. W. Holderness of the India Office, Admiral Sir H. B. Jackson of the Admiralty, Major-General C. E. Callwell of the War Office, Sir M. Sykes and Sir Ll. Smith of the Board of Trade. There is a copy of its *Report* in the *Austen Chamberlain Papers* (Box AC 19) at Birmingham University.
5 *W.P.*, file 135/3.
6 Telegram from Wingate, Khartoum, to Clayton, Cairo, 15 October 1915, *W.P.*, file 135/4.
7 *W.P.*, file 135/1, note of 24 July 1915.
8 *W.P.*, file 135/4, letter to Gen. C. E. Callwell at the War Office, London, 19 October 1915.
9 *W.P.*, file 135/5, telegram from Wingate to Clayton, 14 November 1915.
10 *W.P.*, file 135/4, letters from Clayton to Wingate, 9 and 27 Oct. 1915, and file 135/5, telegram from Clayton to Wingate, 13 Nov. 1915.
11 Storrs to Col. O. A. G. FitzGerald, 8 March 1915, quoted in J. Nevakivi, 'Lord Kitchener and the Partition of the Ottoman Empire', K. Bourne and D. C. Watt (eds), *Studies in International History*, 1967, p. 320.
12 *W.P.*, file 139/6.

13 *W.P.*, file 135/2, telegram from Wingate to Clayton, 30 Aug. 1915, and file 135/4, letter from Wingate to Clayton, 20 Oct. 1915.

14 *W.P.*, file 470/2, Wingate to Clayton, *Very Private*, 15 June 1916.

15 *W.P.*, file 135/6, where the English translation of the letters is preserved.

16 See E. Kedourie, *England and the Middle East*, 1956, p. 54.

17 Commander D. G. Hogarth, 'Position and Prospects of King Husein', *Arab Bulletin Supplementary Papers No. 2*, 1 March 1918.

18 Lt.-Col. C. E. Wilson, 'King of the Arabs', *Arab Bulletin Supplementary Papers No. 5*, 24 June 1918.

19 *W.P.*, file 135/5. Wingate advanced the same argument in a letter to General Callwell of 23 December, file 135/7.

20 *W.P.*, file 135/5, telegram from McMahon to Foreign Office repeated to Wingate in Clayton's telegram of 13 November 1915, and letter from Clayton to Wingate on 12 November.

21 *W.P.*, file 135/7, McMahon's telegram repeated to Wingate in Clayton's telegram of the same date.

22 See Kedourie, *England and the Middle East*, p. 36.

23 *W.P.*, file 135/4, Clayton's letter to Wingate of 9 October 1915, cited above.

24 See S. G. Haim, 'Islam and the Idea of Arab Nationalism' in W.Z. Laqueur (ed.), *The Middle East in Transition*, 1958.

25 See N. Bentwich, *Wanderer Between Two Worlds*, 1942, p. 75.

26 *W.P.*, file 135/6. Kitchener, it is interesting to remember, himself proposed buying the French out in the Levant in the autumn of 1915. On this and on the Alexandretta schemes, see Kedourie, *England and the Middle East*, pp. 43–6, and Nevakivi, *loc. cit.*

27 *W.P.*, file 135/6, letter from Parker to Clayton, 18 November 1915.

28 *W.P.*, file 135/6, *Results of Second Meeting of Committee to discuss Arab Question and Syria*.

29 *W.P.*, file 135/6, Parker to Clayton, 28 November 1915.

30 *W.P.*, file 135/7.

31 On this allocation of territory to the future Arab state see the illuminating paper by E. Marmorstein 'A Note on "Damascus, Homs, Hama and Aleppo"', in *St. Antony's Papers no. XI*, 1961, where the author convincingly argues that the plan, originating with Sir Mark Sykes, is an echo of a paragraph in Gibbon's *Decline and Fall* which described the limits of Muslim territory after the initial conquests of the Crusaders. Evidence to confirm Mr Marmorstein's view occurs in a passage by Rashid Rida in which he says that in June 1917 he heard from one of Sir Mark Sykes's Syrian collaborators 'that he understood from Sir Mark Sykes himself that they wanted to give the whole Syrian littoral to France because this was the

territory which the Crusaders had occupied during the famous Crusades'; *al-Manar*, XXII (1921), p. 452.

32 *W.P.*, file 135/2.

33 *W.P.*, file 135/4, dispatch from McMahon to Grey, 26 October 1915.

34 In a letter of 1 November 1915, Wingate informs Clayton that he had discussed the boundaries offered to the sharif with al-Mirghani and explained to him why reservations to the sharif's proposals concerning Syria, Palestine and Mesopotamia had to be made (*W.P.*, file 135/5).

35 *W.P.*, file 136/1, letter to Clayton, 20 January 1916.

36 *W.P.*, file 470/2, Wingate to Clayton, 24 April 1916.

37 *W.P.*, file 136/6, letter to Wingate, 22 May 1916.

38 D. G. Hogarth, 'Wahabism and British Interests', *Journal of the British Institute of International Affairs*, IV (1925), pp. 72, 73.

39 *W.P.*, file 135/5, note by Storrs, 12 November 1915.

40 *W.P.*, file 143/3, telegram from C. E. Wilson, Jedda, to Wingate, 13 November 1916; file 143/1, telegram from McMahon to Wingate, 14 November, and file 143A/6, letter from Clayton to Wingate, 23 November.

41 *W.P.*, file 136/2, verbal message attached to note by Storrs, 26 February 1916.

42 *W.P.*, file 136/5, telegram from Wingate to Clayton, 23 April 1916.

43 *W.P.*, file 136/1.

44 *W.P.*, file 136/1, letter to Wingate, 17 January 1916.

45 *W.P.*, file 136/6, letter to Wingate, 8 May 1916.

46 *W.P.*, file 136/2, letter to Ibrahim Dimitri, 28 February 1916. A note by Storrs of 5 December 1915 (file 135/7) records that Rashid Rida called at the residency in Cairo and was given details of the offer to Husain, of the ambiguity of which he complained.

47 *W.P.*, file 135/9. The note is unsigned and undated.

48 See Kedourie, *England and the Middle East*, p. 62.

49 *Ibid.*, pp. 113–5.

50 *W.P.*, file 145/3, note by Clayton, 10 March 1917, commenting on a request by Sykes to assemble Arab delegates to meet him on a forthcoming journey to Cairo.

51 *W.P.*, file 139/5, letter of 7 August 1916.

52 *W.P.*, file 145/3, telegram from Foreign Office to high commissioner, Cairo, 14 March 1917.

53 *W.P.*, file 145/4, memorandum by Clayton, 3 April 1917.

54 See Kedourie, *England and the Middle East*, pp. 37–8 and 97–8.

55 *W.P.*, file 145/7, memo. by Clayton for Symes, 27 May 1917.

56 *W.P.*, file 139/3, telegram from Wilson, Jadda, to Wingate, 9 August 1916.

57 The sharif's words recorded in a note by Fuad al-Khatib, the deputy

foreign minister, taken down by Lieutenant-Colonel Newcombe, *W.P.*, 145/7.

58 *W.P.*, file 145/7, memo. by Wilson, 24–7 May 1917.

59 This was apparently the length of the last interview. Sykes and Picot saw the sharif in Jadda on 18 and 19 May, but Sykes had seen both Faisal and the sharif on 2 and 5 May respectively, and explained to them the topics which would be discussed on his return with Picot (*W.P.*, file 145/7, telegram from high commissioner, Cairo, to Foreign Office, 8 May 1917).

60 *W.P.*, file 145/7, note by Lieutenant-Colonel Newcombe, 20 March 1917.

61 *al-Manar*, XXXIII (1933), p. 797.

62 *W.P.*, file 148/8, letter to Wingate, 21 April 1918.

63 *W.P.*, file 146/1, note on the *Anglo–Franco–Russian Agreement about the Near East*, by D. G. Hogarth, 9 July 1917; a letter from Wingate to Hogarth of 12 August 1917 (file 146/3) indicates that the note was written to be shown to the authorities in London.

64 See *W.P.*, file 145/8, particularly dispatch from Wingate to Balfour, 11 June 1917.

65 *W.P.*, file 146/10, telegram to Foreign Office, 28 November 1917.

66 *W.P.*, file 149/1, dispatch from Clayton, 1 July 1918.

67 See Kedourie, *England and the Middle East*, pp. 111–2.

68 *W.P.*, file 148/12, telegram to Foreign Office, 16 June 1918.

69 Dispatch of 21 September 1918 from Wingate, Cairo (*W.P.*, file 149/7).

70 *Austen Chamberlain Papers* (Box AC 20). Sir Keith Hancock in his *Smuts*, vol. I, 1962, indicates (pp. 498–9), that both L. S. Amery, then a member of the war cabinet Offices, and Smuts himself, were opposed to the Sykes–Picot Agreement. Smuts considered it 'a hopeless blunder of policy'. See also W. K. Hancock and Jean van der Poel (eds.), *Selections from the Smuts Papers*, 1966, vols III and IV, which reproduce letters from Amery to Smuts dealing with the middle eastern settlement: nos 820 and 848 in vol. III, and particularly no. 861 in vol. IV, a letter of 19 November 1918 where Amery insists on the necessity of taking French acquisition of Alsace–Lorraine into account: 'It may be justice that she should get it. But the fact remains that she gets an asset of very great value for which all the rest of us have fought and suffered enormous losses. If France gets nothing but Alsace–Lorraine and the rest of us divide up the German colonies and the near east, we shall still be heavy losers financially, and it doesn't seem to me equitable that France should claim, in addition to Alsace–Lorraine, a share in such small "profits" as there may be, unless she is also prepared to pool the total expenses'; in another letter of 17 December (no. 866 in vol. IV)

Amery writes: 'I see no reason . . . why Palestine, the Arab state [in Syria] and Mesopotamia should not find their welfare in permanent association with the British League of Free Nations . . .'.

71 *W.P.*, file 151/2.

72 U.S. Department of State Archives, telegrams from Laughlin to Lansing, London, 10 and 14 October 1918 (767.90b14/1 and 2).

73 *W.P.*, file 148/10, note by G. S. Symes, 13 June 1918.

74 *Tour of Duty*, 1946, p. 50.

75 G. Puaux, *Deux années au Levant*, 1952, p. 176.

76 K. D. D. Henderson (ed.), 1953. The quotation is from a letter to J. W. Robertson, dated Cairo, 11 May 1943, p. 326.

3 The Capture of Damascus, 1 October 1918

1 Terence Rattigan: *Ross: A Dramatic Portrait*, 1960, p. 72.

2 *Ibid.*, p. 105.

3 Robert Graves, *T. E. Lawrence to his Biographer*, 1938, p. 104.

4 Monroe, p. 62. Miss Monroe gives neither the date nor the provenance of Clayton's report. The report is dated 8 October 1918; a copy of it is found in the *Milner Papers*, New College, Oxford, and in *W.P.*

5 Zeine, pp. 25–7.

6 Longrigg, p. 63.

7 See E. Kedourie, *England and the Middle East*, p. 121.

8 I am grateful to the Australian Army Headquarters, Canberra, for permission to consult these War Diaries and to the director, Australian War Memorial, for help in this connection. See appendix for a précis of events based on the diaries and compiled by me.

9 *Official History of Australia in the War 1914–1918*, vol. VII, *Sinai and Palestine*, by H. S. Gullett, 1935, p. 752.

10 *Official History of the War, Military Operations in Egypt and Palestine from June 1917 to the end of the War*, by Cyril Falls, part II, pp. 573–4.

11 Gullett, p. 752.

12 Gullett, pp. 758–62; Kedourie, *England and the Middle East*, pp. 120–1.

13 Gullett, p. 764.

14 Kedourie, *England and the Middle East*, pp. 113–7.

15 Muhammad Kurd Ali, *Khitat al-Sham* (History of Syria), Damascus, 1925, vol. III, pp. 149 fn., and 154.

16 *Seven Pillars of Wisdom* (1935 ed.), p. 675.

17 See Kedourie, *England and the Middle East*, p. 121, where the bulletin is quoted from the Yale Papers. This bulletin seems to have been issued by Allenby's G.H.Q. in a news summary on 2 October. I am indebted for this information to Dr M. Vereté, Hebrew University, Jerusalem.

18 U.K. Admiralty, *The International Situation and General Intelligence*,

NOTES

no. 336, 1 to 3 October 1918, p. 10, Bodleian Library, Oxford.

19 U.S. National Archives, Department of State, *Weekly Report on Matters Relating to Near Eastern Affairs*, 17 October 1918, no. 37, p. 40.

20 Falls, p. 591 fn. In a popular account of Allenby's campaign, *Armageddon 1918*, 1964, p. 145, Captain Falls repeats the account of the official history, writing, 'Australians and Arabs both claim to have entered first, but the issue remains undecided'. The book throws no light on the events here discussed.

21 House of Commons *Debates*, 31 October 1918, col. 1640.

22 A detail mentioned in the British war history (p. 591) is curious. Lawrence, it says, went into Damascus at 7.30 in the morning and General Macandrew with the 14th Cavalry Brigade followed him into the city at 10.30. Why, if 'we, the Arab leaders had waited for the slower British', Macandrew should, in the end, still be preceded into Damascus by the Sharifians is not clear. Can this be the origin of 'the oft-repeated story' that the entry of the British troops was delayed, which Mr Longrigg, as has been seen, refuses to credit?

23 *Seven Pillars*, pp. 600, 684, 636, 664, 668–9.

24 *Ibid.*, pp. 664–6.

25 *Ibid.*, p. 664.

26 W. F. Stirling, 'Tales of Lawrence of Arabia', *The Cornhill*, vol. 74, 1933, p. 509: 'Lord Allenby had allowed Lawrence twenty-four hours to organise and instal a provisional government before the British troops were to be permitted into Damascus'.

27 Wajih al-Haffar, 'Al-hukamāt allati ta'aqabat 'ala al-hikm fi Suriya – I' (The Successive Governments of Syria), in *Majallat al-shurta wa'l-amn* (Police and Public Security Magazine), vol. I, no. 6, 15 June 1953, pp. 18 ff. I am grateful to Professor Salah al-Din al-Munajjid for drawing my attention to this valuable series of articles of which the first is quoted here. The author draws on local knowledge and unpublished papers.

28 Note by Captain C. D. Brunton, General Staff Intelligence, Palestine, 13 August 1921, Palestine Government file Pol/2223, Israel State Archives.

29 'An Autobiography' by General Chauvel, typescript, pp. 142–5, Australian War Memorial, Canberra. I am grateful to the Director of the Memorial for allowing me to consult this typescript. The Director states that there is no record of the date on which it was written, or of that on which it was deposited at the Memorial. The same story emerges from a report by Chauvel of 2 October 1918 in W.O.95/4371, file Z/96 which makes it utterly clear that Ayyubi was Lawrence's nominee.

30 Haffar, *ibid*, and Anis al-Nusuli, '*Ishtu wa shahhadtu* (I Have Lived and Seen), Beirut 1951, p. 16.

31 *Seven Pillars*, p. 672.

32 Alec Seath Kirkbride, *A Crackle of Thorns*, 1956, pp. 8–9. See also the report of an eye-witness, Ali al-Tantawi, *Fi bilad al-Arab* (In the Arab Countries), 1939, p. 53: 'We said, Who is the sharif? They said, Faisal son of al-Husain, so hasten to give him welcome. We rose up, but we did not go to welcome him. We went to slaughter the fleeing army. When we finished with them we wiped their blood off our hands and went to welcome the sharif'. Also, Abd al-Fattah abul-Nasr al Yafi, *Mudhakkirat qa'id arabi* (Memoirs of an Arab Commander), n.p., n.d., who states, p. 207, that the Ottoman commander had undertaken not to destroy anything in Damascus and had been promised that his troops would not be molested during their retreat through Damascus. He goes on to say that this promise was not kept, that the soldiers were 'butchered' in many places, and that but for the Jaza'iris' intervention none of the Ottoman troops would have escaped. 'An eye-witness has told me', he goes on to say, 'that Damascenes were throwing the weak and wounded, who were in a lamentable condition, over the balcony of the military hospital'.

33 A pamphlet published in Beirut in 1921, Hanna abu Rāshid, *Layali al-'id fi waqa'i' al-Amir Sa'id* (Festival Nights in Celebration of Amir Sa'id's Exploits), may throw some light on this enmity. The author states that Lawrence's enmity towards the Jaza'iris stemmed from the fact that he suspected them of having friendly relations with the French, and feared that if they were in a position to gain Faisal's ear, they would influence him in favour of the French connection. It seems a likely explanation.

34 Haffar, *loc. cit.*, gives the text of Nasir's mandate to Amir Sa'id al-Jaza'iri.

35 Copy in *W.P.*, file 149/7. The reference to French liaison officers is explained by a telegram from the War Office dated 25 September (a copy of which is found in the same file) in which they tell Allenby that they had informed the French that 'it would be desirable if General Allenby advances to Damascus, that, in conformity with Anglo–French agreement of 1916, he should, if possible, work through an Arab administration by means of a French Liaison Officer'.

36 Letter reproduced in Muhammad Jamil Bayhum, *Suriya wa Lubnan 1918–1922* (Syria and Lebanon 1918-1922), Beirut, 1968, pp. 74–5.

37 Anwar al-Rifa'i, *Jihad nisf qarn* (Half a Century of Struggle), Damascus, n.d., p. 93.

38 *Arab Bulletin*, no. 64, 27 September 1917.

39 Anwar al-Rifa'i, *Jihad nisf qarn*. This book contains an interesting collection of documents relating to the Jaza'iri brothers and their relations with Faisal and the Sharifians. Faisal's war-time letters to Sa'id and the Ottoman commander of the Fourth Army in 1917 are

reproduced on pp. 87–92; the affair of the Sharifian standard is
mentioned on p. 79, and the text of the proclamation issued when the
Jaza'iris took over from the Ottomans in Damascus is reproduced on
pp. 99–101.

40 See appendix, below, and Kedourie, *England and the Middle East*,
pp. 122–7. W. T. Massey, a journalist accompanying Allenby's
forces, deserves great praise. His narrative in *Allenby's Final
Triumph*, 1920, sober and unpretentious, is confirmed in all essentials
by the other sources and official documents. This is all the more
worth saying that in *Seven Pillars* Lawrence dismisses with a contemptuous tone the journalists' reports about the Damascus
disorders.

41 Kirkbride, *A Crackle of Thorns*, p. 9.

42 Sir Hugh Foot, *A Start in Freedom*, 1964, p. 72.

4 Sir Herbert Samuel and the Government of Palestine

1 Quoted in John Bowle, *Viscount Samuel*, 1957, p. 171.

2 Quoted in Bowle, *Viscount Samuel*, p. 176.

3 Viscount Samuel, *Memoirs*, 1945, p. 148.

4 F.O. 800/215, Balfour Papers, Samuel to Balfour, 27 March 1919.

5 *Report of the High Commissioner on the Administration of Palestine
1920–1925, Colonial no. 15*, 1925, p. 27.

6 pp. 150–1.

7 p. 168.

8 113 H.L. Deb. 5s., col. 99.

9 See memo. by Middle East Department of the Colonial Office,
16 February 1923, in Cab.27/222.

10 *P.P. vol. XV (1921), An Interim Report on the Civil Administration of
Palestine during the period 1st July 1920–30 June 1921*, Cmd. 1499.

11 106 H.L. Deb. 5s. col. 807.

12 Telegram from Allenby to Curzon, Very Urgent, Private and very
Confidential. Cairo, 6 May 1920; *Documents on British Foreign Policy,
1919-1939* First Series, vol. XIII, 1963, no. 246.

13 Chief Political Officer, Cairo, 9 October 1919, to Chief Administrator,
Occupied Enemy Territories (South), Palestine Government file
Pol/2108, Israel State Archives.

14 F.O. 371/5121, file E 9379/85/44, which contains the full Report of
the Court of Enquiry.

15 See the Report of the Court of Enquiry mentioned above and
Allenby's telegrams, 8 and 18 Mar. 1920, reproduced in *Documents
on British Foreign Policy 1919–1939*, First Series, vol. XIII, nos 216
and 223. In an undated draft memorandum on the Jerusalem riots
of May 1920, Storrs mentioned the presence in Jerusalem at that time

of unauthorised Sharifian officers in close touch with the local authorities, whose activities no attempt was made to shackle. *Storrs Papers*, Pembroke College, Cambridge, box III/1.

16 See E. Kedourie, *Afghani and 'Abduh*, 1966, pp. 37–8.

17 In view of Hajj Amin's subsequent connection with the Nazis, and of their sponsorship of the 'Gross-Mufti' as a leader of all the Arabs, this remark by Grobba, the German minister at Baghdad in the 1930s, is of interest: 'Although', he writes in his memoirs (*Männer und Mächte im Orient*, 1967, p. 9), 'I know that the rank of a Grand Mufti does not exist in Islam, I have nevertheless described Hajj Amin al-Husaini as Grand Mufti because he is known as such in Germany'.

18 Summary of the law in an address by Samuel of July 1921, copy of which is found in C.O. 733/54 appendix to a dispatch, secret, Jerusalem, 9 August 1921. The law dates from 1326; presumably this is the Ottoman financial, and not the *hijri* year and therefore corresponds to *c.* 1910.

19 Palestine government file Pol./2287, for texts and translations of these petitions.

20 These two dates are given by Hajj Amin in two different applications for a passport; Palestine government file no. H/582, Israel State Archives.

21 *Report* of the Royal Commission on Palestine, cmd. 5479 (1937), p. 177; Report of the Court of Enquiry into the Easter Disturbances, Jerusalem 1920, F.O. 371/5121.

22 Palestine government file C.S. 106/1, Israel State Archives. A note by Storrs's 'little Persian agent Ruhi' (see Ronald Storrs, *Orientations*, definitive ed., 1943, p. 149) states that it was at his suggestion that Samuel pardoned Hajj Amin. Ruhi, it would seem, either accompanied Samuel or was sent ahead of him to Salt; *Storrs Papers*, box III/5.

23 Palestine government file Pol./2223, Israel State Archives.

24 Pol./2287

25 Pol./2287.

26 Storrs, *Orientations*, p. 334. An entry in Storrs's Diary of 22 December 1917 speaks of the mufti Kamil as being a 'Mufti by right of descent'; *Storrs Papers* Pembroke College, Cambridge, box II/5.

27 N. and H. Bentwich, *Mandate Memories*, 1965, p. 191, suggest that the lay members of the electoral college cast their votes under the influence of Raghib al-Nashashibi. The number of votes cast for Hajj Amin is indicated in a note by Dr M. D. Eder of the Zionist Commission giving details of an interview with the Civil Secretary on 21 April; it was the Civil Secretary who informed Eder that the government was surprised by Jarallah's election; D. M. Eder, Notes from Letters and Reports, 1919–21, Zionist Central Archives, Jerusalem, Collections 11/41.

28 Pol./2287, and C.O. 733/3 dispatch no. 92, Secret, 9 May 1921 (Political Report for April).

29 Translation of the notice in Pol/2287.

30 C.O. 733/3, dispatch no. 52, secret, cited above.

31 Storrs, *Orientations*, p. 313.

32 There is a hint of this in Storrs, *Orientations*, p. 320.

33 F.O. 371/5267, file E. 9433/8343/44 and F.O. 371/5268, files E.11720, 11835/8343/44.

34 C.O. 733/28, private letter from Samuel to Shuckburgh enclosed with confidential dispatch, 27 December 1922.

35 C.O. 733/47, Dispatch, Confidential, from Clayton, 6 July 1923.

36 C.O. 733/28, minutes on conference, dispatch of 27 December 1922, cited above.

37 Samuel Correspondence, Israel State Archives. I am very grateful to Sir John Richmond for permission to quote from this letter.

38 Pol./2287.

39 Pol./2287, letter of 10 May 1921, in Arabic signed by Jarallah, on behalf of the legal secretary, informing Hajj Amin that in view of Jarallah's withdrawal the high commissioner had appointed him mufti of Jerusalem. The document was probably to be used if the high commissioner proved agreeable but it is clear that no use was made of it since, as will be seen, Hajj Amin never received a letter of appointment.

40 Pol./2287. It may be that Storrs seconded Richmond's efforts on behalf of the mufti for the memo ends: 'It is worth noting that notwithstanding that it is known that your Excellency and Mr Deedes have both assured Hajj Amin of his appointment, Ragheb Nashashibi continues to state openly that at all costs this shall be prevented. Mr Bentwich confirms the continued efforts of Ragheb Nashashibi in this direction. I have informed the governor of Jerusalem who has spoken to him on the subject', Bentwich, *Mandate Memories*, p. 191, declare that Storrs, with Richmond, persuaded Samuel to appoint Hajj Amin.

41 Palestine Royal Commission, *Report*, p. 177.

42 Pol./2287, Richmond's letter of 20 October 1921 to the high commissioner. See also his note to the financial secretary of 2 August 1921 and his letter to the civil secretary of 25 October 1921. Richmond's argument for the primacy of the mufti of Jerusalem was that in Ottoman times the *sanjak* of Jerusalem was not subordinated to any *vilayet* and was attached directly to Istanbul. This of course established no more than that the mufti of Jerusalem was on a par with the mufti of any other *vilayet*. Richmond also had recourse to a piece of rhetoric which he attributed to Storrs to the effect that Jerusalem was a place of 'some special renown and honour'.

43 Palestine government file Pol./445/A, Israel State Archives.

44 111 H.L.Deb. 5s., 8 December 1938, col. 423.

45 p.167.

46 R. Meinertzhagen, *Middle East Diary, 1917–1956*, 1959, p. 58.

47 F.O. 800/215. Balfour Papers.

48 C.O. 537/855.

49 C.O. 537/852. Deedes to Shuckburgh, Jerusalem, 22 November 1921. In his evidence before the cabinet committee set up in 1923 to consider Palestine policy Samuel stated that before the mandate went through he considered whether Art. 4 (which gave the Zionist organisation a special and privileged status) 'ought not to be eliminated'. Weizmann however was 'excessively alarmed and said that their prestige would be gone'. If Art. 4 were removed, the movement would 'almost come to an end' as this would be taken to mean that the British government had gone back on its promises. Therefore, Samuel added, nothing was done at the time: See Cab. 27/222, meeting of 9 July 1923.

50 Palestine Government Gazette, no. 43, p. 4.

51 C.O. 738/8, dispatch no. 551, 29 December 1921.

52 p. 181. In a letter of 10 April 1937 to the secretary of the Royal Commission on Palestine, the chief secretary of Palestine stated that the income from *awqaf* properties amounted then to LP67,799; in addition the president of the Supreme Moslem Council controlled some LP50,000, being funds administered on behalf of minors and orphans. The president also controlled 'considerable' amounts of money donated by Muslims abroad for the repair of Muslim holy places and the relief of poor Muslims: for instance, the money collected for the repair of the Aqsa mosque amounted to LP120,000. The council appointed seventeen judges of Shari'a courts, five muftis, thirty-eight clerks, and twenty-eight process-servers. The council also appointed marriage officers in towns and villages who received fees rather than salaries. See C.O. 733/347, file 75550/57. In addition of course, the council had in its gift numerous posts relating to the management of the religious endowments.

53 The *Report* of the Royal Commission on Palestine describes briefly (pp. 179–81) how this situation was allowed to develop from 1921 to 1936.

54 *Op. cit.*, 1938, pp. 168–9.

55 Israel State Archives, file no. 2630.

56 See for instance, Friday sermons by Shaikh Abd al-Qadir al-Muzaffar and Shaikh Sai'd al-Khatib quoted in appendix D.I. to the Political Report for March 1923, C.O. 733/44.

57 Colonial no. 15 (1925), p. 45.

58 Letter from Jamal al-Husaini, 30 March 1923, enclosed with dispatch

from Samuel, no. 596, 15 June 1923, included in Cab. 27/222.

59 *P.P. vol. XXV (1923), Palestine: Papers relating to the Elections for the Palestine Legislative Council 1923*, Cmd. 1889, p. 9.

60 C.O. 733/42.

61 C.O. 733/43, minute of 13 March 1923 on telegram dated 10 March reporting on the boycott.

62 Samuel's dispatch, no. 596, 15 June 1923, in Cab. 27/22.

63 C.O. 733/50, Samuel's telegram of 11 October 1923.

64 Note of an interview with officials of the Arab executive, 30 November 1931, Israel State Archives, *'Awni Abd al-Hadi Papers*, box 155.

65 This scheme with which Colonel Waters-Taylor, Bols's chief-of-staff, was connected may have been a factor in precipitating the Easter riots at Jerusalem shortly afterwards; see the report of the Court of Enquiry into the Easter disturbances, F.O. 371/5121.

66 Samuel to Curzon, 2 April 1920, *Documents on British Foreign Policy 1919–1939*, first series, vol. XIII, no. 235.

67 Samuel to Curzon, 14 May 1920; Samuel Correspondence, Israel State Archives.

68 The correspondence between Samuel, the Colonial Office and the Foreign Office is quoted from Palestine government file Pol./435/1, Israel State Archives.

69 C.O. 733/320, telegram from chief Secretary, 23 November 1936.

70 C.O. 733/320, copy of telegram from Foreign Office to Sir A. Clark Kerr, 28 November 1936.

71 C.O. 733/20, copy of telegram to Sir M. Lampson, 16 November 1936.

72 Ormsby-Gore to Samuel, 15 September 1936; Samuel Correspondence, Israel State Archives.

73 Alan Houghton Brodrick, *Near to Greatness: A Life of the Sixth Earl Winterton*, 1965, pp. 183–4.

74 106 H.L.Deb. 5s., 20 July and 21 July 1937, cols. 642 and 815.

75 Samuel to the colonial secretary, 7 April 1938, Samuel Correspondence, Israel State Archives.

76 Note by Samuel of a meeting with MacDonald at the Colonial Office, 17 October 1938; Samuel Correspondence, Israel State Archives.

77 111 H.L.Deb., 5s., 8 December 1938, cols. 427–8.

5 Sa'd Zaghlul and the British

1 The article is reproduced in Abbas Mahmud al-'Aqqad, *Sa'd Zaghlul*, Cairo, 1936, pp. 65–6.

2 In his *Report* on Egypt for 1905, Egypt No. 1 (1906), Cmd. 2817, *British Parliamentary Papers*, vol. CXXXVII, 1906, pp. 15–6.

3 See Muhammad Rashid Rida, *Tarikh al-ustadh al-imam* (History of the Teacher and Leader [i.e. Muhammad Abduh]), vol. I, 1931, p. 593.

NOTES

4 Ahmad Shafiq Pasha, *Mudhakkirati fi nisf qarn* (My Memoirs of Half a Century), 1936, vol. II, part 2, p. 72.
5 Ahmad Shafiq, Memoirs, pp. 102, 112 and 129.
6 C. C. Adams, *Islam and Modernism in Egypt*, 1933, p. 229.
7 The address is printed in 'Aqqad, pp. 154–5.
8 Kitchener's letter to Grey, 7 March 1912; F.O. 800/48, Grey Papers.
9 This is suggested by F. Charles-Roux, 'L'Egypte de l'occupation anglaise á l'independence egyptienne', in G. Hanotaux, *Histoire de la nation egyptienne*, vol. VII, 1940, p. 228. This was also the opinion of the nationalist leader Muhammad Farid; see Muhammad Subayh, *Mawaqif hāsima fi tarikh al-qawmiyya al-arabiyya* (Decisive Episodes in the History of Arab Nationalism), 1964, vol. 2 (which reproduces large extracts from Muhammad Farid's memoirs), p. 271.
10 Muhammad Farid memoirs in Subayh, Decisive Episodes, p. 271.
11 Later on in the session, Zaghlul was taxed by fellow-members with raising a hue and cry about the *awqaf*, while he made no objection of any kind to the setting-up of a Ministry of Agriculture which raised identical issues. His rejoinder was lame, laboured and sophistical; see Government Egyptien, Assemblée legislative, *Recueil des comptes-rendus des séances, session 1913–14*, Cairo, 1914, *passim* and Ahmad Lutfi Hafiz, *Sa'd Zaghlul fi hayatihi al-niyabiyya* (Sa'd Zaghlul's Parliamentary Life), Cairo, 1927, vol. I, pp. 148–62.
12 Memorandum reproduced in *Documents Collected for the Information of the Special Mission Appointed to Enquire into the Situation in Egypt*, vol. I, pp. 89 ff., F.O. 848/1.
13 F.O. 407/182, nos. 21 and 23, telegrams of 28 March and 4 April 1914.
14 Ahmad Shafiq, Memoirs, pp. 272, 350.
15 *Documents Collected for ... the Special Mission ...*, vol 2, p. 138, telegrams from Cheetham to Grey, 12 December 1914, and Grey's answer, 15 December F.O. 848/1.
16 *Documents Collected for ... the Special Mission ...*, vol. 2, p. 24, note by Sir W. Brunyate enclosed with dispatch from Wingate, 24 Nov. 1918, F.O. 848/1.
17 Letter from Wingate to Hardinge, 29 November 1917, *W.P.*, 146/8.
18 *Documents Collected for ... the Special Mission ...*, vol. I, pp. 193–5, telegram from Wingate, 9 December 1917, and telegram from Balfour, 13 December, F.O. 848/1.
19 Wingate's letter to Sir R. Graham, 9 June 1918, *W.P.*, box 163.
20 'Since these two interviews [with Zaghlul and with Husain Rushdi on 13 November] which were evidently part of a pre-arranged plan of campaign of which the sultan was – at any rate to some extent – cognisant ...'. Wingate's dispatch, confidential, 20 November 1918, F.O. 407/183, no. 147.

21 *Documents Collected for . . . the Special Mission . . .*, vol. 1, pp. 165–6, F.O. 848/1, dispatch from Wingate, 23 July 1917.

22 As Lord Lloyd put it in *Egypt since Cromer*, 1933, vol. I, p. 259.

23 F.O. 848/2, letter from Wingate to Hardinge, 3 November 1917.

24 Minute by Cheetham, 31 August 1918, on a note by Greg, director-general of the Egyptian Ministry of Foreign Affairs, enclosed with confidential dispatch from Wingate, of same date, F.O. 407/183, no. 133.

25 Letter from Wingate to Graham, 24 March 1918, *W.P.*, and dispatch, very confidential, from Wingate, 31 August 1918, F.O. 407/183, no. 134.

26 Dispatch of 31 August 1918, F.O. 407/183, no. 134.

27 Letter from Wingate to Hardinge, 19 October 1918, *W.P.* In a dispatch of 8 October previous Wingate wrote: 'Since Sultan Fuad succeeded I have observed a tendency on his part both to deprecate the authority of his ministers and to neglect some of the essential facts of the protectorate.'

28 F.O. 407/183, no. 134.

29 Letter from Wingate to Hardinge, 6 November 1918, *W.P.*

30 Sir Charles Petrie, *Life and Letters of Sir Austen Chamberlain*, 1940, vol. 2, p. 341.

31 'Note on the Main Points which have given rise to the Present situation in Egypt', October 1919, *W.P.*

32 Wingate to Hardinge, 31 January 1917, *W.P.*

33 *Documents Collected for . . . The Special Mission . . .*, vol. 1, pp. 198, 201ff., note by Brunyate 14 November 1917, enclosed with dispatch from Wingate, 15 December; and letter from Wingate to Hardinge, 24 December. F.O. 848/1.

34 F.O. 407/184, no. 246, note by an anonymous Englishman, enclosed with dispatch from Allenby, 7 April 1919, W. G. Hayter, a legal adviser both to the residency and to the Egyptian government, in the course of a letter dealing with Brunyate's pension, stated that Brunyate's memo. was 'improperly' publicised by Rushdi together with his reply; F.O. 371/3729, file 139282, letter from Hayter to Sir J. Tilley, 19 October 1919.

35 See for instance his conversation with Haines, 8 December 1918: 'He said that for four years he had been reproached with having been a traitor to his country . . .', *Documents Collected for . . . the Special Mission . . .*, vol. 2, p. 57, F.O. 848/1.

36 'Umar Tusun, *Mudhakkira bima sadara 'anna mundh fajr al-haraka al-wataniyya al-misriyya min sanat 1918 ila sanat 1928* (Memorandum on our activities since the dawn of the Egyptian national movement from the year 1918 to the year 1928), 1942, pp. 4–10.

37 Fu'ad asked Cheetham to deport 'Umar Tusun, calling him undesirable 'as he felt he was an aspirant for the throne and was
   plotting against him'; Wingate's letter to Hardinge, 18 November
   1918, *Documents Collected for . . . the Special Mission . . .*, vol. 2,
   p. 12, F.O. 848/1.

38 *Documents Collected for . . . the Special Mission . . .*, vol. 2, p. 37,
   dispatch from Wingate, 28 November 1918, F.O. 848/1.

39 See memo. by the Coptic notable Gallini Fahmi, no. 8A, in F.O.
   848/8.

40 Abd al-Aziz Fahmi, *Hadhihi hayati* (This is my life), 1963, pp. 72–3.
   Zaghlul himself confirmed Rushdi's and Aldi's encouragement in an
   interview of 1926 with Ahmad Shafiq; see his *A'mali ba'd mudhakkirati* (My activities after [the publication of] my memoirs), Cairo
   1941, pp. 251–2. Ahmad Shafiq also states (*loc. cit.*) that according
   to Lutfi al-Sayyid, Zaghlul was terrified of the possibility of being
   executed by the British under martial law, and asked for a society
   to be formed which would defend them if they were arrested. See
   also al-Manar, vol. xx (1921), pp. 499–500.

41 Note by Husain Rushdi Pasha, 13 December 1918, *W.P.*

42 Muhammad Husain Haikal, *Mudhakkirat* (Memoirs), vol. 1, Cairo
   1951, p. 82.

43 Letter from Sir R. Graham to Wingate, January 1919, F.O. 848/2;
   also telegrams from Wingate 25 November 1918 and from Balfour
   to Wingate 2 December., F.O. 407/183, nos. 144 and 146.

44 He and his immediate subordinates in the residency possibly had a
   shrewd suspicion of the purpose of the visit, see note by Captain
   Alexander, Wingate's *aide-de-camp*, 25 March 1919, F.O. 848/2.

45 Residency, Cairo, to Foreign Office, telegram, 11 January 1919,
   W.P.

46 Wingate to Balfour, 5 December 1918; Wingate to Graham, 22
   December; note of meeting with sultan, 1 January 1919, *W.P.* A
   typical interview with Fu'ad is recorded by Wingate in a note of
   13 December. 'Again and again', wrote Wingate, 'he affirmed with
   much heat that it was contrary to liberal British ideas to stifle this
   legitimate struggle for freedom and I became more and more convinced that he must have lent considerable support to the views of
   the Extremists.

   I was confirmed in this impression by the fact that when I used the
   word "extremist" in speaking of the pretensions of Zaghlul and his
   party, His Highness affirmed that they represented the truly patriotic
   Egyptian spirit.' Fu'ad, Wingate also wrote, 'continued to insist on
   the birth of real patriotism throughout the length and breadth of the
   land and the necessity of satisfying these national aspirations.' *W.P.*

47 This is what 'Aqqad states, *Sa'd Zaghlul*, p. 205.

NOTES

48 *Egypt Since Cromer*, vol. I, p. 281. A letter of 31 January 1917 in the *Storrs Papers* which seems by Storrs himself contains some very derogatory remarks about Haines, box II/4.

49 Haines to Wingate, 25 November 1918, *W.P.*

50 vol. I, p. 86

51 Ahmad Shafiq, *Hauliyyat Misr al-siyasiyya, Tamhid* (Annual Survey of Egyptian Politics, Introduction), 1926, vol. 1, p. 177.

52 Residency, Cairo, to Foreign Office, telegram of 5 December 1918, *W.P.*

53 Brunyate to Wingate, 15 December 1918, *W.P.*

54 'Note on Unrest in Egypt', by Sir Ronald Graham, 9 April 1919, F.O. 407/184, no. 152*.

55 The instances are found in Tawwaf (pseud.), *Egypt, 1919*, 1925, who records incidents in Bani Suef and Aswan; in Ahmad Shafiq, *Hauliyyat, Tamhid*, vol. 1, p. 508, who records the arrest of the vice-governor of Minia Province, its director of the Parquet and judge, who were accused of rebellion against the government; and in a note sent by a notable of Bani Mazar to Milner while he was in Egypt with his mission, which records with circumstantial detail the incitement of a government official, who encouraged the people to attack British troops. Cf. *Milner Papers*, New College, Oxford.

56 Wingate's telegram of 17 November 1918, F.O. 407/183, no. 142.

57 Wingate's telegram of 16 January 1919, F.O. 407/184, no. 23.

58 *Documents Collected for . . . the Special Mission . . .*, vol. 2, pp. 68–70, F.O. 848/1.

59 Gertrude Bell's Egypt Diary, entry for 30 September 1919, *Gertrude Bell Papers*, University of Newcastle.

60 F.O. 407/184, no. 55.

61 Quoted in Ahmad Baha' al-Din, *Ayyam laha tarikh* (Historic Days), Cairo 1954 (1959 edn.), p. 113. French text of the letter enclosed with Cheetham's dispatch of 15 March 1919, F.O. 407/184, no. 74.

62 F.O. 407/184, nos 64, 65 and 69; telegrams from Cheetham, 6 March 1919, from F.O., 7 March, and from Cheetham, 9 March respectively.

63 *Documents Collected for . . . the Special Mission . . .*, vol. 2, pp. 115–6, 119, F.O. 848/1.

64 *Documents Collected for . . . the Special Mission . . .*, vol. 1, p. 247, F.O. 848/1. In a letter to Milner of 29 December 1919, Wingate admitted that the recruitment of volunteers and the requisition of supplies 'must invariably partake of the nature of exactions'. F.O. 848/2.

65 See the numerous memoranda on the grievances of the fellaheen in the papers of the Milner Mission, particularly a memorandum by Rennell Rodd (a member of the mission) summarising evidence on

these grievances submitted to the mission, in F.O. 848/8. See also the memoranda and letters sent by Somers Clarke in F.O. 848/4 and F.O. 848/11. Clarke's views were also published in a pamphlet, *The Unrest in Egypt*, Cairo 1920, which is one of the best descriptions of the impact of the war on the Egyptian peasant.

66 *Economic Effect of the War in Egypt – Review of Financial Effect*, Memorandum by L. G. Roussin, May 1919.

67 F.O. 848/6. See also in F.O. 848/8, a memorandum entitled 'Suggestions for a note on social relations in Egypt'. The title is sufficient indication of the drop in the standards of British administration which the war brought about. In his *Reminiscences* (1923) the archaeologist A. H. Sayce also remarks (p. 455), on the bad impression which the proletarian manners of the conscript armies made on the Egyptians.

68 F.O. 407/184, no. 87.

69 F.O. 407/184, no. 82.

70 F.O. 407/184, no. 83.

71 F.O. 407/184, no. 87 quoted above.

72 Telegram from Gary, Cairo, 18 March 1919, 883.00/97.

73 F.O. 407/184, no. 84.

74 F.O. 371/3714, file 41615.

75 F.O. 608/213, file 662/1/8, minute dated 17 March.

76 F.O. 608/213, file 662/1/8, minute of 17 March.

77 F.O. 608/213, file 662/1/8.

78 *Balfour Papers*, British Museum Add. Ms. 49734, telegram of 18 March.

79 Curzon's strictures are quoted in Leonard Mosley, *The Glorious Fault: the Life of Lord Curzon*, 1960, pp. 236–7.

80 F.O. 848/2.

81 F.O. 371/3714, file 42439.

82 F.O. 407/184, nos 92 and 103.

83 F.O. 371/4714, file 44711.

84 F.O. 848/3, memorandum by Sir W. Brunyate, 1 March 1920. A letter from Storrs meant for the Foreign Office, dated 8 August 1914, warns in very strong terms against Edward Cecil taking charge of Egypt, since he is on notoriously bad terms and unpopular with both Egyptians and Englishmen. A secret addendum to the letter, meant possibly for his parents attributes the scheme to an intrigue of Kitchener's and the Salisbury family; *Storrs Papers*, box II/3.

85 F.O. 371/3204, file 186090.

86 Private letter from Stewart Symes, 12 March 1919, *W.P.*

87 F.O. 800/215, Balfour Papers.

88 F.O. 371/3714, file 42905.

89 Lord Hardinge of Penshurst, *Old Diplomacy*, 1947, pp. 233–4.
90 F.O. 608/213, file 662/1/8, telegram no. 540 of 20 March 1919.
91 F.O. 371/3714, file 44175, telegram no 542 of 20 March 1919.
92 F.O. 848/2.
93 F.O. 800/217, Balfour Papers.
94 'G.H.Q's Historical Summary of Events during Unrest in March, April and May 1919', pp. 51ff., F.O. 848/10.
95 Clayton to Wingate, 21 April 1919, *W.P.*
96 So he told Miss Bell when she visited Egypt in September 1919; see her 'Egypt Diary', *Gertrude Bell Papers*, entry of 30 September.
97 F.O. 407/184, no. 87.
98 F.O. 407/184, no. 206.
99 F.O. 407/184, no. 339.
100 F.O. 407/184, no. 123.
101 F.O. 800/216, Balfour Papers.
102 Hardinge, *Old Diplomacy, loc. cit.*
103 F.O. 407/184, no. 131.
104 F.O. 407/184, no. 134, note by Wingate, 3 April 1919.
105 F.O. 800/216, Balfour Papers, Curzon to Balfour, 3 April 1919.
106 F.O. 800/216, copy of Bonar Law's letter to Lloyd George, 3 April 1919.
107 F.O. 407/184, no. 144.
108 F.O. 608/213, file 662/1/8, minute by Sir Henry Wilson, 7 April 1919.
109 F.O. 407/184, no. 148, Curzon's telegram to Allenby, 5 April; and no. 150, Allenby's telegram, 6 April.
110 F.O. 371/3714, file 53358.
111 F.O. 848/101.
112 *Documents Collected for . . . the Special Mission . . .*, vol. 2, p. 290; F.O. 848/1.
113 F.O. 608/213, file 662/1/8.
114 Ahmad Shafiq, Annual Survey . . . Introduction, vol. 1, pp. 326–7.
115 Ahmad Mahir acted as the link between the Supreme Council and Abd al-Rahman Fahmi. Details of the *Wafd*'s terrorist apparatus are found in Muhammad Anis, *Dirasat fi watha'iq thawrat 1919* (Studies in the Documents of the 1919 Revolution), vol. 1, Cairo 1963, which publishes the secret correspondence between Zaghlul in Paris and Abd al-Rahman Fahmi in Cairo, also in a series of articles by Mustafa Amin (Madame Zaghlul's nephew) in *Al-Akhbar*, Cairo, July–September 1963, which quote from unpublished memoirs and documents. See in particular the issues for 20 and 22 August and 4 and 9 September 1963 concerning Nuqrashi's and Ahmad Mahir's complicity in organising attempts on the lives of ministers.
116 Allenby's telegram of 20 April 1919. On it, Vansittart shrewdly minuted: 'The extent of his [Zaghlul's] "representativeness" is

considerable at present, but we should not seal it.' F.O. 608/213, file 662/1/8.

117 F.O. 407/187, no. 33.

118 G.H.Q.'s 'Historical Summary, F.O. 848/10, p. 185.

119 *Balfour Papers*, British Museum, Add. Ms. 49750. A letter from Curzon to Balfour of 28 April (F.O. 800/216, Balfour Papers) speaks of Milner's reluctance to go out to Egypt if his mission was to be treated 'as a further step in Allenby's hitherto most ill-fated policy of concession'. 'I should add', Curzon continued, 'that the various officers and officials who are fresh home from Egypt and of whom several have been to the Foreign Office are united in deploring the policy which has been pursued since Allenby's arrival and which has apparently been adopted without the approval of Cheetham and our other leading men.' The reference to Cheetham is quite piquant.

120 See his declaration to *Le Temps*, Paris, 21 July 1919, and an editorial in *The Egyptian Gazette*, Cairo, 20 October 1919, stating that the prime minister had declared the previous week that he was opposed to the coming of the Milner Mission which 'would be received, with the open hostility of the great mass of the population', and if the mission were sent he would have no alternative but to resign.

121 F.O. 407/185, no. 29, telegram from Allenby 17 November 1919.

122 F.O. 407/185, no. 100.

123 See particularly Anis, Studies, pp. 42–4 and 181. See also J. A. Spender, *Life, Journalism and Politics*, 1927, vol 2, pp. 93–5, for his experiences in Egypt as a member of the Milner Mission.

124 *Documents Collected for . . . the Special Mission . . .*, vol. 3, p. 112, F.O. 848/1.

125 Letter from Milner to Curzon 10 December 1919, F.O. 848/11. See also a memo. by Milner of 22 December (F.O. 848/8) in which he envisages a settlement which would maintain the army of occupation, British control over the Sudan, and over certain parts in the Egyptian administration.

126 F.O. 848/5. Milner's conversation with Fischer took place on 31 January.

127 Spender, *Life* . . ., vol. 2, p. 91.

128 Milner, *England in Egypt* (13th ed.), 1920, pp. iv–v.

129 H. L. Debs, 5s, 4 November 1920, col. 213.

130 F.O. 848/8, 'Some General Observations by Mr J. A. Spender'.

131 F.O. 848/8. A memo. by Spender, undated (also in F.O. 848/8), makes the same points.

132 F.O. 848/6. Evidence before sub-committee A, 11 February 1920, p. 7. On the intimidation of *'omdas* by the Zaghlulists see further F.O. 848/5, memoranda of conversations between notables from Asiut and Girga, and Spender, Rodd and Lloyd (the secretary of the mission).

133 The text of the General Conclusions of the Milner Mission is found, conveniently bound together with the Report of the mission (issued in 1921) in F.O. 371/4978, file 5168/6/16.
134 F.O. 848/5, Milner's diary.
135 F.O. 848/11.
136 *J. A. Spender Papers*, British Museum, Add. Ms. 46,393.
137 Anis, Studies, pp. 88, 187, 194 and 218; Aqqad, *Sa'd Zaghlul*, pp. 293–4 and 299.
138 F.O. 848/5. See also Haikal, Memoirs, vol. 1, p. 100.
139 F.O. 848/20.
140 F.O. 848/20.
141 F.O. 371/4984, file 3939/93/16.
142 F.O. 848/20, letter to Walrond, 10 May 1920.
143 F.O. 848/20.
144 F.O. 848/20, Walrond to Milner, 10 May 1920.
145 F.O. 848/20, Milner's telegram of 11 May 1920.
146 F.O. 848/27, memo by Hurst, 13 May 1920.
147 F.O. 848/20, Walrond to Milner, 13 and 14 May 1920.
148 F.O. 848/27, memo by Hurst, 15 May 1920.
149 F.O. 848/20, Walrond to Milner, Paris, 19 May 1920.
150 F.O. 371/4980, file 12578/6/16. When the so-called Zaghlul–Milner Agreement was revealed in the press in August 1920, Duff Cooper, who was then in the Egyptian Department of the Foreign Office, noted in his diary: 'I wonder that Milner did not get some measure of cabinet concurrence before going so far'; *Old Men Forget*, 1953, p. 102.
151 F.O. 371/4979, file 9763/6/16.
152 F.O. 371/4988, file 12961/93/16, Scott's telegram of 13 October 1920.
153 F.O. 371/4981, file 14430/6/16, telegram to Allenby 24 November 1920.
154 F.O. 371/4978, file 5178/6/16, telegram to Allenby 21 May 1920.
155 The whole story may be followed in F.O. 371/4985, files 7269/93/16, 7453/93/16, 8421/93/16 and 8482/93/16.
156 F.O. 371/4987, files 12440/93/16 and 12447/93/16.
157 F.O. 371/4988, file 12618/93/16.
158 F.O. 371/3988, file 13180/93/16.
159 Anis, Studies, reproduces (pp. 221–2) a letter from Russell, commandant of the Cairo City Police, dated 10 July 1922, in which he complains of the great freedom given to Abd al-Rahman Fahmi in prison; he is 'living in hospital like a duke, with uncontrolled visits and uncensored post'. He can discover no written orders prescribing such treatment and presumes that the orders were verbal. He points out the futility of imprisonment under such conditions, and refuses to take responsibility for controlling political crime in Cairo if a con-

victed criminal like Abd al-Rahman Fahmi 'is free to plot what crimes he likes from inside the protecting walls of the prison'.

160 F.O. 371/4988, file 13100/93/16.

161 F.O. 371/4989, file 1474/93/16.

162 F.O. 848/11.

163 F.O. 848/20.

164 These are the words of a minute by Hurst of 8 October 1918, F.O. 371/4980, file 12578/6/16.

165 F.O. 848/5, Milner's diary, p. 27, 21 December 1919.

166 F.O. 848/20. Minutes of meetings between Milner Mission and Egyptian Delegation of 21 and 22 June, and 5 July 1920.

167 Egypt no. 1 (1921) cmd. 1131, *British Parliamentary Papers*, vol. xlii, 1921, p. 21.

168 *Ibid.*, p. 23.

169 *Ibid.*, p. 24.

170 A draft telegram of 19 August to Cairo, approved by Milner, declared that all the men proceeding to Egypt could do was 'to create a public opinion favourable to the proposed arrangement', and it went on to say that 'if they act up to their professions, which the mission believes to be sincere, they will conduct their campaign with that end in view'. F.O. 371/4979, file 10237/6/16.

171 Text of Zaghlul's letter of 22 August 1920 in Ahmad Shafiq, Survey . . . Introduction, vol. 1, pp. 746–7. The delegates whom Zaghlul sent to Egypt were Hafiz 'Afifi, Wisa Wasif and Mustafa al-Nahhas.

172 F.O. 371/4979, file 11054/6/16.

173 F.O. 371/4987, file 12140/93/16. Reports on the situation in Egypt compiled by the Department of Public Security for the period 7–21 September 1920.

174 F.O. 371/4979, file 11466/6/16.

175 Abd al-'Aziz Fahmi, Life, p. 117.

176 *Ibid.*, pp. 105ff.

177 F.O. 371/4980, file 12530/6/16.

178 F.O. 848/20, minutes of meeting between the Milner Mission and the Egyptian Delegation, 25 October 1920.

179 F.O. 371/4980, file 11542/6/16.

180 F.O. 371/4979, file 10456/6/16, Scott's telegram of 25 August 1920.

181 Allenby was telegraphing to Curzon on 2 July 1920: 'On one point sultan laid particular emphasis. He hopes that with a view to his own prestige in the country he may be given credit, personally, for some of the concessions to be made by H.M.G. to Egypt.' F.O. 371/4979, file 7628/6/16. And in his telegram of 25 August just mentioned Scott reported that the Egyptian prime minister had asked 'that H.M.G. should reserve some concession to sultan as suitable recogni-

tion of his loyalty, and to repair damage to his prestige done by Zaghlul's success'.

182 F.O. 371/6292, files 603, 727, 858/260/16, Allenby's telegrams of 12, 15 and 17 January 1921; F.O. 371/6295, file 4919/260/16, Curzon's cabinet memo. of 21 February; F.O. 371/6292, file 2463/260/161, cabinet conclusion, 22 February, and file 2083/260/16, Curzon's telegram to Allenby of same date.

183 F.O. 371/4981, minute of 23 November 1920.

184 F.O. 371/4981, file 14430/6/16.

185 F.O. 371/6293, file 2849/260/16, Lindsay's minute of 4 March and telegram to Allenby of 8 March.

186 F.O. 371/6294, file 3853/260/16, Allenby's dispatch of 18 March 1921.

187 F.O. 371/6294, file 3549/260/16, Allenby's telegram of 21 March 1921, and file 4237/260/16, Allenby's telegram of 8 April.

188 F.O. 371/6295, Allenby's telegram of 30 April 1921, giving Boyle's account of a visit to Zaghlul.

189 Egypt no. 3 (1921), Cmd. 1527, *British Parliamentary Papers*, vol. xlii, 1921.

190 *Ibid.*, pp. 239–40.

191 Egypt no. 1 (1907, Cmd. 3394, *British Parliamentary Papers*, vol. C, 1907, pp. 5–6.

192 F.O. 371/6297, file 7039/260/16, Walrond's telegram of 14 June 1921.

193 F.O. 371/6295, file 4736/260/16, Allenby's telegram, urgent, 21 April 1921.

194 F.O. 371/6295, file 5352/260/16.

195 F.O. 371/6310, file 14377/260/16, minute of 17 October 1921.

196 F.O. 371/6307, file 12611/260/16, reply of the Egyptian Delegation, 15 November 1921.

197 F.O. 371/6307, file 12696/260/16, Allenby's telegram of 18 November 1921.

198 F.O. 371/6310, file 14377/260/16, minute by Lindsay, 7 November 1921.

199 F.O. 371/6307, file 12842/260/16, Curzon's telegram of 19 November 1921.

200 F.O. 371/6306, file 11909/260/16, minute by Lindsay, 25 October 1921.

201 F.O. 371/4980, file 12578/6/16, minute of 4 October 1920.

202 F.O. 371/6310, file 14377/260/16.

203 F.O. 371/6305, file 11225/260/16.

204 F.O. 371/6305, file 11225/260/16 *loc. cit.*

205 F.O. 371/6298, file 7320/260/16.

206 F.O. 848/6, Hayter's evidence of 5 February 1920.

207 F.O. 407/185, Allenby's telegram of 22 June 1919.

208 F.O. 371/3729, file 139282, Allenby to Curzon, London 25 September 1919.

209 U.S. National Archives, records of the Dept. of State, 883.00/184, telegram from Gotlieb, Cairo, 20 July 1919.

210 H. E. Bowman, *Middle East Window*, 1942, pp. 243–4.

211 *Egyptian Gazette*, Cairo, 24 November 1927.

212 F.O. 371/6307, file 10042/260/16, minute by Lindsay, 5 September 1921.

213 Firmin van den Bosch, *Vingt années d'Egypte*, 1932, pp. 44–5. After his retirement, Sir Sheldon Amos stood (unsuccessfully) as a Liberal for Cambridge; see Bertrand Russell, *Autobiography*, vol. I, 1967, p. 141.

214 F.O. 371/6302, file 8857/260/16.

215 Miss Bell's letter, Cairo 29 September 1919 in Elizabeth Burgoyne, *Gertrude Bell . . . 1914–1926*, 1961, pp. 112–3.

216 F.O. 371/6306, file 11503/260/16, memo. by Clayton, 8 October 1921, and F.O. 800/153, Curzon Papers, memo. by Clayton, 21 October 1921.

217 F.O. 371/6306, file 11260/260/16.

218 F.O. 371/6298, file 7320/260/16, Allenby's dispatch of 17 June 1921.

219 F.O. 371/6306, file 11705/260/16; Allenby's note of 22 October 1921.

220 F.O. 371/6306, file 11908/260/16, minutes of the first meeting of the cabinet sub-committee on the situation in Egypt, 24 October 1921, no. C.P. 3458.

221 F.O. 371/6307, file 12388/260/16, cabinet conclusions, 4 November 1921.

222 F.O. 371/6307, file 12465/260/16.

223 F.O. 371/6307, file 12696/260/16, telegram of 18 November 1921, previously cited.

224 F.O. 371/6307, files 12656–12666/260/16.

225 F.O. 371/6308, files 13374 and 13461/260/16.

226 F.O. 371/6308, file 13587/260/16.

227 F.O. 371/6308, files 13654 and 13687/260/16.

228 F.O. 371/6308, file 13997/260/16.

229 F.O. 371/6308, file 14016/260/16.

230 F.O. 371/6308, file 14075/260/16.

231 F.O. 371/6309, file 14182/260/16.

232 Zaghlul's removal was being canvassed by Selby some two months earlier in his letter to Tyrrell, quoted above.

233 In his memoirs, Isma'il Sidqi claims to have himself suggested the main lines of Allenby's proposals, and reproduces a first draft in French in his own handwriting. See his *Mudhakkirati* (Memoirs), 1950, pp. 25–6.

234 F.O. 371/7730, file 467/1/16.

235 F.O. 371/7731, file 1482/1/16, Allenby's dispatch of 2 February 1922.

236 F.O. 371/7730, file 467/1/16.

237 F.O. 371/7730, file 652/1/16, cabinet memorandum no. C.P. 3616.
238 F.O. 800/153, Curzon Papers, Curzon to Allenby 18 January 1922.
239 *Ibid.*
240 F.O. 371/7730, file 970/1/16, draft cabinet conclusions, 18 January 1922; and file 652/1/16, Curzon's telegram to Allenby of same date.
241 F.O. 371/7730, file 767/1/16, and F.O. 800/153, Curzon Papers.
242 F.O. 371/7730, file 971/1/16, cabinet conclusions, 23 January 1922.
243 F.O. 371/7730, file 767/1/16. This telegram was accompanied by a personal one from Curzon (the draft of which is in the same file) in which he informed Allenby that he had argued his case 'with all my energy and power', but that the cabinet would go no further.
244 F.O. 371/7730, file 921/1/16.
245 F.O. 371/7730, file 1031/1/16, Amos to Murray 26 January 1922.
246 F.O. 371/7730, file 1040/1/16, conclusions of cabinet, 26 January 1922; and F.O. 371/7731, file 1121/1/16, conclusions of cabinet, 27 January.
247 A proof of this White Paper, which remained unpublished, is in F.O. 371/7731, file 1380/1/16.
248 F.O. 371/7730, file 1040/1/16.
249 Minutes of the two meetings of 15 February in F.O. 371/7731 files 1964 and 1965/1/16.
250 F.O. 371/7732, file 2205/1/16, cabinet conclusions, 16 February 1922,
251 Allenby's scheme was set out in his telegram no. 19 of 12 January 1922 in F.O. 371/7780, file 468/1/16. It is reproduced in Cmd. 1592 (1922) cited above, p. 22.
252 F.O. 371/6292, file 877/260/16, Allenby's telegram of 18 January 1921.
253 F.O. 371/6292, file 1365/260/16, Scott's telegram of 29 January 1921.
254 F.O. 371/8962, file 4888/10/16, dispatch of 5 May 1923.
255 Aqqad, *Sa'd Zaghlul,* pp. 421–2.
256 F.O. 371/8968, file 8594/85/16, report from S.I.S., 23 August 1923.
257 Mustafa Amin in *al-Akhbar,* Cairo, 16 September 1963, quoting the unpublished memoirs of Zaghlul's confidential secretary, Muhammad al-Ansari.
258 Haikal, Memoirs, vol. 1, p. 171. The Liberal Constitutionalists accused Zaki al-Ibrashi who was then assistant under-secretary of s.ate at the ministry of the interior of having worked the elections against them. Ibrashi as is well-known, was a palace man. See his short biography in 'List of Leading Personalities in Egypt' in F.O. 407/217, no. 12.
259 This was the language held by his confidant Robert Rolo; F.O. 371/8963, memo by E. M. B. Ingram reporting a conversation with him, 28 December 1923.
260 In his Report for 1906, Cmd. 3394 (1907), p. 7.

261 Lloyd, *Egypt since Cromer*, vol. 2, ch. 6.

262 Sir Charles Petrie, *Austen Chamberlain*, vol. 2, p. 337.

6 The Genesis of the Egyptian Constitution of 1923

1 Sir David Kelly, *The Ruling Few*, 1952, p. 226.

2 U.S. National Archives, Dept of State records, 741.83/10, undated dispatch no. 43 from Alexandria (received 10 October 1928).

3 Brian Gardner, *Allenby*, 1965, p. 16.

4 C. F. Adam, *Life of Lord Lloyd*, 1948, p. 197, quoting a letter from Lloyd to a friend, written in 1927.

5 Dispatch from Allenby to Curzon, 20 January 1922, see Ch. 5, above.

6 Allenby to Curzon, 12 January 1922, F.O. 371/7730, file 467/1/16, quoted p. 153 above.

7 Adam, *Life of Lord Lloyd*, p. 197.

8 Quoted in Ahmad Biyali, *Adli Pasha*, Cairo 1922, p. 256.

9 Document reproduced in Muhammad Khalil Subhi, *Tarikh al-hayat al-niyabiyya fi Misr* (Parliamentary History of Egypt), vol. V, Cairo 1939, p. 459.

10 The list of members is printed in Subhi, Parliamentary History, vol. V, pp. 493–4; Muhammad Husain Haikal was a member of the secretariat and his Memoirs give valuable glimpses of the working of the commission; see his Memoirs, vol. I, chapter 3.

11 883.00/436, telegram from Cairo, 2 October 1922.

12 The debates of the commission and of a sub-committee of eighteen members drawn from the full commission in order to consider first principles have been published: *Mahadir al-lajna al-'amma li-wad' al-dustur* (Minutes of the General Constitutional Commission), and *Mahadir lajnat wad' al-mabadi' al-'amma li'l-dustur* (Minutes of the Commission Set Up to Lay Down the General Principles of the Constitution), Cairo 1924; they have been substantially reproduced in a valuable commentary on the constitution, Muhammad al-Sharif, *'Ala hamish al-dustur* (On the Margin of the Constitution), Cairo 1938, 2 vols. in which the debates have been rearranged to follow the order of the articles as they appear in the constitution of 1923.

13 Haikal, Memoirs, p. 134.

14 *Ibid.*, p. 137.

15 The draft constitution is printed in Subhi, Parliamentary History, pp. 495ff.

16 Printed in *ibid*, pp. 466–92.

17 In his *Report* for 1906, Cmd. 3394 (1907), p. 7.

18 A. P. Wavell, *Allenby, Soldier and Statesman*, 1946, p. 316; Subhi, Parliamentary History, p. 498.

19 Memoirs, pp. 155–6.

20 Wavell, *Allenby, Soldier and Statesman*, p. 309.

21 Haikal, Memoirs, pp. 141–2.

22 883.00/436, previously cited.

23 883.00/438, dispatch from U.S. minister, Cairo, 1 December 1922.

24 Wavell, *Allenby, Soldier and Statesman*, p. 318. For the events leading to Tharwat's resignation see Haikal, Memoirs, pp. 155–6 and *al-Kashkul*, 8 January 1926, p. 4; also dispatch from U.S. minister, 1 December, 883.00/438.

25 Wavell, *Allenby, Soldier and Statesman*, p. 320.

26 So the U.S. minister reported in a dispatch from Cairo, of 21 October 1929; 741.8311/53.

27 Wavell, *Allenby, Soldier and Statesman*, p. 320. Subhi, Parliamentary History, vol. IV, 1947, pp. 53–4 purports to give the gist of a note dated 2 February 1923 from Allenby to the king objecting to the mention of the Sudan in the constitution and threatening that if British wishes were not met within twenty-four hours, the Declaration of 28 February 1922 would be revoked.

28 Albert Shuqayr, *al-Dustur al-misri wa'l-hikm al-niyabi fi Misr* (The Egyptian constitution and representative government in Egypt), Cairo 1924, reproduces, pp. 67–88, an article in *al-Muqattam*, of 23 March 1923 giving details of the amendments suggested by Tawfiq Nasim before his resignation. See also, Biyali, *Adli Pasha*, p. 316; Ahmad Shafiq, Survey . . ., Introduction, vol. 3, Cairo 1926, pp. 468ff.

29 883.00/460, dispatch from U.S. minister, Cairo, 22 February 1923.

30 Text of letter dated 27 December 1922, in Ahmad Shafiq, *ibid.*, pp. 378–80.

31 Nash'at, as is well known, was mentioned in the assassination trials which followed Sir Lee Stack's murder as having had a connection in 1922–3 with the *Wafd*'s apparatus; see the deposition before the *juge d'instruction* of Sulaiman Fawzi, editor of *al-Kashkul* (who knew Nash'at) printed in this periodical in its issue of 12 February 1926; see also a most interesting article on Nash'at in *al-Kashkul*, 18 December, 1925, where it is stated that during the period when 'Adli was considering the formation of a cabinet, the authorities seized the manuscripts of Wafdist manifestos translated into Arabic by the (publicist) Manfaluti, who had been dismissed from his government post by the Tharwat administration and been employed subsequently by Nash'at in the palace; these translations were further stated to have been corrected by Nash'at, and to have been originally drafted in French by another Palace official, (Achille) Sayqali (Sekaly).

32 Wavell, *Allenby, Soldier and Statesman*, p. 321.

NOTES

33 Text in Ahmad Shafiq, Survey, p. 518.
34 Subhi, Parliamentary History, p. 542
35 Text in Subhi, Parliamentary History, pp. 517–43.
36 Article 43, compared with Article 41 of the draft.
37 Article 46, compared with Article 42 of the draft.
38 Article 49, compared with Article 45 of the draft.
39 Articles 74 and 80, compared with Articles 71 and 75.
40 Article 153, without a counterpart in the draft.
41 Article 156, compared with Article 146 of the draft.
42 Abd al-Aziz Fahmi, Life, p. 143.
43 Text of the Law of 30 April 1923, in Subhi, Parliamentary History, pp. 621ff.
44 Haikal, Memoirs, vol. I p. 171. See p. 418, fn. 258 above.
45 Conversation towards the end of 1924 with the managing director of the Suez Canal Co., *Austen Chamberlain Papers*.
46 Directed successively by 'Abd al-Rahman Fahmi and Shafiq Mansur, two prominent *Wafdists*.

7 Egypt and the Caliphate, 1915–52

1 There is a short and scrappy biography by Anwar al-Jundi, *al-Imam al-Maraghi*, no. 115 in the *Iqra'* series, 1952.
2 Shaikh al-Zawahiri, Maraghi's rival and successor in 1929, states in his Memoirs that Maraghi's appointment in 1928 was against the king's wishes. But this does not necessarily mean that Fu'ad objected to Maraghi personally; more likely, he disliked giving an appointment to his minister's nominee. See Fakhr al-Din al-Ahmadi al-Zawahiri, *al-Siyasa wa'l-Azhar* (Politics and al-Azhar), Cairo 1945, p. 55.
3 See S. G. Haim, 'State and University in Egypt', in C. D. Harris and M. Horkheimer (eds.), *Universität und Moderne Gesellschaft*, 1959.
4 *Oriente Moderno*, vol. XVI, 1936, p. 475, quoting *al-Ahram* of 5 May 1936. The lessons were for three hours a week.
5 al-Jundi, pp. 116, 164.
6 *W.P.*, file 134/7, contains a translation made in Wingate's office, for the text of which see appendix. I have not been able to trace the Arabic original. The letter is undated, but seems to have been written at the end of April or the beginning of May 1915. al-Jundi, p. 112, erroneously calls the letter a *fatwa*.
7 See, for instance, the exposition of the classical view by Muhammad Rashid Rida, printed in *al-Manar*, vol. XXIII, 1922, pp. 729–52, and translated in H. Laoust, *Le Califat dans la doctrine de Rashid Rida*, 1938, pp. 29–42, where the authorities are cited. Rashid Rida wrote this article to refute the views of Maulana Abu'l Kalam Azad

who, in defence of the Ottoman caliphate, asserted that Quraishite descent was not necessary; see his treatise on the caliphate published serially in translation in *al-Manar*, vol. XXIII; his views on Quraishite descent are printed pp. 753ff. When Rashid Rida replied to Abu'l Kalam Azad he had fallen out with and was opposed to the claims of King Husain so that it cannot be said that his argument is an advocate's brief. On the necessity for a caliph to be a descendant from Quraish see the authoritative discussion in E. Tyan, *Institutions du droit public musulman*, vol. I, *Le Califat*, 1954, pp. 361–70.

8 Letter from Wingate to Cromer, 14 May 1915, *W.P.*, file 134/6. Maraghi's earlier note in support of the sharif is here said to have been dated 22 April.

9 *W.P.*, file 153/6.

10 *W.P.*, file 153/8.

11 Letter from Fuad al-Khatib to Muhammad Sharif al-Faruqi, 14 Muharram 1335 H./10 November 1916 in translation in *W.P.*, file 143A/1.

12 *Documents Collected for the Information of the Special Mission Appointed to Enquire into the Situation in Egypt*, vol. I, p. 155, F.O. 848/1.

13 Dispatch from Allenby, 12 April 1920, F.O. 371/4984, file E.3592/93/16.

14 *Ibid.*, vol. II, p. 54.

15 Dispatch from Cairo, 11 March 1924, no. 867.404/79.

16 Ahmad Shafiq, Survey, 1926, 1929, pp. 149–50.

17 Translations and reports from the Arabic press in the *Egyptian Gazette*, 8 March 1924, enclosed with the dispatch cited above.

18 Survey 1924, 1928, pp. 118–9.

19 *Revue du Monde Musulman*, vol. LXIV 1926, pp. 29–33, where the statement is translated in full.

20 Shakib Arslan, *al-Sayyid Rashid Rida . . .*, Damascus, 1938, p. 367.

21 *Majallat al-mu'tamar al-islami al'amm li'l-khilafa fi Misr* (Review of the General Islamic Congress for the Caliphate in Egypt) no. 1, October 1924, pp. 3–12. Rashid Rida's epithets for the fallen Husain are: '*madh'uman, madhuran, ma'funan, mathburan, manbudhan, mahjuran.*' Abd al-Mut'al al-Sa'idi, *Al-Mujaddidun fi'l Islam . . .* (Reformers in Islam . . .), Cairo n.d. [after 1952], states, p. 542, that Rashid Rida responded favourably to Fu'ads ambition to be caliph.

22 Ahmad Shafiq, Survey 1927, 1928, p. 60.

23 *Al-Manar*, vol. XXVIII, 1927–8, pp. 319–20, quoting Fikri Abaza's speech.

24 *Egyptian Gazette*, 1 April 1927, translating article in *al-Ittihad* newspaper.

25 Survey, 1924, p. 119.

26 Ahmad Shafiq, Survey, 1925, 1928, pp. 1,053–5 and 917–8.

27 The phrases are E. W. Lane's, see *The Manners and Customs of the Modern Egyptians* (Everymans Library ed.), pp. 445–6. See also article 'Mahmal', in *The Encyclopaedia of Islam*, and Jacques Jomier, O.P., *Le Mahmal*, Cairo 1953.

28 Ahmad Shafiq, Survey, 1924, p. 300. The other bone of contention related to the Egyptian medical mission which it was customary to send with the pilgrims. Husain forbade them to attend to the sick, even though they were Egyptian. Himself a man of overweening ambition, he may have considered such a mission a reflection on Hijaz facilities and an easy pretext to diminish and humiliate him.

29 Lane, *The Manners and Customs of the Modern Egyptians*, p. 144.

30 Muhammad Husain Haikal, *Memoirs*, vol. 1, 1951, p. 258.

31 *Majallat al-mu'tamar* ..., no. 1, October 1924, p. 19 and no. 2, November 1924, p. 48.

32 Haikal, Memoirs, vol. I, pp. 402 and 231, says that initially Ibn Sa'ud was favourable to Fu'ad's views, but that when he conquered the Hijaz, he began increasingly to oppose them.

33 Dispatch from the U.S. minister, Bulkeley, 20 August 1931, no. 883.00/711.

34 Arslan, *Al-Sayyid Rashid Rida* ..., p. 352.

35 *Revue du Monde Musulman*, vol. LXIV, pp. 34–6, for the text of the statement. The *ulama* alleged elections in Egypt, disturbances in the Hijaz, and the necessity to reach closer understanding among Muslims as reasons for the delay.

36 *Al-Manar*, vol. XXVI, 1926, pp. 190–1.

37 Article in *al-Mahrusa* newspaper, translated in the *Egyptian Gazette* of 8 March 1924, enclosed with the U.S. minister's dispatch no. 867.404/79 cited above.

38 Ahmad Shafiq, Survey 1926, pp. 149–50, and Survey 1925, p. 1055.

39 Dispatch from U.S. high commissioner, Admiral Mark Bristol, Constantinople, 23 January 1925, no. 867.00/1844. See also the shaikh's obituary in *al-Manar* vol. XXXIII, 1933, where it is also stated, p. 134, that he had been offered the spiritual caliphate.

40 Ahmad Shafiq, Survey 1926, p 107, quoting *al-Siyyasa* of 2 February 1926.

41 Translated into French: 'L'Islam et les bases du pouvoir', in *Revue des études islamiques*, vols. VII and VIII, 1933 and 1934, pp. 353–91 and 163–232.

42 Report in *al-Siyyasa* newspaper, 12 March 1926, quoted in Ahmad Shafiq, Survey 1926, pp. 148–9.

43 My Activities ..., pp. 181–2. The reference to a republic is interesting. The tribunal did not deal with this issue, confining itself to purely theological and academic points, but Shaikh Yusuf al-Dijwi, a

member of the Areopagus of the Grand *Ulama*, who had instigated the trial, in an attack on the book accused Ali Abd al-Raziq of desiring to destroy the monarchy and to promote rebellion by telling the reader that religion does not forbid it while, in fact, it is considered one of the greatest sins; 'if the government understood the real purpose of the book', he wrote, 'they would be the first to combat it'. This is probably the nearest that any of Ali Abd al-Raziq's opponents came to say or hint publicly that the tract had some connection with current Egyptian politics; see al-Dijwi's *al-Islam wa usul al-hukm wa'l-radd alayhi* (Islam and the Foundations of Authority and its Refutation), Cairo n.d., pp. 59 and 121–3.

44 Haikal, Memoirs, vol. I, pp. 232–3 and 165–6.

45 al-Aqqad, *Sa'd Zaghlul*, p. 480.

46 *Radd hay'at kibar al-ulama ala kitab al-islam wa usul al-hukm li'l-shaikh Ali Abd al-Raziq* (Refutation by the Areopagus of the Grand Ulama of the Book, Islam and the Foundations of Authority, by Shaik Ali Abd al-Raziq), n.d. The pamphlet ends with the sentence: 'This is the *ratio decidendi* of the judgment against Shaikh Ali Abd al-Raziq issued by the General Administration of Religious Establishments'. [Signed: the Party of] Union. The judgment is analysed by L. Bercher in *Revue des Etudes Islamiques*, vol. IX, 1935, pp. 75–86.

47 Ahmad Shafiq, Survey, 1926, pp. 40 and 105ff; *Revue du Monde Musulman*, vol. LXIV, p. 126. The congress at Mecca met from 7 June to 5 July 1926. The Egyptian government ignored entirely the Mecca congress and did not even deign to reply to the invitation to attend; see *al-Kashkul*, 18 June 1926, p. 12.

48 Ahmad Shafiq, Survey 1926, p. 203.

49 Al-Siyyasa wa'l-Azhar, pp. 215–6.

50 Ahmad Shafiq, Survey 1926, pp. 280–1.

51 The minutes of the meetings and resolutions are translated in *Revue du Monde Musulman*, vol. LXIV, pp. 46–122.

52 See S. G. Haim, 'Alfieri and al-Kawakibi' and 'Blunt and al-Kawakibi', in *Oriente Moderno*, vols. XXXIV and XXXV, and *ibid.*, *Arab Nationalism*, 1962, pp. 28–29.

53 Rashid Rida to Antonius, 10 January 1935; *Antonius Papers*, Israel State Archives.

54 Dispatch from the U.S. minister, Cairo, 28 December 1941, no. 883.00 General Conditions/7.

55 Dispatch of 20 August 1931, no. 883.00/711, cited above.

56 Dispatch from Cairo, 21 December 1931, no. 865C 00/67.

57 *Nur al-Islam*, vol. II, no. 6, Jamada al-akhira, 1350H/October 1931, p. 464, and no. 8, sha'ban 1350H/December 1931, pp. 590ff. Rashid Rida wrote, shortly after the Jerusalem congress, that Shawkat

Ali was rumoured to have wanted to use the congress to proclaim Abd al-Majid the true caliph and that this aroused the strenuous opposition of Turkey; see *al-Manar*, vol. XXXII, 1932, p. 120. On Turkish objections, see *Oriente Moderno*, vol. XI, 1931, p. 579. Shawkat Ali was hostile to Ibn Sa'ud, and this may have encouraged Fu'ad at one point to seek his support. Shawkat Ali visited Cairo in August 1931 and saw the king; he was then thought to be working for him; dispatch from U.S. minister, Cairo, 9 September 1931, no. 883.00/714. On Shawkat Ali's hostility to Ibn Sa'ud, see *Revue du Monde Musulman*, vol. LXIV, p. 15, and *al-Manar*, vol. XXIX, 1929, pp. 162ff.

58 Dispatch from Cairo, 29 March 1932, no. 883.00 General Conditions /12.

59 See details in *Oriente Moderno*, vol. XI, 1931, pp. 527–8.

60 Private information.

61 *Oriente Moderno*, vol. XII, 1932, p. 25. Azzam was eventually expelled from Palestine for making an anti-Italian speech; see *ibid.*, p. 42. The occasion of the anti-Italian agitation was the recent execution of the rebel leader Umar al-Mukhtar in Cyrenaica. There may be a significant connection between Azzam's attack on Italy and the reports, mentioned above, of Italian support for Fu'ad in the caliphate question. In his dispatch of 28 December 1931, no. 833.00 General Conditions/7, cited above, the U.S. minister reported the appearance of an outspoken article by Azzam entitled 'Sidky Pasha continues to be friendly to the Italians but offending to the Moslems and Arabs'.

62 *Al-Manar*, vol. XXXII, pp. 120 ff. contains an interesting account of the intrigues and manoeuvres behind the Jerusalem congress; him mufti's letter to Sidqi is printed p. 126; see also *Oriente Moderno*, vol. XI, 1931, p. 529, for translation of the mufti's letter.

63 Dispatch from Cairo, 25 September 1933, no. 883.00 General Conditions/30.

64 Dispatch from Cairo, 20 October 1933, no. 883.00 General Conditions/31.

65 Haikal, Memoirs, vol. I, p. 402, who writes that he agreed with Ali Mahir that the caliphate was a burden which Egypt did not have the strength to shoulder.

66 Article dated 8 May 1936, published in *The Egyptian Gazette* of 20 May, enclosed with dispatch from the U.S. minister, Cairo, 23 May 1936, no. 783.90f/10.

67 Al-Jundi, *al-Imam al-Maraghi*, p. 109, mentions Maraghi went on a mission to Ibn Sa'ud 'on matters pertaining to the caliphate'.

68 Muhammad al-Tabi'i, *Min asrar al-sasa wa'l-siyyasa* (Secrets of Politicians and Politics), Cairo n.d. [after 1952], pp. 57–8, 62, and 78.

69 Reported by *al-Lahab*, Jerusalem, 27 February 1938.

70 Reprinted in *Sawt al-Sha'b*, Jerusalem, 20 February 1938.

71 See Haikal, Memoirs, vol. II, 1953, chapter 2, *passim*.

72 Dispatch from Cairo, 17 March 1938, no. 383.1163/46. The newspaper report was taken from *La Bourse Egyptienne* of 9 March.

73 Report in *The Egyptian Mail*, 5 March 1938, translating interview appearing in *al-Balagh*, and in *La Bourse Egyptienne* of the same date, enclosed with dispatch no. 383, 1163/46, cited above.

74 Dispatch from Cairo, 27 April 1938, no. 883.00 General Conditions/73.

75 According to Jewish and Greek traditions respectively, both Moses and Plato also died on the anniversary of their birth.

76 Dispatch from Cairo, 21 February 1938, no. 383.1163/45, enclosing a translation of the rector's broadcast taken from *al-Ahram* of 12 February.

77 al-Jundi, *al-Imam al-Maraghi*, pp. 109–10. The date of the sermon is not given, but the author mentions that Maraghi was taken to task by the prime minister and that he answered by threatening to arouse the population against him. The prime minister in question was probably Husain Sirri, whose period in office ran from November 1940 to February 1942; his predecessor Hasan Sabri himself had favoured a neutral policy for Egypt. A. A. Michie, *Retreat to Victory*, 1942, p. 145, tends to confirm that it was during Sirri's ministry that Maraghi preached his sermon; this author also provides more details of the sermon than al-Jundi, who is content with a bare mention of its subject.

78 Haim, 'State and University...', p. 100, quoting the Memoirs of Maraghi's rival, Shaikh al-Zawahiri.

79 G. Kirk, *The Middle East in the War*, 1952, p. 257, quoting contemporary Egyptian, English and German press reports.

80 al-Jundi, *al-Imam al-Maraghi*, p. 110.

81 The episode is described in Haim, 'State and University...', pp. 100–1.

82 See E. Nune, 'L'Idea dell'Unita Araba in Recenti Debattiti della Stampa del Vicino Oriente', *Oriente Moderno*, vol. XVIII, 1938, pp. 411–2, where the author quotes contemporary Egyptian press reports.

83 *Oriente Moderno*, vol. XVII, 1937, p. 575, giving details of an interview in *al-Ahram*, 26 September 1937.

84 *Oriente Moderno*, vol. XVIII, 1938, p. 222.

85 Dispatch from Cairo, 23 December 1938, no. 883.00 General Conditions/82.

86 E. Rossi, 'Il Congresso Interparlamantare Arabo e Musulmano pro Palestina al Cairo (7–11 Ottobre)', in *Oriente Moderno*, vol. XVIII,

1938, p. 589 and *Oriente Moderno*, vol. XIX, 1939, p. 104. The delegates in January included Sa'udi princes and the Yemeni heir to the throne.

87 Haikal, Memoirs, Vol. II, pp. 156–7. It appears from the context that Bindari aspired to Ali Mahir's place, and that this was his way of insinuating himself in Faruq's good graces.

88 Al-Ittihad al-Arabi fi'l-Qahira, *al-Kitab al-thani* (The Arab Union in Cairo, Second Book), Cairo 1950, p. 10. The king subsequently sent Abd al-Rahman Azzam on a mission to Ibn Sa'ud. Azzam was a long-standing advocate of Arab unity, had many connections in the Arab world, had by then abandoned the *Wafdists* and become a king's man, and was the son-in-law of Khalid al-Qarqani, an influential adviser of Ibn Sa'ud.

89 *United States Weekly Review of Official Foreign Broadcasts*, no. 110, 8 January 1944, p. 21.

90 Musa Sabri, *Qissat malik wa arba' wizarat* (The Story of a King and Four Ministries), Cairo, 1964, p. 142.

91 See article 'Sharif' in *The Encyclopaedia of Islam*.

92 Details of this committee were given by Hafiz Afifi, at the time chief of the royal cabinet, in his evidence in Karim Thabit's trial before the revolutionary court in 1953; see Kamal Kira (ed.), *Muhakamāt al-thawra* (Trials of the Revolution), vol. 4, Cairo 1954, p. 672. See also E. Kedourie, 'Revolutionary Justice in Egypt: The Trials of 1953', in *The Political Quarterly*, 1958, p. 393, also Abd al-Rahman al-Rafi'i, *Muqaddimāt thawrat 23 yulyu* (Preliminaries of the 23 July Revolution) Cairo 1957, pp. 134–5.

8 Pan-Arabism and British Policy

1 P. W. Ireland (ed.), *The Near East: Problems and Prospects*, 1942, p. 70.

2 Published as *Arab Independence and Unity*, 1943. Extracts included in J. C. Hurewitz, *Diplomacy in the Near and Middle East*, vol. II, 1956, pp. 236–7.

3 See chapter 7 above, pp. 198–207

4 Haikal, Memoirs, vol. II, p. 319.

5 *Ibid.*, p. 330.

6 *Ibid*, p. 155.

7 *Ibid.*, p. 156. See above, pp. 204–5.

8 In an interview of some two years before Ali Mahir expatiated on the benefits of regimenting and indoctrinating the young; see Rom Landau, *Search for Tomorrow*, 1938, pp. 28–9. See also Abd al-Rahman Azzam, 'al-Tarbiyya al-'askariyya wa atharuha fi'l sha'b'

(Military Training and its Effect on the People), *al-Hilal*, Cairo, November 1939, pp. 6–9.

9 *Oriente Moderno*, vol. XX, 1940, p. 39, stated, quoting *al-Bashir* of Beirut (22 November 1939) that the Egyptian government had officially asked Iraq for a copy of the Futuwwa regulations in order to adopt them in Egyptian schools.

10 *Oriente Moderno*, vol. XIX, 1939, p. 512.

11 J. Heyworth-Dunne, *Religious and Political Trends in Modern Egypt*, 1950, p. 36.

12 Ishaq Musa al-Husaini, *al-Ikhwan al-muslimun* (The Muslim Brethren), Beirut 1955, pp. 108–9.

13 The head of the British military mission to Egypt 1938–40, Lieutenant-General Sir Gordon Macready, has recorded in his memoirs (*In the Wake of the Great*, 1965, pp. 118–9) that Aziz al-Misri was telling Egyptian officers at the Staff College in 1940 that the Germans were superior and certain to win the war. Macready reported this to Wavell and the British ambassador. Aziz was then dismissed at the request of the British.

14 Haikal, Memoirs, vol. II, pp. 180–1.

15 Ali Mahir's speech is extensively quoted in Salah al-Aqqad, *al-Arab wa'l-harb al-'alamiyya a,-thaniyya* (The Arabs and the Second World War), Cairo 1966, pp. 19–20.

16 A letter from Husain Sirri, Ali Mahir's successor as Egyptian prime minister to Rashid Ali al-Gaylani, Iraqi prime minister, dated 28 December 1940, refers to talks having taken place between Nuri al-Sa'id and Ali Mahir concerning an Arab alliance negotiations for which were to be resumed that year; Abd al-Razzaq al-Hasani, *al-Asrar al-khafiyya fi hawadith sanat 1941 al-taharruriyya* (Hidden Secrets of the Liberatory Events of 1941), 2nd ed., Sidon, 1964, p. 67.

17 Husaini, The Muslem Brethren, p. 119. Compare the prayer of Muslim schoolboys cited in appendix D of Lane's *Manners and Customs of the Modern Egyptians*: 'O God, destroy the infidels and polytheists, thine enemies and the enemies of the religion. O God, make their children orphans, and defile their abodes and cause their feet to slip, and give them and their families and their households and their women and their children by marriage and their brothers and their friends and their possessions and their race and their wealth and their lands as booty to the Muslims: O Lord of the beings of the whole world'.

18 At a meeting between Jewish Agency officials and Foreign Office officials on 21 March 1945, and in a letter from Dr Weizmann to the secretary of state for Foreign Affairs, of 27 March. I am indebted

for this information to the Weizmann Archives, Rehovoth, Israel.

19 The expression is curiously un-English; it seems, rather, a literal translation of a phrase which occurs frequently in modern Arabic political rhetoric: *'Mufakhiru al-arab'*. One wonders how it got to figure in Mr Eden's brief.

20 The list is reproduced in *al-'Irfan*, Sidon, August 1951.

21 Compton Mackenzie, *Eastern Epic*, vol. 1, 1951, p. 93.

22 *History of the Second World War: the Mediterranean and the Middle East*, vol. II, 1956, p. 334. See also L. Hirszowicz, *The Third Reich and the Arab East*, 1966, chapters 5–8, and E. Kedourie in *Middle Eastern Studies*, vol. 3, 1966–7, pp. 190–4.

23 Harold Macmillan, *The Blast of War, 1939–1945*, 1967, p. 423; Duff Cooper, *Old Men Forget*, 1953, p. 323, and Sir Llewellyn Woodward, *British Foreign Policy in the Second World War*, 1962, pp. 120–2, 257 and 274.

24 W. S. Churchill, *The Second World War:* vol. III *The Grand Alliance* 1950, pp. 294 and 714.

25 Great Britain, Foreign Office, Statements of Policy by the United Kingdom in respect of Syria and the Lebanon, 18 June–9 September 1941, Cmd. 6600 (1945), p. 2.

26 Charles de Gaulle, *Mémoires de guerre*, vol. I, *L'Appel*, 1954, p. 468.

27 Letter from de Gaulle to Sir Miles Lampson, Cairo, 3 June 1941, *ibid.*, pp. 413–4.

28 Cmd. 6600 (1045), pp. 2 and 4.

28a Memorandum of a conversation between Mr Casey and State Department officials, Washington 8 January 1943, *Foreign Relations of the United States, 1943*, vol. IV p. 954.

29 Georges Catroux, *Dans la bataille de Mediterranée*, 1949, pp. 176–8.

30 *Ibid.*, p. 262.

31 De Gaulle, *Mémoires*, vol. I, pp. 599–600; Jacques Soustelle, *Envers et contre tout: De Londres à Alger*, 1947, p. 360.

32 Charles de Gaulle, *Mémoires de guerre*, vol. II, *L'Unité*, 1956, pp. 350–1: telegrams of 9 and 11 August 1942 from de Gaulle in Cairo to the Free French delegation in London. A dispatch from the U.S. consul at Beirut, William M. Gwynn, dated 12 August 1942, in which he reported a conversation with General Holmes, commander of the Ninth Army, is of interest in this connection: 'I expressed the view', wrote Gwynn, 'that no greater folly could be imagined than to attempt to hold elections at a time when no one dared to express his mind for fear of an English or French concentration camp or a Lebanese or Syrian prison . . . when there was no popular demand for elections, the population thinking of nothing but bread, and when, finally, no elections were being held in Iraq, Palestine, or England itself. He said he quite agreed. I asked him if he could explain why then

NOTES

General Spears was so insistent on having them held in the immediate future; he replied that the insistence came from London but could not explain why'. See *Foreign Relations of the United States 1942*, vol. IV, 1963, p. 609. A telegram from Consul Gwynn a month earlier stated: 'Syrian and Lebanese officials are being urged by British Minister Spears to press their claim for independence and ignore so far as possible Free French. In public pronouncements he appears to take independence of two countries seriously but in private conversation he laughs at the idea'. Gwynn to Secretary of State, 13 July, *ibid.*, p. 598

33 The amendments are listed in Bshara Khalil al-Khuri, *Haqa'iq Lubnaniyya* (Lebanese Truths), vol. 2, 1960, pp. 300–2.

34 This is Catroux' opinion; see dispatch from Lebanese minister in Moscow, 4 December 1946, recording a conversation with Catroux on the 1943 events, printed in Khuri, vol. 2, pp. 318–21.

35 Camille Chamoun, *Marahil al-istiqlal* (The Stages of Independence), 1949, pp. 186–7.

36 At the end of the crisis, Camille Chamoun declared that it was not a question of numbers, but of a principle, that five hundred men were the same thing as ten thousand (or one hundred). See his declaration quoted in *Correspondance d'Orient*, no. 515, July 1945, p. 54. Happy the politician who can so easily and successfully insist on principle!

37 Answer by foreign secretary (Eden) to question by Spears, 29 May 1945, H.C. Debs. 5s. Vol. 411, cols. 39–41.

38 It is most likely that the French allegations are correct. Such evidence as can be gathered indicates that before the disturbances the French were on the defensive and the Syrians provocative. See dispatches in *The Times* and *Le Monde* for the period, and for Hama in particular a valuable compilation by Uthman Haddad, Hasan al-Qattan and Abd al-Hasib al-Shaikh Sa'id, *Thaurat Hama 'ala al-taghayan al-faransi* (Hama's Revolt against French Oppression), vol. I, Hama, 1945.

39 Terms of the British ultimatum of 31 May in H.C. Debs. 5s., vol. 411, cols. 378–380. Text of ultimatum from the British army authorities to the French commander in Damascus in *Correspondence d'Orient*, n. 515, pp. 16–7.

40 H.C. Debs. 5s. vol. 130, co. 47, 24 November 1943.

41 Duff Cooper, *Old Men Forget*, p. 323.

42 The address is printed in *Politique etrangère*, July 1947.

43 F. Stark, *Dust in the Lion's Paw*, 1961, pp. 12 and 83.

44 Henderson, *Life and Letters of Sir Douglas Newbold*, 1953, pp. 430–1.

45 Major-General Sir Edward Spears, K.B.E., M.P., 'The Path to Arab Unity', *Great Britain and the East*, April 1945, p. 72.

430

46 *The Times*, 24 March 1945, third leader.

47 The question is discussed at greater length in my article, 'Islam and the Orientalists', *British Journal of Sociology*, September 1956.

48 Ireland (ed.), *The Near East: Problems and Prospects*, p. 62.

49 'Toward Arab Unity', *Foreign Affairs*, October 1945, p. 129.

50 Ireland, *The Near East*, pp. 95 and 98.

51 *Oriente Moderno*, vol. XXI, 1944, p. 2.

52 Stark, *Dust in the Lion's Paw*, p. 130.

53 'I have urged', wrote Hugh Dalton in his diary in January 1947 (*High Tide and After*, 1962, p. 190), 'that instead of trying to make a synthetic glue of all the Arab states, including Egypt, we should try to split them'. But such an outlook was highly unusual in British official circles. Similarly unusual was Isma'il Sidqi's outlook when, in the negotiations of 1946, he refused to involve Egypt with her fellow-members in the Arab League in a multilateral defence treaty: 'He personally', stated a memorandum summing up his conversations with the British in April 1946, 'did not support the notion of making treaties comprising political and military undertakings between Egypt and the states of the Arab League'. See *al-Qadiyya al-misriyya 1882–1954* (The Egyptian Question 1882–1954), Cairo 1955, pp. 499–500. This work is an official collection of documents.

54 Sir Edward Grigg, *British Foreign Policy*, 1944, pp. 149–50.

55 Folke Bernadotte, *To Jerusalem*, 1951, pp. 24. The meeting with Nuqrashi took place on 29 May.

56 Abdullah's proposal was put before a meeting of Arab League delegates at Amman at the beginning of December (before a meeting of the League at Cairo which took place on 8 December). Abdullah's proposal is described by Haza' al-Majali, *Mudhakkirati* (My Memoirs), 1960, p. 63, who was present at the meeting.

57 Z. Sharef, *Three Days*, 1962, p. 72. The author was secretary of the provisional government of Israel, and well placed to report on negotiations between Abdullah and the Zionists.

58 Muhammad Mahdi Kubba, *Mudhakkirati* ... (My Memoirs ...), Beirut, 1965, pp. 260–1.

59 Sharef, *Three Days*, pp. 72–3 and 205ff. Michel Bar-Zohar, *Ben Gourion*, 1966, states (p. 171) that the interview took place on 10 May.

60 See Muhammad Amin al-Husaini, *Haqa'iq 'an qadiyyat Filastin* (Truths on the Palestine Question), 1954, pp. 174–5, for Nuqrashi's statement at Aley. Sir J. B. Glubb has stated (*A Soldier with the Arabs*, 1957, p. 66), that up to the end of February 1948 there was no thought of armed intervention in Palestine by the Arab League. Arif al-Arif, *al-Nakba* (The Disaster), vol. 2, Sidon, n.d. [c. 1950],

states (p. 381) that Azzam, the secretary-general of the Arab League, was surprised to hear on 14 May that Egyptian troops were going to invade Palestine.

61 Glubb, *A Soldier with the Arabs*, pp. 63–6.

62 Abd al-Razzaq al-Hasani, *Tarikh al-wizarat al-iraqiyya* (History of Iraqi Cabinets), vol. 7, 3rd ed., Sidon, 1968, p. 276; Khalil Kanna *al-Iraq amsuhu wa ghaduhu* (Iraq Yesterday and Tomorrow), Beirut 1966, pp. 82–3.

63 In a conversation with the Syrian diplomat Armanazi in May 1951; see Najib al-Armanzi, *'Ashr sanawat fi'l-diblumasiyya* (Ten Years in Diplomacy) vol. 1, Beirut, 1964, p. 251.

64 Text of the broadcast in *al-Zaman*, Baghdad, 17 December 1956.

65 Iraq's adventurous and aggressive policy in Syria and the Lebanon during this period was amply documented in the various trials which took place in Baghdad following the *coup d'état* of 14 July 1958; see in particular the evidence and documents presented at the trial of Ghazi al-Daghistani, Rafiq Arif, Ahmad Mar'i, Yusuf Mahmud and Sayyid Amin Bakr (who were high army officers involved in subversive operations against Syria), and Fadil al-Jamali and Tawfiq al-Suwaidi (who were ministers directing policy under the regent), in vols. I–IV and VI of *Muhakamāt al-mahkama al-askariyya al-khassa* (Trials of the Special Military High Court), 1958–9.

9 The Kingdom of Iraq: A Retrospect

1 The best account of these events to be published so far is *Majzarat Qasr al-Rihab* (The Massacre of Qasr al-Rihab), compiled by *al-Hayat*, Beirut, 1960.

2 The events of 1935 in Jabal Sinjar are described in Roger Lescot, *Enquête sur les Yazidis de Syrie et du Djebel Sindjār*, 1938, pp. 190–5.

3 A fortnight before the *coup d'état* Abd al-Latif Nuri addressed a letter to the minister of Defence saying that if he was not relieved of financial worries he would fall into a despair the consequences of which would be unpleasant. For text see Hasani, Iraqi Cabinets, vol. 4, 1st ed., pp. 181–2.

4 His intermediary seems to have been the notorious Sab'awi, later executed after the failure of Rashid Ali's movement. See abd al-Razzaq al-Hasani, Hidden Secrets, 1st ed. 1958, p. 20.

5 *Documents on British Foreign Policy*, series 1, vol. VII, 1959, pp. 720–1. Proceedings of the Third Conference of Hythe, 8–9 August 1920.

6 John Bowle, *Viscount Samuel*, p. 206.

7 Dispatch from Consul Thomas R. Owens, Baghdad, 10 May 1923, 741.90g/23.

NOTES

8 Letter from Austen Chamberlain to L. S. Amery, Geneva, 11 June 1925, *Austen Chamberlain Papers* (Box AC 53).

9 Letter from Dobbs to Shuckburgh, Baghdad, 15 January 1929, Sudan Archive, University of Durham, file 472/13.

10 Elizabeth Burgoyne, *Gertrude Bell from her Personal Papers 1914–1926*, 1961, pp. 270–1.

11 Burgoyne, *Gertrude Bell*, pp. 273, 279–80, 294 and 302.

12 Private information; Hasani, Iraqi Cabinets, vol. 3, p. 96; Gerald de Gaury, *Three Kings in Baghdad*, 1961, p. 86.

13 The remark, on p. 212, occurs in an anonymous note on 'King Faisal as a Political Factor in the Emancipation of Iraq from the Mandatory Regime' which in its short sentences and clipped prose and in its familiarity with local conditions, contrasts strongly with the treatment of middle eastern questions in the Surveys of those years.

14 Dispatch from Sloan, Baghdad, 22 July 1932, 890 g.001 Faisal/36.

15 B. H. Bourdillon, 'The Political Situation in Iraq' (read to the British Institute of International Affairs, 7 October 1924), *Journal of the British Institute of International Affairs*, vol. III, 1924, p. 278.

16. Kedourie, *England and the Middle East*, pp. 207–12.

17 Hasani, Iraqi Cabinets, vol. 1, 2nd ed., 1965, p. 43 fn. 1.

18 Dispatch by Consul Thomas R. Owens, Baghdad, 7 July 1921, 890g.00/37.

19 Letter from Miss Bell to the American diplomat E. van H. Engert, then Chargé d'Affaires at Tehran, Baghdad, 1 August 1921, enclosed with Engert's dispatch from Tehran, 5 September 1921, 890g.00/40.

20 The artificial deference towards Faisal which the British imposed and encouraged, the deliberate and diligent build-up of a monarchical court and its trappings, comes out well in Miss Bell's leters from 1922 until her death in 1926. A different attitude is disclosed in L. E. O. Charlton's autobiography, *Charlton*, 1931. Charlton, who served as chief of air staff in Iraq, wrote of himself, p. 273: 'He dined out now and then with officials of the civil administration and sat at one or two banquets given by Faisal on various occasions of Arab ceremony. For some reason or other, it was distasteful for him to see English ladies curtsey before this trifling potentate, who, at that time, was supported entirely by the force of British prestige'.

21 Miss Bell to Engert, 25 September 1921, enclosed with Engert's dispatch from Tehran, 16 October 1921, 890g.00/41; Consul Owens' dispatch from Baghdad, 1 November 1921, 890g.00/41 and his dispatch of 20 January 1922, 890g.00/45.

22 Consul Owens' dispatch from Baghdad, 23 August 1923, 890g.00/77.

23 See dispatch from American consul Thomas R. Owens, Baghdad, 1 September 1922, and enclosures, 890g.00/57. A biographical sketch

of al-Mudarris by Khairi al-Umari is published in *al-Aqlam*, Baghdad, vol. 1, no. 4 (December 1964), pp. 76–87.

24 Abbas Ali, *Za'im al-thaura al-iraqiyya* (The Leader of the Iraqi Revolution), Baghdad, 1950, p. 151. In a contemporary dispatch, the U.S. Consul wrote: 'It is said that he [Faisal] met a number of Shi'ite Mujtahids shortly after his arrival and in their presence took an oath on the Koran that he would never accept the mandate or anything else less than complete independence'. Dispatch from Owens, Baghdad, 18 August, 1922, 890g.00/55.

25 Abd al-Aziz al-Qassab, *Min dhikrayati* (Recollections), Beirut 1962, pp. 221–6 and 231–2. See also Ali Jawdat, *Dhikrayat* (Recollections), Beirut 1967, pp. 148–157, for his activities in Hilla and Najaf; and John Batatu, *The Shaikh and the Peasant in Iraq 1917–1958*, Ph.D. thesis, Harvard University, 1960, pp. 80–1, quoting secret British reports. Batatu mentions (p. 82) similar tactics adopted by Jamil al-Midfa'i in 1927 when *mutasarrif* of Diwaniyya.

26 *Report on the Administration of Iraq, April 1922–March 1923*, Colonial No. 4, 1924, pp. 17–8. See also the exchange of letters between the cabinet and king printed in Hasani, Iraqi Cabinets, vol. 1, pp. 87–90.

27 Burgoyne, *Gertrude Bell*, pp. 271–2.

28 'Open defiance of the authority of government such as presented a dangerous likelihood of insurgence is the sole ground on which the R.A.F. has been called upon to fulfil its legitimate role in assisting the local administration to preserve internal peace'. Colonial No. 4, p. 22.

29 Sati' al-Husri, *Safahat min al-madi al-qarib* (Pages from the Recent Past), 1948, p. 16.

30 Dispatch from Sloan, Baghdad, 3 February 1932, 890g.00/176.

31 Dispatch from Sloan, Baghdad, 2 December 1931, 890g.00/167.

32 890g.00/176 and 890.00 Faisal/36, both cited above, and dispatch from Sloan, Baghdad, 25 September 1931, 890g.00/165.

33 Letter from A. K. Sloan (who had been Chargé d'Affaires in Baghdad) to Wallace Murray, Department of state, Jerusalem, 18 March 1933.

34 Text of telegrams in Hasani, Iraqi Cabinets, vol. 3, pp. 158–9, and 171–6.

35 *Oriente Moderno*, vol. 13, 1933, p. 472.

36 Dispatch by Knabenshue, Baghdad, 30 August 1933, 890g.00 Ghazi/3, telegram from Knabenshue, Baghdad, 4 September, 890g.00/265, and dispatch by him, Baghdad, 19 September, 890g.00 General Conditions/14.

37 Maurice Peterson, *Both Sides of the Curtain*, 1950, p. 138. Sir Maurice Peterson is perhaps the only English writer with official connections who, when dealing with Iraqi politics under the monarchy, did not choose to disguise and palliate.

38 J. M. Keynes, *Two Memoirs*, 1949, pp. 41–2.
39 Husri, Pages from the Recent Past, pp. 19–22. Al-Husri, whom Faisal consulted regarding his son, decided that Ghazi was not congenitally backward but merely retarded. On Ghazi's boyhood and schooldays in England see de Gaury, *Three Kings in Baghdad*, pp. 52–3.
40 *Ibid.*, p. 103.
41 Dispatch from Jerusalem, 30 October 1933, 890g.oo/80.
42 *Mudhakkirat Taha al-Hashimi 1919–1942* (Diaries of Taha al-Hashimi 1919–1942), Beirut 1967, pp. 148, 151, 224 and 472. According to Naji Shawkat – an ex-prime minister – as reported by Hasani (Iraqi Cabinets, vol. 5, 2nd ed., 1967, p. 76 fn. 1), Nuri al-Sa'id, Rashid Ali, Rustum Haydar and Taha al-Hashimi were full of joy at the news of Ghazi's death, 'these four having sustained harm through Bakr Sidqi's movement'.
43 Yunus Bahri, *Sab'at ashhur fi sujun Baghdad* (Seven Months in the Prisons of Baghdad), Beirut, 1960, p. 119.
44 890g.415/6, dispatch from Knabenshue, Baghdad, 30 March 1939.
45 Ali al-Tantawi, *Baghdad mushahadat wa dhikrayat* (Baghdad: Scnes and Memories), Damascus 1960, pp. 84–6.
46 Bahri, Seven Months in the Prisons of Baghdad, p. 119.
47 'Reports dating from May 1920, indicated that hostile organisations well supplied with funds existed for the purpose of collecting and forwarding arms and ammunitions to Iraq'. *Report on Iraq Administration October 1920–March 1922* (Colonial Office), n.d., p. 31.
48 An amendment to the penal code passed in June 1923 gave the Iraqi government the right to deport foreigners for political offences. On the strength of this law shaikh Mahdi al-Khalisi was soon afterwards arrested and deported: *Report on the Administration of Iraq April 1923–December 1924*, Colonial No. 13, 1925, p. 11. Faisal himself, 'hunting with the hounds and running with the fox', as Miss Bell put it, intrigued with these divines while agreeing to their deportation. See Burgoyne, *Gertrude Bell*, pp. 313, 317 and 321.
49 Colonial No. 4, pp. 4–5.
50 Article by Salman al-Safawani, quoted in Abd al-Rahman al-Bazzaz, *Muhadarat 'an al-Iraq min al-ihtilal hatta al-istiqlal* (Lectures on Iraq from Occupation to Independence), Cairo 1954, p. 41.
51 Ali al-Bazirgan, *al-Waqa'i' al-haqiqiyya fi'l-thaura al-iraqiyya* (The True Events of the Iraqi Revolt), Baghdad, 1954, p. 240.
52 Dispatch from Sloan, Baghdad, 16 January 1941, 890g.oo/138; dispatch from the same, Baghdad, 21 July 1931, 890g.oo/154; and letter from him to W. Murray, Dept. of State, Jerusalem, 12 December 1932.
53 Bazirgan, The True Events of the Iraqi Revolt, p. 70.
54 Document enclosed with dispatch from Sloan, Baghdad, 11 February

1932, 890g.00/179; for complete text, see appendix. An interesting account of the Sunni-Shi'ite rift in the last years of the mandate may be found in the autobiography of the well-known Egyptian writer, Ahmad Amin, *Hayati* (My Life) (2nd ed.), Cairo, 1952, pp. 238ff. Another interesting outside reaction is that of Reza Shah's famous minister Teymourtache who in 1929 complained to the U.S. Chargé d'Affaires that Iraq refused to recognise the capitulatory rights of Persia which might protect Persian subjects 'against the Sunnite fanaticism of the Iraqi'; dispatch from R. A. Wallace Trent, Tehran, 2 February 1929, 741.91/108.

55 Hasani, Iraqi Cabinets, vol. 4, pp. 71–3.

56 *Ibid.*, vol. 3, p. 191. Official attitudes towards the Shi'ite position may be illustrated by a conversation between the U.S. consul and Faisal's assistant private secretary, Abdullah al-Hajj. Commenting on Kurdish demands of autonomy in 1930, the latter remarked that the Kurds were 17 per cent of the population but had 22 per cent of government posts, whereas the Shi'ites, forming 60 per cent of the population were content with only 15 per cent of government posts and 25 per cent of seats in Parliament; what then had the Kurds to complain of? Dispatch from Sloan, Baghdad, 890g.00/127.

57 *Oriente Moderno*, vol. xv, 1935, p. 326.

58 In a dispatch of 4 December 1928, Sir Henry Dobbs stated that the enforcement of conscription would cause widespread risings, and that unrest had already been caused in Basra by a census which was feared to be a prelude to conscription. A Kurdish deputy, Ismail Rowanduzi, declared in a letter published in *The Baghdad Times*, 12 November 1927, that both Shi'ites and Kurds were equally opposed to military conscription; see Hasani, Iraqi Cabinets, vol. 2, pp. 96–7. The following August a deputy, Shaikh Abd al-Abbas al-Farhud of the bani Rabi'a declared at a meeting of government deputies that he had a following of 3000 men and 'would rather go over to Ibn Sa'ud than have them conscripted'; see John Batatu, *The Shaikh and the Peasant in Iraq 1917–1958*, p. 56, quoting a contemporary secret report in the Security Library, Baghdad.

59 *Report on the Administration of Iraq 1927*, Colonial no. 35, p. 18. *Oriente Moderno*, vol. 7, 1927, p. 609; Hasani, Iraqi Cabinets, vol. 6, p. 146, for text of tribesman's letter.

60 *Oriente Moderno*, vol. 9, 1927, pp. 88 and 129; Colonial no. 35, p. 159.

61 Abd al-Razzaq al-Hassan, *Al-Uruba fi al-mizan* (Arabism in the Balance); see C. A. Nallino, *Recentissimi publicazioni di polemica politico-religiosa musulmana nell'Iraq*, Oriente Moderno, vol. 13, 1933, pp. 596–604, also reprinted in his *Raccolta di Scritti editi e*

inediti, vol. 3. See also *Muhawarat al-imam al-muslih Kashif al-Ghita al-Shaikh Muhammad al-Husain ma' al-safirain al-britani wa'l-amerki fi Baghdad* (Conversation of Shaikh Muhammad al-Husain Kashif al-Ghita with the British and American Ambassadors), Najaf, 1954, pp. 36–8, where the Shi'ite divine describes the disorders occasioned by this book.

62 Text of Basra petition in Hasani, Iraqi Cabinets, vol. 1, 2nd ed., pp. 77–80.

63 Mosul Commission Report, 1925, p. 38.

64 Qassab, Recollections, pp. 248ff., 259ff.

65 *Review of the Civil Administration of Mesopotamia*, Cmd. 1061, 1920, p. 94: 'The Jewish community in the city of Baghdad is a very important section of the community, outnumbering the Sunnis or Shi'iahs'. According to the last Ottoman official yearbook of the Baghdad vilayet as quoted in the *Arab Bulletin*, no. 66, 21 October 1917, the population figures for the city of Baghdad were as follows:

Arabs, Turks and other Moslems except Persians and Kurds	101,400
Persians	800
Kurds	8,000
Jews	80,000
Christians	12,000

The importance of Baghdad Jewry may be gauged by other indices. For instance a proclamation of the military governor in 1919 fixed the number of sheep to be slaughtered daily in Baghdad east, the more populous part of the city, at 220 for Jewish butchers and 160 for Muslim butchers; *Baghdad Times*, 24 March 1919. Again, when the Baghdad Chamber of Commerce was set up in 1926, the administrative council was composed as follows: 1 member representing the banks, 3 members representing British merchants, 1 member for the Persian merchants, 1 member for the Christian merchants, 5 for the Jewish and 4 for the Muslims. Dispatch from U.S. consul J. Randolph, Baghdad, 10 November 1926, 890g.00/108.

66 Sulaiman Faidi, *Fi ghamrat al-nidal* (In the Midst of the Struggle), Baghdad 1952, pp. 218–9.

67 Instructions by the Acting Civil Commissioner to Major Noel, *Precis of Affairs in Southern Kurdistan during the Great War*, Office of the Civil Commissioner, Baghdad, 1919.

68 On Kurdish affairs generally in this period, see C. E. Edmonds, *Kurds, Turks and Arabs*, 1957.

69 Bourdillon, *loc. cit.*, p. 287.

70 Clippings from *The Baghdad Times* enclosed with dispatch from U.S. consul Randolph, Baghdad, 12 June 1964, 741.90g/45.

71 Iraq Government, Ministry of the Interior, *Majmu'at mudhākarāt al-majlis, al-ta' sisi al-iraqi* (Debates of the Iraq Constituent Assembly), Baghdad, n.d., p. 440.

72 See Edmonds, *Kurds, Turks and Arabs*; he describes (p. 415) how he did his best to calm the fears of a member of the commission regarding the results of a decision in favour of Iraq. The Anglo-Iraqi treaty was due to expire within three years, but this, said Edmonds, was a concession to 'extremist opinion' in both England and Iraq and 'nobody seriously contemplated the possibility that, before the expiry of four years, the treaty would not be renewed for a further period'.

73 Miss G. Bell to Lady Bell, 12 March 1925, Gertrude Bell Papers, University of Newcastle.

74 *Austen Chamberlain Papers*, Box AC57.

75 British pressure on the Kurds continued unremitting up to the last. The prospect of independence aroused discontent among the Kurds in the summer of 1930. A delegation composed of the acting Iraqi prime minister and the acting British high commissioner visited Kurdish areas in order to impress on the Kurds that Baghdad and the British were at one in resisting demands for Kurdish autonomy. The delegation was not well received and was followed by riots in Sulaimaniyya; dispatch from U.S. consul R. Y. Brown, Baghdad, 15 September 1930, 890g.00/131. In 1931 the Kurdish leader Shaikh Mahmud started a rebellion which the Iraqi army was left to tackle so that it might be 'blooded' before independence; it did not prove very successful and the royal air force had to intervene; dispatch from Sloan, Baghdad, 11 June 1931, 890g.00/150.

76 See *Oriente Moderno*, vol. 11, 1931, p. 107, for the outspoken remarks of a Kurdish deputy.

77 *Mudkākarāt al-majlis al-ta'sisi*, pp. 1266–7; the debate on separate representation for the communities is found on pp. 1,246ff.

78 Colonial No. 44, 1929, pp. 9–10. In a dispatch of 21 May 1928 (890g.03/9) Randolph stated that the *mutasarrifs* in the provinces were the government's election agents to whom were circulated lists of secondary electors and members who had to be elected.

79 Khalil Kanna, a minister under the monarchy, put forward in his *Memoirs* the original argument that electoral contests in the provinces would have endangered public security, and that the 'election' of government nominees protected the people against violence between various factions. This should count as an argument against parliamentary assemblies in places like Iraq, not so much as one in favour of packing them. See Kanna, Iraq; its Yesterday and To-morrow, p. 80.

80 See article *Hizb* (Arab countries) by E. Kedourie, *Enycyclopaedia of Islam* (new edition), 1968.
81 Muhammad Mahdi Kubba, Memoirs, p. 352.
82 A. D. MacDonald, *Euphrates Exile*, 1936, pp. 54–6.
83 His biographer remarks on the diminished grasp of public affairs which Curzon showed in this period; Ronaldshay, *Life of Curzon*, vol. III, chapter 15.
84 *Policy in Iraq, Memorandum by the Secretary of State for the Colonies*, Cmd. 3440 (1929).
85 Miss Bell's letters to Engert, Baghdad, 3 May 1921, enclosed with Engert's dispatch from Tehran, 1 June 1921, 890g.00/39.
86 Review in *The Iraq Times*, 21 March 1938, enclosed with dispatch from Knabenshue, Baghdad, 9 April 1938; in the accompanying dispatch the anonymous author is stated to have been Judge Lloyd, then a judge of the Iraq Court of Appeal.
87 'Current Affairs in Iraq', from a correspondent in Baghdad, *Journal of the Royal Central Asian Society*, vol. 10, 1923, part 2, p. 142.
88 MacDonald, *Euphrates Exile*, p. 81.
89 Draft dispatch in *Austen Chamberlain Papers* (Box AC57).
90 Dispatch by Dobbs, Baghdad, 4 December 1928, in *Sudan Archive*, University of Durham, file 472/13.
91 Historical Summary by Sir H. Dobbs in *The Letters of Gertrude Bell*, vol. II, 1927, p. 545.
92 There was, among other things, an attempt on the life of two pro-British deputies who were grievously injured: see Burgoyne, *Gertrude Bell*, pp. 340–1.
93 Burgoyne, *Gertrude Bell*, p. 343.
94 The text of the British ultimatum is given in Hasani, Iraqi Cabinets, vol. 1, 2nd ed., p. 185.
95 Dispatch from U.S. consul Randolph, Baghdad, 24 May 1928, 890g.03/2, and 2 August 1929, 890.002/20. In a dispatch of 2 May 1935 (890.g002 General Conditions/53) the U.S. minister Knabenshue reported that Cornwallis (who had been the senior adviser at the interior in 1928) did not have his contract renewed because of opposition by Yasin al-Hashimi, then prime minister. It may be that Yasin remembered and did not forgive Cornwallis's role in the elections of 1928 which had led to the defeat of his faction.
96 *Policy in Iraq, Memorandum by the Secretary of State for the Colonies*, Cmd. 3440 (1929).
97 *The Arab of Mesopotamia*, 1919, pp. 10–2.
98 For instance, a tribal leader, Hajj Abd al-Wahid Sikar whose tribe had risen in support of Yasin al-Hashimi had a fairly large sum of money due for land and water taxes written off when the latter came to power in 1935; dispatch from Knabenshue, Baghdad, 2 May 1935, 890g.00 General Conditions/53.

NOTES

99 Colonial No. 4, p. 10.

100 Colonial No. 4, pp. 71–2.

101 *An Inquiry into Land Tenure and Related Questions*, p. 27. An excellent anonymous note on 'The Middle Euphrates District of Iraq', in *The Survey of International Affairs 1934*, pp. 213–6, which betrays detailed local knowledge states that a 'notoriously unjust decision in an important land case in 1933 had effectively destroyed the trust of the tribes in the justice of the government' and that in Muntafiq 'a land settlement commission, consisting entirely of Iraqis, failed badly in 1931–2'.

102 See Salah al-Din al-Nahi, *Muqqadima fi al-iqta' wa nizam al-aradi fi'l-Iraq* (An Introduction to Feudalism and the Land System in Iraq), Baghdad, 1955. There is no satisfactory published study of land settlement in Iraq under the monarchy. D. Warriner, *Land and Poverty in the Middle East*, 1948, and *Land Reform and Development in the Middle East*, 1957, touch on some aspects of the question. S. Haider, *Land Problems of Iraq*, University of London unpublished thesis, 1942, an excellent piece of work which deals with the period before 1914, is indispensable for understanding subsequent developments. Batatu's *Shaikh and Peasant* is a most competent study of landownership and land policy under the monarchy. A recent work, useful but hardly adequate, is Muhammad Taufiq Husain, *Nihayat al iqta' fi'l-Iraq* (The End of Feudalism in Iraq), Beirut, 1955. See also Ja'far Khayyat, *al-Qarya al-iraqiyya* (The Iraqi Village), n.p., 1950.

103 Dispatch from Randolph, Baghdad, 26 May 1928, 890g.03/3.

104 The confiscatory legislation of 1951 is conveniently set out in *The Baghdad Chamber of Commerce Journal*, nos. 3–6, 1951. The *Official Report* of the Chamber for 1950–1, gives details, pp. 169–179, of two meetings between the Council of the Chamber and the Secretary-General of the Department of Frozen Property, and of the help given by the Chamber to facilitate an inventory of confiscated goods.

105 When Ghazi died Nuri al-Sa'id, then prime minister, let it be known that unless the Parliament elected Abd al-Ilah regent, the army would intervene; see Hasani, Hidden Secrets, 1st ed., pp. 27–9. Hasani also reports (Iraqi Cabinets, vol. 5, 2nd ed., p. 75 fn. 1) that Taha al-Hashimi informed Ali Jawdat – an ex-prime minister – that if Abd al-Ilah were not elected the army would intervene.

106 Hasani, Iraqi Cabinets, vol. 8, pp. 155–7.

107 Fadil Husain, *Tarikh al-hizb al-watani al-dimiqrati 1946–1958* (History of the National Democratic Party 1946–1958), Baghdad 1963, pp. 304–5.

108 C. L. Sulzberger, 'German Preparations in the Middle East', *Foreign*

Affairs, 1942, p. 667. In his Recollections (p. 241) Ali Jawdat admits that Hajj Amin received official subsidies.

109 Salah al-Din al-Sabbagh *Fursan al-'uruba fi'l-Iraq* (The Knights of Arabism in Iraq), Damascus, 1956, p. 119. These are the posthumous memoirs of one of the prominent army officers behind Rashid Ali.

110 Rumours of the impending offer to Ali of the Syrian throne were intermittently heard in the late 1920s and early 1930s. One such rumour is recorded by a report from U.S. vice-consul B. Livingston, Baghdad, 28 February 1931, 890g.00/142.

111 Hasani, Hidden Secrets, 1st ed., pp. 27–9.

112 Amin al-Mumayyiz, *al-Mamlaka al-arabiyya al-su'udiyya kama 'araftuha* (The Sa'udi Kingdom as I Knew It), Beirut, 1963, p. 33. The author was Iraqi ambassador in Saudi Arabia 1954–6. He remarks elsewhere (p. 620) in his memoirs: 'What have we Iraqis to do with the Hijaz? When we accepted Faisal I as king of Iraq we did not undertake to restore the throne of the Hijaz to his brother or his nephew. Why then these enmities between us and the Saudis today . . .?'

113 See the evidence presented in the People's Court at Baghdad at the trial of Abd al-Jalil al-Rawi in October 1958; Trials of the Special Supreme Military Court, vol. 4, 1959, pp. 1,620ff. (evidence of Muhammad Salman Hasan, Jabir 'Umar, Salim al-Nu'aymi and of the accused, and the documents cited by the prosecution), also Kanna, Memoirs, pp. 130–1, and King Husain of Jordan, *Uneasy Lies the Head*, 1962, p. 190.

114 See Patrick Seale, *The Struggle for Syria*, 1965, *passim*. Ample evidence concerning Iraqi policy in Syria and Abd al-Ilah's active role in its formulation and conduct was presented at the trials of the People's Court in Baghdad after Qasim's *coup d'état*; see Trials, vol. 1 (trial of Ghazi al-Daghistani), 1958, vo. 3 (Trial of Fadil al-Jamali), 1959, vol. IV (trials of Burhan-al-Din Basha'yan, Ahmad Mukhtar Baban and Abd al-Jalil al-Rawi), 1959, and vol. 6 (trial of Tawfiq al-Suwaidi), 1959.

115 Kanna, Iraq Yesterday and To-morrow, p. 286.

116 Text of address in Sati'al-Husri, *Ara' wa ahadith fi'l-tarbiyya wa'l-ta'lim* (Opinions and Addresses on Pedagogy and Education), Cairo, 1944, pp. 68–75.

117 Sati' al-Husri, *Mudhakkirati fi'l-Iraq* (My Iraq Memoirs), vol. 1, Beirut, 1967, p. 80.

118 *Ibid.*, pp. 167ff. The official apologia for the refusal to provide subsidies to communal schools appears in the *Report on the Administration of Iraq 1927*, Colonial No. 35, 1928: 'A feature of the last year has been the attempts made by the Jewish community to get a government school in Baghdad for Jews. The Jews have a moral

claim to be heard because, by providing so many schools of their own, they relieve to that extent the pressure on government schools. But under the present financial stringency it is difficult for government to maintain a school for a community which already provides, though at its own expense, proportionately more primary schools for its children than the government provides for Mohammedan children'.

119 Husri, My Iraq Memoirs, p. 10.

120 *Ibid.*, pp. 479–80.

121 Mahmud Azmi, Jabha min shu'ub al-arabiyya (A Front of Arabic-speaking Peoples), *al-Hilal*, November 1938, p. 3. Azmi taught for a period at the Law College in Baghdad.

122 Husri, My Iraq Memoirs, pp. 215–6.

123 Tantawi, Baghdad: Scenes and Memories, p. 112.

124 Colonial No. 35, p. 159.

125 Kanna, Iraq Yesterday and To-morrow, p. 52. It was precisely then that Sab'awi established his first contacts with the officers Salah al-Din al-Sabbagh and Fahmi Sa'id – contacts which assumed much importance in the military *coups d'état* of the late 1930s, and particularly in Rashid Ali's movement of 1941. See Hasani, Hidden Secrets, 1st ed. p. 12.

126 Tantawi, Baghdad: Scenes and Memories, pp. 84–6.

127 Hasani, Iraqi Cabinets, vol. 4, p. 48.

128 Abdal-Rahman al-Bazzaz, *Safahat min al-ams al-qarib* (Pages from the Recent Past), Beirut, 1960, pp. 71–2.

129 Fahmi al-Mudarris, *Maqalat Siyasiyya* (Political Essays), 1931, pp. 122, 92–3 and 130.

130 de Gaury, *Three Kings in Baghdad*, p. 49.

131 Burgoyne, *Gertrude Bell*, pp. 291, 286 and 346.

132 Hasani, Iraqi Cabinets, vol. 1, 2nd ed., pp. 154–5. See also Mumayyiz, The Sa'udi Kingdom as I Knew It, p. 277.

133 Text of his instructions in Hasani, Hidden Secrets, 1st ed., pp. 52–3. See also M. Khadduri 'General Nuri's Flirtations with the Axis Powers', *Middle East Journal*, vol. XVI, 1962.

134 *Fursan al-'uruba*, pp. 70–1.

135 Hasani, Iraqi Cabinets, vol. III, p. 54.

136 *Oriente Moderno*, vol. XX, 1940, p. 302. See also Hasani, Iraqi Cabinets, vol. 8, p. 108; 'Sami is considered one of the most intimate of Sayyid Nuri al-Sa'id's entourage'.

137 Peterson, pp. 141–3; Peterson refers to Nuri's 'restless brain' and detects in him 'a certain instability'. In this, too, he stands alone among British writers – academic or official – who have always painted Nuri in the most admirable colours.

138 Clément Huart, *Histoire de Baghdad dans les temps modernes*, 1901, p. 154.

139 Abbas al-Azzawi, *Tarikh al-Iraq bayn ihtilalain* (History of Iraq Between Two Occupations), vol. vii, Baghdad, 1955, p. 50.

10 'Minorities'

1 H. G. O. Dwight, *Christianity in Turkey*, 1854, p. 93.

2 *Ibid.*, p. 112.

3 *Ibid.*, p. 244.

4 Turkey (no. 6), Cmd. 8108 (1896).

5 Dwight, *Christianity in Turkey*, p. 110.

6 E. M. Bliss, *Turkey and the Armenian Atrocities*, 1896, p. 335.

7 Dwight, *Christianity in Turkey*, pp. 148–9. For a detailed account of the schism see Leon Arpee, *The Armenian Awakening*, 1909.

8 F. Macler, *Autour de l'Arménie*, 1917, pp. 68–72, On the reorganisation of the Armenian community in the 1860s see R. H. Davison, *Reform in the Ottoman Empire 1856–1876*, 1963.

9 A. O. Sarkissian, *History of the Armenian Question to 1885*, 1938, p. 137. See also G. Young, *Corps de droit ottoman*, 1905–6, vol. II, pp. 76–78, for the defeat of the hierarchy.

10 The Armenian revolutionaries seem to have reasoned that Russian would be a lesser evil than Ottoman domination; also perhaps they could not bring themselves to believe that Russia, hostile as it was to the Ottoman Empire, might be just as hostile to them. In an article written in 1932 (and republished in 1958) Martin Shatirian, who is described as a 'charter member' of the Armenians Revolutionary Federation, wrote that 'some of us even thought that Russia's attitude was one of those inexplicable, temporary enigmas'; see M. Shatirian, 'The Founders of the A.R.F. on National Independence', *Armenian Review*, vol. XI (1958), no. 2, pp. 93–107. Russian hostility to the Armenian revolutionaries is well known; the official Ottoman Report, *Aspirations et agissements révolutionnaires des societes armeniennes avant et aprés la proclamation de la constitution ottomane*, 1917, gives, pp. 40ff., a useful account of this Russian hostility in the two decades preceding the first world war.

11 There is an excellent account of the diplomacy of the Armenian Question in W. L. Langer, *The Diplomacy of Imperialism*, 1951, pp. 145–66, 194–212 and 321–50.

12 They could not cross it; witness the fate of the Armenian Republic in 1920.

13 Dispatches from Layard, Constantinople, no. 365, Confidential, 18 March 1878, and no. 383, Confidential, 20 March, F.O. 78/2782; see also no. 401, Confidential, 25 March F.O. 78/2783. In a

dispatch, no. 1152 of 19 September 1878, Layard reports an interview with the Armenian Patriarch who demands an Armenian vali for Armenia. The Patriarch, Layard reported, said that the Armenians were accusing him of having misled them and of having prevented their availing themselves of a Russian offer to join in the war which, had it been accepted would have secured for them complete independence, or at least autonomy; F.O. 78/2799. On the intricacies of the Armenian Question at San Stefano see B. H. Sumner, *Russia and the Balkans 1870–1880*, pp. 416–17.

14 Bliss, *Turkey and the Armenian Atrocities*, p. 334.

15 *Documents diplomatiques francais*, 3eme serie, tome VII, p. 151.

16 For Russian discouragement of Armenian nationalism in the Caucasus see H. F. B. Lynch, *Armenia*, 1901; Sir Charles Eliot, *Turkey in Europe*, 1908, pp. 398-3; and Lord Warkworth, *Notes from a Diary in Asiatic Turkey*, 1898, pp. 99ff.

17 G. W. E. Russell, *Malcolm MacColl*, 1914, p. 153. See also A. O. Sarkissian, 'Concert Diplomacy and the Armenians, 1890–1897', in A. O. Sarkissian (ed.), *Studies in Diplomatic History and Historiography in honour of G. P. Gooch*, 1961.

18 Gooch and Temperley, *British Documents*, vol. X, part I, p. 488.

19 In a letter to Mme Novikoff quoted in H. W. V. Temperley, 'British Policy in Turkey', *Cambridge Historical Journal*, 1933, p. 185.

20 Eliot, *Turkey in Europe*, p. 13.

21 For a *rationale* of bribery as a method of government see *ibid.*, pp. 137–8, and especially the witty introduction. See also Curzon, *Persia*, vol. I, pp. 438–48.

22 See Lynch, *Armenia*, vol. I, p. 84; and the comments of Vice-Consul Fitzmaurice at Urfa in 1896, Turkey (no. 3), Cmd. 8303 (1897), p. 102, on the use of the telegraph by the central Ottoman government to keep the provincial valis informed of Armenian incidents in the empire to prevent the spread of harmful rumours: 'The motive appears at first sight a good one, but the result, as generally happens in Turkey, was and is disastrous. For the Porte, generally, either willingly or unwillingly misinformed, telegraphs the first garbled account, and this becoming known through the officials to the Mussulman population, tends to poison and excite the minds of the latter against the unsuspecting Christians, who are, in most cases, innocent of any treasonable intentions'.

23 This can be illustrated from a whole range of liberal writing and comment of all shades and colours on foreign affairs; see for instance *The Life and Letters of Jowett*, vol. II, p. 118; Duke of Argyll, *Our Responsibility for Turkey*, 1896; Malcolm MacColl, *The Sultan and the Powers*, 1896; and an interesting quotation from J. D. Bourchier

in *History of The Times*, vol. IV, part I, p. 75. This was of course, the creed which sustained both Stratford Canning and Cromer.

24 A. Nazarbek, *The Voice of the Armenian Revolutionaries* ..., 1895, p. 11.

25 See for instance the case of the Armenian notable in Erzerum who was dissuaded 'by advice not unmixed with menace' from serving on a reform commission set up by the Turks. *British Parliamentary Papers*, vol. XCV, 1896, p. 283.

26 Macler, *Autour de l'Arménie*, p. 140.

27 *Aspirations et agissements*, p. 16; G. V. Cardishian, 'The Armenian Revolutionary Federation', *The Armenian Review*, vol. II, 1949, no. 4, p. 65.

28 Shatirian, 'The founders of the A.R.F. . . . .', states that the Dashnaks learnt from the example of Narodnaya Volya, the Russian populist and terrorist group.

29 This point is made by K. S. Papazian, *Patriotism Perverted*, 1934, p. 21.

30 Turkey (no. 1), Cmd. 5723 (1889), p. 71.

31 Turkey (no. 5), Cmd. 8015 (1896), p. 99.

32 *British Parliamentary Papers*, vol. XCVI, 1890–91, p. 523, see also *Aspirations et agissements*, pp. 310–1.

33 *Ibid.*, vol. XCVI, 1896, p. 99.

34 Turkey (no. 6), Cmd. 8108 (1896), p. 14. The picture which emerges from the British Blue Books is confirmed by the French reports; see Ministère des affaires etrangères, *Documents diplomatiques, Affaires arméniennes, Projets de réforme dans l'empire ottoman 1893–7*, 1897.

34a Layard's dispatch, no. 1145 of 16 September 1878; F.O. 78/2799.

35 Turkey (no. 3), Cmd. 8015 (1896), p. 196.

36 Massacres were quite easy to organise. Sir Mark Sykes has described very well how the thing is done; '. . . it is the work of a mob acting under the following impulses:

'First degree: Hate Armenians; have been told the Armenians intend a revolution; have been told so by Armenians; have heard it hinted that the government wish a massacre; rumour goes that the Armenians have concealed weapons; they desire to plunder; they desire to fight; they massacre.

'Second degree: Say twenty-five per cent are loafing about, hear shots; cry of "Ho, ye Muslims!"; run to see what is the matter, strike for the faith; the Armenians have risen and they massacre.

'Third degree: the remainder! Fire! Blood! Murder! Kill! They massacre'. (*Dar ul-Islam*, p. 126, fn. 1.)

37 *British Parliamentary Papers*, vol. CVI, 1898, p. 274; W. A. and E. T. A. Wigram, *The Cradle of Mankind*, 1922, pp. 247–75.

38 Dispatches from Leishman, Istanbul, nos. 8170/1 and 8170/4.

39 *L'Action du Parti S. R. Arménien dit Daschnaktzoutioun, 1914–23*.

445

40 Gooch and Temperley, *British Documents*, vol. X, part I, pp. 450, 470; F. Valyi, *Spiritual and Political Revolutions in Islam*, 1925, pp. 205–63; *Aspirations et agissements*, pp. 90ff.

41 A. Emin, *Turkey in the World War*, 1928, pp. 218–9; R. Nogales, *Four Years Beneath the Crescent*, 1926; and a series of eight articles on 'The Defence of Van' by O. Mekhitarian, *The Armenian Review*, Boston, vols. I and II (1948–9).

42 See above, pp. 436-7 fn. 65.

43 R. Coke, *The Heart of the Middle East*, 1925, p. 220.

44 He was James Saumarez Mann (1893–1920). See *An Administrator in the Making*, 1921, pp. 258–61.

45 Miss Bell quotes one of them, Ja'far al-Askari (*Letters*, II, p. 569) as follows: 'Complete independence is never given, it is always taken'. Which, she informed her father, was 'a profound saying'. This debased rhetoric represents the limit of their political wisdom.

46 John Joseph, *The Nestorians and their Muslim Neighbours*, 1961, chapter 8.

47 Permanent Mandates Commission, *Minutes of the Twentieth Session*, p. 140.

48 League of Nations, *Official Journal*, 1933, p. 1,792.

49 Letter dated 3 November 1930 to an unnamed correspondent – probably Captain H. Rassam – cited in Yussif Malek, *The British Betrayal of the Assyrians*, 1935, p. 46.

50 League of Nations, *Official Journal*, 1933, p. 1,792.

51 *Ibid*. See also Royal Government of Iraq, *Correspondence Relating to Assyrian Settlement*, Baghdad, 1933. Documents nos. 29, 31, 32, 35, 38 and 40 in this collection are particularly useful in setting out the position of the two parties.

52 *Ibid*., p. 1,805.

53 Dispatch from the British administrative inspector at Mosul, Colonel R. S. Stafford, 2 September, 1933. Summaries of several of his dispatches are contained in a report from U.S. legation, Baghdad, 890g.4016, Assyrians/147. See also, R. S. Stafford, *The Tragedy of the Assyrians*, 1935, chapters 11 and 12.

54 Telegram from U.S. minister Knabenshue, Baghdad, 26 August 1933, 890g.4016 Assyrians/63. When his predecessor asked the British high commission at the end of 1931 what clause in the new Anglo–Iraqi treaty enabled the British to intervene should circumstances require, he was bidden to consider rather what clause of the treaty prohibited intervention; dispatch from Sloan, Baghdad, 19 December 1931, 890g.01/287. It would seem that the British demanded that Bakr Sidqi, the army commander who organised the massacre, should be put on trial, but obviously nothing came of this, much to the subsequent regret of Taha al-Hashimi, who reported this in his

NOTES

Diaries (p. 153), at the time when he and his brother were the victims of Bakr's *coup d'état* in 1936.

55 The number of the murdered given above is the official figure which was kept confidential at the time; see Hasani, Hidden Secrets, 2nd ed., p. 245n., The *farhud* (as this incident was locally known), is described in Hayyim J. Cohen, 'The Anti-Jewish *Farhud* in Baghdad, 1941', *Middle Eastern Studies*, vol. 3, 1966–7, pp. 2–17. See also Hasani, *ibid.*, 1st ed. pp. 223–4, and *ibid.*, 2nd ed., p. 244, where it is stated that after long discussions on 2 June, between the mayor, the regent and other officials, the regent finally issued an order for the Iraqi army to intervene. See also Hashimi, Diaries, p. 455. Two references to the *farhud* in the literature are worth noting. M. Khadduri in *Independent Iraq*, 1951, pp. 203–4, writes that 'those extreme elements who regretted the collapse of the Rashid Ali regime gave free vent to their feelings by making the Jewish community in Baghdad the scapegoat for their failure, and pillaged Jewish shops on 2 June'. How is it possible, one wonders, to have heard of the pillage and not of the murders? G. de Gaury, who was the British representative with the regent, gives in *Three Kings in Baghdad*, pp. 128–9, an even more curious account. He states that the mob 'set out to loot the Christian and Jewish shops in the main street, some of whose owners had the temerity to fly British flags and banter the defeated Muslims'. This story appears in no other account, and certainly not in the report of the official committee of enquiry (published in Hasani, Hidden Secrets, 1st ed., pp. 226–36). We note again the discreet silence concerning the murders. This author also complains that 'representations in London' arising out of the 'disturbances', 'led the good names of the regent and those with him being blackened'.

56 S. de Chair, *The Golden Carpet*, 1944, p. 118.

57 F. Stark, *East is West*, 1945, p. 162.

58 See E. Kedourie, 'Wavell and Iraq, April–May 1941', *Middle Eastern Studies*, vol. II, 1965–6, pp. 373–88. That the curious behaviour of the British troops was the result of Wavell's determination that they should not enter Baghdad except at the request of the Iraqis is perhaps implied by Miss Stark's statement (*East is West*, p. 160) that 'the British troops . . . were anxious not to enter the town unless invited'. In her later autobiographical work, *Dust in the Lion's Paw*, 1966, Miss Stark quotes an entry in her diary for 2 June 1941 which confirms such an interpretation: 'I see H.E. [Cornwallis] with the war correspondents in the evening. He surprised me by saying he thought the town looked friendly'. This was indeed surprising, since rioting had been going on for the last twenty-four hours. 'I feel it very much to the contrary', Miss Stark continued, 'and think it is a

447

pity we did not bring the regent in with a good show of troops or
aeroplanes. Always the choice between placating one's enemies or
encouraging one's friends. But the pretence that this is an Iraqi
spontaneous Restoration is just nonsense . . .'. Miss Stark also states
that the oriental secretary, Vyvyan Holt, tried twice to urge the
intervention of British troops at a meeting between Cornwallis and
British generals at the embassy, 'and dare not go a third time, and
one realises why battles can be lost by a sheer inability to get the
data to the people who make the decisions'.

59 C. E. Callwell, *Life of Maude*, 1920, p. 275.

60 C. L. Sulzberger, 'German Preparations in the Middle East', *Foreign
Affairs*, 1942, p. 664. Colonel W. G. Elphinston remarked at the time
on the parallel between Damascus in October 1918 and Baghdad in
1941; see his letter in *Royal Central Asian Society Journal*, vol.
XXVI, part I, 1944, p. 107.

61 But at least Lawrence, though later he chose to disguise the events
in the *Seven Pillars*, decided after an interval to call in the British
troops; see above, chapter 3.

62 E. Kedourie, *England and the Middle East*, 1956, p. 158.

63 See H. E. Sereni, *ha-Abib ha-qadosh* (Sacred Spring), 1951, pp. 68–70,
and Clara Urquhart and Peter Ludwig Brent, *Enzo Sereni, A Hero
of Our Times*, 1967, pp. 156ff. Sereni began organising the Zionist
underground in Baghdad in 1942.

64 See, for instance, Wilson, *Loyalties*, p. 305.

65 For a similar incident involving the Jews of Constantinople in 1862,
see M. Franco, *Histoire des israélites de l'empire ottoman*, 1897, p. 164.

66 *Bulletin des écoles de l'Alliance israelite*, January 1910, pp. 9–10.

67 To cite but one of a multitude of examples: Jews in Muslim countries,
declared Ben-Gurion in the Parliament in 1960, had 'lived in a society
that was backward, corrupt, uneducated and lacking in independence and self-respect'; the older immigrants from these countries
would never change fundamentally, but the younger ones had to be
imbued with the 'superior moral and intellectual qualities' of those
who created the state of Israel. 'If, heaven forbid, we do not succeed',
he continued, 'there is a danger that the coming generation may
transform Israel into a Levantine state', *New York Times*, 25 October
1960.

68 The Hagana sent one of its men to set up a branch in Iraq to organise
military training and set up a clandestine wireless transmitter; see
Munya M. Mardor, *Strictly Illegal*, 1964, chapters 10 and 11. The
author states that Sereni was opposed to these activities.

69 See J. B. Schechtman, *Population Transfers in Asia*, 1949, for a
Zionist view of the subject.

70 *Manchester Guardian*, 12 March 1952, reporting a statement by M. Shertok.

71 *Observer*, 11 September 1949.

72 A list of these outrages is set out in Hasani, Iraqi Cabinets, vol. VIII, p. 192. The author also states (p. 151) that prior to these incidents it was estimated that no more than eight thousand Jews would leave the country. The Iraqi government brought to trial a number of young Jews who were accused of throwing these bombs. But the evidence adduced is not always convincing, and it must remain an open question whether Zionists were responsible for some or all of the incidents which stretch over a period from April 1950 to June 1951. From some remarks made by the presiding judge, a chief purpose of their trial seems to have been to prove that it was the Jews of Iraq who had brought all their sufferings on themselves, and the Iraq government was in no way to blame.

73 'Nobody in Palestine believes that the *Patria*, which blew up in Haifa harbour in 1940 loaded with illegal immigrants who were being taken by the British to Mauritius, was destroyed by its own passengers or by "refugees resolved to bring their hopeless odyssey to an end". The blowing up of the ship, in which some 250 Jews died, was a political action in a "cold war".' R. Weltsch, in *Commentary*, February 1952, p. 198. The 'Lavon Affair' is also relevant in this connection.

74 Quoted in *Mideast Mirror*, vol. II, no. 44, 17 March 1951.

75 The attitude of the Iraqi government then and since is exemplified by the answer of the prime minister to a suggestion made in 1953 that Palestinian refugees might be given loans out of frozen Jewish funds. He stated in Parliament that the matter had been discussed in the council of ministers and that it was found that the law relating to frozen properties did not allow loans to be made; and furthermore, such loans might prejudice the interests of the Palestinians; *al-Sha'b*, Baghdad, 18 May 1953.

76 Article VI of the constitution prohibited legal discrimination against any group of Iraqis, and para. 3 of Article IX prohibited the general confiscation of movable or real property. These anti-Jewish laws seem to have stimulated the appetite of the rulers of Iraq. In 1954, Nuri, once again prime minister, issued a decree whereby Iraqis convicted of Communism could be deprived of their nationality and deported abroad; on that occasion Salih Jabr, who was then in opposition, publicly stated that such a measure was repugnant to the constitution; *al-Sha'b*, Baghdad, 21 August 1954. And, of course, the *coup d'état* of 14 July 1958 inaugurated a whole series of proscriptions and confiscations, the first victims of which were the leading politicians and officials of the monarchy.

77 487 H.C. Deb. 55, written answer by Mr Younger, 23 April 1951.

78 Permanent Mandates Commission, *Minutes of the Twentieth Session*, p. 135.

79 'The prime minister [of Egypt] recognised the extent of Jewish economic power, since it controlled the economic systems of many countries, including the U.S., England, France, Egypt itself, and perhaps even Sweden'. 'The King [of Egypt] then struck a more personal note. King Gustaf of Sweden, he said, was regarded in Egypt as being strongly pro-Jewish. And was he not also a Free-manon?' F. Bernadotte, *To Jerusalem*, pp. 27 and 70; the Iraqi prosecutor in the Zionist trial referred to above quoted from the protocols of the Elders of Zion (attributing them to Herzl) to prove the immensity of the Zionist peril; Abd al-Jabbar Fahmi, *Sumum al-af'a al-sihyawni* (The Poisons of the Zionist Snake), Baghdad, 1952, p. 529; this work contains a transcript of the various trials of Iraqi Zionists and Israeli agents held in Baghdad. See S. G. Haim 'Arabic Antisemitic Literature', *Jewish Social Studies*, 1955, and below, pp. 334-7.

80 Wilson, *Mesopotamia 1917–1920*, p. 335.

81 R. Montagne, 'Modern Nations and Islam', *Foreign Affairs*, July 1952, p. 592.

11 Religion and Politics

1 A. Bertram and J. W. A. Young, *Report of the Commission Appointed by the Government of Palestine to inquire and report upon certain controversies between the Orthodox Patriarchate of Jerusalem and the Arab Orthodox Community*, 1926, pp. 57–8.

2 W. K. Hancock, *Country and Calling*, 1954, p. 159.

3 See *al-Manar*, vol. XIX, 1916, pp. 185ff., for a brief biographical account.

4 *Kadha ana ya dunya* (Such I am, O World), selected and edited by his daughter Hala Sakakini, Jerusalem, 1955. Sakakini was born in Jerusalem in 1878 and died a refugee in Cairo in 1953.

5 Marun Abbud, *Saqar Lubnan* (The Eagle of the Lebanon), Beirut 1950, p. 38, quoting a contemporary chronicle; F. J. Bliss, *The Religions of Modern Syria and Palestine*, 1912, p. 326.

6 See 'Public Statement of Asaad Shidiak', *Missionary Herald*, Boston, vol. 23, 1827.

7 *Ibid.*, pp. 136, 170–1, and 177 and 370.

8 Ahmad Faris al-Shidiaq (1804–87), *al-Saq 'ala al-saq fi ma huwa al-Fariaq*, or to use the translation provided on the title page, *La vie et les aventures de Fariaq, relation de ses voyages avec ses observations critiques sur les Arabes et sur les autres peuples*, Paris, 1855 (Cairo ed. 1919), p. 103.

9 See his collection of articles, *al-Durar* (The Pearls), ed. by his brother, 'Awni Ishaq, 1909, pp. 189 and 329.

10 Bliss, *Religions of Modern Syria and Palestine*, who states (p. 112) that the Maronite hierarchy was then being 'threatened by the activity of the societies of Freemasons and other popular benevolent associations which have sprung up in the Lebanon since the beginning of the century in consequence of the liberal ideas brought back from the New World of returned emigrants'. In the journal *al-Mashriq* which he edited, the Jesuit Louis Cheikho ran a series of articles in 1910 and 1911 in which he virulently attacked freemasonry; see in particular vol. 14 (1911) for his discussion of freemasonry in Egypt, Syria and Turkey; the articles were collected and published in a book, *al-Sirr al-maṣun fi shi'at al-māsun* (The Well-Protected Secret Concerning the Sect of the Masons), 1911.

11 I have not been able to see a copy of *al-Muhalafa al-thulathiyya* (The Triple Alliance), which was published in New York in 1903 and which is now very rare. There are summaries of its theme and quotations from its text in various works devoted to Rayhnai; see in particular Marun Abbud, *Amin al-Rayhani*, Cairo, 1955, and Muhammad Ali Musa, *Amin al-Rayhani*, Beirut, 1961.

12 *Al-Makari wa'l-kahin* (The Muleteer and The Priest), Beirut, 1929. The first edition was published in New York in 1904.

13 Letter to Na um Labaki, 1901, in Albert Rayhani (ed.), *Rasa'il Amin Al-Rayhani 1896–1940* (Letters of Amin al-Rahani, 1896–1940), Beirut, 1959, p. 26.

14 He was excommunicated by his bishop before the first world war; see Amin al-Rayhani, *Qalb Lubnan* (The Heart of the Lebanon), Beirut (2nd ed.), 1958, p. 84. The columns of *al-Mashriq* contain over the years bitter and violent denunciations by its editor, Louis Cheikho, of one whom he considered a traitor to his community and infected with what Cheikho called 'anti-religious rabies' (*al-kalab al-ladini*); see *al-Mashriq*, 1924, pp. 478–9.

15 Letter to the poet Bahara al-Khuri, dated probably 1910; *Rasa'il*, pp. 167–8.

16 *Rasa'il*, p. 298, letter to Marun Abbud, November 1926.

17 He tells us that a brief period of teaching at the Jesuit College of St Joseph at Beirut was terminated at the instance of the papal nuncio 'because I am a danger to the Maronite community and the Catholic religion'. See his work, *Ruwwad al-nahda al-haditha* (Pioneers of the Modern Renaissance), Beirut, 1952, p. 177.

18 Marun Abbud, *al-Nabi Muhammad*, Sidon 1353/1934 the quotations above are from pp. 23–4.

19 Passage quoted in Musa, *Amin al-Rayhani*, pp. 72–3.

20 A *sāqiya* or water-wheel 'mainly consists of a vertical wheel, which

raises the water in earthen pots attached to cords, and forming a continuous series; a second vertical wheel fixed to the same axis, with cogs; and a large horizontal, cogged wheel, which, being turned by a pair of cows or bulls, or by a single beast, puts in motion the two former wheels and the pots. The construction of this machine', observes E. W. Lane, 'is of a very rude kind; and its motion produces a disagreeable creaking sound'. *The Manners and Customs of the Modern Egyptians* (Everyman ed.), p. 336.

21 See the preface to vol. I of his *Muluk al-arab* (The Kings of the Arabs), Beirut 1924, pp. 6ff.

22 Quotations in Musa, *Amin al-Rayhani*, p. 77.

23 Rayhani's political testament is extensively cited in Marun Abbud, *Amin al-Rayhani*, p. 41.

24 *Rasa'il . . .*, p. 285.

25 This kind of rebellion was even rarer among Arabic-speaking Jewish communities. There is one well-known case, that of the Baghdadi Jew Nissim Susa who became a convert to Islam in the 1930s under the name of Ahmad Nasim Susa. He published an apologia, *Fi tariqi ila'l-Islam* (On My Way to Islam) (2 vols.), Cairo and Najaf, 1936–8. This graduate from an American university presents many similarities to the Maronite and Orthodox rebels in his revulsion from the religion and traditions of his community and in his fervid desire to identify with and be accepted by the Muslim majority; the only convincing way for a Jew to prove his solidarity with the Arabs in the struggle against Zionism, he says (vol. I, p. 163), is 'by deserting Judaism, including the religion, the customs, the traditions, and the fellow-feeling'; in vol II (p. 183) he reprints an article which he had contributed to a newspaper in which he had argued that non-Muslim civil servants should not be allowed leave of absence on the occasion of their religious feasts.

26 T. E. Dowling, *The Orthodox Greek Patriarchate of Jerusalem* (3rd ed.), 1913, p. 50.

27 Bertram and Young, *Report*, p. 338, Articles 11 and 12 of the Brotherhood Regulations.

28 Bliss, *Religions of Modern Syria and Palestine*, pp. 55 and 58.

29 R. Janin, *The Separated Eastern Churches*, 1933, pp. 80–1.

30 Bertram and Young, *Report*, p. 25.

31 Uspensky's autobiography was published posthumously, *Kniga Bytja Mojego* (The Book of my Life) (P. A. Syrku, ed., Academia Scientiarum Impierialis, for the Imperial Orthodox Palestine Society, 4 vols, St Petersburg, 1894–6). I am indebted to Dr Andrew Mango for these bibliographical details.

32 The pamphlet from which this passage is quoted, *Lamha tarikhiyya fi akhawiyyat al-qabr al-muqaddas al-yunaniyya* (Historical Outline of

the Greek Brotherhood of the Holy Sepulchre), was published in a first edition in 1893, the pseudonymous author being stated to be al-Shaikh Abd al-Ahad al-Shafi, the work being printed at the press of Sam the son of Noah. Its reading was forbidden to the faithful; see Shḥada Khuri and Nicholas Khuri, *Khulasat tarikh kanisat Urshalim al-arthudhaksiyya* (Brief History of the Orthodox Church of Jerusalem), Jerusalem, 1925, pp. 235–6. It was reprinted in 1909 by Girgis Abdulla al-Isa al-Yafi. The British Museum *Catalogue of Arabic Printed Books* attributes the work to Salim Mikha'il Shahhada. If correct, the attribution would be highly significant, since Salim Mikha'il Shahhada (1848–1907) was in fact the dragoman of the Russian consulate in Beirut (see Martin Hartmann, *The Arabic Press of Egypt*, 1899, p. 38, and the relevant entry in Sarkis, *Mu'jam* . . .), and the pamphlet makes extensive use of Russian works. The passage translated above occurs in what seems an extended quotation (pp. 72 –8) from Uspensky's autobiography. It is also quoted in P. Deplaissan 'La Politique russe dans la Palestine et la Syrie', *Echos d'Orient*, vol. IV (1901), p. 297. Isma'il Kemal Bey who was governor of Beirut in 1891–2 states that Shahhada was involved in anti-Greek agitation on behalf of the Russians in the affair of the See of Antioch; see Somerville Story (ed.), *The Memoirs of Ismail Kemal Bey*, pp. 196–7.

33 Bertram and Young, *Report*, pp. 138–9; A. Fortescue, *The Orthodox Eastern Church*, 1907, p. 288; Khuri, Brief History, pp. 205ff. See a long dispatch by the British Consul in Jerusalem, no. 1 of 7 January 1887 (F.O. 195/1581), describing the 'chronic struggle between Greeks and Russians.'

34 Bertram and Young, *Report*, p. 215; Bliss, *Religions of Modern Syria and Palestine*, gives an account of the incident. Alphonse d'Alonzo, *La Russie en Palestine*, 1901, makes the point (p. 17) that though Russia had only negligible interests in Damascus it yet established at the time a consulate there. He also mentions (p. 45 fn. 1) that the Russians made an annual allowance to the Arabic-speaking bishops of the patriarchate of Antioch. The publisher of the second edition of the *Lamha* stated in an Afterword (p. 139) that the pamphlet was instrumental in wakening the native communities in the see of Antioch to the oppression of the Greeks. This again throws an interesting light on the origin and character of this pamphlet. See a memorandum on Russian influence in the Greek Orthodox community enclosed with dispatch from the British Embassy, Constantinople, 27 April 1899 in F.O. 429/198, no. 76; also a dispatch of 9 November (F.O. 424/199, no. 53) describing Ottoman acquiescence in Russian dominance in the see of Antioch.

35 See *Echos d'Orient*, vol. III, (1899–1900), pp. 177–181; IV (1901), p. 281; VIII (1905), pp. 160–2, and XVI (1913), p. 30; J. Richter,

A History of Protestant Missions in the Near East, 1910, p. 57;
Shukri Khalil Swaidan, *Tarikh al-jam'iyya al-imberatoriyya al-
arthudhaksiyya al-filastiniyya* (History of Imperial Orthodox
Palestine Society), Boston 1912.

36 Mikha'il Nu'ayma, *Sab'un: qissat 'umr 1889–1959* (Seventy Years:
the Story of a Life 1889–1959), vol. I, Beirut, 1959, pp. 74–5.

37 *Ibid.*, p. 142.

38 Sakakini, 26, entry of 15 May 1908.

39 *Ibid.*, 38, entry of 21 September 1908.

40 *Ibid.*, 180, entry of 30 April 1919.

41 *Ibid.*, 170, entry of 21 March 1909.

42 A. Bertram and C. Luke, *Report of the Commission appointed by the
Government of Palestine to inquire into the Affairs of the Orthodox
Patriarchate of Jerusalem*, 1921, appendix C; *Echos d'Orient*, vol.
XII (1909), pp. 112, 242–3; vol. XIII (1910), p. 42; vol. XIV (1911),
p. 239. The disturbances of 1908–9 are discussed extensively in
Khuri, Brief History, and in dispatches and telegrams from the
British consul in Jerusalem, E. C. Blech; dispatch no. 61 of 10
November 1908 and telegram of 31 December, F.O. 195/2287; and
dispatch no. 1 of 1 January 1909, and no. 13 of 26 February 1909,
F.O. 195/2321. Blech's conclusion on the disturbances as expressed
in his telegram of 31 December 1908 seems sensible: 'Though native
party is usually considered as in Russian interest I think present
situation is not due to Russian instigation'. See also dispatch by
U.S. consul T. R. Wallace, 15 March 1909, for a graphic description
of a riot which took place following the murder – probably for
robbery – of two Arabic-speaking Orthodox on 24 February. Greek
shops were attacked, another native Orthodox being killed in the
disturbance. At the funeral, bloody sheets were displayed and a
Muslim orator pledged the support of his community in the struggle
against the Greeks.

43 This mixed council, set up in 1911 did not function at all. The
patriarchate was reluctant to cooperate and the outbreak of war
provided an opportunity to suspend its sittings. After the war it
was not revived; but the irregular appointment of a metropolitan for
Nazareth in 1922 led to the formation of the Arabic Orthodox
Congress at Haifa which renewed the demand for such a council.
'The Haifa Congress Party', wrote Bertram and Young, *Report*,
p. 102, 'undoubtedly represents the majority of the active members
of the community', and it is interesting to note that the mixed
council this party demanded was to be two-thirds lay in membership and only one-third ecclesiastical; further, in all matters political,
administrative and economic, the patriarch was not to speak on
behalf of the community, except with the express permission of the

mixed council. He was not to appear in public for the purpose, unless accompanied by two members of the mixed council; Bertram and Young, p. 274. The temper of the Congress Party may be gathered from a comment of the newspaper *Filastin* of 16 October 1931. *Filastin*, discussing the election of a new patriarch, spoke of three mandates oppressing Palestine, the English, the Zionist and the Greek, 'which is not the lightest'. The patriarchate, wrote *Filastin*, was siding with the Zionists against the Arabs, and the cause of the Palestinian Orthodox ought to be the cause of all the Arabs, Muslim as well as Christian; *Echos d'Orient*, vol. XXXI (1932), p. 91.

44 Sakakini, 26, entry of 15 May 1908.

45 Sakakini, 53, entry of 3 January 1912.

46 *Ibid.*, 34, entry of 25 July 1908.

47 *Ibid.*, 39, entry of 30 September 1908.

48 Khuri, Brief History, p. 247.

49 *Ibid.*, pp. 54–5.

50 Sakakini, 37.

51 *Ibid.*, 57–8, entry of 12 January 1914. The year before he had published a pamphlet, *al-Nahda al-arthudhaksiyya fi Filastin* (The Orthodox Renaissance in Palestine), full of defiance and rhetoric.

52 Sakakini, 147, entry of 29 April 1918.

53 *Ibid.*, 89, entry of 26 March 1915.

54 *Ibid.*, 151, entry of 28 May 1918.

55 Sakakini, 109 and 117, entries of 21 December and 24 December 1917.

56 Elderly, presumably, because a young man in a Muslim society would not have been rich enough to afford such a choice piece.

57 Bashir Ka'dan and Shafiq Shalati, *Ha'ula al-sahyuniyyun* (Those Zionists), Damascus, 1946, pp. 15, 27 and 70.

58 Ibrahim Izzat, *Kuntu fi Isra'il* (I was in Israel), Beirut, 1957, pp. 42–3. This obsession with Jewesses may also be noticed in Anwar al-Sadat, *Revolt On the Nile*, 1957, pp. 18–9. The immodesty of the Zionist women colonists and the temptations of Tel-Aviv in this respect have of course been long-standing beliefs in Palestine and the neighbouring countries.

59 *Khitab maftuh ila al-bimbashi al-sabiq Jamal Abd al-Nasir* (Open letter to ex-Colonel Jamal Abd al-Nasir) n.p., n.d., p. 39.

60 Muhammad al-Ghazali, *Al-ta'asub wa al-tasamuh bayn al-masihiyya wa al-islam* (Fanaticism and Tolerance between Christianity and Islam), Cairo, n.d. (after 1952), pp. 164–5. The book seems a reply to J. Tagher's *Coptes et musulmans*.

61 Traian Stoianovich, 'The Conquering Balkan Orthodox Merchant', *Journal of Economic History*, vol. XX (1960), p. 245, quoting from and

summarising *Memoires du Prince Nicholas Soutzo Grand Logothète de Moldavie 1798–1871*, 1899.

62 M. Franco, *Essai sur l'histoire des Israelitèes de l'empire ottoman*, pp. 158, 160–1, 220–32; Narcisse Leven, *Cinquante ans d'histoire*, vol. I, 1911, pp. 233–6, 388–292 Jacob M. Landau, *Ha-Yehudim be-misrayyim be-meath ha-tesha'asra* (The Jews in Nineteenth-century Egypt), 1967, pp. 160ff.

63 Abraham Mitrie Rihbany, *A Far Journey*, 1914, pp. 81–2.

64 *al-Mashriq*, vol. XX, (1922), pp. 1,061–2. The book reviewed was Jean Drault's *Une cause célebre: l'assassinat in P. Thomas et le Talmud*, 1922. Cheikho's polemical style is violently outspoken and *al-Mashriq* under his editorship contains many diatribes against Judaism and the Jews in the traditional theological style.

65 Marun Abbud, *Naqdāt 'abir* (Criticisms of a Passer-by), 1959, p. 43.

66 Unless, of course, it was influenced by the Marcionite heresy.

67 See S. G. Haim, 'Arabic Anti-Semitic Literature'. *loc. cit.*

68 Correspondence between Crane and Antonius, and reports of meetings with Muslim notablities in *Antonius Papers*.

69 Sakakini, 64–6, entry of 23 February 1914.

70 *Ibid.*, 178, entry of 17 April 1919.

71 *Ibid.*, 331, entry of 30 October 1940.

72 Fu'ad Ammun, in *Dirasat 'an hukum at Lubnan* (Studies in Lebanese Government), Beirut, 1956, p. 302. Franklin's alleged speech is discussed in the *Franklin Institute News*, vol. 13 (1938), no. 4, pp. 1 and 2, cited in *Commentary*, vol. 22 (1956), p. 537.

73 Sakakini, 39–453, entries of 8 and 23 October 1908.

74 *Ibid.*, 46–8, entries of 12, 14 and 21 November 1908.

75 *Ibid.*, 80, entry of 3 November 1914.

76 *Ibid.*, 166, entry of 26 January 1919.

77 *Ibid.*, 277.

78 *Antonius Papers*, Israel State Archives.

79 The articles were published in the Egyptian periodical *al-Fath* and later brought together in a pamphlet from which extensive extracts are given in the appendix.

80 Israel State Archives, Record Group 65, file no. 2646.

81 Sakakini, 71, entry of 14 March 1914.

82 *Ibid.*, 67, entry of 25 February 1914.

83 *Ibid.*, 99–100, entry of 18 December 1917.

84 Khalil al-Sakakini, *Filastin ba'd al-harb al-kubra* (Palestine After the War), Jerusalem, 1925, pp. 24–5. One form which this Christian Orthodox identification with Arabism took was what may be called Ghassanism, i.e. the notion that the Arabic-speaking Orthodox were really the descendants of the Arab tribe of banu Ghassan who had adopted Christianity in pre-Islamic times and

become the clients of Byzantium. See for instance the transparently autobiographical novel by Najib Nassar, an Orthodox from Haifa who was one of the earliest and most uncompromising opponents of Zionism, *Riwayat Miflih al-Ghassani aw safha min safahat al-harb al-'alamiyya* (The Story of Miflih the Ghassanid, or a Page from World War History), Haifa, n.d. Miflih, be it noted, is a name used by Beduins, hardly ever by townspeople and certainly not by Christians. Marun Abbud recounts a conversation with Najib Nassar in which he tells Nassar: 'May God prosper banu Ghassan. They stood for Arabism and for its sake fought the imperialist Romans. May God save them from these other [imperialists – i.e. the Zionists]'. *Naqdāt 'abir*, p. 43.

85 Sakakini, 165–7, entries of 26 and 29 January 1919.
86 *Ibid.*, 194, entry of 23 June 1920. In spite of having publicly given this reason for his resignation, he was allowed to rejoin the Department after Samuel left, in 1926.
87 *Ibid.*, 296, entry of 4 May 1937.
88 *Ibid.*, 66, entry of 25 February 1914.
89 Ishaq Musa al-Husaini in his foreword to Sakakini's *Diary*.
90 *Ibid.*, 264–5, entry of 6 December 1934.
91 See the comment of H. E. Bowman, sometime director of Education in Palestine. Writing of the Arabic-speaking schools (which were supported and administered by the government) he stated that the Arab leaders in Palestine 'did their utmost to make the schools the nucleus of nationalist inspiration. Their aim was to embarrass the government by giving the schools a nuisance value; and, at the same time, to inculcate in the Arab youth a passionate nationalism which would show itself in overt acts whenever an opportunity served'. *Middle East Window*, p. 311. The same, of course, holds true, *mutatis mutandis*, of the Zionist schools.

12 The Chatham House Version

1 *Report of the Provisional Committee appointed to prepare a Constitution and select the original members of the British Branch of the Institute of International Affairs*, 1920, pp. 2 and 10–1.
2 Royal Institute of International Affairs, *Annual Report*, 1939–40, p. 8.
3 *Annual Report*, 1942–3, pp. 3–5.
4 *Ibid.*, pp. 24–5.
5 *Ibid.*, p. 32.
6 *Ibid.*, p. 47.
7 *A Study of History*, vol. 10, 1954, p. 139.
8 A. J. Toynbee, 'A Study of History: What I am trying to do', in

International Affairs, 1955, reprinted in M. F. Ashley Montagu (ed.), *Toynbee and History*, Boston, 1956, p. 3. See also *A Study of History*, vol. 10, p. 241.

9 *A Study of History*, vol. 10, p. 166.

10 *Ibid.*, vol. 12, p. 139.

11 *Ibid.*, pp. 77–8.

12 Vol. 4, pp. 281–2; vol. 9, p. 431 n. 2; vol. 10, p. 136.

13 *A Study of History*, vol. 4, pp. 257–8.

14 *Ibid.*, vol. 3, p. 216.

15 *Ibid.*, vol. 3, p. 191 and vol. 10, p. 140.

16 *Ibid.*, vol. 4, p. 128.

17 *Ibid.*, vol. 5, p. 200.

18 *Ibid.*, vol. 9, p. 334.

19 *Ibid.*, vol. 12, p. 309 n. 2.

20 *Ibid.*, vol. 7, p. 710.

21 W. Den Boer, 'Toynbee and Classical History: Historiography and Myth', in M. F. Ashley Montagu, *Toynbee and History*, pp. 232, 242.

22 *A Study of History*, vol. 8, p. 451.

23 *Ibid.*, vol. 5, p. 174.

24 *Ibid.*, vol. 5, p. 175.

25 *Ibid.*, vol. 5, pp. 173–4.

26 *Ibid.*, vol. 12, p. 617.

27 *Ibid.*, vol. 5, p. 588.

28 *Ibid.*, vol. 4, pp. 566, 548.

29 *Ibid.*, vol. 8, p. 291.

30 *Ibid.*, vol. 6, p. 196; and see in general pp. 178–213 for a discussion of the saviour with the sword.

31 *Ibid.*, vol. 1, p. 474; vol. 7, p. 56; vol. 2, p. 183; vol. 12, p. 204 n. 1.

32 *Ibid.*, vol. 8, p. 191.

33 *Ibid.*, vol. 3, pp. 47, 28.

34 *Ibid.*, vol. 10, p. 143.

35 *Ibid.*, vol. 3, p. 80.

36 See the dictionaries of Lane, Kazimirski and Dozy; also H. A. R. Gibb and H. Bowen, *Islamic Society and the West*, vol. 1, part 2, pp. 252–3.

37 The misunderstanding of the word *ra'īyeh* – as Toynbee writes it – illustrates one minor but interesting aspect of the Chatham House Version. Chatham House publications during Toynbee's tenure are marked by a finicky quest for exactitude in using and in transliterating Arabic words. Misplaced as it is, this desire for exactitude might have been excusable had there been competence enough to achieve accuracy. As it is, mistakes abound, the result of ignorance or half-knowledge. Thus Toynbee insists on giving us the modern Arabic word for Philistia and writes فِلَسْتِين (*Study*, vol. 2, p. 54 n. 3),

when as everyone knows Palestine in Arabic is spelled فلسطين
Or he actually coins a word which he alleges to exist in Arabic; he
states (*Study*, vol. 12, p. 59) that in Arabic there is a word for self-
centredness in the plural, the word *nahniyah*; this word is in fact
unknown to the dictionaries. Ibn Khaldun's *Muqaddima* becomes
Muqaddamāt (*Study*, vol. 4, p. 131 n. 3); *Karbalā* becomes *Qarbalā*
(*Study*, vol. 9, p. 100); Ali Abd ar-Rāziq becomes Ali Abdur-Razzaq;
the Egyptian town of Asiūt becomes As-Siyūt; the Berber ḍahīr
becomes the dāhir; the Baghdad suburb of Kazimayn is described
as 'the Shi'ī Holy Cities of Karbalā and Najaf, on the right bank of
the Euphrates' (*Survey of International Affairs*, vol. 1, *The Islamic
World* . . ., pp. 16, 88, 127 and 333.); the Syrian family of Bayhum
becomes Bayḥum; Nasīb al-Bakri becomes Naṣib; Hananu becomes
Hananu, the title of a publication is given as *al-Lubnan ba'd el harb*
(S. H. Longrigg, *Syria and Lebanon under French Mandate*, pp. 205,
217, 121 and 382); etc.

38 *A Study of History*, vol. 3, pp. 455–7.
39 *Ibid.*, p. 456.
40 *Ibid.*, vol. 12, pp. 90, 458–9.
41 *Ibid.*, vol. 1, pp. 348, 353, 370–1; vol. 9, p. 159.
42 *Ibid.*, vol. 4, pp. 112–3.
43 *Ibid.*, vol. 1, pp. 398, 396; vol. 9, pp. 95–6.
44 See his *Nationality and the War*, published in 1915, where he states
(p. 411) that 'we have identified ourselves' with the principle 'that
peace can only be secured by giving free play to every manifestation
of the spirit of Nationality'.
45 A. J. Toynbee, *The Western Question in Greece and Turkey*, 1922,
pp. 1–2.
46 *A Study of History*, vol. 3, pp. 151–2.
47 In *The Islamic World since the Peace Settlement*, published in 1927
Toynbee had still not worked out the law whereby the penetration
of one society by the ideas of another is the result of sickness in the
latter, for he writes there (p. 1): 'Possibly this violence was a passing
phase – an aftermath of the General War – but for the time being it
gave the contact between civilisations a distinctly hostile turn and
tended to divide mankind into two camps: the camp in which
western civilisation was indigenous and was therefore taken for
granted, and the camp in which it was an intrusive and therefore
subversive force.'
48 *A Study of History*, vol. 3, pp. 151, 153.
49 *Ibid.*, pp. 150–1.
50 *Ibid.*, vol. 12, pp. 154–6.
51 Another illustration of the shakiness of Toynbee's laws occurs in
volume 2 where he states (p. 123): 'In the writer's belief, the recent

transfer of the Chinese capital from Peking to Nanking is likely to be perpetuated, and this just because, so far from invalidating our "law", it actually illustrates and confirms it'. The law in question asserts that marches develop a political power which gives them a predominance over the interior; Nanking being a march, the prophecy follows.

52 *A Study of History*, vol. 5, pp. 493–4.

53 *Ibid.*, vol. 8, pp. 529–30.

54 *The World and the West*, 1953, pp. 2–3.

55 *The Western Question*, p. 40.

56 *Ibid.*, pp. 58–61.

57 *A Study of History*, vol. 1, pp. 33, 36 n.1, 161–3.

58 *Ibid.*, p. 210.

59 *Ibid.*, vol. 2, pp. 6–7.

60 *Ibid.*, p. 127.

61 *Ibid.*, vol. 4, p. 239.

62 *Ibid.*, vol. 5, p. 40.

63 *Ibid.*, vol. 12, p. 278 and vol. 8, pp. 148–9.

64 *Ibid.*, vol. 12, p. 627.

65 *Ibid.*, pp. 596–7.

66 *The Islamic World since the Peace Settlement*, p. 350.

67 *A Study of History*, vol. 2, p. 55 n. 4; see also *ibid.*, pp. 10, 14, 24.

68 In 1954 he was still declaring: 'The sin of which I feel that we westerners need to repent is Pharisaism' (in a letter to *The Times Literary Supplement*, reprinted in *Counsels of Hope: The Toynbee–Jerrold Controversy*, 1954, p. 38). In 1961 he was praising 'Pharisaic-Christian pacifism' and stating that the 'Pharisees' pacifism saved Judaism from perishing with the Zealots' (*A Study of History*, vol. 12, p. 505).

69 *A Study of History*, vol. 1, p. 214; vol. 5, p. 182; vol. 7, pp. 474 n. 1, 438–9; vol. 12, pp. 541–2.

70 *Ibid.*, vol. 8, p. 405.

71 See A. J. Toynbee, *Acquaintances*, 1967, p. 203.

72 F.O. 371/4368, file 577/480.

73 'Memorandum on the Exclusion of Palestine from the Area Assigned for Arab Independence by the McMahon–Husein Correspondence of 1915–16' by W. J. Childs, 24 October 1930, pp. 53–4; F.O. 371/14495, file 4691/427/65.

74 *The Western Question* . . ., pp. 48–9.

75 See his article 'The Present Situation in Palestine', in *International Affairs* (The Chatham House Quarterly), vol. 10, no. 1, January 1931, pp. 45, 67–8. See also an article of his in *The New Republic* of 6 September 1922, where he states, (p. 40) that Palestine was

included in the British promise to Husayn; he reiterates this belief as late as 1967; see *Acquaintances*, p. 196.

76 'The Present Situation in Palestine', *International Affairs*, pp. 40–1.
77 *A Study of History*, vol. 8, p. 257. Another Arab Nationalist assertion which Toynbee took for granted is that Syria 'in the wider popular meaning of the term' had constituted at some time – when has never been made clear – a political unit which the Allies cruelly carved up after 1918. See *Survey* for 1928, p. 322, and *Survey* for 1930, pp. 222–3.
78 'Britain and the Arabs: the Need for a New Start', *International Affairs*, vol. 40, no. 4, October 1964, p. 639.
79 *Encounter*, October 1967, p. 68. The statement occurs in an open letter from Toynbee to J. L. Talmon on the subject of the Six Day War of June 1967.
80 *Survey* for 1930, p. 169.
81 *Survey* for 1934, pp. 110–1.
82 *A Journey to China or Things Which Are Seen*, 1931, pp. 111–5.
83 *The Islamic World since the Peace Settlement*, p. 510.
84 *Survey* for 1934, p. 211.
85 *A Study of History*, vol. 8, p. 291 n. 1.
86 'Great Britain and France in the East', *The Contemporary Review*, January 1922, p. 31.
87 *A Journey to China*, p. 111.
88 *The Islamic World since the Peace Settlement*, p. 20.
89 *Survey* for 1928, p. 212.
90 *Survey* for 1928, p. 278; *Survey* for 1930, p. 310.
91 *The Western Question*, p. 181.
92 *Survey* for 1936, pp. 789–91.
93 *Great Britain and Egypt*, 1952, p. 94.
94 *Ibid.*, p. 76 n.1.
95 *Survey* for 1934, p. 101.
96 *The World in March 1939*, pp. 127, 134–5.
97 *Survey* for 1938, vol. 1, p. 425.
98 *Independent Iraq* (2nd ed.), 1960 (1st ed., 1951), p. 30.
99 *Ibid.*, chs. 3, 4.
100 *The World in March 1939*, p. 133 n. 4.
101 *Syria and Lebanon Under French Mandate*, pp. 3, 5–6.
102 *Ibid.*, pp. 84, 90, 94; *Survey* for 1937, vol. 1, p. 552.
103 *Syria and Lebanon Under French Mandate*, pp. 107–8, 367.
104 *Ibid.*, pp. 116–7.
105 *International Affairs*, vol. 15, 1936, pp. 474–5. Gibb was closely connected with Chatham House. As early as 1932–3 he and Harold Bowen were invited to examine the 'Reaction of the Islamic World to the Impact of Western Civilisation'. In 1943–4 he became a

member of the editorial committee of *International Affairs*, and the following year a member of the Council of Chatham House and vice-chairman of the publications committee.

106 *Syria and Lebanon Under French Mandate*, pp. 182–3.

107 *International Affairs*, vol. 10, 1931, pp. 63–4.

106 'Introduction', in R. N. Frye (ed.), *The Near East and the Great Powers*, 1951, pp. 9–10.

109 'The Case for the Arabs', *The Spectator*, 25 November 1938, p. 912, a review of G. Antonius, *The Arab Awakening*, 1938.

110 'The Case for the Arabs'.

111 *Syria and Lebanon Under French Mandate*, pp. 54, 59–60. It is of interest to read a review of C. Weizmann's *Trial and Error*, signed S.H.L., which appeared in *The Arab World*, October 1949, p. 17: 'It would obviously be over-optimistic or merely foolish', declares the reviewer, 'to expect more than a certain degree of "loyalty" to Great Britain, its policies and its people from immigrant foreigners of alien blood, background and ambitions such as are the foreign Jews to whom H.M.G. so readily accords the privilege of British nationality.'

112 Another account of the origin of the Balfour Declaration appears in *A Study of History*, vol. 8, p. 303, where Toynbee declares that 'the Western Powers were tantalisingly inhibited from playing this Palestinian card so long as they had any hope of keeping their Anti-Semitic Russian partner in the firing-line, and it is no wonder that the Balfour Declaration was published as soon as the last Western hopes of further Russian military collaboration had expired'. This is hopelessly confused and fanciful, for the Balfour Declaration was not a 'Western' but a British enterprise, and there is no evidence of a Tsarist veto having delayed its appearance.

113 *The World in March 1939*, p. 138.

114 *International Affairs*, vol. xx, October 1944, pp. 467–9, 472.

115 *Great Britain and the Middle East*, pp. 5–6.

116 *Politique étrangère*, 1947, p. 47.

117 T. S. Eliot, *East Coker*.

List of Works Cited

The following is a list of the published works cited in this book, with the exception of British Parliamentary Papers and Debates, and of newspapers and periodicals referred to for news items and the like. Place of publication is London unless otherwise indicated.

Abbas al-Azzawi, *Tarikh al-Iraq bayn ihtilalain* (History of Iraq Between Two Occupations), vol. VII, Baghdad 1955

Abbas Ali, *Za'im al-thaura al-iraqiyya* (The Leader of the Iraqi Revolution), Baghdad 1950

Abbas Mahmud al-Aqqad, *Sa'd Zaghlul*, Cairo 1936

Abbott, E., and Campbell, L., *Life and Letters of Benjamin Jowett*, vol. II, 1897

Abd al-Ahad al-Shafi, (pseud.), *Lamha tarikhiyya fi akhawiyyat al-qabr al-muqaddas al-yunaniyya* (Historical Outline of the Greek Brotherhood of the Holy Sepulchre), 2nd ed., n.p. 1909

Abd al-Aziz al-Qassab, *Min dhikrayati* (Recollections), Beirut 1962

Abd al-Aziz Fahmi, *Hadhihi hayati* (This is my Life), Cairo 1963

Abd al-Fattah abul-Nasr al-Yafi, *Mudhakkirat qa'id arabi* (Memoirs of an Arab Commander), n.p., n.d.

Abd al-Jabbar Fahmi, *Sumum al-af'a al-sihyawni* (Poisons of the Zionist Snake), Baghdad 1952

Abd al-Rahman Azzam, 'al-Tarbiyya al-'askariyya wa atharuha fi'l sha'b' (Military Training and its Effect on the People), *al-Hilal*, Cairo 1939

Abd al-Rahman al-Bazzaz, *Muhadarat 'an al-Iraq min al-ihtilal hatta al-istiqlal* (Lectures on Iraq from Occupation to Independence), Cairo 1954.

———, *Safahat min al-ams al-qarib* (Pages from the Recent Past), Beirut 1960

Abd al-Rahman al-Rafi'i, *Muqaddimāt thawrat 23 yulyu* (Preliminaries of the 23 July Revolution), Cairo 1957

Abd al-Razzaq al-Haṣṣan, *al-Uruba fi al-mizan* (Arabism in the Balance), Baghdad 1933

Abd al-Razzaq al-Hasani, *al-Asrar al-khafiyya fi hawadith sanat 1941 al-taharruriyya* (Hidden Secrets of the Liberatory Events of 1941), 1st ed., Sidon 1958, 2nd ed., Sidon 1964

L'Action du parti S.R. arménien dit Daschnaktzoutioun 1914–1923, n.p., n.d.

Adams, C. C., *Islam and Modernism in Egypt*, 1933

Adib Ishaq, *al-Durar* (The Pearls), Beirut 1909

Ahmad Amin, *Hayati* (My Life), 2nd ed., Cairo 1952

Ahmad Baha' al-Din, *Ayyam laha tarikh* (Historic Days), Cairo 1954

Ahmad Biyali, *Adli Pasha*, Cairo 1922

Ahmad Faris al-Shidiaq, *al-Saq 'ala al-saq fi ma huwa al-Fariaq* (*La vie et aventures de Fariaq, relation de ses voyages avec ses observations critiques sur les Arabes et sur les autres peuples*), Paris 1855

Ahmad Lutfi Hafiz, *Sa'd Zaghlul fi hayatihi al-niyabiyya* (Sa'd Zaghlul's Parliamentary Life), Cairo 1927

Ahmad Nasim Susa, *Fi tariqi ila'l-Islam* (On my Way to Islam), vol. I, Cairo 1936; vol. II, Najaf 1938

Ahmad Shafiq Pasha, *A'mali ba'd mudhakkirati* (My Activities after [the publication of] my Memoirs), Cairo 1941

———, *Hauliyyat Misr al-siyasiyya* (Annual Survey of Egyptian Politics), 10 vols., Cairo 1926–1933

———, *Mudhakkirati fi nisf qarn* (My Memoirs of Half a Century), vol. II, part 2, Cairo 1936

Albert Rayhani (ed.), *Rasa'il Amin al-Rayhani 1896–1940* (Letters of Amin al-Rayhani 1896–1940), Beirut 1959

Albert Shuqayr, *al-Dustur al-misri wa'l-hikm al-niyabi fi Misr* (The Egyptian Constitution and Representative Government in Egypt), Cairo 1924

Ali Abd al-Raziq, *al-Islam wa usul al-hikm*, Cairo 1925; translation: 'L'Islam et les bases du pouvoir' in *Revue des études islamiques*, vols. VII and VIII, Paris 1933–4

Ali al-Bazirgan, *al-Waqa'i al-haqiqiyya fi'l-thaura al-iraqiyya* (The True Events of the Iraqi Revolt), Baghdad 1954

Ali al-Tantawi, *Baghdad mushahadat wa dhikrayat* (Baghdad: Scenes and Memories), Damascus 1960

———, *Fi bilad al-Arab* (In the Arab Countries), Damascus 1939

Ali Jawdat al-Ayyubi, *Dhikrayat* (Recollections), Beirut 1967

d'Alonzo, Alphonse, *La Russie en Palestine*, Paris 1901

Amin al-Mumayyiz, *al-Mamlaka al-arabiyya al-su'udiyya kama 'araftuha* (The Sa'udi Kingdom as I Knew It), Beirut 1963

Amin al-Rayhani, *al-Makari wa'l-kahin* (The Muleteer and the Priest), Beirut 1929

———, *Muluk al-Arab* (Kings of the Arabs), 2 vols., Beirut 1924

Amin al-Rayhani, *Qalb Lubnan* (The Heart of the Lebanon), 2nd ed., Beirut 1958

Anis al-Nusuli, *'Ishtu wa shahhadtu* (I Have Lived and Seen), Beirut 1951

Anonymous, *Kitab maftuh ila al-bimbashi al-sabiq Jamal Abd al-Nasir* (Open Letter to ex-Colonel Jamal Abd al-Nasir), n.p., n.d.

Anwar al-Jundi, *al-Imam al-Maraghi*, Cairo 1952

Anwar al-Rifa'i, *Jihad nisf qarn* (Half a Century of Struggle), Damascus, n.d.

Anwar al-Sadat, *Revolt on the Nile*, 1957

Duke of Argyll, *Our Responsibility for Turkey*, 1896

Arif al-Arif, *al-Nakba* (The Disaster), vol. II, Sidon n.d. [c. 1950]

Arpee, Leon, *The Armenian Awakening*, Chicago 1909

Bashir Ka'dan and Shafiq Shalati, *Ha'ula' al-sahyuniyyun* (Those Zionists), Damascus 1946

Batatu, John, *The Shaikh and the Peasant in Iraq 1917–1958*, unpublished Ph.D. thesis, Harvard University, 1960

Bell, G. L., *The Arab of Mesopotamia*, Basra 1919

Lady Bell, (ed.), *The Letters of Gertrude Bell*, 2 vols., 1927

Bentwich, N., *Wanderer Between Two Worlds*, 1942

Bernadotte, Folke, *To Jerusalem*, 1951

Bertram, A., and Luke, C., *Report of the Commission appointed by the Government of Palestine to inquire into the Affairs of the Orthodox Patriarchate of Jerusalem*, 1921

Bertram, A., and Young, J. W. A., *Report of the Commission Appointed by the Government of Palestine to inquire and report upon certain controversies between the Orthodox Patriarchate of Jerusalem and the Arab Orthodox Community*, 1926

Bliss, E. M., *Turkey and the Armenian Atrocities*

Bliss, F. J., *The Religions of Modern Syria and Palestine*, 1912

Bourdillon, H. B., 'The Political Situation in Iraq' in *Journal of the British Institute of International Affairs*, vol. III, 1924

Bowle, John, *Viscount Samuel*, 1957

Bowman, H. E., *Middle East Window*, 1942

Brodrick, Alan Houghton, *Near to Greatness: A Life of the Sixth Earl Winterton*, 1965

Bshara Khalil al-Khuri, *Haqa'iq Lubnaniyya* (Lebanese Truths), vol. II, Beirut 1960

Burgoyne, Elizabeth, *Gertrude Bell from her Personal Papers 1914–1926*, 1961

Callwell, C. E., *Life of General Maude*, 1920

Cardishian, G. V., 'The Armenian Revolutionary Federation', *The Armenian Review*, vol. II, Boston 1949

Catroux, Georges, *Dans la bataille de Mediterrannée*, Paris 1949

de Chair, S., *The Golden Carpet*, 1944

Chamoun, Camille, *Marahil al-istiqlal* (The Stages of Independence), Beirut 1949

Charles-Roux, F., 'L'Egypte de l'occupation anglaise à l'indépendance égyptienne' in G. Hanotaux, *Histoire de la nation égyptienne*, vol. VII, Paris 1940

Charlton, L. E. O., *Charlton*, 1931

Cheikho, Louis, *al-Sirr al-maṣun fi shi'at al-māsun* (The Well-Protected Secret Concerning the Sect of the Masons), Beirut 1911

Churchill, W. S., *The Second World War*, vol. III, *The Grand Alliance*, 1950

Clarke, Somers, *The Unrest in Egypt*, Cairo 1920

Cohen, Hayyim J., 'The Anti-Jewish *Farhud* in Baghdad 1941' in *Middle Eastern Studies*, vol. III, 1966–7

465

Coke, R., *The Heart of the Middle East*, 1925
Cooper, Duff, *Old Men Forget*, 1953
Counsels of Hope: The Toynbee-Jerrold Controversy, 1954
Curzon, G. N., *Persia and the Persian Question*, vol. I, 1892
Dalton, Hugh, *High Tide and After*, 1962
Davison, R. H., *Reform in the Ottoman Empire 1856–1876*, Princeton 1963
Den Boer, W., 'Toynbee and Classical History: Historiography and Myth' in M. F. Ashley Montagu (ed.), *Toynbee and History*, Boston 1956
Deighton, S. H., 'Les relations anglo-egyptiennes' in *Politique étrangère*, Paris March 1947
Deplaissan, P., 'La Politique russe dans la Palestine et la Syrie', *Echos d'Orient*, vol. IV, Paris 1901
Dirasat 'an hukumat Lubnan (Studies in Lebanese Government), Beirut 1956
Documents on British Foreign Policy, First Series, vol. XIII, 1963
Dowling, T. E., *The Orthodox Greek Patriarchate of Jerusalem*, 3rd ed., 1913
Dowson, Sir Ernest, *An Inquiry into Land Tenure and Related Questions*, Baghdad 1931
Dwight, H. G. O., *Christianity in Turkey*, 1854
Edmonds, C. E., *Kurds, Turks and Arabs*, 1957
Egyptian Government, *al-Qadiyya al-misriyya 1882–1954* (The Egyptian Question 1882–1954), Cairo 1955
——, Legislative Assembly, *Recueil des comptes-rendus des séances, session 1913–14*, Cairo 1914
Eliot, Sir Charles, *Turkey in Europe*, 2nd ed., 1908
Emin, A., *Turkey in the World War*, 1928
Fahmi al-Mudarris, *Maqalat siyasiyya* (Political Essays), Baghdad 1931
Fakhr al-Din al-Ahmadi al-Zawahiri, *al-Siyasa wa'l-Azhar* (Politics and al-Azhar), Cairo 1945
Falls, Cyril, *Armageddon 1918*, 1964
——, *Official History of the War, Military Operations in Egypt and Palestine from June 1917 to the end of the War*, 1928–30
Firmin van den Bosch, *Vingt années d'Egypte*, Brussels 1932
Foot, Sir Hugh, *A Start in Freedom*, 1964
Forbes Adam, C., *Life of Lord Lloyd*, 1948
Fortescue, A., *The Orthodox Eastern Church*, 1907
France, *Documents diplomatiques*, Affaires arméniennes, *Projets de réforme dans l'empire ottoman 1893–7*, 1897
——, *Documents diplomatiques français*, 3ème série, tome VII, Paris 1934
Franco, M., *Histoire des israélites de l'empire ottoman*, Paris 1897
Gardner, Brian, *Allenby*, 1965
de Gaulle, Charles, *Mémoires de guerre*, vols. I and II, Paris 1954–6
de Gaury, Gerald, *Three Kings in Baghdad*, 1961
Gibb, H. A. R., 'Introduction' in R. N. Frye (ed.), *The Near East and the Great Powers*, Cambridge, Mass. 1951
——, 'Middle Eastern Perplexities' in *International Affairs*, 1944
——, 'The Case for the Arabs', in *The Spectator*, 25 November 1938

466

Gibb, H. A. R., 'Toward Arab Unity' in *Foreign Affairs*, New York October 1945

――――, and Bowen, Harold, *Islamic Society and the West*, vol. I, pt. 2, 1957

Glubb, J. B., *A Soldier with the Arabs*, 1957

Gooch, G. P., and Temperley, H. W. V., *British Documents on the Origin of the War*, vol. X, pt. 1, 1938

Graves, Robert, *T. E. Lawrence to his Biographer*, 1938

Grigg, Sir Edward, (Lord Altrincham), *British Foreign Policy*, 1944

――――, 'Les problèmes du Moyen-Orient' *Politique étrangère*, Paris July 1947

Grobba, F., *Männer und Mächte im Orient*, Göttingen 1967

Gullett, H. S., *Official History of Australia in the War 1914–1918*, vol. VII, *Sinai and Palestine*, Sydney 1935

Haider, S., *Land Problems of Iraq*, unpublished Ph.D. thesis, University of London 1942

Haim, S. G., 'Alfieri and al-Kawakibi' in *Oriente Moderno*, vol. XXXIV, Rome 1954

――――, 'Arabic Antisemitic Literature' in *Jewish Social Studies*, New York 1955

――――, 'Blunt and al-Kawakibi' in *Oriente Moderno*, vol. XXXV, Rome 1955

――――, 'Islam and the Idea of Arab Nationalism' in W. Z. Laqueur (ed.) *The Middle East in Transition*, 1958

――――, 'State and University in Egypt' in C. D. Harris and M. Horkheimer (eds.), *Universität und Moderne Gesellschaft*, Frankfurt 1959

Hancock, W. K., *Country and Calling*, 1954

――――, and Jean van der Poel (eds.), *Selections from the Smuts Papers*, vols. III and IV, 1966

――――, *Smuts*, vol. I, 1962

Hanna abu Rāshid, *Layali al-'id fi waqa'i' al-Amir Sa'id* (Festival Nights in Celebration of Amir Sa'id's Exploits), Beirut 1921

Lord Hardinge of Penshurst, *Old Diplomacy*, 1947

Hartmann, Martin, *The Arabic Press of Egypt*, 1899

al-Hayat (newspaper), *Majzarat Qasr al-Rihab* (The Massacre of Qasr al-Rihab), Beirut 1960

Haza' al-Majali, *Mudhakkirati* (My Memoirs), n.p. 1960

Henderson, K. D. D. (ed.), *Life and Letters of Sir Douglas Newbold*, 1953

Heyworth-Dunne, J., *Religious and Political Trends in Modern Egypt*, Washington 1950

Hirszowicz, L., *The Third Reich and the Arab East*, 1966

History of the Times, vol. IV, pt. I, 1952

Hogarth, D. G., 'Wahabism and British Interests' in *Journal of the British Institute of International Affairs*, IV (1925)

Huart, Clément, *Histoire de Baghdad dans les temps modernes*, Paris 1901

Hurewitz, J. C., *Diplomacy in the Near and Middle East*, vol. II, Princeton 1956

King Husain of Jordan, *Uneasy Lies the Head*, 1962

467

Husain, Fadil, *Tarikh al-hizb al-watani al-dimiqrati 1946–1958* (History of the National Democratic Party 1946–1958), Baghdad 1963

Ibrahim Izzat, *Kuntu fi Isra'il* (I was in Israel), Beirut 1957

Iraq Government, *Correspondence Relating to the Assyrian Settlement*, Baghdad 1933

Iraq Government, Ministry of the Interior, *Mudhākarat al-majlis al-ta'sisi al-iraqi* (Debates of the Iraqi Constituent Assembly), Baghdad, n.d.

Ireland, P. W. (ed.), *The Near East: Problems and Prospects*, Chicago 1942

Ishaq Musa al-Husaini, *al-Ikhwan al-muslimun* (The Muslim Brethren), Beirut 1955

Isma'il Sidqi, *Mudhakkirat* (Memoirs), Cairo 1950

al-Ittihad al-Arabi fi'l Qahira, *al-Kitab al-thani* (The Arab Union in Cairo, Second Book), Cairo 1950

Jomier, Jacques, O. P., *Le Mahmal*, Cairo 1953

Ja'far Khayyat, *al-Qarya al-iraqiyya* (The Iraqi Village), n.p. 1950

Janin, R., *The Separated Eastern Churches*, 1933

Joseph, John, *The Nestorians and their Muslim Neighbours*, Princeton 1961

Kamal Kira (ed.), *Muhakamāt al-thaura* (Trials of the Revolution), vol. 4, Cairo 1954

Kedourie, E., *Afghani and 'Abduh: An Essay on Religious Unbelief and Political Activism in Modern Islam*, 1966

———, *England and the Middle East: The Destruction of the Ottoman Empire 1914–1921*, 1956

———, '*Hizb* (Arab Countries)' in *Encyclopaedia of Islam* (new ed.), Leiden 1968

———, 'The American University of Beirut' in *Middle Eastern Studies* vol. III (1966–7)

———, 'Islam and the Orientalists' in *British Journal of Sociology*, September 1956

———, 'Revolutionary Justice in Egypt: The Trials of 1953' in *The Political Quarterly*, 1958

———, 'Wavell and Iraq, April–May 1941' in *Middle Eastern Studies*, vol. II, 1965–6

Kelly, Sir David, *The Ruling Few*, 1952

Keynes, J. M., *Two Memoirs*, 1949

Khadduri, M., *Independent Iraq*, 1st ed., 1951; 2nd ed., 1960

———, 'General Nuri's Flirtations with the Axis Powers' in *Middle East Journal*, vol. XVI, Washington 1962

Khairi al-Umari, 'Fahmi al-Mudarris', in *al-Aqlam*, vol. 1, no. 4, Baghdad 1964

Khalil al-Sakakini, *Filastin ba'd al-harb* (Palestine after the War), Jerusalem 1925

———, *Kadha ana ya dunya* (Such I am, O World), Jerusalem 1955

———, *al-Nahda al-arthudhaksiyya fi Filastin* (The Orthodox Renaissance in Palestine), Jerusalem 1913

LIST OF WORKS CITED

Khalil Iskandar Qubrusi, *Da'wa nasara al-Arab ila'l-dukhul fi'l-islam* (A Call to the Arab Christians to Embrace Christianity), Cairo n.d.

Khalil Kanna, *al-Iraq amsuhu wa ghaduhu* (Iraq Yesterday and Tomorrow), Beirut 1966

Kirk, G., *The Middle East in the War*, 1952

Kirkbride, Alec Seath, *A Crackle of Thorns*, 1956

Landau, J. M., *Ha-Yehudim be-misrayyim be-meath ha-tesha' 'asra* (Jews in Nineteenth-century Egypt), Jerusalem 1967

Landau, Rom, *Search for Tomorrow*, 1938

Lane, E. W., *The Manners and Customs of the Modern Egyptians*, 1836

Langer, W. L., *The Diplomacy of Imperialism*, New York 1951

Laoust, H., *Le Califat dans la doctrine de Rashid Rida*, Beirut 1938

Lawrence, T. E., *Seven Pillars of Wisdom*, 1935

League of Nations, *Mosul Commission Report*, Geneva 1925

Lescot, Roger, *Enquête sur les Yazidis de Syrie et du Djebel Sindjār*, Beirut 1938

Leven, Narcisse, *Cinquante ans d'histoire*, vol. 1, Paris 1911

Lord Lloyd, *Egypt since Cromer*, 2 vols., 1933–4

Longrigg, S. H., *Syria and the Lebanon under the French Mandate*, 1958

————, Review of C. Weizmann's *Trial and Error* in *The Arab World*, October 1949

Lynch, H. F. B., *Armenia*, 2 vols, 1901

MacColl, Malcolm, *The Sultan and the Powers*, 1896

MacDonald, A. D., *Euphrates Exile*, 1936

Mackenzie, Compton, *Eastern Epic*, vol. I, 1951

Macler, F., *Autour de l'Arménie*, Paris 1917

Macmillan, Harold, *The Blast of War, 1939–1945*, 1967

Macready, Sir Gordon, *In the Wake of the Great*, 1965

Mahmud Azmi, 'Jabha min shu'ub al-arabiyya' (A Front of Arabic-speaking Peoples), *al-Hilal*, Cairo 1938

Majallat al-mu'tamar al-islami al-'amm li'l-khilafa fi Misr (Review of the General Islamic Congress for the Caliphate in Egypt), Cairo 1924–5

Malek, Yussif, *The British Betrayal of the Assyrians*, Fairlawn, N. J., 1935

Mann, J. S. *An Administrator in the Making*, 1921

Mardor, Munya M., *Strictly Illegal*, 1964

Marmorstein, E., 'A Note on "Damascus, Homs, Hama and Aleppo" ' in *St. Antony's Papers*, no. XI, 1961

Marun Abbud, *Amin al-Rayhani*, Cairo 1955

————, *al-Nabi Muhammad*, (The Prophet Muhammad), Sidon 1934

————, *Naqdāt 'abir* (Criticisms of a Passer-by), Beirut 1959

————, *Ruwwad al-nahda al-haditha* (Pioneers of the Modern Renaissance), Beirut 1952

————, *Saqar Lubnan* (The Eagle of the Lebanon), Beirut 1950

Massey, W. T., *Allenby's Final Triumph*, 1920

Meinertzhagen, R., *Middle East Diary 1917–1956*, 1959

Mekhitarian, O., 'The Defence of Van' in *The Armenian Review*, vols. I–II, Boston 1948–9

Michel Bar-Zohar, *Ben Gourion*, Paris 1966

469

Michie, A. A., *Retreat to Victory*, 1942

Milner, Lord, *England in Egypt*, 13th ed., 1920

Mikha'il Nu'ayma, *Sab'un: qissat 'umr 1889–1959* (Seventy Years: the Story of a Life 1889–1959), vol. I, Beirut 1959

Monroe, Elizabeth, *Britain's Moment in the Middle East 1914–1956*, 1963

Montagne, R., 'Modern Nations and Islam' in *Foreign Affairs*, New York 1952

Mosley, Leonard, *The Glorious Fault: The Life of Lord Curzon*, 1960

Muhammad al-Ghazali, *al-Ta'asub wa al-tasamuh bayn al-masihiyya wa al-islam* (Fanaticism and Tolerance Between Christianity and Islam), Cairo n.d.

Muhammad Ali Musa, *Amin al-Rayhani*, Beirut 1961

Muhammad al-Sharif, *'Ala hamish al-dustur* (On the Margin of the Constitution), 2 vols., Cairo 1938

Muhammad al Tabi'i, *Min assar al-sasa wa'l-siyasa* (Secrets of Politicians and Politics), Cairo n.d.

Muhammad Amin al-Husaini, *Haqa'iq 'an qadiyyat Filastin* (Truths on the Palestine Question), Cairo 1954

Muhammad Anis, *Dirasat fi watha'iq thaurat 1919* (Studies in the Documents of the 1919 Revolution), vol. I, Cairo 1963

Muhammad Husain Haikal, *Mudhakkirat* (Memoirs), 2 vols., Cairo 1951–2

Muhammad Jamil Bayhum, *Suriya wa Lubnan 1918–1922* (Syria and Lebanon 1918–1922), Beirut 1968

Muhammad Khalil Subhi, *Tarikh al-hayat al-niyabiyya fi Misr* (Parliamentary History of Egypt), vol. V, Cairo 1939

Muhammad Kurd Ali, *Khitat al-Sham* (History of Syria) vol. III, Damascus 1925

Muhammad Mahdi Kubba, *Mudhakkirati* (My Memoirs), Beirut 1965

Muhammad Rashid Rida, *Tarikh al-ustadh al-umam* (History of the Teacher and Leader [i.e. Muhammad Abduh]), vol. I, Cairo 1931

Muhammad Subayh, *Mawaqif hasima fi tarikh al-qawmiyya al-arabiyya* (Decisive Episodes in the History of Arab Nationalism), Cairo 1964

Muhammad Taufiq Husain, *Nihayat al-iqta' fi'l-Iraq* (The End of Feudalism in Iraq), Beirut 1955

Muhawarat al-imam al-muslih Kashif al-Ghita al-Shaikh Muhammad al-Husain ma' al-safirain al-britani wa'l amerki fi Baghdad (Conversation of Shaikh Muhammad al-Husain Kashif al-Ghita with the British and American Ambassadors in Baghdad), Najaf 1954

Musa Sabri, *Qissat malik wa arba' wizarat* (The Story of a King and Four Ministries), Cairo 1964

Najib al-Armanazi, *'Ashr sanawat fi'l-diblumasiyya* (Ten Years in Diplomacy), Vol. I, Beirut 1964

Najib Nassar, *Riwayat Miflih al-Ghassani* (The Story of Miflih the Ghassanid), Haifa n.d.

Nallino, C. A., 'Recentissimi publicazioni di polemica politico-religiosa musulmana nell 'Iraq' in *Raccolta di scritti editi e inediti*, vol. 3, Rome 1939

Nazarbek, A., *The Voice of the Armenian Revolutionaries*, 1895

Nevakivi, J., 'Lord Kitchener and the Partition of the Ottoman Empire' in K. Bourne and D. C. Watt (eds.), *Studies in International History*, 1967

Nogales, R., *Four Years Beneath the Crescent*, 1926

Nune, E., 'L'Idea dell'Unita Araba in Recenti Debattiti della Stampa del Vicino Oriente' in *Oriente Moderno*, vol. XVIII, Rome 1938

Ottoman Government, *Aspirations et agissements révolutionnaires des sociétés arméniennes avant et après la proclamation de la constitution ottomane*, Istanbul 1917

Papazian, K. S., *Patriotism Perverted*, Boston 1934

Peterson, Sir Maurice, *Both Sides of the Curtain*, 1950

Petrie, Sir Charles, *Life and Letters of Sir Austen Chamberlain*, 2 vols., 1940

Proceedings of the First Muslim-Christian Convocation, n.p., n.d. (1955?)

Puaux, G., *Deux années au Levant*, 1952

Radd hay'at kibar al-ulama ala kitab al-islam wa usul al-hukm li'l-shaikh Ali Abd al-Raziq (Refutation by the Areopagus of the Grand Ulama of the Book, Islam and the Foundations of Authority by Shaikh Ali Abd al-Raziq), Cairo, n.d.

Rattigan, Terence, *Ross: A Dramatic Portrait*, 1960

Republic of Iraq, *Muhakamāt al-mahkama al-askariyya al-khassa* (Trials of the Special Miltary Court); 22 vols., Baghdad 1958–1962

Richter, J., *A History of Protestant Missions in the Near East*, 1910

Rihbany, A. M., *A Far Journey*, Cambridge, Mass. 1914

Ronaldshay, Lord, *Life of Lord Curzon*, vol. III, 1928

Rossi, E., 'Il Congresso Interparlamantare Arabo e Musulmano pro Palestina al Cairo (7–11 October)' in *Oriente Moderno*, vol. XVIII, Rome 1938

Royal Institute of International Affairs, *Annual Reports* (various dates)

———, *Report of the Provisional Committee appointed to prepare a Constitution and select the original members of the British Branch of the Institute of International Affairs*, 1920

Royal Institute of International Affairs, Cairo Group, *Great Britain and the Middle East*, 1944

Russell, Bertrand, *Autobiography*, vol. I, 1967

Russell, G. W. E., *Malcolm MacColl*, 1914

Salah al-Aqqad, *al-Arab wa'l-harb al-'alamiyya al-thaniyya* (The Arabs and the Second World War), Cairo 1966

Salah al-Din al-Nahi, *Muqqadima fi'l-iqta' wa nizam al-aradi fi'l-Iraq* (An Introduction to Feudalism and the Land System of Iraq), Baghdad 1955

Salah al-Din al-Sabbagh, *Fursan al-uruba fi'l-Iraq* (The Knights of Arabism in Iraq), Damascus 1956

Samuel, Viscount, *Memoirs*, 1945

Sarkissian, A. O., *History of the Armenian Question to 1885*, Urbana 1938

———, 'Concert Diplomacy and the Armenians, 1890–1897' in A. O. Sarkissian (ed.), *Studies in Diplomatic History and Historiography in honour of G. P. Gooch*, 1961

Sati' al-Husri, *Ara' wa ahadith fi'l-tarbiyya wa'l-ta'lim* (Opinions and Addresses on Pedagogy and Education), Cairo 1944
——, *Mudhakkirati fi'l-Iraq* (My Iraq Memoirs), vol. I, Beirut 1967
——, *Safahat min al-madi al-qarib* (Pages from the Recent Past), Beirut 1948
Sayce, A. H., *Reminiscences*, 1923
Schechtman, J. B., *Population Transfers in Asia*, New York 1949
Seale, Patrick, *The Struggle for Syria*, 1965
Sereni, H. E., *ha-Abib ha-qadosh* (Sacred Spring), Tel Aviv 1951
Shakib Arslan, *al-Sayyid Rashid Rida*, Damascus 1938
Sharef, Z., *Three Days*, 1962
Shatirian, M., 'The Founders of the A[rmenian] R[evolutionary] F[ederation] on National Independence' in *Armenian Review*, vol. XI, Boston 1958
Shhada Khuri and Nicholas Khuri, *Khulasat tarikh kanisat Urshalim al-arthudhaksiyya* (Brief History of the Orthodox Church of Jerusalem), Jerusalem 1925
Shukri Khalil Suwaidan, *Tarikh al-jam'iyya al-imberatoriyya al-arthudhaksiyya al-filastiniyya* (History of the Imperial Orthodox Palestine Society), Boston 1912
Simpson, H. J., *British Rule, and Rebellion*, 1938
Soustelle, Jacques, *Envers et contre tout: De Londres à Alger*, Paris 1947
Spears, Sir Edward, 'The Path to Arab Unity', *Great Britain and the East*, April 1945
Spender, J. A., *Life, Journalism and Politics*, 2 vols., 1927
Stafford, R. S., *The Tragedy of the Assyrians*, 1935
Stark, F., *East is West*, 1945
——, *Dust in the Lion's Paw*, 1966
Stirling, W. F., 'Tales of Lawrence of Arabia' in *The Cornhill*, vol. 74, 1933
Stoianovich, Traian, 'The Conquering Balkan Orthodox Merchant' in *Journal of Economic History*, vol. XX, New York 1960
Storrs, Ronald, *Orientations*, definitive ed., 1943
Story, Somerville (ed.), *The Memoirs of Ismail Kemal Bey*, 1920
Sulaiman Faidi, *Fi ghamrat al-nidal* (In the Midst of the Struggle), Baghdad 1952
Sulzberger, C. L., 'German Preparations in the Middle East' in *Foreign Affairs*, New York 1942
Sumner, B. H., *Russia and the Balkans 1870–1880*, 1937
Sykes, Sir Mark, *Dar ul-Islam*, 1904
Symes, Sir Stewart, *Tour of Duty*, 1946
Taha al-Hashimi, *Mudhakkirat* (Diaries), Beirut 1967
Temperley, H. W. V., 'British Policy Towards Parliamentary Rule and Constitutionalism in Turkey' in *Cambridge Historical Journal*, vol. IV, 1932–3
Toynbee, A. J., *Acquaintances*, 1967
——, *A Journey to China or Things Which Are Seen*, 1931

Toynbee, A. J., *Nationality and the War*, 1915
———, *A Study of History*, 12 vols., 1934–1961
———, (ed.) *Survey of International Affairs*, (various dates)
———, *The Western Question in Greece and Turkey*, 1922
———, 'Britain and the Arabs: the Need for a New Start' in *International Affairs*, 1964
———, 'Great Britain and France in the East' in *The Contemporary Review*, 1922
———, 'The Present Situation in Palestine' in *International Affairs*, 1931
———, 'A Study of History: What I am trying to do' in *International Affairs*, 1955
———, 'The Trouble in Palestine', in *The New Republic*, New York 6 September 1922
Tyan, E., *Institutions du droit public musulman*, vol. I, *Le Califat*, Paris 1954
Umar Tusun, *Mudhakkira bima sadara 'anna mundh fajr al-haraka al-wataniyya min sanat 1918 ila sanat 1928* (Memorandum on our activities since the dawn of the Egyptian national movement from the year 1918 to the year 1928), Alexandria 1942
United Kingdom, *(Official) History of the Second World War: the Mediterranean and the Middle East*, vol. II, 1956
Urquhart, Clara, and Brent, Peter Ludwig, *Enzo Sereni, A Hero Of Our Times*, 1967
Uthman Haddad, Hasan al-Qattan and Abd al-Hasib al-Shaikh Sa'id, *Thaurat Hama 'ala al-taghayan al-faransi* (Hama's Revolt against French Oppression), vol. I, Hama 1945
Valyi, F., *Spiritual and Political Revolutions in Islam*, 1925
Wajih al-Haffar, 'Al-hukumāt allati ta'aqabat 'ala al-hikm fi Suriya' (The Successive Governments of Syria) in *Majallat al-Shurta wa'l amn* (Police and Public Security Magazine), Damascus 1953
Warkworth, Lord, *Notes from a Diary in Asiatic Turkey*, 1898
Warriner, Doreen, *Land and Poverty in the Middle East*, 1948
———, *Land Reform and Development in the Middle East*, 1957
Wavell, A. P., *Allenby, Soldier and Statesman*, 1946
Wigram, W. A. & E. T. A., *The Cradle of Mankind*, 1922
Wilson, A. T., *Loyalties, Mesopotamia*, 2 vols., 1930–1.
Woodward, Sir Llewellyn, *British Foreign Policy in the Second World War*, 1962
Young, G., *Corps de droit ottoman*, vol. II, 1905–6
Yunus Bahri, *Sab'at ashhur fi sujun Baghdad* (Seven Months in the Prisons of Baghdad), Beirut 1960
Yusuf al-Dijwi, *al-Islam wa usul al-hukm wa'l-radd alayhi* (Islam and the Foundations of Authority and its Refutation), Cairo, n.d.
Zeine N. Zeine, *The Struggle for Arab Independence*, Beirut 1960

Index

Abaza, Fu'ad, *see* Fu'ad Abaza

Abbas Hilmi, khedive of Egypt, 89, 90; attaches Zaghlul to himself, 86; clashes with Zaghlul, 85; condoles with Zaghlul on death of his father-in-law, 87; his opinion of Muhammad Abduh, 84; seeks throne in Levant, 196

Abbas Mahmud al-Aqqad, 192

Abbud, Marun, *see* Marun Abbud

Abd al-Aziz Fahmi, 84, 88, 165; complains of Hasan Nash'at's power, 185–6; dismissed as minister of justice, 192; protests against amendment of draft constitution, 172, 174

Abd al-Aziz ibn Sa'ud, quarrels with Egypt, 187; his views on caliphate, 188

Abd al-Ilah, regent of Iraq, 238, 249; ambitions in Syria and Jordan of, 272–3; Hijazi nationality of, 272; increases power of Iraqi monarchy, 270

Abd al-Khaliq Tharwat, 89, 98; Allenby committed to support of, 158; becomes Prime Minister, 158; defines task of his ministry, 164–5; in favour of Zaghlul's deportation, 152; resigns office, 171; his views on government of Egypt, 151–2; unable to oppose proclamation of Fu'ad as king of Sudan, 170

Abd al-Qadir al-Jaza'iri, Amir, 43

Abd al-Rahman al-Bazzaz, defends political activities of students, 276

Abd al-Rahman al-Kawakibi, 195

Abd al-Rahman al-Naqib, 243; poor opinion of Faisal of, 255

Abd al-Rahman Azzam, 197, 216, 218, 426 fn. 88; organises 'Territorial Army', 217; on Palestine war, 233

Abd al-Rahman Fahmi, organises terrorism, 117; dilatory manner of dealing with, 130; freed by Zaghlul, 132; organises boycott of Milner mission, 119; treatment in prison of, 414 fn. 159

Abd al-Raziq, Ali, *see* Ali Abd al-Raziq

Abd al-Raziq, Mustafa, *see* Mustafa Abd al-Raziq

Abd al-Razzaq al-Hasani, 232

Abduh, Muhammad, *see* Muhammad Abduh

Abdullah, second son of sharif Husain, (later amir and king), 23; policy over Palestine, 230–1

Abdullah al-Qassab, organises pro-Iraq movement in Mosul, 254

Abu'l-Huda, Tawfiq, *see* Tawfiq abu'l-Huda

Adib Ishaq, 321

Adil Arslan, 188, 196

Adli Yakan, supports demand for autonomy, 94; advises against commutation of Abd al-Rahman Fahmi's sentence, 131; asked by British to endorse Milner-Zaghlul agreement, 135; declines to form administration, 172–3; fails to reach agreement with British, 142; in favour of constitutionalism in Egypt, 164; forms ministry, 139; professes satisfaction at Zaghlul's deportation, 152; proposes negotiations with Zaghlul, 125–6; resigns as minister, 97, 118; takes part in new ministry, 117

Ahmad al-Sanusi, proposed for spiritual caliphate, 189–90

Ahmad Lutfi al-Sayyid, 95

Ahmad Mahir, member of supreme council for assassinations, 117

Ahmad Nasim (Nissim) Susa, on his conversion to Islam, 451 fn. 25

Ahmad Shafiq, 98; on proceedings of caliphate congress, 193–4

Alexandria, affray at, 140

Ali Abd al-Raziq, publishes *Islam and the Foundations of Authority*, 190; similarity of his views to Maraghi's, 190; trial of, 191

Ali al-Bazirgan, 251

Ali al-Mirghani, Sayyid, 17; deprecates discussing frontiers of Arab state, 22; as intermediary between British and Sharif Husain, 18

Ali al-Tantawi, 249, 275; on disorders in Damascus, 401, fn. 32

Ali Jawdat al-Ayyubi, 237; incited by Faisal to rouse Shi'ites, 244

Ali Mahir, 117, 165; British demand dismissal of, 218; negotiates recognition by Egypt of Sa'udi Arabia, 198; his pan-Arab policy, 216; replaces Abd al-Aziz Fahmi as minister of justice, 192; takes anti-monarchical line, 166

Ali Sha'rawi, 84

Allenby, Field Marshal, 37; adopts policy of concessions in Egypt, 112, 114; agrees with Clayton and Hayter, 148; allows Sharifian troops to enter Damascus, 51; appointed special commissioner in Egypt, 110; compels Fu'ad to give up claim to Sudan, 172; defends his policy against Foreign Office, 154; deports Zaghlul, 152; dismisses British officials in Egypt, 145–6; favours constitutionalism in Egypt, 158, 169; imposes appointment of Adli as prime minister, 139; insists in releasing Zaghlul from Malta, 115–16; miscalculates effects of Zaghlul's release, 117; objects to appointment of Samuel, 56–7; objects to Fu'ad becoming king of Sudan, 169–70; his opinion of Adli, 170; opposes commutation of Abd al-Rahman Fahmi's sentence, 131; persuades Fu'ad to issue constitution, 173–4; plans for capture of Damascus of, 46; his policy in 1922, 162–3; professes ability to form moderate government in Egypt,

148–9; proposes unilateral abrogation of protectorate, 151, 153; recalled to London, 157; regrets Tharwat's fall, 171–2; reports that British advisers in Egypt demand Egyptian independence, 149–50; resigns as high commissioner in Egypt, 159; supports Tharwat, 164; threatens to resign as high commissioner, 155–6; his treatment compared with Wingate's, 156; warns against wide modification of Milner scheme, 137; warns of difficulty of negotiating with Adli, 141

Alliance israélite universelle, the, views of schoolmasters sent by, 309–10

Altrincham, Lord, see Grigg, Sir Edward

Amery, L. S., on end of Iraq mandate, 257–8; on middle eastern settlement, 398 fn. 70

Amin al-Husaini, see Muhammad Amin al-Husaini

Amin al-Rayhani, anti-clericalism of, 321–2; acquires Arab identity, 324–5; pro-Muslim sentiment of, 323–4

Ammun, Fu'ad, see Fu'ad Ammun

Amos, Sheldon, 416 fn. 213; threatens resignation of British advisers in Egypt, 156; views on Egypt of, 146–7

Anti-semitism, among Eastern Christians, 335–7; in Arab world, 449 fn. 79

Antonius, George, 195, 337; believes in primacy of Muslims in Arab nationalism, 339; influence of, 5; reviewed by Gibb, 391; significance of career of, 318

Aqqad, Abbas Mahmud al-, see Abbas Mahmud al-Aqqad

Arab League, 215, 219; and Palestine problem, 229–30; record of, 228

Arab movement, beginnings of in 1914–18 War, 15; amorphous character of, 25

Armenians, position of, in Ottoman Empire, 287, 290; attacks by Armenians on, 296; Britain and, 292; communal reforms among, 290; demand for autonomy by 291, 443 fn. 13; effect of missionary activity

INDEX

Armenians—*contd*

among, 287–9; massacres of, 297–9, 445 fn. 36; nationalism among, 294–5; Ottoman reforms and, 294; Protestant community formed among, 289; Russia and, 290–2, 443 fn. 10

Arslan, Adil, *see* Adil Arslan

Arslan, Shakib, *see* Shakib Arslan

As'ad al-Shidiaq, conversion to Protestantism of, 321

Askari, Ja'far al-, *see* Ja'far al-Askari

Assyrians, massacred by Iraq army, 237, 306; Gibb on, 389; problem in Iraq of, 246, 303–4; Toynbee on, 378

Axis powers, their attitude to pan-Arab demands, 220–1

Ayyubi, Ali Jawdat al-, *see* Ali Jawdat al-Ayyubi

Ayyubi, Shukri al-, *see* Shukri al-Ayyubi

Aziz Ali al-Misri, 217, 427 fn. 13

Azmi, Mahmud, *see* Mahmud Azmi

Azzam, Abd al-Rahman, *see* Abd al-Rahman Azzam

Baghdad, predominance of Jews in, 254–5, 436–7 fn. 65; its British occupation in 1917 and 1941 contrasted, 308; character of history of, 281–2

Baghdad Pact, 234

Bakr Sidqi, 237–8; acclaimed for victory over Assyrians, 247; demand by British for trial of, 446 fn. 54; massacres Assyrians, 246

Bakri, Nasib al-, *see* Nasib al-Bakri

Balfour, Arthur, agrees to Allenby's policy, 114; concedes *Wafd* demands, 106–7; Curzon's judgment of, 107; refuses permission for Egyptians to visit London, 100; his views on Wingate's dismissal, 111–12

Balfour Declaration, 53; as interpreted by Samuel, 55; Longrigg's view of, 391; non-publication in Palestine of, 57; Toynbee's view of, 461 fn. 112

Banna, Hasan al-, *see* Hasan al-Banna

Barrow, Major-Gen. Sir G. de S., 37

Basir, Muhammad Mahdi al-, *see* Muhammad Mahdi al-Basir

Basra, refusal to be included in Iraq of, 254

Bazirgan, Ali al-, *see* Ali al-Bazirgan

Bazzaz, Abd al-Rahman al-, *see* Abd al-Rahman al-Bazzaz

Beeley, H., on Amin al-Husaini, 385; on growing unity of Arab national feeling, 387

Bell, Gertrude, 262, 301; confesses representative government in Iraq a mistake, 266; has emotional scene with Faisal, 244–5; on Faisal's imposition over Iraq, 262–3; foresees early end of Iraq mandate, 257; on Nuri al-Sa'id, 279; on position of shaikhs in Iraq, 267; on pro-Ottoman sentiment in Iraq, 242; her view of Cheetham, 100; her view of Faisal, 240–1, 263

Bentwich, Norman, 67, 404 fn. 40

Bernadotte, Folke, 230

Bethman, Erich W., 2

Bevin, Ernest, his policy in Palestine, 231–2

Bidault, Georges, 229

Bindari, Kamil al-, *see* Kamil al-Bindari

Birthdays, in Islam, 201

Bourchier, Col., quells disorders in Damascus, 40, 50

Bourdillon, B. H., 241, 256, 263

Bowman, Humphrey, on Patterson, 146; on Arab schools in Palestine 456 fn. 91

Boyle, Harry, his opinion of Zaghlul, 140

Britain, policy in Egypt of, 96, 102; attitude to Iraqi intervention in Palestine, 233; attitude to Palestine problem of, 231–2; attitude to pan-Arabism of, 221; attitude toward Assyrians of, 303–4, 306; character of postwar foreign policy of, 107; colonial experience of, 262; consequences of bringing Faisal to Iraq to, 265–6; consequences of declaration of February, 1922 to, 163; declares Egyptian protectorate unsatisfactory, 138; difficulties of Middle Eastern policy of, 228–9; establishes centralised regime in Iraq, 258–9; and Iraqi anti-Jewish legislation, 312–13; and pan-Arabism, 225; policy in Levant of, 222–4; policy towards Iraq mandate of,

476

Khalil Kanna—*contd*
Palestine, 233; on Abd al-Ilah's Syrian ambitions, 272; on elections in Iraq, 438 fn. 79

Khatib, Fu'ad al-, *see* Fu'ad al-Khatib

Khuri, Bshara al-, *see* Bshara al-Khuri

Kirk, G. E., on Egyptian politics, 385; on Middle Eastern frontiers, 386; on Zionist factor in Middle East politics, 391–2

Kirkbride, A. S., testimony on Damascus events by, 45, 47

Kitchener, Lord, reports clash between Abbas Hilmi and Zaghlul, 85; and Abbas Hilmi, 86

Kurds, of Iraq, refusal to be included in Iraq of, 254; autonomy promised by British to, 256; opposition to pan-Arabism of, 258; revolt against Iraq of, 237, 238–9

Kuwait, invasion attempt by Ghazi of, 249

Law, Bonar, 115

Lawrence, T. E., 262, 301; hostility towards Jaza'iri brothers of, 45–6; on Robert Graves's account of capture of Damascus, 34–5; treatment of Druzes in *Seven Pillars* by, 40; treatment of fall of Damascus in *Seven Pillars* by, 41–3, 45, 47

Lebanon, the, political events in, 223–4

Levant, the, elections demanded by British in, 223; British policy in, 221–2

Liberal Constitutionalist party, in Egypt, 164; embarrassed by Ali Abd al-Raziq's trial, 193; opposes Fu'ad's becoming Caliph, 190; protests against amendment of constitution, 172

Lindsay, Sir Ronald, expects Fu'ad to behave as constitutional monarch, 139; approves Allenby's policy, 154; argues for leaving internal affairs of Egypt to Egyptians, 144–5; reports on negotiations with Adli, 141–2

Lloyd, George (Lord Lloyd), 29–30, 161; his opinion of Haines, 97

Lloyd George, David, 52, 262; gives in to Allenby, 157; interviews Adli, 142; offers Wingate peerage as condition of silence, 112

Longrigg, S. H., on capture of Damascus, 36; criticises French policy in Levant, 388; praises British policy in Iraq, 389; reviews Weizmann's *Trial and Error*, 461 fn. 111; his view of Syrian history, 386–7; on Zionist influence over British, 391

Lutfi al-Sayyid, Ahmad, *see* Ahmad Lutfi al-Sayyid

Macandrew, Major-Gen. H. J. M., 37

MacDonald, A. D., on character of Iraqi regime, 261; on position of British officials in Iraq, 263–4

McMahon, Sir Henry, gives account of beginning of Arab movement, 14; describes Arab movement as national not religious, 19; as high commissioner in Egypt, 91–2; on his pledge to sharif Husain, 22; his reliance on E. Cecil, 108

MacMichael, Sir Harold, his view of Sykes-Picot Agreement, 31

Macmillan, Harold, urges Spears' recall, 221

Mahir, Ahmad, *see* Ahmad Mahir

Mahir, Ali, *see* Ali Mahir

Mahmal, the, quarrel over, 186, 187

Mahmud Azmi, opposes Fu'ad's ambition of becoming caliph, 189; on Husrism in Iraq, 274

Mahmud Fahmi al-Nuqrashi, member of supreme council for assassinations, 117, 135; his attitude to Palestine problem, 216; and Egyptian intervention in Palestine, 230–1

Makram Ubayd, 135; Muslim attacks on, 199

Mann, J. S., on self-determination in Mesopotamia, 302–3

Maraghi, Muhammad Mustafa al-, *see* Muhammad Mustafa al-Maraghi

Maronites, and Western influence, 320

Marun Abbud, pro-Muslim sentiment of, 323–4; anti-semitism of, 337

Massey, W. T., 402 fn. 40

Meinertzhagen, R., 70

Meyerson, Golda, 230, 231

Middle class, in middle east, 8–9

Midfa'i, Jamil al-, see Jamil al-Midfa'i

Mikha'il Nu'ayma, on Russian influence among Orthodox, 328–9; on

Mikha'il Nu'ayma—*contd*
  inculcation of Arab nationalism in
  Russian college at Nazareth, 330
Mills, Eric, on Weizmann's attitude to
  Arabs, 71
Milner, Lord, mission to Egypt headed
  by, first mooted, 115; aims at a
  treaty with Egypt, 132; believes in
  negotiating with Adli, 138; breaks
  negotiations with Zaghlul, 136;
  change in his views on British policy
  in Egypt, 120–1; concedes control
  of foreign affairs to Egypt, 133; his
  conduct of negotiations with Zaghlul, 129; disappointed with Egyp-
  tion politicians 125; his manner of
  dealing with terrorism, 130–1, 132;
  optimism over negotiations with
  Zaghlul, 126; preface to his *England
  in Egypt* quoted, 121; reaches
  agreement with Zaghlul, 134; his
  view of Allenby's policy, 118; his
  views on timing of mission, 119;
  see also Milner mission
Milner mission, general conclusions of,
  123–4; defines Milner-Zaghlul Agree-
  ment, 134; justifies negotiations
  with Zaghlul, 133
Minyawi, Muhammad Faraj al-, *see*
  Muhammad Faraj al-Minyawi
Mirghani, Ali al-, *see* Ali al-Mirghani
Misri, Aziz Ali al-, *see* Aziz Ali al-Misri
Missionaries, U.S. Protestant, view of
  Islam of, 2; activities among
  Armenians of, 287–8; reaction of
  Maronites to proselitysing by, 320–1
Monroe, Elizabeth, 35
Montagu, Edwin, 89
Moody, R., on elections in Palestine, 75
Mosul commission, recommendations
  of, 256, 257
Mosul, pro-Iraq sympathies of, 254;
  British hold out to Iraq promise of
  support over, 256–7
Moyne, Lord, urges Spears's recall, 221
Mudarris, Fahmi al-, *see* Fahmi al-
  Mudarris
Mufti, position in Islam of, 58–9;
  election in 1921 of – of Jerusalem,
  62–3, 66; Ottoman regulations con-
  cerning election of, 60; use of
  epithet 'Grand' to describe – of
  Jerusalem, 59

Muhammad Abduh, 81, 84, 178
Muhammad al-Gharabli, 184
Muhammad al-Sadr, 244
Muhammad Amin al-Husaini, Hajj,
  record of, 60–1; allowed to assume
  post of mufti, 67; H. Beeley on preference for democracy of, 385;
  controls Supreme Muslim Council,
  72; effects in Palestine of appointment as mufti of, 69; gives Samuel
  pledge of good behaviour, 61–2;
  organises congress in Jerusalem,
  195–6; Samuel's pardon of, 403 fn.
  22; subsidised by Iraq, 272
Muhammad Faraj al-Minyawi, 186
Muhammad Farid, on Zaghlul's relations with nationalist party, 85
Muhammad Haidar, 216
Muhammad Husain Haikal, 95; declares Maraghi used for political
  purposes, 200; defends Ali Abd
  al-Raziq, 191; discusses Egyptian
  delegation to Palestine conference,
  216; on Husain Rushdi's constitutional views, 167–8; on Inshass
  meeting 215–16; his misgivings over
  Arab unity, 228; on Nuqrashi's
  attitude to Palestine, 216; on pro-
  Axis sympathies of Egyptian ministers, 218; reports conversation with
  Bindari on caliphate, 204–5, 217;
  on *Wafd* petition, 98
Muhammad Mahdi al-Basir, 243
Muhammad Mahmud, appointed prime
  minister by Faruq, 199; dismissed
  as prime minister, 217; superseded as
  delegate to Palestine conference, 216
Muhammad Murad, mufti of Haifa, 74
Muhammad Mustafa al-Maraghi,
  career of, 178–9; advocates neutral-
  ity in war for Egypt, 202, 426 fn. 77;
  agitation by *Wafd* against, 202;
  appointed tutor to king Faruq, 198;
  celebrates Faruq's birthday, 201;
  claims political participation Islamic duty, 200–1; his opinions on
  caliphate, 179–81, 208–12; proposes
  adjournment of caliphate congress,
  193; seeks to obtain caliphate for
  Faruq, 203–4; similarity of his
  views on caliphate to Ali Abd al-
  Raziq's, 190; takes part in anti-
  Coptic campaign, 199

Errata

p. 3, line 18: *for* "unsubstantial" *read* "insubstantial"

p. 3, line 23: *for* "doctrins" *read* "doctrines"

p. 23, line 18: *for* "unsubstantial" *read* "insubstantial"

p. 51, line 32: *for* "enterç" *read* "enter?"

p. 76, line 28: *for* "representative" *read* "representatives"

p. 102, line 38: *for* "*corvée*" *read* "*corvée*"

p. 165, line 10: Add a comma after "again"

p. 165, line 14: *for* "counoil" *read* "council"

p. 165, line 27: *for* "*ahqiya*" *read* "*ashqiya*"

p. 177, line 22: *for* "*rechtstaat*" *read* "*Rechtstaat*"

p. 195, line 15: substitute a comma for the period after "*Awakening*"

p. 197, line 35: delete comma after "d'affaires"

p. 214, line 37: *for* "kingdoms" *read* "kingdom"

p. 241, line 33: *for* "Tauriq" *read* "Tawuq"

p. 243, line 35: delete comma at end of line

p. 245, last line: *for* "has" *read* "had"

p. 254, line 26: *for* "Abdullah" *read* "Abd al-Aziz"

p. 306, line 4: *for* "woman" *read* "women"

p. 348, line 43: *for* "throughout" *read* "through"

p. 349, line 29: *for* "god" *read* "gods"

p. 360, line 9: *for* "*nauseum*" *read* "*nauseam*"

p. 362, line 39: *for* "ra'īyya" *read* "ra'iyya"

p. 363, lines 5, 20: *for* "ra'īyya" *read* "ra'iyya"

p. 366, line 13: *for* "enthsuiastically" *read* "enthusiastically"

p. 370, line 33: *for* "affluents" *read* "effluents"

p. 375, line 34: *for* "Storrs" *read* "Storr"

p. 393, line 12: *for* "out" *read* "our"

p. 400, line 25: *for* "hikm *read* "hukm"

p. 432, line 35: *for* "abd" *read* "Abd"

p. 433, line 28: *for* "leters" *read* "letters"

p. 435, line 18: *for* "Scnes" *read* "Scenes"

p. 438, line 2: delete comma after "*al-majlis*"

ERRATA

p. 443, line 32: *for* "Armenians" *read* "Armenian"; *for* "*societes*" *read* "*sociétés*"; *for* "*armeniennes*" *read* "*arméniennes*"; *for* "*aprés*" *read* "*après*"

p. 444, line 11: *for* "*francais*" *read* "*français*"

p. 448, line 27: *for* "*israelite*" *read* "*israélite*"

p. 451, line 23: *for* "Na um" *read* "Na'um"

p. 451, line 33: *for* "Bahara" *read* "Bshara"

p. 456, line 6: *for* "*tesha'asra*" *read* "*tesha'esre*"

p. 456, line 10: *for* "*célebre*" *read* "*célèbre*"; *for* "*in*" *read* "*du*"

p. 459, line 14: *for* "Hananu" *read* "Hananu"

p. 464, line 26: *for* "*hikm*" *read* "*hukm*"

p. 465, line 20: after "*Atrocities*" add comma and "1896"

p. 469, line 7: *for* "'*asra*" *read* "'*esre*"

p. 473, line 28: *for* "hikm" *read* "hukm"